THE EUROPEAN PARLIAMENT

For "**The European Parliament**" Facebook page, and details of our other books on the Parliament, visit our dedicated website:

http://www.europesparliament.com/

Any corrigenda and addenda to this 8th edition will be published on this website.

The European Parliament

8th edition

RICHARD CORBETT
FRANCIS JACOBS
MICHAEL SHACKLETON

JOHN HARPER
PUBLISHING

The European Parliament
8th edition

Published by John Harper Publishing
27 Palace Gates Road
London N22 7BW, United Kingdom.

www.johnharperpublishing.co.uk
www.europesparliament.com

First edition 1990
2nd edition 1992
3rd edition 1995
4th edition 2000
5th edition 2003
6th edition 2005
7th edition 2007
8th edition 2011

ISBN 978-0-9564508-5-2

Printed and Bound in Malta by Gutenberg Press Ltd

TABLE OF CONTENTS

I: THE FRAMEWORK

II: THE ACTORS AND WORKING STRUCTURES

III: THE POWERS OF THE PARLIAMENT

IV: APPENDICES

TABLES AND FIGURES

Figures

ABOUT THE AUTHORS

Dr. Richard Corbett is the advisor on constitutional questions to the President of the European Council, Herman Van Rompuy. He handles the President's relations with the European Parliament. From 1996 to 2009 he was a Member of the European Parliament (MEP). He was spokesperson on constitutional affairs and EU reform for the Socialist Group. He was Parliament's rapporteur on the European Constitution and on the Treaty of Lisbon, as well as on several revisions of Parliament's Rules of Procedure. He represented Yorkshire & Humber, was Deputy Leader of the European Parliamentary Labour Party (EPLP) and a member of Labour's National Policy Forum. Prior to his election, he was Deputy Secretary-General of the Socialist Group. He has written widely on European affairs, his publications including *The Treaty of Maastricht: from conception to ratification*, and *The Role of the European Parliament in closer EU Integration*.

Francis Jacobs is Head of the European Parliament's Information Office in Ireland. Before moving to Ireland he was the Head of Unit responsible for the Committee on the Environment, Public Health and Consumer Protection. He had previously worked on the European Parliament Committees on Constitutional Affairs, Rules and Economic and Monetary Affairs, as well as on its Temporary Committee on German Unification. He was the editor and principal author of *Western European Political Parties: A Comprehensive Guide*, has lectured extensively on EU matters and has contributed various articles and chapters on European Union matters, notably on the work of the European Parliament. He has also worked on the Rules of Procedure of the Scottish and Albanian Parliaments.

Dr. Michael Shackleton is Head of the European Parliament Information Office in the United Kingdom. Before moving back to Britain, he was responsible for the setting up of europarltv, the Parliament's webTV channel, launched in September 2008. He had previously been the Head of Unit responsible for conciliations and co-decision. His earlier jobs included working in the secretariat of the Committee on Budgets, in the division for relations with national parliaments and as head of the unit responsible for the Committee of Inquiry into the Community Transit System. He has co-edited *The Institutions of the European Union* and has published a broad range of articles on co-decision, the EU budget, interparliamentary relations and the democratic deficit. He has lectured widely on the role of the Parliament, including as a Visiting Fellow at the University of Berkeley (California), the College of Europe (Bruges), the University of Sussex (UK) and the Institut des Études Politiques (Paris), and is now a Visiting Professor at the University of Maastricht (Netherlands).

ACKNOWLEDGEMENTS

The authors have continued to rely on the help of friends and colleagues in the Parliament and outside to keep abreast of the rapid pace of change within the institution and for helping to update statistics.

For this eighth addition, they would like to pay particular tribute to Bent Adamsen, Auke Baas, Lucinia Bal, Alexander Beels, Sarah Blau, Kieran Bradley, Robert Bray, Roger Brawn, Paul Broos, Eduardo Bugalho, Sarah Clarkson, Maria D'Alimonte, Pietro Ducci, Andrew Duff, Simon Duffin, Paul Dunstan, Javier Fernandez, Bob Fitzhenry, Ben Fox, Fabio Galatioto, Pekka Hakala, Geoff Harris, Katrin Huber, Rik Hugelier, Maria Jose Martinez, Kent Johannson, Fiona Kearns, Gay Kavenagh, Sophie Kerr, Bjorn Kjellstrom, Nikolas Lane, Jose Luis Linazasoro, Andrea Lovei, David Lowe, Andreas Maurer, Claire Meyer, Ute Muller, Dietmar Nickel, Niall O'Neill, Pekka Nurminen, Una O'Dwyer, Gergely Polner, Sir Julian Priestley, Patrizia Prode, Loreta Raulinaityte, Derek Reed, Jacek Safuta Sarah Sheil, Peter Schiffauer, Anthony Teasdale, Juan Urbieta, and Libby Vannet. They have also had technical assistance from Anne McEvoy, Elaine Agius, and Lol Kirkwood. Finally, thanks are due to Michelle Kneeshaw for her work on the proofs and Caroline Wilding for the compilation of the Index.

Any errors remain, as ever, the responsibility of the authors alone. They would also emphasise that the views expressed are theirs alone, and do not necessarily reflect those of the Parliament.

NOTE ON THE TREATIES

The European Union is now governed by two main treaties: the **Treaty on European Union (TEU)**, which sets out (in a brief and relatively readable way) the main principles, competences, powers and institutions of the EU as well as the general provisions relating to the Common Foreign and Security Policy, and the **Treaty on the Functioning of the European Union (TFEU)**, which contains the detailed policy and institutional provisions.

This relatively clear situation is the result of the Treaty of Lisbon. Prior to that, things were more complex.

The first treaty, the European Coal and Steel Community treaty (ECSC), came into force in 1952 (for a duration of 50 years – it expired in 2002). In 1958, two further treaties entered into force, the European Economic Community (EEC) treaty and the European Atomic Energy Community treaty, known as EURATOM. Together these treaties constituted the European Communities, commonly referred to as the European Community (EC).

These treaties were amended a number of times, most notably: the Single European Act (which entered into force in 1987), Maastricht (1993), Amsterdam (1999), Nice (2003) and Lisbon (2010). As a result of Maastricht, a European Union was established, composed of the European Community, supplemented, in a largely separate legal framework, by a Common Foreign and Security Policy and Cooperation on Justice and Home Affairs. Amsterdam and Nice transferred the bulk of the latter into the European Community treaty.

The complexity of this situation led the Member States to the idea that all the treaties should be repealed and replaced by a single "constitution". Such a constitution was drafted in a Convention in 2003-2004 and finalised in an intergovernmental conference in 2004. Although a majority of Member States ratified it, it was rejected in 2005 by France and the Netherlands, with concerns expressed in the latter about the very term "constitution".

As a result, Member States abandoned the idea of a new constitution and reverted to amending the pre-existing treaties. In doing so, they retained a large number of the specific reforms that had been envisaged in the constitution, but lost the codification into a single document. Nonetheless, the Lisbon Treaty did restructure the basic treaties into just two.

FOREWORDS

Over eight editions, *The European Parliament* has established itself as an important landmark in the literature on the European Union. The book provides an invaluable guide to the institution's history, power and politics. It explains both what drives the Parliament internally and the dynamics of its increasingly central role in the EU political system as a whole. For academics and practitioners alike, Corbett, Jacobs and Shackleton offer a superb starting-point for any serious understanding of the world's only elected transnational parliament.

Jerzy Buzek
President of the European Parliament

★ ★ ★

One of the distinguishing features of the European Union is that it possesses a directly elected Parliament. Through successive changes to the treaties, member states have granted it a powerful role within the EU system, both as legislator with the Council in the Union's bicameral legislature and in providing scrutiny and control over all the Union's activities. It ensures that the full pluralism of the political diversity within each member state is brought into the heart of EU decision taking.

No one can seek to understand the functioning of the European Union without understanding its Parliament. This book – now in its eighth edition – is recognised in academia and among practitioners as the authoritative guide to the European Parliament.

Herman Van Rompuy
President of the European Council

"On my first visit to Strasbourg in 1979 as a Member of the European Parliament, I went for a walk across the bridge from Strasbourg to Kehl. Strasbourg is in France. Kehl is in Germany. They are very close. I stopped in the middle of the bridge and I meditated. There is Germany – there is France. If I had stood on this bridge 30 years before at the end of the Second World War when 25 million people lay dead across our continent and if I had said: 'Don't worry. In 30 years time we will all be together in a new Europe, our conflicts and wars will be ended and we will be working together in our common parliament', I would have been sent to a psychiatrist. But it has happened and it is now clear that the European Union is the best example in the history of the world of conflict resolution."

John Hume MEP
Acceptance speech upon winning the Nobel Peace Prize Oslo, 10 December 1998

I: THE FRAMEWORK

1. The Parliament in context

Every parliament has its own history, culture and powers, and operates within a particular political environment. In the case of the European Parliament, some special characteristics set it apart.

First, it is the world's most far-reaching experiment in transnational democracy, where international diplomacy is replaced – or at least complemented by – transnational democracy.

Second, it forms part of a unique and historically unprecedented institutional system: the European Union, with its mixture of supranational powers and intergovernmental cooperation.

Third, its very existence is controversial, with some politicians in some Member States having opposed its creation and further development.

Fourth, it is evolving quickly. Elected for the first time in 1979, the European Parliament is still a young parliament but has developed its role and powers considerably in the 32 years that have passed since then.

Fifth, it is obliged by the Member States to operate in three different locations rather than have a single seat.

Sixth, it is multilingual to a degree unknown elsewhere (only the Indian and South African parliaments are even remotely comparable) with interpretation at meetings and translation of all documents.

Seventh, like the US Congress, but unlike the national parliaments of all the EU Member States, no government emerges directly from a majority in Parliament and elections to it are not therefore about keeping or changing an executive.

Eighth, the Parliament continues to expand in size, from 410 members from 9 countries when it was first elected to 734 from 27 now and a scheduled 751 soon.

Ninth, its Members come from a vast number (nearly 200) political parties, though they are affiliated to a handful of European groupings

Tenth, unlike most national parliaments in European countries, it has a fixed term of office and cannot be dissolved for early elections

For all these reasons, the European Parliament defies easy categorisation. Moreover, it cannot be understood without reference to the European Union as a whole and the unique characteristics that mark it out from any other international organisation in the world.

The EU can be traced back to the European Coal and Steel Community, set up after World War II "as a first step to a European Federation" (Schuman Declaration) – a bold attempt to bring together former enemies and to establish a lasting framework of binding cooperation among the states of Europe to ensure peace and stability.

But there is also a pragmatic driving force behind European integration, namely the practical concern to manage the growing economic interdependence of European countries. The creation of a single European market, with goods and services flowing freely from one country to another, has reinforced this, requiring a degree of common policy-making. A common market needs common rules and the assurance that everyone will apply those rules. It needs a level playing field and some harmonisation of the ways in which public authorities intervene in the market. It generates pressure for common European-level rules in areas such as consumer protection, environmental standards, external trade, assistance to less prosperous regions, competition policy, and workplace standards, and for common policies in areas where all governments intervene in the market, notably transport and agriculture.

There is also a growing cooperation in areas other than those which arise from the single market, such as combating transnational crime and in foreign policy, or where Member States can gain by pooling resources, such as in research programmes.

From fig-leaf to co-legislature

The recognition of the need for common policies and rules in such matters led national parliaments, when ratifying the founding treaties, to confer legislative power on the EU in limited but important areas. Initially, these powers were given to the Council, composed of ministers representing national governments, acting on a proposal of the Commission, a collegial European executive appointed by national governments but charged with acting in the overall European interest. The Council could approve Commission proposals in most matters by a "qualified majority" of about 71 per cent of the votes, each Member State having a weighted vote according to its size but unanimity was required to modify Commission proposals. On some issues, unanimity was required to adopt a proposal. Application of European legislation was to be a matter for Member States, but subject to monitoring by the Commission, which could, if necessary, take a Member State to the Court of Justice, composed of judges appointed by national governments to rule on disputes concerning the interpretation of the treaties and European legislation.

Under this initial system, the European Parliament was essentially a forum, composed until 1979 of delegations from national parliaments. It was merely consulted on a small range of legislative proposals prior to their adoption by Council and given the right to dismiss the Commission in a vote of censure by a two-thirds majority.

These powers were, not surprisingly, considered to be too limited, especially by those called upon to serve in the European Parliament, who claimed that a system whereby ministers alone could adopt legislation suffered from a "democratic deficit". Parliament had to fight for its powers, and it has done so with considerable success.

Over four decades, the Parliament has moved from being a largely consultative assembly to being a genuine co-legislator in a European Union that has itself evolved considerably beyond the original European Communities, both in scope and in powers. Parliament and Council now form a bicameral EU legislature.

This change has come about step by step, notably as Member States approved new treaties supplementing or amending the original treaties:

First, the **budget treaties** of 1970 and 1975 provided for Council and Parliament to be the "budgetary authority", jointly thrashing out the annual budget within a fixed revenue limit. These budget procedures were complicated, but they allowed Parliament scope to amend the budget as well as take the final vote on its adoption or rejection.

Second, in 1975 a **conciliation procedure** was agreed between the institutions for dealing with legislation with budgetary consequences where there was a need to avoid potential conflict between Council's legislative powers and Parliament's budgetary powers. The procedure laid down that, should Council wish to diverge from Parliament's opinion, the matter should be referred to a conciliation committee composed of the members of Council and an equal number of MEPs, although it would still be up to the Council to adopt the legislation in question.

Third, in 1979, Parliament was **elected by universal suffrage** for the first time. This was designed to generate greater democratic legitimacy and more public debate on European issues, but also provided Parliament with full-time members (and more of them – the nominated Parliament had 198 members, the first elected Parliament 410), focussed on European issues.

Fourth, in 1980 the *Isoglucose* **judgment of the Court of Justice** (cases 138 and 139/79) struck down legislation because Council had adopted it before Parliament gave its opinion. This ruling gave Parliament a de facto delaying power, which it could use to bargain for amendments. Clearly, Parliament's bargaining position was stronger when there was pressure for a rapid decision than where there wasn't, but it helped get Council used to the need to negotiate with Parliament.

Fifth, in 1987, the **Single European Act** came into force, introducing two new procedures for the adoption of Community acts. The *cooperation procedure,* applied initially to only ten treaty articles, in effect adding a second reading to the traditional consultation procedure by requiring that Council's position be referred back to Parliament, which then had three months to approve it, reject it (in which case it would fall unless Council overruled Parliament by unanimity within three months) or press for amendments (which, if supported by the Commission, could only be rejected unanimously in Council, whereas a qualified majority could approve the revised text). The *assent procedure* gave Parliament equal rights with Council in requiring Parliament's approval as well for the ratification of accession treaties and association agreements.

Sixth was the **Treaty of Maastricht**, which came into force on 1 November 1993. This brought in a number of increases in the powers of the European Parliament:

–   It introduced, for ten treaty articles, the co-decision procedure, whereby texts would need the approval (or, at least, non-rejection) of both Council and Parliament, with up to three readings in each institution and a conciliation committee to negotiate a compromise if agreement has not been reached after two readings.

- The cooperation procedure was extended to most of the other areas where Council acts by a qualified majority.
- The assent procedure was extended to a wider category of international agreements and a number of other areas.
- Parliament was given the right to vote on a number of appointments. Its vote on the nominations for President of the Commission and President of the European Monetary Institute/Central Bank were formally consultative but, many felt, politically binding. Its vote to allow (or not) the Commission as a whole to take office through a vote of confidence was legally binding and the normal term of office of the Commission was changed to match the five-year term of the Parliament. In addition, the Parliament was given the task of selecting an Ombudsman whose five-year term of office also coincides with that of the Parliament.
- Various powers of scrutiny were enhanced, notably by a provision in the Treaty for parliamentary committees of inquiry.

Seventh, was the **Treaty of Amsterdam**, which came into force on 1 May 1999. This greatly extended the scope of co-decision so that most non-agricultural legislation became subject to it. It also modified the procedure to Parliament's advantage in ways that are described in Chapter 11. At the same time, the treaty made Parliament's vote on the candidate for Commission President a legally binding one. If a Commission President designated by the European Council fails to gain majority support in the Parliament, he or she cannot take office.

Eighth, was the **Treaty of Nice**, which came into force in 2003. This extended further the scope of co-decision, and gave the Parliament a general right to take the other institutions to the European Court of Justice.

Ninth, was an agreement between Parliament and Council in 2006, to introduce a new method, called **Regulatory Procedure with Scrutiny**, for controlling Commission implementing decisions under the so-called "comitology" procedures. This allowed Parliament to veto certain categories of Commission decisions.

Tenth, was the **Treaty of Lisbon** which entered into force on 1 December 2009. This:

- turned co-decision into the ordinary legislative procedure, applicable to almost all areas in which the EU can legislate.
- extended the assent procedure, the name of which was changed in English to the consent procedure, to ordinary trade agreements and to six legislative matters not subject to the ordinary legislative procedure.
- provided for the President of the Commission to be elected by the European Parliament – still on a proposal of the European Council, but with the latter obliged to take account of the results of the European elections and to consult to see who is capable of securing a parliamentary majority.
- introduced a new budgetary procedure to require the approval of all EU expenditure by both the Council and the European Parliament without any exceptions, thus bringing all expenditure under parliamentary control.
- extended the new system of supervision of Commission implementing

measures, entrenching the 2006 agreement between Parliament and Council and in addition giving Parliament the right to revoke any delegation of legislative powers to the Commission.

–   laid down that future treaty changes will be prepared, prior to an Intergovernmental Conference (IGC), by a Convention involving national and European parliament representatives, unless the European Parliament decides that this is not necessary. It gave Parliament a formal right to propose treaty revisions.

As regards the adoption of legislation, we now have in the EU "a classic two chamber legislature: in which the Council represents the states and the European Parliament represents the citizens" (Hix, 1999). Whether it is "classic" or not, the pooled policy making at EU level is not just a matter for governments alone, but for the directly-elected Parliament as well.

The Parliament also has a role in scrutinising the executive in the form of the European Commission. Commissioners are politicians nominated (like national ministers) by Prime Ministers or Presidents. The team of Commissioners as a whole requires the approval of a majority in Parliament to take office and, once in office, can be dismissed by (and only by) a vote of no confidence taken in the European Parliament – and both these aspects have been dramatically illustrated in recent years.

The latter – the power to dismiss the Commission, which Parliament enjoyed from the beginning, seemed rather theoretical until early 1999 when it was illustrated in a spectacular way with the dramatic resignation of the Santer Commission, described in more detail in Chapter 15. As a result of an investigation into the Commission by a committee of independent experts set up by Parliament, it became clear that there was the necessary majority in Parliament for a vote of no-confidence, and within two hours the Commission pre-empted this and resigned.

The former – the vote to approve an incoming Commission, referred to in Parliament's rules as the "election" of the Commission, was illustrated in an equally dramatic way in the autumn of 2004. The team of Commissioners put together under President-designate Barroso came before Parliament for the public hearings that Parliament insists on for every commissioner prior to its vote. It became clear that there was not a majority willing to approve the Commission without changes being made to the team, as described in detail in Chapter 14. Despite initial attempts to face down Parliament, Barroso withdrew his team just before the vote and returned three weeks later with three changes meeting Parliament's main concerns.

All this makes the EU radically different from a traditional intergovernmental organisation. Indeed, it is only necessary to imagine what the EU would be like without the Parliament: it would be a system dominated by bureaucrats and diplomats, loosely supervised by ministers flying periodically into Brussels. The existence of a body of full-time representatives in the heart of decision-taking in Brussels, asking questions, knocking on doors, bringing the spotlight to shine in dark corners, in dialogue with their constituents back home, makes the EU system more open, transparent and democratic than would otherwise be the case. MEPs are drawn from governing parties and opposition parties and represent not just capital cities but the regions in their full diversity. In short, the Parliament brings pluralism into play and brings added value to the scrutiny of EU legislation.

It also takes the edge off national conflict. Council can all too often give the appearance of decision-taking by gladiatorial combat between those representing "national interests". Reality is more complex and the fact that the Parliament organises itself not in national delegations but in Political Groups shows that the dividing line on most concrete subjects is not so much between nations but between different political viewpoints or between various sectoral interests.

A federal system in the making?

Common policy-making through common institutions in such a wide area has led many to conclude that the European Union is, or is becoming, a federal system. This conclusion depends entirely on what is meant by "federal".

Some use the term to mean a centralised super-state. In fact, this has never been the aim of the European Union and it is, indeed, far from becoming such a super-state. The European budget represents a mere 2 per cent of public expenditure, with 98 per cent remaining national or sub-national. European legislation can only be adopted in the areas defined by the treaties, which can themselves only be amended with the unanimous agreement of each and every Member State. Even within that area, no major legislation or policy can be adopted without the agreement of the Council, composed of national ministers who are members of national governments accountable to national parliaments. Disputes are settled by a Court whose members are appointed by national governments, not by the European Commission. The Commission itself, far from being the gargantuan bureaucracy of tabloid mythology, has fewer employees than an average medium-sized city and does not itself decide key policies: it simply proposes and implements.

These structural and legal safeguards against the creation of an over-centralised system are reinforced by the diverse emotional ties and commitments of European peoples. There is little danger of a Euro-nationalist hyperbole carrying people away. Furthermore, most key issues of political life are national rather than European in character: health service provision, education, housing policy, pensions, social security, law and order, the level of income tax, and so on. All these issues will remain mainly national rather than European in focus.

But if the term "federal" simply means, as in much continental usage, multi-level governance, as decentralised as possible, but centralised where necessary by means of exercising limited competences through common institutions with their own powers, then the European Union has always had a number of federal characteristics. In its field of competence, European law prevails over national law. Qualified majority voting, rather than consensual intergovernmental agreements, is the norm for adopting legislation within that field of common policy making. It has an executive, the Commission, which, once appointed, is independent of national governments, has a virtual monopoly on initiating proposals for new legislation and is given the responsibility for managing existing policies and verifying the application of Union law. It has a directly elected supra-national Parliament. It has a common Court to settle differences in interpreting

Union law. It has a budget financed by revenues which belong to the Union as of right under the treaty, not by national subscriptions. Rights are conferred directly on individual citizens by the treaty. Last but not least, the wide scope of the field of competence of the European Union goes far beyond any traditional international organisation, and most Member States share a common currency. All these are federal characteristics and it would not be distorting the meaning of the word federal to claim that the European Union is already a system of federal type (albeit a decentralised one, and without the usual competences of a federation in foreign affairs and security). In that sense, the European Parliament and the Council together constitute a federal style bicameral legislature, though with a limited field of responsibility.

Rather than argue about the theology of federalism, most governments and MEPs avoid using the term and focus more on the practicalities: what are the areas in which we need to or want to adopt common policies? What should the content of such common policies be? In those areas, how can we organise a European institutional system that is both efficient and democratic? What legislation is necessary at European level and what should it lay down? This is the stuff of day-to-day discussion and debate in the Parliament.

Table 1: *Some main events in the Parliament's history*

---

10 September 1952	ECSC Parliamentary Assembly with 78 members holds its first meeting.
1 January 1958	Treaty of Rome enters into force. Assembly (common to ECSC, EEC and EAEC) enlarged to 142 members.
30 March 1962	European Assembly decides to describe itself as European Parliament.
22 April 1970	Treaty changes give the Parliament certain budgetary powers.
16 January 1973	First meeting of enlarged Parliament following accession of the UK, Ireland and Denmark.
22 July 1975	Treaty changes giving further budgetary powers to the Parliament.
20 September 1976	Adoption by Council of act providing for direct elections.
7–10 June 1979	First direct elections to the European Parliament. Repeated every 5 years.
17 July 1979	First meeting of directly elected European Parliament of 410 members.
13 December 1979	Parliament rejects budget for the first time.
14 February 1984	European Parliament adopts Spinelli Draft Treaty on European Union.
1 July 1987	Entry into force of Single European Act allocating new powers to the Parliament and giving treaty status to the name European Parliament.
1 November 1993	Entry into force of Maastricht Treaty on European Union allocating further new powers to the European Parliament.

15 March 1999	Commission resigns when faced with probable adoption of a vote of censure by Parliament.
1 May 1999	Entry into force of Amsterdam Treaty extending Parliament's powers. Parliament and Council now effectively a bicameral legislature for most EU legislation.
1 February 2003	Entry into force of the Treaty of Nice adjusting allocation of seats for the future enlarged Parliament and further marginally increasing its powers.
July 2004	First proposed team for Barroso Commission forced to withdraw when clear no majority for it in Parliament.
July 2006	Agreement between Parliament and Council gives Parliament the right to veto certain types of Commission decision on legislative implementing measures.
1 December 2009	Entry into force of the Treaty of Lisbon, giving full co-legislative powers to Parliament in virtually all areas of EU legislative activity, the right to elect the President of the Commission and some other enhanced powers.

The style of Parliament

The European Parliament is not a "sexy" Parliament in media terms. Compared to many national parliaments, it lacks the cut and thrust of debate between government and opposition. Like the US Congress, its real work is done in committee. The plurality of languages used makes the debates far from spectacular. For these reasons among others, it gets far less coverage in the media.

But when it comes to the detail of legislative or budgetary work, MEPs shape legislation in a way that members of many national parliaments do not. In the national context, when a government publishes a bill, it is usually clear what will come out of the procedure. It is headline news if the parliament amends it against the will of the government. This is not the case in the European Parliament. A draft directive really is a draft – MEPs go through it paragraph by paragraph amending it and rewriting it. So do the ministers in the Council – and ultimately the positions of the two must be reconciled – but the net effect is that every year, thousands of amendments to draft legislation put forward by ordinary back-bench MEPs end up on the statute book and apply in 27 different countries. In national parliaments, being a back-bencher, or an opposition party MP, often offers very limited power and little job satisfaction other than the prospect of, perhaps, one day wielding ministerial power. MEPs, on the other hand, whilst not having a career path to a ministry (though a surprising number do become ministers in their Member States) can play a significant role in shaping legislation – a classical parliamentary function almost forgotten by some national parliaments.

The nature of day-to-day work is also different. One measure of a good MP in a national context is someone who is a good debater, able to score points over his or her opponents. An effective MEP is someone who is good at explaining, persuading and negotiating with colleagues from 27 different

Figure 1: *Growth in number of Members of the European Parliament*

1.	1952 – 1957	78 members
2.	1958 – 1972	142 members
3.	1973 – 1979	198 members
4.	1979 – 1981	410 members
5.	1981 – 1985	434 members
6.	1986 – 1994	518 members
7.	1994 – 1995	567 members
8.	1995 – 2004	626 members
9.	2004 – 2006	732 members
10.	2007 – 2009	785 members
11.	2009– now	736 members

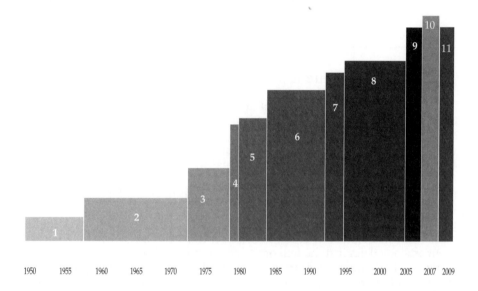

countries. This is done at three levels. First, within Political Groups, as MEPs from different national parties work towards developing a common position as a Group. Second, with other Groups in the Parliament, as no Group has an overall majority and coalitions must be built. Indeed, the type of majority can vary from one issue to another as there is no predetermined coalition, but instead a general willingness to work by means of achieving substantial majorities on most issues. Third, once Parliament has a position, there is a need to negotiate with Council for the final outcome. Such a parliamentary style leaves ample scope for an active MEP, providing that he or she is good at building the necessary majorities.

Despite the significant and growing role of the European Parliament, turnout in European elections has remained low, and even declined to less than half the electorate in the 21st Century elections. Although comparable to turnouts in mid-term congressional elections in the USA, it remains below that commonly experienced in EU Member States for national parliamentary elections (although these too have been declining in several countries by just as much). This is likely to remain the case, for a number of reasons. First, European elections will remain less significant for day to day issues than national elections, for the reasons alluded to above and because even when Parliament does deal with high profile issues, the impact on citizens is not usually immediate as most legislation is in the form of directives which will be transposed into national law some time later. Second, there is no government directly at stake in European elections and the bulk of the electorate is used to voting in national elections to keep or throw out a national government. Third, the EU institutions are inevitably more distant than national or local institutions and, as in other federal-type systems, will usually have a lower turnout (e.g. USA, Switzerland). Fourth, the lower media coverage of the European Parliament alluded to earlier. Fifth, the consensus-style decision-making at EU level, which often prevents partisan alternatives from being highlighted to the electorate. Sixth, the fact that the European Parliament only relatively recently acquired the sort of decisive powers over legislation that are normally expected of parliaments and still has a lingering reputation of being just a "talking shop".

Finally, however, there is the widespread lack of understanding of how the EU institutions actually operate. In some countries, a significant proportion of the press is overtly hostile to the EU, but in all countries there is an abundance of incorrect information, false assumptions and numerous misunderstandings in the media and among national politicians. We hope that this book can help fill the gap by improving understanding of how the European Parliament works and the contribution it makes to ensuring that the EU is open, transparent, accountable and democratic.

2.   How it is elected

Nearly all international parliamentary assemblies consist of representatives nominated from members of national parliaments. This was true of the European Parliament itself up to 1979, but since then it has been directly elected. This status is not unique – the Central American Parliament is also now directly elected – but the much greater powers of the European Parliament set it apart.

The treaties laid down that elections to the European Parliament should be by a uniform electoral procedure. After years of failing to agree such a procedure, the treaties were amended (through the Amsterdam Treaty of 1997) to allow for the adoption of "common principles" as an alternative to a totally uniform procedure. This was finally done in 2002 so as to apply from the 2004 elections. So, although elections are organised trans-nationally, the Member States have used different electoral systems, albeit with a degree of convergence in recent years.

Unlike other areas of Community law where it is the Commission that has the right of initiative, in this case it is the European Parliament itself that enjoys the right to propose a common system or common principles. Its proposal must then go to the Council, which must adopt a procedure by unanimity (and since the Maastricht Treaty of 1992 with the assent of Parliament).

Progress on moving to direct elections and then devising a uniform electoral system was slow. It was not until 1976 that the Council finally agreed on the form of direct elections, 16 years after Parliament had first submitted proposals for such elections. Moreover, Parliament submitted proposals in 1983 and 1992 for a uniform system but these remained blocked in the Council. Parliament's 1998 proposals for common principles were eventually enacted in 2002.

The present chapter is divided into five sections. The first deals with the period preceding direct elections and the Council Decision which finally enacted them. The second examines the variety of national systems in force, and the main differences between them. The third looks at the consequences of the current diversity, and at the main issues tackled in trying to draw up a uniform electoral system. The fourth examines the proposals made so far to draw up such a system. The final section surveys the seven sets of elections held so far.

Moving towards direct elections

Direct elections to a European Assembly were envisaged in the original treaties. Article 21 of the 1951 ECSC Treaty gave Member States the option of electing their own members. Article 138 of the1957 EEC Treaty stated that "the Assembly shall draw up proposals for elections by direct universal suffrage in accordance with a uniform procedure in all Member States. The Council shall, acting unanimously, lay down the appropriate procedures which it shall recommend to the Member States for adoption in accordance with their respective constitutional requirements". Parliament first put forward such proposals on 17 May 1961 (Dehousse report), and further resolutions on this subject were adopted in 1963 and 1969, but to no avail (although some national parliaments such as that of Italy considered bills unilaterally to elect their own MEPs by universal suffrage). In 1973 Parliament decided to prepare new proposals and appointed Dutch Socialist, Schelto Patijn, as rapporteur. The following year, the Paris Summit of Heads of Government decided to institutionalise their meetings in the form of the European Council, and to meet three times per year. To balance this reinforcement of the intergovernmental side of the Community, they also agreed that direct elections to the Parliament "should be achieved as soon as possible" and stated that they awaited Parliament's new proposals, on which they expected Council to act in 1976 with a view to holding direct elections in or after 1978.

Parliament's new proposals were adopted in January 1976. One of the main stumbling blocks had been the treaty requirement for a uniform electoral procedure. Patijn's strategy was to overcome this by allowing each country to use its own procedure for the first elections, and providing for the elected Parliament to make new proposals for a uniform system thereafter.

The draft put forward by Parliament suggested a five-year term of office, for members to vote on an individual and personal basis and not be bound by any instructions or mandate and for membership to be compatible with membership of the parliament of a Member State, but not membership of a national government or of the European Commission. Parliament would have 355 members, ranging from six from Luxembourg, to 67 from the UK and 71 from West Germany. Elections were to be held in principle on the same day, although individual Member States could have them a day earlier or later than the fixed date or spread them over two consecutive days. Other elements of the electoral system, including the method of filling seats that became vacant, were provisionally left to individual Member States until a uniform electoral system was adopted.

The Council Decision 76/787 (OJ 278 of 8.10.1976) approved an "Act Concerning the Election of the Representatives of the Assembly by Direct Universal Suffrage". It followed the Parliament's proposal in most respects. The most important difference concerned the sensitive issue of the number and distribution of seats between the individual Member States. The Parliament was now to have 410 members. Compared to Parliament's draft, the more populous Member States were given higher representation. Moreover, the four largest Member States, West Germany, the UK, Italy and France, were given the same total of 81 members each, even though the population of West Germany was a bit higher. Another difference from Parliament's draft was that the elections would take place over a four-day period, starting on a Thursday morning and ending on the following Sunday.

Although Council reached agreement in October 1976, it still took a further three years before the first direct elections were held (they were originally scheduled for May/June 1978, but had to be postponed for a year). The first direct elections in 1979 were thus fought under differing national legislation, although the systems chosen for the European elections were not necessarily the same as those used for national elections. France, for example, used a proportional system for the European elections with the whole country as one constituency and with a 5 per cent threshold, rather than the majority system in two rounds within single member constituencies which has been the traditional system for French domestic elections. Germany, too, created a unitary proportional system for the European elections (although retaining the traditional 5 per cent threshold) rather than the mixed constituency-list system used in national elections. Belgium and Italy introduced specific constituencies for the European elections different from national elections, as did Ireland and the UK. The last two countries retained, however, their distinctive national electoral systems: the single transferable vote (STV) in the case of Ireland, and the majority "first past the post" system in single member constituencies in the case of Great Britain (after the House of Commons had rejected the 1978 Labour government's initial proposal for a regional list system). Even the UK, however, did make an exception to its normal practice by permitting the three Northern Ireland seats to be contested under the much more proportional system of STV. Finally Denmark and Luxembourg also made substantial breaks with national practice, by having only one national constituency for the European elections rather than the smaller units used for national elections. Only the Netherlands was essentially unaffected, with one national constituency with fully proportional results being the practice for both European and national elections.

Attempts to draw up a uniform electoral system

After the 1979 elections the new Parliament set to work on achieving a uniform system, but it took over 20 years and four more sets of European elections before decisive progress was finally made. During this long period the temporary rules became increasingly entrenched, compounded by the fact that new Member States with their own national rules were continuing to join the EU, and were adding to the already considerable complexity. The most serious problem, however, remained the first-past-the post majority system that was used only in the United Kingdom (and even then not Northern Ireland), since this was not just of national significance, but had considerable effects on the overall political balance within the whole European Parliament (see below).

In 1979 the first elected Parliament established a special sub-committee of its Political Affairs Committee to deal with the issue and appointed Jean Seitlinger (EPP, France) as rapporteur. He put forward two main options, firstly a mixed system as in elections to the German Bundestag (in an attempt to reconcile proportionality with a strong constituency element and also to win over the then 60-strong British Conservative contingent) and secondly a system of proportional representation within multi-member constituencies of between three and nine members.

In March 1982 the full Parliament (by 158 votes to 77 with 27 abstentions) opted for proportional representation in multi-member constituencies of between three and 15 seats. There would be the option of preferential voting (within a list). Member States could make exceptions to take account of special geographical or other factors recognised by the constitution of a Member State. Nationals of a Member State would be able to vote and to stand for election there irrespective of their place of residence. One anomalous feature of the text, however, was that it conferred the right to stand for election on those who had been resident in a country for at least five years, but did not similarly confer the right to vote. The text was submitted to the Council, which examined it within a working party for a year, without finding the necessary unanimity, with the British posing the main, but not the only, obstacle. Eventually the Council abandoned any attempt to agree on a system for the 1984 elections, but undertook to continue this work with a view to the 1989 elections.

The 1984–89 Parliament drew up another report. Reinhold Bocklet (German CSU), the rapporteur, favoured a step-by-step approach, with agreement on a few essential issues rather than uniformity in the details. He suggested proportionality in small multi-member constituencies or in a single national constituency. Thresholds could be maintained as long as they did not exceed 5 per cent. He even mooted the idea of Member States being granted a temporary exemption from applying the agreed system. The report was adopted in committee, but only by the unconvincing majority of 16 to 8, with 13 abstentions. This was considered insufficiently strong support to bring the report to the House, and it was referred to a special working party under the chairmanship of the rapporteur. In view of continuing disagreements, however, the 1984–89 Parliament did not adopt any text. The Council was not, therefore, forced to consider any new proposal.

In the 1989–94 Parliament, responsibility was transferred to the Committee on Institutional Affairs, which chose Karel de Gucht (Flemish Liberal, later, from 2007 to 2009, Belgian Foreign Minister and since 2009 a Member of the European Commission) as rapporteur. After first adopting an interim resolution in October 1991, Parliament adopted a new set of proposals on 10 March 1993, by 216 to 79 with 19 abstentions. The basic premise was that uniformity did not require a completely identical electoral procedure but only a harmonisation of its main elements, notably the principle of proportional representation, taking account of the votes cast throughout the territory of the Member State. However, lists could be drawn up either for the whole territory of a Member State or for regional constituencies. A concession was made to the UK electoral system by enabling a Member State to retain single-member constituencies for up to two-thirds of the seats for that country. The remaining seats would have to be distributed in such a way as to ensure overall proportionality. Preference votes for individuals would be allowed. Member States would also be permitted to institute minimum thresholds of between 3 per cent and 5 per cent for parties to obtain seats. Finally, Member States could also make limited arrangements to take account of special regional features.

The Council again failed to act on the Parliament's proposal. However, the situation changed in 1997 with two crucial developments. The first was the election of a Labour government in the UK, committed to introducing proportional representation for European elections. The second was the Amsterdam Treaty agreement, providing that any European system need no longer be uniform but only "in accordance with principles common to all Member States."

To take advantage of this new flexibility, a report was drawn up by Parliament's Institutional Affairs Committee with Giorgios Anastassopoulos (Greek EPP) as rapporteur. His report (A4–0212/98) was adopted by Parliament on 15 July 1998, and included a draft act containing the basic principle that all MEPs should be elected by a list system of proportional representation. Otherwise it went into little detail. On sensitive matters, such as whether there should be electoral thresholds (of not more than 5 per cent), preferential voting and special arrangements to take account of "specific regional characteristics", it suggested that these should be optional rather than mandatory. However, Member States with more than 20 million inhabitants would have to establish regional constituencies.

The rapporteur also proposed that a certain percentage of seats should be filled on the basis of Europe-wide lists, thus strengthening the role of the transnational parties and stimulating a European campaign rather than just a series of national ones. This idea met with considerable opposition, so the compromise adopted by Parliament suggested that only 10 per cent of the total number of seats should be allocated to such a Europe-wide constituency, and that it should only be considered in 2009. (This has still not advanced, as outlined below.)

This time, Parliament's proposal was approved by Council, with only a few modifications (outlined below); Parliament gave its assent to this in June 2002 (Gil Robles Report A5-212/2002) by 399 votes to 111, and the June 2004 European elections took place on this basis. The key legal texts are thus Council Decision 2002/772/EC modifying the original 1976 Decision 76/787, that sets out the general principles of the system, as well as Council Directive 93/109/EC that governs the rights of EU citizens to vote or stand as a candidate in their country of residence. Finally, the sensitive issues of the overall size of the EP, and of the number of seats in each member state, have been tackled in successive Intergovernmental Conferences revising the treaties (see below).

As a result of these changes all the national systems used in the 2004 and 2009 elections were proportional. Nevertheless there still remain considerable differences between them. Some countries have one national constituency, whereas others have several regional constituencies. In some countries there are de jure electoral thresholds below which no seats can be won. Some countries' electoral laws provide for simple (or "closed") party lists, whose order cannot be changed by the voter, while others provide for different forms of preferential voting in which the order of candidates can be modified by the voter. In a couple of countries, voters can even vote for individual candidates from different parties. Eligibility rules for candidates still vary considerably, as do procedures for filling vacancies, national lists of incompatibilities, and a number of other issues.

Key issues in drawing up the electoral system

(i) The nature of the electoral system

A first and fundamental issue over the years has been whether there should be an obligation to have a system of **proportional representation** in all countries. The main exception in this regard was the majority system used in the

UK from 1979-1999, which could alone alter the entire political balance in the European Parliament. A small swing in votes can produce a magnified swing in seats in a "first past the post" system. This was all the more so in the large constituencies that were used for European elections with relatively fewer "safe seats". As a result the overall balance in the European Parliament could be changed more by a small swing of votes in some 40 marginal seats in Britain than by a large swing across the rest of Europe. Whichever one of the two main British parties was ahead of the other could take a near clean sweep of the British (i.e. UK excluding Northern Ireland) seats, as the Conservatives did in 1979 winning 60 of the 78 seats available, and Labour did in 1994 winning 62 out of 84. Other British parties were squeezed out entirely: the Liberal Democrats won no seats at all until 1994, despite being Europe's largest Liberal party with as much as 19.5 per cent of the vote in 1984, and the UK Greens obtained no seats with 14 per cent in 1989. This system affected the overall balance of Groups across Europe. In 1984, the European Democratic Group, of which the Conservatives were the main component, won 50 seats with 6 million votes across Europe compared with only 32 seats obtained by the Liberal Group with 10 million votes. In 1994, the Socialist Group received the bonus, keeping them larger than the EPP, despite having obtained fewer votes. The British electoral system was thus not only a British matter, but one of concern for the whole Parliament.

Table 2: *Electoral system used for 2009 European elections*

Member State	Constituency	Preference voting	Voting day for individuals	Type of proportional calculation
Austria	National	Yes, within list	Sunday	D'Hondt
Belgium	Regional	Yes, within list	Sunday	D'Hondt
Bulgaria	National	Yes, within list	Sunday	Hare-Niemeyer
Cyprus	National	Yes, within list	Saturday	Droop method/ largest remainder
Czech Rep.	National	Yes, within list	Friday-Sat.	D'Hondt
Denmark	National	Yes, within list	Sunday	D'Hondt
Estonia	National	No, simple list	Sunday	D'Hondt
Finland	National	Yes	Sunday	D'Hondt
France	Regional	No, simple list	Sunday	D'Hondt
Germany	Nat/Reg	No, simple list	Sunday	Sainte-Lagüe
Greece	National	No, simple list	Sunday	Droop/largest remainder
Hungary	National	No	Sunday	D'Hondt
Ireland	Regional	Yes, STV Variable	(Friday in 2004/2009)	Single Transf. Vote
Italy	Regional	Yes, within list	Saturday/Sunday	Hare-Niemeyer
Latvia	National	Yes, within list	Saturday	Sainte-Lagüe
Lithuania	National	Yes, within list	Sunday	Hare/largest remainder
Luxembourg	National	Yes	Sunday	Hagenbach-Bischoff
Malta	National	Yes	Saturday	Single Transf. Vote
Netherlands	National	Yes, within list	Thursday	D'Hondt
Poland	Regional	Yes	Sunday	D'Hondt (overall national result)+ Hare-Niemeyer (distribution among regional candidates)
Portugal	National	No, simple list	Sunday	D'Hondt
Romania	National	No	Sunday	D'Hondt
Slovenia	National	Yes, within list	Sunday	D'Hondt

Member State	Constituency	Preference voting	Voting day for individuals	Type of proportional calculation
Slovakia	National	Yes, within list	Saturday	Droop
Spain	National	No, simple list	Sunday	D'Hondt
Sweden	National	Yes, within list	Sunday	Modified Sainte-Lagüe
UK-GB	Regional	No, simple list	Thursday	D'Hondt
UK-NI		Yes, STV	Thursday	Single Transf. Vote

The Irish system of the single transferable vote (STV), which is also used in Northern Ireland and in Malta, is also not entirely proportional. The Irish Labour Party, for example, could be said to have been over-represented in 1979 with four of the 15 seats on 14.5 per cent of the first preference vote but under-represented in 1984 with none on over 8 per cent. Nevertheless the distorting impact of STV is much less.

There has been a wide range of electoral systems used in the other countries, but whatever their other shortcomings they were all broadly proportional in their effects, and have had little or no disproportionate impact on the political balance of the Parliament.

There was, thus, broad support within Parliament for the principle of proportional representation to be introduced as a central element of any uniform electoral system. A simple majority voting system was generally felt to be inappropriate for the European Parliament, where the objective is to achieve fair representation of major currents of opinion rather than to form a stable government majority as in national parliaments.

Once the UK had changed over to a regional list system in 1999, there was no longer any serious obstacle to reaching agreement on this issue. The 2002 Council Decision thus now sets out the clear principle that "in each Member State, members of the European Parliament shall be elected on the basis of proportional representation, using the list system or the single transferable vote". There are several other references in the text to the need for an essentially proportional system but there is no requirement for a single system of proportional representation. Apart from the three above mentioned cases of STV, all use a list system, but with various methods of calculating proportionality, some being more favourable to smaller parties than others. The most common is the d'Hondt system but Hare-Niemeyer is used in several countries, Sainte-Lagüe and modified Sainte-Lagüe in Latvia and Sweden respectively, Hagenbach-Bischoff in Luxembourg and the Droop Quotient in Cyprus and Slovakia. Poland even uses two systems, d'Hondt for the nation-wide outcome, and Hare-Niemeyer for the subsequent attribution of seats to specific lists.

A second important issue has been the **size of constituencies**. There has been considerable (and probably growing) recognition of the advantages of regional rather than national constituency representation in terms, in particular, of strengthening links between the electors and the elected, and of bringing local or regional concerns more to the forefront. However, only a few countries have such systems (see above). In other countries it is sometimes implicit, in that individuals on party lists may well represent particular regions or interest groups, but there is no guarantee of this.

The most purely proportional systems, those where the entire country is the electoral area, are those where the constituency element is inevitably weakest. On the other hand, the more constituencies there are, and the smaller the electoral areas, the less proportional is the overall result.

There has been considerable discussion of other ways of reconciling these elements such as through a mixed system as used in German federal elections (and now for the Scottish Parliament and Welsh Assembly), in which a number of members are directly elected in single member constituencies and others are elected on national lists to "top up" the parties and provide a more proportional overall outcome.

Another possibility, the STV system used in Ireland, Northern Ireland and Malta, appears to be too unfamiliar to win widespread support.

Many continue, however, to support national list systems. Certain central governments, for example, such as that of Spain, have been concerned about the effect regionally-based systems might have for regional parties such as those in Catalonia and the Basque country, which might be expected to use such systems to further their case for greater regional autonomy or independence. Opposition has also come from certain small national parties able to win, say, 5–10 per cent of the vote, which would give them seats in a national constituency, but not enough to win seats in small regional constituencies. Thus the Green and Communist parties in France were able to help block the proposals of their Socialist coalition partners in the Jospin government to move to regional lists for the 1999 elections. However, France did subsequently move from a single national constituency to a regional constituency list system in time for the 2004 elections.

It was on this issue of national or regional constituencies that there was one of the few significant differences between the principles advocated by the Parliament on the basis of the Anastassopoulos report and the final Decision that was adopted by the Council. The Parliament had advocated making a system of territorial constituencies compulsory for all Member States whose population exceeded 20 million, which would thus have forced Spain, for example, to abandon its single national constituency.

The Council Decision, however, only left this as an option. "In accordance with its specific national situation, each Member State may establish constituencies for election to the European Parliament or subdivide its electoral area in a different manner, without altering the essentially proportional nature of the electoral system". 20 of the 27 Member States have currently opted for a single national constituency, whereas Belgium, France, Ireland, Italy and the UK have opted for regional constituencies. Germany and Poland have hybrid systems with constituency elements. Of course, six Member States elect fewer than ten MEPs and are unlikely to sub-divide into constituencies.

A third contentious issue has been whether **preferential voting** should be allowed. There has been some criticism of simple or closed lists (especially those at national level), where the voters have no possibility of altering the order of the lists of candidates put up by the parties by expressing a preference between individual candidates (and in 1998 in the UK the proposal for closed lists became the main reason – or rather excuse! – for the conflict between the Commons and the Lords over the proposed electoral system). It is felt by some to give too much power to the parties, as a candidate placed by a major party at the top of the list is certain to be elected (although no more so than a candidate in a "safe seat" in a single member constituency).

There has thus been some support for allowing voters to express a preference for individual candidates within a party list, or even (as where STV is used, or under the system of "panachage" in Luxembourg) between candidates of different parties, but others are concerned that such systems turn the electoral battle into fights within parties instead of between them. The Council Decision of 2002 thus leaves preferential list voting only as an option for a Member State. A majority have now opted for some kind of preferential voting, although the scope of preferential voting is very different from one system to another, being greatest where STV is used and in Luxembourg, where voters can express preferences not just within one list, but across lists. In Sweden voters can both override the order of lists (if a candidate receives at least 5% of the total number of votes cast for his or her list), and can even add new names on blank ballots. On the other hand nine countries have opted for systems without preferential voting (see Table 2).

A fourth issue has been that of **minimum thresholds** for a party to gain a share of the seats. The main argument against de jure thresholds (there will always be de facto thresholds, especially in more regionally based systems) is that they exclude small but significant elements of public opinion. The argument in their favour is that they can help to avoid fragmentation and make it more difficult for small extremist parties to obtain a political platform. The 2002 Council Decision now permits this as an option for a Member State, which may set a minimum threshold for the allocation of seats, as long as this does not exceed 5% of the votes cast at national level. At present Germany, Hungary, Lithuania, Poland, the Czech Republic and Slovakia all have 5% national thresholds. Sweden, Austria and now Italy have a lower threshold of 4%. Romania has also introduced a national threshold of 5%, but this only applies to parties rather than to independent candidates (thus permitting Elena Basescu, the daughter of the current President, to be elected in 2009 with 4.22% of the vote).The new French system, on the other hand, has introduced 5% thresholds in each of its regional constituencies

A final issue has been whether allowances should be made for specific geographical or **regional circumstances**, such as the seat reserved for the German speaking minority in Belgium. This is apparently now covered by the phrase in the 2002 Council Decision that national electoral provisions "may if appropriate take account of the specific situation in the Member States", as long as the essentially proportional nature of the system is not compromised.

(ii) Conditions applying to candidates

Rules on **eligibility** to be a candidate have also changed. Originally, candidates usually had to be a national of the Member State in which they wished to stand and in some countries they also had to be domiciled in that country. An early exception was Italy which by 1989 was already permitting candidates from any Member State, thus allowing former UK Liberal leader David Steel to stand in the Central Italy constituency and Maurice Duverger, the French political scientist, to be elected on the Italian Communist ticket. The UK was also an exception in permitting any Commonwealth or Irish citizen to stand (as in national elections), thus allowing Christine Crawley (then Irish) and Anita Pollack (Australian) to be elected as Labour MEPs in 1984 and 1989 respectively. Council Directive 93/109/EC of 6 December 1993 (implementing Article 8B of the Maastricht Treaty) now allows any European Union citizen to stand as a candidate in their country of residence under the same conditions as citizens of that country. A temporary derogation was initially permitted for Luxembourg, with its exceptionally high percentage of resident foreigners.

The new law has so far led to only a handful of Members being elected in countries other than their own (see Table 3). The most remarkable case has been Danny Cohn-Bendit, A German citizen elected in Germany from 1994-1999, in France from 1999-2004, in Germany again from 2004-2009, and then again in France from 2009 onwards. In the longer term, and to a degree in practice already, there is a strong case for allowing any EU citizen to stand anywhere in the European elections irrespective of nationality or residence (although they will generally be at a practical disadvantage compared to local candidates).

In other respects eligibility rules for candidates still vary considerably. Age limits, for example, vary between 18 years (Austria, Denmark, Finland, Germany, Hungary, Malta, Netherlands, Portugal, Slovenia, Spain and Sweden), 21 (Belgium, Bulgaria, Czech Republic, Estonia, Ireland, Latvia, Lithuania, Luxembourg, Poland, Slovakia and United Kingdom), 23 (France and Romania) and 25 (Cyprus, Greece, Italy). In some countries candidates must be nominated by political parties, in others independents can also stand. Some countries require deposits, others lists of signatures. There are differing rules on the length of campaign and on election expenses, and on whether public money is available to meet certain party expenses. As some feel strongly about these issues no consensus has yet emerged to include common rules, although the persistence of national rules has led to some significant differences in practice, such as those regarding independent candidacies, or prisoners' entitlements to vote.

Table 3: *Non-nationals elected to European Parliament (date first elected)*

Year	Name	Nationality	Member State of Election	Group/Party
1984	Christine Crawley	Irish	UK	Socialist
1989	Anita Pollack	Australian	UK	Socialist
	Maurice Duverger	French	Italy	GUE
1994	Wilmya Zimmermann	Dutch	Germany	Socialist
	Olivier Dupuis	Belgian	Italy	Radical
1999	Daniel Cohn-Bendit	German	France	Green
	Monica Frassoni	Italian	Belgium	Green
	Frédérique Ries	Luxemb.	Belgium	Liberal
2001	Miguel Mayol i Raynal	French	Spain	Green
2004	Bairbre de Brun	Irish	UK	GUE
	Willem Schuth	Dutch	Germany	Liberal
	Daniel Stroz	German	Czech Rep.	GUE
	Ari Vatanen	Finnish	France	EPP-ED
2009	Marta Andreasen	Spanish	UK	EFD
	Anna Maria Corazza Bildt	Italian	Sweden	EPP
	Derk Jan Eppink	Dutch	Belgian	ECR

Note: (1) Dual-nationals not included in table. (2) Members re-elected not repeated.

One issue where some aspects are covered by common rules and others not is that of **incompatibilities**. The existing list in the 1976 Act was extended by the 2002 Act to cover additional EU posts such as the EU Ombudsman and the members of the Board of the European Central Bank. National law still varies greatly as regards certain other incompatibilities. In a country like Italy it has been possible to be the mayor of a big city at the same time as being an MEP, whereas in others this is not possible. Claude Desama, for example, a long-serving Belgian MEP, had to resign in 2001 when he was elected as mayor of the small city of Verviers, which was only just over the permitted Belgian threshold of 50,000 inhabitants.

A related issue where there has been increasing impetus to act has been that of the **dual mandate**, and whether an MEP could also be a member of a national parliament. There have been differing points of view on this subject. The main and progressively more powerful argument against the dual mandate was that membership of the European Parliament was becoming a very demanding full-time job, and could not be combined with another such job without the member's performance and attendance being undercut in both parliaments. The main arguments in favour were that the dual mandate, if used sparingly, permitted a number of very well known national politicians to stand for, and hence give publicity to, the European Parliament, and that it enabled stronger links to be maintained between the European Parliament and national parliaments.

As mentioned above, the Council's 1976 Act expressly permitted members of national parliaments also to be members of the European Parliament, but three Member States (Belgium, Portugal and Spain) went against this and began to forbid it (possibly illegally) in their national legislation, and a further country (Greece) only allowed it on a very limited scale. Moreover, even in countries where there were no such formal restrictions, it was often informally discouraged and a large number of political parties either began to forbid it in their statutes or in practice. Over time, France and especially Italy became the only countries to have a large number of dual mandate MEPs.

In 1988 the European Parliament adopted a report by its Committee on Legal Affairs prepared by the British Labour MEP, Geoff Hoon, in favour of prohibiting dual membership of the European Parliament and national parliaments (although not of regional assemblies), a position Parliament later reiterated when working out proposals on a uniform electoral procedure and on a members' statute. (Ironically, Hoon himself later became a dual mandate member for two years, after being elected to the House of Commons in 1992 and before standing down from the European Parliament at the 1994 elections).

The issue was finally settled in the 2002 Council Decision which provided that, "from the European Parliament elections in 2004, the office of Member of the European Parliament shall be incompatible with that of member of a national parliament". Two limited derogations to this were granted to the UK (for members of the UK Parliament who had been MEPs during the 1999-2004 Parliament, and who, if re-elected in 2004, could keep their dual mandate until 2009) and to Ireland (for members of the Irish Parliament elected to the European Parliament at the subsequent poll and who could keep their dual mandate until the next Irish Parliamentary elections).

As a result of these derogations there were 7 dual mandate MEPs in the

2004-2009 Parliament, two British members of the House of Lords and 5 members of the Irish Parliament (4 members of the Dáil and 1 Senator). After the 2009 elections there were no longer any dual mandate members. Sarah Ludford, a life peer in the British House of Lords, was re-elected to the European Parliament as a Liberal Democrat, but is subject to the European Parliament (House of Lords Disqualification) Regulations of 2008, whereby she is disqualified from sitting or voting in the House of Lords, or in any of its committees during her term of office as MEP.

Another controversial issue in the past was that of **rotation**, where candidates give an undertaking to their political parties to give up their seat after a certain time so they can be replaced by another candidate on the list. This was first used on a major scale by the French Gaullist party (the RPR) in 1979: their MEPs were meant to stand down after one year, so that in theory about 70 of their candidates would have entered the European Parliament in the course of the Parliament's five-year term. This so-called "tourniquet" or "turnstile" system was challenged by some MEPs who considered that it violated the terms of the 1976 Act which stipulated that members were elected for five-year terms, and were not to receive any binding instructions from outside. The issue was twice examined by Parliament's competent committee (Sieglerschmidt reports), which concluded that the system was legally acceptable but politically objectionable. This, and the fact that the system did not work smoothly in practice, with some RPR members refusing to resign, led the RPR to abandon the "tourniquet". Rotation of members has only been very sparingly used by other parties (e.g. the German Greens from 1984 to 1989; the French Greens from 1989 to 1994, who practically all stood down after two-and-a-half years to make way for the next members in their list; and the Italian Greens, who devised a more complicated system of rotation). This practice has now been generally abandoned.

Another important set of differences is on **methods of filling vacancies**, for example by the next candidate on the list (the most common system), by designated substitutes (for example, Belgium and, optionally, Germany) or through special by-elections (UK until 1999). Ireland found itself in particular trouble in this regard, as it had a system of nomination by the party holding the vacant seat, which cut out the voter completely. This has now been replaced by a system of designated substitutes.

(iii) The right to vote

Rights to vote also differed until 1994. In some countries it followed the nationality principle without qualifications, so that all citizens of that country could vote in the European elections irrespective of where they lived in the world or, for some countries, in the Union. In other countries, such as Ireland, voters lose their rights if they live outside their country. On the other hand, Ireland was quick to give the vote in European elections to resident citizens of other European Union countries. Similar rights were granted in Belgium and the Netherlands, provided that a foreign resident's home country had not given them the right to vote. The UK permitted resident Irish and Commonwealth citizens to vote as well as stand for election with the latter still being the only non-EU citizens allowed to vote in EP elections.

As a result of the Maastricht Treaty, a major reform was introduced

(Council Directive of 6 December 1993, see above). Besides being able to stand as a candidate, any European Union citizen is now allowed to vote in his or her country of residence. The conditions for exercising this new right, however, have by no means been uniform. In some countries (Denmark, Ireland, Netherlands), resident EU citizens were automatically entered on the electoral register. In others an EU citizen had to register in person, sometimes on the basis of full and timely information from the national government concerned, and sometimes not. In one country (Slovenia) a minimum of 5 years residence was first required, in another (Malta) a Maltese ID card was needed, and initial declarations might have to be subsequently renewed. In practice, therefore, a certain measure of discrimination still remains in a number of EU countries between local nationals and other EU citizens.

Another factor is that whereas the residence principle has been considered by many to be the more "European" option, some EU citizens still have much more interest in, and understanding of the political system of their country of origin than that of their country of residence, and would thus prefer to continue to vote on the basis of their nationality.

Whether for these reasons, apathy, or lack of awareness of this new right, or because they could still vote in their own country, relatively few of the nearly 9 million EU citizens resident in EU countries other than their own have availed themselves of their new legal rights since the possibility was first introduced in 1994.

In some countries non-national EU citizens are now very numerous in absolute and/or percentage terms, with almost 2 million resident in Spain and 77,000 in Cyprus. The percentage of these who were actually registered to vote in 2009 remains relatively low, but increased sharply between the 2004 and 2009 elections in certain EU countries, such as France (from 145,000 to over 200,000) and in Spain (from 130,000 to 284,000).

In others there was less progress. In Denmark, for example, there was a 66% increase from 2004 to 2009 in resident non-national EU citizens of voting age (from 58,000 to 97,000), but only a 7% increase (from 15,600 to 16,800) in those actually registered to vote. Although the figures provided in some countries are not sufficiently detailed, the Commission, from whom the above figures all stem, has calculated that the proportion of citizens living in another Member State and registered to vote there had gone up to 11.6% by 2009 compared to only 5.9% in 1994. The Commission and Parliament are now looking at ways in which this figure can be further increased in the future, and current obstacles reduced.

Several other issues related to voting should also be mentioned. The **minimum age to vote** is uniformly 18, with the exception of Austria where it has been lowered to 16. **Compulsory voting** is the law in four countries (Belgium, Cyprus, Greece and Luxembourg), and has been deemed a civic duty in Italy. A more problematic matter has been that of the **polling day** for European elections. This has had two aspects, the month in which they are held, and the actual day on which voting takes place in different countries. As regards the first issue, all the elections so far have taken place in June. In its resolution approving its draft Act on the Uniform Electoral Procedure the European Parliament suggested that the elections be held, instead, in May, in order to avoid the school holidays beginning in June in a number of Member States, and thus helping to raise turnout. This was not followed by the Council, not as a matter of principle, but because all alternative dates seemed to pose a problem for one Member State or another. The European elections in 2004 and 2009 thus again took place in June, albeit earlier in the month in 2009. The 2002 Act, however, does provide scope for a change to May, if an acceptable date can be found in the future.

The other issue of the actual voting day has been left to national custom. Some have argued that having a single voting day for the whole of Europe would help to increase the profile of the elections, but this point of view has not prevailed, and the elections have always taken place within a four day time span. In the majority of countries voting day in the 2009 elections was on Sunday, but the Netherlands and UK kept their traditional voting day of Thursday. In Ireland voting day is variable but was Friday on this occasion. In the Czech Republic the elections took place on Friday afternoon and Saturday morning, in Cyprus, Latvia and Slovakia on Saturday, and in Italy on Saturday afternoon and Sunday.

One practical problem posed by this staggered voting over four days concerns the need to keep the outcome secret until after the last countries have voted on Sunday. In 2004 and 2009 the pattern of the Dutch results was already clear by Thursday evening, and was then publicised in the media. Exit polls were also available early in other countries, such as Latvia, which voted on Saturday. Tougher definitions may thus be required in the future of the term "officially made public".

Finally a special problem has been that of **Gibraltar**, and whether its inhabitants should have the right to vote in European Parliament elections. Because of the sensitive status of Gibraltar no voting rights were given to Gibraltarians in the five elections from 1979-1999, in spite of numerous protests. In 2004, however, and after a judgement in their favour in 1999 in the European Court of Human Rights (Matthews case) they were finally allowed to vote, not in a separate constituency, but by being attached to the south-west constituency in the UK.

(iv) Finance

Should there be public financing of parties' election campaigns for the Parliament? If so, there are further questions about the extent to which such support should be granted before election day on the basis of a party or Group's size, or afterwards on the basis of results actually achieved. This is a matter of great sensitivity, not only because some Union countries provide for public funding of elections, whereas others do not, but also because of the extent to which the system might favour established parties rather than new ones.

The above issues came to the fore when the French Greens challenged the Parliament's budgetary allocations for information campaigns which were distributed to individual political parties through the Political Groups (see Chapter 5). The sums involved were substantial, and the whole system was felt by many parties with few or no members in the Parliament to discriminate strongly against their interests. The European Court of Justice eventually found in favour of the French Greens, primarily on the grounds that it was *ultra vires* for Parliament to have developed what amounted to public financial support for parties in the absence of a uniform electoral system. Since then the Groups' funds cannot be used for electoral campaigning.

(v) The number of seats

The **overall composition** of the European Parliament has changed greatly since before direct elections, when it only had 198 members, fewer than either of the two largest Political Groups in the 2009 Parliament. It continued to grow steadily after the successive enlargements from 410 after the first direct elections to 626 in the 1999-2004 Parliament. Parliament had itself suggested that the upper limit on its size should be 700, and this was accepted by the Member States and incorporated into the Amsterdam Treaty, but later revised upwards to 732 in the Treaty of Nice (see final chapter), and subsequently adjusted to 736. After the accession of Bulgaria and Romania the number rose to 785 members for the second half of the 2004-09 parliamentary term, since the number of MEPs from the existing Member States remained the same until the next elections (as happened in May 2004, when the 626 existing MEPs were joined by 162 MEPs from the 10 new Member States, and the total number briefly went up to 788 until after the June elections).

The Lisbon Treaty provides for 751 MEPs, with 12 countries gaining a total of 18 seats (4 more from Spain, 2 more from Austria, France and Sweden, and 1 more from Bulgaria, Italy, Latvia, Malta, the Netherlands, Poland, Slovenia and the United Kingdom), and one country (Germany) losing 3 seats. It had been hoped that the Lisbon Treaty would be in force by the 2009 elections, but it was only ratified afterwards, and 736 MEPs were thus elected under Nice Treaty rules. The European Council later agreed that a Protocol be adopted, and then ratified by all Member States, in order to implement this increase during the lifetime of the 2009-2014 Parliament, but without penalising Germany, so that it can be allowed to keep its current total of 99 MEPs until the next elections in 2014. The EP decided in principle that, after signature of the Protocol, but pending its ratification, the additional Members would be able to take their seats already as observers (non-voting Members).

How the additional MEPs are chosen has proved to be controversial. Most Member States are simply taking the person(s) who would have been elected had the extra seat already been in place at the time of the election – and indeed the extra seat often featured in the 2009 election campaign. France, however, announced its intention to nominate the two extra MEPs from the French Parliament. There were strong objections to this by many in the EP as a matter of principle, which held up the procedure for several months in an ultimately unsuccessful attempt to make the French government think again. In the Italian Parliament a vote had to be taken on which method of calculation would be used, as each would give the additional Italian seat to a different party.

Once this is implemented, and with 3 additional German Members elected under Nice Treaty rules being allowed to stay until the end of the legislature, there will then be 754 MEPs until the 2014 elections, maintaining the EP's place as one of the largest chambers not just in the EU but in the world, just smaller than the UK House of Lords.

What will happen after future EU enlargement, notably if large countries like Turkey or Ukraine enter, is unclear. Under the treaty, they must fit within the ceiling of 751 members, with a consequent re-distribution of seats. Previous experience, however, suggests that Member States may prefer to change the treaty to increase the size of the EP. This would pose difficult questions about the logistics and functioning of an ever larger Parliament.

Difficult questions are also posed about the related issue of the **distribution of seats** between the different countries, large, medium and small, within the European Union. In theory one of the central elements of a uniform electoral system should be approximate equality between the number of people per seat in each country. However, this is balanced by the need to ensure that smaller countries have adequate representation. These two divergent concerns are often met in bi-cameral systems with one chamber elected proportionally to population and another representing the component states equally (e.g. US Senate) or with only slight weighting (e.g. German Bundesrat). In the Union, it is in the Council that the Member States are represented as such, and originally Member States were indeed represented with only a slight weighting (2 to 10 votes, according to size). However, the Council now includes both elements within its own voting rules, with two scales, a population key and another key of one vote per state. In Parliament, the weighting is described as "degressive proportionality" with an advantage to small countries. The result is that Luxembourg has one MEP per 81,000 inhabitants, and Malta one per 82,000 whereas Spain has one per 906,000 inhabitants and France one per 885,000. Germany, which has the most MEPs, and one MEP per 830,000 inhabitants, is actually better off in this respect than Spain, France and the UK, and in a very similar position to Italy (see Table 4 below). Compared to the pre-enlargement Parliament, this discrepancy has declined considerably, but others have opened up among some of the smaller countries. Slovenia, for example, has only one more MEP than Luxembourg, and a Slovene MEP represents almost four times more people than his or her Luxembourg or Maltese equivalent. Once the Lisbon Treaty corrections are made (see Table 4), the existing discrepancies will be mitigated, but a few will still remain.

A particularly controversial issue in the past, however, has been the balance between the largest Member States. As we saw above, the EP's own proposals before direct elections would have given a few more seats to Germany, to reflect its slightly larger population, but the Council opted, instead, for equality in the number of seats between the four largest countries, Germany, UK, Italy and France. In 1990–91 this equality of treatment was put into question when Germany's population increased by 16 million as a result of unification with the former East Germany. There was also the immediate issue of representation of the 16 million East Germans within the European Parliament. West German members could hardly resign to make way for them, since all members had been elected for a five-year term and they naturally felt that extra seats should be created for the new German citizens (and even if they did resign, their seat would go to the next candidate on their party list). But creating new members of the European Parliament for the former East Germany could not be done overnight, since it necessitated a controversial treaty change that would have to be negotiated and then ratified by the Member States.

The ad hoc solution that was adopted (on 12 July 1990) was to nominate 18 observers ("Beobachter") from the former East Germany (who came initially from the former East German Parliament but were later chosen by the German Bundestag). These observers could attend plenaries (where they sat in special seats at the back) and committees and were also integrated into their respective Political Groups. They had speaking rights in committee and in their Groups but not in plenary, and had no voting rights nor the right to become Parliament office-holders. They could not table questions, resolutions or amendments, and could only take part in the work of the interparliamentary delegations in Brussels, Luxembourg or Strasbourg.

This unsatisfactory situation was only intended to be a temporary solution since the case for German membership to be increased was unanswerable. In 1991 the European Parliament voted by 241 votes in favour to 62 against (38 of which were French) and 39 abstentions to support an increase of German membership to 99. However, this solution was not accepted by the European Council meeting at Maastricht in December 1991, despite being endorsed by the preparatory meeting of foreign ministers. The issue was then postponed with a view to taking a decision in 1992. Parliament then proposed (De Gucht Report, June 1992) a solution that not only increased the number of German seats but also, to a lesser degree, those of the other large and medium-sized Member States (especially the Netherlands, which was curiously under-represented before). Parliament's new proposal was endorsed without modification by the December 1992 Edinburgh European Council and ratified by the Member States. As a result, the increase of 18 in the number of German seats was accompanied by an increase of six seats each for the three next largest countries, the UK, France and Italy. Five other countries were also given more seats, so that the result of increasing German representation by 18 seats was an overall increase of 49 seats in the size of the EP.

This balance between the biggest Member States was again changed in the Treaty of Nice to prepare for forthcoming enlargements to twelve new countries. Germany retained 99 seats but all other EU countries (except Luxembourg) were given reduced representation. The Czech Republic and Hungary were given two fewer seats than Belgium, Portugal and Greece in spite of their similar number of inhabitants, but this obvious anomaly was subsequently corrected in their Accession Treaty. France, UK and Italy went down to 72 seats each, and all other "old" Member States also lost seats, albeit in two stages (2004 following the accession of ten new countries, and 2009 following the accession of Romania and Bulgaria).

The Lisbon Treaty made a further significant change, first by lowering the number of German members from 99 to the new maximum figure of 96, but also by breaking the equality between the next biggest countries of France, the UK and Italy. France, which now has a considerably larger population than Italy, in particular, will have 74 seats. It had originally been intended that the UK would have 73 seats and Italy 72, but Italy fought to keep an extra seat, and this was eventually achieved, so that both countries have 73 seats. At the other end of the spectrum, a new minimum has been established of 6 seats, so that Malta will move up from 5 to 6 seats.

The EP has itself played a key role in these issues concerning its own composition, and has put forward, most recently in its 2007 resolution on this issue, the concept of "degressive proportionality" as its key guiding principle in this respect. The ratio between the population and the number of seats of each Member State must thus vary in relation to their respective populations. There should also be respect for the principle of "solidarity", "whereby the more populous states agree to be under-represented in order to allow the less populous States to be represented better". An upper ceiling needs to be established under the principle of "efficiency" and a minimum number of seats under the principle of "plurality", "by allowing the main constituents of the spectrum of political opinion in each Member State – particularly the majority and the opposition – to be represented". This whole issue is again being re-examined within the Parliament, and one of the likely recommendations is that the number of seats per Member State should be re-evaluated, in the light of population and other changes, before each new set of elections. In the meantime the likely forthcoming accession of Croatia will immediately put the existing system to the test; with its 4.4 million inhabitants, it would be entitled, under the present key, to 12 seats in the Parliament.

Table 4: *Number of MEPs per country and ratio to population*

(2009 figures, from table in working document of 19 May 2010 by Andrew Duff on a proposal for a modification of the Act concerning the election of the members of the European Parliament)

Country	Population (million)	Seats in 2009 elections	Seats in line with Lisbon Treaty	2009 elections Inhabitants per MEP	Lisbon Treaty allocation Inhabitants per MEP
Germany	82.0	99	96(-3) (99 until 2014)	830,000	854,000 (830,000 until 2014)
France	64.4	72	74(+2)	885,000	862,000
UK	61.6	72	73(+1)	850,000	838,000
Italy	60.0	72	73(+1)	828,000	817,000
Spain	45.8	50	54(+4)	906,000	839,000
Poland	38.1	50	51(+1)	762,000	747,000
Romania	21.5	33	33	653,000	653,000
Netherlands	16.5	25	26(+1)	656,000	631,000
Greece	11.3	22	22	510,000	510,000
Belgium	10.7	22	22	485,000	485,000
Portugal	10.6	22	22	483,000	483,000
Czech Republic	10.5	22	22	472,000	472,000
Hungary	10.0	22	22	457,000	457,000
Sweden	9.3	18	20(+2)	510,000	459,000
Austria	8.4	17	19(+2)	490,000	439,000
Bulgaria	7.6	17	18(+1)	449,000	424,000
Denmark	5.5	13	13	421,000	421,000
Slovakia	5.4	13	13	415,000	415,000
Finland	5.3	13	13	408,000	408,000
Ireland	4.4	12	12	367,000	367,000
Lithuania	3.3	12	12	281,000	281,000
Latvia	2.3	8	9(+1)	284,000	252,000
Slovenia	2.0	7	8(+1)	289,000	253,000

[continues over]

Country	Population (million)	Seats in 2009 elections	Seats in line with Lisbon Treaty	2009 elections Inhabitants per MEP	Lisbon Treaty allocation Inhabitants per MEP
Estonia	1.3	6	6	223,000	223,000
Cyprus	0.8	6	6	132,000	132,000
Luxembourg	0.5	6	6	81,000	81,000
Malta	0.4	5	6(+1)	82,000	68,000
EU	499.7	736	751 (754 until 2014)		

Besides the number of seats per country, a further sensitive issue has been whether there should be an additional **Europe-wide constituency**, in order to provide a more European and not just national dimension to the elections. This option had been forcefully advocated by Giorgios Anastassopoulos in his 1998 report on the uniform electoral system, although Parliament's final resolution (see above) eventually called for a European constituency of 10% of the total number of seats only to be considered as a possibility to be introduced from the 2009 European elections. Even this proposal was not followed by the Council; Parliament's subsequent resolution accepted this, but called for the issue to be examined at a later date. Indeed, the Constitutional Affairs Committee of the Parliament is now re-examining this issue in its review of the Act concerning the election of the Members of the Parliament. UK Liberal Democrat Andrew Duff is its rapporteur, and he has advocated a Euro constituency of 25 seats, which would be added to the existing total. The idea will continue to be highly controversial, not least because it would require a treaty amendment ratified by every Member State.

A final word should be added on transitional solutions to EP membership, namely the creation of **observer status** within the European Parliament for parliamentarians from countries about to join the European Union. As we have seen above, this was originally devised in the context of German unification to deal with the problem of unrepresented East German citizens. It has since been extended to provide for limited participation within the EP for national parliamentarians from candidate countries in the period immediately preceding their accession to the EU. From 2003 to 2004, therefore, there were 162 observers from the 10 candidate countries. In the plenary they were literally observers, being given seats but without the right to speak or vote, whereas they had fuller rights in their Political Groups and in committee meetings, where they could speak but not vote. They also had limited office facilities. After enlargement had taken place they then became full members of the European Parliament, for one session in May 2004. Relatively few of the 162 observers, however, went on to become full members of the European Parliament after the June 2004 elections. Observer status was again created for 35 national parliamentarians from Romania and 18 from Bulgaria for a year prior to their accession, and the possibility of observer status was envisaged again in 2010, as described above for the additional members arising from the Lisbon Treaty, pending them taking up their seats.

The European elections so far

Seven sets of European elections have been held so far, in 1979, 1984, 1989, 1994, 1999, 2004 and 2009. (For a detailed analysis of results by country, see the tables in Appendix 1.) A few brief general observations can be made. European elections can still more accurately be characterised as a set of different national elections than as coordinated Europe-wide campaigns. The issues have tended to be primarily domestic, and the elections used to test governments' (and oppositions') popularity or unpopularity. In some countries the European elections have been on the same day as national elections, making it even more difficult to separate the issues and provide a distinctly European identity to the European elections.

Nevertheless, European issues have gradually come more to the forefront, be it specific issues such as EU environmental and social legislation and regional policy, or else the EU's general development, with some parties or lists opposing, for instance, the Maastricht and Amsterdam Treaties or the euro. Moreover, certain political families have campaigned on common manifestos throughout Europe, such as the Party of European Socialists, the European People's Party, the European Liberals and the Greens. National party use of these manifestos is still very variable, but they have generally grown in importance from one European election to the next.

The **turnout** in the elections has also varied greatly from country to country. Overall, it has gradually declined (see Figure 2 below), but not uniformly (for example the turnout in Denmark and Sweden was higher in 2009 than in any EP election since they joined). It is generally lower than for national elections in Europe for the reasons outlined above, but, as pointed out, is now roughly similar to the turnout in mid-term congressional elections in the United States. The downward trend (loss of over 20 percentage points from 1979 to 2009) mirrors a trend in national and local elections in many Member States over the same period. For example, there was a drop of 20 percentage points in the German Bundestag elections between 1976 and 2009; and of 21 percentage points in French Assembly elections between 1973 and 2007.

The decline is therefore not peculiar to the European Parliament, but is a challenge faced by democracy at all levels. A matter of particular concern is the continuing low turnout in most of the new Member States in central and eastern Europe in both national and European elections. In the 2009 European elections, turnout was below 30% in 6 out of the 10 countries, and below the EU average of 43% in 8 of them. On the other hand turnout also went up in 6 out of the 10, including the two biggest increases in turnout in any EU country in Latvia and Estonia.

The Commission carried out a post-election public survey to measure possible variables to increase turnout. Responses indicated that the three top measures that could boost citizens' motivation to vote were: more information provided on the impact of the European Union on their daily life (84%), more information provided on the programmes and objectives of candidates and parties in the European Parliament (83%) and more information provided on the European Parliament elections themselves (80%). These three suggestions were supported by a majority of respondents in every single Member State.

Figure 2: *Turnout in European Parliament elections*

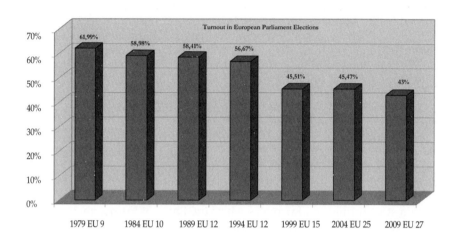

But there are other factors besides lack of information (always an easy answer in surveys). Like local elections, European elections are considered to be of secondary importance compared to national elections: no government is at stake, merely the political balance in the Parliament. Some have suggested that the composition of the Commission should depend entirely on the majority in Parliament, thus making European elections more like national elections, in that an executive would be at stake, and turnout might thus rise. Others argue that the EU is too heterogeneous to permit this kind of majoritarian system comparable to those in Member States, but the choice of at least the President of the Commission is now likely to depend on the majorities in the EP, with European political parties putting forward candidates ahead of the election campaigns (see Chapter 15). In any event, the issue of electoral participation will continue to be a major challenge for political parties.

Table 5: *Turnout in European Parliament elections (%)*

Year	1979	1981	1984	1987	1989	1994	1995	1996	1999	2004	2007	2009
EU	62	-	59	-	58.4	56.7	-	-	49.5	45.5	-	43.0
Luxembourg	88.9	-	88.8	-	87.4	88.6	-	-	87.3	91.3	-	90.8
Belgium	91.4	-	90.7	-	90.7	90.7	-	-	91	90.8	-	90.4
Malta	-	-	-	-	-	-	-	-	-	82.4	-	78.8
Italy	85.6	-	82.5	-	81.1	73.6	-	-	69.8	71.7	-	65.0
Denmark	47.8	-	52.4	-	46.2	52.9	-	-	50.5	47.9	-	59.5
Cyprus	-	-	-	-	-	-	-	-	-	72.5	-	59.4
Ireland	63.6	-	47.6	-	68.3	44.0	-	-	50.2	58.6	-	58.6
Latvia	-	-	-	-	-	-	-	-	-	41.3	-	53.7

Year	1979	1981	1984	1987	1989	1994	1995	1996	1999	2004	2007	2009
Greece	81.5		80.6	-	80	73.2	-	-	70.2	63.2	-	52.6
Austria	-	-	-	-	-	-	-	67.7	49.4	42.4	-	46.0
Sweden	-	-	-	-	-	-	41.6	-	38.8	37.8	-	45.5
Spain	-	-	-	68.5	54.7	59.1	-	-	63	45.1	-	44.9
Estonia	-	-	-	-	-	-	-	-	-	26.8	-	43.9
Germany	65.7	-	56.8	-	62.3	60.0	-	-	45.2	43.0	-	43.3
France	60.7	-	56.7	-	48.8	52.7	-	-	46.8	42.8	-	40.6
Bulgaria	-	-	-	-	-	-	-	-	-	-	29.2	39.0
Finland	-	-	-	-	-	-	-	57.6	30.1	39.4	-	38.6
Portugal	-	-	-	72.4	51.1	35.5	-	-	39.9	38.6	-	36.8
Netherlands	58.1	-	51	-	47.5	35.7	-	-	30	39.3	-	36.7
Hungary	-	-	-	-	-	-	-	-	-	38.5	-	36.3
UK	32.3	-	32.6	-	36.4	36.4	-	-	24.0	38.5	-	34.7
Slovenia	-	-	-	-	-	-	-	-	-	28.3	-	28.4
Czech Republic		-	-	-	-	-	-	-	-	28.3	-	28.2
Romania	-	-	-	-	-	-	-	-	-	-	29.5	27.7
Poland	-	-	-	-	-	-	-	-	-	20.9	-	24.5
Lithuania	-	-	-	-	-	-	-	-	-	48.4	-	21.0
Slovakia	-	-	-	-	-	-	-	-	-	17.0	-	19.6

Note: *there are various ways to calculate turnout: do you count numbers voting or numbers expressing a valid vote? As a percentage of registered voters or of population of voting age? Such discrepancies account for different figures on the above from different sources, including past editions of this book. The above table uses the figures now used by both Parliament and the Commission, calculated by dividing the number of voters by the number of registered voters, except for the UK which divides the number of recorded votes by the number of registered voters.*

3.   Where, when and in quale lingua

The seat issue: where the Parliament meets

It is a hazardous business, on the Friday before Strasbourg plenary sessions, to walk in the corridors of the European Parliament's buildings in Luxembourg and Brussels, blocked as they are by trunks stuffed with files and office equipment about to be transported to Strasbourg. This is one of the most visible signs that the European Parliament is nomadic, obliged to operate in three countries, with its seat officially in Strasbourg, the bulk of parliamentary activity in Brussels and much of the secretariat in Luxembourg.

Under the treaties, the decision on its seat belongs not to the Parliament, but to the national governments. They reached agreement at the Edinburgh summit in December 1992, chaired by John Major, "on the location of the institutions and of certain bodies and departments of the European Communities" (OJ C-341 23/12/1992), later incorporated into a protocol to the Amsterdam Treaty. This states that: "The European Parliament shall have its seat in Strasbourg where the twelve periods of monthly plenary sessions, including the budget session, shall be held. The periods of additional plenary sessions shall be held in Brussels. The committees of the European Parliament shall meet in Brussels. The General Secretariat of the European Parliament and its departments shall remain in Luxembourg." This text can now be found in Protocol 6 of the Lisbon Treaty.

The majority of plenary sessions are indeed held for four days a month in Strasbourg, but several short additional sessions are now held in Brussels. On the other hand, whilst committees normally hold their meetings in Brussels, some often meet during the plenaries in Strasbourg. Around half of Parliament staff are based in Luxembourg but most of the remainder are now based in Brussels, including almost all the staff who deal directly with MEPs and the political work of the parliament (notably in committees, research and press & information), as well as Political Group staff and MEPs' own assistants, making Brussels the primary location.

However, Parliament is legally obliged to maintain facilities in all three cities. There are now two plenary debating chambers (or "hemicycles") in use, one in Strasbourg and one in Brussels (as well as two no longer used in Luxembourg: a small one which housed the Parliament before direct elections in 1979 and a larger one, built by the Luxembourg authorities in the 1980s, which was only used by Parliament on four occasions, the last time in 1986). The hemicycle of the Parliamentary Assembly of the Council of Europe in Strasbourg that Parliament used until 1999, now only serves for meetings of that Assembly.

The duplication extends still further: MEPs have offices in Strasbourg and

Brussels and members of the secretariat have their own offices in Luxembourg or Brussels, and share a smaller number of offices in Strasbourg. Parliament now spreads over fourteen buildings in Brussels (the largest named after Paul-Henri Spaak, Altiero Spinelli, Willy Brandt and Jozsef Antall), four in Strasbourg (named after Louise Weiss, Winston Churchill, Salvador de Madariaga and Pierre Pflimlin) and six in Luxembourg, most notably the Robert Schuman, the Konrad Adenauer and two Tower buildings. Although Luxembourg is the official home of the secretariat, it contains only 18 per cent of the total surface area of Parliament's buildings, as compared to 49 per cent for Brussels and 33 per cent for Strasbourg. In terms of meeting rooms, the domination of Brussels is even clearer with 97 meeting rooms compared to 51 for Strasbourg and 8 for Luxembourg.

The lack of a single fixed seat is costly not just in terms of buildings, but also in terms of travel, with a proportion of the staff "commuting" between cities. For part-sessions in Strasbourg, additional temporary staff and equipment have to be hired and a large number of trunks of documents have to be transported from Brussels and from Luxembourg, despite the fact that information technology has lessened the problem in recent years.

It is not surprising, therefore, that the cost to the Parliament of its geographical dispersion is considerable, amounting to some 15 per cent of its budget. Supporters of Strasbourg point out that this extra cost constitutes only about 0.13 per cent of the whole EU budget, that whether MEPs travel to Brussels or to Strasbourg from their constituency is not very different in cost and that only a proportion of the staff needs to travel. Even with this extra burden (and that of multilingualism), the cost per citizen of the European Parliament is about half that of the House of Commons. But Strasbourg also imposes a cost on the other institutions: the Commission has estimated its own costs relating to having to go to Strasbourg at over €2 million every year.

Such considerable expenditure is difficult to justify, especially in more straitened economic times. Parliament undoubtedly loses effectiveness and therefore influence and its public image is also harmed. For most MEPs (and visitors, including press), Strasbourg is far more difficult to travel to than Brussels. It has direct air links to only seven of the 27 national capitals (Brussels has direct flights from all of them, other than nearby Luxembourg). Such is the inconvenience of getting to Strasbourg that most members have to make complicated connections (which, if missed due to a delayed flight, will result in hours wasted in airport lounges or even unplanned stopovers in hotels) and some have to leave home by Sunday afternoon if they are to be in Strasbourg for the start of the session on Monday afternoon.

Many members have a flat or a house in Brussels where they work three weeks out of four, but few do the same in Strasbourg where they spend only three nights a month, normally in a hotel room (though these are hard to find during sessions, with many MEPs and assistants having to stay well out of town). For all these reasons, Strasbourg will therefore remain unpopular with many members and staff alike. An on-line poll organised by MEPs in the "Campaign for Parliamentary Reform" at the start of 2005 showed 72 per cent of respondents (staff and members) in favour of holding all plenary sessions in Brussels. In 2006 over one million EU citizens signed an online petition for a single seat in Brussels. In the same year Parliament wrote to the European Council asking whether Member States had any plans to review the situation. The reply from the President of the European Council (then Chancellor Schüssel of Austria) was that "consultations with Member States – in particular with France, the host state – have made it clear .... that the unanimity required for a decision changing the seat of the European Parliament could not at present be secured". There is nothing to suggest that this situation will change in the near future, although 171 MEPs signed a letter to European Council President Van Rompuy in March 2010 calling for action and a working party under Vice President McMillan-Scott was set up in 2010 to look further into the issue.

Historical background

How did the present situation come about, what has been done to remedy it, and what are the prospects for change in the future?

The treaties laid down that the seat of the institutions should be determined by common accord of the governments of the Member States. Until 1992 no such common accord was reached and the initial working places of the institutions and bodies were only provisional.

The ECSC Assembly began to meet in Strasbourg (with only two extraordinary sessions held elsewhere) as Strasbourg was the seat of the Parliamentary Assembly of the Council of Europe to which most of its initial members belonged and which had the only fully-equipped, multilingual parliamentary hemicycle. The secretariat, however, was installed in Luxembourg, the then site of the Council and Commission (High Authority).

Sessions continued to be held in Strasbourg with the entry into force of the EEC and Euratom Treaties in 1958. However, parliamentary committees began meeting on a regular basis in Brussels where the bulk of the new Community institutions were now based. The staff remained in Luxembourg.

The 1965 Merger Treaty, whereby the three separate Communities (ECSC, EEC and Euratom) were given a common Council and Commission, did not come up with a solution for the seat. Instead, an accompanying decision by the governments of the Member States confirmed that Luxembourg, Brussels and Strasbourg would remain the provisional places of work of the Community and that the General Secretariat of the Assembly and its departments would remain in Luxembourg. No mention was made of the Assembly's meetings, and the status quo (plenaries in Strasbourg, committees in Brussels) was left untouched.

From 1967 onwards, on its own initiative, and simply for the convenience of holding the sittings at the working place of the secretariat, Parliament began to hold part-sessions in Luxembourg. The number was gradually increased until in 1976 and 1977 more were held in Luxembourg than in Strasbourg.

The situation changed rapidly after direct elections in 1979. For the first few months after the elections only Strasbourg had a hemicycle big enough to seat the enlarged Parliament, in the new building of the Council of Europe. By the time Luxembourg had completed its own new hemicycle the members had got used to going to Strasbourg where they were given their own offices (facilities unavailable in Luxembourg). The majority of members had come around to the belief that it was preferable to have to travel regularly to only two cities, Brussels and Strasbourg, than to three. This evolution was of great concern for the Luxembourg-based staff who went on strike over the issue.

The solution that most wanted was a single seat, and the directly elected members began to call more insistently on national governments to take such a decision. However, in March 1981 the European Council meeting only decided to reiterate the status quo. There followed various attempts to revise the situation.

On 7 July 1981, Parliament adopted a resolution (based on a report by an Italian Socialist, Mario Zagari), by 187 votes to 118 with seven abstentions, in which it again called for a decision on a single working place but, pending such a decision, for plenary sittings to be held in Strasbourg, committee meetings to take place in Brussels and the operation of the Parliament's secretariat to be reviewed to meet these new requirements. In August 1981 the Luxembourg government challenged this resolution (Case C-230/81) but in February 1983 the Court of Justice found in the Parliament's favour. It stated that Luxembourg could not prevent the Parliament giving up the practice of meeting in Luxembourg, which it had only introduced on its own initiative and was not an integral part of the status quo.

In February 1983, Parliament voted by 130 to 99 with 11 abstentions that an additional part-session, which could not be held in Strasbourg, should take place in Brussels (at the Palais des Congrès) rather than in Luxembourg. It took place on 28 April 1983 and was the only sitting in Brussels, apart from one ECSC Assembly meeting in 1956, until the two meetings in early 1991 (described below). The sitting did show, however, that unless held in a properly equipped parliamentary chamber, such sittings were particularly vulnerable to filibusters (e.g. by requests for roll-call votes in the absence of voting machines).

In July 1983, Parliament went a step further by adopting a resolution (by a written declaration of over half its members rather than by a formal vote in plenary) to divide up the secretariat with services concerned with the functioning of part-sessions in Strasbourg and with those of the parliamentary committees in Brussels. This resolution was again challenged by the Luxembourg government (Case C-108/83), on this occasion successfully, when the Court of Justice annulled the Parliament's resolution as a violation of the Member States' decision to provisionally maintain the status quo.

On 24 October 1985, a resolution, adopted by 132 votes to 113 with 13 abstentions, called for the construction of a new Parliament building in Brussels, including a chamber with seating for no less than 600 people. The resolution stated that Parliament needed a large meeting room in Brussels for many of its routine meetings (such as those of the larger Political Groups) but also for any supplementary plenary sittings that might be held in Brussels. The resolution's opponents argued that this was the opening step in a process that would lead to the abandonment of Strasbourg in favour of Brussels. The French government called for the resolution to be declared null and void (Case C-258/85). The Advocate-General of the Court found in the French government's favour, but the full Court rejected the request in September 1988, thus acknowledging that Parliament would be within its rights to hold some sittings outside Strasbourg.

In January 1989, Parliament adopted, by 222 to 176 with four abstentions, a new resolution on its working place (based on a report by Derek Prag, a British Conservative) calling for a reduction in the dispersal of its work and staff. It again called for a final decision on a single seat but expressed pessimism that such a decision would be taken after more than 30 years of failure to do so by the national governments. Meanwhile, it provided for staff dealing with certain activities, such as committee and information work, to be based in Brussels and declared that it was now necessary to hold additional plenary sittings during the weeks traditionally set aside for committee or Group meetings. The resolution had particularly strong support from Belgian, British, Dutch and Spanish members, but was contested by French and Luxembourg members, with the vast majority of EPP members also opposed. Luxembourg again took Parliament to the Court (see below).

While the case was pending, French members, in particular, called for a guarantee that the holding of plenary sessions in Strasbourg would continue after the new Brussels building came on-stream, and that a new hemicycle would be built in Strasbourg. In March 1990 a compromise on these lines was adopted by Parliament's Bureau, but was challenged by back-bench supporters of Brussels. At the April 1990 plenary a bitter debate culminated in a final vote in which the Parliament supported the Bureau's text.

A further episode was prompted by a decision to hold two supplementary sittings in Brussels, so that the Parliament could hear a statement and debate developments in the Gulf War and in the Baltic States, but without any formal votes being taken on motions for resolution. These sittings were held on 30 January and 6 February 1991, in the presence of the Commission but not of the President of the Council, the Luxembourg Foreign Minister, whose refusal to attend was condemned by the Parliament in a resolution of 14 March 1991 as a mark of disrespect for the Parliament. This controversial precedent of holding debates in Brussels was subsequently pursued, but, until the new buildings were ready, such meetings were known as "open meetings of the enlarged Bureau" (see Chapter 9).

On 28 November 1991, the Court of Justice (in joined cases C-213/88 and C-39/89) dismissed the Luxembourg government's challenge to the Parliament resolution of January 1989 (cited above), as well as to other decisions of Parliament's Bureau of June 1988. The Court found, inter alia, that the Parliament's objectives as regards its internal organisation justified its building projects in Brussels, and that the transfer of a number of Parliament officials to Brussels was not on such a scale as to be in breach of prior government decisions on the seat.

Shortly afterwards, on 8 January 1992, President Barón signed the lease for the new Parliament buildings in Brussels. Parliament began to plan sittings in Brussels and to cut the number in Strasbourg. This prompted a vigorous reaction from the French government, which put pressure on the other governments, leading to the Edinburgh Council Decision of December 1992 and ultimately to the Amsterdam Treaty protocol cited at the beginning of this chapter. This requires Parliament to hold 12 plenary sessions in Strasbourg, but allows additional sittings in Brussels.

Conflict has continued, however, over the implementation of these decisions. In 1993, the French Assemblée Nationale delayed the procedures for ratification of the increase in the number of MEPs agreed by the Member States in 1992, until the Parliament's President agreed to sign the lease for a new building and hemicycle built by the French authorities in Strasbourg. The lease was finally signed by President Klepsch, amid some controversy, in the spring of 1994, a signature later questioned by the Court of Auditors.

The new building was inaugurated at the July 1999 part-session with further argument about its cost and design.

An additional source of conflict has been over the number and length of part-sessions in Strasbourg, in particular whether there should be twelve such sessions per year which, given the August recess, means holding two plenary sessions in one other month. A second session in October had traditionally taken place to hold Parliament's first reading of the budget, which took up too much time for a normal part session. Streamlined procedures for considering the budget within the Parliament meant that the second session in the same month was no longer necessary, and Parliament held only 11 Strasbourg sessions in 1992, 1993 and 1996 and 10 in the election year of 1994, all with only one session in October. The French government sought to annul the Parliament's 1996 decision, and the Court of Justice found in its favour (case C-345/95) on 1 October 1997. The Court ruled that Parliament could only hold additional sessions in Brussels if it had first provided for 12 sessions in Strasbourg, and that if it did not hold a session in August, then it would have to hold an extra session during one of the other months of the year. The Court conceded, however, that the Parliament need only hold 11 sessions during election years. For other years, Parliament had to re-introduce two plenary sessions during the month of October (or recently, September).

Unable to eliminate Strasbourg sessions or to cut their number, Parliament instead cut their length. In October 1999, when adopting Parliament's calendar of meetings for 2000, amendments for Strasbourg part-sessions to last only from Monday to Thursday were narrowly rejected, but approved a year later for 2001 and again for every year since. Friday sittings now seem to be definitively abolished. The latest development came when Parliament voted, in March 2011, on its calendar of plenary sessions for 2012 and 2013, and voted by secret ballot, and by a majority of over 100 in both cases, to hold two sessions in the same calendar week in October, with a technical break between the two on the Wednesday. This provoked a challenge from the French authorities.

A final issue has been the location of Parliament's staff. Luxembourg is no longer a venue of parliamentary activity, but its government insists on respect for the Amsterdam Treaty protocol, which refers to the secretariat and its departments being based in Luxembourg. Yet the practical needs of the Parliament have meant that many officials have been transferred to Brussels to avoid incessant commuting between the two cities. The increase in staff numbers, notably in response to EU enlargement, has given the Parliament some margin in reconciling these different needs. In 2000, an agreement was reached between the Luxembourg government and Parliament permitting a transfer of staff to Brussels, in return for a guaranteed minimum number of staff (at least 50%, excluding Group staff and staff appointed to external national offices, and a minimum of 2060) in Luxembourg. Parliament thus has to face up to the costs (financial and human) of having staff based in Luxembourg when all the Parliament's meetings are elsewhere. It also has an increasingly divided secretariat, with Luxembourg based staff mainly dealing with translation, administration and other matters not requiring close proximity to members.

In theory, the problem of the seat has been settled: any change requires further treaty revision. In practice, however, the unnecessary travel, the far greater difficulty of access to Strasbourg (accentuated following the 2004 and 2007 enlargements with none of the twelve new Member States having direct flights), the continuing cost of having three working places for the Parliament, the renting or ownership of extra buildings, and the dispersal of Parliament's secretariat, indicate that the question is likely to remain controversial. The flashpoints are likely to focus on the remaining ambiguities concerning the length of sittings in Strasbourg, on the number and duration of additional sittings in Brussels and on possible future reform of Parliament's own timetable of activities.

When: Parliament's cycle of activities

Parliament's timetable traditionally followed a monthly cycle of a plenary week in Strasbourg followed, in Brussels, by two "committee weeks" devoted mainly to meetings of the various committees and "Group week" when the Political Groups meet, to prepare their stance at the next plenary session and other business. There is a one-month recess in August. During election years, the outgoing Parliament winds up its activities by May, and the new one assembles in July.

The traditional timetable has always been less simple in practice. There is the extra plenary week in September or October referred to above (and in the early 1980s, there was occasionally an extra plenary in March to deal with agricultural prices). Political Groups and committees have always held additional meetings during plenary weeks. Committees sometimes meet during Group weeks.

In recent years the timetable has been modified further. The growth of Parliament's legislative control and other activities has made it necessary to organize more frequent plenary sittings and more committee meetings, as well as to provide time for Conciliation Committee meetings with the Council (see Chapter 12). The availability from 1993 of the hemicycle in Brussels provided an opportunity for more flexibility, by enabling plenary sittings in Brussels during what were normally committee weeks. Since such sittings began in Brussels on a regular basis in autumn 1993, the typical pattern has been for them to last two half-days. Five or six such Brussels plenary sessions have been scheduled every year since 2000.

In October 1999 (and occasionally again since then) an attempt was made by some members to have weekly sittings on Wednesday afternoons in Brussels to allow the President of the Commission to report directly to Parliament on the decisions taken by the Commission at its weekly meeting. The idea of doing this in the course of such micro-plenaries every week was rejected by the Parliament, but is sometimes implemented in another form as "meetings of the Conference of Presidents open to all members". In 2010 Parliament started holding short extra sittings in Brussels, convened during the year and not scheduled in advance in the annual timetable, to enable the President of the European Council to report to Parliament on the outcome of its meetings, without having to wait until the next scheduled meeting. In 2011, however, this was again designated as a "Conference of Presidents open to all members", in order not to upset the Strasbourg lobby.

More time has been found for committee meetings by allowing them to meet on the Monday afternoon and Tuesday morning of Group weeks.

Holding committee meetings in Strasbourg remains controversial (they can conflict with the plenary or other meetings, and also they are not envisaged in the Amsterdam Treaty protocol), but in practice has become inevitable, especially for matters related to the current plenary. Such Strasbourg meetings require special authorisation from the President and normally take place at one of two times: Monday 7:00 p.m. to 9:00 p.m. or Tuesday 5:30 p.m. to 7:00 p.m.

Many members have complained that the rhythm of Brussels and Strasbourg meetings has been such as to give them inadequate time to remain in touch with their home political base or constituency. As a result, meetings on Fridays have been phased out and three or four weeks are reserved for external activities enabling members to work in their constituencies or to take part in overseas visits with delegations.

More radical changes to Parliament's cycle of activities, such as holding committee meetings in the mornings with plenary sessions in the afternoons, have fewer prospects since the incorporation of the protocol in the Treaties laying down where and how often the Parliament should meet.

Table 6: *Time spent in plenary sittings*

	1990	1992	1994*	1996	1998	2000	2001	2002	2003	2004*	2005	2006	2007	2008	2009*
No. of sittings (days)	60	56	57	71	73	71	55	61	61	50	60	62	62	63	51
No. of hours	420	411	366	483	492	467	421	430	439	314	417	440	426	467	367

* election years

In quale lingua: languages within the European Parliament

The language regime within the European Parliament is one of its most unusual features. It is of the European Union institutions the one most affected by the linguistic variety of the Union, and it is unique amongst world parliaments in the number of its working languages. The situation was complex enough before 2004 with 11 working languages being used, but the arrival of twelve more states in 2004 and 2007 and the addition of Irish has led to more than a doubling of the number of official languages to 23: Bulgarian, Czech, Danish, Dutch, English, Estonian, Finnish, French, German, Greek, Hungarian, Irish, Italian, Latvian, Lithuanian, Maltese, Polish, Portuguese, Romanian, Slovak, Slovene, Spanish and Swedish.

Why does the European Parliament have to have nearly four times more working languages than the six used in the United Nations? Is this multilingualism really necessary? There are a number of reasons why it is still considered to be so important.

First, the Parliament is directly elected, and its elected members, unlike career diplomats, cannot automatically be expected to be competent linguists, although many are. The electorate should be free to choose a popular trade unionist from Germany or farmer from Latvia even if he or she cannot speak or understand a foreign language.

Second, protection of Europe's cultural diversity is considered to be of great political importance. Many members, especially from the smaller countries, feel that they must defend their country's language, even if they speak other languages, since it is central to their country's identity and culture. The Bureau's 2001 report on the implications of enlargement put it succinctly: "If Parliament does not recognize their language, it is less likely that citizens will recognize it as being their Parliament."

Third, unlike the United Nations, the European Parliament adopts legislation that is directly binding on citizens. The principle of equality between languages is thus fundamental. Amending texts requires full understanding of their meaning, and members should then have the right to put forward proposed changes in their own language. Legal precision is not easy to achieve, and is even more difficult in someone else's language. The same 2001 Bureau report went on to sum up: "For Parliament, enlargement cannot be at the expense of equal treatment for all members. The right of an elected member to speak, read and write in his or her language lies at the heart of Parliament's democratic legitimacy."

These principles have been regularly reaffirmed in Parliament resolutions, for example in the Parliament resolution of 6 May 1994 "on the right to use one's own language" which stated that it was "undesirable for an institution composed of elected members to introduce restrictions on the use of languages", and that "all of the Union's official languages must be used on a strictly equal basis, whenever necessary, for any meetings of the European Parliament whether they are used actively or passively, orally or in writing".

The principle of multilingualism has also been strongly asserted in the EP's Rules of Procedure. Rule 146.1 states that "All documents of Parliament shall be drawn-up in the official languages." Rule 61.1 provides that, in the context of legislative procedures, Parliament will only announce receipt of the Council position when all the necessary documents have been "... duly translated into the official languages". Rule 156.6 states that untranslated texts may not be put to a vote if 40 members object. As regards interpretation Rule 146.2 states that "all members shall have the right to speak in Parliament in the official language of their choice. Speeches delivered in one of the official languages shall be simultaneously interpreted into the other official languages and into any other language the Bureau may consider necessary." Rule 146.3 provides for interpretation to be "provided in committee and delegation meetings from and into the official languages used and requested by the members and substitutes of that committee or delegation" and Rule 146.4 for interpretation to be provided even at committee and delegation meetings away from the usual places of work from and into the languages of those members who have confirmed that they will attend the meeting.

Multilingualism imposes a major burden on the Parliament. Every additional language creates a large number of additional language combinations (the formula is n x (n-1) where n equals the number of working languages). Before Spanish and Portuguese accession there were "only" 42 combinations: it is now 506. About 1,500 posts are earmarked for linguists (translators, lawyer-linguists and interpreters), and around a third of these posts deal with the 10 new enlargement languages, with much interpreting and translation work also being done freelance. The direct and indirect costs of all this is very great, and it complicates and slows down Parliament's working methods.

The volume of translation and the resources devoted to it are impressive. In 2008, for example, the total number of pages translated amounted to 1,807,384, of which 303,522 were the verbatim debates (see Table 7). To cope with all this there are about 1250 officials in the Translation Directorate General with 750 posts set aside for translators as well as a substantial pool of freelancers who account for around 39% of the pages translated. Interpretation needs are also great, with Parliament having the highest requirement for interpreters of all the EU institutions. Parliament employs some 320 permanent interpreters, joined by as many as 600 freelancers during peak periods.

Taking interpreters and translators and linked staff together, around one third of Parliament's staff are in its linguistic services. The direct cost of multilingualism has thus amounted to a very substantial share of the Parliament's total budget. Together with the percentage due to the geographical dispersion of the Parliament these two cost centres alone amount to over half the Parliament's budget. While these figures need to be put into perspective (the cost per EU citizen per year for both translation and interpretation needs has been estimated at around 2 euros, and will probably not rise significantly), they are still very high, especially after the recent enlargements.

They are, however, not the whole story, since multilingualism also has indirect costs, and has a significant wider set of impacts on the Parliament. First, translation requirements slow down the work of the Parliament, since a considerable time elapses between the transmission of a text and the moment when it emerges from translation in all the languages, with knock-on effects on the timing of their consideration in committee and in plenary. Texts for consideration in committees and delegations now have to be submitted no later than 10 working days before the meeting (one of which is for legal verification by the tabling office) enabling the text to be available 48 hours before the meeting. For plenary, texts must be tabled by the Friday of the 3rd week before the session (for initiative and legislative reports in single or first reading it is the 4th week before). This will normally mean they will be ready at the start of the week before the part-session. It is thus more difficult than it was for a committee to submit a report for the next plenary after its adoption in committee. The constraints can also be considerable in those cases, notably in the case of second reading texts, involving tight treaty-imposed timetables. Any subsequent modifications to texts can add to these problems. Moreover, even when the text is ready in most languages, one or two may still be missing. If there is goodwill by the members affected, this may not further delay matters, but it can hand a new weapon to a determined filibusterer, who can use translation gaps to delay further progress. Amendments also have to be translated into all languages, and further delays ensue. While in committee meetings the practice can be more informal, with oral amendments or untranslated written amendments often being put to the vote, this cannot be done if only a single member objects.

Table 7: *Number of Pages Translated Per Language in 2008*

Language	By EP translation	By freelance translators	Total (excl. debates)	Debates	Grand Total
Bulgarian	52,209	9,401	61,610	2	61,612
Czech	42,706	18,498	61,204	15,675	76,879
Danish	45.867	27,170	73,037	16,590	89,627
German	64,256	26,073	90,329	13,973	104,302
Greek	53,063	21,656	74,719	16,111	90,830
English	36,747	9,786	46,533	15,166	61,699
Spanish	58,139	19,886	78,025	15,976	94,001
Estonian	41,140	17,802	58,942	15,943	74,885
Finnish	54,361	18,454	72,815	16,457	89,272
French	59,019	28,528	87,547	15,021	102,568
Hungarian	46,221	20,564	66,785	16,694	83,479
Irish	2,071	6	2,077	0	2,077
Italian	46,514	33,301	79,815	15,950	95,765
Lithuanian	45,395	15,974	61,369	16,913	78,282
Latvian	45,697	17,491	63,188	17,023	80,211
Maltese	43,250	12,321	55,571	2	55,573
Dutch	50,339	24,122	74,461	16,020	90,481
Polish	53,486	14,657	68,143	14,844	82,987
Portuguese	58,760	13,548	72,308	15,539	87,847
Romanian	48,705	13,830	62,535	2	62,537
Slovakian	51,837	8,067	59,904	16,794	76,698
Slovene	49,631	9,683	59,314	16,531	75,845
Swedish	53,348	19,758	73,106	16,297	89,403
Others	16	509	525	0	525
Total	**1,102,777**	**401,085**	**1,503,862**	**303,522**	**1,807,384**

A second impact is that restrictions have had to be introduced as regards the length of texts sent for translation, with the length of explanatory statements and preparatory working documents not meant to exceed 7 pages for non-legislative reports, 6 pages for legislative reports and 3 pages for opinions (a page being defined as 1,500 characters). Motions for a resolution (including recitals, but excluding citations), are not meant to exceed 4 pages, conclusions to non-legislative opinions not more than one page and justifications for amendments no more than 500 characters. Each parliamentary committee is given an annual reserve of 45 pages, which it can allocate to texts which it considers need to be longer than the standard limits, but once it has used up this margin for flexibility, it must then apply to Parliament's Bureau for any further derogation. Moreover, certain potentially useful documents cannot be translated at all. Transcripts of US Congressional hearings or House of Lords inquiries are valuable documents, but translation of the full proceedings of all European Parliament hearings would be too costly.

A further impact is that the quality of texts can also suffer, not least because texts are often produced in English or French by non-native speakers. In addition, some texts may not be translated directly, but through another pivot language. This may lead to misunderstandings and unnecessary amendments. To improve quality it is best to have a collation of texts between the different language sections, ideally in the presence of the person who drafted the initial text, who knows best why a text was drafted in a particular way. This is often difficult to put into practice, however, not just because of tight deadlines but also because the translation service is in Luxembourg, whereas the vast majority of texts are produced in Brussels. One important change, however, has been the establishment of a Tabling Office incorporating lawyer-linguists and other officials, many of whom are in Brussels, and whose main objective is to help members and staff in ensuring the better linguistic quality of texts.

The constraints imposed by interpretation in meetings are of a different nature, such as on the number of committee meetings that can be held in parallel (no more than 18), and more generally on when committees can meet. Parliament also has a number of other meetings, such as working groups, committee coordinators' meetings or between rapporteurs and shadow rapporteurs, and it is often hard or impossible to provide interpretation for such meetings, with considerable implications for Parliament's work when those involved in the meeting are unilingual or have no common language.

Adapting Parliament's meeting rooms to extra languages has also required costly changes, including reducing the space available for the public and, in some cases, blocking out the windows in existing rooms. Moreover, although Parliament's hemicycles have now been equipped for 27 booths, a number of Parliament's other meeting rooms still do not have enough interpreting booths for all languages,

One constraint, for which the interpreters are primarily responsible, is regarded as beneficial by many members. This is the limitation on Parliament's working hours, with plenary and committee meetings needing to have special permission to go past certain fixed hours. Committee meetings, for example, cannot exceed seven hours a day (9:00 to 12:30 and 15:00 to 18:30). If the committee wishes to go on longer without prior authorisation, it has to do so without interpretation. This is because of agreed limits to interpreters' working hours, with longer meetings requiring costly additional teams of interpreters.

A further constraint is on the quality of communication at Parliament's meetings. However excellent the interpretation, it is a brake on spontaneity and comprehension. Words can be successfully interpreted but cultural differences may not. The indirect irony or criticism of an Italian member may well be completely lost in interpretation whereas the directness of a Dutch or Danish member may only seem like rudeness to a southern or eastern member. A joke may result in laughter from some members and perplexed silence from others. As a result, when members wish to direct a point to a specific member, they may address them in the latter's language.

Many of these problems have been present for a long time but they have been considerably reinforced by the recent enlargements, which has not just doubled the number of languages but also brought in many difficult new languages (for the first time even many interpreters do not always know which language is being spoken). Moreover, some of these languages are used by relatively few people, and there are generally very few translators and interpreters. Hence Rule 147 which allows exceptions to the general commitment to multilingualism.

For all these reasons Parliament has had to look hard at its traditional working methods, and to develop both formal and informal adjustment mechanisms. In the 1999-2004 Parliament a report was drawn up by then

Vice-President Podesta which looked at some of the possibilities. The working party's final report put forward a number of options, some of which have been implemented (such as the provision of more booths in meeting rooms), and some of which have not (such as removing interpreters from the meeting rooms and having them interpret at longer range while looking at the speakers on screens: some experiments of this kind have been tried, but so far have appeared to impose new strains on interpreters, to lower quality and generally not to be very cost-effective).

Following on from this report, a Code of Conduct on Multilingualism was adopted by the Bureau on 19 April 2004, came into force on the day of enlargement on 1 May 2004 and was revised in 2006 and 2008. With the objective of achieving "controlled full multilingualism", it sets out a series of principles and procedures, including more careful planning of demand for translations and for interpretation (for example three months' notice for meetings requiring interpretation and three weeks' notice for any changes in the required language regime), establishment of an order of priority for the allocation of language facilities and the extension of certain other key deadlines. A particularly controversial element was the requirement to draw up language profiles for each user, both for interpretation and translation needs. A committee, for example, which had no Estonian members or substitutes, was not meant to include Estonian in its language profile, and would thus not normally have Estonian interpretation at its meetings, even if an Estonian member from elsewhere in the Parliament was interested in a committee agenda, and turned up, even with some prior notice, at the meeting in question. In addition, if there was an Estonian member on the committee but it was demonstrated that he or she was not using the Estonian booth, then this too would have to be reflected in a revised language profile for the committee, so that the languages provided properly reflected real needs. The new wording of Rule 146.2 allows this by referring to "official languages used and requested" by members or substitutes on a committee. The implications of such profiles for a committee's translation needs are potentially problematic, as interpretation and translation requirements may vary for the same member. Committees are also meant to submit monthly estimates of their translation needs, something that is very hard to calculate in advance. But despite the difficulties, the system has started to settle down and become a part of the way Parliament manages multilingualism.

In any case, a number of pragmatic solutions are being used as regards interpretation. One of these is the use of pivot languages. One radical outcome of the Podesta working group report was to give up the matrix system of interpretation (whereby each language is interpreted into every other language), and to develop, instead, a radial system, with interpretation from all languages into a pivot language and then out of that to other languages. This "relay" system has proved inevitable, due to the sheer number of combinations. When there are not enough trained interpreters for a particular language, those interpreters who are available may not only have to interpret into their mother tongue, but out of it into another pivot language (particularly English), from which they are interpreted into other languages. This breaks the old rule that interpreters should essentially interpret into their own language, but it began, and has remained the case for Finnish, and is now also being used for the post-2004 languages. Its necessity is shown by the fact that, since there are still only 3 interpreters per booth after enlargement, there are now only 67 interpreters to deal with 23 languages and 506 language combinations at a meeting requiring full language coverage (such as a plenary or big committee meeting), compared to 33 interpreters for 11 languages and 110 language combinations before enlargement.

Attempts are also being made to cut back on interpretation in other ways. Rule 146.4 now provides that members at meetings away from the usual working places will only get interpretation if they have confirmed that they will be attending the meeting and "these arrangements may exceptionally be made more flexible where the members of the committee or delegation so agree." In practice no more than five languages can be made available at such meetings. Informal meetings are increasingly conducted in English or French, if all concerned agree.

Moreover, within the Political Groups, a less rigid system applies. Some Groups do not have a membership requiring all languages anyway, but even the Socialist Group, which is the second largest Group, only uses four languages (English, French, German and Spanish) for most internal documents. English and French are used within the Liberal Group for documents, although English is currently dominant for spoken purposes. This, however, is only feasible in the context of non-public meetings among colleagues of the same political family. Another feature of Groups is that their secretariats often do a lot of their own translation because of time constraints. The code of conduct provides for Groups to have active interpretation only up to a ceiling of seven along with passive interpretation provided it does not require an increase in the number of booths or interpreters.

Most debates in plenary and in committee are conducted with members using their own language, but an increasing number of members use other languages, especially English. At informal meetings, use of other languages is even greater, with English becoming increasingly dominant. A survey in 2006 by Marios Matsakis MEP, covering 402 MEPs and their assistants, showed 92.9 percent of respondents able to communicate in English. Besides English, a substantial number of members also speak French and German (and Russian, although fewer admit it) as second or third languages. Some members are truly multilingual, with one even claiming to speak 14 languages!

Language use is also more flexible within the Parliament secretariat. French is not the main internal working language to the same extent as it is in certain other institutions (for example the Court of Justice). Its *primus inter pares* position has slowly been replaced by English over the years, although French is still more widely used among staff than it is among the MEPs. Among Parliament's staff, a practice of conducting meetings in French and English, with all speakers obliged to speak a language other than their own (British officials would therefore have to speak French and French ones English) grew up, but has become less common, with a substantial number of new officials not able to work on this basis.

Translation constraints have also been affected by the increasing dominance of the major languages and, in particular, English. Until the late 1990s there were considerably more French than English original texts, but English overtook French in 1998, and is now well ahead of it. In 2009 almost 54% of the texts sent for translation were in English, compared to around

17% in French and only around 6% in German and 4% in Spanish, with all the others below 3.5% (Italian 3.2%, Dutch under 2.5% and down to 0.23% in Maltese). The dominance of English has, if anything been further reinforced since enlargement, with almost 75% of texts sent to translation in some committees being in English, and with not a single one of Parliament's committees using more French than English.

Even this mixture of formal and informal adjustments has not been enough to cope fully with the challenges of the latest enlargements. Many committee meetings have had to begin with an apology from the chairman that certain of the new languages were not being made available, even if they had been included in a committee's "language profile". Committee minutes have to be adopted in the absence of certain languages. Some of the newer languages have proved to be particularly problematic, such as Maltese, where there is a lack of trained translators and interpreters. The distinction made in the past between "active" and "passive" languages is now proving harder to sustain. The backlog of untranslated texts has become much greater and the gap between the adoption of Council common positions on legislation and their transmission as fully translated common positions to the Parliament has gone up to an estimated average of around six months.

Anticipating some of these problems, the Parliament, on the basis of a report by Mr Dell'Alba, adopted a special transitional arrangement in its Rules of Procedure (Rule 147) that provides for account to be taken of the availability in real terms and sufficient numbers of the requisite interpreters and translators, and thus for some flexibility in the application of Parliament's normal rules. These arrangements were prolonged in March 2009 but are subject to constant review and can be repealed at any time. Already some hard decisions have had to be taken, such as the fact that the verbatim records of plenary sessions are not being translated into all the new languages.

In addition, there are increasing calls for more favourable treatment for regional languages, which may be used by substantial numbers of people (Catalan, for example, is spoken by more people than speak many official EU languages), but which are not recognised as official languages. Parliament's Bureau agreed on 6 July 2006 to deal with citizens' correspondence in Basque, Catalan and Galician (which have constitutional status in Spain).

The prospects for the future are further complicated by the linguistic implications of further EU enlargement, with the possible addition of Croatian, Icelandic and Turkish in the near and medium term. As a result of all these factors, the tension between the conflicting criteria of democratic fairness and logistical practicality is likely to become ever more acute.

II: THE ACTORS AND WORKING STRUCTURES

4. The individual members

Any examination of Parliament's key "actors" must begin with its individual members. This chapter looks at the background of the individual members, their role within the Parliament, their capacity for independent action, the position of back-benchers, and finally their rights and obligations (including the questions of the members' statute and the status and role of their assistants).

Background of the individual members elected in 2009

Turnover and length of service

A remarkable feature of the European Parliament has been the high turnover in its membership at each election and, to a lesser extent, between elections (see Table 8). The 2009 elections confirmed this trend, though with considerable variations in it at both Political Group and national level. Three Groups had a majority of re-elected members (ECR 56%, EPP 53% and S&D 52%), ALDE had an equal number of new and re-elected members, and three other Groups had a clear majority of new members (EFD 69%, Greens/EFA 62% and GUE/NGL 57%).

Table 8: *Number and proportion of MEPs elected in European elections who were outgoing members*

1989	266/518	51.4%
1994	241/567	42.5%
1999	286/626	45.7%
2004	308/570 [counting 15 old M.S. only*]	54.0%
2009	365/736	49.6%

* In 2004 direct comparisons of turnover were complicated by the fact that a considerable number of MEPs from the 10 new Member States had previously been MEPs for only one session after EU enlargement in May 2004. Whereas some of these new MEPs had been Observers at the EP (without voting rights in committee or plenary and without speaking right in the plenary) for the year before they became full members, the large majority had not. In total, nearly 52% of all the members elected in June 2004 were entirely new to the Parliament, and just over 48% were outgoing members; however, if the May 2004 session is discounted, the figures change to over 58% entirely new members, and to under 42% re-elected members. Taking the 15 "old" Member States, 54% of the MEPs elected in June 2004 were outgoing MEPs and 46% were new. Taking the 10 new Member States, under 28% of the 162 elected MEPs had been members in May 2004 (with many, if not all, of these having been Observers) and over 72% were new. The overall effect of EU enlargement, therefore, was that there was a very high number of new MEPs in the 2004-9 Parliament, but not much more so than after previous EP elections.

Another facet of high turnover is that there are relatively few very long-serving MEPs. There is now only one current MEP who served in the pre-1979 nominated Parliament (Astrid Lulling from Luxembourg, who was an MEP from 1965-1974 but only returned to the EP in 1989). Only one of the current MEPs (previous outgoing EP President, Pöttering) has served continuously since 1979, and one other (Brok) from 1980. Yet another, Newton-Dunn was first elected in 1979, and has been re-elected on all but one occasion, being absent from the EP between 1994 and 1999. Five others (Hughes, Martin, McMillan-Scott, Elles and Le Pen) have been re-elected continuously since 1984. In all, only 15 current MEPs have served without a break since the first edition of this book in 1990; another 5 were MEPs when it was first published, but have not served continuously since that time.

Germany and the UK have provided a disproportionate number of those MEPs with very long service in the Parliament, contrasting with others, such as France and Italy, which have generally had very high rates of turnover. German influence and their number of office-holders within the EP is thus, perhaps, less dependent on the fact that they are the largest delegation than on their often lengthy experience, although the 59% of their MEPs who were re-elected in 2009 was, in fact, a lower figure than usual. Moreover, the lengthy service of a number of UK MEPs, originally reinforced by the single member constituency system, has persisted even after the transition to a regional list system. 5 of the 9 MEPs with over 25 years service in the EP are from the UK, and over 72% of the British MEPs elected in 2009 were outgoing members. A third large country which has had considerable continuity in its MEPs has been Spain. In spite of losing a number of long-serving MEPs in 2009 (such as Baron Crespo and Medina Ortega), 56% of its MEPs were still re-elected.

At the opposite end of the spectrum, Italy and France continue to have exceptionally low average lengths of service among their MEPs, and among the highest turnovers in membership: 55 of the 81 French members elected in 1989 were new to the Parliament, as were 56 of the 87 French members in 1994 and 60 out of 87 in 1999. There was slightly greater continuity in 2004 when 36 of the 78 French members were re-elected, and in 2009 when the figure was 30 out of 72 (42%). Very few of these (with the notable exception of Wurtz, who was an MEP from 1979-2009) have had lengthy periods in the Parliament.

The figures for Italy are even more striking. Some 58 of the 81 Italian members elected in 1989 were new, as were 68 of the 87 Italian members in 1994 and 66 of the 87 in 1999. There was relatively greater continuity in 2004 when 45 of the 78 Italian members were new, and 33 were re-elected, but the figure was down again in 2009, when 51 of the 72 were new, and only 21 (29%) were re-elected. The average length of service of Italian MEPs has again been very low, with only a few exceptions, such as Pannella. Comparisons between length of service in some other countries are often harder to make, either because of the small size of a country, or the limited period of time in which they have been in the European Union. It was striking, however, that there were a considerable number of countries where under 40 % of their previous MEPs were re-elected in 2009, including long-standing Member States such as Greece (27%) and Portugal (32%), as well as more recent Member States, such as Poland (38%), Latvia (37.5%), Cyprus (33%) and Lithuania (25%).

Gender Balance

With 35% of the total, the proportion of women members of the European Parliament is substantially higher than the 24% average in the national parliaments of EU countries (September 2009 figures) The current number of women MEPs also reflects an almost continuous increase since the first direct elections (see Figure 3) despite the initially lower percentage of women members in the several new Member States.

Figure 3: *Growth in proportion of women MEPs*

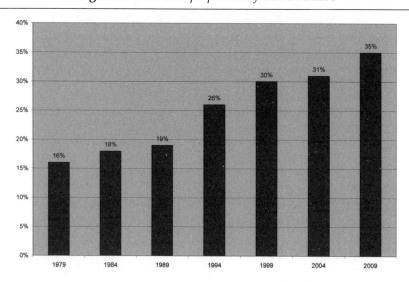

The difference between old and new Member States is now less marked, with half of the 12 Member States joining since 2004 having higher than average numbers of women MEPs, for example in Estonia (where the figure is 50%), Slovakia, Latvia, Romania, Hungary and Bulgaria. On the other hand, only 22% of Polish MEPs and 18% of Czech MEPs are women, and there has still never been a woman MEP elected in Malta since it joined in 2004.

There are, of course, great variations among the old Member States as well. The highest percentages of women MEPs are in the Nordic countries (Finland 62%, Sweden 56%, Denmark 46%) and in the Netherlands (48%), but there is also a very high percentage in France (46%), and to a lesser extent in Austria (41%) (see Table 9). On the other hand, Italy has always had the lowest percentage of women MEPs among the larger Member States, and only 22% were elected in 2009. The UK has also had a lower than average number of women MEPs, but the introduction of a regional list system in 1999 contributed towards an increase from 18% to 24% women members, and the percentage rose again to over 33% in 2009.

There are also considerable variations between the percentage of women MEPs in the different Political Groups. The highest percentages of women are in the Green/EFA Group (55%), ALDE (45%) and the S&D Group (40%).

They are substantially fewer women MEPs in the EPP (33%), GUE/NGL Group (29%),and especially in the EFD (16%) and ECR (13%) Groups.

Table 9: *Women MEPs as of August 2009*

Country	No. Women MEPs	Total No. MEPs	Women as a % of MEPs
Finland	8	13	61.5
Sweden	10	18	55.6
Estonia	3	6	50.0
Netherlands	12	25	48.0
Denmark	6	13	46.1
France	33	72	45.8
Austria	7	17	41.2
Slovakia	5	13	38.5
Latvia	3	8	37.5
Germany	37	99	37.4
Romania	12	33	36.4
Belgium	8	22	36.4
Hungary	8	22	36.4
Portugal	8	22	36.4
Spain	18	50	36.0
Bulgaria	6	17	35.3
Cyprus	2	6	33.3
United Kingdom	24	72	33.3
Greece	7	22	31.8
Slovenia	2	7	28.6
Ireland	3	12	25.0
Lithuania	3	12	25.0
Italy	16	72	22.2
Poland	11	50	22.0
Czech Republic	4	22	18.2
Luxembourg	1	6	16.7
Malta	0	5	0.0
Total	**257**	**736**	**35.0**

National parliamentary and ministerial experience

While so many of the current MEPs are newcomers and their average length of service in the European Parliament is limited, many of them have nevertheless had considerable experience in their own national parliaments, and/or as office-holders in their national governments or in their own party.

The percentage of MEPs with former national parliamentary experience has fluctuated greatly since direct elections (see Table 10). Unsurprisingly, it was at the high level of 45% in the first directly elected Parliament, with a considerable number having been nominated MEPs from their national parliaments before direct elections, and many, notably in France and Italy, also having a dual mandate. It then dropped sharply until 1989, as careers in the

European Parliament increasingly became alternatives to those in national politics, most strikingly in the UK and in Germany. The percentage then remained fairly stable from 1989 until the major enlargement in 2004, one impact of which was a sharp increase in the number of MEPs with national parliamentary experience, from the 28% figure of former or current national parliamentarians who had been elected as MEPs in 1999 to a 36.6% figure in 2004. No less than 90 (55.5%) of the 162 MEPs elected in 2004 from the 10 new Member States were former national parliamentarians. In certain of them, Latvia (8/9), Estonia (5/6) and Cyprus (5/6), practically all their new MEPs had such experience, and even in a much larger delegation, such as that of Poland, with its 54 members, there were 23 former members of the Sejm and 4 former Senators. In contrast only 178 (31.2%) of MEPs from the 15 old Member States elected in 2004 had had national parliamentary experience, although even this figure had gone up slightly since 1999. In 2009 the figures for MEPs with national parliamentary experience hardly went down at all compared to 2004, and remained at 35.7%. The figures from the 12 new Member States went up, with 114 of the 201 (56.7 %) having such experience. In contrast, the percentage of MEPs with national parliamentary experience from the older Member States went down to 27.9% (149 of the 535 MEPs).

The sharp differences in the percentage of former national parliamentarians between different EU countries is shown in Table 10 below, which indicates that certain of the older Member States, such as the UK, Germany, Netherlands and France have particularly low numbers in this regard. In the case of the first two, in particular, this seems to coincide with a low turnover among their MEPs, considerable seniority for many of them, and the consequent creation of a European rather than national parliamentary career for such MEPs. In other countries, especially the new Member States, but also in older Member States like Finland, Ireland or Portugal there has been greater fluidity, and more of a premium seems to be put on former national parliamentary experience.

Table 10: *Previous parliamentary and governmental experience of MEPs (1979-2009)*

	1979	1984	1989	1994	1999	2004	2009
MEPs with national parliamentary experience	45%	35%	26%	30%	28%	36.6%	35.7%
MEPs with national ministerial experience	16.7%	13%	14.1%	10.5%	10.2%	16%	17.1%

Until recently the above figures for national parliamentary experience would also have included a considerable number of MEPs who had dual mandates and were thus members of both the European Parliament and of their national parliament. The dual mandate has long been formally or informally discouraged in most Member States or parties (see Chapter 2) but by the 1999 elections there were still 40 MEPs (6.4% of the total) who were also members of a national parliament, of whom no fewer than 22 were from Italy. Seven others were from the UK, two being the long-standing dual mandate members John Hume and Ian Paisley from Northern Ireland, the remainder all coming from the House of Lords. By 2004 the dual mandate had been for-mally abolished, with two limited derogations for outgoing British MEPs re--elected in 2004 who were also members of the UK House of Lords (there were only two members in this category, Baronesses Nicholson and Ludford) and for members of the Irish Parliament elected to the European Parliament, who were allowed to keep a dual mandate until the next Irish parliamentary elec-tions, when they would have to make a choice. After the 2004 elections there were 6 Irish MEPs in this category (Ryan, Aylward, Mitchell, Coveney and Harkin from the Dail and Jim Higgins from the Seanad), but after the 2007 national elections when only Coveney opted for the Irish Parliament and the others opted to stay in the European Parliament, this derogation came to an end. After the 2009 elections there are no longer any dual mandate MEPs (although Sarah Ludford was re-elected in the UK, but on the basis of taking leave from the House of Lords)

Table 11: *National parliamentary and Ministerial experience of MEPs elected in 2009*

Country (MEPs)	Ex National Parliament	Ex national Minister
Austria 17	5 (29.4%)	1 (5.9%)
Belgium 22	10 (45.5%)	6 (27.3%)
Bulgaria 17	9 (52.9%)	4 (23.5%)
Cyprus 6	4 (66.7%)	2 (33.3%)
Czech Republic 22	11 (50%)	3 (13.6%)
Denmark 13	5 (38.5%)	1 (7.7%)
Estonia 6	5 (83.3%)	3 (50%)
Finland 13	9 (69.2%)	5 (38.5%)
France 72	15 (20.8%)	8 (11.1%)
Germany 99	13 (13.1%)	-
Greece 22	6 (27.3%)	2 (9.1%)
Hungary 22	10 (45.4%)	6 (27.3 %)
Ireland 12	8 (66.7%)	5 (41.7%)
Italy 72	24 (33.3%)	9 (12.5%)
Latvia 8	8 (100%)	6 (75%)
Lithuania 12	9 (75%)	8 (66.7%)
Luxembourg 6	3 (50%)	2 (33.3%)
Malta 5	1 (20%)	1 (20%)
Netherlands 25	4 (16%)	-
Poland 50	27 (54%)	16 (32%)
Portugal 22	13 (59.1%)	8 (36.4%)
Romania 33	15 (45.4%)	11 (33%)
Slovakia 13	10 (76.9%)	3 (23.1%)
Slovenia 7	5 (71.4%)	5 (71.4%)
Spain 50	21 (42%)	7 (14%)
Sweden 18	7 (39%)	2 (11.1%)
UK 72	6 (8.3%)	2 (2.8%)
TOTAL 736	263 (35.7%)	126 (17.1%)

A second significant impact of enlargement has been the considerable increase in MEPs with both senior and junior ministerial experience, as again shown in Tables 10 and 11. Whereas only 64 or a little over 10% of the

MEPs elected in 1999 had held such ministerial office, this figure went up in 2004 to 117 or 16% of the total, and further rose to 126 or 17.1% of the total in 2009, the highest figure for any of the Parliaments since 1979. Again there is a sharp difference between MEPs from the 15 old and the 12 new Member States, with only 58 or 10.8.% of the former having such experience, compared to 68 or 33.8% of the latter. No fewer than 6 of the 8 Latvian MEPs, 5 of the 7 Slovenes and 8 of the 12 Lithuanians are former ministers, and there are significant numbers from most of the other new Member States as well (50% of the Estonians, 43% of the Slovenes, a third of the Hungarians, etc). In the old Member States the figures are generally much lower, with, in particular (and as in 2004) not a single former senior or junior national minister from among the 99 German MEPs or the 27 Dutch MEPs, only 1 among the 17 Austrians and 13 Danes, and only 2 former junior ministers among the 72 British MEPs.

Another interesting feature is the number of former Prime Ministers and Presidents who have been elected to the EP. This has varied from election to election, but in 2004 and 2009 it has been at a higher level than in any election since the first in 1979 (see Table 12). Several of these former leaders have held important office in the Parliament: Emilio Colombo (Italy) as President just before direct elections, Pierre Pflimlin (France) from 1984–87 and Jerzy Buzek, the current EP President; Mariano Rumor and later Giovanni Goria (both Italy) as chairs of the Political Affairs Committee; Leo Tindemans and Wilfried Martens (both Belgium) as chairs of the EPP Group; Valéry Giscard d'Estaing (France) and Guy Verhofstadt (Belgium) as chairs of the Liberal Group; Poul Schluter (Denmark) as an EP Vice-President; and Michel Rocard (France) as chair of three different committees. After the 2009 elections there are now two former Presidents (Landsbergis and Paksas of Lithuania) and 8 former Prime Ministers, as well as one former acting Prime Minister, with the majority of these from the new Member States.

Besides these, the current set of MEPs include a considerable number of former Deputy Prime Ministers (8), Foreign Ministers (15), as well as many other former senior ministers.

Table 12: *Former Presidents and Prime Ministers elected to the European Parliament*

Year	Name & Nationality
1979-84	Willy Brandt (D), Leo Tindemans (B), Gaston Thorn (Lux), Edgar Faure (F), Pierre Pflimlin (F), Michel Debré (F), Jacques Chirac (F), Emilio Colombo (I), Mariano Rumor (I), Giulio Andreotti (I), Pierre Messmer (F)
1984-89	Pierre Pflimlin (F), Leopoldo Calvo Sotelo (E), Maria de Lourdes Pintasilgo (P), Francisco Balsemão (P),
1989-94	Valéry Giscard d'Estaing (F), Laurent Fabius (F), Giovani Goria (I), Emilio Colombo (I), Bettino Craxi (I), Arnaldo Forlani (I), Leo Tindemans (B)
1994-99	Paul Schluter (DK), Wilfried Martens (B), Michel Rocard (F), Leo Tindemans (B)

Year	Name & Nationality
1994-99	Poul Schluter (DK), Wilfried Martens (B), Michel Rocard (F), Leo Tindemans (B)
1999-04	Michel Rocard (F), Mario Soares (P), Jacques Santer (Lux), Ciriaco De Mita (I), Silvio Berlusconi (I), Hans Modrow (GDR)
2004-9	Vytautas Landsbergis (Lithuania), Michel Rocard (F), Guntars Krasts (Latvia), Alojz Peterle (Slovenia), Jean-Luc Dehaene (B), Massimo D'Alema (I), Poul Nyrup Rasmussen (DK), Anneli Jäätteenmaki (Finland), Jerzy Buzek (Poland), Andres Tarand (Estonia) and Eugenijus Gentvilas (Lithuania)
2009-14	Jerzy Buzek (Poland), Anneli Jäätteenmaki (Finland), Vytautas Landsbergis, Rolandas Paksas and Zigmantas Balcytis (Lithuania), Alojz Peterle (Slovenia), Jean-Luc Dehaene and Guy Verhofstadt (Belgium), Ciriaco De Mita (Italy), Ivars Godmanis (Latvia), Theodor Dimitru Stolojan (Romania)

NB. For MEPs who left to become Prime Minister or President in their country, see Table 48

Other political experience

There are three former members of the European Commission in the new Parliament (the same number as in the last two), Danuta Hubner of Poland, Sandra Kalniete of Latvia and Louis Michel of Belgium. A fourth, Michel Barnier, was a member for six months until elected to the Commission. Another Commissioner, Meglana Kuneva was elected, but decided not to take the seat but to serve out the rest of her mandate as a Commissioner.

A considerable number of current MEPs have held other important posts in their countries. There are several former regional presidents, such as Mathieu Grosch (former President of the Council of the German-speaking Community in Belgium) and Amalia Sartori and Guido Milana (respectively former Presidents of the Veneto and Lazio regional governments in Italy). Among the other former regional office-holders are former members of regional executives, former Marshals of Polish regions (Voivods), a former Northern Ireland minister (Bairbre de Brun), as well as a number of former or serving mayors, notably from France and Italy. The French delegation, for example, includes two former mayors of major cities (Dominique Baudis of Toulouse and Catherine Trautmann of Strasbourg) and the Italian delegation Gabriele Albertini of Milan and Sergio Cofferati of Bologna. With many of the MEPs being from former Communist countries, it is unsurprising that a number of them played a role during the transitional period. A number of Polish members (including the current EP President Buzek) were active in Solidarnosc, and a Romanian member, Laszlo Tokes, (currently an EP Vice President), as a Protestant pastor and then Bishop from the Hungarian minority, played a crucial part in the events leading to the fall of Ceausescu. On the other hand, another MEP, Alfreds Rubiks, had been a leading figure in the Latvian Communist Party during the Soviet period, and was then sentenced to a lengthy prison sentence in 1991 on accusations of seeking to overthrow the new Latvian Rebublic.

In addition to the above, a number of the MEPs elected in 2009 come from well-known political families, including Vittorio Prodi (brother of the former Commission President and Italian Prime Minister), Luigi Berlinguer (cousin of the former Italian Communist leader Enrico Berlinguer, whose brother Giovanni had been in the 2004-2009 Parliament), Marine Le Pen (who now serves with her father in the French Front National delegation), Indrek Tarand (son of fomer Estonian MEP and Prime Minister Andres Tarand), Elena Basescu (daughter of the current Romanian President) and Jaroslaw Walesa (son of Lech Walesa). Ana Maria Corazza Bildt (wife of Swedish politician Carl Bildt), and Carmen Romero (wife of former Spanish Prime Minister Felipe Gonzalez) are also both MEPs.

Other experience

The MEPs elected or re-elected in 2009 include members with a wide range of other experience, including celebrated judges and magistrates (such as Antonio Di Pietro of Italy and the Norwegian-born Eva Joly elected in France), anti-Mafia campaigners (such as Rosario Crocetta and Sonia Alfano of Italy), trade union leaders (such as Sergio Cofferati of Italy), the 1968 student leader Daniel Cohn-Bendit (initially a German Green, then French Green, then German and now again French Green MEP), anti-globalization campaigner Jose Bové of France, Egyptian-born and former Moslem convert to Catholicism Magdi Allam of Italy, and Christian Engstroem, a Swedish computer programmer and lobbyist for copyright and patent law reform, elected as a Pirate Party MEP. There is a former Under Secretary General of the United Nations, Pino Arlacchi and a former Secretary General of the Czech Trade Union Confederation, Richard Falbr. One of the two MEPs of Roma origin in the last Parliament, Livia Jaroka of Hungary, was re-elected in 2009, when the first ever deaf MEP, Adam Kosa of Hungary, was also elected. The range of other experience includes former diplomats, academics (including an archaeologist and a prominent seismologist), doctors, engineers and scientists.

Non-political celebrities in other spheres are now comparatively rare, but there are a number of media personalities, journalists and former TV film stars, such as the actor Michael Cashman (British Labour) from the TV series "Eastenders" as well as former TV presenters (such as Dirk Sterckx, Yvo Belet and Frédérique Ries from Belgium, Jean Marie Cavada from France and actress/presenters Barbara Matera and Elisabetta Gardini among the Italian delegation, which also includes the pop singer, Iva Zanicchi).

Among those with sporting backgrounds who were elected in 2009 were an Olympic fencing champion (Pal Schmitt of Hungary); a member of the Ice Hockey Hall of Fame (Peter Stastny of Slovakia), a European and world race walking champion (Sari Essayah of Finland) and a Taekwondo champion (Slavi Binev of Bulgaria).

Finally, one of the two cosmonauts elected in 2004, Vladimir Remek of the Czech Republic (the other had been Umberto Guidoni of Italy), was re-elected as a Czech Communist MEP in 2009, and remains the only MEP to have an asteroid (2552 Remek) named after him!

Post-MEP experience

Those MEPs who leave the Parliament to move on to other things frequently remain active in political life. A stint as an MEP is a not infrequent part of a successful political career. In France, for instance, 11 of the last 20 Prime Ministers have, at one stage or another in their careers, been MEPs (as have several Presidents). Many post-war Belgian and Italian Prime Ministers have similarly been MEPs. A large number of MEPs have gone on to become national or regional ministers in their own Member States (see Table 48).

In the three years following the 1999 elections, no fewer than 18 MEPs were appointed ministers in nine Member States. In the last year of the 1999-2004 Parliament 4 members of one committee alone (the Environment Committee) were appointed as national or regional government ministers (Jorge Moreira da Silva and Frédérique Ries in the Portuguese and Belgian governments, Laura Gonzalez Alvarez and Emilia Muller in the Asturian and Bavarian regional governments respectively).

This pattern has continued. Toomas Hendrik Ilves left the European Parliament in 2006 to become the President of Estonia. Valdis Dombrovskis similarly left the European Parliament in 2009 in order to become the Latvian Prime Minister. Since the 2009 elections a considerable number of elected MEPs have left to take up other roles. Pal Schmitt of Hungary left to become President of Hungary; four others (Eniko Gyori of Hungary, Giorgos Papakonstantinou of Greece, Ramon Jauregui of Spain and Alan Kelly of Ireland) became national government ministers; and yet another, Jean-Claude Marcourt, became a regional government minister. Several others were nominated as Commissioners (Viviane Reding of Luxembourg, Michel Barnier of France, Janusz Lewandowski of Poland and Rumiana Jeleva of Bulgaria, although the latter was subsequently not confirmed). Six others went to their national parliaments.

In some countries more MEPs have gone on to their national parliament than the reverse. Whereas there have been relatively few British ministers who have become MEPs, many former MEPs have become ministers. Indeed, every single one of the eight British MEPs first elected to Westminster in 1983/84 and of the five elected in 1987, was later promoted to positions in government or on the opposition front-bench. Furthermore, many went on to play a prominent part in European affairs, such as by serving on the Commons Select Committee on European legislation (in 2002, a quarter of its members were former MEPs) or by playing an important role in major European debates (e.g., Geoff Hoon in the Maastricht ratification procedure). Some became ministers in roles where their European experience would be likely to be relevant (David Curry – Ministry of Agriculture, and Eric Forth – Department of Trade and Industry). Three (Joyce Quin, Geoff Hoon (twice) and Glenys Kinnock) became European ministers in the 1997-2010 Labour government, and among several other former MEPs in that Labour Government were the Deputy PM (John Prescott) and a Sports Minister (Dick Caborn). In the current Conservative-Liberal Democrat coalition government both the Deputy Prime Minster (Nick Clegg) and the Secretary of State for Energy and Climate Change (Chris Huhne) are former Liberal Democrat MEPs, and Transport Minister of State Theresa Villiers is a former Conservative MEP.

In the UK, seepage back to national politics has been complicated by the constituency system and by the fact that both major British parties have frowned upon MEPs standing for selection as Westminster candidates. In other Member States, the osmosis between the European Parliament and national politics has often been easier, thanks notably to the list system and, in some Member States, to the fact that ministers do not have to be MPs.

Some MEPs who became ministers in their own Member State were later re-elected to the European Parliament, such as Hanja Maij-Weggen, Hedy d'Ancona and Piet Dankert from the Netherlands, Jacques Santer of Luxembourg, Alain Lamassoure of France, Giorgio Napolitano of Italy, Frédérique Ries of Belgium and Pat the Cope Gallagher of Ireland.

All these factors imply that MEPs are not simply an isolated political group with no links or inter-connections with the rest of the political class. The osmosis with national politics has not eroded its identity, nor the commitment of the majority of MEPs to strengthening the Parliament in its own right, but has given the Parliament the added advantage of being an integral part of Europe's political networks. Indeed, it is the place *par excellence* where politicians from different Member States are in regular contact. No other group of politicians in Europe is in such constant contact with colleagues from other Member States.

The role of individual members within Parliament

Parliament's rules state that MEPs "shall not be bound by any instructions and shall not receive a binding mandate" and this is now further reinforced by the Members Statute of 28 September 2005, which reiterates the above, and further states (in its Article 2) that "Members shall be free and independent" and that (Article 3) " Members shall vote on an individual and personal basis". They are therefore free from any external constraint as to how they vote, how they organise their work and what they say.

As in any Parliament, most members submit themselves to the discipline required of belonging to a Political Group and the pressure to follow the collective position adopted by the Group. Group whipping and discipline are discussed in the next chapter, but they are less strict than in most national parliaments. In any case, individual members can play an important role in defining a Group position, as positions are defined by the Group itself, rather than being handed down from above by ministers or a party leader. Individual members can also (and occasionally do) opt out of the Group position if they are not satisfied. As a result, individual "back-bench" members do play a considerable role in the life of the Parliament.

There are also a number of maverick or "outsider" members who have made a considerable impact within the Parliament by effective use of the relevant Rules of Procedure, beginning with Marco Pannella in the first directly elected Parliament in 1979. And occasionally there are back-bench revolts against Group leaderships, especially when members from different Groups are angered by what they see as a cosy deal cooked up by the Group leaders, most often on procedural or timetable issues.

Parliament's Rules of Procedure provide for numerous rights for individual members, or for several members acting together outside the normal Political Group or committee framework.

A very important recently-acquired right is the catch-the-eye system that is now used in plenary debates after the rapporteurs and Group spokespersons have had their say. This was introduced primarily to permit a more spontaneous discussion, but it also gives greater scope for backbenchers. From the

2009 elections until the end of October 2010 there were over 2700 requests to speak by individual members in the catch-the-eye section of plenary debates, of which almost 80% (over 2150) were able to be accommodated.

In addition, a single individual member may put questions to the Commission or Council (for question time or for a written answer), table a motion for resolution or a written declaration, table and move amendments to any text in committee, make explanations of vote, ask questions related to the work of Parliament's leadership (Conference of Presidents, Bureau and Quaestors), table amendments to the Rules of Procedure, raise points of order, or move the inadmissibility of a matter (both of these latter rights entailing a prior claim over other requests to speak). Individual members may also make personal statements, notably when derogatory comments have been made about them by other speakers.

The use of some of these powers is described in greater detail elsewhere in this book. A few comments, however, can be made at this stage, regarding some of these powers and their value for individual members.

The value of Question Time in plenary, for example, which was initiated before British entry into the Community, but which for many years was dominated by British members, has often been questioned in the European Parliament context, in that it has little of the cut and thrust of its original model, is often very poorly attended, and yet takes up valuable plenary time. Nevertheless, all attempts to reduce its duration are met with strong resistance from certain MEPs (not exclusively British), who claim that it is of great importance for individual MEPs. At most sessions there is now Question Time to the Commission, and there are also regular if less frequent Question Times to the Council and also to the President of the Commission. The greatest users of Question Time are now the 12 Irish MEPs, who not only ask the most questions, but frequently ask supplementaries as well. 6 of the 13 questions to the Commission, for example, in May 2010 were asked by Irish members, and no less than 10 of the 19 questions to the Council in September and October 2010.

Written questions, too, can be of considerable value in enabling an individual member to put down a marker on an issue of constituency or other importance. Another such device is by tabling a motion for resolution. Although such motions only rarely lead to a committee report, members can, nevertheless, gain publicity from their initiative, and show their constituents or other groups that they are active (thus these motions are comparable to "early-day motions" in the UK House of Commons). A similar function is provided by written declarations (see Chapter 15).

Another individual right is to make explanations of vote in plenary. These used to precede the final vote on a text and, although limited to one minute per member, cumulatively delayed it by up to half an hour or more. Considerable pressure was often exerted for them not to be made orally, but converted into written explanations (cheers often greeted members' calls of "in writing" and groans when they actually started to speak!). Members often did assert their right to an oral statement, however, and these statements were often more concise and passionate than those made in the preceding debate, and made before a much fuller, if often noisy, house. In 1994, however, a rule change allowed the President to place these explanations of vote after the final vote (when most of the members have left the chamber) in order to speed up voting time. Some members have made considerable use of this, including Carlo Fatuzzo of the Italian Pensioners' Party, whose statements on a huge range of issues became a regular feature of plenary sessions during the 1999-2004 and 2004-09 Parliaments.

Both oral and written explanations of vote are still frequently given in the current Parliament, with 792 oral explanations being given from the July 2009 elections until October 2010, and 5618 written explanations. From January to early November 2010 alone, no fewer than 635 oral explanations of vote were given, with the British Conservative MEP, Dan Hannan giving 46 of these. Other MEPs who often give such oral explanations of vote include some from the new Member States (Czech Republic, Lithuania, Poland, Estonia, and Latvia) as well as a considerable number of Italian and Irish MEPs.

As in any parliament, points of order and procedural motions are also often used (and sometimes abused) by individual members. They are particularly frequent at the beginning of sittings, or after controversial rulings have been made by the President, or in order to continue a terminated debate by other means. They are also often used to make isolated points of constituency or sectoral concern.

In order to provide greater discipline as regards points of order the Rules were changed in January 1992, limiting individual points of order to one rather than three minutes, and requiring the members concerned to specify which rule or rules were not being respected. The 2002 Rules revision (Corbett Report) also set aside half an hour at each plenary week for members to make "one minute speeches" on any matter they chose, thus obviating the need to make bogus points of order. It immediately became much used by members, and this has continued to be the case at both Strasbourg and Brussels sessions. From the 2009 direct elections to early November 2010, 642 statements were made under this rule (150), an average of over 30 per session, and with up to 40 being made on occasion (and with up to 86 requests per session). It is currently very much used by MEPs from the new Member States, notably Poland and Romania (8 of the 30 speeches in June 2010 were by Romanian MEPs), and among the older Member States by Spanish, Portuguese, Greek, Irish and UK members, with the 12 Irish MEPs making practically as many statements as the 72 from the UK.

Parliament's Rules of Procedure also grant rights to individual members acting together with a certain specified number of other members. This is done wherever the Rules confer such rights on Political Groups, and even in a few cases where Political Groups have no such rights (such as a request for a quorum to be ascertained). The actual number of members required to assert such rights is currently set at 40. In some special cases, one-tenth, one-fifth, one-quarter, or one-third of MEPs is required.

40 members may, for example, table an amendment in plenary, nominate candidates for President, Vice-President, Quaestor or Ombudsman; table those types of motions for resolution dealt with directly in plenary (to wind up debates on statements or on oral questions or on human rights); propose to reject or to amend legislative "common positions" of the Council or the draft budget; request roll call votes; and oppose the adoption of reports without debate.

The Rules thus give considerable scope for dissident members within a

Political Group, or coalitions of individual members across Groups, to trigger different procedures.

The work of an individual MEP: choice of priorities

The main constraint on members is time. Parliamentary business takes up one week a month in plenary session in Strasbourg and much of the next three weeks by committee, plenary and Group meetings in Brussels (especially if an MEP is active on two committees), and with occasional meetings in other countries as well. This is compounded by the time it takes to travel between these various locations and the member's home country.

In addition, members are expected to keep in touch with their political base at home. Members with geographical constituencies (such as UK and Irish members) typically spend a couple of days each week dealing with individual constituents, NGOs, local government leaders and staff, businesses, trade unions, development agencies, MPs, party bodies, etc. in their areas and taking up invitations to speak at universities, schools, organisations, chambers of commerce, clubs and, last but not least, local media. They will also have a vast amount of correspondence to deal with. All this may relate to their work in the Parliament, to the local application of European legislation, to European grants and assistance or to problems encountered by constituents travelling or working in other Member States. Even if members do not have a geographical constituency to nurse, they may have some similar activities or have sectoral (e.g., trade union) or other specific responsibilities within their party.

Within Parliament, there are further conflicting pressures. The meeting of their main committee may coincide with a hearing or debate in another committee that is of greater political importance to them. Intergroup meetings (see Chapter 10) may take up time, as does speaking to visitors' groups. MEPs may well be involved in their own national party committees or working groups or liaison with government ministers. Lobbyists wish to meet members, and to invite them to presentations and receptions. The member will also have requests for interviews from the media and will anyway wish to cultivate these contacts on a regular basis.

Time pressure is even greater on the President, the leaders and co-ordinators of the Political Groups, leaders of national party delegations, committee chairs and rapporteurs on controversial policy issues who have fuller agendas because of their specific role. Members who have established a reputation in a particular field are also in particular demand, especially if they are proficient linguists.

Members can, of course, count on the assistance of Parliament staff, Group staff or their own assistants, though not nearly to the same extent as members of the US Congress.

All this shows that an individual MEP is faced with tough choices. An active member may well gain greater influence within the Parliament, with prestigious rapporteurships, and so on, but lose touch with his or her own political base at home, and risk not being re-elected. While the choice is not usually as stark as this (members who have built up their reputations within the Parliament may well gain domestically as well), a member must select an appropriate balance of priorities. How much time should they spend in

Parliament and at home? Should they remain generalists or seek to become policy specialists? What activities should they concentrate on?

A number of factors condition these choices. Geographical proximity to Brussels or Strasbourg makes it easy for certain members to come and go frequently, whereas this is more difficult for other members, such as those from Ireland, Southern Italy, Spain, Portugal, Greece, Cyprus, Finland or the Baltic states.

Secondly, some types of electoral system, and party selection system, may put more pressure on some members than on others to spend a lengthy period of time at home base, though all systems require cultivation of some sort of base if they want to ensure that they remain a candidate the next time around. Another factor is the nature of a member's interests and responsibilities. Moreover, whilst individual members cannot be mandated, some of them retain close links with particular sectors or interest groups which will help to condition their choice of priorities. Whether a member is from a mainstream or a fringe party is yet another factor. Members from small Groups and non-attached members may well find it easier, for example, to make an impact in plenary where they can make a well publicised speech, than in committee where they may find it extremely hard to get major rapporteurships.

Differences in national culture also play a role, with different emphasis being put on different aspects of a parliamentarian's role, and even on the importance attached to attendance at meetings. Examples of such differences in national culture abound. Members from northern European countries have generally been more prepared to spend time, for example, on the details of technical legislation than many members from southern Europe; British and Irish members have traditionally put more of an emphasis on Question Time in plenary, and so on.

As a result of all these factors, the priorities of individual members are very different, as are their profiles within the European Parliament. Some become known as men or women of the House, and are constantly present in plenary. Others are more effective within committee, or in their Group or their national party delegation; others concentrate more on their national or regional political image. Some members remain generalists, whereas others become specialists, and are always allocated reports or opinions within a particular policy area. Some even develop functional rather than policy specialities (e.g. the Rules of Procedure). Some only pay short visits to Brussels or Strasbourg, whereas others are always present. Many but by no means all, have even bought accommodation in Brussels and some make that their family home rather than have their family compete for the member's precious time in the constituency.

Compared to the United States, for example, where individual Senators and Congressmen are subject to ratings and numerical rankings by a wide variety of interest groups and lobbies, this has been much less developed for Members of the European Parliament, although some organisations, such as environmental NGOs, have begun to attempt it. An interesting initiative has been that of Votewatch, which analyses the records of individual MEPs on the basis of formally published public information, including their committee reports and opinions, speeches in plenary and attendance records. It also looks at individual sensitive votes in the Parliament, and at the breakdown of such votes by national party, Political Group and Member State, as well as attempting an analysis of overall voting cohesion under these different categories. It will be instructive to see whether there will be further follow-up to such initiatives, and whether the performance and priorities of individual MEPs will become more of a matter of public comment.

Rights and obligations of individual members

The adoption of the Members' Statute

MEPs used to be paid quite different salaries by their own national parliament. For many years, progress on eliminating the main differences in treatment of MEPs from different Member States was hampered by the lack of a formal legal basis in the treaties for the adoption of a members' Statute. This was finally remedied in 1997 with the Amsterdam Treaty, which added provisions whereby the European Parliament shall "with the approval of the Council acting unanimously lay down the regulations and general conditions governing the performance of the duties of its members." The issue of individual members' salaries and allowances was particularly controversial until agreement was finally reached on a uniform Statute for MEPs. The application of national rules had led, inter alia, to huge differences in the basic salaries of members from different countries, as well as to divergent treatment mentioned elsewhere in this chapter in such matters as incompatibilities and immunity requests.

Until the Statute came into force in July 2010 a member's basic salary was paid by his or her Member State and was (except for the Netherlands) the same as the salary paid to a national parliamentarian from that country. This difference in national treatment resulted in basic annual salaries varying enormously. The best paid were members from Italy, followed by those from Austria and Ireland. Those from Spain received less than a third as much, but after enlargement this was no longer the lowest with most of the MEPs from the new Member States having still lower salaries, with the Bulgarians on 7% of what an Italian got!

Correcting this anomaly was a matter of great sensitivity. In those Member States where salaries were lower, a sharp rise in MEPs' salaries could have had a negative effect on public opinion and on relations with national parliamentarians. In countries where salaries were higher, there was a natural reluctance to favour a large drop in salary. The battle to adopt a common Statute was thus a long one.

Parliament's Legal Affairs Committee, with Willi Rothley, a German socialist, as rapporteur, had begun work in the 1994-1999 Parliament, and proposed a common and transparent salary for all MEPs. This would be based, pending an external study by independent experts, on the weighted average of the existing salaries of the then 15 Member States. All MEPs would be subject not to national taxation but to a common European tax, so that, as is the case for EU staff, the establishment of a common salary would not be undercut by great differences in tax treatment. He also covered the complex issue of pensions and other benefits and proposed that the Statute should cover issues such as the independence of MEPs and rules of conduct on their financial interests.

Rothley's report was easily adopted in committee but had a tougher passage in plenary on 3 December 1998, when his basic approach was supported by Parliament, but with some close votes on some of his key recommendations. The finally adopted text included a number of new points on non-financial matters, such as a list of incompatibilities, immunity and verification of credentials, and the filling of vacant seats.

Parliament's text was then examined by a Council working party, which met on several occasions with Parliament representatives. Common tax for MEPs was opposed by certain Member States, notably the Nordic countries and the UK. On 26 April 1999, only shortly before the Parliament's final plenary before the elections, the Council adopted its own version of the Statute, which followed the Parliament's draft on certain issues but took a different approach on others. It eliminated the proposed transitional arrangements, permitted derogations from a common tax regime for MEPs (so that some but not all members would continue to be subject to national taxation regimes) and proposed a different regime as regards pensions. The Council also sought to include detailed rules on the reimbursements of MEPs' expenses within the Statute.

On 5 May 1999 the EP decided, on a vote of 336 to 140 with 31 abstentions, on Rothley's recommendation, not to accept the Council's text. He argued not just on the substance, but on the procedure: it was not up to Council to make a counter-proposal when the treaty provided for Parliament to elaborate and adopt a text with the assent of the Council. After all, Parliament did not elaborate counter-proposals when it had to give assent to Council texts! Instead the Parliament sought to pursue negotiations with the Council on the basis of the Parliament's original draft, with a view to a decision "if possible before the end of this parliamentary term".

This timetable was not met, and the 1999-2004 Parliament was still confronted with the issue. It seemed that the Nice Treaty, by introducing qualified majority voting on the Statute (except for tax matters, which would still require unanimity) would facilitate the obtaining of Council's assent. The Legal Affairs Committee (with Willy Rothley again rapporteur) consulted a group of outside experts on the level of salaries (whose recommendation was based on salaries in comparable jobs) and led to the committee adopting a recommendation that MEPs should be paid 50% of the basic salary of a judge at the Court of Justice. A package thought capable of obtaining Council's assent was approved by Parliament (by 294 votes to 171 with 59 abstentions) in June 2003. The Council, however, announced that it objected to three points: the retirement age for MEPs, the tax arrangements for their salaries and questions to do with privileges and immunities, which it said should not be part of the Statute but reviewed through a revision of the 1965 Protocol on Immunities (a matter for governments alone).

Parliament responded by voting again in December 2003 and deciding by a very large majority (345 to 94 with 88 abstentions) to eliminate these bones of contention. Accepting the wish of several governments to be able to levy national income tax on MEPs' salaries (even though they were now to be paid from the EU budget), Parliament agreed that they could be subject not only to European tax but also to national tax. Its only condition was that there should be no double taxation (a point accepted by the Council). Parliament proposed a compromise on the retirement age, which the then

Italian Presidency of the EU had indicated would be acceptable: MEPs would be entitled to a pension from the age of 63 (instead of 65 as the Council wanted or 60 as proposed by Parliament in June). Finally, Parliament agreed to deal with the immunities and privileges separately, asking the Member States to revise the 1965 Protocol.

Unexpectedly and at the very last minute – during the Council meeting of 26 January 2004 which was due to give final approval to the Statute – ministers from Germany, Sweden, France and Austria objected to the level of the proposed salaries for MEPs, set at half that for a judge of the European Court of Justice and which until then had been unopposed. The new Parliament elected in 2004 decided (Gargani Report A6-0189/2005) to concede to Council's demands, accepting in June 2005 to reduce the level of the common salary to 38.5 percent of that of a judge at the Court of Justice. It was thus able finally to adopt the Statute, with the assent of the Council, and it entered into force at the beginning of the 2009 Parliament.

Incompatibilities and verification of credentials

A few incompatibilities were established in the original 1976 Council Act on direct elections. It laid down a list of posts that were held to be incompatible with the job of MEP: minister in a government of a Member State, European Commissioner, a member or the Registrar of the Court of Justice or an active (i.e. not on leave) official of an EU institution. Member States were permitted to lay down additional incompatibilities, pending the entry into force of a uniform electoral procedure. The common principles for European elections adopted in 2003 and applied since 2004, lay down additional incompatibilities, notably for bodies set up since 1976 (European Central Bank, Committee of Regions, Ombudsman, etc) and phase out the dual mandate with national parliaments (see Chapter 2).

The 1976 Act also provided for the Assembly to verify the credentials of members. This is carried out by the Parliament's competent committee (at present, the Legal Affairs Committee) and is normally just a matter of taking note of the results communicated by the competent authorities of the Member States. Pending verification, newly elected members have the same rights as other members.

Verification has not always been a formality. The credentials of Irish members, nominated in 1981 to replace colleagues who had become ministers, was challenged because in Ireland, at the time, it had been provided for the national parliament to choose a replacement MEP in the event of a midterm vacancy. Some MEPs challenged this as an infringement of the principle that MEPs should be directly elected. Although unsuccessful, the challenge did eventually lead to a change in the Irish system with designated replacements being put up at the time of the elections. Only one member has actually had her election invalidated (in 1979), and had to stand again (successfully) for election, the late Dame Shelagh Roberts: she had been deemed to occupy a post of profit under the Crown, which was incompatible with being an MEP under the relevant UK rules.

The acceptance of resignations from Parliament has also been challenged, on the grounds that these may have resulted from outside pressure. This was notably the case with the French Gaullist party in the 1979-84

Parliament, which had concocted a system whereby most of its MEPs stood down after a year in favour of the next on the list, who then did likewise. Their system was found to be technically legal, but the embarrassment was sufficient to ensure that it was not repeated.

In March 1994, Parliament's competent committee ruled that, in circumstances where freedom to exercise the mandate was not guaranteed, Parliament could reserve the right to declare the mandate invalid, even where the member in question had already been involved in Parliament's work. Parliament adopted more systematic rules on the verification of credentials (now Rule 3) and on the term of office of members (Rule 4) in May 1994. In 1999 the Rules were further reinforced as regards the examination of cases where the election of a member is due to the withdrawal of a higher-placed candidate from the same list.

Facilities

Once elected, new members are given an initial background briefing, receive a pass, a voting card for use in electronic votes at the plenary sessions, and also a special *laisser-passer*, which allows them to travel freely around the European Union without any other documents. They are also given offices in Brussels and Strasbourg. These offices are broadly equal in size and facilities, with only Parliament's Presidents and Vice-Presidents, former Presidents, Quaestors and Political Group and committee chairs getting larger offices. Members also have some working space available to them collectively in the European Parliament's office in their own national capital. They may make use of the shuttle minibus and cars for travel to and from the airport or station in Brussels and Strasbourg or to their hotel. Former MEPs may join the Former Members' Association, which keeps them informed of events, and offers a small "transit" office for former members visiting the Parliament.

Salaries and allowances

After the July 2009 elections, all newly elected MEPs came automatically under the regime of the new Statute. All MEPs coming within its scope have the same salary, which, as described above, is paid out of Parliament's budget, and has been fixed at 38.5% of the basic salary of a judge at the European Court of Justice. In 2010 this monthly pre-tax salary amounted to €7.807.12. The salary is reduced to €6.083.91 after imposition of the EU tax, but, as described above, individual Member States can subject the salary to additional national taxes.

MEPs who were already members in the 2004-09 Parliament and who were re-elected were given the option of retaining instead the previous national system for salary, as well as transitional allowances and pensions, for the duration of their time as MEPs. They were given until 13 August 2009 to make their decision, which was irreversible. If they then opted to retain their national system, they continued to be paid from the budget of their own Member State.

Again as mentioned above, pension entitlement, to be paid from the European Parliament budget, is now from the age of 63, with the level being fixed at 3.5% of the salary for each full year of service as an MEP, and with a maximum ceiling of 70%. Community tax is deducted by Parliament from this sum, but Member States also retain the right to make this pension subject to national taxation, as long as there is no double taxation. The EP old age pension is compatible with other pension schemes, but MEPs entitled to both an old age pension and a transitional allowance are given 3 months to decide which one they wish to opt for. There is also scope for an invalidity pension if MEPs have to resign on the grounds of no longer being able to perform their duties. Parliament had previously set up a voluntary pension fund for its members. It will be maintained for re-elected members or former members who had already acquired rights or future entitlements in that fund, but members opting for the common salary under the Statute may not acquire any new rights, and the fund is not open to newly elected members.

In spite of the long-standing differences in basic salary, MEPs from different countries have long been treated equally, however, in the size of the five main allowances to which they are entitled.

Members receive daily allowances for attendance at Parliament to cover accommodation and subsistence, provided they sign a register to prove their presence. This is currently fixed at €298 per day but during plenaries can be reduced by half if an MEP misses more than half the roll-call votes. The allowance is set at €149 for meetings outside the EU, but exclusive of reimbursement for hotel bills.

MEPs are also reimbursed for travel expenses to and from their constituencies or places of residence to EP plenary, committee, group or other meetings. This used to be on a flat rate lump sum basis upon presentation of proof that the journey had been made, but this became a matter of considerable controversy, lacking in transparency, and clearly being capable of abuse. The system has thus changed since the 2009 elections. Members are now reimbursed for the actual cost of their tickets, and on presentation of the actual receipts, subject to a maximum ceiling of a business class air fare, a first class rail fare, or else €0.49 per kilometre for car journeys. Certain ancillary expenses are also taken into account.

In addition members may now be reimbursed for up to 24 return journeys within their own Member State by air, rail or boat, and also a certain number of journeys by car up to a fixed number of kilometres (in three bands of 8,000, 16,000 and 24,000 kilometres according to the size of the country). Previously they did not have any special funding for travel costs within their own Member State, which can be very high in the case of MEPs whose regional constituencies are large (a constant gripe, for example, of former Scottish National Party MEP, Winnie Ewing, when she represented the Scottish Highlands and Islands). Finally they can also claim up to €4,148 per annum for other work-related travel outside their own Member State.

Members are given a monthly general expenditure allowance of €4202 for office, IT, telephone and postage costs. Any member attending fewer than half of the plenary days in the course of a parliamentary year has to reimburse half of their general expenditure allowance, unless there are valid medical or family reasons or unless the member has been absent on other official Parliament business. This happened to four MEPs in 2007/08, two in 2008/09 and one in 2009/10. Finally, members can make use of a budget for staff for one or more secretaries or assistants, though this money is not handled by them (see section below on members' assistants).

In addition, members are given insurance cover, are reimbursed for two thirds of their medical expenses, and are provided with offices in Brussels and Strasbourg. They have access to Parliament cars under certain circumstances (primarily to and from the airport or railway stations in Brussels and Strasbourg), and may also attend language and computer courses.

When MEPs leave the Parliament, they are also entitled to a transitional allowance, which lasts for a period of one month for every year of a member's service, but for no less than 6 months or longer than 24 months. It is to be discontinued if a member takes up certain posts, such as in a national parliament, national or regional government, or as an EU official.

Immunities

This is another area where the lack of a uniform Statute for members had led to considerable diversity between nationalities. Members' immunity is covered by the protocol on the privileges and immunities of the European Union. This provides for MEPs to enjoy the same immunities in their own country as national parliamentarians and, while in other countries of the Union, to be immune from any measure of detention and from legal proceedings. Members are in any case immune while travelling to and from the Parliament. Immunity does not apply when caught in the act of committing a criminal offence. Immunity can only be waived by the European Parliament, upon application from the legal authorities in the Member States, thus allowing the MEP in question to appear in court.

Parliament called in 1983 for the protocol to be amended, and the Commission subsequently tabled a proposal to this effect, which would have provided uniform rules. This has still not been adopted.

Requests by the national authorities of the Member States for members' immunity to be waived are a regular feature at plenary sessions, as are requests as to whether a member's immunity applies as well as requests by the concerned members for the Parliament to defend their immunity. Such requests are transmitted to the competent committee, which submits its report recommending in favour of or against the waiving of immunity, but without, of course, pronouncing on or even examining the member's guilt, which is a matter for the courts. The committee has traditionally nominated one or two specialist rapporteurs for such requests for a number of years.

In its many reports on requests for the waiving of immunity the Parliament has established a number of basic principles, the most important of which is not to waive immunity if the acts of which a member is accused form part of his or her political activities. In the majority of cases, mostly concerning controversial statements by members or participation in unauthorised demonstrations, Parliament has not acceded to requests to waive immunity. Between 1979 and the 2009 elections, some 157 immunity cases were decided upon in the plenary. On 45 of these occasions immunity was waived or a member's immunity not defended, a figure that has risen sharply, however, in recent years.(see Table 13). Allegations of corruption or serious criminal activities (e.g., embezzlement or fraud, membership of the Camorra, provision of assistance to criminals, etc.) constituted some of these latter cases, as did more minor and non-political offences such as parking in a prohibited area or failure to report a road accident.

A striking feature is that 71 (over 45%) of the cases treated in plenary to 2009 concerned Italian members (including no less than 15 concerning Marco Pannella). So many problems have arisen in the Italian context that Parliament adopted a specific resolution in June 2002 on the legal situation concerning Italian members. A more recent resolution, in April 2009, looked at the specific situation as regards legal immunity in Poland. There have been a considerable number of cases concerning German and French members (19 and 16 respectively), as well as Greek and Portuguese members. On the other hand, there have been a number of countries – including some which have been in the EU since before 1979 – like the Netherlands, Luxembourg or Ireland, which have never been concerned by immunity requests. The only ones concerning the UK both related to Ashley Mote, elected for the United Kingdom Independence Party and charged with housing benefit fraud, who was subsequently jailed.

From the 2009 elections to the end of 2010 there were only 5 cases treated in the plenary, with 3 others having been dropped, and with 8 still pending. Of those already treated all but one concerned new Member States, and all but one ended up with Parliament waiving or else deciding not to defend the immunity of the member concerned.

Table 13: *Immunity cases treated in EP plenary*

Legislature	Cases treated in plenary	Decision to waive or not to uphold Member's immunity	Decision not to waive or to uphold Member's immunity	No recommendation
1979-84	8	1	7	-
1984-89	36	9	27	-
1989-94	33	5	28	-
1994-99	9	2	7	-
1999-2004	27	4	20	3
2004-2009	44	24	20	-

Some controversial cases do arise. In December 1989, Jean-Marie Le Pen's immunity was waived by a large majority after a passionate debate on whether the particularly controversial nature of remarks for which he was being prosecuted justified abandonment of Parliament's customary concern to protect members' expression of political opinions. Parliament thus over-ruled its relevant committee's narrow decision (ten to nine with two abstentions) not to waive Le Pen's immunity. Le Pen's immunity was waived in similar circumstances on another charge at the March 1990 plenary, and yet again on 6 October 1998, on this latter occasion on a request submitted not by the French but by the German authorities.

A request from a Spanish court to waive Silvio Berlusconi's immunity, not long before he became Prime Minister of Italy, was not acted upon when the then President of Parliament, Nicole Fontaine, ruled that it had not been for-warded to Parliament by the correct governmental authority. This led to controversy in the Parliament, with many on the left in particular believing that she had sought to avoid dealing with the issue. Precedents were found on both sides of the argument, but the procedural matter was only settled after Berlusconi had left Parliament to become Prime Minister.

Declaration of financial interests

Rule 9 of Parliament's Rules of Procedure states that Parliament may lay down a code of conduct for its members. The only implementing provision so far is that contained in Annex I of the Rules providing for a declaration of financial interests. National traditions on this issue vary greatly, with some countries such as the UK and Germany having fairly rigid rules, others much weaker ones, and some none at all.

Parliament first adopted a report in March 1983 on the issues involved, drawn up by Hans Nord (Dutch Liberal, former Parliament Secretary-General). It opted for brief general provisions rather than a set of very detailed rules. Over time, these have been tightened up and Annex I now provides that each member make a detailed declaration of professional activities and list any other paid functions or activities (Article 2). Members are also meant to disclose orally any direct financial interest in a subject under discussion in Parliament or in one of its bodies, and, in a recent reform of the rule, irrespective of whether this interest is obvious from their written declaration (Article 1). Finally, members' declarations are to be contained in a register. The register is available for public inspection in the offices in Luxembourg, Strasbourg (during plenary sessions) and Brussels of the members' activities unit of the Directorate General for the Presidency. Since 2001 (Corbett Report interpreting the rules) it can also be consulted on the internet (where each MEP's entry can be found under their own page on the Parliament's website).

Complaints about insufficient information provided by some members, and the lack of sanctions against members not in compliance, resulted in the rules being made more rigorous, with sanctions introduced for the first time. If a member persists in not submitting a declaration, the President shall give two months to comply, after which the member is "named or shamed" in the minutes of the first day of each part-session after expiry of the time limit. In case of further non-compliance the President is to take action to suspend the member concerned.

Moreover, members must now have duly completed their financial declaration before they may be validly nominated as an office-holder of Parliament or one of its bodies, or as a member of any delegation representing Parliament externally. Indeed one of the first tasks that has to be carried out at the constituent meetings of Parliament's committees is to verify that the various Group nominees for chair or vice-chair have filled in such a declaration! The considerable effectiveness of the new measures was shown by the fact that all members now comply.

Members' assistants

As indicated earlier, members are given a budget for the employment of personal assistants. At the time of writing, this secretarial allowance amounted to

€19,364 per month. None of this money is handled by members, as Parliament now directly employs the assistants selected by the member.

Members are allowed considerable freedom in the deployment of these assistants. Some members prefer to have more assistance in Brussels, others in their own constituencies, and a few in their national capital. However, the general norm is to have one or two well paid full-time assistants and one or more less well paid or part-time assistants in Brussels, and two or three in the constituency office. A number of members choose to have a stagiaire on an internship for six months or for an academic year from September to July, usually in Brussels. There are also some members who make little use of assistants.

The role of assistants varies greatly, with some given considerable political responsibilities, and others concentrating more on office tasks, such as typing, booking tickets or running other errands. Typical tasks are to arrange meetings with Commission officials or representatives of trade associations, to manage the considerable volume of correspondence (including several hundred emails per day!) received by members, to draft letters, articles, press releases or parliamentary questions, amendments to parliamentary reports and to carry out background research. Some assistants help to draft reports when their boss becomes a rapporteur. Brussels-based assistants also often attend meetings when the member is elsewhere engaged, and brief the member on what took place. Some help service the intergroups in which their member is active (see Chapter 10).

Assistants based in the member's home country tend to deal with constituents' enquiries, handle mail and have a liaison function with national or regional interests, the party and the press – all matters of considerable importance in view of the large amount of time spent travelling by the average MEP.

While there are some exceptions, assistants tend to be less well paid (although there are great variations between them) than Parliament or Political Group staff, and there has tended to be a far higher turnover, although this is expected to change as a result of the new Assistants' Statute which came into force following the 2009 elections. They tend to be younger (often recent university graduates), and take on the job as their first or second job. A minority, however, remain assistants for many years, and when they leave the employment of one member may then start working for another. Some even work for two or more members at once. In at least one case (both before and after the introduction of the Statute) assistants formed a consortium with a number of MEPs on their books, as well as members from the respective national parliament. In other cases several members have pooled some of their resources and run a joint secretariat. The Spanish Socialist Party (PSOE), the Dutch Labour Party (PVA) and the Swedish Social Democrats (SSD) are among those who have established such an arrangement, with assistants being allocated to focus on a particular parliamentary committee.

A handful of part time assistants have their own careers (in consultancy or as freelance writers, for example) or pursue further university education usually through Masters degrees or PhDs, and have a part-time role as assistants in order primarily to widen their range of contacts and knowledge. In this context, assistants must declare in writing any additional remuneration from sources outside the Parliament. This is included in a special register on the financial interests of members' assistants, which is available for public consultation.

A number of assistants have gone on to political careers in their own right, such as the current UK Labour MEPs Stephen Hughes (who worked for Roland Boyes), Arlene McCarthy (Glyn Ford), and former MEPs such as Gary Titley (Terry Pitt and then John Bird) Anita Pollack (Barbara Castle), Simon Murphy (also John Bird) or the former MPs Oona King (Glyn Ford and then Glenys Kinnock), and John Grogan. On the Conservative side, in 2009 Emma McClarkin (also representing the East Midlands region) joined her former employer Roger Helmer as a Tory MEP. Other former assistants include a number of current MEPs: the Belgian Derk Jan Eppink of the Lijst Dedecker, the Dutch Liberal Sophia In't Veld, German CSU MEP Bernd Posselt, the German Green MEP Rebecca Harms, German SPD MEPs Jens Geier and Petra Kammerevert of Germany, the Irish Fine Gael member Paul Murphy and non-attached MEPs Bela Kovacs of Hungary and Martin Ehrenhauser of Austria, as well as several former MEPs, Italian Radical MEP Gianfranco Dell' Alba, German SPD MEP Axel Schaefer, Spanish Socialist MEP, Javier Moreno, and Dutch Green MEP Kathalijne Buitenweg.

Most members have an assistant who travels regularly to Strasbourg plenary sessions, but many assistants remain in Brussels or in their national base. On the other hand, their access to meetings, which was once a problem in certain committees and Groups, is now normally unrestricted with rare exceptions.

The Assistants' Statute

Prior to the adoption of the Assistants' Statute, the status of parliamentary assistants was subject to lengthy discussion and controversy. For a long time, the Parliament remained unwilling to take over the role of employer, leaving this to the members. This resulted in a wide divergence of terms and conditions and diverging legal situations as assistants were employed under various national laws. Even many of the Brussels assistants were employed not under Belgian law, but national law and (perfectly legally, but sometimes with enormous bureaucratic complications) posted to Brussels.

In the 1990s, a general Assistants' Association was created specifically to campaign for a Statute for Assistants. However, despite having several hundred paying members and an active board including members from across the Political Groups, the Association was never officially recognised by the Parliament, although it held meetings with several Secretaries-General of the Parliament and with the Parliament Vice-Presidents responsible for assistants.

In May 1998, in response to a request from Parliament, the Commission put forward a proposal for a Council Regulation (COM (1998) 312.fin.), designed to provide for assistants to be covered by the Conditions of Employment of Other Servants and Auxiliary Staff in the existing EU Staff Regulations, but allowing MEPs to retain some autonomy in determining the level of their assistants' remuneration. Although Parliament subsequently adopted this proposal (on the basis of a Report by Klaus-Heiner Lehne (A4-0018/99)) in 1999, it failed to make headway in the Council.

In September 2006, pending progress on the legislative side, Parliament's Bureau adopted a Codex for Parliamentary Assistants. It laid down a number of items that were required to be included in contracts between members and assistants and spelled out the rights and duties of assistants within the Parliament.

In July 2008, the Parliament's Bureau adopted measures aimed at making payments to parliamentary assistants more traceable and transparent, bringing an end to a legal grey area that had led to some cases of abuse. Moreover, the conclusion of staff contracts with relatives was to be banned – with the proviso that existing contracts would be allowed to be extended for one parliamentary term.

Having been reticent about taking the role of employer from the MEPs, Parliament's position changed, in part following the presentation in March 2008 by a confidential committee of a summary giving details of numerous payment abuses, particularly through the use of "service provider contracts". To tackle such payments, as part of the Assistants' Statute the Parliament decided to amend its procedures for local assistants. For a local assistant to be employed requires a contract signed by both the employer and employee and approval by an approved paying agent, before the Parliament will release the payments for local assistants. The aim is to avoid conflicts of interest, such as cases in which members authorised relatives to take care of the payment.

These requirements were consolidated, at Parliament's request, into a new Commission proposal, which Parliament approved (on the basis of a Report for the Legal Affairs Committee by Giuseppe Gargani (A6-0483/2008) in December 2008 by 598 votes in favour, 19 against and 47 abstentions. The Statute is officially known as Council Regulation (EC) No 160/2009 of 23 February 2009 amending the Conditions of Employment of Other Servants of the European Communities.

The Assistants' Statute came into force (at the same time as the Members' Statute) following the 2009 European elections. The Statute puts assistants on a similar legal footing to other European civil servants. They are paid directly by the Parliament, pay the same EU tax rates, and have the same rights with regard to pensions and medical treatment; although unlike other EU staff they can be subject to summary dismissal without warning and usually have a lower remuneration.

Members maintain the exclusive right over who they wish to employ and setting the remuneration level of each one. For example, the Statute provides for 19 different pay levels and defines two different types of assistant. Assistants performing largely secretarial duties can be placed within grades 1-13, while assistants classified as "political advisors" who help draft amendments, reports and closely follow their MEPs' legislative committees should be placed within grades 7-19. However, the interpretation of whether an assistant is a "secretary" or an "advisor" is entirely at the discretion of the MEP, so in practice these pay levels are indicative rather than binding, though the total budget per member cannot be exceeded.

It is worth noting that a number of the Brussels-based assistants of British MEPs are members of the GMB (one of only two British trade unions with a branch in Brussels), which has been active on their behalf and also campaigned for an Assistants' Statute. Following the adoption of the Assistants'

Statute, the GMB started to recruit assistants from other Member States, and now have members from approximately 10 Member States.

The impact of the Statute is likely to change the career progression of parliamentary assistants' based in Brussels. Many politically inclined assistants used to see natural career progression by moving into political consultancy either in Brussels or by moving back into domestic politics in their home Member State, with a few moving to the Political Group secretariats. Now the pay scales in the Statute put more emphasis on assistants being more permanent, and on a comparable footing with Political Group staff.

Conclusion

The MEPs elected in 2009 are more diverse than ever. Around half of them are new MEPs, and more of them than ever before are women. They come from a wide range of backgrounds, some directly political (with many former national and regional parliamentarians, and many former government ministers), and others less so, or not at all.

There seems to be a distinction between countries whose MEPs tend to have longer-term careers in the European Parliament, and others where being an MEP is much more inter-changeable with a national or regional political career.

Whatever their background, however, individual MEPs within the European Parliament play a particularly important role. In a Parliament with so many parties and Political Groups, where there are no permanent majorities or minorities, and where the outcomes of votes are decided on very different bases, national, sectoral, ethical or ideological, they have more freedom of manoeuvre than backbenchers in practically all national parliaments, with the exception of the US Congress.

5. The Political Groups

The Political Groups are of central importance in the work of the Parliament. It is through them that political majorities are built on legislation, the budget and every other vote in Parliament, as MEPs vote predominantly along Group lines. Groups play the decisive role in choosing the President, Vice-Presidents and committee chairs. They set the parliamentary agenda, choose the rapporteurs and decide on the allocation of speaking time. They have their own staff, receive considerable funds from the Parliament and often influence the choice of the Parliament's top officials. The power of the Groups is also shown by the powerlessness of those non-attached members who are not in Political Groups, who are highly unlikely, for example, ever to hold a powerful post within the Parliament, or be a major rapporteur.

Parliament's Rule 30 states that members "may form themselves into groups according to their political affinities". The minimum number of members required to form a Group has now been raised to 25, but they must also be drawn from at least one quarter of the Member States, with the current figure thus being seven. There had previously been a more complex rule, with it being possible but more difficult to form a Group if its members were drawn from a small number of Member States. Indeed, before 1999 it had even been possible to form a Group with 29 members from one country. Berlusconi's Forza Italia was the only national party to take advantage of this rule, when they founded the Forza Europa Group in 1994.

In spite of the recent changes, the current thresholds to set up a Group within the Parliament are still relatively low by national parliamentary standards, but attempts to raise these thresholds meet with strong resistance from the smaller Groups.

A second sensitive issue with regard to the formation of a Group is that of definition of "political affinities". During the constituent session in July 1999, a varied group of non-attached members, ranging from Emma Bonino's Italian Radicals to the French Front National, tried to create a new "Technical Group", but its existence was quickly challenged by the other Groups on the grounds of lack of political affinity. Parliament decided that the new Group did not, by its own admission, meet the test of Rule 29-1 as regards the need for political affinity. This decision was, however, challenged at the Court. Although unsuccessful, the Group was allowed to exist (by order of the President of the Court of First Instance), pending the court hearing, for almost two years. The Group lost the case, and was then dissolved. As a result of this episode a new interpretation was added to Parliament's relevant rule, stating that Parliament need not normally evaluate the political affinity of members of a Group, since it is implicit in the act of formation of a Group. "Only when this is denied by the Members concerned is it necessary for Parliament to evaluate whether the group has been constituted in conformity with the Rules."

Rule 30 also provides that the President shall be notified in a statement when a Group is set up. This statement must specify the Group's name, its members and its leadership, or bureau. As a result of the problems that had been faced by the Technical Group in 1999, newly established Groups have placed a greater emphasis on also submitting a declaration of principles. The statement provided by a short-lived Identity, Tradition and Sovereignty (ITS) Group in January 2007, for example, not only complied with the minimum conditions laid out in the relevant rule but also included a set of shared principles. The European Conservatives and Reformist Group that was established after the 2009 elections announced that it had signed up to a declaration, originally negotiated in Prague, setting out the aims and values of the new Group, and another Group, the Europe of Freedom and Democracy Group, adopted a political programme with 4 basic principles.

An important adjunct to Rule 30 concerns what happens when a Group no longer fulfils the threshold requirements. "If a group falls below the required threshold, the President, with the agreement of the Conference of Presidents, may allow it to continue to exist until Parliament's next constitutive sitting, provided the following conditions are met:

- the members continue to represent at least one-fifth of the Member States;
- the Group has been in existence for a period longer than a year.

The President shall not apply this derogation where there is sufficient evidence to suspect that it is being abused".

As of the moment of writing, this provision had not yet been applied, but it provides a safeguard for those Groups just above the threshold who could otherwise be put under undue pressure by just one or two members threatening to leave.

There are now seven Political Groups within the Parliament, some with familiar names, others whose titles do not immediately indicate the nature of their membership or even their position in the ideological spectrum.

This chapter examines the historical evolution and current position of the Groups. It surveys their structures and working methods, assesses their cohesion and examines the balance of power between them.

Figure 4: *Seats in 2009 Parliament*

From left to right:

1 – *European United Left – Nordic Green Left (35);*

2 – *Progressive Alliance of Socialists and Democrats (184);*

3 – *European Greens – European Free Alliance (55);*

4 – *Alliance of Liberals and Democrats for Europe (84);*

5 – *European People's Party (265);*

6 – *European Conservatives and Reformists (54);*

7 – *Europe of Freedom and Democracy (32);*

8 –*Non-attached members (27)*

Source:
http://en.wikipedia.org/wiki/File:2009_European_Parliament

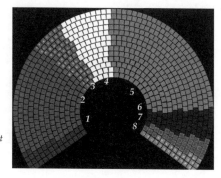

Figure 5: *Evolution of the Political Groups*

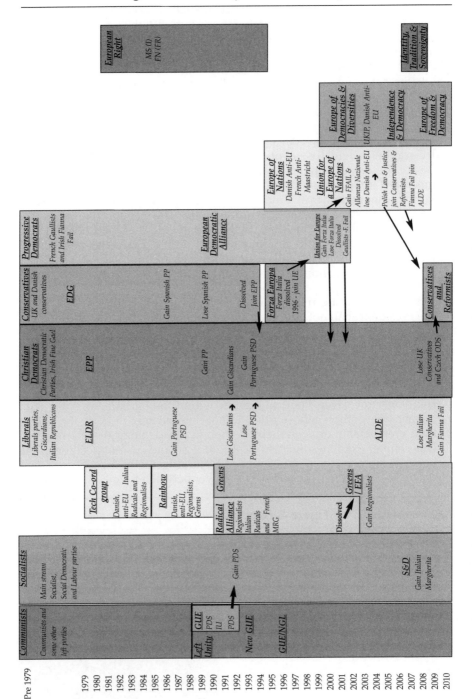

Historical evolution

The evolution of the Groups has blended continuity and change. Since before direct elections, the Socialists and the Christian Democrats (EPP) have been the two large Groups with a constantly changing pattern of smaller Groups, some of which have been absorbed by them, particularly by the EPP. Even among the smaller Groups, there are some consistent patterns: there has always been a Liberal Group (under various names), which has often been the third-largest Group. There has always been a Group (briefly two) to the left of the Socialists (originally called the Communist Group), and a Group with Greens and/or Regionalists (for ten years, two). There has also almost always been two groups to the right of the EPP, usually with one moderately eurosceptic (in the sense of most of its members broadly accepting the EU, but opposing any federal developments) and one radically eurosceptic (in the sense of most of its members opposing the EU's existence or wanting their country to leave it): their composition and names have, however, constantly changed, with component parties switching between them, or leaving to join a mainstream Group or the non-attached, or simply disappearing. For ten years (and fleetingly again for a few months), the extreme right constituted a Group.

Groups were first formally established in 1953 by the Common Assembly of the European Coal and Steel Community (ECSC), which set the minimum membership for a Group at nine (out of 78). This was the first international assembly whose members sat according to political affiliation.

The first three Groups to be founded, all in June 1953, were those representing the Socialists, the Liberals and the Christian Democrats. From 1953 to 1965 these remained the only three Political Groups, and they are the only ones that have existed continuously to the present. Until 1975 the largest was the Christian Democrats, often close to an absolute majority (38 out of 77 in 1953, 39 out of 78 in 1955 and 1956, 67 out of 142 after the Assembly was enlarged in 1958). The Socialists were generally the second largest Group, and the Liberals the third, apart from the years 1959/60 to 1961/62 when the Liberals overtook the Socialists (43 Liberals to 33 Socialists in 1961/62).

After the **enlargement of the Assembly in 1958** the rules for forming Groups were also changed, with the minimum membership raised to 17. This was again lowered to 14 in 1965, to enable the French Gaullists to break away from the Liberals and form the European Democratic Union.

British, Irish and Danish accession to the Community in 1973 led to the creation by British and Danish Conservatives of a new Group, the European Conservatives, with 20 members. The European Democratic Union was joined by members from the Irish party, Fianna Fáil, and the name of the Group was changed to European Progressive Democrats. The Socialist Group was reinforced and would have become the largest Group if the British Labour Party had not refused to nominate the members to which it was entitled until after the 1975 referendum on whether the UK should remain a member of the Community. When Labour did join in 1975, the Socialist Group became the largest Group, and remained so until 1999.

In 1973 there was another rule change. A Group could now be formed by as few as ten members (out of 198), if they were from three or more Member

States. The last Group created in the old nominated Parliament was the Communist Group, in October 1973. This began with only 14 members.

With the first **direct elections in 1979,** the number of members more than doubled to 410. An attempt was immediately made to adapt proportionally the minimum threshold for the creation of Groups. This would have prevented the formation of a "Group for the Technical Co-ordination and Defence of Independent Groups and Members", comprising a heterogeneous mixture of small parties and individuals (the Italian Radicals and two small Italian parties of the left, Belgian Regionalists, Danish anti-Europeans and an Irish independent, Neil Blaney), who had no common platform but recognised that it was more advantageous to be in a Group than to be non-attached. Filibustering techniques (notably by Marco Pannella of the Italian Radicals) were then successfully used to stop any rule change. The Technical Group was able to survive. Unlike the other Groups it had not one but three co-presidents who took turns to represent the Group.

While no other new Groups were created immediately after direct elections there was a change in the balance between the Groups. The Christian Democrats (who changed their name to the Group of the European People's Party, EPP) won seats but remained narrowly second to the Socialists. The European Conservatives moved from being the fifth to the third largest Group with 64 seats, as a result of the British Conservatives winning 60 of the 81 UK seats on 48 per cent of the vote. They also changed their name to the European Democratic Group (EDG). Besides the British Conservatives (and for a while also an Ulster Unionist) they included three members from the Danish Conservatives and one from the Danish Centre Democrats, though the latter subsequently joined the EPP Group.

The Communists also did well, advancing from being the sixth largest Group, to being the fourth largest. Their full name was the "Communist and Allies Group". Besides the French, Italian and Greek Communists, they also included the non-Communist Socialist People's Party from Denmark and a number of left-wing independents elected on Communist lists (such as Altiero Spinelli). The Liberals slipped from being the third to become only the fifth largest Group. The European Progressive Democrats obtained only 22 members. They again included the French Gaullists and the Fianna Fáil members from Ireland but also recruited a Dane from the anti-tax Progress Party, and Winnie Ewing of the Scottish National Party, who had previously sat as an independent.

Greek accession in 1981 reinforced the Socialist Group, who were joined by PASOK members, and the EPP Group, who recruited members from New Democracy. The Communists also gained three new members.

The **second elections in 1984** led to the creation of an eighth Group, the European Right, with members from Le Pen's Front National in France, the Italian Social Movement (MSI) and one from the Greek EPEN. The heterogeneous Technical Group was transformed into a larger and slightly more structured Rainbow Group, consisting of the first set of Greens to be elected to the Parliament (from Die Grünen in Germany and Agalev and Ecolo in Belgium), left alternative parties (such as Democrazia Proletaria in Italy and the Groen Progressief Akkoord in the Netherlands), regionalist parties of the European Free Alliance (such as the Flemish Volksunie and the Italian alliance of Union Valdôtaine–Partito Sardo d'Azione) and the anti-european

Danes in the Danish People's Movement. The Italian Radicals did not participate in the new Rainbow Group, partly because of the Group's suspicion of what they saw as the overpowering personality of Marco Pannella. The other Groups remained unchanged in structure, with the Socialists and European Progressive Democrats gaining seats and the others all losing some.

Spanish and Portuguese accession in 1986 was of greatest advantage to the Socialist Group, which gained 42 new members. The European Democrats (EDG) recruited the main Spanish party of the centre-right (Alianza Popular). Significant gains were also made by the Liberals, in particular through the adhesion of the Portuguese Social Democrats (for whom the Group changed their name yet again to Liberal, Democratic and Reformist Group). The other Groups all made lesser gains.

One of the main parties that entered the Parliament was the Social Democratic Centre (CDS) of former Spanish Prime Minister Adolfo Suárez, who remained non-attached. In late 1987 an attempt was made to create a new Technical Group, based on the CDS members, the Italian Radicals and one or two other non-attached members. The Group had only 12 members but quickly lost its Dutch Calvinist member, who decided, in particular, not to be associated with the Radical party of Pannella and "Cicciolina" (the "porno star", Ilona Staller, elected to the Italian parliament on the Radical list). An attempt was made to "lend" two Italians from the Socialist Group to keep the new Group in existence, but this failed, and the new Group collapsed after a few days.

A final development that took place in the second directly elected Parliament was that the Group of the European Progressive Democrats renamed itself the Group of the European Democratic Alliance.

The **third direct elections in June 1989** saw the reinforcement of the two largest Groups, the Socialists and the EPP (which the Alianza Popular MEPs now joined), and the fragmentation of the smaller Groups. There were ten Groups in number instead of eight, as a result of the creation of two completely new Groups. A separate Green Group was formed for the first time, and the divided Communist and Allies Group finally split into two separate Groups, one dominated by the reformist Italians and the other by the orthodox French Communists, but neither calling itself Communist.

Two of these Groups soon disappeared. In May 1992, the remaining EDG members (largely UK Conservatives) joined the EPP and in January 1993 the majority of the former Italian Communists (renamed the PDS) joined the Socialist Group. In consequence, the Group of the United European Left, of which the Italians had been the largest component, no longer had enough members to survive as a Group. By the end of the 1989-94 Parliament, the Socialist Group had grown to 198 members and the EPP to 162. The two largest Groups had over 69% of the Parliament's membership, compared with 54% before the 1989 elections, and this is still the largest combined percentage that these two Groups have enjoyed throughout the history of the Parliament.

After the **1994 elections** the Socialists and the EPP were roughly the same size as before, but in an enlarged Parliament their combined membership as a percentage of the total was reduced to under 63%. The Liberals, Greens and European Democratic Alliance also continued. A further Group, the

Confederal Group of the European United Left, was not entirely new, in that it was primarily based on former or continuing Communist parties of the Left Unity Group, but it also absorbed the surviving reformist parties from the former Group of the United European Left, whose acronym (GUE) it revived.

On the other hand, three entirely new Groups were founded. One of the main reasons for this was the political fragmentation among the French MEPs, with the list led by Bernard Tapie ("Energie Radicale") taking away votes from the French Socialists, in particular, and the nationalist list of Philippe de Villiers harming the mainstream centre-right list. Energie Radicale, with several regionalist parties and the Italian Radicals, formed the nucleus of a new Group called the European Radical Alliance, and the members elected on the de Villiers list helped to establish, along with some Danish members, a Eurosceptic Group called Europe of Nations. The final new Group, Forza Europa, was based on Berlusconi's new Forza Italia party in Italy. Of the other Groups that had existed in the 1989-94 Parliament, the former members of the Rainbow Group were either not re-elected or went into the Europe of Nations or European Radical Alliance, and the Group of the Right could not be reconstituted, because it did not have enough members, and because the Italian right-wing Alleanza Nazionale would not join them. As a result, there was an exceptionally high number of non-attached members (27) at the beginning of the 1994-99 Parliament, 25 of them from the far-right.

Austrian, Finnish and Swedish accession in 1995 saw gains relatively proportional to their size for the Socialist, EPP, Liberal, Green and GUE Groups.

The main change during the 1994-99 Parliament was the substantial increase in the size of the EPP Group. The main reason for this was the controversial adherence to the EPP (after a transit for three years via the EDA Group, which changed its name to Union for Europe) of most of the members of the Forza Europa Group, which was dissolved. Nine Portuguese Social Democrats also left the Liberal Group and joined the EPP Group, whose numbers had thus risen to 201 by the time of the June 1999 elections, only 13 fewer than the Socialist Group. Most of the Lega Nord members also left the Liberal Group, and became non-attached.

The **1999 elections** saw the EPP (now joined also by the French Gaullists) overtake the Socialists to become the biggest Group with 233 members, whereas the latter shrank from 214 to 180 members. The combined numbers of the two big Groups was just under 66% of the total number of MEPs.

The Liberal Group, the GUE and the Greens all had significant increases in their membership. The Green Group joined forces with a number of regionalist parties to form the combined Group of the Greens/European Free Alliance. The Union for Europe disappeared as most of its members (French Gaullists) joined the EPP. The European Radical Alliance also dissolved (the French Radicals not being re-elected and the regionalists joining the Greens). The Europe of Nations Group changed into the Union for a Europe of Nations, recruiting notably the Irish Fianna Fáil members of the dissolved Union for Europe Group, but losing its Danish Eurosceptics and Dutch ultra-Calvinists to a new Europe of Democracies and Diversities Group set up with the new UK Independence Party and French members elected on a hunting, fishing, nature and traditions platform. For a while, as described above, there was also a Technical Group, containing many of the non-attached members.

 The other important development during the 1999-2004 Parliament was the arrival in 2003 of 162 observers from the national parliaments of the ten countries who were due to join the European Union in 2004. Their role was a limited one (see Chapter 2) but 150 of them joined the existing Political Groups, with only 12 remaining non-attached. In some cases it was obvious to which Group they would affiliate, and in others it was much less so. Moreover, there were some inter-group transfers between the initial arrival of the observers and the date of enlargement. The final outcome, however, by the first post-enlargement plenary in May 2004, when the observers became full members, was that 121 of the 150 joined the two largest Groups (64 the EPP/ED and 57 the PSE) and only 29 joined the other 5 Groups (14 the Liberals, 7 the UEN, 6 the GUE, 2 the Greens and none at all the EDD). The overall share of the two largest Groups in Parliament's membership thus went up from 65.1% to 67%.

The **2004 elections** and their aftermath of Group realignment did not, however, confirm this trend. Instead of increasing, the share of the two largest Groups actually decreased slightly from 67% in May 2004 down to 63.9% in the new Parliament, but with the EPP-ED slipping less than the PES. The biggest gainers were the Liberals, whose name was changed to the Alliance of Liberals and Democrats for Europe (ALDE), and who were now not only the third largest Group, but had over double the number of members of the fourth largest Group. Predictions that the Green/EFA Group would fare badly as a result of enlargement were confirmed, with only one MEP from a new Member State, but they were now again the fourth largest Group, although far behind the Liberals. The GUE/NGL Group was just behind them in fifth position. The former Europe of Democracies and Diversities (EDD) Group was renamed as the Independence and Democracy Group (IND/DEM) and overtook the UEN Group in size. Finally the latter, whose continued existence had been in question for some time after the elections, managed to survive, but only as the smallest of the seven Groups. There were also 30 non-attached members from 11 separate parties.

In the first half of the 2004-2009 legislature a number of members left the parties for which they had been elected, and there were considerable shifts of membership between the Groups. The main beneficiary of these changes was the UEN Group which rose from 27 to 44 members, and went from being the smallest Group to the fourth largest, ahead of both the Green/EFA and GUE/NGL Groups. The main loser was the IND/DEM Group which dropped from 36 to 23 members.

The **accession of Romania and Bulgaria** to the EU in January 2007 also had an impact on the Political Group balance within the European Parliament. As described in Chapter 2, the number of seats rose temporarily (until 2009) to 785, with 35 Romanian and 18 Bulgarian MEPs being initially nominated from their national parliaments, but with direct elections in both countries scheduled for later in 2007.

The three largest Groups all gained from the initial nominations, with the EPP gaining 4 Bulgarians and 9 Romanians and rising to 277 members, the Socialists 6 Bulgarians and 12 Romanians and increasing to 218 members and the ALDE Group 7 Bulgarians and 9 Romanians and going up to 106 members. Romanian and Bulgarian accession also permitted the creation of a new Group in January 2007 on the far right of the political spectrum, the ITS Group, with

21 members from 7 Member States, including 6 Romanians and 1 Bulgarian. None of the other Groups gained any Romanian or Bulgarian members. There were only 14 non-attached members, a much lower figure than before, in considerable measure as a result of the creation of the ITS Group.

The ITS Group was short-lived. It was dissolved in November 2007 after its Romanian members walked out in protest against remarks made by fellow Group colleague, Alessandra Mussolini, granddaughter of the "Duce". On the eve of the 2009 elections there were thus again 7 Groups, as well as 30 non-attached members.

In the aftermath of the **2009 elections**, in which the size of the European Parliament dropped from its temporary figure of 785 to 736 members, 7 Groups were established, but with one of the former Groups disappearing (the UEN), and a new one (the ECR Group) being set up.

The combined total of the two largest Groups further slipped to only 61% of the total. The EPP generally polled well, but went down from 288 to 265 members because of the departure of the British Conservatives to found the ECR. The Socialist Group slipped from 217 to 184 members, and would have fared worse without the adhesion of all 21 members from the Italian Partito Democratico, in consequence of which the Socialist Group changed its name to the Progressive Alliance of Socialists and Democrats. The ALDE Group went down from 100 to 84 members, but the Greens/EFA Group actually increased its number of seats, and went up from 43 to 55 members. It thus became the fourth largest group just ahead of the new European Conservatives and Reformists Group (ECR), formed by a mixture of parties coming from the EPP (such as the British Conservatives and the Czech ODS Party) and from the now dissolved UEN (such as the Polish Law and Justice Party). In sixth place came the GUE/NGL Group with 35 members, and the smallest Group, initially with 30 members, was the Europe of Freedom and Democracy Group (EFD), a re-constituted version of the former Independence and Democracy Group and featuring UKIP. There were also 28 non-attached members, of whom most were from parties of the far right.

Composition of the Groups

Group of the European People's Party (Christian Democrats) (EPP)

Chair	Joseph Daul
Secretary-General	Martin Kamp
Current membership	265
Current Parliament posts	1 President, 5 Vice-Presidents, 2 Quaestors, 9 committee chairs and 1 subcommittee chair
Group founded	23 June 1953 (Christian Democratic Group until 1979)

Current member parties (2010) with number of members:

Austria: Österreichische Volkspartei (Austrian People's Party) (6)

Belgium: Christen Democratisch & Vlaams (Christian Democrat and Flemish Party) (3):

	Centre Democrate Humaniste (Humanist and Democratic Centre) (1) (plus the Christliche-Soziale Partei (Christian Social Party)(CSP-EVP) (1)
Bulgaria	Grazhdani za Evropeisko Razvitie na Bulgaria (GERB) (Citizens for European Development of Bulgaria)(5) Sajuz na Demokratichnite Sili (Union of Democratic Forces) (1)
Cyprus:	Demokraticos Synagermos (DISY) (Democratic Rally of Cyprus) (2)
Czech Republic:	Krestansko Democraticka Unie (Christian Democratic Union) (2)
Denmark:	Det Konservative Folkeparti (Conservative People's Party) (1)
Estonia:	Isamaa ja Res Publica Liit (Pro Patria and Res Publica Union) (1)
Finland:	Kansallinen Kokoomus (National Coalition Party) (3) Suomen Kristillisdemokraatit (Finnish Christian Democrats (1) (observer member)
France:	Union pour un Mouvement Populaire (Union for a Popular Movement) (29) (includes 2 members from Nouveau Centre and 1 from Gauche Moderne)
Germany:	Christlich Demokratische Union (Christian Democratic Union) (34); Christlich-Soziale Union (Christian Social Union) (8)
Greece:	Nea Dimokratia (New Democracy) (8)
Hungary:	FIDESZ, Magyar Polgári Szövetség – Kereszténydemokrata Néppárt (Alliance of Young Democrats, Hungarian Civic Union – Christian Democrats) (14)
Ireland:	Fine Gael (4)
Italy:	Il Popolo della Liberta (People of Freedom)(PdL) (25) Ex PdL (Futuro e Liberta)(Future and Freedom) (4) Unione di Centro (UDC) (4); Südtiroler Volkspartei (South) Tyrol People's Party) (1) (Observer status within Party) Independent ("Io amo l'Italia")("I love Italy") (1)
Latvia:	Jaunais Laiks (New Era) (1); Pilsoniska Savieniba (PS) (Civic Union) (2)
Lithuania:	Tevynes Sajunga - Lietuvos krikscionys demokratai (TS-LKD) (Homeland Union – Lithuanian Christian Democrats) (4)
Luxembourg:	Chrëschtlech Sozial Vollekspartei (Christian Social People's Party) (3)
Malta:	Partit Nazzjonalista (Nationalist Party) (2)

Netherlands: Christen Democratisch Appel (Christian Democrat
                   Appeal) (5)
Poland: Platforma Obywatelska (Civic Platform) (25)
                   Polskie Stronnictwo Ludowe (Polish People's Party) (3)
Portugal: Partido Social Democrata (Social Democratic Party) (8)
                   Partido Popular (CDS-PP) (Popular Party) (2)
Romania: Partidul Democrat Liberal (Liberal Democratic Party) (11)
                   Uniunea Democrata Maghiara din Romania (Romaniai
                   Magyar Demokratak Svovetsege) (Hungarian Democratic
                   Union of Romania) (3)
Slovakia: Krestanskodemokraticke hnutie (Christian Democrat
                   Movement) (2)
                   Slovenská Demokraticka a Krestanska Unia –
                   Demokraticka Strana (Slovak Democratic and Christian
                   Union) (2)
                   Magyar Koalicio Partja–Strana madarskej koalicie (Party
                   of Hungarian Coalition) (2)
Slovenia: Nova Slovenija (New Slovenia-Christian People's Party) (1)
                   Slovenska Demokratska Stranka (Slovenian Democratic
                   Party) (2)
Spain: Partido Popular (PopularParty) (23)
Sweden: Moderata Samlingspartiet (Moderate Party) (4)
                   Kristdemokraterna (Christian Democrats) (1)

Total: 265

The EPP Group remains by far the largest Group, as it has been since 1999, and many of its parties, such as those in France and Italy, polled well in the 2009 European elections. The German CDU-CSU delegation, while it lost a few seats, remains by far the largest national delegation within the Parliament. The EPP also dominates in many of the new EU Member States. It would have done even better without the departure from the Group of two substantial parties from its former European Democrat component, the UK Conservative Party and the Czech ODS, who went off to create the ECR Group (see below). Without this, the Group would have had around 300 members. The Group is now without representation in the UK, and thus no longer has MEPs in all EU Member States. On the other hand there is no longer the European Democrat subgroup, and there is now much greater linkage between membership of the EPP Group and membership of the European People's Party.

Over time the Group had not only grown considerably but also changed its character. Its original nucleus was parties of Christian Democratic inspiration, which generally regarded themselves as centrist, and were keen European federalists. They were represented in all six original Member States, and were traditionally the largest parties in five of them (the exception being France where they were represented by the relatively small CDS, the Centre des Démocrates Sociaux). The largest and most dominant parties within the Group were the CDU/CSU in Germany and the DC in Italy. These parties were all full members of the European People's Party, a federation of

Christian Democratic parties in the EC (see below) which sought to evolve into a European political party, with its own programme and direct membership. They did, however, vary in their views on economic and social issues, and in their positioning within their national political spectrum.

This original Christian Democratic core has now been considerably modified, and the balance within the Group has changed considerably. They recruited widely from parties of the centre-right, often from outside the Christian Democratic tradition, and the position of the German delegation as the largest and most dominant force within the Group was considerably reinforced, not least after the collapse of the Italian Christian Democrats, who had been the second force within the Group. An early recruit was the Irish Fine Gael party, which joined the Group (and the Federation of the EPP) after Irish accession, and thus pre-empted its larger rival party, Fianna Fáil, from joining the same Group. Since direct elections a large number of other centre-right parties also joined the Group, some of Christian Democratic provenance (the Austrian People's Party, the Finnish and Swedish Christian Democrats), but some from very different backgrounds. Certain of these parties came directly into the Group (the Greek New Democracy Party, the Finnish and Swedish Centre-Right and Moderate Parties), whereas others transited through other Groups (the Spanish Partido Popular and the British and Danish Conservatives from the former European Democratic Group, the Portuguese Social Democrats and certain French UDF members from the Liberal Group, the French Gaullist party and the Italian Forza Italia from the former Union for Europe Group). Some of these new recruits to the Group became full members of the party, whereas others remained outside.

Most of the parties within the Group are now full members of the European People's Party. Non-EPP member parties may also join the Group under Rule 3(2) of its Rules of Procedure if they subscribe to the political programme of the European People's Party. Both of these categories of member are formally "committed to a policy, which on the basis of a Constitution, pursues the process of federal unification and integration in Europe, which is a constituent element of the European Union as a Union of citizens and States". Finally there is a third category who may become allied members of the Group under Rule 4 of its Rules of Procedure if they subscribe to the basic policies of the Group.

The former version of this Rule also permitted such allied parties to have the right to "promote and develop their distinct views on constitutional issues in relation to the future of Europe". Prominent among the allied members invoking this Rule were the British Conservatives, who, with the Danish Conservatives and (for a while only) the Spanish Alianza Popular, had been in their own separate Group from British entry in 1973 until 1992 (see under ECR below). The Spanish members in the renamed Partido Popular then left the EDG to join the EPP Group and later to become a full EPP member party. There were mixed views within the EPP about their relations with the remaining EDG members, but the latter were eventually (in April 1992) admitted into the Group of the EPP on the basis of acceptance of the Group's programme.

The British Conservatives then remained within the Group until the 2009 elections. To accommodate them, the Group was later renamed as the "Group of the European People's Party (Christian Democrats) and

European Democrats", with the latter not having to share the federalist objectives of the other EPP parties. The British Conservatives were the largest of the four parties within the European Democrat component of the group, with the Czech ODS being the other substantial party in this category. This degree of flexibility within the largest EP Political Group still did not satisfy many within the British Conservative party, and a commitment made by David Cameron to leave the Group (made during his campaign to win the party leadership) was eventually implemented after the 2009 elections, with both the British Conservatives and the Czech ODS leaving the EPP-ED Group to form the ECR (see the separate entry below).

The second controversial application to join the Group of the EPP was that of Forza Italia. As mentioned above, the former Italian Christian Democratic Party (DC) had been one of the pillars of the EPP and its Group, but its disintegration in the early 1990s left only smaller successor parties within the EP. Silvio Berlusconi's new Forza Italia dwarfed them in size but initially formed its own Group, Forza Europa. They later joined the Union for Europe Group. In the end most of the Forza Italia members joined the EPP Group, and have since closely followed the mainstream Group line. Following the 1999 elections there were 34 Italian members in the EPP Group from 8 separate parties, including 22 from Forza Italia. After the 2004 elections these numbers dropped to 24 Italian members from only 5 parties, with 16 from Forza Italia. The other recent Italian addition to the group were the members from the former Alleanza Nazionale (National Alliance). This was the successor party to the Italian Social Movement (MSI), which had had MEPs since 1979, and which had been in the Group of the European Right between 1984 and 1989. After 1989 the MSI left this Group, partly over differences of general political emphasis, but more specifically because of differences with the German Republikaner over the political situation in the South Tyrol (where the MSI had been the most vocal defenders of the Italian-speaking minority). They thus became non-attached, and retained this status during the 1994-99 Parliament, by which time the MSI's successor, Alleanza Nazionale, was seeking new respectability as a mainstream party of government, and did not wish to join up with far-right parties. In the 1999 elections Alleanza Nazionale made a common list with Mario Segni, a dissident Christian Democrat who had been in the EPP at the start of the 1994 Parliament. They were later in the UEN Group but then joined up with Forza Italia members in the renamed and enlarged Popolo della Liberta (People of Freedom, PdL). This obtained 29 seats in the 2009 elections. In 2010, however, the split between Sivio Berlusconi and the former Alleanza leader Gianfranco Fini led to four MEPs leaving the PdL, and adhering to Fini's new party Futuro e Liberta (Future and Freedom), although remaining within the EPP. In spite of this development, there is still somewhat less fragmentation than in the past among the Italian parties of the right and centre-right, and there are only two other Italian parties within the EPP Group, the Union of the Centre with 4 seats, and the regional party SVP with 1 seat. There is also one independent, the Egyptian-born Magdi Allam, who has founded a political movement called "I love Italy".

A third complex situation within the Group has been that of its French members. The mainstream parties of the French right have tended to be seriously divided within the Parliament, with only the UDF members from the

CDS tradition consistently within the EPP, with the other UDF members in the Liberal Group, and with the Gaullists in their own RDE and later UFE Groups. After the 1999 elections they were finally re-united in the Group of the EPP (even including a member from a Green party, Génération Écologie).

These successive changes in the composition of the Group and of the original balance between its Christian Democratic founding parties were not to the taste of all of its members. In April 2000, several members (largely from the Benelux and France with some Spanish and Italian members) set up the Schuman study group to bring together more centrist and federalist members. After the 2004 elections the French UDF members, along with a few others (such as Gérard Deprez, the former long-serving leader of the Francophone Christian Democrats in Belgium), left the EPP for the ALDE Group, although the subsequent creation of the MODEM party in France by Francois Bayrou led to some former UDF members joining up with the UMP and thus the EPP. After the 2009 elections, there were 29 French members in the Group, 26 from the UMP and 3 from allied parties.

The EPP-ED greatly benefited from EU enlargement, successfully recruiting parties in all the 10 new Member States that joined the EU in 2004, and then generally doing well in those countries in the subsequent European elections. Six new parties and 13 new members then joined the Group after Bulgarian and Romanian accession in January 2007. There are now 85 members in the Group (almost a third of the total), who come from the 12 new Member States. The largest national delegation from the new Member States is that of Poland, with one party, the PO (Civic Platform) alone accounting for 25 MEPs after the 2009 elections, as well as providing the current EP President, Jerzy Buzek. Other substantial parties from new Member States after the 2009 elections include the Hungarian FIDESZ (12 members) and the Liberal Democratic Party from Romania (10 members).

The EPP Group has provided over half the Presidents of the Parliament, including the previous incumbent, Hans-Gert Pöttering, who had led the Group from 1999-2007, as well as the current President, Jerzy Buzek (see Table 20).

Group of the Progressive Alliance of Socialists and Democrats (S&D)

Leader	Martin Schulz
Secretary-General	Anna Colombo
Current membership	184
Current Parliament posts	5 Vice-Presidents, 1 Quaestor and 6 committee chairs
Group founded	23 June 1953 (known as Socialist Group until 1993)

Current member parties (2010) with number of members:

S&D Member Parties:

Austria: Sozialdemokratische Partei Österreichs (Social Democratic Party of Austria) (4)

Belgium: Parti Socialiste (PS) (Socialist Party) (3)
                    Socialistische Partij Anders (SP.A)/Spirit (SP) (Socialist
                    Party/Spirit) (2)

Bulgaria: Balgarska Socialisticeska Partija (Bulgarian Socialist Party) (4)

Czech Republic: Ceska Strana Socialne Demokraticka (Czech Social Democratic
                    Party) (7)

Cyprus: EDEK (Movement of Social Democrats) (1)

Denmark: Socialdemokratiet (Social Democratic Party) (4)

Estonia: Sotsiaaldemokraatlik Erakond (Social Democratic Party) (1)

Finland: Suomen Sosialidemokraattinen Puolue (Finnish Social Democratic
                    Party) (2)

France: Parti Socialiste (Socialist Party) (14)

Germany: Sozialdemokratische Partei Deutschlands (Social Democratic Party
                    of Germany) (23)

Greece: Panellinio Sosialistiko Kinima (PASOK) (Pan-Hellenic Socialist
                    Movement) (8)

Hungary: Magyar Szocialista Párt (Hungarian Socialist Party) (4)

Ireland: Labour Party (3)

Lithuania: Lietuvas Socialdemokratu Partija (Lithuanian Social Democratic
                    Party) (3)

Luxembourg: Letzeburger Sozialistesch Arbechterpartei (Luxembourg Socialist
                    Workers' Party) (1)

Malta: Partit Laburista (Labour Party) (3)

Netherlands: Partij van de Arbeid (Labour Party) (3)

Poland: Sojusz Lewicy Demokratycznej – Unia Pracy (Democratic Left
                    Alliance) (7)

Portugal: Partido Socialista (Socialist Party) (7)

Romania: Partidul Social Democrat (Social Democratic Party) (10)
                    Ex Romania Mare (1)

Slovakia: SMER-SD (Smer-Socialna demokracija) (the Direction-Social
                    Democrats) (5)

Slovenia: Socialni Demokrati (Social Democrats) (2)

Spain: Partido Socialista Obrero Español (PSOE) (Spanish Socialist
                    Workers' Party) (21)

Sweden: Socialdemokratiska Arbetarepartiet (Social Democratic Labour
                    Party) (5)

UK: Labour Party (13)

(ii) Others:

Cyprus: Dimokratiko Komma (Democratic Party) (1)

Italy: Partito Democratico (PD) (Democratic Party) (22)

Latvia: Tautas Saskanas Partija (National Harmony Party)

(Socialdemokratiska- Saskanas) (Social Democratic Party-
Harmony) (1)

Romania: Partidul Conservator (Conservative Party 1)

Total: 186

The Group remains the second largest in the European Parliament in the
aftermath of the 2009 elections, but has lost 33 seats compared to the outgoing Parliament, in spite of a number of new Italian recruits who have led to
it being re-named (from Group of the Party of European Socialists, PES). It
is, however, now the only Group to be represented in all EU Member States.

The Socialist Group was the largest Group in the directly elected Parliament
until the 1999 elections, when it fell to 180 members and had 53 fewer members than the EPP. The greatest single reason for this fall in numbers (there
had been 221 after Austrian, Finnish and Swedish accession) was the loss of
33 members from the UK, largely but not exclusively because of the change of
electoral system. EU enlargement left the PES still far behind the EPP but by
the May 2004 plenary the Group had recruited 57 new members from all 10 of
the new Member States, and its numbers had gone back up to 232.

The 2004 elections, however, led to a number of severe losses in certain of
the old and new Member States, in particular in Poland (minus 17),
Germany (minus 12), and in the UK (minus 10). These were only partially
compensated by gains in some other countries, most obviously in France
(plus 13). It now only had 33 members from the new Member States, and
none from Cyprus and Latvia. As a result the PES only had 202 seats, 66
fewer than the EPP-ED. Moreover, the balance of power within the Group
had also changed, with the two parties that had long been the largest in the
Group (British Labour and the German Social Democrats) overtaken in size
by both the French and Spanish Socialists.

Between 2004 and 2007 there were only minor adjustments to the compo-
sition of the Group, with a net loss of two members from Poland and from
Italy. The PES was, however, the biggest beneficiary of Romanian and
Bulgarian accession to the EU in January 2007, gaining 12 members in
Romania from the Social Democratic Party and 6 in Bulgaria from the
Bulgarian Socialist Party. Its overall numbers were thus 217 members before
the 2009 elections.

The 2009 elections led to considerable losses for many of the parties in the
Group, with particularly heavy losses for the French Socialists (minus 17),
and other substantial ones for the British Labour Party (minus 6), the
Portuguese and Hungarian Socialists (each minus 5), the Dutch PvdA
(minus 4) and the Austrian and Spanish Socialists (each minus 3). These
were partially compensated by 5 gains for the Czech Socialists, and a few
more modest gains, including for the Irish Labour Party, which went up
from 1 to 3 seats, and is at its highest level since the 1979-84 Parliament.
Another party which gained a couple of seats was SMER-SD, the Slovak
party led by then Prime Minister Robert Fico. During the previous
Parliament its affiliation to the PES had been suspended over Fico's government coalition with right wing populist parties, but its MEPs had been
allowed to join the Group on an individual basis. The party has now
rejoined the PES. Other parties retained their position, like PASOK in

Greece, and the German Social Democrats, who kept 23 seats, the same as their very poor result in 2004, but which enabled them again to become the largest single party in the Group.

The biggest change affecting the Group came, however, in Italy, which led to its gaining a significant number of Italian seats, but also led to a historic change in the name of the Group.

The composition of the Group had always been the most straightforward of the European Parliament Groups, consisting of the mainstream Socialist/Social Democratic parties in the Member States. Almost all the parties in the Socialist Group had thus been full members of the Party of European Socialists (PES). There had already been an unusual situation in Italy where two parties, the Socialist Party (PSI) and the Social Democrats (PSDI), both long-standing members of the Socialist International, had traditionally co-existed within the Group. During the 1989-94 Parliament, however, the former Italian Communist Party (PCI), the dominant force within what was then the Group of the United European Left, not only changed its name to the Partito Democratico della Sinistra (PDS: Democratic Party of the Left), but also transferred allegiance to the Socialist Group. With the collapse of the Italian Socialist and Social Democratic parties, the PDS subsequently provided the great majority of Italian members of the PES. In October 2007 the situation further evolved with the creation of the Partito Democratico (PD, Democratic Party), which brought together the PDS and also the Margherita coalition, whose members came from Christian social and liberal rather than socialist traditions, and whose European Parliament MEPs were primarily in the ALDE Group and in the European Democratic Party. The PD went on to win 21 seats in the 2009 elections, and all of its MEPs, including those from the former Margherita component, joined the Socialist Group, which changed its name in consequence to the Group of the Progressive Alliance of Socialists and Democrats (S&D). The PD is still not, however, a full member of the PES. It is now, along with PSOE in Spain, the second largest party in the Socialist Group after the German SPD.

Unlike in the last Parliament the Group is now again represented in all EU Member States. In Cyprus a member was elected from the socialist party EDEK, and a member from the DIKO (Democratic Party) also joined the Group (having previously been in the ALDE Group). Finally, in Latvia a member was elected from the then National Harmony Party (now the Social Democratic Party-Harmony) component of the Harmony Centre coalition, and also joined the Group (unlike the member from the other main component party of the coalition, who joined the GUE Group)

Alliance of Liberals and Democrats for Europe (ALDE)

Chair	Guy Verhofstadt
Secretary-General	Alexander Beels
Current membership	85
Current Parliament posts	3 Vice-Presidents, 1 Quaestor, 2 committee chairs and 1 temporary committee chair
Group founded	23 June 1953 (as Liberal Group; became Liberal and Democratic Group in November 1976; Liberal, Democratic, and Reformist

Group in 1986; Group of the European
Liberal, Democrat and Reform Party in 1995;
and Alliance of Liberals and Democrats for
Europe in 2004)

Current member parties (2010) with number of members:

(i) European Liberal Democrat and Reform Party (ELDR) member parties:

Belgium: Vlaamse Liberalen en Demokraten (VLD) (Flemish Liberals and
                 Democrats) (3)
                 Mouvement Réformateur (MR) (2)

Bulgaria: NDSV/HACB (National Movement for Stability and
                 Progress) (2)
                 Dvizenie za Prava i Svobodi (Movement for Rights and Freedoms)
                 (3)

Denmark: Venstre (Danmarks Liberale Parti) (Liberal Party) (3)

Estonia: Eesti Reformierakond (Estonian Reform Party) (1)
                 Eesti Keskerakond (Estonian Centre Party) (2)

Finland: Suomen Keskusta (Centre Party of Finland) (3)
                 Svenska Folkpartiet (Swedish People's Party) (1)

Ireland :   Fianna Fáil (3)

Germany: Freie Demokratische Partei (FDP) (Free Democratic Party) (12)

Italy: Italia dei Valori-Lista Di Pietro (Italy of Values-Di Pietro List) (6)

Latvia: Latvijas Pirma Partija-Latvijas Cels (LPP/LC) (Latvia's First Party-
                 Latvia's Way) (1)

Lithuania: Lietuvos Respublikos Liberalu Sajudis(LRLS) (Liberals Movement
                 of the Republic of Lithuania) (1)

Luxembourg: Demokratesch Partei (Democratic Party) (1)

Netherlands: Volkspartij voor Vrijheid en Democratie (VVD) (People's Party for
                 Freedom and Democracy) (3)
                 D66 (Democrats 66) (3)

Romania: Partidul National Liberal (National Liberal Party) (5)

Slovenia: Liberalna Demokracija Slovenije (Liberal Democrats of Slovenia) (1)
                 Zares-Nova Politika (1)

Spain: Convergencia i Unio-Convergència Democràtica de Catalunya
                 (CDC) (Convergence and Union-Democratic Convergence of
                 Catalonia) (1)

Sweden: Centerpartiet (Centre Party) (1) Folkpartiet Liberalerna (Liberal
                 People's Party) (3)

UK: Liberal Democrats (12)

(ii) European Democratic Party member parties:

France: Mouvement Democrate (MODEM) (Democratic Movement) (6)

Ireland: Independent (Marian Harkin) (1)

Lithuania: Darbo Partija (Labour Party) (1)
Slovakia :   Ludova Strana-Hnutie za demokraticke Slovensko (LS-HZDS) (1)
                  (People's Party-Movement for a Democratic Slovakia)
Spain: Partido Nacionalista Vasco (Basque National Party) (1)

Total: 84

The ALDE Group has remained the third largest Group in the aftermath of the 2009 elections, and continues to have a pivotal role within the political spectrum of the Parliament. The composition of the Group has changed considerably over the years. After the 1994 elections, there had been a considerable shift in the Group's internal balance of power from its southern to its northern members, a shift symbolised by the loss of most of its French and Spanish members, election of two UK Liberal Democrats for the first time, and by the choice of a Dutch Liberal to be its new chair. This was further reinforced during the 1994-99 Parliament by the departure of the Portuguese Social Democrats to the EPP, and by the adhesion of Finnish and Swedish parties from the Liberal and Centre Party traditions. The stronger northern emphasis of the Group was largely confirmed after the 1999 elections, not least because the UK Liberal Democrats won ten seats, making them the single largest component in the Group. The main exception to the northern emphasis of the Group was its fluctuating Italian component, with the traditional Italian Liberal parties (the Partito Liberale and the Partito Repubblicano) being essentially replaced first in 1994 by Umberto Bossi's Lega Nord, and then, after the latter was eased out of the Liberal Group as a result of the extreme positions later taken up by that party's leadership, by members elected in 1999 on the list led by Romano Prodi.

The other result of these shifts was that the ELDR Group, as it was then called, became very weak in a majority of the larger Member States, apart from the UK and, to a lesser extent, Italy, with no French or German members, and very few members from Spain (where the Catalan regionalist party Convergència has been the only long-standing member of the Group).

After the 2004 elections there was again a considerable shift. The UK Liberal Democrats maintained their position as the largest single party within the Group, going up to 12 seats, and again providing the leader of the Group. The Group also won 14 seats in 7 of the new Member States, and returned after a long absence in Germany, where 7 FDP members were elected: they had previously won seats in the 1979 and 1989 elections, but had fallen below the necessary 5% threshold in 1984, 1994 and 1999.

The Group subsequently did very well in the post-election negotiations. In particular, the 11 elected members of the French UDF, who had been in the Liberal Group up to the 1989-94 Parliament (and had even provided several leaders of the Group), but had left it for the EPP, rejoined the Group, where they now provided the second largest delegation. In addition, the Group made a considerable number of Italian recruits, notably from the Margherita List, but also including members from the Italian Radicals. The new Lithuanian Labour Party, which had won 5 seats, also joined the Group. Furthermore talks were held aimed at the Irish Fianna Fáil Party joining the Group though in the end they decided to stay with the UEN Group, leaving the independent Marian Harkin as the only Irish member of the Group.

(There had been a long tradition of Irish independents in the Group, starting with T.J. Maher, and including Pat Cox, who became leader of the Group, and then of the Parliament, making him the only Political Group leader in the history of the EP not to be a member of a national political party.)

As a result of these changes, a number of non-ELDR parties were now in the Group, which subsequently changed its name to that of Alliance of Liberals and Democrats for Europe (ALDE). It thus now included members from two separate European political parties, the pre-existing European Liberal Democrat and Reform Party and the newly-constituted European Democrat Party (EDP).

Between 2004 and 2007 the ALDE Group had a net gain of two members, with a new recruit from Poland (a dissident member from the Civic Platform), and one from the Martin list in Austria, who again gave the Group a representative from Austria after a gap of several years. In January 2007 Romanian and Bulgarian accession gave the Group a further initial boost of 16 new members, three more than had the EPP-ED. Seven of these were from two separate parties in Bulgaria, the National Movement Simeon II and the Movement for Rights and Freedoms, giving the ALDE Group more members from Bulgaria than any other Group. The other 9 were from two parties in Romania, the National Liberal Party and the Conservative Party, although one of the nominated National Liberal MEPs then left the party and joined the new right-wing ITS Group.

The Group had already grown more than any other Group in the aftermath of the 2004 elections, and after Bulgarian and Romanian accession it rose to 105 members, with its share of the total membership of the Parliament going up from 8.4% in May 2004 to 13.5%. It was represented in 22 of the 27 Member States, being without representation only in Greece and Portugal among the old Member States, and in the Czech Republic, Slovakia and Malta among the new Member States.

After the 2009 elections the Group ended up with over 20 fewer seats. Although the German FDP had done particularly well, rising from 7 to 12 seats, and a number of other parties held their own, or made slight gains or losses, including the UK Liberal Democrats, who lost their position as the largest party in the Group but still returned with 11 (rather than 12) seats, there were significant losses in a number of countries, including Italy (the solid performance of the Di Pietro list with 7 seats being offset by the loss of the former Margherita members to the Socialist Group), France (where Francois Bayrou's MODEM returned with only 6 seats compared to the 11 of the UDF in 2004), Poland (where the Group lost all its seats), Lithuania, Romania and Bulgaria. The Group is now present in 19 of the 27 Member States. Besides Poland, the Group is now no longer represented in Austria, Cyprus and Hungary. Of the countries where it was formerly not represented, it is still not present in Greece, Portugal, the Czech Republic and Malta, although it has gained one representative in Slovakia.

Since the elections the Group has gained one more member, Edward McMillan-Scott, a long serving British Conservative who was unhappy with his party's move away from the EPP-ED Group, and stood successfully for a Vice Presidency of the Parliament against the official candidate of his new Group. He was subsequently expelled from the party, and became first non-attached and then an ALDE member after he joined the Liberal Democrats.

The ALDE Group remains one of only two Groups (the other being the Green/EFA Group) to have members from two separate European political parties co-existing within its ranks. 24 of its 28 parties (and 75 of its 85 members) are within ELDR, and 4 of its parties and 9 members are within the EDP with one independent.

Group of the Greens/European Free Alliance

Co-Presidents	Daniel Cohn-Bendit and Rebecca Harms
	Jill Evans (President of EFA Group and 1st Vice-President of the Greens/EFA Group)
Secretary-General	Vula Tsetsi and José-Luis Linazasoro (deputy secretary-general and EFA secretary-general)
Current Membership	55
Current Parliament posts	1 Vice-President, 1 committee chair and 1 chair of subcommittee
Group Founded	July 1989 (previously in Rainbow Group from 1984)

Current member parties (2010) with number of members:

(i) Green Parties:

Austria:	Die Grünen (The Greens) (2)
Belgium:	ECOLO (Ecologist Party) (2) Groen (Green) (1)
Denmark:	Socialistisk Folkeparti (Socialist People's Party) (2)
Finland:	Vihreät (Green Union) (2)
France:	Europe Ecologie (Europe Ecology) (13)
Germany:	Bündnis 90/Die Grünen (Alliance 90–The Greens) (14)
Greece:	Oikologoi Prasinoi (Ecologist Greens) (1)
Luxembourg:	Dei Greng (The Greens) (1)
Netherlands:	Groen Links (Green Left) (3)
Spain:	Iniciativa per Catalunya Verds (Initiative for Catalonia/Greens) (1)
Sweden:	Miljopartiet de Grona (Green Ecology Party) (2)
UK:	Green Party (2)

(ii) European Free Alliance Parties (or allies):

Belgium:	Nieuw-Vlaamse Alliantie (NVA) (New Flemish Alliance) (1)
France:	U Partitu di a Nazione Corsa (Party of the Corsican Nation, elected on Europe Ecology list) (1)
Latvia:	Par Cilveka Tiesibam Vienota Latvija (For Human Rights in United Latvia) (1)
Spain:	Esquerra Republicana de Catalunya (Republican Left of Catalonia) (1) (elected on list Europa de los Pueblos/Verdes, Europe of the Peoples/Greens)

UK: Scotland: Scottish National Party (SNP) (2)
                  Plaid Cymru–The Party of Wales (1)

(iii) Others

Estonia :   Independent (I. Tarand) (1)
Sweden: Piratpartiet (Pirates Party) (1)
Total: 55

The Greens polled well in the 2009 elections, and the Green EFA Group is now the fourth largest Group in the Parliament, and has more seats than ever before. It has still failed, however, to make a breakthrough in the new Member States.

The Greens were founded as a Group in their own right after the June 1989 elections, although they had already been allied with regionalist parties in the Rainbow Group in the 1984-89 Parliament. In 1989 they had 29 members, with the two largest delegations (with 8 members each) coming from France and Germany. After the 1994 elections, the Green Group had only 23 members, with no members from France and a reinforced German presence of 12 members. Following the 1995 enlargement, the Greens were considerably reinforced by additional members from the Austrian, Finnish and Swedish Green parties.

The Greens did well in the 1999 elections. The French Greens returned to the Parliament with nine seats, and the two Belgian Green parties, Ecolo and Agalev, did very well in the immediate aftermath of the dioxin scandal, and went up from one seat each, to three and two seats respectively. The Dutch Groen Links, which went up from one to four seats, also enjoyed considerable success and for the first time two British Greens were also elected.

The position of the Group was further reinforced by the inclusion of a number of parties belonging to the European Free Alliance (EFA), and was renamed, in consequence, as the Greens/European Free Alliance Group. Since its first general assembly in Brussels in 1981, when it adopted its initial declaration of fundamental principles, the EFA has been a framework for cooperation between a number of regionalist parties seeking to build Europe on the basis of the peoples and regions, and thus aiming for the maximum degree of decentralization or outright independence for their regions. It subsequently became a federation of parties in 1994 and a fully-fledged European Political Party in 2004. While its members have been in different Groups within the Parliament their main homes had previously been the two Rainbow Groups from 1984-1994, and the European Radical Alliance from 1994-1999.

As a result of this joining of forces the Greens/European Free Alliance Group had 48 members and became the fourth largest group, though later on in that Parliament, they suffered a number of defections, and were overtaken by the GUE Group.

After the 2004 elections the Greens and the European Free Alliance, both of which had now become fully-fledged European political parties, decided to remain together within the same Group. They now had only 42 members, and their overall share of total MEPs had slipped from 7.2% before enlargement to only 5.7%. They narrowly overtook the GUE Group, however, and were again the fourth largest Group. They were particularly strong in Germany, where they won 13 seats, but also managed to hold on to 6 Green seats in France, in spite of a potentially unfavourable change in the electoral system.

In late 2005 the expansion of the UEN Group pushed them back again into fifth place. They gained no new members as a result of Bulgarian and Romanian accession, and slipped further behind the biggest Groups.

The Group made considerable gains in the 2009 elections, especially in France where the Europe Ecology list elected 13 Green members, and 1 EFA member from the autonomist Party of the Corsican Nation. They also gained 1 seat in Germany, where they now have 14 Green MEPs, and also gained additional Green seats in Belgium, Finland, Greece (for the first time), the Netherlands and Sweden, and EFA seats in Denmark and in Belgium (where the New Flemish Alliance had previously been allied with the Flemish Christian Democrats in the EPP-ED Group and were now elected separately with the EFA). Of their 55 members 44 are from 12 Green parties, 9 are from 7 EFA parties and two others are in neither, the independent Estonian MEP, Indrek Tarand and an MEP from the Swedish Pirates Party (which advocates total copyright and patent reform). They are represented in 12 of the 15 old Member States, but not in Ireland (where they won seats in both 1994 and 1999, but not in 2004 or 2009), nor in Italy (where they lost the two seats that they had held in 2004) or Portugal.

The Greens have benefited less than any other Group from EU enlargement, with only 2 seats (an EFA seat in Latvia and the independent seat in Estonia) from the 12 new Member States. Not a single Green has been elected in these countries, although there are a number of parties from these countries within the European Green Party.

The group traditionally has one male and one female co-chair, currently Rebecca Harms of the German Greens and the outgoing co-chair, Daniel Cohn-Bendit, the 1968 student leader, who had been a German Green MEP during the 1994-99 Parliament, a French Green MEP from 1999-2004, a German MEP from 2004-2009 and who has again been a French MEP since 2009. The EFA component of the Group also has a President, currently Jill Evans of the Welsh nationalist Plaid Cymru. A further distinctive feature of the Group is that the Secretary General of the EFA is the Deputy Secretary General of the Group.

European Conservatives and Reformists Group (ECR)

Chair	Michal Kaminski
Secretary-General	Frank Barrett
Current membership	54
Current Parliament posts	1 committee chair
Group founded	July 2009

Current member parties (2010) with number of members:

Belgium   Lijst Dedecker (LLD, Dedecker List) (1)

Czech Republic: Obcanska Demokraticka Strana (ODS, Civic Democratic Party) (9)

Hungary: Magyar Demokrata Fórum (MDF, Hungarian Democratic Forum) (1)

Latvia: Tevzemei un Brivibai/LNNK), (TB/LNNK, For Fatherland and Freedom) (1)

Lithuania: AWPL, Electoral Action of Poles in Lithuania (1)

Netherlands: ChristenUnie (Christian Union) (1)

Poland: Law and Justice (11)
                 Dissident Law and Justice (4)

UK: Conservative Party (24); Ulster Conservatives and Unionists-New
                 Force (UCUNF) (1)

Total: 54

The ECR is a new centre-right group, founded in July 2009, with most of its members from parties which had previously been either in the EPP-ED or UEN Groups. The ECR prefers to describe itself as "Eurorealist" rather than Eurosceptic, though its founding declaration of principles (the Prague Declaration) emphasises "the sovereign integrity of the nation state, opposition to EU federalism and a renewed respect for true subsidiarity".

Its largest component party is the British Conservative Party, whose members have reverted to being in their own separate group after an 18 year period when they had been in the EPP Group. From British entry in 1973 until 1992 they were the largest party within the European Conservative Group until 1979, renamed the European Democratic Group (EDG) from 1979-92. This was the third largest Group in the Parliament from 1979-89, and even provided one EP President, Lord Plumb. The Spanish members in the group then left the EDG to join the EPP Group. After this, the remaining EDG members first sought a close working relationship with the EPP Group and then to join it directly. Although there was majority support for their joining from within the EPP (notably from the German members), there was also opposition from other members who preferred to keep the EDG at arm's length. In April 1992, however, the EPP Group finally voted by 66 to 28 with five abstentions to admit the individual EDG members into the Group of the EPP on the basis of acceptance of the Group's programme.

After the 1999 elections the British Conservatives all remained within the Group, but were instrumental in changing its official name to a new and longer form of the "Group of the European People's Party (Christian Democrats) and European Democrats" and reaching an understanding that they would issue a separate whip on integration issues (as permitted by the EPP-ED Rules of Procedure – see above). In view of the divisions within the British Conservative Party on European issues, their continued presence in the Group remained controversial, both within the Conservative Party itself and amongst certain of the EPP member parties but it was decided that they should remain as members of the Group after the 2004 elections. Primarily because of the success of UKIP, they lost 9 members in those elections, but were still the second largest national delegation in the Group. After David Cameron became leader of the party he was again forced to review its membership of the EPP-ED Group as a result of commitments made during his campaign. Contacts were again established with a number of other parties, primarily from the new Member States, to explore the creation of a new Group. This did not prove to be immediately possible, nor was it popular with many Conservative MEPs, but a new commitment was made that the Conservatives would aim to leave the Group after the next European elections. In the meantime, Roger Helmer, one of their existing MEPs most keen on the policy of leaving the Group, who had been expelled from the EPP-ED, sat as a non-attached member.

After the 2009 elections the British Conservatives, who had 25 elected MEPs, finally implemented Cameron's commitment to leave the EPP-ED when they succeeded in gaining sufficient allies to form the new ECR Group. The second largest party in the new group was the conservative Law and Justice Party from Poland with 15 MEPs, which had previously been the largest party in the former UEN Group. One other former UEN party also joined the ECR Group, the Fatherland and Freedom Party from Latvia, with 1 MEP.

Three former EPP-ED parties joined the British Conservatives in the ECR. Two of these were from its former ED component, the Civic Democratic Party (ODS) from the Czech Republic, with 9 MEPs and the Ulster Unionist party with 1 MEP, which had now forged a new alliance with the British Conservative Party in the Northern Ireland electoral context. The third party, the Hungarian Democratic Forum with 1 MEP, had actually been a full EPP member party.

Finally three other MEPs joined the ECR, one from the Christian Union from the Netherlands, which had previously been part of the Dutch Calvinist coalition within the former IND-DEM Group, another from the Electoral Action for Poles in Lithuania and finally one from the Dedecker list from Belgium, a right wing breakaway from the VLD, the Flemish Liberal Party. In addition, the outgoing secretary-general of the former UEN Group became the secretary-general of the ECR Group

Initial tensions concerning the creation of the new Group were reflected in the outcome of the elections to the Parliament's new Bureau. The ECR Group was to be led by a British Conservative (Timothy Kirkhope), but had put forward a candidate for a Vice Presidency (Michal Kaminski) from the Polish Law and Justice Party. Another British Conservative (Edward McMillan-Scott), a long standing MEP and former Parliament Vice-President who was deeply unhappy about the decision to leave the EPP-ED Group, stood against the ECR's official nominee, and succeeded in defeating him. McMillan-Scott was then forced to leave his party and his Group, first becoming non-attached and then becoming a Liberal Democrat and joining the ALDE Group. On the other hand the unsuccessful official candidate Kaminski became the leader of the ECR Group instead of Timothy Kirkhope, thereby leaving the group without a Vice-Presidency of the Parliament. The ECR's other candidate (Malcolm Harbour), however, was successfully elected as the chair of the Internal Market Committee. In November 2010 Michal Kaminski left the Law and Justice Party, and joined a dissident grouping of former party members. Three other former Law and Justice MEPs followed him. He subsequently resigned as leader of the Group. In the election to succeed him in early 2011, Jan Zahradil (Czech ODS) defeated Timothy Kirkhope, the UK Conservative.

Confederal Group of the European United Left/Nordic Green Left (GUE/NGL)

Chair	Lothar Bisky
Secretary-General	Maria d'Alimonte
Current membership	41
Current Parliament posts	1 Quaestor and 1 committee chair

| Group founded | July 1994 (but one of the successor Groups to the Communist Group founded in 1974) |

Current member parties (2010) with number of members:

(i) Party of the European Left:

(a) full member parties:

France:	Parti Communiste Français-Indépendants (French Communist Party and Allies) (2)
	Parti de Gauche (Left Party) (1)
Germany:	Die Linke (the Left) (8)
Greece:	SYRIZA (Synaspismos tis Rizospastikis Aristera) Greek Coalition of the Radical Left) (1)
Portugal:	Bloco de Esquerda (Left Bloc) (3) (also member of network of European Anticapitalist Left)
Spain:	Izquierda Unida (United Left) (1)

(b) observer parties:

| *Cyprus:* | Anorthotiko Komma Ergazomenou Laou (AKEL) (2) |
| *Czech Republic:* | Komunisticka Strana Cech a Moravy (Czech and Moravian Communist Party) (4) |

(ii) Nordic Green Left Alliance member parties:

| *Sweden:* | Vänsterpartiet (Left Party) (1) |

(iii) other member parties:

Denmark:	Folkebevaelgelsen mod EU (People's Movement against the European Union) (1)
France:	Parti Communiste Réunionais (Communist Party of Reunion) (1)
	Independent (Marie-Christine Vergiat, elected on Left Front list) (1)
Greece:	Kommounistiko Komma Ellados (Communist Party of Greece) (2)
Ireland:	Socialist Party(1) (member of network of European Anticapitalist Left)
Latvia:	Latvijas Socialistiska Partija (Latvian Socialist Party)(part of Saskanas Centrs alliance) (1)
Netherlands:	Socialistische Partij (Socialist Party) (2)
Portugal:	Partido Comunista Portugués (Portuguese Communist Party) (2)
UK:	
Northern Ireland:	Sinn Féin (1)

Total: 35

After the 2009 elections the GUE/NGL Group lost a number of seats, and is now the second smallest Group in the European Parliament. It is essentially drawn from Communist, former Communist and left Socialist parties from 12 countries, and its history is a complex one.

From its foundation in October 1973 until 1989, the only Group to the left of the Socialist Group was the Communist and Allies Group. During the 1984-89 legislature, in particular, it operated with two very distinct wings. One was led by the Italian Communist Party, the largest single party within the Group, which always provided the President of the Group. The Italians were supported by the member from the Eurocommunist party in Greece (the smaller of the two Greek Communist parties, and which itself later split in two), by the member from the Danish Socialist People's Party, and later by members from Spain. The more traditional Communist faction was dominated by the French Communists, and also included the larger and more orthodox of the two Greek Communist parties and later the Portuguese Communist Party. As a result of these divisions the Group seldom agreed on a common line.

After the 1989 elections, the two factions formally divided and created two new Groups with confusingly similar names, the Italian Communist-led Group taking on the name "European Unitarian Left" (GUE after its French initials) and the more hard-line Group the name "Left Unity", "Coalition des Gauches" in French, and which also included a member from the Irish Workers Party.

The Italian Communist Party later changed its name to that of the Partito Democratico della Sinistra (PDS: Democratic Party of the Left). A considerable minority of its membership refused to accept the party's change of direction and of name and started a new Communist party under the name Rifondazione Comunista, along with members from another left-wing Italian party, Democrazia Proletaria (Proletarian Democracy). The vast majority of the MEPs remained in the PDS, but two joined Rifondazione Comunista at the end of 1991. The PDS members subsequently joined the Socialist Group, leaving the six remaining members of the United European Left on their own, and without enough members to keep the Group going. After the 1994 elections, some members (the Spanish members of Izquierda Unida, United Left) favoured the creation of a large Red/Green Group with the Greens. In the end, however, they opted to join up with the remaining Communist parties of the Left Unity Group, but under a new name. The new GUE Group was born, with the English language name having become "European United Left" in 1992.

The largest single force in the Group, with 9 members, was the Spanish Izquierda Unida, which included members from the mainstream Spanish and Catalan Communist parties, but also from the left Socialist party PASOK and from Green and other backgrounds. With the exception of the Greek party Synaspismou tis Aristeras (Coalition of the Left), most of the other parties in the Group still explicitly called themselves Communist, and included members from the French, Greek and Portuguese parties as well as from the Italian Rifondazione Comunista which, in spite of its name, was less hard-line and more pro-European than the others. Divided over internal tactics in Italian politics, Rifondazione Comunista later itself split in two, with the veteran Italian Communist, Armando Cossutta, creating yet another party, the Partito dei Comunisti Italiani.

After enlargement in 1995, the Group gained Swedish and Finnish members, with the Swedish party being anti-EU, but with the Finnish party more divided on this issue. At the insistence of its new members the Group added a new reference to "Nordic Green Left" at the end of its existing name.

After the 1999 elections the GUE Group enlarged to include members from two additional countries, Germany, with six members from the PDS (the successor to the East German Communist Party), and the Netherlands, with one member from the left-wing Socialistische Partij. In France the Communist Party's attempt to broaden its traditional base was unsuccessful, but the Trotskyist alliance of Arlette Laguiller and Alain Krivine managed to elect five members, who were accepted into the Group as associate members. In Italy both of the continuing Communist parties, Rifondazione and the Comunisti Italiani, obtained seats and entered the Group. The two Greek parties in the former Group (the KKE and Synaspismos) were joined by two new members from the breakaway Socialist DIKKI party, and the Group also had eight members from the three Nordic countries. The main setback for the Group was the poor performance of Izquierda Unida, which went into the 1999 elections internally divided, and went down from nine to four seats.

In 2001-2, the GUE/NGL Group benefited from defections from the Socialists, from the Greens and from the EDD to overtake the Greens to become the fourth largest Group with its highest ever total of 49 MEPs.

The Group had very mixed results in the 2004 elections, going from fourth to fifth in size, and its share of total EP members falling from 7.8% before enlargement to 5.6% in the new Parliament, in spite of its excellent result in the Czech Republic.

In France the two parties of Trotskyist orientation lost all their seats, and the French Communists only won 3 seats. In Spain Izquierda Unida went down to only one seat, and some ground was also lost in the Nordic countries. On the other hand the two Italian parties held their own, with 5 and 2 seats respectively, and the German PDS successfully crossed the 5% threshold and returned with 7 seats, making it the single largest delegation within the Group.

The Czech Communists polled extremely well and won 6 seats, making them the second largest delegation within the Group. AKEL in Cyprus also won two seats. In the other 8 new Member States the Group was unrepresented.

The other distinctive new recruit to the Group was Sinn Féin, which now had members both from Ireland and from the Northern Ireland constituency within the United Kingdom.

By the end of 2005 the Group had fallen further to sixth in size, and it gained no new recruits as a result of Bulgarian and Romanian accession in January 2007.

The 2009 elections saw very mixed fortunes for the Group. The Left Party in Germany, the broader-based successor to the former PDS, polled well, and won 8 seats, making it by far the biggest party in the Group. In France 5 MEPs were elected, 4 of them on the "Front de Gauche pour changer d'Europe" (Left Front to Change Europe), including 2 from the French Communist Party, 1 from the new Parti de Gauche (Left Party, created by dissidents from the Socialist Party), and 1 independent. The Czech Communists won 4 seats, two fewer than in 2004, but still enough to make them the third largest delegation within the Group. 5 MEPs were elected in Portugal, 3 from the Left Bloc (which surpassed the Communists for the first time) and 2 from the Portuguese Communists. The Group also gained a new member from Latvia, the former Latvian Communist leader, Alfreds Rubiks, elected as a Latvian Socialist member on the list of the alliance of parties of the Harmony Centre.

The biggest loss for the Group was the failure to win any seats in Italy, compared to the 7 won by two parties in 2004. The Finnish Left also lost their one seat, and the Swedish Left lost one of their former two seats. Sinn Féin's MEP was re-elected in Northern Ireland (with the party topping the constituency poll for the first time), but it lost its seat in the Republic of Ireland to Joe Higgins of the Socialist Party, who then joined the Group.

The parties within the Group now fall into several categories. Six parties with 16 members are in the Party of the European Left, and an additional two parties with 6 members are observers. One other party with 1 member is in the Nordic Green Alliance component of the Group. Finally there are a further 8 parties with 12 members, who are in neither of these categories. Several of the Group parties are, however, also in the more informal network of the European Anticapitalist Left.

The long-serving chair of the Group, Francis Wurtz (French Communist), who had been an MEP since 1979, finally retired at the 2004 elections, and was replaced as Group leader by Lothar Bisky of the German Left Party.

Europe of Freedom and Democracy Group (EFD)

Co-chairmen	Nigel Farage and Francesco Speroni
Secretary-General	Emmanuel Bordez
Current membership	30
Group founded	July 2009

Current member parties (2010) with number of members:

Denmark:	Dansk Folkeparti (Danish People's Party) (2)
Finland :	Perussuomalainen (True Finns) (1)
France:	Mouvement pour la France (Movement for France) (1)
Greece:	Laikos Orthodoxos Synagermos (LAOS) (Popular Orthodox Rally) (2)
Italy :	Lega Nord (Northern League) (9)
Lithuania :	Partija Tvarka ir teisungumas (Order and Justice) (2)
Netherlands:	Staatkundig Gereformeerde Partij (Dutch Reformed Political Party, SGP) (1)
Slovakia:	Slovensko narodna strana (Slovak National Party, SNS) (1)
UK:	UK Independence Party (11)

Total: 30

The Europe of Freedom and Democracy Group (EFD) is a Group of Eurosceptic orientation, emphasising the role of individual nation states, and opposing further European integration. It was founded in July 2009, but is a successor to two previous Eurosceptic Groups, the Europe of Democracies and Diversities Group (EDD) and the Independence and Democracy Group (IND/DEM). Both of these, however, included a few left of centre as well as right of centre Eurosceptic parties, whereas the EFD has a much clearer right wing orientation.

The Europe of Democracies and Diversities Group (EDD) was a new Group established after the 1999 elections and consisting of mainly Eurosceptic parties from four EU countries. The Group's Dutch and Danish parties were in the former Europe of Nations Group, whereas its French and British (UKIP) components were new to the Parliament.

There had long been four Danish members from the anti-EU movement (which only stands in European, not national, elections). In 1994 the movement split, with two competing lists. The People's Movement against the European Union remained opposed to Danish membership in the EU, whereas the June Movement (Junibevaegelsen) no longer opposed Danish EU membership "per se", but resisted further integration. They continued to sit in the same Group until 2002 when two left to join the GUE/NGL Group, where the sole representative of the People's Movement remained after the 2004 and 2009 elections.

The Group also contained three MEPs from a coalition of three separate fundamentalist Calvinist parties in the Netherlands, the inspiration of which is primarily religious rather than nationalist, and whose emphasis is placed more on respect of subsidiarity principles than strong Euro-scepticism.

The French list, Chasse, Pêche, Nature et Traditions, represented hunters, fishermen and other rural voters (especially in south-west France) opposed to certain EU directives, notably those on protecting birds. After narrowly falling below the 5 per cent threshold in 1994 they won six seats in 1999. Three other French members also defected to the EDD from the UEN Group during the first half of the 1999-2004 Parliament.

Finally the UK Independence Party advocated British withdrawal from the EU, and was able to win three seats after the change in the electoral system in 1999; however, one member subsequently left the party and the Group to become non-attached.

The 2004 European elections gave very mixed results to these four components of the former EDD Group. The well-financed UK Independence Party got huge publicity, and won 12 seats at the expense of other British parties, especially the Conservatives. The Dutch Calvinists and the Danish June Movement both lost seats, and the French hunters failed to win any. On the other hand potential new recruits polled very well in other countries, notably in Poland where the Catholic conservative League of Polish Families won 10 seats, and in Sweden where a new June List on the lines of the June Movement in Denmark won 3 seats. The EDD was thus reconstituted as the Independence and Democracy (IND/DEM) Group, initially with 38 members from 10 countries, and thus much bigger than the former EDD Group. Besides the parties mentioned above, it also included 4 members from Umberto Bossi's Lega Nord from Italy and 3 members from Philippe de Villiers' Eurosceptic Mouvement Pour la France, as well as one member from the Popular Orthodox Rally Party in Greece, another from a list in the Czech Republic and finally an independent elected in Ireland (Kathy Sinnott).

In the course of the 2004-9 Parliament the Group lost 16 of its initial 38 members, including 8 Poles from the League of Polish Families and 4 members from the Italian Lega Nord, as well as members from the Swedish June

List and a number from UKIP. The departing members went to several Groups or became non-attached, although the largest single beneficiary was the former UEN Group.

After the 2009 elections, four of the component parties of the IND/DEM Group had members who had been re-elected to the European Parliament. UKIP had increased its seats in the UK from 12 to 13, the Greek LAOS had two seats, the Dutch Calvinist SGP had one seat and the French Movement for France, led by Philippe de Villiers, also had one seat. The latter had allied himself with the Irish anti-Lisbon Treaty campaigner, Declan Ganley, during the run-up to the European elections but when he was the only Ganley ally elected to the European Parliament, again turned to his former Group colleagues.

In addition to these former IND/DEM parties the new Group recruited two parties from the defunct UEN Group, the Italian Lega Nord (which had once been an IND/DEM party) and the right wing Danish People's Party. Two newly elected parties also joined the Group, the one member from the True Finns Party of Timo Soini and the one member from the Slovak National Party. They were later joined by the two members of the Lithuanian Order and Justice Party of former Prime Minister and President, Rolandas Paksas.

Since the Group was formed it has already lost two of its UKIP members, Nikki Sinclaire, who left in March 2010, and Mike Nattrass in June 2010. Both have become non-attached.

While more right wing than its predecessors, the Group is not homogeneous on EU institutional issues. The largest component party (UKIP) would like the UK to leave the EU whereas others, while generally highly critical of the EU, put more emphasis on national sovereignty and on slowing down further European integration rather than their country leaving. Indeed differences on this issue was one of the reasons cited by Mike Nattrass for leaving the Group while remaining a member of UKIP. Another strand within the Group is that of conservative religious orientation, shared by several of its component parties.

The Group is co-chaired by MEPs from its two largest parties, Nigel Farage of UKIP and Francesco Speroni of the Lega Nord.

The non-attached members

Current parties not attached (2010), with number of members:

Listed below are the parties represented in the 2004-2009 European Parliament that are not in any Group.

Austria:	Liste Dr Hans-Peter Martin–Für Echte Kontrolle in Brussel (Hans-Peter Martin List for Tight Control in Brussels) (2)
	Independent originally elected on Martin list (Angelika Werthmann) (1)
	Freiheitliche Partei Osterreichs (Freedom Party of Austria) (2)
Belgium:	Vlaams Belang (Flemish Interest) (2)
Bulgaria:	Nacionalem Sajuz Ataka (Attack National Union) (2)
France:	Front National (National Front) (3)
Hungary:	JOBBIK Magyarországért Mozgalom (Movement for a Better Hungary) (3)

Netherlands: Partij voor de Vrijheid (PVV) (Freedom Party) (4)

Romania: Partidul Romania Mare (Greater Romania Party) (1)
               Partidul Noua Generatie-Crestin Democrat (New Generation-
               Christian Democrat Party) (1)

Spain: Union, Progreso y Democracia (UpyD) (Union, Progress and
               Democracy Party) (1)

UK: Northern Ireland Democratic Unionist Party (1)
               British National Party (BNP) (2)
               Former UKIP (2)

Total: 27

The successful struggle led by Pannella and others at the beginning of the directly elected Parliament in 1979, prevented the numbers required for forming a Political Group from increasing significantly to reflect the much higher membership of the Parliament. As a result, and because of the great advantages accorded to membership of a Political Group, only a small number of members have remained non-attached. These have tended to be members of small political parties or individual personalities sharing little common political ground with any of the existing Groups, or who have positively preferred the complete freedom of movement given them by non-attached status.

As of 1994, a disproportionate number of the non-attached members came from parties on the right or far right of the political spectrum (the French Front National, the Belgian Vlaams Blok and Front National, the Italian Alleanza Nazionale and later the Austrian Freedom Party), which, for a variety of reasons, were unable to agree on forming a Group of their own to succeed the Group of the Right that had existed from 1984-1994.

After the 1999 elections Alleanza Nazionale joined the UEN Group, but the French, Belgian and Austrian parties of the far right remained as non-attached members. They were joined by 10 Italian members (7 Radicals and 3 from the Lega Nord), Ian Paisley of the Democratic Unionist Party of Northern Ireland (who had been a non-attached member since 1979), a member of the extremist Basque Movement Euskal Herritarrok, and an independent French member, Marie France Garaud, who had been elected on Pasqua's RPFIE list, but did not join the others on the list in the UEN Group. Later on, six other members from that list left the UEN to join her and one British UKIP member also became non-attached.

Shortly after the elections an attempt was made to form a Technical Group in order to take advantage of the benefits of a Group within the Parliament. Those wishing to participate consisted of a variety of non-attached members and parties of very different orientation, ranging from the Lista Emma Bonino to the French Front National, but not all the non-attached members (e.g. the representatives of the Austrian Freedom Party, as well as Ian Paisley) wished to join such a Group. As described above, the Technical Group was eventually dissolved after it lost a lengthy struggle in the courts, primarily because it was considered, by its own admission, not to have the necessary political affinities required in Parliament's Rules. A proposed Rules change tabled by Italian non-attached members in order to permit a "Mixed Group" that would incorporate all non-attached members, and that would enjoy the normal rights of a Political Group (a possibility that exists, for example, in the Italian and Spanish parliaments) received little support.

After the 2004 elections there were 28 non-attached members, of whom almost half were from French, Flemish, Italian and Austrian right-wing parties that had not managed to form a Political Group. After Romanian and Bulgarian accession in January 2007 a new right-wing group, the Identity, Tradition and Sovereignty (ITS) Group, was established, and as a result of this, there were, for a time, only 14 non-attached members, primarily Slovak, Polish, Italian and UK MEPS. The ITS Group lasted less than a year, and collapsed in November 2007 after the departure of the members from the Romania Mare party, protesting after remarks made by one of their erstwhile colleagues, Alessandra Mussolini, the grand-daughter of the Duce. The ITS members again became non-attached.

As a result of the 2009 elections, there are again 28 non-attached members, the vast majority of whom are from very diverse parties of the populist and far right. Several of these were in the former ITS Group, namely the French Front National (down from 7 to 3 members), Romania Mare, the Flemish Vlaams Belang, the Austrian Freedom Party, and the Bulgarian party, Ataka, each with 2 members. They were also joined by three right-wing parties that had not previously won seats in the European Parliament, the Dutch Freedom Party (PVV) led by Geert Wilders with 4 members, the Hungarian JOBBIK with 3 and the British National Party with 2.

The largest of the other contingents among the non-attached members is that led by Dr Hans-Peter Martin from Austria, a journalist first elected in 1999 on the Austrian Socialist list, but later expelled from the group. In 2004 he was re-elected with one other colleague on a populist programme of control of members' expenses and perks, but his colleague subsequently joined the Liberal Group, leaving Martin alone among the non-attached members. In 2009, however, his list did very well, and returned with 3 MEPs, one of whom, however, has since become independent.

There are also 3 British non-attached members, including Diane Dodds of the Democratic Unionist Party (DUP) from Northern Ireland. The DUP has continuously elected members to the EP since 1979 (with Ian Paisley from 1979 to 2004 and Jim Allister, who subsequently left the DUP to form the Traditional Unionist Voice, from 2004-2009), and has always been non-attached.

The other two British members are Nikki Sinclaire and Mike Nattrass, both elected on the UKIP list in 2009, but who subsequently left the EFD Group to become non-attached. The other two non-attached members are from the Christian nationalist New Generation Party from Romania and from the Union, Progress and Democracy Party from Spain, a centrist party opposed to the fragmentation of Spanish politics, and whose most prominent member is Rosa Diez, a former leading figure in PSOE.

Parliament's Rules lay down certain rights for the non-attached members. They are entitled to a secretariat (Rule 33), and the 14 MEPs have been allocated staff by the Bureau, which has also decided to set aside rooms for their disposal on an occasional basis at Parliament's normal working places. One of the non-attached members attends meetings of the Conference of Presidents as an observer, and without the right to vote (Rule 24.2). The decision as to who this should be used to be taken by the non-attached members themselves, but there was controversy as to how this delegate should be chosen, and in the absence of consensus, it is now the President of Parliament who invites the member who is entitled to attend. Non-attached members may also nominate members to committees and delegations (Rules 186 and 198) and an equal number of substitutes (Rule 187). Finally, they are allocated an overall speaking time in plenary based on the fractions previously allocated to the different Political Groups (Rule 149-4(c)). The non-attached members are allocated seats at the very back of the hemicycle.

As a general rule non-attached members have been able to make more of an impact in plenary than in committees, through participation in debates, points of order or even demonstrations and challenges to the authority of the presiding officer (see section on order in the chamber in Chapter 9). Their protests are rarer in committee and non-attached members are rarely allocated the more significant rapporteurships. Whether they obtain any reports or opinions depends very much on their party or personality, and on the size and culture of their committee. It is more likely to occur in a large committee with a lot of legislative and other work to distribute. In the Environment Committee, for example, Mr Kronberger of the FPO took part in committee coordinator meetings and obtained several reports and opinions including a technical but not insignificant legislative report on air quality.

Changing Groups

MEPs may change Political Group or become non-attached members. This happens more frequently than in most national parliaments, and occurs at all times during the legislative period, especially around and after the mid-point of the legislature. Italian and French MEPs have been particularly prone to switch groups, as have Polish MEPs more recently, but many other nationalities have also been involved, including British members. On the other hand there have been very few switches in certain other countries, such as Germany, and none at all in 10 others.

If a member changes Group, they retain Parliament posts such as committee chair, Vice-President or Quaestor, to which they may have been elected as a member of their original Group. This is because such posts are formally elected by members and only informally based on a share-out among Groups at the time of the election. One member, Antoni Gutierrez, even retained his committee chair (Regional Affairs) after his Group no longer existed. Similarly, the member concerned will retain full membership of a committee, but not any substitute membership (as members can only substitute for a missing member of their own Group). Although the Rules have been interpreted to provide that "if a member's change of Political Group has the effect of disturbing the fair representation of political views in a committee, new proposals for the composition of that committee shall be made by the Conference of Presidents" (interpretation of Rule 186), no major problem has yet been caused in this regard.

Support provided by Parliament to Political Groups

Parliament's budget allocates certain appropriations directly to the Political Groups (€53.75 million in 2010). Each Group's share (and that of the non-attached members) is determined by a complex formula: 12.5% in fixed ratios

(1 point for every 40 members in a Group, the total divided by 2 and increased by one), 45.5% proportionally to the number of members of each group, but with its size augmented by an additional 5% for each language the Group uses, and 42% proportionally to the number of members of each Group with no further adjustment. In 2010 this gave overall sums of €20.0m to the EPP-ED, €14.0m to the S&D, €6.2m to ALDE, €3.9m to the Greens/EFA, €3.6m to the ECR, €2.5m to the GUE/NGL and €2.3m to the EFD Group. The non-attached members got around €40,000 per member. Such funds must be externally audited by an external audit firm (which Groups can choose from 11 approved by the Bureau) even before the routine EU auditing takes place.

The relevant budgetary heading is item 4000 of Parliament's budget, which covers the secretariat and administrative expenditure of the Groups and their own political activities. Formerly, information activities by the Groups were in a separate item 3708. This latter item was originally used for European election campaigns but this was challenged in the Court of Justice by the French Green Party, Les Verts, in 1983 and the Court ruled that financing of party election campaigns was a national competence until the adoption of a uniform electoral system. As a result, the rules were changed so that the item only funded information activities and could no longer be used for any election campaign or for any information activity in the 30 days prior to European elections. It has now been moved into item 4000.

The Groups also obtain support from the Parliament in terms of their staff entitlements (see below), office space, meeting rooms and technical facilities. Altogether, the Groups can be said to account for around 15 per cent of Parliament's budget.

Political Group staffing

Precise rules have been established regarding the numbers of staff to which Political Groups are entitled.

Each Group receives a small basic allocation of posts irrespective of size, while the great majority of posts are then allocated roughly according to size. In detail, 15% of AD (political advisor/administrator) posts set aside for the political Group are distributed evenly to all political Groups (this currently amounts to 7 per Group). Additional AD posts are distributed to larger Groups on the following basis: 13 AD posts for Groups of 250 members and more, 10 AD posts for Groups of 200 members or more, 8 AD posts for Groups of 150 members or more, 5 AD posts for Groups of 100 members or more and 3 AD posts for Groups of 80 members or more. The remaining AD posts (actually the bulk, 226) are then distributed proportionately between all political Groups. Regarding AST (assistant) posts, these are in the first instance distributed on the basis of 1.4 AST posts per AD post, with any remaining AST posts distributed among political Groups in proportion to their size. Clearly, each nationality within the Group will want to have one or more members of staff from that country, so that the relevant political, cultural and linguistic skills and knowledge are represented on the Group staff. This calculation produces a quota of total staff for each Group that, in 2009, ranged from 46 (EFD) to 264 (EPP), with 19 posts allocated to non-aligned members. In total, the combined staffing of all Political Groups, plus non-aligned members, accounted for 862 posts out of an overall

European Parliament establishment plan of 6081 (i.e. some 14.0%). This compares to only 285 Group posts in 1982, and the rate of increase has been considerably greater than for Parliament's permanent staff.

The great majority of these are temporary, not permanent officials, and do not have the same job security enjoyed by permanent officials. They are recruited directly by the Groups, and do not have to pass the same open competitions which Parliament's permanent officials have been through. In practice, however, the majority of Group staff do enjoy *de facto* if not *de jure* job security, and relatively few of them are made redundant as a result of election defeats, political disappointments or Group reorganisations, a notable exception being the redundancies of virtually the entire staff of the EDA Group in 1999 when the bulk of its MEPs (French Gaullist) joined the EPP Group. Furthermore there are a number of permanent officials working within the Groups who have passed an open external competition. These may be Group officials who passed an exam but then remained with a Group, or they may be seconded officials at a later stage in their careers.

At one time, recruitment of staff within a Group was often based on political and personal contacts and patronage, but more objective methods are now the norm, at least in the large Groups, with both written and oral exams and language tests modelled on the open competitions of European institutions for civil servants – though, of course, candidates must normally also have a political affinity with the Group and political experience is taken into account.

Group staff have both general and sectoral responsibilities, examples of the former being administrative or press work, or responsibility for urgency debates in plenary. Some staff work directly to assist the Group leader, whereas others follow particular policy areas. The larger Groups are able to have up to three officials to follow a busy committee, whereas an official in a smaller Group may have to follow three committees at once. They must prepare the discussions within their Group meetings, and help their members to formulate a Group position before a committee meeting or a Parliament session. They prepare background information for the Group. They help to draw up whips both in committee and in plenary. They sometimes have to round up Group members to help in tight votes in their committee. They help maintain contacts with national parties, national governments where their party is in power, Commissioners of their own tendency and civil society organizations. They must take account of the various national, sectoral, or constituency considerations that are of importance to individual members.

Group staff sometimes move on to political careers. Among those who have become MEPs are Florus Wijsenbeek and Jessie Larive of the Liberals, Raymonde Dury, Carole Tongue, Javier Moreno and Richard Corbett of the Socialists, Caroline Jackson and Anne McIntosh of the Conservatives, Bruno Boissière, Alexander De Roo, Kathalijne Buitenweg and Monica Frassoni of the Greens, Gianfranco Dell'Alba (non-attached, formerly in the Green Group secretariat) and Hanne Dahl of IND-DEM. Others have gone on to national parliaments.

Structures of Groups

Each Political Group has its own internal structures, notably a Bureau composed of a chair, vice-chairs, treasurer and others. Bureaux vary considerably in size and responsibilities, and are obviously more important in the larger Groups where they play a role in preparing the political discussions and positions of the Group as a whole. They normally also take the decisions regarding the administration and management of the Group and its secretariat.

Group chairs provide political leadership for their Group. They speak on its behalf in major debates and to the outside. They represent the Group in their party, in Parliament's Conference of Presidents, and in negotiations with other Groups, notably in informal meetings of Group chairs in which many deals are struck.

Group chairs are elected by their Group and in most cases remain in office for some years. After the 2004 elections only the Socialists and the UEN chose a new chair. At the halfway point in the legislature in January 2007, with the exception of the new ITS Group, only the EPP-ED Group had to elect a new chair, as a result of Pöttering's election to the EP Presidency. After the 2009 elections, only the ALDE and GUE replaced their leaders (Greens and EFA replaced one and kept one of their co-leaders).

The longest-serving chair was Christian de la Malène of the RDE (Gaullist) Group who was chair from 1975 to 1994. The Greens, and occasionally other smaller Groups, have had two co-chairs.

Table 14: *Leaders of those Political Groups that have lasted more than two parliaments*

Date	No. of Years	Name	Country

1. Christian Democrats (EPP)

Date	No. of Years	Name	Country
1953-58	5	Emmanuel SASSEN	NL
1958-59	1	Pierre WIGNY	B
1959-66	7	Alain POHER	F
1966-70	4	Joseph ILLERHAUS	D
1970-75	5	Hans A. LÜCKER	D
1975-77	2	Alfred BERTRAND	B
1977-82	5	Egon KLEPSCH	D
1982-84	2	Paolo BARBI	I
1984–92	8	Egon KLEPSCH	D
1992–94	2	Leo TINDEMANS	B
1994–99	5	Wilfried MARTENS	B
1999–2007	7	Hans Gert PÖTTERING	D
2007-		Joseph DAUL	F

2. Socialists

Date	No. of Years	Name	Country
1953–56	3	Guy MOLLET	F

1956–58	2	Henri FAYAT	B
1958–59	1	Pierre O. LAPIE	F
1959–64	5	Willi BIRKELBACH	D
1964–67	3	Kate STRÖBEL	D
1967–74	7	Francis VALS	F
1974–75	1	Georges SPENALE	F
1975–79	4	Ludwig FELLERMAIER	D
1979–84	5	Ernest GLINNE	B
1984–89	5	Rudi ARNDT	D
1989–94	5	Jean-Pierre COT	F
1994–99	5	Pauline GREEN	UK
1999–2004	5	Enrique BARON	E
2004-		Martin SCHULZ	D

3. Liberals

1953–57	4	Yvon DELBOS	F
1957–69	12	Rene PLEVEN	F
1969–73	4	Cornelis BERKHOUWER	NL
1973–78	4	Jean DURIEUX	F
1978–79	1	Jean PINTAT	F
1979–84	5	Martin BANGEMANN	D
1984–89	5	Simone VEIL	F
1989–91	2	Valéry GISCARD D'ESTAING	F
1991–94	3	Yves GALLAND	F
1994–98	4	Gijs DE VRIES	NL
1998–2002	4	Pat COX	IRL
2002-2009	7	Graham WATSON	UK
2009-		Guy VERHOFSTADT	B

4. Greens

1989–90	2	Alexander LANGER &	D
		Maria SANTOS	P
1991–93	3	Adelaide AGLIETTA &	I
		Paul LANNOYE	B
1994–95	1	Alexander LANGER &	D
		Claudia ROTH	D
1995–96	1	Claudia ROTH	D
1997		Claudia ROTH &	D
		Magda AELVOET	B
1998		Magda AELVOET	B
1999–2002	3	Heidi HAUTALA &	FIN
		Paul LANNOYE	B
2002-09	7	Daniel COHN-BENDIT &	F/D
		Monica FRASSONI	
2009-		Daniel COHN-BENDIT &	F/D
		Rebecca HARMS	D

5. European Democratic Group
(Founded 1973, until 1979 called European Conservative Group)

1973–77	4	Sir Peter KIRK	UK

1977–78	1	Geoffrey RIPPON	UK
1979–82	3	Sir James SCOTT-HOPKINS	UK
1982–87	5	Sir Henry PLUMB	UK
1987–93	6	Sir Christopher PROUT	UK

(Absorbed into EPP Group in 1993)

6. Communist Group *(founded 1973)*

1973–79	6	Giorgio AMENDOLA	I
1979–84	5	Guido FANTI	I
1984-89	5	Giovanni CERVETTI	I

(Split in 1989 into two Groups, the United European Left, led by Luigi COLAJANNI (I) until absorbed into Socialist Group in 1994, and the Left Unity Group – see below)

7. European United Left / Nordic Green Left
(Founded in 1989 from split in the Communist Group. Called Left Unity Group 1989–94)

1989–91	2	Rene PIQUET	F
1991-92	1	Alexandros ALAVANOS	GR
1992-93	1	Rene PIQUET	F
1993-94	1	Joaquim MIRANDA	P
1994-99	5	Alonso PUERTA	E
1999-2009	10	Francis WURTZ	F
2009-		Lothar BISKY	D

8. "Gaullist" Group, *called*
Union for Europe Group (1995–1999)
Group of the European Democratic Alliance (1988–95)
Progressive Democrats (1973–1988)
European Democratic Union (1965-73)

1965	1	Jacques VENDROUX	F
1965-66	1	Andre BORD	F
1966-1967	1	Alain TERRENOIRE	F
1967-68	1	Jean DE LIPKOWSKI	F
1968-72	4	Raymond TRIBOULET	F
1973-75	2	Yvon BOURGES	F
1975-94	19	Christian DE LA MALENE	F
1994-99	5	Jean Claude PASTY	F

Majority joined EPP Group in 1999, minority joined UEN, which was then dissolved in 2009 (see below)

9. Union for a Europe of Nations *(called Europe of Nations Group 1994-99)*

1994-97	3	Sir James GOLDSMITH	F
1997-99	2	Jens-Peter BONDE	DK
1999-2004	5	Charles PASQUA	F
2004-2009	5	Brian CROWLEY & Cristina MUSCARDINI	IRL, I

10. Europe of Freedom and Democracy Group
(called Europe of Democracies and Diversities 1999-2004 and Independence and
Democracy Group 2004-9)

1999-2004	5	Jens-Peter BONDE & Hans BLOKLAND	DK, NL
2004-2008	4	Jens-Peter BONDE & Nigel FARAGE	DK, UK
2008	1	Kathy SINNOTT & Nigel FARAGE	IRL, UK
2008-2009	1	Hanne DAHL & Nigel FARAGE	DK, UK
2009-		NIGEL FARAGE & FRANCESCO SPERONI	UK, I

11. Far Right (called the European Right from 1984-1989 and Technical Group of
the European Right from 1989-1994 and Identity, Tradition and Sovereignty Group
in 2007)

| 1984-94 | 10 | Jean-Marie LE PEN | F |
| During 2007 | ½ | Bruno GOLLNISCH | F |

Working methods within the Groups

Groups generally convene during the "Group week" in Brussels (and occasionally other locations, normally at the invitation of one of the member parties of the Group). Meetings last two or three days, and are primarily
devoted to examining the next week's plenary agenda. They are also used
for discussion of the Group's own activities (campaigns, conferences, publications etc.), for development of Group positions on major political issues or
debates or broader political strategy, and for receiving visiting delegations
or leaders of national parties or other personalities (Commissioners, ministers or personalities from third countries). These meetings are both preceded
and followed by a variety of Group working parties of both a political and
technical nature, as well as meetings of national party delegations.

Groups also meet in Strasbourg during plenary week: before the beginning of the plenary on Monday, and also for up to two hours between 6.30
pm and 8.30 pm on Tuesday and Wednesday evenings. They occasionally
meet on Thursday mornings in the increasingly rare event of the plenary
only beginning at 10:00 am. Each Group has its own meeting room and its
own rules and practices concerning the confidentiality of its meetings.

The Groups do not normally meet during the committee weeks, except
when there is a Brussels plenary sitting the same week, but the Group members within a committee (especially from the two largest Groups, the
Socialists and the EPP) get together before the start of the committee meeting to discuss the positions that they will adopt. These meetings are generally led by the Group's co-ordinator on the committee, who is elected by the
Group's members on the committee. Groups also appoint a shadow rapporteur where another Group has the rapporteurship.

The Group's coordinators are the Group's leader in each committee, act as
spokesperson in the subject area concerned and play a key role in formulat-
ing Group policy. Their role is further described in Chapter 7. The current
Group coordinators are set out below.

Table 15: *Group Coordinators (spokespersons)*

Committee	EPP	S&D	ALDE	Greens	ECR	GUE/NGL	EFD
Foreign Affairs	Salafranca/ Brok	Vigenin	Neyts	Lunacek& Brantner	Tannock	Meyer	Belder
Constitutional Affairs	Mendez de Vigo	Guerrero	Duff	Hafner	Fox	Sondergaard	Messerschmidt
Agriculture	Dess	Capoulas Santos	Lyon/ Reimers	Hausling	Nicholson	Rubiks	Fontana
Budgets	Garriga Polledo/ Surjan	Farm	Jensen	Trupel	Bokros	Portas	Andreasen
Budgetary Control	Grassle	Geier	Chatzimarkis	Staes	Czarnecki	Sondergaard	Andreasen
Culture& Education	Scurria	Honeyball	Takkula	Benarab-Attou	McClarkin	Vergiat	Soini
Development	Mitchell& Kaczmarek	Berman	Goerens	Greze	Deva	Zimmer	Speroni
Economic &Monetary	Gauzes	Bullman	Goulard/ Schmidt	Giegold	Swinburne	Klute	Bloom
Employment	Csaba	Cercas	Harkin/ Bennahmias	Lambert	Cabrnoch	Zimmer	Bizzotto
Environment	Liese/ Seeber	McAvan	Davies	Hassi	Ouzky	Liotard	Rossi
Internal Market	Schwab	Gebhardt	Busoi	Ruhle	Bielan	Trianta-phyllides	Salvini
International Trade	Caspary	Arif	Kazak	Jadot	Sturdy	Scholz	Dartmouth
Industry	Castillo-Vera	Riera Madurell	Ek	Turmes	Chichester	Matias	Tzavela
Legal	Zwiefka	Rapkay	Wallis	Lichtenberger	Hannan	Mastalka	Speroni
Civil Liberties	Busuttil	Moraes	Hennis-Plasschaert	Romeva i Rueda	Kirkhope	Tavares	Batten
Fisheries	Antinori	Rodust	Gallagher	Lovin	Grobarczyk	Ferreira	Farage
Petitions	Gruny	Bostinari	Valean	Auken	Helmer	De Brun	Salavrakos
Regional	van Nistelrooi	Krehl	Manescu	Schroedter	Vlasak	Hoarau	Bufton
Transport	Grosch	El Khadraoui	Stercks/ Meissner	Cramer/ Lichtenberger	Zile	Kohlicek	Imbrasas
Women	Bauer	Thomsen	Parvanova	Cornelissen	Vannakou-dakis	Figueiredo	Bloom
Human Rights SC	Tokes/ Vaidere	Howitt	Donskis	Lochbihler	Tannock	Meyer	-
Security/ Defence SC	Gahler	Gualltieri	van Baalen	Butikofer	Van Orden	Losing	Campbell-Bannerman

Own activities of the Groups

Apart from work directly related to Parliament, Groups have developed their own political activities. They form an important channel of communication between corresponding parties in different countries and also between the European Union and national politics. In this, they complement

Parliament's role as a forum and channel of communication described in Chapter 16.

Groups receive a constant stream of visitors from national parties, including ministers and front-bench spokesmen in national parliaments. They also send delegations to national parties, and Group chairs or vice-chairs often address the congress or conference of national parties in the Group. Groups also publish brochures, studies and newsletters aimed in part at national parties. Groups organise seminars and conferences with national parties on European themes.

A particular effort may be made by a Group on behalf of one of its national parties when that Member State holds the Presidency of the Council, especially when that party is in government. Some Groups organise special meetings and briefings for the ministers or shadow ministers concerned and these can provide ministers with a valuable alternative source of information to national civil servants. As such, they are of particular assistance to parties in the smaller Member States.

The Socialists, Christian Democrats and Liberals organise "summits" of their Group chair, national party leaders, prime ministers of the countries where they are in government and Commission members, prior to meetings of the European Council. This is done through their party federations (see page 124).

National party delegations

Group members of the same nationality (normally from one political party) form national delegations that serve as an important link to national parties. Most national delegations within the large Groups meet once during "Group week" and again during plenaries. They will sometimes take a collective decision and try to act as a bloc in Group discussions. On important issues, Groups will try to negotiate compromises among their national delegations before taking a decision. When Groups fail to vote cohesively, it is usually because one or more national delegations have decided to opt out of a Group position. Posts within the Group structures (Bureau of Group and Group nominations for posts in Parliament) are often shared among the delegations within a Group using the same proportional method (d'Hondt) as for posts among Groups in Parliament, albeit with greater flexibility.

Most national delegations, especially those from large parties, have their own officers (chair, treasurer, etc.) and their own staff, partly financed from Group funds, some of whom can be employed in the national capitals (e.g. press officers, liaison officers with national parties). These staff are relatively few in number (even major parties from large Member States will have less than half a dozen). It is also through national delegations that the bulk of the "information money" is spent.

In the Socialist Group, for instance, some €7.5m is allocated to the national delegations (19 per cent of which is shared equally and 81 per cent in proportion to the number of MEPs). Delegations do not have absolute discretion on how they use money for information purposes: there are strict Parliament rules preventing the responsibility being delegated any further (e.g. to national parties) and all sums must be spent according to Socialist Group priorities and relate to the activities of the Group and its members.

Any printed matter must specify that it is on behalf of the Group and any reference to a national party or an individual member must not be larger in size than the reference to the Group. Accounts are subject to inspection by the Court of Auditors.

Delegations are normally represented within the structures of their national parties (e.g. national executive committees, back-bench committees in the national parliamentary Groups etc.) where they will be involved notably, but not exclusively, in discussions with a European dimension (often alerting them to that dimension). Some national party leaders have sat in the European Parliament instead of in the national parliament, e.g. Gérard Deprez, leader of the PSC (Walloon Christian Democrats), Karel van Miert, SP (Flemish Socialist), Caroline Lucas (UK Greens), Nigel Farage (UKIP) or in both parliaments (many Italian, French, Belgian and Northern Irish party leaders). In other cases, the European parliamentary leader will be in close contact with the national leader and meet regularly. In the UK, for instance, Conservative, Labour and Liberal MEPs attend their party conferences as of right. Labour MEPs have the same rights as Westminster MPs in the electoral college for electing the Labour Party leader (Conservative MEPs have only a consultative vote in their leadership elections). Labour gives a place to the EPLP leader on the Labour National Executive Committee (since 2010 with the right to attend shadow cabinet) and six places on the National Policy Forum. In 1997, the new Labour Government set up a system of "link members" so that each government department's ministerial team involves an MEP from the appropriate parliamentary committee, ensuring close cooperation at an early stage on policy formulation. A similar system has been established by the coalition government.

Naturally, frequent contacts are not a guarantee of identity of views. MEPs and MPs will inevitably have different perspectives and, on occasion, will accuse each other of, respectively, "having gone native" or being "parochial". However, this does not detract from the utility of such contacts: on the contrary, it makes them more useful for both sides. Leadership of a national delegation is usually occupied for several years by the same person. As regards the UK, the leaders of the two main parties in the European Parliament are shown in Table 16. The high turnover of Labour leaders in the 1984-89 Parliament and of Conservative leaders since 2001 is in part a reflection of hotly contested elections at a time when pro- and anti-europeans were evenly divided. Pauline Green's tenure from 1993-94 was brief because she became leader of the whole Socialist Group after the 1994 elections.

Table 16: *Leaders of the UK Conservative and Labour MEPs*

Conservatives	*Labour*
Sir Peter Kirk (1973-77)	
Geoffrey Rippon (1977-79)	Sir Michael Stewart (1975-76))
Sir James Scott-Hopkins (1979-81)	John Prescott (1976-79)
Sir Henry (later Lord) Plumb (1982-86)	Barbara Castle (1979-85)

Conservatives	*Labour*
Sir Christopher Prout (1986-94)	Alf Lomas (1985-87)
Lord Plumb (1994-95)	David Martin (1987-88)
Tom Spencer (1995-98)	Barry Seal (1988-89)
Edward McMillan Scott (1998-2001)	Glyn Ford (1989-93)
Jonathon Evans (2001-04)	Pauline Green (1993-94)
Timothy Kirkhope (2004-07)	Wayne David (1994-98)
Giles Chichester (2007-08)	Alan Donnelly (1998-99)
Philip Bushill-Matthews (2008)	Simon Murphy(1999-2002)
Timothy Kirkhope (2008-2010)	Gary Titley (2002-2009)
Martin Callanan (2010)-	Glenis Willmott (2009-)

The Liberal Democrat MEPs, first elected in 1994, had Graham Watson as their leader until he was elected President of the whole ELDR (now ALDE) Group in 2002, since when leadership of the delegation has been held successively by Diana Wallis (2002-04), Chris Davies (2004-06), Diana Wallis again (2006-07), Andrew Duff (2007-09) and now Fiona Hall (2009-).

Group discipline & whipping

Groups issue voting instructions to their members, both in terms of how to vote on each amendment and text as well as indicating which votes are important (where a number of Groups have taken up the British tradition of issuing one-, two- or three-line whips). Most members follow their Group's voting recommendation most of the time. As the Group's position is defined not by instructions from above but by a process of discussion and negotiation within the Group involving the Group's coordinator in the relevant committee, the leadership, and often the leaders of component national party delegations, it is usually acceptable to most members.

Group "whipping" systems are, however, less strict than in most national parliaments, for a number of reasons. First, there is no government emerging from the Parliament demanding systematic support from its majority. Second, the diversity of regional, national party and sectoral interests within a Group make it difficult to agree on a common Group line on some issues. Most Groups accept that, in practice, individual members or whole national party components can occasionally opt out of the Group whip on particular votes and either abstain or not take part in the vote, or even vote the other way. Third, Groups have fewer effective sanctions against dissident members than are usually available in national parliaments. They can give a member a less favourable committee or delegation allocation, but only at the next 2 ½ year allocation. They can deny new rapporteurships, but not withdraw existing ones. They can decline to offer speaking time in plenary for debates, but not for points of order, question time or explanations of votes. The ultimate sanction of not re-nominating a member for election is a prerogative of the national or local party, not the Group.

It is indeed the national party delegation that is in a stronger position to "discipline" individual members, even on matters such as committee allocations when the Group will usually base its nominations on proposals from its national delegations. A national delegation is likely to be able to ask its national party to discipline a member (e.g. to suspend him/her from membership), and in cases of differing views between a national party delegation and the rest of its Group, it is the national party pressure that is usually stronger on a member in those (relatively few) cases where it is crucial. In practice, however, even this discipline is less than in most national parliaments and it is only members who persistently vote against the party line on important issues who are likely to find themselves in trouble.

Despite the above, Group cohesion is strong in most Groups and has got stronger over time, as illustrated by the following table, drawn on calculations and research by Votewatch.eu, examining every single roll call vote in the 2004-09 Parliament and the first year of the 2009-14 Parliament. The four Groups sometimes characterised as mainstream all have over 90 percent cohesion, while those on the relative extremes have less cohesion, especially the EFD.

Table 17: *Voting Cohesion of Political Groups*

(Scale: 0 = split down middle every vote, 100 = all members vote same way in every vote)

	EPP	PES/S&D	ALDE	Green/EFA	GUE	UEN	CER	ID/EFD
2004-09	88	91	89	91	85	76		47
2009-10	93	93	91	96	84		86	47

Most members realise that their main policy and political objectives are more likely to be obtained by coordinated action with those who are close to them politically and with whom they have developed an effective structure. Group whips also sometimes entrench unity in that individual members do not have the time or experience to take their own position on every amendment on every issue and usually follow the Group line on the voting list prepared by the Group coordinator, or his/her upturned or downturned thumb. Thus, most Groups can count on well over 80 per cent of their members supporting the Group line in most votes, and this in turn means that it is the positions taken by Groups that are usually decisive in determining Parliament's position.

Power balances and relationships between the Groups

After each European election much of the attention has focused on whether Parliament has had a left-of-centre or right-of-centre majority. This is, of course, of great significance, but it is not the whole story. There are a number of reasons for this, relating both to diversity and to the search for unity.There is no parliamentary divide between government and opposition, so alliances vary from issue to issue. Some 170 national political parties are represented in the 7 Political Groups and among the non-attached members, so Groups are not always cohesive. With a huge range of different national, regional and sectoral interests, voting patterns are sometimes more related to these factors than to ideological divisions. (Coalitions, for example, of those representing agricultural areas, are often forged across

Group boundaries.) The division between federalists and Eurosceptics sometimes appears within Groups, and is at times more striking than party differences. At the same time, in a Union of diverse Member States, it is common to seek widespread agreement rather than force things through by a narrow majority. Many members come, anyway, from countries with more of a consensual political tradition than, say, the UK or France and certain political situations also reinforce the search for consensus, such as the need for a common front to defend Parliament's institutional prerogatives, or the need for an absolute majority in certain votes in the legislative and budgetary procedures (see Chapters 12 and 13). Much of the EP's work is highly technical, often making left-right arguments less relevant. The "rapporteur" system that lies at the heart of the Parliament's work is oriented towards finding a consensus.

All the above factors lessen the coherence of the Groups and blur left-right divisions, but research on Group voting patterns (such as that carried out by Simon Hix of the LSE, Tapio Raunio of Tampere, Amie Kreppel of the University of Florida or by Votewatch.eu) indicates that the most common political divisions in the Parliament are nonetheless on traditional left-right lines, and that each Group's votes most frequently coincide with those of the Groups next to them on the left-right spectrum. The EP is, in that sense, a "normal" parliament where political views are confronted.

A crucial factor is the nature of the balance of power within the Parliament. Currently, the EPP Group is easily the largest, but is still over 100 members short of an overall majority. Even the combined forces of the EPP and ALDE are still short of such a majority. A right-of-centre majority, therefore, can only be constructed if there is great voting cohesion within these two Groups, and if allies are found within the two right wing Groups (ECR and EFD), which are generally Eurosceptic, and also contain some very right-wing parties. This is thus not an easy option. The converse was true before the 1999 elections when the Socialist Group was the largest, but could only attempt a purely left majority if it could rely on solid undivided support from the Greens, Communists, former Communists and regionalists. A purely left-of-centre majority is now even more difficult to construct, with the S&D, Green and GUE-NGL Groups being far short of a majority, and not even being sure to reach it if they join forces with ALDE.

The sort of majorities required to amend Council's position under certain legislative and budgetary procedures are therefore difficult to achieve on a narrow left or right basis. To do so, usually the Socialists and the EPP must negotiate compromises with each other. They are the only two Groups that alone can combine to obtain an overall majority and have been since before direct elections. Their combined forces have always represented over 54% of the members of the Parliament, reaching a peak of 69.5% in 1993 (currently 61%) and any deal struck between them is likely to achieve the necessary majority, unlike fragile left or right coalitions. The relationship between the Socialists and the EPP is therefore of central importance. Representatives of the two Groups meet with each other to strike deals over political or patronage issues without smaller Groups to left or right always being consulted. These latter may then be forced to conform on a take-it or leave-it basis.

Certain general rules of operation can be observed. When consensus or special majorities are not of prime importance, the Socialist Group turns initially to the left and the EPP to the right in terms of deal-making . This often leaves ALDE in the pivotal position, and often means that there is a centre-left major-ity on civil liberties issues and the environment, and a centre-right majority on economic issues. However, in the more usual cases when consensus is impor-tant or when special majorities are required, the Socialists and the EPP try to find compromises, often bringing the Liberals and others on board too.

This gives an interesting result in terms of how often each Group is on the "winning" side in votes, as illustrated in Table 18, also drawn on calcula-tions and research by Votewatch.eu, examining every single roll call vote in the 2004-09 Parliament and the first year of the 2009-14 Parliament. The fig-ures should, however, be handled with care: voting for the final outcome of a compromise is not necessarily a measure of the degree of influence in shaping that compromise.

Table 18: *How often each Group is in the majority on a recorded vote*

	EPP	PES/S&D	ALDE	Green/EFA	GUE	UEN	CER	ID/EFD
2004-09	86	81	86	60	52	75		46
2009-10	85	84	89	64	51		62	49

The mechanics of inter-group negotiations on plenary resolutions are described in the section "Building majorities: bargaining among Groups" in Chapter 9.

European party federations

Besides the Political Groups in the Parliament, the main political families have set up structures outside Parliament bringing together the national parties belonging to them. Three were established before the first direct elec-tions and gradually developed a significant infrastructure:

–   The Party of European Socialists (PES – until 1992 the Confede-ration of Socialist Parties of the European Community). This brings together the parties affiliated to the Socialist International.
–   The European People's Party (EPP). This brings together the Christian Democrats and other centre-right or conservative par-ties
–   The European Liberal, Democratic and Reformist Party (ELDR), bringing together a variety of liberal and allied parties

Between 1979 and 2004, two more emerged, namely the European Federation of Green Parties (which subsequently became the European Green Party) and the Democratic Party of the Peoples of Europe–European Free Alliance (DPPE-EFA), which brought together regionalist and nation-alist parties such as the Scottish National Party, the Flemish Volksunie, Basque, Corsican, Sardinian, Catalan and Welsh nationalists), and whose name was later shortened to the European Free Alliance.

The development of the party federations has been gradual and is still rather limited, but through regular working parties they are adopting common policies in a growing number of areas. They organise regular congresses composed of delegates from their member parties and involving, where appropriate, their Group in the European Parliament. They adopt policy, such as common manifestos for European elections. Their decision-taking tends in practice to be by consensus among the member parties, which means that the content of their policies tends to the lowest common denominator and is, therefore, often less precise than the policies of their corresponding Group in the European Parliament, which can adopt policy by a majority vote. However, the pressure to reach consensus, particularly before elections, is considerable and the effort of convergence does have an impact on the positions of individual parties. The main parties have become more cohesive over the years, in particular the Socialists who, in the 1970s and early 1980s, often had great difficulties in reaching any consensus at all. Most now allow majority voting in their constitutions, though this is not frequently used.

The holding of a "summit" of heads of state and government, party leaders, the chair of the Political Group in the European Parliament and Commissioners belonging to their political family is perhaps one of the most significant activities of the PES, the EPP and more recently the ELDR. Most such summits are arranged as pre-meetings for European Council meetings. These can be significant, as in October 1990 when the EPP leaders agreed to press the case for a strict timetable for monetary union at the subsequent European Council in Rome. This was the so-called "ambush" of Margaret Thatcher, who was left isolated at the summit with all the other Member States agreeing on a timetable for EMU. Increasingly, the PES and the EPP organise meetings of their ministers prior to ordinary Council meetings as well, in which the corresponding Group coordinator and Commissioner will also participate. This can be an important opportunity for each of those Groups to influence "its" ministers in the Council.

The groupings do occasionally collaborate, and there have been summits of the Presidents of the PES, EPP and ELDR. It was as a result of a joint initiative of the three that the Treaty of Maastricht introduced a new article recognising the importance of European political parties. A further initiative resulted in the Treaty of Nice providing for the adoption of a European Party Statute to give such parties legal personality, provide for their transparency and openness of their accounts and give them access to funding. Attempts to agree such a statute ahead of ratification of the Nice Treaty, which would have required unanimity, were abandoned in 2001 when the Austrian government, which included Haider's FPO, insisted on very lax conditions for creating a party (only two Member States and few auditing requirements). However, following the entry into force of the Nice Treaty, providing for co-decision between Parliament and Council, with the latter acting by qualified majority, efforts resumed and Parliament and Council agreed in 2003 on a regulation on "political parties at European level", which became operational in July 2004, and which has subsequently been further amended. Political parties are now explicitly recognized in Article 10-4 of the Treaty on European Union which states that: "Political parties at European level contribute to forming European political awareness and to expressing the will of citizens of the Union".

The Regulation on political parties lays down that, to achieve recognition and hence EU funding, a European party must be represented in at least one quarter of Member States, in the European Parliament or in the national parliaments or regional assemblies; alternatively, it must have received in at least one quarter of the Member States, at least three per cent of the votes cast at the most recent European elections. A European party also must respect the principles of the EU, i.e. liberty, democracy, respect for human rights and fundamental freedoms, and the rule of law (but does not have to support the EU itself). A European party must publish its accounts and have them audited by an external auditor (as well as being subject to checks by the EU Court of Auditors). It must publish the names of any donors contributing more than €500, and not accept donations of more than €12,000 from any single donor, nor accept anonymous donations. Of the sums made available for funding European political parties, 15% is distributed in equal shares among the parties, while the rest is distributed in proportion to the number of members elected to the European Parliament. To receive such financing, a European-level political party must file an application with the European Parliament each year. Any money thus received may only be used to cover expenditure directly linked to the objectives set out in its political programme and may not be used for the direct or indirect funding of national political parties.

One reason for providing European-level parties with specific and transparent funding was that they previously relied heavily on the secretarial and logistic support of their corresponding Group in the European Parliament. This had been criticised by the Court of Auditors as lacking transparency. Under the new system, they now all have secretariats located outside of Parliament's premises and employ their own staff.

A further feature of the new system, following revision of the EU Regulation in 2008, is that permitting the creation and financing of European political foundations linked to European political parties, and which are meant to back up the work of that party. They have to meet certain criteria to be eligible for European Parliament grants, such as having legal personality separate from that of the European political party to which they are affiliated, and observing certain principles of respect for democracy, human rights and fundamental freedoms. If they meet these criteria, they then receive annual operating grants of up to 85% of the expenditure of a foundation for such items as conferences, publications, research studies, advertisements or administrative, personnel and travel costs. That part of the expenditure not covered by the Parliament grant has to be covered by other sources of finance, such as membership fees or donations. Grants made to foundations cannot be used for such purposes as campaign costs, or direct or indirect funding of national candidates, parties or foundations, nor to pay off debts or debt service charges.

Following the adoption of the statute, thirteen parties have applied for registration under the new system. Five of these were the parties that had already existed before the new statute, and that were outlined above. The others were new parties. More were created following the adoption of a system for financing such parties in 2004. Three such parties were set up in 2004, the Party of the European Left (which includes a number of the parties in the GUE-NGL Group, see above), the European Democratic Party (which includes several of the non ELDR parties in the ALDE Group, see above) and the Alliance for Europe of the Nations (based on the parties within the former UEN Group and now defunct after the ending of the UEN Group in

2009). Two separate Eurosceptic European political parties were set up in 2006, the still existing EU Democrats and the now defunct Alliance of Independent Democrats in Europe (largely based on the former ID Group). The latter party would have been partially subsumed in the proposed Libertas Party of Declan Ganley, which was briefly recognized in 2009, but then suspended following controversy over its composition. Finally two other European parties were recognized in 2010, the Alliance of European Conservatives and Reformists (based on the parties in the new ECR Group- see above) and the European Christian Political Movement, which has a number of members in national parliaments, but only one in the European Parliament, Peter Van Dalen from the Dutch Christen Unie, who sits in the ECR Group.

The maximum sums made available for 2010 for the European political parties listed below (the final grant may remain the same, or be adjusted downwards) were just under €5 million for the European People's Party (EPP), €3.4 million for the Party of European Socialists (PES), €1.5 million for the European Liberal Democrat and Reform Party (ELDR), €1.05 million for the European Green Party, €1 million for the Alliance of European Conservatives and Reformists, €700,000 for the Party of the European Left, €500,000 for the European Democratic Party, €340,000 for the European Free Alliance (EFA) and around €210,000 for each of the EU Democrats and the European Christian Political Movement.

All of the above, apart from the European Christian Democratic Political Movement, have established separate political foundations which are now the recipients of grants from the European Parliament. The maximum grants awarded in 2010 (again subject to possible subsequent downward adjustment) were €3.3 million to the Centre for European Studies (EPP), €2.15 million for the Foundation for European Progressive Studies (PES), €820,000 for the European Liberal Forum (ELDR), €680,000 for the Green European Institute (European Green Party), €660,000 for New Direction- Foundation for European Reform (Alliance of European Conservatives and Reformists), €475,000 for Transform Europe (Party of the European Left), €340,000 for the Institute of European Democrats (European Democratic Party), €210,000 for the Centre Maurits Coppieters (EFA) and €150,000 for the Foundation for EU Democracy (EU Democrats)

The currently recognized parties have the following office-holders, and number of MEPs:

Table 19: *European Political Parties*

European People's Party (EPP)

President	Wilfried Martens (Belgium)
Secretary-General	Antonio Lopez Isturiz (Spain)
Foundation	Centre for European Studies (CES)
Number of MEPs in the Party:	*261 from full EPP Member Parties (with 2 others from observer parties)*

Party of European Socialists (PES)

President   Poul Nyrup Rasmussen (Denmark)
Secretary-General   Philip Cordery (France)
Foundation   Foundation for European Progressive Studies (FEPS)
Number of MEPs in the Party: 162

The European Liberal Democratic and Reformist Party (ELDR)

President   Annemie Neyts Uyttebroeck (Belgium)
Secretary-General   Federica Sabbati (Italy)
Foundation   European Liberal Forum (ELF)
Number of MEPs in the Party: 73

European Green Party (EFGP)

Spokespersons   Monica Frassoni (Italy) & Philippe Lamberts (Belgium)
Secretary-General   Jacqueline Cremers (Netherlands)
Foundation   Green European Institute
Number of MEPs in the Party: 44

Alliance of European Conservatives and Reformists

President   Jan Zahradil MEP (Czech Republic)
Secretary-General   Dan Hannan MEP (UK)
Foundation   New Direction-Foundation for European Reform
Number of MEPs in the Party :   44

Party of the European Left

President   Pierre Laurent (France)
Foundation   Transform Europe
Number of MEPs in the party :   *22 (16 from full member parties and 6 from observer parties)*

European Democratic Party

Co-Presidents   Francois Bayrou (France) & Francesco Rutelli (Italy)
Honorary President   Romano Prodi
Co-Secretaries-General   Marielle de Sarnez and Josep Broz
Foundation   Institute of European Democrats (IED)
Number of MEPs in the party :   10

European Free Alliance (EFA)

President   Eric Defoort (Flanders)
Secretary-General   Marta Rovira (Catalonia)
Foundation   Centre Maurits Coppieters
Number of MEPs in the party :   9

EU Democrats

President   Soren Wibe
Foundation   Foundation for EU Democracy
Number of MEPs in the party :   0

European Christian Political Movement (ECPM)

President   Peeter Vosu (Estonia)
Secretary-General   Guido van Beusekom (Netherlands)
Number of MEPs in the party :   1

6.　Leadership structures

At the beginning of, and halfway through, each term of office (i.e. every two-and-a-half years) the Parliament elects its formal office holders: the President, 14 Vice-Presidents and five Quaestors (temporarily increased to six between 2007 and 2009). At the same time, some Political Groups take the opportunity to renew their leaderships which, although elected from within their Groups and not by the Parliament as a whole, play a key role in Parliament's leadership structures. Committee chairs and Vice-chairs are also up for re-election.

The two main decision-making bodies within the Parliament (other than the full plenary) are the Conference of Presidents (consisting of the President and the Political Group chairs) and the Bureau (consisting of the President and the 14 Vice-Presidents). In addition, the Quaestors play an important role in managing a number of issues directly concerning members' interests.

The present chapter looks first at the role of the President, Vice-Presidents and Quaestors, and how they are elected. It then examines the different responsibilities of the Conference of Presidents, the Bureau and the Quaestors, their working methods, and the relationships between them. Finally, it provides some brief background on the Conference of Committee Chairs and the Conference of Delegation Chairs.

The President

There have been 27 different Presidents of the Parliament since the establishment of the Common Assembly in 1952. As Table 20 below indicates, they have come from eight countries and four Political Groups, most regularly the Socialists and Christian Democrats.

The President's formal duties, under Rule 20 of the Rules of Procedure, are: "to direct all the activities of Parliament and its bodies"; "to open, suspend and close Parliament's sittings,... to ensure observance of (the) Rules, maintain order, call upon speakers, close debates, put matters to the vote and announce the results of votes, and to refer to committees any communications that concern them" as well as to represent the Parliament "in international relations, on ceremonial occasions and in administrative, legal and financial matters".

These tasks involve the President in an enormous variety of activities inside and outside the Parliament, some of which can be delegated. In practice, for example, the President does not chair all sittings. He or she chairs the opening sitting of each part-session, formal sittings (when visiting heads of state or political leaders address the Parliament) and important debates or votes. For the remainder of the Parliament's business, the Vice-Presidents are invited to chair. Similarly, the President can invite a Vice-President to represent the institution abroad but all Presidents have a punishing schedule of visits to countries inside and outside the Union, combining a protocol side (audience with the head of state, participation in ceremonies) and a functional side (meetings with the head of government, foreign minister, trade minister etc.) as well as an opportunity to make the European Parliament better known to a wider public through the media.

At the same time, the President's role is wider than Rule 20 suggests. He or she signs into law the Union budget and co-signs with the President-in-Office of Council all legislation adopted under the ordinary legislative procedure (codecision). The President chairs the Conference of Presidents and Bureau meetings, unless there are exceptional circumstances, and has a casting vote in the Bureau. He or she enjoys the right to chair the Parliament's delegations in conciliation meetings with the Council, though this task has normally been delegated to one of the Vice-Presidents responsible for conciliation. In addition, the Lisbon Treaty gives him the task of convening the Conciliation Committee now provided for in the budgetary procedure and of leading the Parliament delegation to that committee.

Table 20: *Presidents of the Parliament*

Date	*Name*	*Political Group & Nationality*
1952–54	Paul-Henri Spaak	Socialist/B
1954–	Alcide De Gasperi	Christian Democrat/I
1954–56	Giuseppe Pella	Christian Democrat/I
1956–58	Hans Furler	Christian Democrat/D
1958–60	Robert Schuman	Christian Democrat/F
1960–62	Hans Furler	Christian Democrat/D
1962–64	Gaetano Martino	Liberal/I
1964–65	Jean Duvieusart	Christian Democrat/B
1965–66	Victor Leemans	Christian Democrat/B
1966–69	Alain Poher	Christian Democrat/F
1969–71	Mario Scelba	Christian Democrat/I
1971–73	Walter Behrendt	Socialist/D
1973–75	Cornelis Berkhouwer	Liberal/NL
1977–79	Georges Spenale	Socialist/F
1977–79	Emilio Colombo	Christian Democrat/I
1979–82	Simone Veil	Liberal/F
1982–84	Pieter Dankert	Socialist/NL
1984–87	Pierre Pflimlin	Christian Democrat/F
1987–89	Lord Plumb	Conservative/UK
1989–92	Enrique Barón	Socialist/E
1992–94	Egon Klepsch	Christian Democrat/D
1994–97	Klaus Hänsch	Socialist/D
1997–99	José Maria Gil-Robles	Christian Democrat/E
1999–02	Nicole Fontaine	Christian Democrat/F
2002–04	Pat Cox	Liberal/IRL
2004–07	Josep Borrell	Socialist/E

Date	Name	Political Group & Nationality
2007-09	Hans-Gert Pöttering	Christian Democrat/D
2009–	Jerzy Buzek	Christian Democrat/PL
N.B.	1952–58	Common Assembly of the ECSC (nominated)
	1958–79	European Assembly/Parliament (nominated)
	1979–	European Parliament (elected)

Furthermore, the President has acquired the right, since the late 1980s and the Presidency of Lord Plumb, to attend and address the opening of all European Council meetings. In addition, working with Parliament's Secretary-General, the President has an important internal role within the Parliament, in overseeing its day-to-day running and administrative structures.

The President (like members of the Commission) is assisted by a personal private office (known by the French term "cabinet"), with a head and deputy head, and around fifteen other administrators, covering a number of nationalities and languages and carrying out a variety of specific functions, such as relations with the press and the preparation of speeches. These cabinet members are drawn from the Political Group staff, from Parliament's own civil service or from outside, such as the Commission or a national civil service: most cabinets contain a mix of all three. For the head of office, many Presidents have felt most at home with someone from their own political background and/or nationality and most have preferred someone with a longer experience of Parliament's working methods and traditions, individuals most easily found from within Parliament's own staff. Of the heads of the private offices of the last nine Presidents, six had long experience inside the Parliament secretariat and/or had worked as a secretary-general of a Political Group, while three came from outside, one from the Commission and the other two from the diplomatic service of the President's own country.

The way in which each President approaches their job varies. Some adopt a direct style of leadership, others a more consensual one. Presidents also differ in the emphasis they put on the various functions and duties mentioned above. Some have attached a particular importance to their external functions, such as relationships with other Union institutions or their activities in the international sphere; others have taken a greater interest in Parliament's internal administration; and others again have devoted more energy to improving the image of the institution in the media.

The Vice-Presidents

Parliament has 14 Vice-Presidents, whose main formal role is three-fold: to preside over the plenary sessions when the President is not in the chair, to replace the President in representing the Parliament externally and to take part in the work of the Bureau.

Although the Vice-Presidents enjoy an order of precedence, determined by the number of votes they receive at their election, this numerical ranking is of limited significance. The importance of their role is more likely to depend on other factors, such as whether they are members of a large Political Group, or whether they are particularly representative of their own nationality (they may be, for example, the only MEP of a particularly nationality in Parliament's leadership structure). But above all, a Vice-President with a strong personality and determination can become very influential in shaping the wide range of decisions taken by the Bureau.

There is some specialisation among the Vice-Presidents, with each entrusted with general or specific tasks as indicated in Table 21, sometimes shared, and sometimes with other institutions, such as membership of the interinstitutional working party on information policy. Others may have special aptitudes that are put to use. Certain Vice-Presidents, for example, have been known for their particularly speedy handling of votes in plenary.

Table 21: *The Vice-Presidents: 2009-2012 term of office and their responsibilities within the Bureau (in order of precedence)*

Giovanni PITTELLA	*Socialists and Democrats/I*	Conciliations (in cooperation with Ms Kratsa-Tsagaropoulou and Mr Vidal-Quadras) Budget (primary responsibility, in cooperation with Mr Vidal-Quadras) Buildings (in cooperation with Mr Vidal-Quadras) Euro-Mediterranean Parliamentary Assembly (EMPA) (in cooperation with Ms Kratsa-Tsagaropoulou and Ms Angelilli) Latin America (in cooperation with Mr Martínez Martínez) Statutes of Members and Assistants and the Voluntary Pension Fund (with Mr Wieland, Ms Roth-Behrendt & Mr Vidal Quadras)
Rodi KRATSA-TSAGAROPOULOU	*EPP/EL*	Conciliations (in cooperation with Mr Pittella and Mr Vidal-Quadras) Information Policy, Press and Citizens Relations (Primary responsibility and in cooperation with Mr Lambrinidis) Chair, Working Party on Information & Communication Policy Chair, Interinstitutional Working Group on Communication EMPA (in cooperation with Mr Pittella and Ms Angelilli) Network of Mediterranean Universities
Stavros LAMBRINIDIS	*Socialists and Democrats/EL*	Euro-Atlantic Relations and the UN (except UNESCO) Multilateral Bodies (Non-Security) European Political Parties EP Information Offices Chair, Working Party External Relations Member, Interinstitutional Working Group on Communication
Miguel Angel MARTINEZ	*Socialists and Democrats/E*	Multilingualism Candidate countries and Enlargement (together with Mr Tökés) National Parliaments/COSAC (in cooperation with Mr McMillan-Scott and Ms Koch-Mehrin) Chair, Contact Group for the House of European History

		Latin America (in cooperation with Mr Pittella) ACP countries (in cooperation with Mr Roucek and Mr Wieland)
Alejo VIDAL-QUADRAS	*EPP/E*	Conciliations (in cooperation with Mr Pittella and Ms Kratsa-Tsagaropoulou) Buildings (primary responsibility, in cooperation with Mr Pittella) Budget (in cooperation with Mr Pittella) Chair Working Party on Buildings, Transport and Green Parliament Member, Interinstitutional Working Group on Communication Statutes of Members and Assistants and the Voluntary Pension Fund (with Mr Pittella, Mr Wieland and Ms Roth-Behrendt)
Dagmar ROTH-BEHRENDT	*Socialists and Democrats/D*	Personnel and the Medical Service (in cooperation with Ms Angelilli) Implementation of Parliamentary Reform Chair, Temporary Evaluation Group on Members' and Assistants' Statutes and the Voluntary Pension Fund (with Mr Pittella, Mr Vidal-Quadras and Mr Wieland as members)
Libor ROUCEK	*Socialists and Democrats/CZ*	Citizens' Agora (in cooperation with Ms Durant) Eastern Neighbourhood policy Multilateral Assemblies in the area of security Asia ACP countries (in cooperation with Mr Martínez Martínez and Mr Wieland) Sakharov Network
Isabelle DURANT	*Greens/B*	Citizens' Agora (in cooperation with Mr Roucek) Eco-Management and Audit Scheme (EMAS) Transport European Political Parties LUX Prize Relations with Brussels authorities Lobbying activities (member of the Working Group established by the Conference of Presidents and chaired by Ms Wallis)
Roberta ANGELILLI	*EPP/I*	EMPA (in cooperation with Mr Pittella and Ms Kratsa-Tsagaropoulou) Personnel and the Medical Service (in cooperation with Ms Roth-Behrendt) Children's rights - Mediator
Diana WALLIS	*ALDE/UK*	Transparency Library services Question Time Northern Dimension and Nordic Region (in cooperation with Mr McMillan-Scott) European Law academy, Trier
László TŐKÉS	EPP/RO	Education (incl. European Schools) and sports UNESCO Intercultural Dialogue & Relations with religious faiths Euronest Western Balkans Candidate countries and Enlargement (in cooperation with Mr Martínez Martínez)
Edward McMILLAN-SCOTT	*ALDE/UK*	Human Rights and Democracy Question Time

		Northern Dimension and Nordic Region (in cooperation with Ms Wallis)
		Chair, Audit Panel
		National Parliaments/COSAC (in cooperation with Mr Martínez Martínez and Ms Koch-Mehrin)
Rainer WIELAND	*EPP/D*	Informatics and Telecom
		Chair, Steering Committee on ICT Strategy
		European Political Parties
		Statutes of Members and Assistants and the Voluntary Pension Fund (with Mr Pittella, Ms Roth-Behrendt and Mr Vidal Quadras)
		ACP Countries (in cooperation with Mr Roucek and Mr Martínez Martínez)
Silvana KOCH-MEHRIN	*ALDE/D*	Chair, Working Party on Gender Equality and Diversity
		National Parliaments/COSAC (in cooperation with Mr Martínez Martínez and Mr McMillan-Scott)
		Science and Technology Options Assessment Panel (STOA)

The Quaestors

Quaestors were first established by the Parliament in 1977. At first they formed a sub-group of the Bureau, but they have been separately and directly elected by the Parliament since direct elections in 1979. They are responsible for administrative and financial matters concerning members individually, in accordance with guidelines that were laid down by the Bureau in 1981 and subsequently reviewed in 1996. They take it in turn (for six months) to chair their meetings. The Quaestors also take part in the meetings of the Bureau in an advisory capacity, where they do not have the right to vote but can speak on a wide range of issues, with a strong Quaestor able to have considerable influence.

As Table 22 below indicates, the Quaestors distribute responsibilities amongst themselves:

Table 22: *The Quaestors: 2009-2012 term of office and their responsibilities*

Lidia Geringer de Oedenberg	*Socialists and Democrats/PL*	Cultural and artistic events sponsored by Members
		Artistic Committee
		Reception facilities for visitors'groups
		Members' facilities in EP information offices (with support from the other four Quaestors on the basis of their specific competences)
		Individual requests relating to payments of parliamentary allowances and reimbursement of expenses (Article 72 of the implementing measures of the Members' Statute)
Jim Higgins	*EPP/IRE*	Register of Members' financial interests
		Relations with the Members' Voluntary Pension Fund
		Use by Members of Parliament's library and document management
		Relations with political groups and non-attached members - rules concerning intergroups - use of Parliament's premises
		Contacts with Former Members' Association (with Ms Lulling)
		Support to Ms Geringer de Oedenberg in connection with the

		Information Offices in the following countries: United Kingdom, Luxembourg, Sweden, Denmark, Poland, Belgium and Greece.
Astrid Lulling	*EPP/LUX*	Members' transport facilities, including the car service, the Travel Agency, and facilities at Strasbourg and Brussels airports Members' language and computer courses Relations with national and local authorities in Parliament's three places of work Members' restaurants and bars Mail department and print shop Contacts with Former Members' Association (with Mr Higgins) Support to Ms Geringer de Oedenberg in connection with the Information Offices in the following countries: Latvia, Czech Republic, Malta, France, Romania, Portugal and Austria
Jiri Mastalka	*GUE/CZ*	Services for Members (Medical Service Service, crèche facilities for the children of Members) External services in Parliament's premises (shops and postal services) Telecommunication and information technology (including television facilities) Office equipment for Members Sports centres situated on Parliament's premises in Brussels and Strasbourg Support to Ms Geringer de Oedenberg in connection with the Information Offices in the following countries: Lithuania, Slovenia, Slovakia, Cyprus, Finland, Bulgaria and Germany
Bill Newton Dunn	*ALDE/UK*	Security issues in Parliament's premises Register of lobbyists, long-term visitors' access to restricted areas Use by Members of Parliament's audio-visual facilities Relations with the Ombudsman and the ECJ in cases relating to Quaestors' responsibilities Role and functioning of the Central Register and lists of attendance in the Chamber and in committee and group rooms Support to Ms Geringer de Oedenberg in connection with the Information Offices in the following countries: Ireland, Estonia, Italy, Spain, Netherlands, Hungary

The election of the President, Vice-Presidents and Quaestors

The choice of its officers has always been determined by the Parliament itself, which has always resisted any instructions from outside. Before Parliament became an elected body in 1979, its President was chosen annually. The practice developed of the President being given a second year of office, with election in the second year being by acclamation (only Alain Poher of France was given three years in office). Since 1979, Parliament's officers have been chosen every two-and-a-half years, first in the July session immediately following the June elections and then in mid-term elections which take place in the January session two-and-a-half years later, splitting the five year electoral period into two halves.

The first to be elected is always the **President**. Until he or she has been elected the chair is taken by the outgoing President or one of the outgoing Vice-Presidents or the member with the longest period of office. This is a new arrangement laid down in Rule 14 of the Rules of Procedure and one which replaces the provisions that had applied up to 2009 whereby the task was entrusted to the oldest MEP.

The previous arrangement was one where it was difficult to predict who would be given the task and this proved controversial. In the early days of the Parliament a tradition had developed whereby the oldest member delivered a keynote speech before proceeding with the formal business of supervising the election of the President. The first such speech after direct elections was given by Louise Weiss. The then 86-year-old had been a renowned French suffragette, resistance leader, journalist and fervent supporter of the European cause. In 1989, however, the oldest member was a member of the far right French National Front, the film director Claude Autant-Lara. His speech was boycotted by a large number of members from the outset, and many others walked out as a result of his remarks. Parliament's Rules of Procedure were subsequently amended so that the oldest member could no longer deliver an introductory speech, but merely supervise the election of the President. In 1992 and 1994, Otto von Habsburg should have performed this role, but because he was no longer allowed to make a speech, declined to act as oldest member, and had to be replaced by the second oldest member. In 1999 the sitting was due to be chaired by Mário Soares, former President of Portugal, but as he was a candidate for the post of President, he let the next oldest member (Giorgio Napolitano) chair. In early 2009 there was much speculation that the oldest member after the elections might be Jean-Marie Le Pen, the leader of the French National Front. In order to avoid the risk of his chairing the Parliament (even without the right to make a speech as Autant-Lara had done), it was decided to change the rules. Hence the new provision which enabled Hans-Gert Pöttering to be the first former President to preside at the election of his successor in July 2009.

Nominations for President are generally put forward by a Political Group, but may also be submitted by 40 or more members. The ballot is secret, with members lining up to cast their vote in the centre of the hemicycle, and with the result announced an hour or two later. An absolute majority of the votes cast (not of the total number of MEPs), with abstentions and spoilt ballots not counting, is required for election. If this is not achieved, a second and, if necessary, a third ballot is held, with no obligation on any of the first ballot candidates to stand down, and with the possibility of new candidates (compromise or other) entering the fray. If, however, there is no result in the third ballot, a conclusive fourth ballot is held, in which only the two candidates with the highest votes in the third ballot take part, and in which a simple majority is enough to ensure election.

Thirteen sets of Presidential elections have been held since 1979 (see Table 23), and the circumstances and degree of suspense have varied greatly.

In 1979, Simone Veil was the clear front runner on the centre-right, with support from the Liberals, Christian Democrats and Conservatives. The left was divided, with Socialist and Communist candidates in the field.

In 1982, the election was much more dramatic. The right was divided, with the European Democratic Group (Conservatives) considering that it was their turn for the Presidency. Not only were they unwilling to give a free run to the EPP, but they were also unenthusiastic about Egon Klepsch, the EPP's candidate. The Socialist candidate, by contrast, Piet Dankert, had made his name as Parliament's budget rapporteur on the first occasion that the Parliament rejected the budget in 1979 and then as a Vice-President. He enjoyed the sympathy of some members from outside the ranks of the left. In the decisive fourth ballot Dankert won by 16 votes, clearly gaining support (or abstentions) from certain Conservative and other centre-right members.

In 1984, there was again a clear front runner from the centre-right, Pierre Pflimlin of the EPP, a former French Prime Minister and the long standing Mayor of Strasbourg. Dankert was again the Socialist candidate, the only case in the elected Parliament of an outgoing President seeking re-election. Pflimlin easily beat the by then less popular Dankert on the second ballot.

The 1987 elections were the closest yet. In the third ballot Sir Henry Plumb, supported by the centre right, beat Enrique Barón (Spanish Socialist), supported by the left, by five votes.

In 1989, in contrast, there was a tacit agreement between the two largest Groups, the Socialists and the EPP, to share the two Presidencies of the legislature. The EPP supported Barón in 1989 and in return, the Socialists did not put up a candidate in 1992 against Egon Klepsch, the long-standing chair of the EPP Group and the losing candidate in 1982. Both won an absolute majority on the first ballot, although other candidates clearly obtained a considerable number of votes from outside their own Groups.

In the 1994-99 legislature, the agreement between the Socialist and EPP Groups to share out the Presidency continued, despite the complaints of the smaller Groups. As a result, Klaus Hänsch and José Maria Gil-Robles were both elected on the first ballot, the first with a record majority.

In 1999, the EPP-ED group succeeded in overtaking the Socialists as the largest Group and both these Groups initially indicated their desire to hold the Presidency of Parliament during the first half of the legislative term. Once it became clear that there was no longer scope to continue the previous *alternance*, both Groups sought to build a majority with other Groups. In the end, the EPP-ED negotiated an agreement with the Liberals, under which the EPP-ED would take the Presidency for the first half of the legislature and the Liberals for the second half.

Table 23: *Presidential elections since 1979*

Candidates	1st round	2nd round	3rd round	4th round
1979				
Veil (ELDR/F)	183	192=absolute majority		
Zagari (SOC)	118	138		
Amendola (Comm.)	44	47		
De la Malène (EDA)	26	-		
Bonino (Tech. Grp)	9	-		
	380	**377**		
1982				
Dankert (SOC)	106	114	162	191
Klepsch (EPP)	140	130	156	175
Scott Hopkins (EDG)	63	67	67	-
Chambeiron (Comm.)	43	43	-	-
Pannella (Tech. Grp)	16	18	-	-
	368	**372**	**385**	**366**
1984				
Pflimlin (EPP)	165	221=absolute majority		

Candidates	1st round	2nd round	3rd round	4th round
1984 (cont.)				
Dankert (SOC)	123	133		
Lady Elles (EDG)	44			
Pajetta (Comm.)	37			
Bloch (Rainbow)	17			
Le Pen (Right)	16			
Spinelli (Comm. Ind.)	11	49		
	413	**403**		
1986				
Plumb (EDG)	199	233	241	
Barón (SOC)	206	219	236	
Pannella (Non-Att.)	61	35	-	
Staes (Rainbow)	14	-	-	
	483	**487**	**477**	
1989				
Barón (SOC)	301 = absolute majority			
Von Wechmar (LDR)	93			
Santos (Green)	31			
Ewing (Rainbow)	20			
Le Pen (Right)	18			
Pannella (Non-Att.)	12			
	475			
1992				
Klepsch (EPP)	253 = absolute majority			
Barzanti (U.Eu.Left)	105			
Defraigne (ELDR)	72			
Dillen (Right)	16			
	446			
1994				
Hänsch (SOC)	365 = absolute majority			
Galland (ELDR)	87			
	452			
1997				
Gil-Robles (EPP)	338 = absolute majority			
Lalumière (ERA)	177			
	515			
1999				
Fontaine (EPP-ED)	306 = absolute majority			
Soares (SOC)	200			
Hautala (Green-EFA)	49			
	555			
2002				
Cox (ELDR)	254	277	298=absolute majority	
Martin (SOC)	184	226	237	
Bonde (EDD)	66	76	33	
Wurtz (GUE)	42	-	-	
Onesta (Green)	37	-	-	
	583	**579**	**568**	

Candidates	1st round	2nd round	3rd round	4th round
2004				
Borrell (SOC)	388 = absolute majority			
Geremek (ALDE)	208			
Wurtz (GUE)	51			
	647			
2007				
Pöttering (EPP-ED)	450 = absolute majority			
Frassoni (Green)	145			
Wurtz (GUE)	48			
Bonde (IND/DEM)	46			
	689			
2009				
Buzek (EPP)	555 = absolute majority			
Svensson (GUE)	88			
	643			

As a result, for the first time since 1986, the Socialists and the EPP-ED contested the election. The PES candidate, Mário Soares, could not prevent Nicole Fontaine from being elected on the first ballot, with the support of the Liberals. In return the EPP supported the leader of the Liberal Group, Pat Cox from Ireland, in 2002. He was duly elected, but only on the third ballot against the Socialist candidate, David Martin (a long-serving Vice President), and EDD leader Bonde, who picked up votes from Conservative eurosceptics. This election was the first where the candidates held an open, public debate, outlining their vision for the Presidency and answering questions from the floor in a media-organised event.

In 2004 the EPP-ED and PES once again negotiated an agreement to share the Presidency during the next legislature, thereby ensuring that Josep Borrell and Hans-Gert Pöttering were both elected at the first ballot. However, the size of the votes for Bronislaw Geremek, the former Polish foreign minister and activist in Solidarity, and Monica Frassoni, co-chair of the Green Group, indicated that they had received widespread support outside their own Groups. As in 2002, there were debates between the candidates before the vote in the plenary which thereby became a standard practice continued ever since.

In 2009 there was again speculation that the Liberals would seek an arrangement with one of the two biggest Groups to share the Presidency between 2009 and 2014. The leader of the ALDE group before the elections, Graham Watson, wrote to all members indicating his interest in the post. At the last minute he decided not to stand and the post went to the Polish EPP candidate, Jerzy Buzek, the first time since direct elections that a former Prime Minister had held the post. He was elected in the first round against the only other candidate, the Swedish GUE member, Eva-Britt Svensson. It is understood that a Socialist and Democrat candidate, possibly Martin Schulz, the Group leader, will be supported by the main Groups to serve between 2012 and 2014.

Once the Presidential elections have been settled, they have a bearing on the elections for the **Vice-Presidents** and **Quaestors** (and subsequently on the committee chairmanships, and other posts within the Parliament). These posts are effectively shared out among the Political Groups (and within them among their different national delegations) on the basis of their numerical strength (using the d'Hondt system) after taking into account which Political Group has obtained the Presidency.

To be elected Vice-President on the first ballot a candidate has to receive an absolute majority of the votes cast. If 14 candidates are not so elected, a second ballot for the remaining places under the same rules is held, and finally a third ballot in which those candidates with the most votes win. The "official" nominees of the Groups are almost always elected, although some of them only on the second or third ballot. Some outsider candidates (such as the popular Green candidates Roelants de Vivier in 1987 and Ripa di Meana in 1994) have come close but none succeeded until 2009 when Edward McMillan-Scott, a long-serving member and outgoing Vice President, was elected, while the official candidate of his Group, the newly founded European Conservatives and Reformists, Michal Kaminski, was defeated. This led to the expulsion of McMillan-Scott from the ECR Group and the Conservative party in the UK and, some time later, his joining the Liberal Democrats and the ALDE Group.

Once the Vice-Presidents have been elected, there is a separate ballot for the Quaestors with similar rules, in which there is usually little suspense. Here, however, the "official" candidates from the Groups are not always elected. In 1997, the Irish EDA member, Mark Killilea was elected (eliminating Vincenzo Viola from the EPP) and in 1999 Richard Balfe, an outgoing Quaestor seeking re-election, was re-elected (keeping out Nelly Maes from the Green Group). When the Socialist Group looked unlikely to support him for a further term in 2002, Balfe left the Group, but was again re-elected as an independent before joining the EPP-ED Group (and the UK Conservative party), giving this Group a majority within the college of Quaestors. In 2004 the proposal of the Political Groups was again overturned when the veteran Luxembourgish member, Astrid Lulling, succeeded in preventing the Liberal candidate, Annelli Jäätteenmaki, from being elected in the third round of voting.

Back-bench MEPs clearly feel less inclined to support candidates put forward by Groups following the inter-group share-out in the case of the Quaestors, who are elected last and whose job, after all, is precisely to look after the interests of individual members, rather than those of the Groups.

The Conference of Presidents, the Bureau and the College of Quaestors

In 1993, Parliament reorganised its management structures into three separate bodies, each with a specific set of tasks:

*   the Conference of Presidents composed of the President of Parliament and the chairs of the Political Groups

*   the Bureau composed of the President and the Vice-Presidents, and

*   the College of Quaestors

Prior to 1993, there was an "Enlarged Bureau" instead of the Conference of Presidents. This body brought together the Bureau and the Group chairs (with Quaestors present as well as non-voting members). It was felt to be an unwieldy body and was replaced by the more compact Conference of Presidents. Normally, the Conference of Presidents works by consensus but, where necessary, it votes in accordance with a weighting based on the number of members in each Political Group. As a result, the Conference reflects political strengths inside the Parliament more accurately than did the Enlarged Bureau. The closest such vote was a decision by 298 votes (EPP, UPE, ELDR and EDN) to 297 (SOC, GUE, Green and ARE) in November 1995 (to hold over the awarding of the Sakharov prize, for which see Chapter 16, from December 1995 to January 1996).

The **Conference of Presidents** is responsible for the broad political direction of the Parliament, both internally and externally. Internally, it proposes the membership and competence of parliamentary committees and delegations, adjudicates on disputes of competence between committees, authorises the drafting of reports and draws up the draft agenda of part-sessions. Externally, it decides on inter-institutional relations and relations with Member States and national parliaments, handles matters relating to relations with non-member countries and non-Union institutions and organisations and decides on the sending of delegations to third countries.

The **Bureau** deals with internal financial, organisational and administrative matters as well as staff policy and the management of sittings. Under its financial responsibility, it draws up the preliminary version of the budget of the institution and decides on the size of the establishment plan of the Secretariat, thereby determining how many new staff, if any, can be recruited. It also appoints the Secretary-General. In organisational and administrative terms, it takes decisions on the conduct of plenary sittings, authorises committee meetings away from the usual places of work as well as hearings and study and fact-finding journeys by rapporteurs. In addition, the Bureau often establishes smaller working parties to prepare decisions on sensitive issues, as illustrated in the list of responsibilities found in Table 22.

The **Quaestors**, as described above, are responsible for administrative and financial matters concerning MEPs individually (e.g. members' office equipment, allowances, use of vehicles, etc.). They also deal with day-to-day matters concerning security, passes, the allocation of offices and the use of buildings, including giving permission for the variety of exhibitions that are organised in the Parliament's buildings in and out of session.

The Conference of Presidents meets at least twice, and sometimes three or four times, per month. Its meetings are prepared by meetings of the head of the President's cabinet, the Secretary-General (or Deputy Secretary-General) of Parliament and the Secretaries-General of the Political Groups. The Bureau and the Quaestors normally meet once a month, during part-sessions in Strasbourg, with occasional extra meetings in Brussels.

The meetings of all three bodies are held *in camera*. Meetings of the Bureau tend to be quite formal affairs, with Vice-Presidents actively participating in the wide range of debates on their agenda. Meetings of the Conference of Presidents, on the other hand, tend to be much more brisk, with interventions limited to what is necessary to formalise agreements and to cut deals between the Groups regarding Parliament's business. Meetings of the

Quaestors are robust affairs, often representing a distillation of members' complaints regarding their working environment.

Attendance at all three is limited to their direct membership, though the non-attached members may also send two non-voting members to the Conference of Presidents. When discussing the draft agenda of Parliament, the Conference of Presidents invites a representative of the Commission and of the Council and the chair of the Conference of Committee Chairs within the Parliament (see below). It sometimes receives outside personalities, such as the Presidents of other institutions or a visiting head of state or government, for a political discussion.

On the staff side, attendance at the Conference and the Bureau is normally limited to the Secretary-General, the Secretariat of the Conference and Bureau (four or five Parliament officials), the Directors-General, the head of its Legal Service, and one or two staff from each Political Group. The minutes of meetings are drawn up by the Secretariat and unlike in committees or the plenary, are reviewed and approved before dissemination, given the sensitivity of some of the decisions that are taken and the need to prevent conflicting interpretations.

The Conference of Committee Chairs and the Conference of Delegation Chairs

The chairs of parliamentary committees meet together once a month (usually the Tuesday afternoons of the Strasbourg sessions) to review progress of work in committees and make suggestions to the Conference of Presidents as to forthcoming plenary agendas (for which purpose, the chair of the Conference of Committee Chairs attends the Conference of Presidents). They also hold meetings with the Commission Vice President on legislative timetable issues and (since 2010) an annual meeting with the whole of the Commission about the priorities of the latter's Work Programme. The Conference also serves to discuss organisational matters affecting committees, demarcation disputes and common problems that affect more than one committee. The chair of the meeting is elected by the committee chairs themselves.

The Conference began life as an informal gathering until its existence was formally recognised in the Rules of Procedure in 1993. Since 1979 there have been eight chairs, the longest serving of whom was Ken Collins who served for nearly seven years (see Table 24).

The Conference of Delegation Chairs fulfils a similar function in terms of discussing common organisational and timetable problems. They also elect their own chair, the longest serving of whom was the first, Günter Rinsche, who served for nearly twenty years from 1981, when the body was established (see Table 25). Like the committee chairs, they meet once a month with the chair representing them in the Bureau and Conference of Presidents when issues pertaining to the functioning of delegations are discussed.

Table 24: *Chairs of Conference of Committee Chairs since 1979*

1979 – 1984	Erwin Lange (D – Socialist)
1984 – 1989	Michael Poniatowski (F – Liberal)
1989 – 1993	Henri Saby (F – Socialist)
1993 – 1999	Ken Collins (UK – Socialist)
1999 – 2002	Ana Palacio (ESP – EPP)
2002 – 2007	Joseph Daul (F – EPP)
2007 – 2009	Gerardo Galeote (ESP – EPP)
2009 –	Klaus-Heiner Lehne (D – EPP)

Table 25: *Chairs of Conference of Delegation Chairs since 1979*

1981 – 1999	Günter Rinsche (D – EPP)
1999 – 2001	Claude Desama (B – Socialist)
2001 – 2002	Gary Titley (UK – Socialist)
2002 – 2004	Jan Wiersma (NL – Socialist)
2004 – 2009	Raimon Obiols i Germà (ESP – Socialist)
2009 –	Luis Yáñez-Barnuevo García Garcia (ESP – Socialist)

7.   The Parliamentary committees

As in the US Congress, it is in the parliamentary committees that much of the detailed work of the Parliament is carried out and where individual members can play a crucial role. This chapter examines the structure and functioning of the committees. It looks at the division of responsibilities between them and how members are allocated to them, at the way committee office-holders are chosen, at decision-making structures within the committees, and how they are staffed. It considers where and when committees meet, their workload and working methods, notably how committee rapporteurs are chosen, and how reports and opinions progress through committee.

History, structure and character of committees

Committees were a central part of the Parliament's work from its inception. The Common Assembly of the Coal and Steel Community had already set up seven committees by 1953. In 1958, with the establishment of the EEC and EURATOM, the number of committees increased to 13 in a structure not very different from that which exists today although over the years there have been occasional changes of committee nomenclature and responsibility.

After direct elections in 1979, 16 standing committees were set up. This gradually increased to 20 by 1999 (see Table 26 at the end of this chapter which lists all committee chairs since 1979). By then there was a growing feeling that the number of committees and subcommittees should be reviewed with the primary aim of spreading the new legislative responsibilities arising from the Amsterdam Treaty more evenly. Also, the number of committees was reduced from 20 to 17.

In 2004 EU enlargement provoked a second review of the committee structure and the number was increased back to 20. The Regional and Transport Committees were once again separated (as they had been from 1979 to 1999), the external trade function was taken from the Industry Committee to create an International Trade Committee (thereby effectively reviving the External Economic Relations Committee which had existed up to 1999) and a new Internal Market and Consumer Affairs Committee was established, assuming responsibility for general internal market measures from the Legal Affairs Committee and for consumer protection from the Environment Committee. In addition, the decision taken in 1999 to abolish all subcommittees was reversed with the setting-up of two subcommittees for Security and Defence and for Human Rights, both reporting to the Foreign Affairs Committee. But other decisions taken in 1999 were maintained, with the Industry Committee retaining the responsibility for industrial policy that it had taken over from the Economic Committee and the Constitutional Affairs Committee resulting from the merger of the Institutional Affairs Committee and the Committee on the Rules of Procedure.

The 1999 and 2004 reviews of the committee structure reflected the difficulty of agreeing the way in which responsibility should be divided up between committees. Any changes unravel carefully achieved balances. They confront the *esprit de corps* that develops in committees over the years which makes their members reluctant to see a merger with another committee. Resistance to such a change can be highly successful: in 1999, for example, the Fisheries Committee won a hard-fought battle when threatened with being reunited with the Agriculture Committee. Reforms tend to be agreed by an outgoing Parliament to take effect after the subsequent elections.

The 1999 and 2004 reforms show that it is genuinely difficult to draw up clear demarcation lines between policy areas. Is media policy, for example, a cultural, economic, industrial or legal matter? Are gender issues best dealt with in a separate committee or considered within the mainstream of the work of all committees? Can trade be separated from foreign policy, development and industrial policies? The evolution of Union policy and the stress laid on different aspects of policy are sure to continue to be reflected in calls to modify the organisation of the committees.

Individual committees are not equal in strength and prestige. The Foreign Affairs Committee covers areas where Parliament has relatively few formal powers, yet it has always included a high proportion of the better-known, more influential members. Hence in part its success in ensuring that the two new subcommittees report to it and were not created as separate committees.

The Budgets Committee traditionally had a high profile in an area where the Parliament already had real powers as of the Treaty revisions of 1970 and 1975. It had to adapt to the later reinforcement of the Parliament's legislative role which led to a strengthening of the position of legislative committees, such as the Environment and Transport Committees, and gave the latter a direct role in determining the financial envelope of multiannual programmes in their area of responsibility – though the Budgets Committee again played a critical role in negotiating the financial envelopes for such programmes for the period 2007 to 2013.

There are a number of smaller committees, with fewer legislative proposals to consider and, generally, fewer meetings. Such committees tend to concentrate instead on own-initiative reports on issues of their choice (e.g, the Women's Rights Committee) or else have specialised tasks to carry out (e.g, the Committee on Petitions). Both of these committees – created respectively in 1982 and 1987 – have been very successful up to now in resisting calls to change their character or to merge them with other committees.

Membership of committees

The number, responsibilities and size of committees are initially decided upon during the July session of a newly elected Parliament, and are then confirmed at the half-way point of the Parliament after two-and-a-half years (with, at most, limited changes made to committee sizes rather than structures). In 2009 the 20 committees ranged from a high of 76 members for the

Foreign Affairs Committee and 64 for the Environment Committee, down to 25 for the Legal Affairs Committee and 24 for the Fisheries Committee.

Once the number and size of committees has been determined, the appointments of full members and substitutes are then decided upon by the Political Groups in such a way as to ensure that each committee reflects the overall political balance between the Groups in plenary. Only small exceptions – to the tune of one or two extra members perhaps – are normally accepted, though even this can prove controversial and is now exceedingly rare.

The majority of MEPs serve on one committee as a full member and on another as a substitute. A small number, however, are either full members of two committees and substitute on another, or else are full members of one and substitute on two others. This is largely explained by the existence of so-called "neutralised" committees. These are committees on which an MEP can be a full member without prejudicing his or her chances of being a full member of another committee. These "neutralised" committees have included small technical committees such as the Rules and Petitions Committees, and other committees of specialised interest such as Women's Rights and Budgetary Control. If members were restricted to a single committee, there would be too few who would make these committees their only choice.

Some MEPs have been permitted by their Groups to be full members of two normal "non-neutralised" committees, and a tiny handful have been full members or substitutes on three or more committees. (In the past these have varied from particularly active to apparently inactive MEPs!) At the other end of the spectrum, a small number of MEPs are not full members of any committee. These have understandably included the President of the Parliament and others who have preferred not to be active in committees because of other duties, for example most Group leaders.

The reasons for members' preferences for individual committees vary greatly. In many cases perceived "constituency" advantage is the decisive factor, in others personal interest or expertise play a greater role. Some nationalities and Groups tend to have a preference for certain committees: Irish members, for example, have been keen to sit on the Agricultural and Regional Committees, more Socialists than others want to serve on the Employment & Social Affairs Committee and Green MEPs are particularly keen on the Environment Committee.

However, while these individual preferences do play an important part in the process of committee allocation, the Political Groups cannot always fulfil these wishes, since some committees are over-subscribed and overall political balance must be maintained. Less well-known backbenchers in their first term are often at a disadvantage in this distribution.

One safety mechanism for members who are not completely satisfied with their primary committee assignments as full members is their assignment to a second committee as a substitute. In some cases this is the committee on which they would have preferred to have served as a full member, and they may put more effort into this committee than their main one. Substitutes suffer little disadvantage compared to full members. They have full speaking rights, full voting rights (in the place of an absent full member – and there are usually some absences) and can also be rapporteurs and draftsmen, on occasion drawing up some of the major reports within a committee. Substitutes can even on rare occasions become the coordinators of their Political Groups on a particular committee, as is currently the case with Íñigo Méndez de Vigo, EPP coordinator on the Constitutional Affairs Committee.

Despite the balance generally achieved between Political Groups, committees do tend to develop a corporate identity, and do tend to attract members with a particular sympathy for the sector concerned.

Traditionally committees have witnessed a relatively high turnover in membership from one Parliament to another, even allowing for the high turnover of MEPs at European elections. Only a minority of MEPs stay in one committee for more than ten years. In the Culture Committee, for example, only 3 full members had been members in the previous legislature when it was reconvened after the 1999 elections, 11 (out of 35) in 2004 and 7 (out of 32) in 2009. Very few change mid-term, however.

We may be witnessing a movement towards greater specialisation among members, encouraged by the growth in the legislative responsibilities of the institution. Members can now become experts in a particular field and use that expertise to shape legislation over longer periods of time. There is doubtless less continuity in committee membership than in the US Congress but the contrast may be becoming less stark.

Committee chairs and vice-chairs and their selection

The formal office-holders ("Bureau") within each committee are its chair and the vice-chairs (traditionally three in number, but increased temporarily to four for the second half of the 2004-2009 legislature in order to attribute some such posts to the new Romanian and Bulgarian MEPs who joined mid-term). Since 1 December 2009, the Rules of Procedure have left it to Parliament to determine the number of committee vice-chairs, but for the moment it has been agreed to remain with the (originally temporary) figure of four.

The chair presides over the meetings of the committee, speaks for it in the plenary sessions at a time of sensitive votes or decisions and also represents it at the regular meetings of committee chairs (see Chapter 6). He or she can also have a powerful role in shaping the agenda of the committee, and in acting as its representative outside Parliament.

The chair and the vice-chairs are elected at the committee's constituent meeting, normally during the July plenary of a new Parliament and at the halfway point of the legislature. In practice, all these positions are shared out by agreement among Political Groups on the basis of the number of members within each Group.

The allocation is determined by the d'Hondt system of proportional representation, whereby Groups choose posts in an order determined by the size of the Group. In 2009, for example, the EPP-ED Group had the right to the first, third, fifth, seventh, eleventh, thirteenth, fifteenth, eighteenth and twenty-first choices, the Socialists to the second, fourth, eighth, twelfth, sixteenth and twentieth choices, the Liberals to the sixth, fourteenth and twenty-second choices, the Greens to the ninth choice, the European Conservatives and Reformists Group to the tenth choice, the GUE Group to the seventeenth choice and the EFD Group to the nineteenth choice. This

allocation allowed the Groups to determine a roughly proportional distribution covering the 20 available committees and two subcommittees,

While the choice of chairs is the most important element, an overall package deal is usually prepared by the Groups which also includes the other,
generally less important posts, such as the vice-chairs and chairs of subcommittees. As part of this bargain it is not unknown for a first vice-chair
post of an important committee to be given higher priority than the chair of
a weaker committee. Preliminary agreement on all these matters is reached
by the Groups in the weeks before the first plenary session of a new
Parliament but it is not until the plenary itself that the final decisions can be
taken especially if there is uncertainty as to the size of the Groups and as to
who will become President.

Once a chair has been allocated to a particular Group, its choice of a specific candidate depends on a number of factors including the need to take
into account the size of the national delegations within a Group, and the
experience and expertise of their individual candidates. In contrast with the
US Congress, seniority within the Parliament does not play a major role:
seven (Joly, Moreira, De Magistris, Hübner, De Castro, López Aguilar,
Mazzoni) out of the 20 committee chairs in the first half of the 2009-14 legislature were held by new members of the Parliament (compare six out of 20
in 2004 and four out of 17 in 1999).

Another key factor is the distribution of other posts within a Group. If a
national delegation within a Political Group has already provided a
President, Vice-President or Quaestor of Parliament, or the leader of the
Group, its chances of gaining a major committee chair will normally dimin-
ish since other delegations will want to get their turn. In other cases, a
national delegation may benefit from such distribution, as in 2004 when a
single delegation within the EPP, the German CDU, was able to claim the
chair of the two largest committees. Conversely in 2007 both of these chairs
lost their posts, and were replaced by Polish and Czech members of the
same Group, who had been EP Vice-Presidents in the first half of the legislature, and whose national delegations needed to be compensated for the
loss of these posts.

After the nominations of chairs and vice-chairs have been agreed by the
Political Groups, the formal decisions are taken by the committees at their
constituent meetings. In practice there have rarely been competing candidates, and election of the Political Groups' nominees is normally a formality, by acclamation rather than by vote.

There can sometimes be misgivings among members of a committee, as
happened at the beginning of the 2004 legislative term when the Women's
Committee initially refused to back the nominee of the EPP Group, provok-
ing a reaction in the Economic Committee where the PES candidate was
blocked. Both sides ultimately backed down and the official nominees of the
Groups were confirmed. It is very unusual for a committee to go further and
elect a candidate against the official nominee. It happened, for example, in
June 1993 when Derek Prag was elected as chair of the Institutional
Committee instead of José Maria Gil Robles. Both were members of the same
(EPP) Group but the former was forced by his Group to stand down within
a month in favour of the official Group nominee.

Even rarer is for a candidate from another Political Group to be elected against the official nominee, as this upsets the carefully constructed political balance established between Groups. The one exception so far as regards committee chairs came after the elections in June 1994. Although the then Forza Europa Group was allocated the chair of the Research Committee, the designated nominee, Umberto Scapagnini, lost at the constituent meeting in July, by 12 votes to 13, to the outgoing Socialist committee chair, Claude Desama. The latter had been a popular chair but the main factor in his initial victory was the hostile attitude of many, especially on the left, towards Forza Europa, its leader, the Italian Prime Minister, Silvio Berlusconi, and his government coalition. The result of the vote was stalemate for several weeks. Not only Forza Europa but some other Groups, in particular the EPP, strongly opposed the decision. The re-creation of a monetary subcommittee within the Economic Committee (a chair allocated to a Socialist nominee under D'Hondt criteria) was blocked until the situation in the Research Committee had been sorted out. The committee lost its first few planned meetings. The situation was only resolved well into September, when Claude Desama resigned as chair and Umberto Scapagnini was elected, the whole episode illustrating the strength of political commitment to the proportional allocation of key posts. A comparable set of events occurred in 2004, when the left on the Women's Committee baulked at the prospect of voting for Anna Zaborska, a Slovakian EPP member, and caused the vote to be postponed. The EPP immediately organised retaliation, securing the postponement of the election of Socialist nominee Pervenche Bérès, as chair of the Economic & Monetary Committee. Within a week, the necessary retreats were made and both were elected.

The only occasions when the D'Hondt system has not finally prevailed have been over the less important votes for committee vice-chairs and sub-committee chairs. For example, in 1984, Guy Guermeur, a Gaullist nominee for the chair of the Fisheries subcommittee, who had recently given support to the apartheid government in South Africa, was challenged and an EPP member elected instead with widespread support. At the same time, in the Education & Culture Committee, the official Group nominee for one of the vice-chairs was defeated by a candidate from another Group. In the same committee, two and a half years later, the third vice-chair was supposed to go to a representative of the then Group of the European Right. No nominee was put forward, and there were no representatives of the Group present at the constituent meeting of the committee, which proceeded to elect an Italian Communist as third vice-chair. The Group of the European Right protested strongly, but to no avail, a decisive factor being the "outsider" position that the Group had in the political decision-making structure of Parliament. (In 1987, however, a member of the French National Front, Devèze, was elected to the Bureau of the Agriculture Committee, despite opposition from the left).

The allocation of a position to a Group and within that to a particular national party usually (but not always) means that, in the event of a chair or vice chair standing down midway through their term of office, another member from the same Group and national delegation is nominated to the post – sometimes even when he or she has not been a member of that committee before. Finding a replacement can also cause a hold-up, most spectacularly a several month long vacancy in the chairmanship of the Legal

Affairs Committee in 1992-93, while the German delegation of the EPP deliberated between the competing ambitions of Mr. Bocklet (CSU) and Mr. Alber (CDU), with the former winning out (though only to leave four months later, to the benefit of the latter).

After the 1989 elections the whole system was challenged by the then Group of the European Right, which put up candidates against the other Groups' nominees in most committees. Not only were all these challenges unsuccessful (although prolonging the duration of the constituent meetings of the committees) but the one "official" nominee from the Group of the European Right (Hans Günter Schodruch for the third vice-chair of the Transport Committee), was challenged and defeated. Hence, the Group remained without a single chair or vice-chair. Similarly, in January 2007 the candidates of the newly-formed (and short-lived) Identity, Tradition and Sovereignty (ITS) Group for the first vice-chairmanship of the Culture Committee and the third vice-chairmanship of the Transport Committee were rejected in the committees in favour of nominees from other Groups.

This underlines that the proportional distribution of posts is simply a political agreement, not a right. It can be challenged when its strict application would lead to an allocation to a member from a Group considered by others to be extremist. So far, such Groups have never been large enough to be able to lay claim to a committee chair – only to vice-chairs, where they have indeed normally been challenged.

Once elected, the chairs and vice-chairs have terms of office of two-and-a-half years. Half-way through the five-year term of the Parliament, the whole process is repeated. Fewer changes to the distribution of committees between Political Groups are made at this moment than at the beginning of each Parliament, above all because there is far less change in the numerical balance between the Groups. However, changes have been made to the balance as a result of mid-term enlargements of the Union, and a wish to allocate some posts to members from the new countries. Moreover, certain Groups have felt the need to redistribute posts among their own members for reasons of internal political balance or for other reasons. Even when it remains with the same Group as before, there can be a change of chair. In 2002, for example, eight of the then seventeen committees changed their chair and in 2007 the same happened with eight of the twenty chairmanships.

A really long-serving chair is thus the exception rather than the rule. Perhaps the most striking such exception was Ken Collins, chair of the Environment Committee for 15 out of his 20 years in the Parliament. Other exceptions have been the German SPD member, Erwin Lange, who was chair of the Economic and Monetary Committee for four years and then of the Budgets Committee for seven years (1977–84); the Italian Communist, Pancrazio de Pasquale (Regional Committee from 1979 to 1989); Heinrich Aigner (Budgetary Control Committee from its creation in 1979 to his death in 1988); Michel Poniatowski (Development Committee from 1979-84 and the Energy Committee from 1984-89); Bouke Beumer (Culture Committee from 1982-84 and the Economic Committee from 1987–94), Willy de Clercq (External Economic Relations Committee from 1989 to 1997 and the Legal Affairs Committee from 1997 to 1999) and Diemut Theato (Budgetary Control Committee from 1994 to 2004). Michel Rocard chaired three successive committees for two and a half years each from 1997 to 2004: Development, Employment and Culture.

The result of a system of frequent changes has been that many committees have had a great number of chairs. The Legal Affairs Committee has had 13 chairs since 1979, the Employment/Social Affairs Committee 14 and the Foreign Affairs Committee 12 (see Table 26). Compared to the US Congress, in particular, the European Parliament continues to be characterised by short-term chairmanships.

Group coordinators

A very significant part is played within every committee by the Group coordinators. Each Political Group chooses a coordinator as its main spokesperson on the committee (in most Groups elected by its members of the committee). This role which has evolved in parliamentary practice has finally been officially recognised in the parliamentary reform of 2009 (Corbett Report 2004).

The coordinators of each Group meet together to share out rapporteurships and to discuss the committee's future agenda and outstanding political problems before full discussion in the committee. Coordinators' meetings can also be held to discuss forthcoming votes affecting the committee, possible compromise amendments and so on.

Coordinators lead for their Group on the committee, and allocate tasks among the members of their own Group. Once a report has been allocated to a Group the coordinator often plays the decisive part in the choice of rapporteur from among the members of that Group. They decide which substitute members may vote in place of an absent full member from the Group. The coordinators convene meetings of the members of their Group before the start of the full committee meeting and often act as "whips", maximizing their Group's presence during key votes, and helping to establish the full Group's voting line and speakers' lists for the plenary sessions. They can appoint "shadow rapporteurs" from their group for particular reports to share their workload. (See more on coordinators in Chapter 5, including Table 15 showing who they are.)

The balance of influence between the chair, the bureau and the coordinators differs considerably from committee to committee and over time. Sometimes, the chair is powerful and assertive and can dominate much of the work of a committee. Sometimes the co-ordinators, especially those from the larger groups, are dominant. Sometimes there is a more collective style of leadership of the chair in conjunction with the Group coordinators. The bureau as such rarely plays an important role.

Staff of committees

Compared to the US Congress (but not to the national parliaments of the Member States) the full-time staff of Parliament's committees is small. Committees normally have between four and ten administrators, under a head of unit, all based in Brussels. There are also one or two committee assistants to look after the logistics of the meetings, and a number of secretaries. The committee staff have an important role in briefing members on the past activities and positions adopted within the committee, and help in background research for rapporteurs and in the drafting of texts. They frequently tend to be generalists rather than specialists, largely because there are too few of them to cover what is often a wide range of policy areas, but also because of language constraints. A French-speaking expert on a particular subject area may have to hand over to a German-speaking, but non-expert, colleague if the rapporteur he or she is meant to assist speaks only German.

Besides the committee staff, other officials attend committee meetings. The Legal Service helps committees with specific problems, such as the legal base of legislative proposals, the Directorate-General for Communication is represented and researchers from the policy departments that work alongside the committee secretariats also follow the meetings.

A Political Group also has one or sometimes more of its staff (up to three for a big Group in a large committee) to follow an individual committee. The smaller Political Groups are more stretched in this regard, and their staff may have to follow more than one committee (see Chapter 5 on Political Groups). Finally, there are members' personal assistants (see Chapter 4). In the early days of the directly elected Parliament their presence at committee meetings was disputed in certain committees, but this is no longer the case. Only a minority of the assistants, however, regularly attend committee meetings, although they are quite often used as the "eyes and ears" of a committee member who is elsewhere engaged. They are not generally called upon for drafting of reports, but do frequently draft amendments.

Place, time and character of meetings

The committees' normal meetings are during the two so-called "committee weeks" which immediately follow the plenary session, and precede the Group week. Regular committee meetings typically begin after lunch (to allow members to travel in the course of that morning if necessary) and end before lunch on a subsequent day, although new patterns, with morning starts, have been tried in certain committees. The normal working hours are 3 p.m. to 6:30 p.m. and 9 a.m. to 12:30 p.m. (see Chapter 3). The main exception is the meetings of the Budgets Committee at peak budget time, which often continue until late into the night.

The busier committees meet at least twice a month for two, three or four consecutive half days on each occasion. Other committees may only meet once a month, although often for four half days. The vast majority of these meetings take place in Parliament's buildings in Brussels. For many years, there was a general rule that Parliament's committees could meet once a year outside Parliament's "normal working places" (but within the European Union). This was felt to ensure a good balance between visibility outside Brussels (and learning about national and regional situations) and not indulging in wasteful extra travel. With the growth in size of comittees, this practice has now been ended. Committees are no longer allowed to hold external meetings, but can still send small delegations (inside the European Union or to a candidate country) on missions not normally exceeding three days. No more than 25 members may travel on such missions during any one calendar year and no one delegation may have more than 12 members. No such missions are allowed during election years.

Committees can also meet in Strasbourg, where short extra meetings during plenaries are frequent. They are discouraged in that they compete for scarce room space and interpreters, as well as undercutting plenary attendance, but Parliament's new legislative responsibilities have made them difficult to avoid.

At all meetings, the chair sits up on a raised dais, with the vice-chairs on his or her left and the committee secretariat to the right. The members sit in the central bloc of seats, facing the chair rather than each other, with the Socialists in the front seats on the left, the EPP in the front seats on the right and the smaller Groups behind. The secretariats of the Political Groups, members' assistants and staff sit in the block of seats on one side of the room, with officials of other institutions (normally the Commission or Council) in the block of seats on the other side. Visiting Commissioners or Ministers will be given a seat next to the chair, displacing the vice-chairs.

Before direct elections, committee meetings were closed to the public, but they are now practically always open (see Chapter 16). As for the use of languages, there is a greater informality than in plenary sessions, with members more frequently using a language other than their own. There are also since 2004 new rules on multilingualism whereby only full members are guaranteed the right to speak their own language, with interpretation for less-spoken languages not always being available. For coordinators' meetings, there is sometimes no interpretation, with only English or French being used.

Committee business

The bulk of committee business is concerned with the consideration and adoption of reports and opinions, in fulfilment of Parliament's legislative, budgetary scrutiny and agenda-setting roles. These are normally to consider draft legislative or other texts from the Commission or the Council, but can also be at a committee's "own initiative".

The "committee responsible" and opinion-giving committee(s)

Proposals are referred to the appropriate committee as "the committee responsible", often referred to as the "lead committee", and frequently to one or more of the other committees for their "opinion". Committees may also request that they be asked to give an opinion on a proposal or suggest that another committee give such an opinion to them.

The decision as to where to refer the proposal is prepared by officials in the Directorate General for the Presidency, in cooperation with the committee secretariats, and is then announced by the President of Parliament in the subsequent plenary session. These decisions may be challenged. If so, the question of competence is referred to the Conference of Presidents which must take a decision within six weeks on the basis of a recommendation from the Conference of Committee Chairs, or, if no such recommendation is forthcoming, from the latter's chair. If the Conference of Presidents fails to take a decision within that period, the recommendation is deemed to have been approved.

These streamlined procedures were introduced following a long history of deadlocked disputes between committees. In particular, the default power given to the Chairman of the Conference of Committee Chairs, introduced in 2009 (Corbett Report A6-273/2009), now guarantees that lengthy deadlocks can be avoided. At the same time, the possibilities for shared responsibility or even joint meetings of committees have been enhanced (see below).

Drawing up an opinion for another committee allows for the expression of views, but is less satisfactory than being "the committee responsible". Opinion-giving committees, for example, may table amendments to Commission proposals but are not meant to vote on the Commission proposal as a whole. There is no obligation for the committee responsible to take another committee's amendments on board, though they do have to be voted on. If the amendments are rejected, the opinion-giving committee does not have the right to table amendments in plenary, unless it can obtain the signature of 40 members or the support of a Political Group – any amendment failing to get the support of even one Group is, after all, unlikely to fare well in plenary.

Rule 49 specifies that the main committee must set a fixed deadline for opinion-giving committees, before which date it cannot adopt its own report, but the latter are sometimes given very little time to draw up their opinions, which often have to be abandoned, or else take the form of amendments tabled directly by its members in the responsible committee or are subject to a letter from the chair. Any opinions adopted in time are annexed to main committee reports, though on occasion opinions adopted late are circulated separately.

General dissatisfaction amongst opinion-giving committees with these arrangements led in the 1990s to the development of two procedures, known as "Gomes" and "Hughes" (after the rapporteurs of the original reports), outside the formal Rules of Procedure. The Gomes procedure, which required a decision of the Conference of Presidents, provided for one committee to be responsible, but for (an)other committee(s) to draw up their parts of a report, it being understood that the responsible committee would include in its report without substantial change the entire contribution from the opinion-giving committee(s). The Hughes procedure was invented in 1995 by the Conference of Committee Chairs and became more widely used than Gomes. In this case, the amendments of the opinion-giving committee(s) were not automatically incorporated into the report of the responsible committee but were treated more carefully, on the basis of more systematic and organised contacts between rapporteurs in the different committees and with the name of the draftsman on the cover page of the report along with the main rapporteur.

Neither of these procedures was spelled out in Parliament's Rules of Procedure but elements of both were incorporated into the Rules following the 2002 revision. What is now Rule 50, "Procedure with associated committees" (though often still referred to as the "Reinforced Hughes" procedure), revised again in 2009, provides for the timetable for examining legislative proposals to be agreed jointly by two committees and for the rapporteur and draftsman to endeavour to agree on the texts they propose to their committees and on their position regarding amendments. The responsible committee is supposed to accept without a vote (and thus to integrate directly into its own report to Parliament) amendments from the opinion-giving committee if they are judged to fall within the competence of that committee.

Since 2009, it has been up to the chairs and rapporteurs concerned to jointly identify areas of the text falling within their exclusive or joint competence (previously, the chair of the lead committee always had the final say). In the event of disagreement, one of the committees involved can submit the matter to the Conference of Presidents.

If the lead committee, when finally adopting the report, rejects an amendment that is within the competence of both committees, the opinion-giving committee may table the amendment directly in plenary.

Another innovation in 2009 was to allow the Conference of Presidents, if it is satisfied that the matter is of major importance, to decide that a procedure with joint meetings of committees and a joint vote is to be applied. In that event, the rapporteurs concerned must draw up a single draft report, which shall be examined and voted on by the committees involved at joint meetings held under the joint chairmanship of their respective chairs. The committees involved may set up inter-committee working groups to prepare the joint meetings and votes. This procedure is laid down in Rule 51 as the "Procedure with joint committee meetings", and is starting to be used.

The second basis for committee reports and opinions is when a committee decides that it wishes to draw-up a so-called "own-initiative report" on a particular subject on which it has not been consulted. This might, for example, be an entirely new issue on the policy agenda, or a Commission communication on which Parliament has not been formally consulted, or on the basis of motions for a resolution tabled by individual members.

"Own initiative" reports

Besides legislative or other proposals referred to them, committees may also examine an issue at their own initiative, subject to prior approval. Typical reasons for rejecting requests for approval include that the subject matter is that of another committee, or that the issue has been recently handled by Parliament, or simply that the plenary agenda is getting overloaded. Authorisations dwindled from 1994, when the Conference of Presidents took over responsibility from the Bureau for authorising them,

These tighter controls led initially to a significant drop in the number of own initiative reports: between 1990 and 1994, 528 such reports were adopted, but in the following five years, the number dropped to 212, or around two per committee per year. During the 2004-2009 legislature, it crept back up to 668 (about 130 per year). The Foreign Affairs Committee was responsible for the greatest number (83), followed by the Economic Committee (56).

In December 1999, the Conference agreed that requests for own-initiative reports approved by the Conference of Committee Chairs "shall be deemed to have been approved unless the Conference of Presidents delivers an opinion to the contrary within one month". However, this was in the context of strict quotas (initially two own-initiative reports at any one time for legislative and three for non-legislative committees) and even within the quota, permission was not automatic.

The types of own initiative reports allowed were specified more precisely through a set of criteria adopted by the Conference of Presidents in 2002 (and since amended in 2004, 2006 and 2008). Five types are defined and listed in Annex XVIII of the Rules of Procedure:

(a)   Legislative Own-Initiative Reports, drawn up on the basis of Article 225 TFEU

(b)   Strategic Reports , drawn up on the basis of non-legislative strategic and priority initiatives included in the Commission's annual legislative and work programme

(c)   Non-Legislative Own-Initiative Reports , not drawn up on the basis of a document of another Institution or body of the European Union

(d)   A specific set of Annual Activity and Monitoring Reports (as listed in Annex 1 of Annex XVIII of the Rules)

(e)   Implementation Reports on the transposition of EU legislation into national law and the implementation and enforcement thereof in Member States.

Each parliamentary committee may simultaneously draft no more than six own-initiative reports. For committees with sub-committees (currently only the Foreign Affairs Committee), this quota is increased by one report per sub-committee. Any proposed report must not deal with topics principally involving analysis and research activities which may be covered in other ways, for example by studies. It must not deal with topics which have already been the subject of a report adopted during the previous 12 months, save where new information justifies it on an exceptional basis. To avoid too many reports within these limits, committees may not adopt the report in question within three months of authorisation. Towards the end of the parliamentary term, requests for authorisation to draw up own-initiative reports must be submitted no later than in the July of the year preceding the elections. After that date, only duly substantiated exceptional requests are authorised.

Legislative own-initiative reports are not subject to the ceiling. Conversely, for implementation reports, each committee may draw up one such report a year.

The list in Annex 1 includes such matters as: the annual reports on human rights in the world, as well as those on the application of Union law and the application of the principle of subsidiarity; the annual reports of various EU Institutions and Agencies; the report on equality between men and women in the European Union (Committee on Women's Rights and Gender Equality); and reports in response to various statutory Commission annual reports (such as on competition policy, the internal market and on consumer protection).

Not subject to the ceiling of six reports are four required by Parliament's Rules, namely the annual reports on public access to Parliament documents, on European political parties, on the deliberations of the Committee on Petitions and on the Ombudsman's annual report, Rule 205(2) (Committee on Petitions).

A separate case had been that of motions for resolution tabled by individual members. These are referred to the relevant committee which must then decide whether or not (and by which procedure) such resolutions should be considered. In practice, only a very few such resolutions are taken up. Many raise constituency issues of specific national, regional or sectoral interest only and are not considered appropriate for detailed committee consideration. Moreover, they used to provide a loophole from the requirement for prior authorisation of own-initiative reports, since committees were free to decide as to how to react to them. Now any committee reports drawn up on the basis of such motions have to be authorised like other own-initiative reports and come out of the quota of six. It may be more attractive, therefore, for a committee to consider them, not in a separate report, but in conjunction with a report being drawn up in another context. In both cases, the motions are annexed to the report in question, though the reports themselves may depart quite significantly from the content of the resolution. Such motions are far less common than they were in the past.

Volume and distribution of reports

To measure the total output of the committees, it is necessary to include both legislative and non-legislative work, the latter including issues such as those related to the budget or budgetary control, constitutional issues, waivers of immunity, changes in the rules of procedure, petitions of particular policy interest, "own-initiatives" or any other procedural matters, such as when a proposal's legal base is contested. If these are added together, then between 2004 and 2009, a total of 2096 committee reports were tabled in plenary, 1307 legislative in nature and 789 non-legislative. This is almost the same total, but with a slight shift in favour of legislative reports, compared to the previous legislature's figures of 2077 committee reports (1232 legislative and 845 non-legislative) between 1999 and 2004.

The balance between the different types of legislative and non-legislative reports varied greatly from committee to committee. Some committees had a heavy legislative burden (e.g. the Environment Committee with 219 legislative reports in the 2004-2009 Parliament). Other committees (e.g. the Civil Liberties Committee or the Agriculture Committee) also have a considerable legislative load but, until the entry into force of the Lisbon treaty in December 2009, this consisted primarily of the single reading consultation procedure. A further set of committees is scarcely involved in legislation at all because they have very specific non-legislative tasks (e.g. the Petitions Committee or the Foreign Affairs Committee). In 2004-2009, the Foreign Affairs Committee had 23 assents, 21 consultations and 4 co-decisions but 84 own-initiatives, while the Women's Committee had 9 legislative and 34 non-legislative reports .

Nomination of rapporteurs and draftsmen

Once a committee has decided to draw up a report or opinion, it nominates a rapporteur (when the committee is primarily responsible) or a draftsman (when it has to draw up an opinion for another committee). Only in a few cases are rapporteurs not appointed, namely when a committee decides to approve a legislative proposal without amendment (Rule 46).

Draftsmen of opinions, on the other hand, are quite often dispensed with, because the issue is felt to be of little distinctive interest to the committee or because the timetable of the committee primarily responsible leaves little time for adequate discussion. On such occasions the committee may simply encourage its members to table amendments directly in the main committee in their own name or make a point in a letter to the main committee sent by the chair.

The system of rapporteurs stems from parliamentary practice in a number of mainly southern European countries, and is unfamiliar to those, for example, with British, Nordic or American parliamentary backgrounds (though the possibility is provided for in the Scottish Parliament). It is the job of the rapporteurs (and of draftsmen) to prepare initial discussion on the subject within the committee, to present a draft text, and to amend it, if necessary, to take account of the committee's observations or of new developments. Once the report is adopted by the committee, the rapporteur presents it in plenary, and is asked to give a view on behalf of the committee on any plenary amendments that have been tabled (normally communicated to the President in advance in writing, although the rapporteur may take the floor on complicated points). The rapporteur must also follow developments after the first Parliament reading, and prepare a recommendation for the second reading. Certain other rapporteurships call for continuing follow-up, especially those of an annual nature, such as those on the budget or competition policy. A rapporteur becomes ex officio a member of Parliament's delegation to conciliation with Council (see Chapter 12).

Committees choose rapporteurs and draftsmen by a system whose broad lines are common, but whose details vary considerably from committee to committee. Each Political Group receives a quota of points according to its size. Reports and opinions to be distributed are then discussed by the committee coordinators who decide on the number of points each subject is worth, and then make bids on behalf of their Group, the strength of their claim being based in theory (but not always in practice) on the relationship between the number of points already used by the Group and their original quota. A controversial issue may be the subject of competing bids. Groups may then raise the bid up to a maximum level which varies between three and five points. If two or more Groups are still in contention, the report should go to the Group with the lowest utilization of its notional allocation of points but the Groups concerned often come to an agreement between themselves, possibly in the form of a package deal whereby one Group receives one report and the other is promised a subsequent one. Very occasionally, two co-rapporteurs are appointed, mainly on major reports where the visibility of cross-party support is felt to be an important factor. Such has been the case, for example, within the Constitutional Committee in its reports on the preparations for, or in reaction to, EU treaty changes.

There are certain characteristics of this "auction" system. One is the tendency for Groups not especially interested in a report to try and raise the bids, in order to make other Groups "pay" more for them. A second is that it is often advantageous for a Group to submit the name of a proposed rapporteur as early as possible. If the suggested rapporteur is recognised as a specialist on the issue, it can be easier to get agreement on his or her nomination. Certain technical issues on which there is little political controversy but on which a committee member is a specialist see the same rapporteur appointed again and again, often for very few points. A third feature is the general informality of the system. Trade-offs are common between Groups (as are deals that reports should be allocated for few or no points) and there are very few formal votes to decide on rapporteurships. If a Group occasionally exceeds its total number of points by offering good rapporteurs, a relaxed attitude is often taken by the other Groups. It is generally only for the most politically important issues that a more rigid and partisan stance is taken.

For certain major and regularly recurring reports a rotation system is sometimes developed between the Political Groups. This is the case for Parliament's most obviously prominent rapporteurship, that on the annual budget, and for certain annual reports, such as on competition policy. A particular rotation system between three specialised members from different Political Groups is applied for immunity matters.

One innovation that has been attempted has been to try to name rapporteurs at a much earlier stage on the basis of the annual Work Programme. This is designed to enable rapporteurs to begin their preparatory work in advance of the formal presentation of a legislative proposal by the Commission, thus saving valuable time later on. It provides the possibility for rapporteurs to enter into talks with the Commission, before the latter finalises its proposal, as well as with the Council, not least when there is thought to be a chance of concluding the legislative procedure by agreement at first reading.

The naming of "shadow rapporteurs" by other Groups, especially the larger ones, has become more and more significant in recent years and has been formally recognised in the 2009 Rules reform. Shadow rapporteurs enable Group co-ordinators to spread the burden of speaking and negotiating for their Group. They lead off discussions for their Group when the issue is discussed in committee or plenary or within their Group, and also mobilize their Group in the preparation of amendments. For important reports the rapporteur will have a number of meetings with the "shadows", and they may also be brought along to meetings with the Commission or Council Presidency. In some cases they (or Group co-ordinators) practically constitute informal sub-committees. A particularly striking example of this was the REACH chemicals legislation, where the rapporteur and shadow rapporteurs as well as the draftsmen of the two opinion-giving committees met on an almost weekly basis over an extended period of time to identify the main area of agreement and possible solutions for the key problems at stake.

Choices facing a rapporteur

Once appointed, a rapporteur may proceed in a number of ways. The first element to consider is that of timing. Some legislative reports may be presented quickly, especially where the Commission or Council Presidency has indicated that the matter is an immediate priority (or even formally requested urgent treatment by the plenary), or where the Parliament itself has undertaken (e.g. in the context of the annual legislative programme) to act within a certain time. Other reports, especially own-initiative reports, are often less pressing, and sometimes may not be presented for a year or more. A final deadline is the end of the legislature as all rapporteurships lapse when the five-year Parliamentary term expires and new rapporteurs have to be appointed (or former rapporteurs reconfirmed).

The rapporteur must also decide what assistance to obtain. Some rapporteurs rely heavily on the committee's staff, who are often asked to draft a text on the basis of more or less specific instructions. Other rapporteurs may prefer to write all their reports themselves or to look for assistance in drafting from their own assistants, Group staff, his or her party at home, or other organisations (such as research institutes). Rapporteurs often also seek background information from a wide range of sources, including not only the committee staff and the policy departments in the committee structure but also national governments, employers, trade unions, trade associations, public interest groups and, last but not least, the Commission. They are likely to make use of information provided by various lobbyists. The latter can play a valuable role in this respect, although there is always room for debate as to whether a rapporteur is gaining a balanced picture.

In the course of his or her research a rapporteur may travel to consult people outside Brussels, in the Union or even in third countries. As pointed out in Chapter 4, each member has an annual allowance to be used for travel outside their own country. Some rapporteurs seek to gain additional financial support from the Parliament, although this is only rarely granted.

The structure of the rapporteur's text depends on whether it is legislative or non-legislative. In a *non-legislative report*, the motion for a resolution contains first, a number of procedural citations ("having regard to", for example, any motions for resolution or Commission memorandum on which the report is based, a list of committees drawing up opinions, etc.), then sometimes a number of factual recitals ("whereas...") and concludes with the substance of the matter in a number of paragraphs ("welcomes", "regrets", "deplores", "calls upon the Commission", etc.) The final paragraph is always procedural in that it calls for the resolution to be transmitted to the Commission, Council, or other bodies such as national parliaments.

By contrast, in a *legislative report*, the resolution itself is of a procedural nature only, indicating whether Parliament approves the proposal with or without amendments, or whether it rejects it. It also covers such points as whether Parliament approves the legal base of a proposal (normally a formality, but of considerable importance if Parliament disagrees, such as when it believes that a proposal should come under another procedure, especially where Parliament's powers may be different). Points of substance are addressed by means of amendments to the Commission's proposal or, in second reading, Council's position. They are put forward at the beginning of a report (in the form of a parallel text with the proposal or Council position on the left, and the draft Parliament amendments on the right). The amendments may be accompanied by short justifications. After adoption by Parliament, the legislative texts are now presented in a consolidated version which contains the amendments as well as the non-amended parts of the legislative proposals.

Both types of report are normally accompanied by an explanatory statement, which serves to provide background information on the problem, and outlines why certain recommendations were made. Unlike the draft motion this is not put to the vote in the committee, but is drafted by the rapporteur on his or her own responsibility; it is still supposed to reflect the opinion of the committee. Minority statements may be added to an explanatory statement. In addition, opinions of other committees are annexed to the report, as are any motion for a resolution serving as a basis for the report, or which were considered in conjunction with it.

Opinions from one committee to another are now meant only to consist of proposed amendments to the draft legislation (for legislative reports) or draft paragraphs (for non-legislative texts). Once adopted, they are transmitted to the main committee, which is now required (unless Rule 50 applies, as described above) to put the proposed amendments or paragraphs to the vote.

There are now strict length restrictions on non-legislative texts and the explanatory parts of legislative ones, which have been imposed because of the increasing volume of texts to translate as well as as a result of the dramatic increase in the number of working languages used. As a general rule, motions for a resolution are not meant to exceed four pages, explanatory statements for a legislative report six pages (seven for a non-legislative report) and opinions three pages. Special derogations are required from the Bureau to exceed these limits, a requirement which has served to discourage over-lengthy texts, although committees have a small annual reserve of pages, so that slightly longer texts can be produced on certain priority issues without seeking special authorisation.

The most obvious constraint on a rapporteur is that his or her report should be acceptable to a majority of members of the committee. Formally speaking, rapporteurs are the servants of the committee, not of their Groups. The rapporteur's own personal preferences can more easily be expressed in the explanatory statement, although even here highly partisan statements would be challenged within the committee. On several occasions rapporteurs have lost the confidence of the committee and been replaced by the chair or another member; on others, rapporteurs have chosen to resign when their basic line was rejected, or their draft text was amended out of all recognition. A more common situation is when a rapporteur expresses a point of view which is controversial, but which still has a chance of winning a narrow majority within the committee, with the risk that this will be subsequently overturned in the plenary. Such a strategy, however, runs counter to the pressure which exists on committees to try and achieve the widest possible consensus whenever there is a need for a special majority in Parliament (above all, for votes to amend or reject Council's position in the budget or in second readings of legislation and to approve it in some consent procedures).

The progress of reports through a committee

The process whereby a report goes through committees varies, but there are a number of common stages for most of them. Unless there is particular urgency, or in especially busy periods towards the end of a legislature, in which case these various stages are telescoped into one or two meetings (with a report sometimes being adopted at a special meeting during the plenary), there is normally a period provided for committee discussion before a draft text is produced. Typically the rapporteur will introduce the issue, and give an indication of his or her initial views, and there will then be a possibility for members to give their views. One or more representatives of the Commission will be present to make a statement or answer questions about the Commission's proposals or position. This representative may be the specialist who drafted the proposal, or someone higher up the Commission hierarchy. For more important issues the responsible Director-General or Commissioner will often be present. A Commission representative will normally be present on all occasions when the issue is discussed, although problems are sometimes posed when the committee agenda is changed at short notice. For a committee with a very full agenda there may be ten to 15 Commission officials present at any one moment.

In addition, there is usually a member of the Council secretariat and one or more officials from the ministry or permanent representation of the country holding the rotating Council Presidency present and sometimes those of other Member States as well (typically from the relevant Council working group). Unlike Commission officials, Council or Presidency officials have traditionally been reluctant to speak in committee, except on procedural questions such as timetabling or commenting on the exact status of a text purporting to emerge from the Council. There are signs, however, that this is changing, with chairs of Council working groups sometimes being mandated to give Council's position on issues of substance.

At the end of the initial discussion it is often clearer as to whether the issue is controversial within the committee or not. The rapporteur then undertakes to produce a text by a particular time. Once ready, the text is sent for translation (for which at least ten working days is normally required), and then distributed to all members. There follows a fresh discussion, with committee members and the Commission commenting on the rapporteur's text. A deadline for amendments may then be set. The rapporteur can also decide to make modifications to his or her text or even to draft a new text if there are a large number of amendments.

The committee proceeds to vote at a subsequent meeting, first on the amendments, and then on the proposal as a whole. The rules provide that for legislative reports, after voting on the amendments but before voting on the proposal as a whole, the Commission be asked to state its position on the amendments and the Council to comment. If the Commission is not in a position to make such a statement or declares it is not prepared to accept all the amendments, then the committee may postpone the final vote, in order to put pressure on the Commission. In practice the Commission hardly ever comments at this stage (it has usually made its approach clear in the preceding committee discussions) and the Council never (as it normally has no position at that stage).

Procedures are generally less formal than in the plenary session. Untranslated amendments and even oral amendments are sometimes allowed, especially when the chair, rapporteur or co-ordinators put forward compromises. Voting is normally by show of hands, and sometimes electronic (see below) – the permitted option of standing and sitting being very rarely used. The plenary technique of requesting roll call votes on sensitive issues (by one quarter of the members of the committee) is available to members, but is seldom used. Contrary to the rules applied in plenary, a committee cannot vote where the quorum (also one quarter of the members) does not exist.

Manual counting of votes can be very difficult especially when up to 60 or 70 members are present, when some of them are surrounded by non-members and when others are hardly putting up their hands, perhaps through voting exhaustion or because they do not want to advertise that they are voting against their group whip. A further complication is that too many substitute members from one Group might be taking part in the vote, something that is not always obvious to those counting. As a result, a chair might turn to the secretariat and find that there are two or three variants on the outcome! Electronic voting has thus become increasingly common, especially in the larger committees, where it has had the positive effect of considerably accelerating the handling of votes on complex reports with a large number of amendments, especially when a large committee is evenly divided on sensitive issues. The electronic voting system also indicates whether a Group is exceeding its voting quota, and provides a full printed list of who took part in the final vote on the report.

Once a report has been adopted within a committee it is then collated by the committee secretariat (including any opinions received from other committees) and tabled for final translation into all the languages. It is then submitted to plenary as a sessional document (in the A series of documents). Resolutions and any legislative texts adopted (for plenary procedures, see Chapter 9) are forwarded to the Commission and Council (and often to Member States' governments and parliaments as well) and published in the Official Journal. The committee report with its explanatory statement is not re-issued.

For non-legislative texts, or for legislative texts involving only one reading, that is generally the end of the procedure as far as a committee is concerned. On the other hand, in procedures involving two or more readings by the Parliament, the committee's rapporteur continues to follow developments and may bring the issue up again within the competent committee at any time. Once the Council has adopted its position, this is announced in the plenary, and is then placed on the next agenda of the competent committee. The Rules were amended in 1999 to encourage the Council to present the common position at that meeting and some Council Presidencies have been willing to respond to such requests from committees. Moreover, provision for such a presentation has now been enshrined in the Interinstitutional Agreement on Better Lawmaking adopted at the end of 2003.

The committee adopts a recommendation in second reading, which must go to the plenary within a maximum of three months (four months if extended) of the common position being announced. The recommendation is simply to approve, amend or reject Council's position. Approval or rejection by Parliament brings the procedure to an end, but if amendments are adopted, and these prove unacceptable to Council, the draft legislation is referred to a conciliation between Parliament and Council (see Chapter 12 for more detail).

In such cases, the rapporteur, chair and other members of the committee will participate in Parliament's delegation to the Conciliation Committee. However, the results of conciliation go directly to the plenary for decision without passing through committee, though they are also usually debated within the committee.

A committee's involvement in a report can be maintained over a long period as when it is referred back from the plenary to the committee, or when reconsultation of the Parliament is requested. Occasionally committees which wish to have Parliament pronounce on a certain issue, but do not want to produce a final report until a later date, prepare an interim report.

Alternative and simplified procedures

Parliament has an increasingly full agenda. Until 2002 the Rules contained two alternative procedures intended to lighten Parliament's agenda, and notably to deal with technical legislation, known as the procedure without report (used notably when a legislative proposal could be approved as such without amendment) and the procedure without debate (used in such cases and also for non-legislative reports when requested by the committee). In the 2002 Rules revision (Corbett Report), these procedures were replaced by a single procedure without amendment and debate (now Rule 138) whereby any matter adopted in committee with fewer than one tenth of the members voting against, is taken in plenary as a single vote without amendment, unless MEPs or Groups totalling more than one-tenth of the Parliament request that it be open to amendment. Such matters are also taken without debate unless a Group or 40 members request one.

These possibilities are not restricted just to technical matters. Many rapporteurs who used to seek debates for their reports now accept that this will not necessarily be the case, although she or he can still speak for up to two minutes before the vote, even where is no debate. Removing the right to plenary amendment can be more problematic, not least because what is uncontroversial in the responsible committee may look rather different from the perspective of another committee, but the threshold to revert to standard procedure with amendments (one tenth of Parliament) is low. The procedure has therefore worked rather well and much better than many had suspected.

In the 2009 parliamentary reform, this simplified voting scheme has been made mandatory, subject to some exceptions, for all own-initiative reports. However, in such cases, Groups may table alternative motions for resolution, but still no amendments. This opens the door to Groups bargaining a compromise resolution, but avoids a plethora of amendments.

Also in 2009, the option of a "short presentation" of a report in plenary by the rapporteur was created – somewhat more than a single two-minute speech by the rapporteur, but less than a full debate. This procedure (Rule 139) can only be applied by a decision of Parliament as a whole, on a proposal of the rapporteur or the Conference of Presidents. If so decided, the rapporteur presents the committee's report, the Commission has an opportunity to respond and a ten minute debate may follow in which the floor is given to members who catch the eye of the President for short (one minute) speeches.

Internally, too, committees may use a simplified procedure (Rule 48) whereby the chair may propose to the committee to approve a legislative proposal as it stands, in which case, unless there are objections by at least one-tenth of the members, it is sent to plenary under the procedure without amendment or debate. Alternatively, where there appears to be broad agreement on particular amendments, the chair or rapporteur is asked to prepare a draft which is sent to members of the committee and deemed to be approved unless there are objections (again by at least one-tenth of the members) within a set time limit of at least 21 days. If there are objections, the amendments drafted are put to the vote at the next meeting.

Treatment of confidential documents in committee

The Parliament is generally a very open institution (see Chapter 16). Committee meetings are normally open to the public and even drafts of reports are freely available. Confidentiality is only applied in a limited number of cases. The problem of access to confidential documents first arose in Parliament's Committee on Budgetary Control, which needed to consult confidential documents in the course of its duties. An agreement on handling these documents was negotiated between the Commission and the Parliament, and adopted by Parliament in February 1989. As a result a new Annex (now Annex VIII) was added to Parliament's Rules of Procedure laying down procedures for the consideration of confidential documents communicated to the European Parliament. Confidentialty also applies to procedures concerning the waiver of the immunity of members of Parliament. Individual members may also request application of these procedures to a particular document, but this request must then be accepted by a majority of two-thirds of the members present.

When the confidential procedure is to be applied, attendance at the relevant part of the committee meeting is restricted (to members of the committee, and only those officials and experts who have been designated in advance by the chair and whose presence is strictly necessary). The relevant documents are numbered and distributed at the meeting, but collected again at the end: no notes of their contents or photocopies may be taken. Procedures are laid down for breach of confidentiality, and the committee chair can set down any penalties, including reprimand, or a short-term or even permanent exclusion from a committee (with a possibility of appeal to a joint meeting of Parliament's Conference of Presidents and the bureau of the relevant committee).

The successive Framework Agreements between the Commission and the Parliament built on this to provide for a much wider range of possibilities than those set out in Annex VIII, ranging from light forms of confidentiality through to much more restrictive forms, such as the option of only involving the committee chair. These options were initially rarely used, but are now beginning to be activated, notably for keeping Parliament informed of the progress of negotiations with third countries.

The development of policies in the security and defence fields over the last few years has raised the issue of access to top secret sensitive information in the field of security and defence policy held by Council. In 2002, Parliament and Council reached an Interinstitutional Agreement whereby documents of this kind could be accessed on Council's premises by the President of Parliament and a special committee chaired by the chair of the Foreign Affairs Committee and composed of four members designated by the Conference of Presidents and cleared for security. Information not classified as "top secret", but merely as "secret" or "confidential" may, by agreement, be further distributed to members of the Foreign Affairs Committee meeting, if necessary, *in camera*. These provisions are also laid down in Annex VIII of the Rules of Procedure.

Subcommittees, temporary committees and other ad hoc structures

Although the committee structure is flexible, there are times when strong pressure is exerted to create new structures, either within the standing committee framework (such as subcommittees or working parties) or outside it (such as temporary committees).

Subcommittees

The European Parliament has never had the complex system of subcommittees that has been established within the US Congress. It has been reluctant to create too many new permanent bodies, notably in view of constraints of staff numbers and of members' time. Only a few subcommittees have been established, notably within the Foreign Affairs, Agriculture and Economic Committees. In the 1994–99 legislature, there were three subcommittees: a subcommittee with 26 members on Security and Disarmament and one of 25 members on Human Rights (both of these within the Committee on Foreign Affairs) and a 24 member subcommittee on Monetary Affairs within the Economic Committee. At the end of the legislature, all three subcommittees were disbanded and the new Parliament confirmed this decision. However, in 2004 two subcommittees were re-established in the Foreign Affairs Committee, one dealing with Human Rights, the other with Security and Defence, the former with 35 members, the latter with 36. They were reconfirmed in 2009.

The degree of autonomy of such subcommittees from the main committee has varied. Before it was promoted to a full committee in 1994, the Fisheries Subcommittee, whose area of responsibility was quite distinct from that of the Agriculture Committee as a whole, had a large measure of autonomy, naming its own rapporteurs, voting on reports (though these still had to be ratified formally by the parent committee) and directly receiving the responsible Commissioners and Council President. The subcommittees reporting to the Foreign Affairs Committee, on the other hand, had little autonomy, and acted instead as fora for preparatory discussions before decisions were taken in the main committee. Relations between the Economic Committee and its Monetary subcommittee were in an intermediate category. Disputes over the subcommittee's degree of autonomy (including who it could invite to its meetings) and spheres of responsibility helped to delay its creation for a considerable time in early 1992 and occasionally resurfaced. The subcommittee had a high profile in the run-up to monetary union, inviting eminent personalities and holding major hearings, but its rapporteurs were chosen by the main committee and when it was examining draft reports it could only make recommendations to the main committee, where the formal votes and decisions were taken.

Temporary or special committees

Temporary committees can take the form of committees of inquiry (discussed in Chapter 15 below), whose work is governed by the treaty and provisions agreed between Parliament, the Council and the Commission. Here the discussion will be restricted to those temporary committees which are not committees of inquiry. Such temporary committees have a term of office of up to 12 months that can be prolonged. They can also submit interim and final resolutions on which Parliament formally votes. They have been renamed "Special Committees" in the 2009 rules revision.

There have been 15 such committees since 1979:

1983 – Parliament commissioned two prominent outside experts, Michel Albert and James Ball, to produce a report on ways to stimulate European economic development. Parliament set up a temporary committee on **European Economic Recovery** to provide the necessary follow-up to the Albert-Ball report. This exercise helped to launch the notion of the "cost of non-Europe" (i.e. the cost to the taxpayer, consumer and business of the continuing fragmentation of the internal market), which served to stimulate the 1992 single market programme.

1984 – Temporary committee on **Budgetary Resources**.

1987 – Temporary committee on the Commission's proposals on "**Making a success of the Single Act**" (the "Delors package"). Lord Plumb, the then President of Parliament, chaired the committee, which had two co-rapporteurs, Enrique Barón (PES) and Karl von Wogau (EPP).

1990 – Temporary committee on the Impact on the European Community of **German Unification** was set up with 25 members, with Fernandez Albor (EPP) as chair and with Alan Donnelly (PES) as general rapporteur. Not without some opposition from the permanent committees, it also became the first temporary committee to be made responsible for the consideration of draft legislation (the necessary European legislation to permit German unification) which it completed before the end of 1990.

1992 – Temporary committee on the Delors II package on **future financing** of the European Community. It had 29 members, with Emilio Colombo (EPP) as chair. To minimise friction with the Budgets Committee the latter's chair, Thomas Von Der Vring (PES) was appointed as the temporary committee's rapporteur.

1994/5 – Temporary committee on **Employment** established with a view to making initial recommendations in time for the European Council in Essen in December 1994, and completing its work by the summer of 1995. It had 36 members, with Celia Villalobos (EPP) as chair and Ken Coates (PES) as rapporteur.

1997 – Temporary committee instructed to monitor the action taken on the recommendations made concerning **BSE** (in the report of the BSE Committee of Inquiry). It had 20 members with Dagmar Roth-Behrendt (PES) as chair and Reimer Böge (EPP) as rapporteur.

2000/1 – Temporary committee established to verify the existence of the communications interception system known as **ECHELON** and to asssess its compatibility with European law. It had 36 members with Carlos Coelho (EPP) as chair and Gerhard Schmid (PES) as rapporteur.

2001 –   Temporary committee set up to examine the problems and opportunities offered in the area of **human genetics** and other new technologies of modern medicine. It had 36 members with Robert Goebbels (PES) as chair and Francesco Fiori (EPP) as rapporteur. The report was rejected by the plenary in November 2001.

2002 –   Temporary committee established to analyse the management of the **foot and mouth** epidemic and to suggest ways of preventing similar outbreaks in the future, with particular regard to vaccination. It had 30 members with Encarnación Redondo Jiménez (EPP) as chair and Wolfgang Kreissl-Dörfler (PES) as rapporteur.

2003/4 –   Temporary committee on **Safety at Sea** invited to examine the causes and consequences of martime disasters, including the *Erika* and the *Prestige*. It had 40 members with Georg Jarzembowski (EPP) as chair and Dirk Sterckx (Liberal) as rapporteur.

2004/5 –   Temporary committee on policy challenges and **budgetary means of the enlarged Union 2007-2013** set up to define the Parliament's political priorities for the future financial perspective in budgetary and legislative terms. Josep Borrell, the Parliament's President, was appointed as chair and Reimer Böge (EPP) as rapporteur.

2006/7 –   Temporary committee on the alleged use of European countries by the CIA for the **transportation and illegal detention of prisoners**. Carlos Coelho (EPP) was chair and Claudio Fava (PES) rapporteur in a committee of 46 members. Its report was adopted at the February 2007 plenary amidst enormous media interest.

2009/11 –   Special committee on the financial, economic and social crisis set up to analyse the extent and impact of the **financial crisis** and to propose appropriate measures. The committee comprised 45 members with Wolf Klinz (ALDE) as chair and Pervenche Berès (S&D) as rapporteur.

2010/11 –   Special committee on the policy challenges and for a sustainable European Union after 2013, aiming to define Parliament's political priorities for the **post-2013 Multiannual Financial Framework**. The Committee comprised 50 members, with Jutta Haug (S&D) as Chair and Salvador Garriga (EPP) as rapporteur.

As can be seen from the above list, no fewer than five temporary or special committees have been to consider the medium term financial perspectives or framework of the Union, generally every seven years. Such committees have had a high profile, sometimes being chaired by the

President of Parliament and often with a prominent member (sometimes the chair) of the budget committee as rapporteur.

Other ad hoc structures

Parliament has used other mechanisms for managing its work that are more ad hoc in nature. In the early years after direct elections a favourite mechanism was working parties inside committees. They were relatively easy to establish (they generally had no official status and required no prior authorisation from Parliament's leadership) and to discontinue, and they enabled committees to respond in a rapid and informal way to shorter-term issues.

Around 25 such working parties were established in the first ten years of the directly elected Parliament, within no fewer than 11 committees. Some lasted for a long time, e.g, Human Rights 1980–84 and Fisheries 1977–85, both of which subsequently became subcommittees, the latter even a full committee in 1994. Others were linked to particular events (e.g, those on the Conference on Security and Cooperation in Europe 1979–80 and on the 1986 Year of the Environment). One of them, the STOA working party, has since evolved into a different type of body (see Chapter 15). Many others were set up to help tackle a particular problem (e.g, those set up within the Budgets Committee on Budgetary Discipline in 1985-86 and Future Financing 1986–89).

More recently, this mechanism has ceased to be used but committees have continued to devise more informal mechanisms to improve their functioning, notably through working groups. An example of this was the Health Working Group set up within the Environment Committee during the 1999/2004 Parliament. It was meant to ensure follow-up to the EU Health Action Programme that had been adopted by the committee and then by the Parliament (after conciliation with the Council) but which the main committee had no time to monitor in detail. The working group included 15 members and met on five occasions, and was re-established after the 2004 elections.

In addition, there are regular attempts to improve coordination between committees to deal with specific problems. A good example was the decision taken in November 2004 to create a "temporary coordination structure" responsible for coordinating the work of the Parliament's committees in monitoring the implementation of the Lisbon Strategy. It was designed to enable the institution to provide a "strong and consistent" position on the mid-term review of the strategy, transcending the particularist positions of the committees.

All such ad hoc structures face formidable difficulties to work properly. They have to compete for scarce resources in terms of meeting rooms and interpretation and translation facilities. Nevertheless, they reflect the recognition that the existing committee structures may not be adapted to deal with all issues that arise and that there always has to be openness to alternative organisational mechanisms to the extent that they do not undemine the central role of the committees in processing the Parliament's work.

Conclusion

Committees in the European Parliament are different from committees in many national parliaments in Europe. In some respects, they are more like committees in the United States Congress, assuming a central role in the establishment of the position of the institution on the whole range of issues, legislative and non-legislative, that come before it. The absence of a governmental majority means that the outcome of committee debates is not determined by the executive but as a result of the interplay between the positions of the different Political Groups.

The relationship between Groups in the committees is marked by a subtle mixture of conflict and cooperation. Disagreements can be profound and can be expressed very forcibly but equally, there is often a strong *esprit de corps* which enables members to find a degree of consensus, particularly when the treaty provisions require absolute majorities in plenary that no Group alone can deliver.

Under such circumstances, individual members can play an important part in influencing the direction of discussions. There is a degree of informality and openness within which relations of trust can develop that transcend political divisions, with members from across the political divide getting to know and sometimes like each other and considering that their interests may be closer than those of colleagues in other committees with different priorities.

The importance of the committees draws in outsiders to come and follow their proceedings. There is often no room to accommodate all those who want to watch the emergence of majorities on different issues. Yet it is the principle of openness of committee meetings that has become a hallmark of the institution and played a major part in differentiating it both from most national parliaments and from other institutions of the European Union.

Table 26: *Committee chairs in the elected Parliament 1979-2009*

Date	Name	Group & Country
1. Foreign Affairs (formerly Political Affairs)		
July 79 – April 80	Emilio COLOMBO	EPP/I
April 80 – July 84	Mariano RUMOR	EPP/I
July 84 – Jan. 87	Roberto FORMIGONI	EPP/I
Jan. 87 – July 89	Sergio ERCINI	EPP/I
July 89 – Feb. 91	Giovanni GORIA	EPP/I
Feb. 91 – Jan. 92	Maria Luisa CASSANMAGNAGO	EPP/I
Jan. 92 – July 94	Enrique BARON	SOC/E
July 94 – Jan. 97	Abel MATUTES	EPP/E
Jan. 97 – July 99	Tom SPENCER	EPP/UK
July 99 – Feb. 07	Elmar BROK	EPP/D
Feb. 07 – July 09	Jacek SARYUSZ-WOLSKI	EPP/PL
July 09 -	Gabriele ALBERTINI	EPP/I

2. Development

July 79 – Dec. 79	Colette FLESCH	LIB/LUX
Dec. 79 – July 84	Michel PONIATOWSKI	LIB/F
July 84 – Jan. 87	Katherina FOCKE	SOC/D
Jan. 87 – July 89	Michael McGOWAN	SOC/UK
July 89 – July 94	Henri SABY	SOC/F
July 94 – Jan. 97	Bernard KOUCHNER	SOC/F
Jan. 97 – July 99	Michel ROCARD	SOC/F
July 99 – Jan. 04	Joaquim MIRANDA	GUE/P
Feb. 04 – July 04	Max VAN DEN BERG (acting chair)	SOC/NL
July 04 – Jan. 07	Luisa MORGANTINI	GUE/I
Jan. 07 – July 09	Josep BORRELL	SOC/E
July 09 -	Eva JOLY	GREEN/F

3. International Trade (formerly External Economic Relations)

July 79 – July 84	Sir Fred CATHERWOOD	ED/UK
July 84 – Jan. 87	Dame Shelagh ROBERTS	ED/UK
Jan. 87 – July 89	Jacques MALLET	RDE/F
June 89 – Jan. 97	Willy DE CLERCQ	LIB/B
Jan. 97 – Sept. 98	Luciana CASTELLINA	GUE/I
Sept. 98 – July 99	Philippe A. R. HERZOG	GUE/F

(merged with Industry, Research and Energy Committee in 1999 but recreated in 2004)

July 04 – Jan. 07	Enrique BARON	SOC/E
Jan. 07 – July 09	Helmuth MARKOV	GUE/D
July 09 -	Vital MOREIRA	SOC/P

4. Budgets

July 79 – July 84	Erwin LANGE	SOC/D
July 84 – July 89	Jean-Pierre COT	SOC/F
July 89 – July 94	Thomas VON DER VRING	SOC/D
July 94 – July 99	Detlev SAMLAND	SOC/D
July 99 – July 04	Terry WYNN	SOC/UK
July 04 – Jan. 07	Janusz LEWANDOWSKI	EPP/PL
Jan. 07 – July 09	Reimer BÖGE	EPP/D
July 09 -	Alain LAMASSOURE	EPP/F

5. Budgetary Control

July 79 – March 88	Heinrich AIGNER	EPP/D
June 88 – July 89	Konrad SCHÖN	EPP/D
July 89 – Jan. 92	Peter PRICE	ED/UK
Jan. 92 – March 93	Alain LAMASSOURE	PP/F
April 93 – July 94	Jean-Louis BOURLANGES	EPP/F
July 94 – July 04	Diemut THEATO	EPP/D
July 04 – Jan. 07	Szabolcs FAZAKAS	SOC/HU
Jan. 07 – July 09	Herbert BÖSCH	SOC/A
July 09 -	Luigi DE MAGISTRIS	LIB/I

6. Economic & Monetary Affairs

July 79 – July 81	Jacques DELORS	SOC/F
June 81 – July 84	Jacques MOREAU	SOC/F

July 84 – Jan. 87	Barry SEAL	SOC/UK
Jan. 87 – July 94	Bouke BEUMER	EPP/NL
July 94 – July 99	Karl VON WOGAU	EPP/D
July 99 – July 04	Christa RANDZIO-PLATH	SOC/D
July 04 – July 09	Pervenche BERÈS	SOC/F
July 09 –	Sharon BOWLES	LIB/UK

7. Employment & Social Affairs

July 79 – Jan. 82	Frans VAN DER GUN	EPP/NL
Jan. 82 – July 84	Efstratios PAPAEFSTRATIOU	EPP/GR
July 84 – Jan. 87	Michael WELSH	ED/UK
Jan. 87 – July 87	Rodolfo CRESPO	SOC/P
July 87 – Feb. 88	Jorge CAMPINOS	SOC/P
Feb. 88 – July 89	Fernando GOMES	SOC/P
July 89 – Nov. 89	Hedy D'ANCONA	SOC/NL
Nov. 89 – July 94	Wim VAN VELZEN	SOC/NL
July 94 – July 99	Stephen HUGHES	SOC/UK
July 99 – Jan. 02	Michel ROCARD	SOC/F
Jan. 02 – July 04	Theo BOUWMAN	GREEN/NL
July 04 – Jan. 07	Ottaviano DEL TURCO	SOC/I
Jan. 07 – July 09	Jan ANDERSSON	SOC/S
July 09 -	Pervenche BERÈS	SOC/F

8. Environment, Public Health and Food Safety

July 79 – July 84	Ken COLLINS	SOC/UK
July 84 – July 89	Beate WEBER	SOC/D
July 89 – July 99	Ken COLLINS	SOC/UK
July 99 – July 04	Caroline JACKSON	EPP/UK
July 04 – Jan. 07	Karl-Heinz FLORENZ	EPP/D
Jan. 07 – July 09	Miroslav OUSKÝ	EPP/CZ
July 09 -	Jo LEINEN	SOC/D

9. Industry, Research and Energy (acquired Trade and Industry in 1999 but lost Trade in 2004)

July 79 – July 84	Hanna WALZ	EPP/D
July 84 – July 89	Michel PONIATOWSKI	LIB/F
July 89 – Jan. 92	Antonio LA PERGOLA	SOC/I
Jan. 92 – Sept.94	Claude DESAMA	SOC/B
Sept.94 – July 99	Umberto SCAPAGNINI	FE then EPP/I
July 99 – May 03	Carlos WESTENDORP	SOC/E
May 03 – July 04	Luis BERENGUER	SOC/E
July 04 – Jan. 07	Giles CHICHESTER	EPP/UK
Jan. 07 – July 09	Angelika NIEBLER	EPP/D
July 09 –	Herbert REUL	EPP/D

10. Transport & Tourism (merged with Regional Policy in 1999 and separated again in 2004)

July 79 – July 84	Horst SEEFELD	SOC/D
July 84 – July 89	Giorgios ANASTASSOPOULOS	EPP/GR
July 89 – Jan. 92	Rui AMARAL	LIB/P
Jan. 92 – July 94	Nel VAN DIJK	GREEN/NL
July 94 – Jan. 97	Petrus CORNELISSEN	EPP/NL
Jan. 97 – July 99	Jean-Pierre BAZIN	UPE/F

July 99 – Jan.02	Konstantinos HATZIDAKIS	EPP/GR
Jan. 02 – Sept. 03	Luciano CAVERI	LIB/I
Sept. 03 – July 09	Paolo COSTA	LIB/I
July 09 –	Brian SIMPSON	SOC/UK

11. Internal Market and Consumer Protection

July 2004 – Jan. 06	Philip WHITEHEAD	SOC/UK
Jan. 06 – July 09	Arlene McCARTHY	SOC/UK
July 09 –	Malcolm HARBOUR	ECR/UK

12. Regional Development

July 79 – July 89	Pancrazio DE PASQUALE	COM/I
July 89 – Jan. 92	Antoine WAECHTER	GREEN/F
Jan. 92 – July 94	Antonio GUTIERREZ	GUE/E
July 94 – Jan. 97	Roberto SPECIALE	SOC/I
Jan. 97 – July 99	Miguel ARIAS	EPP/E
(merged with Transport Committee in 1999 and recreated in 2004)		
July 04 – July 09	Gerardo GALEOTE	EPP/E
July 09 –	Danuta Maria HÜBNER	EPP/PL

13. Agriculture & Rural Development

July 79 – Oct. 82	Sir Henry PLUMB	ED/UK
Oct. 82 – July 84	David CURRY	ED/UK
July 84 – Jan. 87	Teun TOLMAN	EPP/NL
Jan. 87 – Jan. 92	Juan Luis COLINO	SOC/E
Jan. 92 – July 94	Franco BORGO	EPP/I
July 94 – Jan. 97	Christian JACOB	RDE/F
Jan. 97 – July 99	Juan Luis COLINO	SOC/E
July 99 – Jan. 02	Friedrich-Wilhelm GRAEFE ZU BARINGDORF	GREEN/D
Jan. 02 – Jan. 07	Joseph DAUL	EPP/F
Jan. 07 – July 09	Neil PARISH	EPP/UK
July 09 -	Paolo DE CASTRO	SOC/I

14. Fisheries (created 1994)

July 94 – Jan. 97	Miguel ARIAS	EPP/E
Jan. 97 – July 99	Carmen FRAGA	EPP/S
July 99 – Jan.02	Daniel VARELA	EPP/E
Jan. 02 – July 04	Struan STEVENSON	EPP/UK
July 04 – July 09	Philippe MORILLON	LIB/F
July 09 –	Carmen FRAGA	EPP/E

15. Culture and Education

July 79 – Jan. 82	Mario PEDINI	EPP/I
Jan. 82 – July 84	Bouke BEUMER	EPP/NL
July 84 – Jan. 87	Winnie EWING	RDE/UK
Jan. 87 – July 89	Eileen LEMASS	RDE/IRL
July 89 – Jan. 92	Roberto BARZANTI	GUE/I
Jan. 92 – July 94	Antonio LA PERGOLA	SOC/I
July 94 – Jan. 97	Luciana CASTELLINA	GUE/I

Jan. 97 – July 99	Peter PEX	EPP/NL
July 99 – Jan. 02	Giuseppe GARGANI	EPP/I
Jan. 02 – July 04	Michel ROCARD	SOC/F
July 04 – Sept. 07	Nikolaos SIFUNAKIS	SOC/GR
Nov. 07 – July 09	Katerina BATZELI	SOC/GR
July 09 –	Doris PACK	EPP/D

16. Legal Affairs

July 79 – Jan. 82	Mauro FERRI	SOC/I
Jan. 82 – July 84	Simone VEIL	LIB/F
July 84 – Jan. 87	Marie-Claude VAYSSADE	SOC/F
Jan. 87 –	Sir Christopher PROUT	ED/UK
Jan. 87 – July 89	Baroness Diana ELLES	ED/UK
July 89 – Nov. 92	Graf STAUFFENBERG	EPP/D
Feb. 93 – June 93	Reinhold BOCKLET	EPP/D
June 93 – July 94	Siegbert ALBER	EPP/D
July 94 – Jan. 97	Carlo CASINI	PPE/I
Jan. 97 – July 99	Willy DE CLERCQ	LIB/B
July 99 – Jan. 02	Ana PALACIO	EPP/E
Jan. 02 – July 09	Giuseppe GARGANI	EPP/I
July 09 -	Klaus-Heiner LEHNE	EPP/D

17. Civil Liberties, Justice and Home Affairs (created 1992)

Jan. 92 – July 94	Amadée TURNER	ED/UK
July 94 – Oct. 95	Antonio VITORINO	SOC/P
Nov. 95 – Jan. 97	Luis MARINHO	SOC/P
Jan. 97 – July 99	Hedy D'ANCONA	SOC/NL
July 99 – Jan 02	Graham WATSON	LIB/UK
Jan.02 – July 02	Ana PALACIO	EPP/E
Sept. 02 – July 04	Jorge HERNANDEZ	EPP/E
July 04 – Feb. 05	Jean-Louis BOURLANGES	LIB/F
Feb.05 – Jan. 08	Jean-Marie CAVADA	LIB/F
Jan. 08 – July 09	Gérard DEPREZ	LIB/B
July 09 –	Juan Fernando LÓPEZ AGUILAR	SOC/E

18. Constitutional Affairs (created Jan. 82 as Institutional Affairs; merged in 1999 with Rules to form Constitutional)

Jan. 82 – July 84	Mauro FERRI	SOC/I
July 84 – May 86	Altiero SPINELLI	COM/I
June 86 – July 89	Sergio SEGRE	COM/I
July 89 – June 93	Marcelino OREJA	EPP/E
June 93 – July 93	Derek PRAG	EPP/UK
July 93 – July 94	José Maria GIL ROBLES	EPP/E
July 94 – Jan. 97	Fernando MORAN	SOC/E
Jan. 97 – July 99	Biagio DE GIOVANNI	SOC/I
July 99 – July 04	Giorgio NAPOLITANO	SOC/I
July 04 – July 09	Jo LEINEN	SOC/D
July 09 –	Carlo CASINI	EPP/I

19. Women's Rights and Gender Equality (created Jan. 1982 as temp. committee, later permanent)

Jan. 82–July 84	Maria CINCIARI RODANO	COM/I
July 84–Jan. 87	Marlene LENZ	EPP/D
Jan. 87–July 89	Hedy D'ANCONA	SOC/NL
July 89–July 94	Christine CRAWLEY	SOC/UK
July 94 – July 98	Nel VAN DIJK	GREEN/NL
July 98 – July 99	Heidi HAUTALA	V/FIN
July 99 – Jan. 02	Maj Britt THEORIN	SOC/S
Jan. 02 – July 04	Anna KARAMANOU	SOC/GR
July 04 – July 09	Anna ZABORSKA	EPP/SK
July 09 –	Eva-Britt SVENSSON	GUE/S

20. Petitions

Jan. 87 – July 89	Raphäel CHANTERIE	EPP/B
July 89 – Jan. 92	Viviane REDING	EPP/LUX
Jan. 92 – July 94	Rosi BINDI	EPP/I
July 94 – Jan. 97	Eddie NEWMAN	SOC/UK
Jan. 97 – July 99	Allesandro FONTANA	EPP/I
July 99 – July 04	Vitalino GEMELLI	EPP/I
July 04 – July 09	Marcin LIBICKI	UEN/PL
July 09 –	Erminia MAZZONI	EPP/I

21. Rules (until 1987 Rules and Petitions; merged with Institutional in 1999)

July 79 – July 84	Kai NYBORG	RDE/DK
July 84 – July 89	Guiseppe AMADEI	SOC/I
July 89 – Jan. 92	Marc GALLE	SOC/B
Jan. 92 – July 94	Florus WIJSENBEEK	LIB/NL
July 94 – July 99	Ben FAYOT	SOC/LUX

Note: *The credentials of new members were verified in a small separate committee from 1981 to 1987 (previously by Legal Committee). Chairs were FERRI (Legal Committee 1981-82), Tom MEGAHY (SOC/UK) 1982-84 and Dieter ROGALLA (SOC/D) 1984-87.The verification of credentials was the responsibility of the Rules Committee from 1987-89 and is now undertaken by the Legal Affairs Committee.*

8. Interparliamentary delegations

Parliament has developed a network of links with countries outside the European Union and in particular, with its counterparts in the parliamentary bodies of those countries. It has a structure of delegations to maintain these links, many of which respond to specific obligations that arise from international agreements between the European Union and third countries. This structure combines five different kinds of delegations:

1.– delegations to joint parliamentary committees (JPCs), formally established as part of association agreements signed by the EU with third countries that include a Joint Council at ministerial level, notably countries that have applied for EU membership;
2.– delegations to parliamentary cooperation committees, also formally established under agreements (partnership & cooperation agreements) signed between these countries and the EU;
3.– delegations designed to foster parliamentary contacts between the EU and the countries concerned and set up by the Parliament itself or as a result of other kinds of agreement between the country and the EU;
4.– delegations to the ACP-EU, EUROMED, EUROLAT and EURONEST Parliamentary Assemblies and other interparliamentary assemblies, such as that of NATO; and
5.– ad hoc delegations, in particular those invited to join election observation missions.

Historical development

At the beginning of the 2009-14 legislature there were 40 parliamentary delegations, linking the institution with parliaments outside the European Union. This reflected a dramatic growth in the importance of the external representation of the Parliament since the first direct elections. In the early 1980s, Parliament's external relations were essentially linked to specific agreements made between the European Community and third countries. There was one joint parliamentary committee (JPC), namely with Turkey, which had been established as a result of the 1963 Association Agreement. Parliament had also been sending delegations to the ACP-EEC Consultative Assembly, set up under the Lomé agreement with the countries of Africa, the Caribbean and the Pacific, since 1976, and indeed to its predecessor under the Yaoundé agreements since 1964. In addition, from 1979 delegations were set up with the Maghreb and Mashreq countries and with Israel as a direct result of agreements between the EU and the countries concerned, which called for the "necessary co-operation and contacts" between parliaments.

The first interparliamentary delegation to be set up independent of any specific international agreement, was to the United States in 1972. It was to be the forerunner of a whole range of such delegations. These were often set up on a proposal from the parliament of the country concerned, such as the Japanese Diet in 1978 or South Korea, which mounted a successful diplomatic effort in 1985–86 with a view to having its parliament accepted as a "partner", in the Parliament's system of interparliamentary delegations.

In the 1990s, with the fall of the iron curtain and the large number of applications to join the EU, JPCs grew in importance relative to other delegations. In 1992, their number rose from one (Turkey) to four when Austria was added following the Commission's favourable opinion on its application to join the EU, and Cyprus and Malta gained JPC status because, like Turkey, they had association agreements with the Community and had also recently applied for membership. JPCs were then set up with Finland, Norway and Sweden, once the Commission had delivered favourable opinions on their applications to join the EU. Although JPCs were disbanded following the relevant accessions, their number continued to grow with the signing of association agreements with the ten Central and Eastern European countries, which all contained "parliamentary clauses", requiring the setting up of JPCs between the European Parliament and the associated countries' parliaments. These lasted nearly a decade, being disbanded once the countries concerned became members of the EU in May 2004 and January 2007. Now, the number of JPCs with applicant countries stands at three: Croatia, Macedonia (FYROM) and Turkey. In addition, there are now JPCs with Mexico and Chile arising from specific EU agreements with those countries as well as with the European Economic Area (EEA). It is likely that the near future will see the establishment of JPCs with Iceland (because of its application to join the EU), Albania (as a result of a provision in its Stability and Association Agreement with the EU) and Morocco (out of its sheer political pressure to have a JPC). The latter two cases will create JPCs inside existing regional delegations for the Western Balkans and the Maghreb respectively.

Similar clauses in the "partnership and cooperation agreements" signed by the EU with various countries of the former Soviet Union provide for the setting up of a new type of body, called "parliamentary cooperation committees". Such committees exist already for Russia, Ukraine, Moldova, Armenia, Azerbaijan, Georgia, Kazakhstan, Kyrgyzstan, and Uzbekistan and are being established progressively for other countries as the agreements enter into force.

Number and composition of delegations

Since the first direct elections in 1979, Parliament has set up its delegations at the same time as (or just after) its committees, by way of formal decision. These decisions lay down the total number and areas of responsibility of delegations, and over time reflect the evolving political situation. As the table below indicates, their size can vary considerably, currently from 10 members on the NATO assembly delegation to 53 members on the delegation to the US Congress, the largest bilateral delegation, and 79 to the multilateral ACP Assembly.

The historical growth in the number of delegations has meant that ever more members of the Parliament have taken part in the work of at least one delegation. In 1989 there were 375 places on 27 delegations in a Parliament of 518 members; by 2004 the figure had increased substantially with 664 places on 34 delegations; by 2009, there were 944 places on 40 delegations. Even without the 273 places on the various Parliamentary Assemblies, many of which deliberately comprise members of delegations to the component countries who are therefore members of both, virtually all MEPs who want to can now have a seat on a delegation.

The number of members on delegations has been a source of controversy. On the one hand, there is a concern to limit numbers, given the cost as well as the sometimes negative impact that large groups of travelling MEPs have had on public opinion; on the other hand, there is a need to avoid offending countries which may see in a reduction in the number of members or of meetings a statement about the attitude of the EU towards them. In 1999 a change was introduced whereby each delegation chair was invited to take a decision as to how many members should travel for "away" meetings. Selection would be on the basis of the areas of activity of each member of the delegation, frequency of participation in preparatory meetings, interest shown, etc. Such a rule does not always reduce the number of participants: in the case of the Joint Parliamentary Assemblies, for example, the number of MEPs has to match the number of delegates from the partner bodies. Nevertheless, it does contribute towards a general reduction in costs and tighter and more focused meetings.

Leadership of the delegations

Each delegation is led by a chair and, in most cases, two vice-chairs who are elected by the delegation in the same manner as committee chairs. In practice, the Groups share out these positions in proportion to their size, using the d'Hondt formula. This achieves a reasonable spread, as reflected in the table below, whereby all but one Group in the Parliament and 15 nationalities (including five new Member States) have delegation chair posts.

Table 27: *Parliamentary delegations, with number of members and chairs (September 2010)*

Delegation	No. of Members	Chair
Delegations to parliamentary Assemblies		
ACP Assembly	79	Michel (ALDE, Belgium)
EUROMED Assembly	49	President of Parliament
EUROLAT Assembly	75	Salafranca (EPP, Spain)
EURONEST Assembly	60	Vigenin (S&D, Bulgaria)
NATO Assembly	10	Saryusz-Wolski (EPP, Poland)
Delegations to Joint Parliamentary Committees (JPCs):		
Croatia	15	Hökmark (EPP, Sweden)
FYR Macedonia	13	Chatzimarkakis (ALDE, Germany)

Turkey	25	Flautre (Greens, France)
Mexico	14	Jauregui (S&D, Spain)
Chile	15	Muniz de Urquiza (S&D, Spain)
Caricorum	15	David Martin (S&D, UK)
EEA	17	Gallagher (ALDE, Ireland)

(the EEA delegation also serves as the interparliamentary delegation for Switzerland, Iceland and Norway and supplies the EP representatives to the Nordic Council, to the Conference of Parliamentarians of the Arctic Region and to the Baltic Sea Parliamentary Conference)

Delegations to Parliamentary Cooperation Committees

Russia	31	Fleckenstein (S&D, Germany)
Ukraine	16	Kowal (ECR, Poland)
Moldova	14	Macovei (EPP, Romania)
Armenia, Azerbaijan, Georgia	18	Cabrnoch (ECR, Czech)
Central Asian countries & Mongolia	19	Bartolozzi (EPP, Italy)

Other Interparliamentary Delegations

Western Balkan countries	8	Kukan (EPP, Slovakia)
Belarus	12	Protasiewicz (EPP, Poland)
Israel	22	Belder (EFD, Netherland)
Palestinian Legislative Council	22	De Rossa (S&D, Ireland)
Maghreb countries & Maghreb Union	18	Panzeri (S&D, Italy)
Mashrek countries	18	David (EPP, Portugal)
Arab peninsula & GCC	15	Niebler (EPP, Germany)
Iraq	12	Stevenson (ECR, UK)
Iran	18	Lochbihler (Green, Germany)
United States	53	Brok (EPP, Germany)
Canada	17	Bradbourn (ECR, UK)
Central America	15	Bozkurt (S&D, Netherlands)
Andean Community	12	Garcia-Margallo (EPP, Spain)
MERCOSUR	19	Yanes-Barnuevo (S&D, Spain)
Japan	25	van Baalen (ALDE, Nethrlands)
China	39	Rivellini (EPP, Italy)
India	20	Watson (ALDE, UK)
Afghanistan	13	Berman (S&D, Netherlands)
South Asia (rest of)	16	Lambert (Greens, UK)
South East Asia and ASEAN	22	Langen (EPP, Germany)
Korean Peninsula	14	Ehler (EPP, Germany)
Australia & New Zealand	16	Bizzotto (EFD, Italy)
South Africa	13	Cashman (S&D, UK)
Pan African Parliament	12	Gahler (EPP, Germany)

(the ASEAN delegation is also responsible for relations with AIPO, the ASEAN Inter-parliamentary Organisation) In addition to the above delegations, the Asia - Europe Parliamentary Partnership (ASEP) offers the opportunity for parliamentarians from the national parliaments of the EU Member States and the EP to meet their counterparts from Asia, meeting roughly every two years since 1996. ASEP has become the parliamentary arm of the Asia - Europe Meeting (ASEM), giving parliamentary guidance to ASEM and involving parliaments in the implementation of ASEM initiatives.

With such a large number of delegations, even very small Groups can claim a post, something that has occasionally resulted in controversy. In 1989 members of the then Group of the Right were nominated as chair of the delegation to Switzerland and vice-chair of the delegation to Israel (a German Republikaner was the nominee for the latter post). These nominations were unpopular with the countries concerned, and were also successfully challenged from within the Parliament itself, to the anger of the Group of the Right (see section on Order in the Chamber in Chapter 9). Subsequently, from

1995 to 1997, the Canadian parliament refused to cooperate with Parliament's delegation. It objected to the fact that the delegation was chaired by a French "Europe of Nations" Group member, Georges Berthu, a vocal supporter of independence for Quebec. The Parliament, in this case, refused to respond to the Canadians' call to find a new chair, taking the view that the choice was a prerogative of the institution and should not be influenced by outsiders. As a result there was a break of more than three years between successive meetings of the delegation with its Canadian counterparts. In the current Parliament, there are no problems of that kind.

The role of delegations

Delegations have a range of tasks. The most obvious of these is to ensure a continuous dialogue and a network of contacts with parliamentary bodies in third countries or in regional organisations, to exchange information on topical issues, to provide parliamentary backing for the Union's external policies, and generally to provide a political counterpart to the work of the Commission and Council in this area. The members concerned also build up knowledge and expertise which may be particularly useful at times of developments of particular importance to the Union, such as possible accession to the EU, or conclusion of an association agreement, or simply a parliamentary debate on a country.

Delegations have regularly monitored the situation regarding the observance of human rights. An EP delegation was the first ever to be permitted to visit Tibet, in late 1991, where it raised questions of human rights violations. The delegation for relations with the Central Asian Republics was active in the 1990s in encouraging the Parliament to delay giving its assent on the Partnership and Cooperation Agreements with Kazakhstan and Uzbekistan, following concerns over human rights. Parliament insisted on specific improvements before going ahead with its vote in March 1999. Subsequently, concerns about the situation in Zimbabwe led to the cancellation of the 5th session of the ACP-EU Joint Parliamentary Assembly in November 2002 following the decision to include in the Zimbabwe delegation two ministers who were on the EU travel ban list.

An EP delegation may also use information it acquires to bring influence to bear on other EU institutions rather than on the partner country. This was the case in 1993, when Parliament's CIS delegation received numerous complaints from various former Soviet republics regarding the administration of the TACIS (Technical Assistance to the Commonwealth of Independent States) programme. Too much of the aid money was allegedly being spent on financing studies, often by European consultants, and not enough was actually going in assistance to the beneficiary countries. The delegation, with the help of the Budgets Committee, put in an amendment to the budget effectively freezing part of the 1994 TACIS funds until the Commission, which administered the programme, had made the necessary changes. The Commissioner responsible, Sir Leon Brittan, appeared before the delegation, and promised to set in train appropriate improvements and changes. These were duly implemented, and Parliament was able to release the funds from the budgetary reserve. Today, it is routine business for delegations to scrutinise budgetary expenditure when visiting a recipient country.

JPCs have in recent years been of particular importance as they operate in the context of association agreements between the EU and third countries, notably but not exclusively for those who are seeking accession to the Union. They examine the workings of the association agreement; receive the Association Council's annual report and make appropriate recommendations linked to the progress of the accession negotiations. The discussions can often be heated as, for example, in the debates on the closure of unsafe units in nuclear power plants in Bulgaria and Lithuania.

Each delegation generally holds an annual interparliamentary meeting, alternately in the Parliament and in the partner country. However, the US delegation traditionally meets twice a year, once in the United States and once in Europe. The same applies to the Russian delegation and to the JPCs. Delegations which deal with a geopolitical region rather than with a single country may try to visit two or more of their partners during a single trip abroad, or send a small working party to each, and may likewise host visits in Europe from more than one parliament in a given year.

Besides the interparliamentary meetings, regular meetings of the delegation are held in Brussels and Strasbourg at which members of the delegation discuss current affairs in the country concerned and, if a joint meeting is due, discuss the agendas of the visits and the issues to be raised. Ambassadors of the countries accredited to the EU, as well as Commissioners and Commission officials, are often invited to these meetings to brief members.

Relations with the rest of the Parliament

The relationship between delegations and Parliament as a whole has not always proved easy. The delegations generally operate in an informal way, and are thus not subject to too many political constraints. They must, however, closely reflect the Parliament's resolutions and policy positions if they make any formal declarations during meetings. Working documents drawn up for delegations follow the same rule, as must those members who are appointed as lead speakers for the delegation on any particular policy issue. Members expressing a purely personal or Political Group point of view are meant to make this clear.

Despite these rules, there is still a concern to avoid the risk of divergence between the official position of the Parliament and what the members of a delegation say or do. Delegations do not formally adopt reports for the attention of the Parliament as a whole. However, the chairs of delegations must always submit a written report to the Foreign Affairs Committee (and where appropriate, the Development Committee). Other interested committees are also informed of the results of the delegation meetings. More generally, coordination between delegations and Parliament's standing committees is now a requirement laid down in Annex VII the Rules of Procedure. When a group of parliamentarians from a third country visits Strasbourg or Brussels, periods of an hour or more are often set aside for joint discussions between them and members of Parliament's relevant committees.

In the same spirit, delegations seek to involve other MEPs in their work. They can, for example, invite rapporteurs or other qualified committee members to accompany them when their visit relates to the work in committee. In March 1999, for example, Terry Wynn accompanied the relevant delegation on its visit to South Africa, after he had been made rapporteur for the Budgetary Control Committee on a report prepared by the Court of Auditors relating to aid to South Africa. In the same year, the delegation for relations with the United States decided to launch the so-called Transatlantic Legislators' Dialogue, with a view to expanding contacts between the EU and the US. This mechanism has been used to set up tele-conferences between members outside as well as inside the delegation inter-ested in discussing topics of mutual concern with their counterparts in the Congress. Thus members of the Environment Committee were able to hold a robust debate with American Congressmen on the response to climate change and the members of Parliament's Working Group with the Middle East had an equally outspoken exchange with their US counterparts.

As the role and number of delegations has increased, their functioning has had to be subject to greater forward planning and to more formalised rules. The activities of the delegations are co-ordinated by a Conference of Delegation Chairs. The chair of this meeting is elected by the other chairs and may be invited to attend the relevant meetings of the Conference of Presidents and the Bureau of Parliament. Amongst the duties of the Conference is the preparation of a calendar of future interparliamentary meetings. The Conference of Presidents then adopts their suggested calen-dar after consulting the Foreign Affairs, Development and Trade Commit-tees. The Conference of Delegation Chairs also draws up implementing provisions for the functioning of delegations, for approval by the Confer-ence of Presidents. These rules codify and formalise the working practices developed over the years and are regularly updated.

Parliamentary Assemblies

The Parliament now participates in four Parliamentary Assemblies:

- the **ACP-EU Joint Parliamentary Assembly**: although formally established only in 2000, this is the culmination of more than forty years of contacts between the ACP and EU countries in a previous "Joint Assembly" first established by the 1963 Yaoundé Convention to provide joint parliamentary scrutiny of the far reaching agreements with developing countries (almost all former colonies of various European countries) in Africa, the Carribean and the Pacific.

- the **Euromed Parliamentary Assembly**: this was formally estab-lished in 2004, emerging from the Euro-Mediterranean Parliamentary Forum set up under the 1995 Barcelona Decla-ration and bringing together parliamentarians from countries neighbouring the Mediterranean, and nowadays considers itself to be the parliamentary institution of the Union for the Mediterranean.

- the **Euro-Latin American Parliamentary Assembly**: this was cre-ated by a summit of Heads of State and government of EU and Latin American countries in Vienna in May 2006. It replaced the biennial EP-Latin American Parliamentary Conference, which had taken place every two years from 1974. It held its constituent meeting in Brussels in November 2006.

- the **Euronest Parliamentary Assembly**: this is the parliamentary layer of the recently established (May 2009 in Prague) Eastern Partnership of the EU , with its constituent meeting in Brussels in 2010.

In addition, in 2002, the NATO Parliamentary Assembly invited the European Parliament to upgrade their mutual relations and to nominate 10 members to a formal delegation. The Parliament representatives enjoy observer status at the Assembly and may take the floor, both in committee and in plenary. Parliament used to send members as observers to the WEU Assembly, but no longer does so, as this body is now redundant.

The ACP-EU Joint Parliamentary Assembly

Parliament's day-to-day work on development issues is carried out by its Committee on Development & Cooperation. However, in the specific context of relations with African, Caribbean and Pacific countries, Parliament nominates a delegation to a wider body, the ACP-EU Joint Parliamentary Assembly. It is a much larger-scale event than any of the bilateral delegation meetings described in the rest of this chapter. In fact, as it is based on the 2000 Cotonou Agreement between the ACP countries and the EU, it is best viewed as an international parliamentary body in its own right and not simply a forum where delegations from the European Parliament and the ACP countries meet. Its treaty basis makes it an international law obligation on the Parliament, unlike other interparliamentary assemblies whose legal bases are less binding.

The two Yaoundé and four Lomé Conventions, followed by the Cotonou Agreement signed in 2000 for a 20 year duration, have set up a unique instrument of cooperation between a group of developed and a group of developing countries. The main features are: access to the European Union for ACP products, notably free access for manufactured products (other than goods in the agricultural sector); financial cooperation and aid; and ongoing dialogue about the ACP countries' economic policies and EU support for those policies.

This Assembly brings together 156 participants, 78 MEPs and 78 representatives of the parliaments of the ACP countries, in the presence of the Council and the EU Commissioner responsible for development policy. It meets twice a year – once in the EU and once in an ACP country. The meetings in ACP countries rotate around the different ACP Regions, of which there are seven (Pacific, Caribbean and five in Africa). In November 2009, for example, the Assembly met in Luanda. The meetings in Europe have recently been held in the country holding the Council Presidency (for example, Prague in March 2009). Plenary meetings have also been held on the premises of the Parliament. However, the last time that this was envisaged, in the autumn of 2002, the meeting had to be cancelled after the European Parliament decided to deny access to members of the Zimbabwean delegation subject to the EU travel ban. In addition, a new departure in the Cotonou Agreement, not included in previous conventions, was a provision allowing the Joint Parliamentary Assembly to hold regional or sub-regional parliamentary meetings. Parliament's and the ACP's secretariat jointly provide the administrative facilities for all these meetings.

A Bureau (each side nominating a co-president and twelve vice-presidents) is elected for a term of one year (frequently renewed: on Parliament's side now for five years, and on the ACP side, for two years) to manage day-to-day affairs and to ensure continuity in the work of the Assembly. Since direct elections Parliament's co-presidents have been as follows:

Table 28: *European Parliament Co-Presidents of ACP Assembly*

1979 –1989	Giovanni Bersani (EPP, Italy)
1989 –1991	Leo Tindemans (EPP, Belgium)
1991 –1994	Marie-Luisa Cassanmagnago (EPP, Italy)
1994 – 1999	Lord Plumb (Conservative, UK)
1999 – 2002	John Corrie (Conservative, UK)
2002 – 2009	Glenys Kinnock (Labour, UK)
2009 –	Louis Michel (Liberal, Belgium)

New rules adopted in 2002 provided for the creation of three standing committees to replace the previous system of ad hoc working parties: a Political Affairs Committee, responsible for promoting democratic processes through dialogue and consultation; an Economic Development, Finance & Trade Committee, responsible inter alia for the implementation of the European Development Fund; and a Social Affairs & Environment Committee.

These committees each adopt resolutions on the basis of proposals drafted by co-rapporteurs, which are then forwarded to the full Assembly for it to consider, amend and adopt. The Assembly also examines two urgency resolutions on themes adopted by the Bureau and appropriate compromises and composites are then negotiated. In addition, there is a question time period with the ACP-EU Council of Ministers (both ACP and EU Council Presidents-in-Office) and the Commissioner for Development being invited to respond, as well as the possibility of written questions.

The Assembly's current priorities include support of democratisation and human rights, conflict prevention, regional cooperation, rural development, the local processing of and trade in commodities, better coordination of the Union's development policies with its other policies and the need to promote training in and technology transfer to the developing countries. From 2003 it extended its activities to informal scrutiny of spending under the European Development Fund, over which democratic control is otherwise weak, and trade, which became a priority with the prospect of the negotiation of the Economic Partnership Agreements (EPAs) provided for by the Cotonou Agreement. Recently, the joint examination of country strategy papers being worked out between the European Commission and a specific country has become a key aspect of its work.

Feedback is provided from the Assembly meetings into Parliament's work as a whole mainly through the Parliament's Development Committee. It can draw up reports on specific problems identified at JPA sessions as well as preparing an annual report on its work. Despite the weakness of the

ACP-EU Council, which is usually attended by very few European ministers (often only the President-in-Office), the Assembly has acquired an importance that goes far beyond the role that it is allotted formally under the text of the Cotonou Convention.

The Euromed Parliamentary Assembly (EMPA)

The European Parliament has been active for a decade in the development of dialogue with the parliaments of countries bordering the Mediterranean as part of the so-called Barcelona process. Initially these efforts were channelled through four interparliamentary delegations (Maghreb, Mashreq, Israel and the Palestinian Council) and one JPC (Turkey). However, in 1998 the EP and parliaments of the signatory countries of the Barcelona process held the first meeting in Brussels of a broader body, named the Euro-Mediterranean Forum. The Forum agreed in 2001 to establish three working parties to ensure the continuity of its activities and from 2002 devoted considerable energy to transforming itself into a Parliamentary Assembly.

Agreement on this transformation was reached by national ministers in Naples in December 2003 and the Euromed Parliamentary Assembly was formally set up in March 2004. It brings together on an annual basis 49 representatives of the European Parliament, 81 from EU Member State parliaments (3 each), ten from five other European Mediterranean countries (2 each), 130 from the ten founding non-European Mediterranean partner country parliaments (13 each) and 10 from Mauritania – a total of 280 (140 from Europe, 140 from North Africa and Asia Minor, Turkey being classified in the latter group for this purpose).

The Presidency of the Assembly is held for one year at a time, alternating between Europe and a partner country (and within Europe alternating between the European and a national parliament). Thus, the Presidents of the Egyptian, European, Tunisian and Greek Parliaments assumed the office successively from March 2004 to March 2008 and those of the European, Jordanian, Italian and Moroccan Parliaments from March 2008 to March 2012. In September 2004 three committees were constituted with formal office holders being appointed, with a fourth committee (on women's rights, previously a temporary committee) being added in 2009. As a result, the parliaments concerned further institutionalised the parliamentary dimension of the Barcelona process and gave themselves a mechanism to exercise democratic control over the Euromed Association Agreements, negotiated by the Commission and national governments.

With the establishment of the Union for the Mediterranean by governments in Paris on 13 July 2008, the EMPA became the parliamentary institution of this process, even if the executive was seemingly slow to recognise this, allowing it only as of September 2009 to participate as an observer at all meetings of the executive.

The Union for the Mediterranean has identified six priority projects which are at the heart of the Partnership's efforts, namely projects for the de-pollution of the Mediterranean Sea; the establishment of maritime and land highways; civil protection initiatives to combat natural and man-made disasters; a Mediterranean solar energy plan; a Euro-Mediterranean University in Slovenia; and a Business Development Initiative focusing on micro, small and medium-sized enterprises.

The Euro-Latin American Parliamentary Assembly

Parliament's delegations responsible for Latin America traditionally took part in the EP-Latin American Parliament Conference. This biennial event (the 17th was held in Lima in June 2005) brought together MEPs with Presidents and high-ranking delegations from all over Latin America, together with representatives of other assemblies from the continent, including the Andean Parliament and the Central American Parliament (Parlacen).

The establishment in November 2006 of the Euro-Latin American Parliamentary Assembly reinforced the relationships between the Parliament and Latin America. At the constituent session in Brussels in November 2006, it was agreed that the Assembly would be composed initially of 120 members – 60 MEPs and 60 parliamentarians from Latin America (figures raised in 2009 to 75 each); that it would meet in plenary in principle once a year, by rotation in Europe and Latin America; and that the work of the plenary would be prepared by three standing committees (Political Affairs, Security & Human Rights; Economy, Finance & Trade; and Social, Migration, Environment, Education & Cultural Affairs). The Latin American representatives come from the national parliaments concerned and from Parlatino (Latin American Parliament), Parlandino (Andean Parliament), Parlacen (Central American Parliament) and, as of April 2009, Parlasur (Mercosur Parliament). The Assembly elects two co-Presidents (currently José Slafranca on the European side) and a bureau of 14 (seven each).

Euronest

On 7 May 2009 in Prague, a summit of heads of state and government launched the "Eastern partnership" between the EU and Armenia, Azerbaijan, Belarus, Georgia, Moldavia and Ukraine, and, inter alia, "invited the parliamentarians from the European Union and the partner countries to come forward with ideas regarding the European Parliament's proposal to establish a EU-Neighbourhood East Parliamentary Assembly" (EURO-NEST PA). After further preparatory work, it was agreed that this should comprise 60 MEPs and 60 MPs from the partnership countries. (The Parliament of Belarus not being recognised as being constituted according to international democratic standards, the possibility of its representatives being nominated by civil society organisations is being examined, in what would be a remarkable departure from standard practice.) It should meet once a year (from 2010), alternating between the EU and a partner country. Its work will be prepared by four committees, roughly corresponding to the platforms for co-operation agreed on the executive side by governments.

Links with other interparliamentary bodies

Parliament maintains contacts with the Parliamentary Assembly of the Council of Europe, inter alia through periodic meetings between delegations of the respective Bureau/Conference of Presidents and cooperation between parliamentary committees. More informally, the Parliament, together with the IPU, plays an active part in the Parliamentary Conference on the World Trade Organisation, organising its sessions in Brussels and Geneva to monitor world trade negotiations and co-organising ad hoc delegations following the ministerial meetings of the DOHA round of trade talks in Seattle, Cancun, Hong Kong and Geneva. The case of NATO was mentioned above. Parliament is also represented on the Nordic Council, the Baltic Sea Parliamentary Conference and the Conference of Parliamentarians of the Arctic Region (CPAR – the parliamentary body of the Arctic Council), via members chosen from and by the EEA JPC delegation.

Election observation and other ad hoc delegations

The Conference of Presidents can set up ad hoc delegations at any time in response to particular political events.

Most often, however, ad hoc delegations have been established specifically to observe elections in particular third countries, with a view to contributing to a judgement as to whether or not they have been free and fair. The teams are small, consisting usually of eight members and assisted by one or two staff members. The first such delegation observed the presidential elections in El Salvador in 1984. Since then the Parliament has observed well over 100 elections (presidential, parliamentary and municipal).

There are two main kinds of election observation missions. The first are those that form part of an EU organised mission (EU-EOMs). Since 2000, the Commission has established such missions, on the basis of Council decisions, for various elections in Asia, Africa, Latin America and Oceania. It appoints a Chief Observer who is a member of the European Parliament and the Parliament delegation operates within the structure that he or she establishes. An example of such a mission was that which observed the National and Provincial Assembly elections in Pakistan at the beginning of 2008. A delegation of 7 members worked closely with a more than 130 strong official EU Election Observation Mission, led by an MEP, Michael Gahler.

The second kind of election mission is that which operates alongside an International Election Observation Mission. In the OSCE area, the Parliament coordinates the work of its delegations with the OSCE Office for Democratic Institutions and Humans Rights (ODIHR), the OSCE Parliamentary Assembly, the Parliamentary Assembly of the Council of Europe and, occasionally, the NATO Parliamentary Assembly. Such missions have been concentrated in the Balkans and the former Soviet Republics, such as the presidential elections in Ukraine in the first half of 2010.

In addition, the Parliament delegation may ensure a presence during elections in a particular country in the form of an ad hoc delegation, as it did with the parliamentary elections in Kosovo in November 2007, or the local elections in Georgia in May 2010.

The growing importance of election observation activity led to a decision in November 2001 to set up an Election Coordination Group (ECG) that examines all general questions related to the planning, organisation, evaluation and follow-up of Parliament's observation missions. It is composed of thirteen members, ensuring an appropriate balance between the Political

Groups, and including representatives of the Committee on Foreign Affairs, the Committee on Development, the ACP, EUROLAT and EUROMED and EURONEST delegations and the Chair of the Conference of Delegation Chairs. On 10 December 2009, the Conference of Presidents adopted a Decision on the "Implementing Provisions Governing Election Observation Delegations" which, inter alia, provides that every member appointed to take part in an election observation delegation shall sign a Code of Conduct and strictly abide by its provisions. The Code particularly emphasises the importance of maintaining strict political impartiality at all times, respecting sovereignty, human rights, and the laws of the country concerned.

The decision establishing the European External Action Service was accompanied by an undertaking (OJ 2010/C/210/01) that the "European Parliament will be consulted on the identification and planning of Election Observation Missions and their follow-up – in keeping with Parliament's budgetary scrutiny rights over the relevant funding instrument, i.e. the EIDHR. The appointment of EU Chief Observers will be done in consultation with the Election Coordination Group, in due time before the start of the Election Observation Mission". This will further enhance the role of the European Parliament as a key player in the field of election observation and more generally, of democracy promotion.

Overall assessment

Parliament has established a highly elaborate system of delegations to enable it to develop relations with countries outside the Union. These links have assumed greater importance as the impact of the Union's own internal decisions on the outside world has grown and as the number of agreements requiring the Parliament's assent has increased. The delegations provide one means for the Parliament to acquire the information it needs to make informed judgments on whether or not to give assent as well as to assist the EU as a whole in the pursuit of its objectives.

Delegations have also served to enhance understanding of the EU amongst parliamentarians of third countries and have helped to establish the EU's democratic credentials around the world. The European Parliament uses its delegations to practice a unique form of parliamentary diplomacy. Its delegations, which are often received at the highest levels of state in the countries they visit, act as political ambassadors for Europe.

9. Plenary

Parliament's plenaries (formally monthly "part-sessions" of an annual session, and divided into daily "sittings") are usually convened for a week each month in Strasbourg with additional days in Brussels (see Chapter 3, including Table 6 for evolution of numbers and hours of sittings). This chapter starts off by examining the setting (what it looks like, the seating arrangements) and the typical timetable of a part-session. It then looks at how the agenda is drawn up, the organisation of debates, voting procedures, common procedural manoeuvres, order in the chamber and so on.

The setting

The Strasbourg sessions took place until May 1999 in the debating chamber or "hemicycle" of the Council of Europe (where the latter's Parliamentary Assembly meets, five times a year). Since then, Parliament uses the debating chamber in the striking, purpose-built building constructed by the French authorities. In Brussels, sessions take place in the Parliament building there. The shape of both these chambers is a compromise between differing national parliamentary arrangements. In the British Parliament, government and opposition face each other across a central alley; in the German Bundestag members face the front in rows and speeches are made from a rostrum; while the French Assemblée Nationale sits in a semi-circle. The European Parliament is essentially semi-circular, but the opposite ends of the political spectrum do face each other. Every seat in the chamber has a desk, a place to keep documents, earphones to listen to interpretation, a microphone and a voting machine.

MEPs sit in the chamber by Political Group (before 1958 they sat alphabetically). The Group leaders sit in the front row of the Parliament in the slice of seats allocated to the Group. Next to them or immediately behind them are the vice-chairs and other members of the bureau of the Group and leaders of the national delegations within the Group. Behind these are other office-holders from the Group (e.g., committee chairs and co-ordinators) and finally the other members of the Group, seated in alphabetical order. Before 2009, small Groups did not necessarily have front row seats and they, including their leaders, sat further back in the chamber, as is still the case for the non-attached members.

As seen from the President's chair, the United European Left Group is on the far left of the hemicycle. Next are the Socialists, then the Greens (who previously sat at the back behind the Socialists), then the Liberals. The EPP is on the centre-right of the chamber, followed by the European Conservatives on the right and the anti-EU Freedom & Democracy Group on the far right. The non-attached members are at the back on the right, reflecting the political views of the majority of the present non-attached members.

The seating plan has in the past been the source of some controversy. Until 1989, the Liberals sat on the right of the hemicycle beyond the then European Democratic Group (EDG) of UK and Danish Conservatives. The Liberals protested, and some wanted the Group to be located between the EPP and the Socialists. In 1989 they were moved over just one place, to sit between the EDG and the EPP. After the members of the EDG joined the EPP in spring 1992, the Liberals again asked to be moved to the centre and were successfully supported in this by the Socialists who wanted to make the point that the EPP, in absorbing the EDG, was becoming more right wing. The EPP were thus shifted further right, but were allowed to stretch across to touch the Socialists (at the back until 1994, subsequently at the front, with the Liberals pushed to the back with other small Groups). In 1999, the Liberals (and the Greens) were given space in the centre all the way from back to front and the EPP, following its absorption of the Gaullists and Forza Italia, was moved completely to the right.

Besides the seats allocated to the members, there are a few other seats in the main body of the chamber. A bloc of seats facing the chamber at an angle on the right is reserved for the members of the European Commission, with its President occupying one of the seats in the front. Commissioners are normally present to take part in debates affecting their own portfolio but on certain major occasions the whole Commission is in attendance.

An equivalent bloc of seats on the left, directly opposite the Commission, is allocated to the Council, with two seats in the front row allocated to ministers from the country currently holding the Council Presidency. The President of the European Council also sits and speaks from here when he comes to Parliament. The High Representative normally sits on the Commission benches, as she is a member (indeed, Vice President) of the Commission, but, curiously, sometimes sits on the Council benches, when reporting on the Foreign Affairs configuration of the Council which she chairs (although she is technically not a voting member of the Council).

Beside the President and behind his chair are a few seats for officials concerned with managing the session and advising the President. At the back of the chamber are other seats for Parliament officials whose duties require their presence in the chamber and for Political Group staff (one per Group). Staff (and MEPs) can also follow proceedings on monitors in their offices. There are screens in the chamber, and at various locations throughout Parliament's buildings, showing what debate is in progress, who is speaking, and who are the next speakers.

Facing the members are a rostrum and a dais. The rostrum is only used for addresses to the Parliament by distinguished visitors (such as Heads of State), since MEPs and the representatives of the Commission and the Council speak from their seats. On the dais, sits the President of the Parliament or one of the Vice-Presidents, flanked by the Secretary-General of the Parliament (on important occasions) and by other administrators who advise the President on procedural points and on matters concerned with the running of the sitting. Other officials keep track of the list of speakers in each debate, and advise members as to how long a debate is likely to last, and roughly when they will be called upon to speak.

Access to the floor is controlled by parliamentary ushers, who wear a special uniform. They also carry out other tasks in the chamber, such as transmitting messages to or from members, or assisting the President if there is disorder.

A large gallery is open to the public and also provides seats for diplomatic observers and the press. All Parliament's sittings are held in public. In 1999, Parliament deleted a provision in its rules, in practice never used, allowing it to decide by a two-thirds majority, to sit *in camera*. Under the gallery, behind glass, are interpreters' booths and positions for television crews and technicians.

As in national parliaments, members of the public may only see a handful of members and wonder where everyone else is. The likelihood is that most are in the building but working in their offices (from which they can follow the debates on their television) or taking part in another meeting in one of the many large and small meeting rooms available on the premises. Each Political Group, for example, has its own meeting room, which can be allocated for other purposes such as for an intergroup (see Chapter 10), when it is free. A member may also be addressing a visitors' group from his or her constituency, or talking to journalists in the press room.

Another frequently used space is the "lobby" immediately outside the chamber, which members must cross to enter or leave it. This space is often occupied by lobbyists, members of trade associations and especially the press, and is also used for quick meetings between Parliament officials and members. Many television and radio interviews are conducted in this space and entire chat shows, panel discussions and news programmes are often made there.

As in all parliaments, the bars are also important meeting places, such as the conveniently located Members' Bar near the hemicycle, the Press Bar and, in Strasbourg, the "Swan Bar", which is reached by a passage over the river.

The typical timetable of a part-session

In a **Strasbourg week**, business begins on **Monday** afternoon, generally with short meetings of the Political Groups, notably to discuss last-minute changes to the agenda, and issues for that day's business.

The sitting in the hemicycle opens at 5:00 p.m., when the President (who normally presides in person at this stage) makes a number of announcements (such as important procedural statements, the death of a member, the arrival of another, or that he has sent a message of sympathy to victims of a disaster, or of congratulations, etc.). A number of other procedural declarations (such as which proposals for legislation have been received) are normally not read out in full, but are included instead in that day's minutes.

The next task is the final fixing of the week's agenda, with Political Groups or numbers of members sometimes trying to make further modifications, which are voted on.

As soon as the agenda is adopted, Parliament proceeds to successive individual debates. If there is a debate needed on a report on whether to lift a member's parliamentary immunity (see Chapter 4), this is normally taken on Monday, as stipulated under Rule 7(8). Monday's sitting used to end at 7 p.m., but now normally goes on until 11 p.m. or, occasionally, midnight. Committees can also meet on Monday evenings (and Thursday mornings). A period is also set aside on the Monday evening for "one minute speeches" (see below).

The number of night sittings lasting until midnight was originally limited to one per week. From 1979 to 1987 these were generally held on Thursdays, but in 1987 they were brought forward to Tuesdays, in order to allow debates on legislation requiring special majorities in second readings (first introduced at that time under the Single European Act) to be taken earlier in the week, and thus to permit votes at a time when the maximum number of members were present. Since 1992 there have normally been two such sittings at each part-session (usually Monday and Tuesday from 1992 to 1994, now Tuesday and Wednesday, in addition to the likelihood of a late finish on Monday).

Tuesday's sitting runs from 9:00 a.m. to 1:00 p.m., 3:00 p.m. to 7:00 p.m., and 9:00 p.m. to 12:00 midnight. It begins with votes on whether to accept Commission or Council requests for urgent procedure to be applied by Parliament on particular pieces of legislation. There are now usually two or three such requests per session, with Council having agreed in July 1995 to limit such requests. The chair of the committee responsible is normally called upon to give the committee's view, and there can then be one speaker in favour, and one against the request. If urgency is then accepted by Parliament (which happens in about half the cases), the item is usually placed on the Thursday's agenda, and if the relevant committee has not already adopted its report on the subject, it will have to hold a special meeting in order to debate and adopt it in the course of the plenary week. (Nevertheless there is nothing to prevent a matter for which urgency has been accepted subsequently being referred back to committee).

The rest of Tuesday's agenda has few particularly distinctive features. There is usually a voting time at 12:00 noon, on reports on which the debate has already closed. Question Hour to the President of the Commission, comprising 30 minutes for free questions and 30 minutes for questions on a pre-defined specific topic, is scheduled from 3:00 p.m. to 4:00 p.m. Question time to the Commission is usually taken from 5:30 to 7:00 p.m.

Each Council presidency introduces its priorities at the beginning of its term of office, and sums up its achievements at the end. The Commission also presents its annual work programme at the beginning of each year. Debates on Commission and Council programmes of this kind thus occur at least five times a year and usually take place on Tuesdays or Wednesdays. Oral questions with debate, and statements by the Commission or Council (which may be wound up with the adoption of a Parliament resolution) are also usually placed on Tuesday's or Wednesday's agenda. Groups meet again from 6:30 to 9:00 p.m. on Tuesdays and Wednesdays.

Wednesday's timetable is the same as for Tuesdays, but is often the window for "key debates" in the presence of both Council and Commission representatives. It also includes a period of voting time, at 11:30 or noon, which sometimes goes on well beyond 1:00 p.m. and includes most votes that may require an absolute majority of Parliament's current members. This is therefore the moment when the highest regular turnout of members must be achieved. Wednesday is also the day most frequently used for major Council statements (though for some countries' Presidency it is switched to Tuesday, for instance if that country's government usually meets on a Wednesday) or statements by the President of the European Council after one of its meetings. Question time to the Council normally takes place from 5:30 to 7:00 p.m.

Thursday's sitting begins at 9:00 a.m. and lasts till the end of a (usually lengthy) voting time that starts at noon, and then from 3:00 p.m. to mid-afternoon. Debates on human rights cases take one hour on Thursday afternoons (until the June 2002 Rules revision, debates on topical and urgent subjects of major importance were held for three hours) with votes thereon at the end of the debate. Turnout of members is much lower that afternoon, especially if, as is often the case, the subject matter is less divisive. Until 2000, Parliament also sat on Friday mornings in Strasbourg, usually for less controversial business.

Parallel to all this are numerous meetings of the Political Group working parties, intergroups, committees, delegations, etc. Furthermore, the typical schedule can, if necessary, be adjusted (e.g., by starting earlier or curtailing a lunch break). The longest sitting ever was on 13 March 1996 when Parliament sat from 8:00 a.m., and finished at 0:45 a.m. with lunch restricted to 20 minutes.

The timetable of **Brussels plenary sittings** is somewhat different. A standard Brussels plenary is normally held six times per year for just two days, in a week otherwise devoted to committee meetings. It starts at 3:00 p.m. on a Wednesday, often with a statement from the Commission, and continues until midnight, resuming the following morning and finishing with votes at 11:00 or 12:00 p.m., which may go on for an hour or more. Groups meet on the Wednesday morning from 11:00 a.m. to 1:00 p.m. and, if necessary, early on Thursday before the sitting. Short additional Brussels plenary sittings can be called at relatively short notice in Brussels, normally for just one or two hours, for instance to hear a statement from the President of the European Council.

"Open" Bureau and Conference of Presidents

In 1991–92, before an equipped hemicycle was available in Brussels, a number of meetings held in similar conditions to plenary sittings took place in Brussels, although they were expressly not described as such. They were referred to instead as meetings of the Enlarged Bureau open to all members. The origins of this innovation are described in Chapter 3. They were used mainly for topical statements by the Commission and, on occasion, for speeches by visiting statesmen. They have now been superseded by Brussels part-sessions. However the practice was revived in 1999 as open meetings of the Conference of Presidents in order to hold what amounted de facto to short notice plenary sittings for these purposes. Other bodies are not allowed to meet at the same time. More recently, Parliament has simply organised sittings at short notice, without pretence that they are not so doing, not least to hear reports from the President of the European Council after its meetings.

How the plenary agenda is drawn up

Unlike some national parliaments, the European Parliament is master of its own agenda. It may discuss (or not) what it likes, when it likes, and according to its own priorities. It cooperates, of course, with the other institutions, notably in dealing with proposals for legislation, and they in turn have a vested interest in cooperating with Parliament in order to ensure smooth passage of proposals. Only as of the second reading of legislative procedures and in the budget procedure is Parliament bound by a formal deadline, laid down in the treaties.

The drawing up of the agenda is therefore an elaborate process. As regards the legislative and non-legislative reports from committees, informal meetings are held between the committee officials to see when items are likely to be ready. The monthly meeting of committee chairs provides a more formal opportunity to discuss which reports are ready, and which reports could be accelerated or held back. This is then submitted to the Conference of Presidents where each Group leader will express a view on the relative priorities of committee reports and also bring other requests (e.g., for oral questions with debate or for Commission or Council statements). The Commission and the Council also try to influence Parliament's agenda and are represented at the relevant meeting of the Conference of Presidents.

The Conference of Presidents must take account of a number of constraints. Parliament may have undertaken to give a legislative proposal priority and, where possible, to deal with it within a certain time frame within the context of the annual legislative programme (see Chapter 12) established with the Commission. Any second or third readings under the ordinary legislative procedure must be completed within three (or a maximum of four) months.

Legislative items are thus given priority on Parliament's agenda. Items adopted in committee by an overwhelming majority (fewer than one-tenth against) are taken in plenary without debate (unless requested by a Group or 40 members) and are subject to a single vote without amendment (unless one-tenth of the members – individually or by Group – request that it be open to amendment).

The Conference of Presidents' meeting on the Thursday before the Strasbourg plenary adopts the final draft agenda which is distributed to all MEPs and voted on by Parliament at the beginning of the part-session on the following Monday. The draft concerns the whole monthly "part-session" (i.e. it includes any subsequent Brussels sittings that month). A Political Group, a committee, or 40 members, may propose changes in writing up to one hour before the opening of the part-session. Each such request is then moved by one member and there is one speaker for and one against, followed by a vote on the request.

The agenda then stands adopted. In practice, however, it can still be subsequently modified, either because urgent requests from Commission or Council are accepted by the Parliament on Tuesday morning, or because unexpected events (e.g., emergency debates on Commission declarations) or straightforward delays mean that items are carried over from one day to the next. To cover unexpected eventualities, the rules allow the President, at any time, to propose to modify the agenda (or take up in his own name suggestions made by others). There can also be, as we shall see, a number of other, procedural manoeuvres to modify the agenda.

Debates on breaches of human rights

Until the June 2002 revision of Parliament's Rules, three hours were set aside each month for debates and votes on topical and urgent subjects of major importance, held in recent years on Thursday afternoons. These are now restricted to one hour on breaches of human rights, democracy and the rule of law, other matters being dealt with under other procedures or taken as an extraordinary debate (see below).

The Conference of Presidents proposes subjects in the draft agenda that may be changed when Parliament adopts the agenda. The main criteria for selection of topics are laid down in Annex III of Parliament's Rules of Procedure. These include the need for Parliament to react quickly or to express a view before a particular event has taken place.

These debates have several distinctive features. There is much less speaking time. There are no explanations of vote. There can be no requests for inadmissibility of a motion, or for motions to be referred back to a committee. No one can call for a debate to be adjourned, though a quorum call can be made. The votes are taken together at the end. Usually, a compromise motion is negotiated between Groups and put to the vote in place of the first resolution that it is meant to replace.

One minute speeches

The adoption of Parliament's agenda on Monday afternoons often gave rise to bogus points of order from individual members, about political, constituency or other matters. As they sometimes led to a mini-debate and could cumulatively take up a considerable amount of time, the 2002 Rules revision (Corbett Report A5-8/2002) provided for half an hour to be set aside for one-minute speeches. These allow members to draw Parliament's attention to any subject, a procedure based on a similar mechanism in the US Congress. They were initially taken just after the adoption of the agenda, but are now taken after the main debates on the Monday, but before the short presentations of own initiative committee reports. Between 20 and 40 such speeches are taken (on average, just under half of the number requested) each month.

Extraordinary debates

Introduced in the 2002 reforms, partly to replace the Topical and Urgent procedure, this procedure allows for short-notice reaction to major events, through a one-hour debate without a resolution. Such debates may be proposed for the vote adopting Parliament's agenda by a Political Group or 40 members, or, in response to events that take place after the adoption of the agenda, by the President after consulting Group chairs.

Formal sittings

Parliament accepts requests by Heads of State of the Member States or of third countries, and occasionally others, to address the Parliament in so-called "formal sittings". These are often held on the Wednesday of the Strasbourg plenary week, and are not treated as a normal sitting in that there can be no points of order, procedural motions, etc. (see Table 49 in Chapter 16).

Table 29: *Duration of debates by type – 6th legislative period 2004-2009*

Debate	Time (hrs &mins)	Percentage
Legislative debates (Codecision procedure)	258h18	12.32%
Legislative debates (Assent procedure)	10h08	0.48%
Legislative debates (Consultation procedure)	112h12	5.35%
Legislative debates (Cooperation procedure)	0h46	0.04%
Own initiative reports	444h34	21.21%
Short presentations	9h44	0.46%
Budget	30h49	1.47%
Budgetary discharge	9h54	0.47%
Interinstitutional agreements	5h40	0.27%
Rules of Procedure	4h25	0.21%
Nonlegislative debates (other)	3h10	0.15%
Other debates	15h39	0.75%
Council /Commission/High Representative statements and debate	497h01	24.12%
Statements by the President of Parliament	14h07	0.67%
Statements (other)	8h11	0.39%
Commission communications	11h19	0.54%
Debate on cases of breaches of human rights, democracy and the rule of law	65h12	3.11%
Formal sittings	28h20	1.35%
One min. speeches on matters of political importance	50h05	2.39%
Question Time (Commission)	80h52	3.86%
Question Time (Council)	53h24	2.55%
Oral questions with debate	141h19	6.74%
Votes	151h28	7.23%
Explanations of vote	47h27	2.26%
Elections	6h11	0.29%
Other (e.g. approval of Minutes, order of business, official welcomes, calendar of part sessions)	35h51	1.71%
TOTAL	2,096h06	

See also Table 6 in Chapter 3 on the total time spent in plenary sessions

NB: At first sight, it might seem surprising that scarcely 20% of time is spent on legislative debates. However, this masks the fact that other categories (votes, initiative reports, statements, question time, etc) can and do also concern legislative activities, and the fact that legislation is prepared in detail in committees, whereas questions, statements, and several other categories have no committee stage. Out of the 2924 documents adopted by Parliament during this period, 1355 were legislative.

The allocation of speaking time in debates

Debates, whatever their origin (legislative or non-legislative reports, oral questions with debate, or debates on statements by the President of the European Council, the Commission or the Council), have many similar features in the way that speaking time is allocated. The President makes proposals after consulting the Political Groups. These proposals are outlined in the draft agenda for the plenary and are divided into speaking time for debates on Monday, Tuesday, Wednesday and Thursday (with the debates on breaches of human rights subject to a separate procedure and thus excluded). Speaking time is allocated to Commission and Council, rapporteurs and draftsmen of opinions, authors of motions; and most of the remaining time is made available to Political Groups to allocate to their members. Finally, some time is set aside for any member (including members who have already spoken but wish to come back on a point) to "catch the eye" of the President for a short (one minute) intervention.

As regards the time allocated to Political Groups, this is calculated according to guidelines laid down in Rule 149 of Parliament's Rules of Procedure: a first fraction of speaking time is divided equally among all Groups, and a further and more substantial fraction is divided among the Groups and non-attached members in proportion to the total number of their members. Once this allocation of speaking time has been made, the Political Groups indicate how much of their overall time they wish to use for each individual debate. They also divide up their speaking time among members within their Group. Some Groups may wish to allocate most of their speaking time to their main spokesperson, while others may prefer to give smaller amounts to several members.

An illustration of what this allocation of speaking time means in practice can be seen in the draft agenda for the afternoon and evening of Wednesday 19 May 2010, when three debates were held, one a joint debate including oral questions. The Commission was given 30 minutes (including replies); Council 10; Parliament's rapporteurs 30 (six minutes each to five rapporteurs); the draftsman of an opinion from another committee, five; authors of oral questions 10, and 195 minutes for individual MEPs distributed among the Groups as follows: EPP 66.5, S&D 47, ALDE 22.5, Greens/EFA 15.5, ECR 15, GUE 10.5, EFD 9.5, and the non-attached members 9. There were also 15 minutes for any member to "catch the eye" of the President.

A typical debate on a legislative proposal begins with the rapporteur giving the view of Parliament's committee and the Commission responding to it (before the 2009 Rules revision, this had been the other way around for a number of years). The rapporteur may be followed by the draftsmen of opinions from other committees, if any, though for a shorter time. The main Group spokespersons for the issue then speak, starting with one from each Group in descending order of their size, and usually followed by other members in new rounds from various Groups. An electronic board shows how much of a member's speaking time has elapsed, and indicates when it has come to an end by means of flashing asterisks. The presiding officer then requests the speaker to stop, and if he or she fails to do so, can cut off the speaker's microphone.

At the end of a debate the Commission will reply and the rapporteur may come back again too. This is the moment when, for legislative resolutions, the

Commission will indicate its position on specific amendments tabled in the report before the Parliament. In some cases the Commission will give a very lengthy reply, which cuts into the time allocated for subsequent debates. The Commission's allocation of speaking time is purely indicative, as the treaty (Article 230) gives the Commission an unlimited right to intervene.

A debate on a Commission or Council statement, or one on foreign policy by the Vice President of the Commission/High Representative, will begin with the statement and be followed by Group spokespersons, as described above. The Commission and/or Council will reply at the very end. However, Parliament can decide instead to have thirty minutes of concise questions and answers instead of a full debate, with members called by the President on a "catch-the-eye" basis.

Time for debates is thus limited, with a corresponding lack of scope for spontaneity, or cut-and-thrust exchanges between individual members, already difficult because of the inevitable time lags involved with interpretation. This is reinforced by a tendency for some members to read out their speeches, repeating set positions that have often already been aired in committee. However, the Rules revision of May 2009 (another Corbett Report) brought in a new innovation to allow for an element of greater spontaneity and interaction between members: any member can now raise a "blue card" to ask to interrupt a speaker and put a short (maximum half a minute) question to him or her. The catch-the-eye period at the end of a debate can also be used for members to intervene a second time in response to others. Finally, members can use their right to give an "explanation of vote" (see Chapter 4) at the end of voting time to make short points (or, alternatively, give them in writing).

Voting

Voting time

Members of the public, lobbyists or journalists who attend Parliament's plenary sessions to follow a particular subject are often surprised to find that the vote on a particular matter does not usually follow the debate, but comes only at voting time, which may be a day later. There are several reasons for this. One is the unpredictability of the duration of votes: if voting followed each debate, it would be even more difficult to plan the organisation of debates within the small number of days available each month. The variety of other meetings that take place during plenary sessions would have to be interrupted every time there was a vote. Most votes are therefore grouped at fixed moments of the week, notably noon on Tuesdays, Wednesdays and Thursdays. At such times, votes under the simplified procedures (without amendments) are generally taken first (starting with the legislative items and then the non-legislative). Items not following a simplified procedure are taken after, again starting with the legislative and then, if any, the non-legislative.

Although members thus have a good indication of when voting time will take place, they are also reminded by division bells, which can be heard throughout the buildings, shortly before a vote will take place (as well as ten minutes before a sitting and when it starts and finishes).

Voting method

Voting is a personal right and no proxy voting is permitted. There are two main ways of voting, by a simple show of hands and by electronic voting. Electronic voting is used when the result of a show of hands is unclear, or if a formal roll call vote has been requested in writing by at least 40 members or a Political Group before voting has begun. The Rules of Procedure do still provide for voting by sitting and standing (when a vote by show of hands is unclear) and also by full roll call with members replying "yes", "no", or "I abstain" in alphabetical order, in the event of the electronic voting system not working. In practice any such (rare) malfunctioning results in a short postponement while the system is fixed.

The electronic voting system was first installed in May 1980. Members must insert their voting card in the voting machine on their desk (or, indeed, any desk as the machine will recognise their card) and press the appropriate button: a green light comes on for a "yes" vote, red for a "no" vote, and yellow for an abstention (unless there is a secret ballot, when a blue light will indicate that a member has voted). When the President announces an electronic vote, a reference to the text being voted (a paragraph, amendment or final text) is displayed on a small screen built in to the voting machine as well as on the electronic scoreboard. Members out of their places must then rush back to them in time, creating a scramble at moments of close and tense voting. Sometimes, before the result is finally announced, members will catch the attention of the President to say that their voting machine was not working and to indicate how they voted. These are then added to the tally.

The final results are first announced by the President and then appear, after about five seconds, on the screens and on the electronic scoreboard. If a roll call vote (RCV) has been requested, the result of each member's vote is formally recorded, first in a special annex to the minutes which appears the next day, and later in the translated minutes which come out in the Official Journal (although unofficially a print-out is available in the press room within half an hour of the vote). All final votes on legislation must in any case be taken by roll call.

Roll call votes tend to be called by Political Groups for three main reasons: to put a Group's position on an issue firmly on record; to embarrass another Group by forcing the latter to take a publicly recorded stance on an issue; and to keep a check on their own members' participation in a vote, and the position they take.

Whatever the reason for a recorded roll call vote, it provides a valuable source for assessing the political positions taken by a Political Group and by individual members. It could, for instance, be used by European interest groups the way American congressmen's voting records are assessed by the Washington-based lobbies. However, it is a tool that must be used with caution. It is easiest, for example, to assess a roll-call vote on the finally adopted text, whereas the most significant vote may have been on a specific amendment. Deciding which vote was significant requires considerable knowledge of the issue at stake.

Results of electronic votes are rarely contested. Sometimes, only one or two votes separate the two sides and members complain that their voting machines did not work, but if they did not catch the eye of the President before the result was announced, they are too late to affect the result. There have been very occasional accusations that certain members have double voted by voting for absent colleagues but no proof has been forthcoming. In fact, the system is generally acknowledged to work remarkably well.

Secret ballots are possible. They are mandatory for certain elections (the President of the Commission, the Ombudsman, the President, Vice-Presidents and Quaestors of Parliament), but are otherwise exceedingly rare and must be requested by at least one-fifth of the members. Only three such requests have been made in recent years: a vote in June 2002 on Parliament's timetable of sittings (where some thought that a secret ballot might make it easier for French MEPs to vote against the holding of certain sittings in Strasbourg), in December 2004 on opening accession negotiations with Turkey and in March 2011 on the timetable of sittings for 2012 and 2013. On all three occasions it was controversial, with some members accusing others of not having the courage of their convictions.

Although simplified by successive reforms, voting time typically lasts about an hour, and can be longer if there are many amendments tabled or if many separate or split votes have been requested. The speed and complexity of votes can be bewildering to outside observers. The sheer numbers are impressive: some 5,249 voting operations took place in 2005, 5,666 in 2006, 6354 in 2007 and 4,647 in 2008.

Voting order

Parliament has laid down standard procedures for the order in which votes are taken, that differ as between non-legislative and legislative texts.

When a **non-legislative text** is put to the vote, Parliament first votes on any amendments tabled to specific parts of a resolution. When there are several amendments on the same point, it normally begins by voting on that furthest removed from the original text, although the President has discretion to do otherwise. He may also put complementary or similar amendments to the vote together (*"en bloc"*). If an amendment is adopted, subsequent contradictory amendments or text fall.

Requests may also be made for a separate vote on a particular paragraph of the original text, or a split vote on parts of a paragraph or an amendment. Such requests must be made by a Group or 40 members the evening before the vote (so that all Groups have advance notice).

Once the voting on amendments is concluded, Parliament then takes a final vote on the motion for a resolution as a whole as it results from the votes on amendments. An opportunity is given for explanations of vote by individual members (orally or in writing, see Chapter 4), normally after this final vote. Oral explanations are limited to one minute for individual members and two minutes for an explanation of vote on behalf of a Group. Written explanations of vote are limited to 200 words, and are included in the verbatim record of proceedings. Explanations are not allowed on procedural matters.

Most votes on non-legislative resolutions require simple majorities for or against. Unless a quorum call is made (see below) or an electronic vote taken there is no check on how many members are actually voting. Certain non-legislative votes of a procedural or decision-making nature, however, do require special majorities. These include amendments to Parliament's Rules of Procedure, which require a majority of the total membership, and censure votes on the Commission, which require favourable votes from a two-thirds majority of the votes cast and a majority of the total membership of Parliament.

Voting on **legislative texts** is similar in terms of the order of voting on amendments, and the possibility of explanations of vote. The main difference is that a distinction is made in first reading between voting on the Commission's text (including amendments to it, specific paragraphs or articles of the text, and the proposal as a whole) and voting on the accompanying (highly formalistic) draft legislative resolution. After voting on the former is completed but before Parliament completes its procedure by voting on the draft legislative resolution, the Commission is asked to react to (and the Council to comment on) Parliament's amendments or, in some cases, its rejection of the proposal. If the Commission gives an unsatisfactory response, or is not in a position to react immediately, the vote on the draft legislative resolution may then be postponed for a period sufficient to allow the responsible committee time to examine the situation. This period may not exceed two months, unless the Parliament decides to extend it. Until Parliament finally votes on the draft legislative resolution, it has not officially spoken.

This possibility of separating votes on a Commission proposal and the accompanying draft legislative resolution that ends the procedure, is an important procedural device developed by the Parliament to reinforce its role in the legislative process. Its significance is described in greater detail in Chapter 12. It applies to legislative procedures in first reading or if there is a single reading by the Parliament.

By contrast, in second or third readings, Parliament votes only on the legislative text, without an accompanying resolution, and it cannot delay, as it must act within three months (or four if extended). For second readings, Parliament has developed rules for determining the moment from which the three-month period is to run, namely when it has received, in all the official languages, the Council's position, its explanation of how it was reached, and the Commission's reaction. Only then does the President of Parliament announce receipt of the common position at Parliament's next plenary session.

In second reading, Parliament may adopt the Council's common position as such, reject it outright or adopt amendments. In the first case there need be no plenary vote at all (with the President of Parliament simply declaring it to be adopted in the absence of any other proposal). In the second and third cases, however, a majority of the total membership of Parliament is required to reject a text or to amend it.

In third reading, Parliament votes on the joint text negotiated in the conciliation committee between Parliament and Council. If agreement has been reached in the committee, a simple majority in Parliament is enough to approve or reject it. There can be no amendments to the text at this stage.

A final word should be added as regards the rules concerning **amendments** that are tabled in plenary. First, they must be tabled by a deadline set down for each report or resolution. In most cases this is set (by the President) as midday Wednesday of the week preceding the plenary session, but for more urgent topics the deadline is set for a moment during the plenary itself, and is announced by the President of Parliament and published in the agenda.

Second, amendments are generally put to the vote only when they have been printed and distributed in all the official languages. Parliament may decide otherwise, but not if 40 members or more object. Inevitably the practice in plenaries is more formal in this respect than in committee meetings.

Third, plenary amendments may only be tabled by a Political Group, the committee responsible for the report (there is a small exception for associated committees whose amendments concerning their field have not been taken up by the committee responsible) or at least 40 members (whereas at committee stage, any member, whether on the committee or not, may table amendments).

Building majorities: bargaining among Groups

The only major exception to the deadline for tabling amendments is where compromise amendments are put forward by Political Groups, or committee chairs or rapporteurs. The President of Parliament must obtain the agreement of Parliament before they are put to the vote. Such compromise amendments would typically entail the withdrawal of texts tabled by different Groups in favour of one composite text. It is relatively difficult to reach last-minute agreement on a compromise amendment that will satisfy all Political Groups, and agreement is often reached between two or three Groups only, notably when these Groups together constitute a majority. It is also common for two or more Groups to agree to support some of each other's amendments.

In the case of resolutions winding up debates on statements by the Commission, Council or European Council, or on oral questions, or on human rights debates, where most Political Groups will have tabled their own motion for resolution, the "compromise amendment" may take the form of a whole compromise resolution tabled by some (or possibly all) Groups. If adopted, the other motions fall.

Political Groups take it in turn for a six-month period to organise the technical aspects of the compromise negotiations: issuing invitations, booking rooms, providing secretarial assistance, and chairing the meetings. Normally, all Groups that have introduced a resolution are invited to participate in the negotiations on the compromise text, even if it is not always possible to get every such Group on board for a compromise. There are no fixed rules as to who represents a Political Group at the meeting (a Group member, a Group member accompanied by a staff member, a staff member) nor about the number of representatives, but in most cases the Group's co-ordinator on the subject will be involved.

Compromise resolutions are often elaborated under considerable time pressure, which does not facilitate the preparation of quality texts. A commitment to sign a compromise text is normally taken at the end of the negotiations. It may happen that concessions are made to a particular Group during the negotiation process on a specific point, without any guarantee that this Group will sign the compromise, or vote for it.

There is no distinct pattern as to the coalitions that are formed during negotiations, but the fact that the EPP and the S&D can together reach a majority means that there is a premium on compromises between them. Some of the smaller Groups then often focus on securing specific points where they have a particular interest. But when the EPP and S&D cannot agree (which is indeed not always easy and, when it happens, can cause unease in their ranks), the ALDE Group is often in the pivotal position and determines whether there will be a left or right leaning coalition on the issue in question (see section on power balances and relations between the Groups in Chapter 5).

A specific problem arises from the fact that Groups have diverse internal working methods. For instance, on general debates (such as ahead of European Council meetings) the EPP elaborates a lengthy resolution, with a number of chapters, each being drafted under the authority of a particular member. Furthermore, all the specialists involved participate in the negotiations, with the result that other Groups' single representatives can be confronted with four or five EPP members during negotiations – though this is not necessarily to the EPP's advantage.

Despite efforts to draft concise texts with clear priorities, texts tend to be made longer during the negotiations, as a compromise can be more easily obtained by including more issues.

Common procedural manoeuvres

Parliament's Rules provide considerable scope for procedural manoeuvres by individual members or by Groups, such as the right to make points of order, request verification of the quorum, request referral back to committee, move the inadmissibility of a matter, the closure or adjournment of a debate or the suspension or closure of the sitting.

By far the most frequently used of these devices are **points of order**. They last for one minute and take precedence over other business. They are meant to refer to the non respect of a specific rule, or to request clarification from the President of Parliament (e.g., pointing out that a text has not been translated). However, bogus points of order are often used to bring totally different subjects onto the agenda, to respond to an event that has just taken place, to make a constituency point, to criticise another member, to criticise a ruling by the President, to participate in a debate when not due to do so, or to continue a concluded debate by other means. On certain occasions, a series of bogus points of order amount to a miniature debate. How flexible the presiding Vice-President or President will be, may depend on the time pressure of the moment and the nature of the points being raised.

The other procedural devices cited above are mainly used for one reason, to get an item off the plenary agenda, and thus to postpone or block Parliament's decision on the matter. The most commonly used rule to achieve this is Rule 175, providing for **referral back to committee**. This is often done by the responsible committee itself, if difficulties have emerged during a debate, or if new developments or an unsatisfactory response by the Commission require reconsideration of the matter within the committee.

A request for referral back, however, may only be made when the agenda is adopted, or at the start of the debate (in these cases it must be notified 24 hours in advance) or at the time of the vote on the report. As on other procedural matters, the President, after having heard the mover of the motion, will then call for one speaker in favour and one against. The committee chair or rapporteur may also speak. Parliament then proceeds to a vote on the request, and if it is adopted, the debate (if applicable) and the final vote are postponed to a future plenary. Requests for referral back are sometimes accompanied by requests that the matter be placed on the next plenary agenda, but this is not automatic.

Another, and more controversial, device to postpone a vote is through a **request to ascertain the quorum**. Most plenary decisions can be taken by simple majority, without any particular number of members being present (unlike committee decisions, where a quarter of the membership must be present), unless there is an objection that the quorum of one-third of Parliament's members is not present. At least 40 members (but not a Political Group) may request that the quorum be checked. The President asks these members to stand up so that they can be counted. The President will then put a particular amendment or point to the vote, and announce whether or not the quorum (246 members) has been attained. If it has not been, the vote is then placed on the agenda of the next sitting.

The 40 or more members who request a quorum count are automatically included in the number of members counted as being present in the chamber for the purpose of establishing the quorum. This interpretation of the Rule was made after an incident when one particular group of members made a quorum call, and subsequently walked out of the chamber to ensure that a quorum was indeed not present. Quorum calls may not be used for preventing debate or for preventing the adoption of the agenda or the minutes. In other words, they cannot bring Parliament itself to a halt.

Other procedural devices are less frequently used. To find that a matter is inadmissible, for example, is relatively rare, since the range of issues debated by the Parliament is so vast. Motions to move closure or adjournment of a debate tend to be used only for genuine timetabling reasons. One other reason used to be to challenge the legal base of a proposal and insist that a report not be voted upon in plenary until the Legal Affairs Committee had given its view as to whether the proposed treaty article for the proposal was the correct one. However, the rules were changed in 1999 to require any such challenges to have been raised already at committee stage.

Order in the chamber

Lack of order is only occasionally a problem within the European Parliament, whose proceedings are usually rather calm compared to some national parliaments, such as the UK House of Commons or the Italian Chamber of Deputies. The variety of languages used, the limited speaking time available and the variety of national parliamentary traditions, means that there tends to be less spontaneous repartee between individual members, and fewer interruptions of members while they are speaking. Nevertheless the European Parliament is livelier than some of the national parliaments in the Member States. When Hanja Maij-Weggen, a long-serving MEP, was appointed as a Minister in the Dutch government, and her aggressive debating style was commented upon in the Dutch Parliament, she claimed to have learnt the technique from British MEPs. Although there are relatively few moments of high drama within the European Parliament, this does not mean that there are not occasionally very lively debates, or periods of unrest in the chamber when a presiding officer's decision is contested.

There have also been a number of individual demonstrations within the chamber, many by the Parliament's "outsider" members. Such incidents have been rare despite threats in 2004 by the new UKIP MEPs to disrupt Parliament. Ian Paisley disrupted the 1988 visit of the Pope and had to be removed from the chamber after having been warned by the President. In October 1989, members of the then Group of the Right protested at their exclusion from leadership posts within Parliament's interparliamentary delegations, eventually causing a scuffle, with the suspension of the sitting and with the lights being switched off in the chamber.

As a result of this last incident, Parliament revised its Rules of Procedure to provide for members to be called twice to order by the President if they create a disturbance in the chamber. On the second occasion their offence is recorded in the minutes. If there is a further repetition, the President may exclude the offender from the chamber for the rest of the sitting (Parliament's ushers are given the delicate task of actually removing the member from the chamber if he or she refuses to leave). Parliament may pass a vote of censure in serious cases of disorder, automatically involving immediate exclusion from the chamber, and suspension for two to five days, including loss of attendance allowance. (This power was used against a Portuguese member, Rosado, who hit a Danish member, Blak, in December 1997 after a vigorous exchange in a debate on tobacco subsidies.) A final such rule provides for closure or suspension of the sitting by the President when disturbances in Parliament threaten to obstruct the business of the house or if an unexpected political situation arises. This rule has only been used sparingly, and more for political deadlocks needing compromise during votes than for disturbances.

Less disruptive demonstrations still take place, usually through members wearing special T-shirts (a speciality of the Green MEPs), waving small placards or such like. However, in January 2005, some British and Polish opponents of the EU waved large banners against the proposed new EU constitution during Parliament's vote on it, refused to lower them when asked by the President, and subsequently disrupted the official launch of Parliament's information campaign on it, with scuffles and fisticuffs causing a subsequent inquiry. In June of the same year, some Lega Nord members disrupted a formal address to Parliament by President Ciampi of Italy.

As a result of these and other incidents, and a growing realisation that Parliament actually had few means to oppose disruptive behaviour or attempts to bring proceedings to a halt, the Rules of Procedure were again revised in 2006 (Onesta Report A6-0413/2005). While specifying that the Rules "shall in no way detract from the liveliness of parliamentary debates nor undermine Members' freedom of speech", and laying down in annexed guidelines that "a distinction should be drawn between visual actions, which may be tolerated, provided they are not offensive and/or defamatory, remain within reasonable bounds and do not lead to conflict, and those which actively disrupt any parliamentary activity whatsoever", the revised Rules empower the President directly, "in exceptionally serious cases of disorder or disruption of Parliament" and after hearing the member concerned, to impose a penalty on the member without needing to go back to plenary for a vote of censure. The member may appeal to the Parliament's Bureau. The possible period of suspension and loss of daily allowance has been extended to ten days (and not necessarily linked), covering all parliamentary activities and not just the plenary. The President may also propose to the Conference of Presidents to suspend or remove the member concerned from one or more of the elected offices he or she holds within Parliament, such as committee chairmanships or places on delegations. The disruptive behaviour need not be on the floor of the House, as the revised rules specify that incidents in committees or other bodies are covered and also specify that "Members shall be held responsible for any failure by persons whom they employ or for whom they arrange access to Parliament to comply on Parliament's premises with the standards of conduct applicable to Members. The President or his representatives may exercise disciplinary powers over such persons and any other outside person present on Parliament's premises." This latter provision was triggered by the involvement of certain members' assistants in the disruptive activities of January 2005 mentioned above.

In February 2010, UKIP leader Nigel Farage was fined for gratuitously insulting the President of the European Council, Herman Van Rompuy at his first appearance in Parliament as President. In November 2010, another UKIP member, Godfrey Bloom, was asked to leave the chamber after shouting the Nazi slogan "Ein Volk, Ein Reich, Ein Führer" at a German MEP and refusing to apologise. He was subsequently fined €2000 by the President.

Record of plenary sittings

Two sets of documents are prepared on a daily basis. First, there are the daily minutes of each sitting, which are divided into two parts. Part I records the business that took place, who spoke, the procedural decisions, the overall results of voting on amendments and texts and the complete register of members present for the day's business (prepared on the basis of lists signed by members at one of two locations within the chamber). Part II contains the texts finally adopted by the Parliament. There is also an annex to the Minutes containing details of the results of all votes taken in plenary. The minutes are distributed in all the official languages at least an hour before the opening of the afternoon period of the next sitting (prior to the 2002 reforms, it was the next morning sitting, involving overnight translation and production which, with increasing workload, members and languages, became ever more costly). They are approved on that occasion, unless objections are raised. The minutes are subsequently published in the EU's Official Journal and on Parliament's website.

Second, there is the verbatim report of the proceedings of each sitting. This is now only published electronically. An initial version, available the following day at around noon, is familiarly known as the "Rainbow" because it contains the members' speeches in the languages in which they were given. Members wishing to make technical corrections to the transcripts of their speeches are required to do so not later than the day following that on which they received them. The "Rainbow" is eventually translated into all the official languages and published electronically as an annex to the Official Journal and more recently on Parliament's website, serving as a full record of what was said. This is important not just in terms of recording for posterity the views of MEPs, but also as an official record of positions taken by the Commission and Council on subjects not always of their own choosing. The website also provides audiovisual records of members' speeches.

Concluding remarks

The European Parliament blends a wide variety of national parliamentary traditions, through its seating arrangements, its procedures and its style. It also has distinctive features of its own arising from the evolution of its powers in the EU system, the linguistic constraints it faces and treaty obligations such as deadlines. Its debates are not as lively or as interesting to the media as those of some other parliaments, but it has developed methods to enhance the role of its members in actually shaping policy outcomes rather than being a rubber stamp or a simple forum. It is to a large degree master of its own agenda and its own procedures and this, as we will see further in other chapters, has been a crucial factor in its development.

10. Intergroups

A striking feature of the Parliament is a large number of informal "intergroups", consisting of members from different Political Groups with a common interest in a particular theme (similar to "all party groups" in the UK House of Commons). This chapter briefly traces the evolution of intergroups, gives an indication of their scale and diversity and examines their advantages and disadvantages, including the rules to which they are subject. By way of example, it looks in more detail at a few specific intergroups.

The evolution of intergroups since 1979

A number of intergroups were established shortly after the first direct elections in 1979 and requested official recognition (i.e. that Parliament provide a meeting room, interpretation or even administrative support). It was quickly realised, however, that Parliament could not provide facilities for all intergroups. The Parliament's Bureau decided to give official recognition only to the Intergroup of Elected Local and Regional Representatives (an institutional rather than political grouping). Intergroups, therefore, had to meet with only restricted facilities, or with facilities provided by sympathetic Political Groups.

This did not, however, prevent a dramatic growth in the number of intergroups. By the end of the 1994-99 Parliament, some 58 intergroups were registered with the EP Secretary-General, of which 12 claimed to have funding, and over 30 their own logo. At the beginning of the 1999-2004 legislature the total figure was around 80. Table 30 gives an indication of the position at the start of 2010, but the list in the second part of that table can only be indicative: it does not necessarily include all intergroups and may include some whose level of activity is very low or sporadic. Nevertheless, it gives a good sense of their diversity. The scale of intergroup activity is also significant, especially during the plenary sessions in Strasbourg where their meetings feature prominently on the list of scheduled meetings on Parliament's notice boards, in meeting rooms often put at their disposal by individual Political Groups.

The importance of the intergroups is far from uniform. Some hold regular meetings, have prominent visiting speakers, large attendances and their own secretariat, sometimes on a full-time basis. Others represent the hobbyhorses of a small number of members and have few resources and infrequent meetings. Rules on membership also vary widely: in some cases, it is limited to MEPs, in others, members can also include trade associations or other external members. An intergroup has even been founded (Global Legislators for a Balanced Environment, GLOBE for short) with members from the US Congress, Japanese Diet, Russian Duma and others. Their sources of support are also extremely varied: some are assisted by Political Groups while others obtain staffing and/or finance from industry or NGOs. For example, the Kangaroo Group, a group which is committed to the elimination of all barriers to the free movement of goods, services and people across the internal frontiers of the European Union, is funded by a corporate membership scheme, as are several EP-industry forums (see below).

A few intergroups have broad-focus political goals (such as the Animal Welfare, Consumer Affairs or Minority Languages intergroups). Some provide a focus for sharing problems and experiences (such as the Intergroup of Elected Local and Regional Representatives) or discussing issues within a particular field (such as the Media Intergroup). Others concentrate on promoting specific interests, be they industrial (such as the now defunct Wings of Europe, concerned with the aeronautical industry, and a High Speed Train Intergroup), regional (mining regions, Atlantic regions, islands and maritime regions), or particular national or political causes (Tibet, Friends of Israel, Friends of Palestine, etc.).

Intergroups have developed because they have a number of major advantages. They permit members to focus on a particular set of issues of specific national, constituency or personal concern. They enable them to specialise, make contacts with outside interest groups on a more informal basis than in committee meetings, and make political contacts outside their own Groups. A member may sometimes find much in common on some issues with certain members in other Groups. Intergroups thus not only help to form cross-Group coalitions on specific issues, but to forge wider political friendships which can be useful in other circumstances, and can help to build that wider consensus which is often essential in the European Parliament. Finally, intergroups can also provide new roles and responsibilities for members and their assistants.

The very success of intergroups, however, has meant that they can constitute a rival centre of attention to official parliamentary activities, and in certain circumstances may undercut the latter. They may cause lower attendances at committee and plenary. There have even been occasions when intergoups have been mistaken by third parties as official organs of the Parliament. And the links of some of them to outside lobbies has been a matter of controversy.

MEP-industry forums

A number of groupings (variously called "forums", "networks", "foundations" or such like) bring together MEPs and specific economic or industrial interests. Most do not consider themselves intergroups, and have not attempted to register as such, though this is entirely a matter of definition. They do, after all, involve MEPs from different Groups.

Most MEP-industry forums focus on specific issues (for example the Sky & Space intergroup or the European Energy Forum), while some (for example the Kangaroo group) are more cross-cutting. Many major industry sectors have "their" MEP-industry forum. Some have only a handful of MEPs involved, while others have up to around seventy.

The agenda of these forums is usually heavily influenced by their business members, who also fund them. Their membership does not normally include NGOs or other representatives of non-commercial interests.

Concerns have been expressed about the funding of such groups, as many of them do not reveal this on their website, if they even have one. Many charge from €5,000 to €25,000 in annual corporate membership and corporate members also sponsor specific lunch or dinner debates or even excursions (such as recent controversial visits to Arctic oil exploration sites or to nuclear power stations). Some are actually run from Brussels corporate offices, such as the Forum for the Automobile and Society (FAS), which is run from the Brussels office of the International Automobile Federation (FIA) or the secretariat of the Sky & Space Intergroup, which is run by the Aerospace and Defence Industries Association of Europe.

Do they have an undue influence on legislation or policy? One is reputed to have weakened legislation intended to regulate industry, such as the rules for testing and approving chemicals (REACH). Another allegedly did the same for software and telecom legislation. On the other hand, on almost every issue, there are likely to be countervailing lobbies and pressures in a highly pluralist environment. Such groups would also argue that they are no different from intergroups supported by public interest lobbies such as the European Consumers' Organisation (BEUC) or the European Public Health Alliance (EPHA), which have acted as the secretariat of corresponding intergroups. What can be said is that cross-party forums are clearly a popular way for all kinds of lobbyists to mingle with and influence select MEPs.

The regulation of intergroups

As a result of fears that some intergroups were too closely linked with certain lobbies, and also of concerns that intergroups can anyway disrupt the work of the Parliament, the governing bodies of Parliament began in the mid-1990s to regulate them. The Political Group chairs reached an agreement in June 1995, formally adopted by the Conference of Presidents in December 1995, in which they reaffirmed that intergroups had no official status, were not organs of the Parliament, could not express the Parliament's point of view, and could not use its name or logo, or any other denominations which could lead to confusion with official organs of the Parliament. At the same time they established specific rules governing the provision of technical facilities to intergroups (which is anyway through Political Groups, not Parliament as such) including:

- the obligation never to meet during a scheduled voting session of the Parliament;
- the communication to the chairs of the Political Groups concerned of the list of persons responsible (who should be from at least three Political Groups), the denomination of the intergroup and its logo, if any, and funding sources; and
- the obligation to comply with the rules concerning the declaration of financial interests of MEPs and assistants and the rules on lobbyists.

In 1998-99, the Rules committee of Parliament examined a report on the financing and operation of groupings of members. This pointed out that it was still not possible to make an adequate assessment of the influence of outside interests on intergroups (for example, several groups were registered as having no external source of finance although they received secretarial aid from outside bodies). It also noted that there was no one consolidated and easily accessible register of groupings (a register at the Secretary-General's office only gave an intergroup's leadership, and did not indicate which MEPs were members or regular participants). As a result of the committee's report, the provisions of Annex 1 of the EP Rules on members' financial interests were tightened up. Chairs of intergroups and other unofficial groupings of members were required to declare any support, whether in cash or kind (e.g. secretarial assistance) which would have to be declared if offered to members as individuals. The Quaestors were also made responsible for keeping a register and drawing up detailed rules for the declaration of outside support by such groupings.

In December 1999 further detailed rules were adopted by the Conference of Presidents requiring the declaration of financial interests to be made on an annual basis, the Quaestors' register to be made public, the precise objectives of each intergroup to be clarified, strict regulation of when they could meet, and their establishment to require the agreement of at least three Groups, each of which could support only a limited number.

This regulation of intergroups, intended to prevent abuse and to limit their number, at the same time meant that those that registered became almost semi-official. It also meant that, besides the registered intergroups, there are a number of unregistered ones, either because they are too small or irregular for their members to consider registering, or because they do not need facilities from the Groups, or because they did not get the sponsorship of three Groups or because they want to avoid publicity. Such unregistered intergroups may not obtain interpretation facilities from Groups nor have their meetings announced on Parliament's screens.

Table 30: *Intergroups*

---

1. Officially Registered Intergroups (list adopted 8 December 2009)

Small and Medium sized Enterprises
Way of Saint James/Camino de Santiago
Family, the rights of the child and bioethics
Sky and space
Youth issues
Urban areas
Mountainous, island and sparsely populated regions and very remote regions
Social economy
Sustainable hunting, biodiversity, countryside activities and forests
Extreme poverty, Fourth World European Committee
Disability
Tibet
Climate change and biodiversity and sustainable development
Water
Baltic Europe
Media
Ageing and intergenerational solidarity
Seas and coastal affairs
Welfare and conservation of animals
Trade union coordination group

New media, free software, open information society
Traditional national minorities, constitutional regions and regional languages
Lesbian, gay, bisexual and transgender (LGBT) rights
Public services
Western Sahara
Anti-racism and diversity
Wine, fruits and vegetables, tradition and quality food

2. Some non-registered Intergroups active or recently active
Kangaroo Group
Global Legislators for a Balanced Environment (GLOBE)
Welfare and Conservation of Animals
Land Use and Food Policy (LUFPIG)
Consumer Forum
Mining
Progressive Women
Roma Rights
Cancer
Ecumenical Prayer Breakfast
Europeans Abroad
Federalist Intergroup
Friends of a Free Iran
Friends of Israel
Friends of Palestine
Law Enforcement, Organised Crime and Terrorism
Sport
Friends of Football
Health
Stateless Nations
Breast Cancer
Sustainable development
Beer Club
Volunteering
Financial Services Forum (EPFSF)
European Energy Forum
Forum for the Automobile and Society
Forum in the European Parliament for Construction (FOCOPE)
Transatlantic Policy Network (TPN)
European Internet Foundation (EIF)

Specific intergroups: some examples

To provide something of the flavour of the way in which intergroups operate, a brief description is given below of the objectives and working methods of five intergroups.

Intergroup on the Welfare and Conservation of Animals

One of the oldest – and largest – this intergroup mobilises cross-party support for animal welfare and conservation. It exists to exchange information
on topical issues, to put pressure on the Commission to come up with new
legislative initiatives, and then to follow these through. It also takes an interest in related conservation and environmental issues.

The RSPCA and similar national societies for the protection of animals set
up a "Eurogroup for Animal Welfare" in 1980. Its first director was Edward
Seymour-Rouse. It then had no special links with MEPs. In 1983, however,
a British Conservative MEP, Stanley Johnson (father of the later London

Mayor, Boris Johnson) along with five other like-minded members, established an Animal Welfare intergroup and served as its first chair. Its secretariat was provided by the Eurogroup.

By the end of the 1984-89 Parliament, the intergroup was significant enough for its chairmanship to be highly sought after. After the 1989 elections, a closely contested election for chair between Hanja Maij-Weggen (Dutch Christian Democrat) and Hemmo Muntingh (Dutch Socialist) was won by the former, with around 90 MEPs taking part in the meeting, and even with party whips being applied – highly unusual for an intergroup. Shortly afterwards, however, Maij-Weggen was appointed as a member of the Dutch government, and left.

Table 31: *Chairs of the Animal Welfare Intergroup*

1983	Stanley Johnson	(UK Conservative)
1984-87	Lieselotte Seibel-Emmerling	(German SPD)
1987-89	Madron Seligman	(UK Conservative)
1989	Hanja Maij-Weggen	(Dutch Christian Democrat)
1989- 92	Mary Banotti	(Irish Fine Gael)
1992-94	Anita Pollack	(UK Labour)
1994-97	Hanja Maij-Weggen	(Dutch Christian Democrat)
1997-99	Michael Elliot	(UK Labour)
1999-2002	José Maria Gil-Robles	(Spanish Partido Popular)
2002-04	Robert Evans	(UK Labour)
2004-07	Paolo Casaca	(Portuguese Socialist)
2007-09	Neil Parish	(UK Conservative)
2009-	Carl Schlyter	(Swedish Green)

The intergroup does not have card-carrying members, and its meetings are open to all MEPs. Turnout at its meetings ranges between a tiny handful and 90, but the average attendance tends to be around 25-35. Some members attend practically all of its meetings, others come occasionally, or when a specific item of interest to them is on the agenda. Sometimes opponents (e.g. supporters of the fur trade, hunting or farming interests, etc.) turn up at meetings, which are thus considerably enlivened.

The most regular attenders tend to be British and Dutch MEPs, who often receive the most constituency mail on animal welfare issues, followed by German, Swedish and Irish members, whereas Spanish, French and Greek members have tended to be less involved. In terms of political allegiance the intergroup has tried to achieve the widest possible spread.

The Eurogroup provides two members of staff dedicated to organising and servicing the intergroup, which is therefore one of the best served intergroups in the Parliament. They can also help individual members in their correspondence on animal welfare issues.

The intergroup's first major success was in obtaining the ban on imports of baby seal products into the Europe. Others have been on limiting animal experimentation, phasing out the battery-cage system for hens, banning the import of certain furs from animals caught in leg-hold traps, and time limitations on the transport of farm animals to slaughter. The intergroup also initiated Parliament's successful request to have animals re-classified as "sentient beings", rather than mere products, in the treaty. The intergroup has been less successful on certain other issues where a consensus approach has proved hard to achieve, such as on some hunting issues.

Intergroup on lesbian, gay, bisexual and transgender (LGBT) rights

This intergroup is an informal forum for MEPs who are interested in issues that impact the lives of lesbian, gay, bisexual and transgender (LGBT) people, as well as their families and employers. Members of the intergroup frequently take a stance on LGBT issues in the Parliament, or when they deal with constituency affairs.

The intergroup has over 100 members. Its work is led by two co-presidents, Michael Cashman (UK Labour), who had previously founded and chaired the Stonewall Lesbian and Gay Rights Group in Britain, and Ulrike Lunacek (Austrian Green), as well as four vice presidents who are members of the Liberal, EPP, Green and GUE Groups.

The work of the intergroup consists in monitoring the work of the European Union (mostly the legislative work of the European Parliament, but also, through questions, the Commission and Council); monitoring the situation of LGBT people in EU Member States and beyond (sometimes involving challenges to national legal situations or active solidarity demonstrations such as high profile attendance at Gay Pride marches where authorities have failed to provide sound and secure surroundings for the event); and liaising with LGTB organizations to relay their concerns at the European level. The treaty provisions providing for EU legislation prohibiting discrimination on grounds of sexual orientation and the reference in the Charter of Rights were both things that the intergroup campaigned for and can now use.

Federalist intergroup

Under various names, a series of intergroups have followed on from the original Crocodile Club established after the first direct elections as an informal discussion group, named after the Strasbourg restaurant where it first met, by Altiero Spinelli, with the aim of getting Parliament to take the initiative in constitutional change aiming to transform the then European Community into a more federal European Union. The Crocodile Club was the initiator of the decision to create a special Committee on Institutional Affairs within Parliament, and it was this committee which prepared Parliament's proposal for a "Treaty on European Union" in 1984, which in turn led to the negotiation of the Single European Act (see Chapter 18).

Re-constituted as the Federalist Intergroup in 1986, soon after the death of Altiero Spinelli, by those who considered the Single Act to be an insufficient response to Parliament's proposal, it sought to continue Spinelli's work for "achieving European Union through the effort of the European Parliament, the only democratically representative institution at Community level". It immediately attracted about 150 members, despite a hefty membership fee, from all Political Groups (except the European Right) and all nationalities. It set up a Bureau whose dozen members rotated monthly in the chair. It appointed a secretary-general, Virgilio Dastoli, the former personal assistant of Spinelli, who was assisted by a volunteer Federalist Intergroup Support Group (FIGS) composed of students in Brussels in the Federalist Youth Movement. It set up federalist intergroups in a number of national parliaments, which held joint meetings. It sponsored several opinion polls in all the Member States (financed by selling exclusive rights to newspapers). These showed clear majorities in all except two Member States (UK and Denmark) for such things as a European government accountable to the European Parliament, legislative powers for the Parliament, and giving Parliament the task of drafting a constitution for European Union. The referendum held in Italy at the same time as the 1989 European elections on this last point was a direct result of the intergroup pressing for this, together with its counterpart in the Italian Parliament and the Federalist Movement in Italy.

After the negotiations for the Maastricht Treaty it became less active but was later revived as "SOS-Europe" by members disillusioned by what they saw as insufficient progress on institutional matters in the Treaty of Amsterdam, seeing itself as a lobby for making more sweeping institutional reforms to better prepare the EU better for its future enlargement.

After the 1999 elections a new European Constitution Intergroup was established with about 100 members expressing an interest in its work. Its initial steering committee consisted of Jo Leinen (PES, Germany), Alain Lamassoure (EPP-ED, France), Andrew Duff (Liberal, UK), Monica Frassoni (Greens, Belgium), Mihail Papayannakis (GUE, Greece), Carlos Carnero (PES, Spain) and Cecilia Malmstrom (Liberal, Sweden). At the start of the 2004-09 Parliament, Jean-Luc Dehaene (EPP, Belgium), Mercedes Bresso (PES, Italy), Thierry Cornillet (Liberal, France) and Alexander Stubb (EPP, Finland) joined the steering committee. Its main objectives were the "constitutionalisation" of the treaty texts, a new and more democratic method of treaty revision and major reform of the EU institutions. These objectives were taken up, to a significant degree, by the Convention and the drafting of the new EU Constitution (see Chapter 18).

Following the adoption of the Lisbon Treaty, which took up much of the substance but not the "constitutional" form of the EU Constitution, the intergroup has reverted to the name Federalist Intergroup and is now chaired by Andrew Duff (ALDE/UK). Its work programme in the Parliament of 2009-14 includes the promotion of full and efficient implementation of the Lisbon Treaty; reform of the EU's financial system; electoral reform for European elections; encouraging participatory democracy; and institutional challenges of EU enlargement.

The Federalist Intergroup has no commercial sponsorship. It is supported by the Union of European Federalists (UEF) and the Young European Federalists (JEF)

European Parliamentary Financial Services Forum (EPFSF)

This is an example of an industry-MEP forum, though one that is transparent with significant information on its own website, including its sources of finance. It promotes a single European market for financial services, provides a focal point and information for MEPs interested in financial services, and is above all a forum for industry-parliamentary dialogue on matters relevant to Europe's financial services industry. It makes its case notably via briefing papers, monthly themed meetings (usually over breakfast or lunch), study visits and training sessions (of which four were held in 2010, on derivatives, banking, insurance & pensions, and investment services).

The Forum's 50 industry members consist of a wide range of leading players (both associations and individual institutions) in the European financial services industry, including representatives from the European Banking Federation, the Association of Mutual Insurance Cooperatives in Europe, the Association of Financial Markets in Europe, and many individual banks. Each pay some €8000 per year for the privilege. MEPs can participate for free.

Its total budget amounts to just over a quarter of a million euros (2008 figures) and is spent on the following:

Staff expenses	161,402
Office expenditures, rent and insurance	27,274
Telecommunication, IT, website	22,217
Events	21,025
Travel and representation costs	2,969
Accounting, audit fees	6,727
Taxes and other financial expenses	1,986
Depreciation office and IT	7,560
Total Costs	**€251,160**

It is run by a steering group, which is chosen by the MEPs, currently consisting of 25 MEPs from the EPP, ECR, Socialist and ALDE Political Groups, and with Wolf Klinz (German Liberal) as chair and Peter Skinner (UK Labour) as its vice-chair.

The Forum is a not-for-profit organisation under Belgian law (ASBL) . It states that it is not a lobbying organisation and that the diversity of its membership means that it is not capable of advocating a position of its own. In its own view, "the value placed on the EPFSF lies in its diverse membership and its position as an acknowledged and reliable source of information, allowing debate and the issuance of impartial commentaries on key issues at the heart of the European legislative agenda. During its debates, all participants, including consumer representatives and other stakeholders, are entitled to voice their opinion. The briefing papers that are prepared in advance of the events are all published on the Forum's website and demonstrate its effort to be as neutral and informative as possible. Since the EPFSF benefits from members of the whole financial industry, which have different point of views, all positions are taken into account, thus helping to ensure neutrality." Critics, however, claim that the 2005 Money Laundering Directive was watered down at least in part due to efforts by the EPFSF.

Disability intergroup

The Disability Intergroup is also one of the oldest intergroups, first established in 1980. Its current chair is Adam Kosa MEP (Hungarian EPP), succeeding the long serving Richard Howitt (UK Labour) who was chair from

1994 to 2009 and remains vice chair along with eight others from different groups and nationalities who constitute its Bureau. The intergroup works closely with the European Disability Forum (EDF) – an independent European non-governmental organisation that represents the interests of 65 million disabled people in the European Union and is actually run by disabled people or family members of disabled people.

The intergroup holds six public meetings a year in Strasbourg to discuss issues of concern to disabled people, disability groups and the EU institutions. It produces a regular newsletter that informs its members and interested parties about its recent work and upcoming issues. Intergroup members take action by tabling amendments to legislation or EU programmes or by putting forward parliamentary questions to the Commission.

The areas of priority for the Disability Intergroup are defined by its Bureau, which meets regularly in Brussels. The Bureau approves the rolling work programme, currently focussing on a number of issues, including making the Parliament itself a model of full accessibility (buildings, documents, websites, hearing loop systems, sign language interpretation and employment procedures) and pushing for swift ratification of the UN Convention on the Rights of Persons with Disabilities (and its implementation in the EU through a comprehensive Disability Pact). It continues to vet EU legislation to check whether the needs of disabled people are catered for.

Indeed, it has had a number of spectacular successes in this regard, not least the 2006 EU Regulation on the rights of persons with disabilities and persons with reduced mobility travelling by air. Previously, persons with disabilities regularly experienced various forms of discrimination when travelling by air or were even simply denied boarding by certain airlines. Now, an airline cannot refuse, on the ground of reduced mobility or disability, to accept the reservation of a person or to deny boarding to a person, except in a limited number of exceptional cases, in which case the disabled passenger has the right to be informed about the reasons thereof, and where appropriate, to receive re-imbursement or re-routing. If notified 48 hours beforehand, a disabled passenger has the right to receive assistance, which must be adapted to his/her specific needs. The regulation entered into force in 2008 and is considered to an important success for the European disability movement.

Conclusion

Intergroups have become an established feature of the European Parliament. Successive generations of members have found such groups to fulfil a useful function beyond the formal structure of committees, Groups and delegations. They may vary considerably in size and significance, but their continued existence is highly likely.

11. The Parliament secretariat

Many are astonished at the size of the Parliament's secretariat. Compared with national parliaments in Europe, it is much bigger, with over 6,000 posts, officials outnumbering MEPs by more than eight to one. This high ratio can only be understood in the light of two particular constraints imposed on Parliament by the Member States, namely that it must devote a very high level of resources to ensuring that parliamentary bodies can operate in all EU official languages and that it is spread over three main places of work (with additional information offices in all Member States). Together these two elements of multilingualism and geographical dispersion account for more than 50% of the annual Parliament budget.

At the same time, few have a very clear understanding of how the secretariat works in practice. Indeed such has been the development of the institution over recent years that even officials of the Parliament have some difficulty in following the enormous range of activities undertaken by their colleagues. And those who were reasonably familiar with its structure some years ago have had to come to terms with a period of revolutionary change marked by three specific developments:

- *first*, all those working for the institution (as well as for all other EU institutions) are subject to a new set of Staff Regulations that came into force in May 2004. It was the first time in 50 years that the system had been completely overhauled and the result was a fundamental revision of the conditions under which Parliament officials now work. The old system of dividing staff into five categories (A for administrative staff, LA for translators and interpreters, B for executive assistants, C for clerical staff and secretaries and D for manual or service staff) was replaced by two "function groups": AD for administrators, including linguists, and AST for "assistants" (i.e. all other support staff), reflecting a move to recruiting staff with higher levels of competence to match new requirements within the institution. The salary structure and terms of conditions of service were also substantially revised in response to calls to modernise the European civil service, particularly in the aftermath of the fall of the Santer Commission in 1999.

- *second*, the increase (resulting from enlargement) from 15 to 27 Member States and from 11 to 23 working languages has led to a major increase in the size of the establishment plan and in the complexity of its operation. Of the new posts for officials from the new Member States, a substantial majority were reserved for linguistic staff, needed to make it possible for all MEPs to participate fully in the work of the institution and for the public to follow it. Recruitment did not prove easy, as most of the new Member States had few, if any, institutes or universities dedicated to language training of the kind required. At the same time, Parliament was confronted by a whole series of additional logistical problems: only so many meeting rooms in the Parliament are equipped to provide interpretation in 23 languages and even in those that are, interpreters have had to learn new ways of working, often using a relay between the original language and the language into which they interpret. To cope with increased demand with only limited resources available, new rules to manage multilingualism were introduced, restricting, for example, the length of written texts that are to be translated and setting priorities for different kinds of text.

–   *third*, the secretariat has been restructured with a view to improving its performance and providing a better service to members, above all in their role as legislators. A whole range of measures has been introduced including a change in the structure and competences of the Directorates-General, the establishment of new structures and working methods and a reinforcement of the mechanisms for financial and personnel management to cope with the growth of the institution and its establishment plan.

Who are the staff of the Parliament?

Parliament's permanent officials are European civil servants, subject to the same terms and conditions as those working in the other EU institutions. They are recruited by the Parliament through open external competitions, now normally organised by the European Personnel Selection Office (known as EPSO). The competitions are generally open to all language groups, although an exception was made for nationals of new Member States in the period immediately after enlargement. Linguistic competence, though not necessarily decisive, is one important factor in recruitment. The minimum requirement is "satisfactory" knowledge of one official language in addition to the mother tongue but extra points are awarded for other languages. In addition, officials are expected to acquire a working knowledge of a second foreign language before their first promotion.

The Staff Regulations lay down that "an official shall carry out his duties and conduct himself solely with the interests of the Communities in mind", and "shall neither seek nor take instructions from any government, authority, organisation or person outside his institution".

The European Parliament now has an establishment plan that provides for 6,135 posts – 5,273 in the General Secretariat and 862 reserved for officials of the Political Groups (2010 figures). This total represents around 15% of the officials employed by the EU as a whole. Of the posts that are inside the General Secretariat, just under half are in Brussels, something over 45% are in Luxembourg and the remainder are spread between Strasbourg and the information offices in the Member States. The 862 temporary officials in the Political Groups, all now working in Brussels, are recruited directly by the Groups (their separate role and status is discussed in Chapter 5). In addition, the Parliament uses free-lance interpreters to complement the full-time interpreters as well as offering short-term contracts to contractual agents for specific jobs where the post cannot be filled by an official, to substitute for staff on maternity leave or to reinforce particular services.

Parliament also offers over 500 short (five-month) traineeships for young people with university backgrounds to become familiar with the working of the institution. Trainees (known as "stagiaires") can be paid or unpaid: the former receive a modest bursary and are known as Robert Schuman scholars. In addition, new traineeships are being developed for young people without university training and exist since 2007 for a limited number of persons with a disability.

Finally, we need to include the "accredited" parliamentary assistants who since 2009 have contracts with the Parliament, although they continue to be selected by MEPs, who can fix their level of responsibility and hence their level of remuneration, as well as terminating their service, if they are not satisfied (see Chapter 4 for more details). By the end of 2009 more than 1,300 accredited parliamentary assistants worked at Parliament, with nearly 70% recruited to work for the duration of the parliamentary term until 2014. A large majority are under 35, with the average age being 32.

Within the newly created two categories of staff (AD and AST), there is a large variety of different kind of posts. The AD category (over 2,500 in total) contains a mixture of administrators, translators and interpreters, with the last two totalling 1,350. The latter figure underlines the effort required to translate documents and interpret speeches into all the languages of the Union. The AST category is larger (over 3400) and includes financial and administrative assistants, secretaries and clerical staff. The category also includes some manual or service staff but officials are no longer being recruited for these tasks, which are now mainly outsourced. Within each career bracket there are a number of grades. New administrators, for example, will normally be recruited at AD5 level, with the opportunity to rise eventually to become a Director or Director-General at AD15 or 16. It is also possible to move from the AST to the AD category by a process known as "certification".

The Staff Regulations also specify that "no posts shall be reserved for nationals of any specific Member State" though they should be "recruited on the broadest possible geographical basis". In fact, in the case of the Parliament, for a range of historical and geographical reasons, there is considerable disparity in the number of officials from different nationalities across the institution as a whole. Such differences are in part the product of the number of applicants from the countries concerned and are not therefore easy to manage. Moreover, they are not equally spread across the grades, with much less disparity visible at higher grades, where significant efforts have been made to improve the balance. Thus the twelve top officials (in late 2010) came from seven different nationalities.

In 2010, 955 posts were occupied by Belgians, 852 by French and 703 by Italians, together making up around one third of all staff. These figures stand in marked contrast to the figure for British officials (382). More generally, nationals of countries that joined the Union earlier tend to be more numerous proportionately than those from countries that joined later. This is particularly evident in the case of the latest entrants, the nationals of each of which formed a very small percentage of the total staff initially, but whose numbers are increasing more quickly than those of the older Member States. As a result a generational change is taking place in the institution. The average age of staff from the new Member States is close to 30, whereas the average age of Danish, Greek, Luxembourg, Dutch and UK officials, for example, is over 50. With a substantial number of the latter due to retire over the next decade, a new balance between new and old Member States can be expected to develop, with the latter ceasing to be so heavily represented.

The permanent staff within the General Secretariat are civil servants carrying out their duties in a politically neutral way. Nonetheless, they are not prevented from being active members of political parties in their spare time, or from standing as candidates in local, national or European elections. To do this they must take leave during the election campaign. If elected, they must take indefinite leave but if subsequently they leave that office, they may return to Parliament's staff.

In practice, few permanent Parliament officials have stood for national or European elections. One who became a senior government minister was Hans Apel, elected to the German Bundestag in the 1970s. He always retained the right to return to Parliament's staff but never exercised it. More recent cases are Ben Patterson, Alain Barrau and Yves Leterme. The first of these worked in the Parliament before 1979, was elected as an MEP in the UK that year and remained a member until 1994 when he lost his seat and returned to the secretariat; the second became a member of the Assemblée Nationale in France, where he was chair of the "Délégation pour les Affaires européennes" before returning to the General Secretariat of the Parliament after losing his seat; and the third has been Belgian Prime Minister and remains a member of the Belgian Senate but remains on leave from the Parliament. Richard Corbett, one of the co-authors of this book, is the only case of someone who has been a trainee ("stagiaire"), a civil servant in the General Secretariat, a senior Group official, an MEP and now an official of another institution, advising the President of the European Council.

There is also movement between the staff of the Political Groups and that of the Parliament as a whole. At the end of the 2004 legislature, three of the Secretaries-General of the Political Groups were appointed to posts in the General Secretariat, one of them, Klaus Welle of the EPP-ED Group, becoming Director-General for Internal Policies and in 2009, Secretary-General. Those Group staff at lower grades who have also passed Parliament's open competitions can be re-deployed as permanent staff without difficulties. Movement from the Groups to the General Secretariat is becoming more common. The Staff Regulations were amended in 2004 to enable Group staff with a minimum of ten years service to participate in an internal competition, organised at least every five years, and if successful, to apply for posts as permanent officials inside the General Secretariat.

A number of long-serving permanent officials have also moved the other way and gone to work in the Political Groups, on a temporary or longer-term basis. The Secretary-General of Parliament from 1997 to 2007, Julian Priestley (who had previously stood on two occasions in Westminster elections as a Labour candidate), was from 1989 to 1994 Secretary-General of the Socialist Group, then head of the Private Office of the President of Parliament. His successor as Secretary-General, Harald Rømer, went from the General Secretariat to become Secretary-General of the old ED Group, then Deputy Secretary-General of the EPP Group, before returning to become the Deputy Secretary-General of Parliament and Director-General for the Presidency.

There is relatively little direct Political Group influence on appointments at lower levels within the Parliament but at higher levels, particularly Directors and Directors-General, where appointments are made by the Bureau of Parliament, political factors do play a significant role alongside nationality, seniority and ability. This has not led to the domination of one political or national interest but certainly has enabled the two largest Groups to make their mark on appointments. Parliament's staff are protected to some degree by those who defend the concept of a neutral European civil service and also by the sheer variety and number of political forces and nationalities represented within the Parliament, which act as counterweights to each other.

The structure of the secretariat

The **Secretary-General** is the highest official within the Parliament and is appointed by the Bureau. In nearly 60 years, there have only been seven Secretaries-General.

Table 32: *Secretaries-General of the European Parliament*

1952–1960	Frits de Nerée tot Babberich
1961–1979	Hans Nord
1979–1986	Hans Joachim Opitz
1986–1997	Enrico Vinci
1997–2007	Julian Priestley
2007–2009	Harald Rømer
2009-	Klaus Welle

The Secretary-General has four main tasks:

- assisting the President, the Bureau, the political bodies and the MEPs;

- ensuring the smooth running of parliamentary business under the leadership of the President and the Bureau;

- with the President, verifying and signing all acts adopted jointly by Parliament and the Council; and

- preparing the basic elements of a report that the Bureau uses to draw up Parliament's draft budget estimates.

To carry out this work he has at his disposal a Private Office which enables him to coordinate the work of the secretariat. With the increasing range and complexity of the tasks assigned to the secretariat, has come an increase in the size of the Private Office, now totalling around 30.

However, the day-to-day work of the institution is in the hands of the **Directorates-General** or DGs. Before 1973 there were four DGs but that number gradually grew to reach the present figure of ten, along with a separate Legal Service (see Figure 6). Their main roles can be described as follows:

Directorate-General for the Presidency responsible for:

– work associated with Parliament's political activity involving the plenary sittings, interinstitutional legislative programming, the Conference of Presidents, the Bureau, the Quaestors and Members' activities;

– assisting Members and the President with the legal-linguistic verification of texts, amendment of legislative texts and the admissibility of amendments;

– relations with national parliaments; and

– the provision of library services, protocol, the mail department, the transmission of documents, the register, archives and security.

The Director General of this DG is also now the Deputy Secretary General of the Parliament.

Directorate-General for Internal Policies of the Union responsible for:

– ensuring the smooth running of parliamentary committees in the field of internal policies,

– coordinating Parliament's legislative activities, notably through the Conference of Committee Chairs;

- supporting committee members, particularly the committee chairs and rapporteurs, in the exercise of their duties

- providing the committees, other parliamentary bodies and the President's office with background notes, briefings and long-term studies on all aspects of Parliament's activities in the field of internal policies;

– helping the committees to develop their work programmes in close cooperation with the Commission and Council; and

– promoting and coordinating all activities relating to better law-making in Parliament.

Directorate-General for External Policies responsible for:

– providing professional support and advice for the committee and delegation chairs in the exercise of their duties;

- helping the committees responsible for external policies develop their work programmes in close cooperation with the Commission and Council;

- ensuring the smooth running of meetings of the committees responsible for external policies and delegations;

- acting as a link between the interparliamentary delegations, non-EU countries and parliaments throughout the world;

– supporting the election coordination group and planning, organising and follow up of election observation missions;

-    providing the President, committees, delegations and other Parliament bodies with information, summary notes and studies;

-    assisting the ACP-EU, Euro-Mediterranean, Euronest and the Euro-Latin American parliamentary assemblies, their committees and working parties as well as special bodies such as the High-Level Group for the Middle East.

Directorate-General for Communication responsible for:

-    liaising with and briefing the press on the activities of the European Parliament;

-    providing information for the general public, the media and opinion leaders on the activities of the Parliament; and

-    managing visitors' groups and establishing a Visitors Centre in Brussels.

The Directorate General has information offices in the capital cities of all Union countries as well as a regional office in Strasbourg. These offices are in almost all cases in the same building as the offices of the European Commission. In the run-up to the 1999 European elections it was decided to set up on a pilot basis, small regional offices alongside the Commission in Barcelona, Edinburgh, Marseilles and Milan. After the elections these offices were made permanent along with a further regional office in Munich. The offices in the capitals usually have two or three administrators and act as national contact points for the European Parliament. Facilities are often also provided at these offices for the respective national delegations of MEPs. In 2010 it was decided to extend these regional offices to include Poland with an office due to be established in 2011 in Wroclaw. In addition, it was decided to set up an office in Washington to liaise with the United States Congress; it began work in the spring of 2010.

The DG has its own audiovisual department, able to deploy television crews, which films and distributes images of Parliament's plenary as well as important events in the committees and other parliamentary activities. The end product is available to national television channels and is broadcast online via the internet. In addition, the DG has responsibility for two specific projects: the establishment of a Visitors' Centre and the running of europarltv, the Parliament's web TV channel.

Directorate-General for Personnel responsible for:

-    managing Parliament's human resources ie. the officials and Political Group and other staff;

-    giving staff access to vocational training (in particular, language training, training in management techniques, IT training); and

-    developing strategies to improve women's working conditions and promoting equal opportunities for each employee.

Directorate-General for Infrastructure and Logistics responsible for:

- technical and administrative management of Parliament's buildings in

Brussels, Strasbourg and Luxembourg and the information offices in the Member States; and

– management of equipment (purchasing, transport, removals, message services, catering, furniture, shops etc.) and practical arrangements for meetings.

With successive enlargements of the EU and the growth of Parliament, this Directorate-General has overseen some of the largest building projects in Europe, and in Strasbourg and Brussels is coping with the complexity of owning rather than renting, following the Parliament's decision not to continue with the expensive practice of renting all its premises.

Directorate-General for Translation responsible for:

– translating documents out of and into the 23 official languages of the European Union;

– organising the translation of documents externally and monitoring their quality; and

– developing appropriate IT tools and terminology databases to aid translators;

This DG, based almost entirely in Luxembourg, is the largest Directorate-General of all, with over 1400 staff, obliged to find ways of responding to clients for its services who are nearly all in Brussels, 200 kilometres away. Despite technological progress, this is not always easy!

Directorate-General for Interpretation and Conferences responsible for:

– organising interpretation for all Parliament's meetings in and outside the three places of work; and

– the administration of Parliament's meeting rooms and providing technical assistance for all meetings organised by Parliament.

Directorate-General for Finance responsible for:

– drawing up Parliament's budget, supervising its implementation, accompanying the discharge procedure, keeping and closing the accounts and managing the treasury;

– providing support for all authorising officers in Parliament;

– managing expenditure related to members' allowances and social entitlements, and implementing financial support for Political Groups, European political parties and foundations and associations of former or current members;

– managing inter-departmental services for the whole of Parliament, such as the inventory and the travel office; and

– administering the Internal Audit Unit that enjoys functional autonomy under the Financial Regulation.

Directorate-General for Innovation and Technological Support responsible for:

–   maintaining and developing Parliament's information systems for the
     members, the Political Groups, the Directorates-General, the European
     Ombudsman and the Data Protection Supervisor so as to allow multi-
     lingual access from all the places of work;

–   managing the computing and telecommunications system;

–   printing and distributing Parliament's working documents; and

–   publishing legislation and documents in the Official Journal.

Legal Service responsible for:

–   providing legal assistance for Parliament's political bodies and for its
     Secretariat;

–   helping the committees with their legislative work and handling legal
     cases taken on behalf of or against the Parliament; and

–   representing the European Parliament in European and national
     courts.

The Legal Service has grown substantially in importance since its founding
in 1985. It now has 89 staff, including nearly 50 lawyers. One particularly
significant development in its work has arisen from the co-decision procedure. Under this procedure, as the next chapter explains, the Parliament is
jointly responsible with Council for adopting, signing and publishing the
final text of European legislation. As a result, the Legal Services of the
Parliament and the Council are obliged to act together in defending the outcome of the co-decision procedure in the event of a case being brought
against it before the European Court of Justice.

Issues affecting the secretariat

Three issues deserve further discussion: the question of the overall size of
the secretariat, its relationship with the Political Groups, and new developments in staff policy, notably mobility and staff reports.

Since the Assembly's beginning in 1952, there has been a dramatic rise in
the number of Parliament staff. A figure of 37 posts in 1952-53 (with staff
preparing documents in the kitchen of the then Secretary-General, who
lived above the Parliament!) rose to 1,995 by 1979, 2,966 by 1984 and is now
just over 6,000. The rate of increase can be compared with that of the
Council, which had almost the same number of officials in the early 1950s
but now is considerably smaller with around 3,500 staff. The rise in the
number of Parliament staff has gone hand in hand with increases in the
number of MEPs from 78 to 736 (soon to be 751), of working languages from
four to twenty three (more than a third of Parliament's officials are in its linguistic services), of nationalities from six to 27 and, last but not least, the
increased range of Parliament's tasks and responsibilities, above all as a co-
legislator.

During the 1990s a concerted effort was made to limit expansion. In 1993
and 1994, for example, the Committee on Budgets insisted on a detailed
screening exercise to establish priorities and to identify areas where there
could be staff cutbacks. For a time, new tasks were met largely through

Figure 6 – *The European Parliament Secretariat*

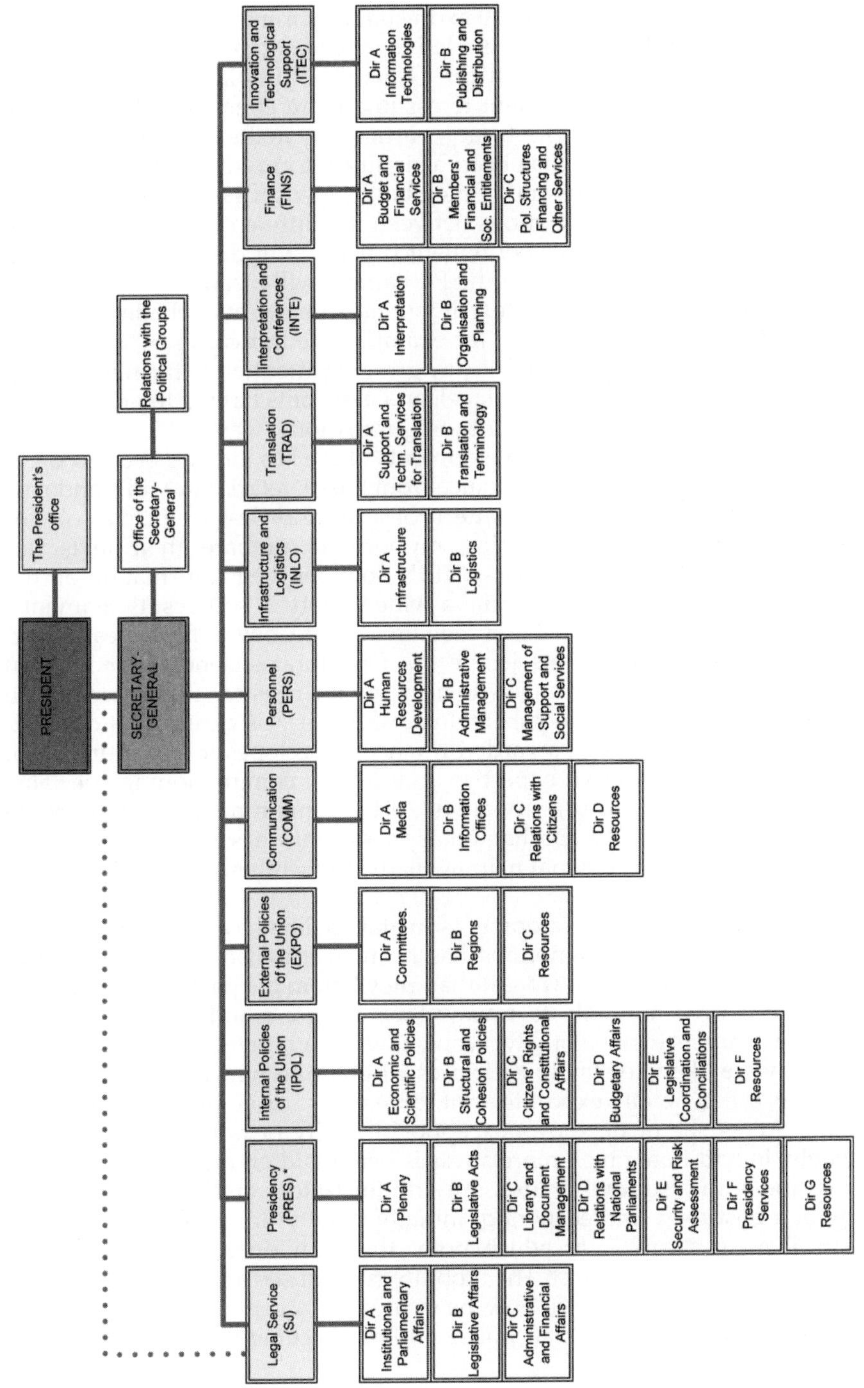

redeployment of existing staff rather than new recruitment. However, the pressures of successive enlargements in 1995, 2004 and 2007 led to an unstoppable pressure to increase the establishment plan, with each new language being calculated to add 120 extra staff as a minimum. Moreover, the entry into force of the Lisbon Treaty led to agreement to create an additional 150 posts, split equally between the General Secretariat and the Political Groups, to enable the Parliament to assume more effectively the new role that it was assigned under the Treaty, particularly in the legislative domain.

At the same time, there has been a significant growth in the number of staff of the Political Groups and of members' personal assistants, raising the question of the future of relations between the different categories of staff. Some argue that the role of permanent officials will decline; others claim that the growth in the powers of the Parliament will mean that there will be room for all to develop their role. All will face a new set of challenges, with the secretariat having to master, for example, the intricacies of new procedures, the Groups being obliged to pay growing attention to the relationship with their parties at the national level, and assistants having to organise the work of their members in an ever more professional way.

Regardless of longer term developments, there has already been recognition of the need to reinforce assistance from the secretariat to MEPs and particularly rapporteurs. The old pattern of a more or less exclusive role for committee secretariats in helping rapporteurs prepare their texts has changed radically in recent years. MEPs now get their information on the subjects they are dealing with from a wide variety of sources. Parliament's Bureau agreed in 2003 to disband the Directorate-General for Research and to create policy departments inside the Directorates-General for Internal and External Policies, with a view to bringing the research function closer to the committees and their members. In addition, it was agreed that committees should themselves be awarded financial envelopes for the purpose of buying in ad hoc external expertise and advice, commissioning specialist research and the like in priority areas. At the same time, it is important to note that the statute for parliamentary assistants has substantially reinforced the system of personal help available to members, independently of the role of the secretariat.

Finally, some recent developments in staff policy have had a significant effect. The system of promotions has been overhauled with annual staff reports assuming a greater weight than they had in the past. All officials are now interviewed annually to review their progress and to see how they wish their careers to develop. Everyone now has a rather clearer idea of how long they are likely to stay in their present grade. A new administrator, for example, can generally expect to wait three years before moving to the next grade, unless she or he shows exceptional ability or fails to perform adequately. In addition, much more stress is being laid on mobility, in particular in the administrative grades. All administrators are only supposed to stay in a post for a limited period, initially three years, extending to seven years later in a career, at which point the individual concerned can be obliged to accept a new post. The mobility rule caused something of a shock in the Parliament but it has now been broadly accepted as introducing a degree of dynamism into staff policy and has become part of the organisational culture. This is a remarkable change in an institution where in the past officials could often spend ten to fifteen years in the same job.

As indicated earlier, Parliament's employees are subject to the same terms and conditions as those that apply to officials in the other institutions. Hence some aspects of staff policy are subject to inter-institutional bargaining and discussion. A good example is staff salaries, which are fixed by the Council on a proposal of the Commission and after consulting Parliament and negotiating with the inter-institutional trade unions. Since 1991, when there was considerable friction and even limited strike action, changes to staff salaries have been linked to the average change in the salary level of national civil servants. This arrangement was confirmed in the package of general staff reform undertaken in 2001 by Commission Vice-President, Neil Kinnock, (although starting salaries for new officials were lowered, provoking concerns that they are no longer competitive with equivalent professions in some Member States).

However, the calculation of the linkage to national salaries is inevitably time lagged. Thus, in 2009, the calculation resulted in an increase of over 3% in salaries, reflecting national increases of earlier years – but now due at a time of economic recession. Council declined to agree to the increase, provoking a challenge in the Court by the trade unions and by the Commission, with the support of the Parliament. In November 2010, the Court ruled against the Council, inviting it to grant the award in full. This is unlikely to put an end to the argument: in 2012 the Staff Regulations and the levels of salary are subject to review and the Council can be expected to adopt a very restrictive position.

The future of the secretariat

The secretariat is in the process of changing very markedly. We have already seen how successive EU enlargements have resulted in an increase in the size of the secretariat. Such an expansion goes hand in hand with a change in the structure of the secretariat. Already a significant number of officials have left with early retirement packages to make way for staff from the new Member States. In any case, many staff recruited in the 1970s and 1980s will be due to retire. Before the end of this legislature 400 officials are anticipated to leave, contributing to a significant drop in the average age of the staff (at present just under 50) and an opportunity for a new generation of staff to make its mark.

It may, however, not be easy to recruit such a large number of new officials. There is some evidence that the somewhat less attractive conditions of employment of the 2004 Staff Regulations, with starting salaries significantly lower than they used to be, has discouraged those who have passed competitions from taking up employment, particularly if they come from richer Member States. Moreover, the slower rate of progress through the grades that can now be expected may lead to fewer staff wanting to spend their whole career inside the Parliament. However, these concerns about the competitiveness of EU salaries need to be set in the context of a much darker economic climate, with many national governments acting to restrict public spending in response to the financial crisis. At least in principle this may serve to make the choice of a career in the Parliament more attractive again.

Finally, there is the issue of the relationship between members of the secretariat and MEPs. The remarkable rise in influence of the Parliament was undoubtedly assisted by a generation of officials who dedicated their professional lives to assisting MEPs to reinforce the institution's role. This task has now been broadly accomplished. As a result, MEPs may wish to rely on the administration for a more limited range of tasks, looking to the Political Groups, their assistants and outside experts for help in their political work. If so, the secretariat will assume a much more technical role than it has done in the past, working under a more clearly defined level of political control.

III: THE POWERS OF THE PARLIAMENT

12.   The Parliament and legislation

The adoption of European legislation now normally requires approval of the European Parliament and of the Council, who together constitute the EU's bicameral legislature. The adoption of legislation under the "ordinary legislative procedure" (historically known as the co-decision procedure) involves up to three readings each in the Parliament and Council. The bottom line is simple: only when both agree on the same text can the legislation be adopted. However, as in national legislative procedures, the detail can be more complex.

There are also a few "special legislative procedures", giving the final say to either the Council or the Parliament instead of co-decision, as well as a "consent procedure", where one institution, usually the Parliament, may either consent to or veto a decision of the other, and, in a few remaining cases, the simple consultation of Parliament, with the Council alone being the final legislator.

All of this is relatively new. Under the original treaties, the European Parliament was given virtually no legislative power, simply being consulted about (some) proposals prior to their adoption by the Council. Although the very first speech of a Council President (Konrad Adenauer) to the Parliament in 1952 compared Council and Parliament to two chambers of a bicameral parliament, this vision took half a century to become reality.

An initial version of co-decision powers was introduced under the Treaty of Maastricht in 1992, but applied to only 15 treaty articles. It was through subsequent treaty amendments (the treaties of Amsterdam, Nice and Lisbon) that the European Parliament has acquired its role as a genuine co-legislature with the Council. Experience under the initial limited scope of the procedure had evidently helped convince Member States that the procedures not only worked and produced results but also reinforced the democratic legitimacy of EU legislation. The IGC (on the proposed EU Constitution) that concluded its work in June 2004 saw Member States agreeing to call co-decision the "ordinary legislative procedure", with Council voting by qualified majority, and to apply it to the vast majority of laws, more than doubling the number of articles covered to reach 85 in total. This was eventually taken up in the Lisbon treaty and became reality in December 2009.

Thus, almost all European Union legislation now has to pass two tests to be enacted: acceptability to a qualified majority of national ministers meeting in the Council and acceptability to a majority of directly elected MEPs in the European Parliament. These two hurdles (or quality controls) mean that European legislation is subject to double scrutiny. Proposals must satisfy two sets of actors – one set looking at them primarily from the perspective of various national interests (as seen by the government of the day of each

Member State) and the other set looking at them primarily from a variety of political perspectives. Both sets must be satisfied that a proposal is necessary, proportionate and suitable for it to become law.

The Ordinary Legislative Procedure

The ordinary legislative procedure provides for up to three readings each in both the Parliament and Council. Only when both agree on an identical text, can it be adopted. Should that happen at first or second reading, the procedure can be concluded at that stage.

Commission proposal

With a few exceptions, legislative proposals begin with a draft submitted by the European Commission. This does not mean that the idea behind a proposal originated with the Commission: most Commission proposals are drawn up in response to requests from the European Council, the European Parliament, individual member states or others or arise from existing legislative or international obligations. However, the authors of the treaties felt that the first formal draft for consideration by Council and Parliament should be prepared by the body which is neutral as between Member States and is obliged to look at the overall interest of all member states – rather than having to consider competing national drafts submitted.

Both the European Parliament (see section below on the right to initiate legislation) and the Council have the right to request the Commission to put forward a proposal. If the Commission refuses to do so, it must formally explain its reasons. Both institutions have significant leverage over the Commission, so outright refusal is unwise.

The European Parliament has a special procedure for formally making such a request to the Commission, but it is couched in the rules as a fall-back procedure if the Commission fails to respond to ordinary requests made in day-to-day parliamentary debates and resolutions. Furthermore, almost all Commission proposals are contained in its Annual Work Programme, which is extensively discussed beforehand with the Council and the Parliament. These aspects are explored further at the end of this chapter.

The Treaty of Lisbon saw a further innovation in the so-called citizens' initiative (Art. 11 TEU) according to which 1 million citizens can invite the Commission to present a proposal on matters they consider necessary. The detailed procedure for this was adopted early in 2011.

Prior scrutiny by national parliaments

Before the Council or the Parliament can take a position on a proposal, there is an eight week period for national parliamentary scrutiny. This is provided for in Protocols 1 and 2 attached to the Treaty of Lisbon. Formally, it is to enable national parliaments to object to a proposal if they consider that it does not comply with the principal of subsidiarity – that is, the proposal should not be a matter for the European Union but for the Member States to regulate, in which case they may adopt a formal objection (see below). In practice, this eight week period gives national parliaments the opportunity to shape the position that their country's minister will take when they attend Council meetings, irrespective of subsidiarity concerns.

How the different national parliaments take advantage of this possibility varies considerably from one to another according to national traditions and constitutional provisions. In the Nordic countries, it is standard practice for a minister to attend the meeting of the relevant parliamentary committee before going to a Council meeting, in order to discuss the agenda and the position he or she intends to take. The committee may even have a formal vote on this, virtually mandating the minister. In the UK, a document-based approach is used, with specialist committees examining every proposal. In Belgium, a broad brush overview is taken by a committee with members of both parliamentary chambers and Belgian MEPs.

If national parliaments do have concerns about subsidiarity (not about the substance), then they can object by adopting a "reasoned opinion" outlining why they think the draft in question does not comply with the principle of subsidiarity. If a third of national parliamentary chambers (one vote per chamber in bi-cameral national parliaments, two votes for a unicameral national parliament) object to a proposal on grounds of subsidiarity, the Commission is obliged to review it ("yellow card"). If half of national parliamentary chambers object ("orange card"), then there is a special vote in the Council and in the European Parliament, either of which may terminate the procedure there and then (by a 55% majority of Member States in Council and a simple majority in the Parliament). Parliament's rules provide for it to act in such cases on a recommendation of its committee responsible, which will have examined the reasoned opinions from the national parliaments.

Although subsidiarity is not normally in question with regard to Commission proposals (and no proposals were subjected to any such procedures in the first year of operation of the Lisbon treaty), the yellow and orange card procedures are an important safeguard, intended to reassure those who fear the European Union has become too interventionist in matters that would best be left to national authorities.

First reading in the European Parliament

The European Parliament then has a period – with no fixed deadline – to adopt its position at first reading and forward it to the Council. Parliament's internal rules require a proposal to be referred to the competent parliamentary committee and for the committee not to adopt a position before the eight week period for national parliamentary scrutiny is complete (unless an urgent procedure is being followed).

Parliament's procedures in committee, the role of the rapporteur and shadow rapporteurs, the procedures in plenary, as well as the way the Groups handle proposals, have all been described in earlier chapters, but it is worth underlining again that the first reading is the one where Parliament has the time to examine a matter in detail, take outside expertise and advice, discuss options internally and with the other institutions, and come to a considered view. The first reading, unless there is pressing urgency, will normally take a matter of some months. It also includes a "cooling off period" of at least one month between the adoption of a position by the committee and the vote in plenary, except in urgent cases.

Parliament votes on the basis of the committee's proposal, but Political Groups or 40 members may also table amendments to the draft legislation or, indeed, motions to reject. The outcome will consist of Parliament voting either to approve the proposal as it stands, or to reject it, or to amend the proposal, in which case it will adopt one or (usually) more amendments. The latter course of action is the most common, as few proposals escape parliamentary amendment, and outright rejection at this early stage is unusual.

As we shall see below (subsection on trilogues), attempts are often made at this early stage to reach agreements with the Council on the desired content of a proposal, and this will involve adopting a package of amendments that result from negotiations between the two institutions.

First reading in the Council

The Council normally starts its work in parallel to the Parliament, but must await Parliament's position before adopting its own. It, too, has an unlimited period to consider the matter. If it approves the Parliament's position, the act is adopted there and then in first reading. If not, it adopts its own position and forwards it to the Parliament, along with an explanation of its reasons for adopting a different position from the Parliament.

The Council's first reading is complicated by two factors. First, the need to find a broad measure of agreement. Even a qualified majority (let alone unanimity) represents a high level of consensus. Until 2014, under the terms of the Treaty of Nice, it requires a triple majority of:

–   255 of the 345 votes (some 74 percent) of the Member States, weighted on a scale of 3 for the smallest (Malta) to 29 for the largest (Germany, UK, Italy and France)

–   a majority of the Member States (one vote per state)

–   62 percent of the population (each state weighted according to its population), if requested

After 2014, under the terms of the Lisbon Treaty, this will be simplified to a double majority of:

–   55 percent of the Member States (one vote per state)

–   65 percent of the population (each state weighted according to its population), though not if only three countries oppose a proposal.

The majority of Member States required is higher if Council is not dealing with a proposal emanating from the Commission. In such (limited) cases, it requires two-thirds (instead of a majority) of Member States until 2014 and 72 percent (instead of 55 percent) thereafter. Furthermore, if a minority opposing a proposal could be outvoted, but comprises a significant number, it can request that discussions continue for a reasonable period of time to find a broader agreement, provided no legal deadlines are missed.

The second complicating factor is that, while Council can approve a Commission proposal by a qualified majority, it can only amend it by unanimity (unless the Commission agrees with the amendment). This is a key part of the dynamics of the legislative procedure that dates from the original treaties. It is easier to approve than to amend a Commission proposal. This was intended to give the Commission some bargaining power in the Council's deliberations, but without going too far, as even approval without amendment requires a high level of support. It was intended to give a slight advantage to the proposal drawn up by the Commission, which is duty bound to consider the interests of the whole Union. Over time, the Commission's advantage in this respect has been both strengthened and weakened: strengthened in that unanimity to amend its proposal is more difficult to achieve with more and more Member States; weakened in that, with the involvement of the European Parliament in the procedure, Council can, at a later stage, agree with the Parliament over the head of the Commission, and this already casts its shadow over the first reading, especially as adopting the Parliament's position means that the act is adopted already at this stage.

In any case, these factors all mean that the Council's first reading can take a long time before a position emerges – sometimes years. Council's internal procedures involve consideration at the level of working groups of national officials, deliberation in COREPER (the Committee of Permanent Representatives – Ambassadors to the EU – of the Member States) and final approval at ministerial level in the Council itself. Sometimes deadlocked discussions are referred to the European Council of heads of state or government, notably under the "emergency break" procedure (provided for in Articles 48, 82 and 83 TFEU, concerning social security and criminal justice, whereby any Member State can ask for a legislative procedure to be interrupted in order to allow a discussion in the European Council, which can terminate the procedure or refer it back, with its own conclusions, to Council to continue the procedure). The European Council does not take any formal legislative decisions, however.

Thus, proposals can take a long time in the Council, or even be blocked indefinitely, and they only formally fall if the Commission eventually withdraws the proposal. In any event, Parliament can sometimes be left waiting for years between its first and second readings, possibly even with an election in between.

Second readings

Internally, Parliament's second reading is prepared by the same committee that dealt with it at first reading (and unless otherwise decided, automatically with the same rapporteur). It makes a "recommendation" to Parliament to approve, reject or amend the Council's position. At this stage, Parliament's internal Rules of Procedure (Rule 66) limit amendments to those which would restore wholly or partly the position adopted by Parliament at its first reading or which seek to reach a compromise with the Council. The only exceptions permitted are to amend a part of the text of a Council's position which was not included in – or differs in content from – the proposal considered at first reading or to take account of a new fact or legal situation which has arisen since the first reading – or if new parliamentary elections have taken place since the first reading.

If Parliament approves Council's position (or takes no action within a three month deadline, extendable to four on the initiative of either institution), it is adopted and no further confirmation by Council is required. If Parliament rejects the Council's position, by a majority of its members, the legislation falls. If Parliament amends the common position, it returns to Council for a second reading there.

The Council can then adopt the proposal only if it accepts each and every Parliament amendment (which it can do by qualified majority, unless the Commission formally opposes an amendment, in which case unanimity is required). Otherwise, the matter is referred automatically to the conciliation committee.

Conciliation and third readings

The conciliation committee is composed of the members of the Council or their representatives and an equal number of members of the European Parliament (thus, at present, 27 on each side). The committee is also attended by the Commission, but Council and Parliament are free to reach an agreement on individual amendments independently of the opinion of the Commission. The treaty provides for a period of up to 8 weeks following the 2nd reading of Council for the 1st meeting of the conciliation committee to take place. The committee then has six weeks (extendable at the request of either institution to eight) to negotiate a compromise text on the basis of the positions of the Council and Parliament at second reading. If it succeeds in reaching an agreement (by a qualified majority on Council's side and by a majority of its delegation on Parliament's side), then within a further six (extendable at the request of either institution to eight) weeks, the text has to be submitted for approval by the committee to the Parliament and to the Council. If they both approve the text (the Parliament voting by simple majority, the Council by qualified majority), it is adopted and the Presidents of the two institutions sign it into law; if either institution fails to support the text, it falls. In practice these formal deadlines of the treaty are often not necessary as conciliation work usually already starts in the phase of the 2nd reading of Council and is often concluded within the 6 months of a particular presidency.

If the conciliation committee fails to reach agreement within the prescribed time, the text automatically falls and cannot become law. This has happened so far, however, only twice – once in the case of the Working Time Directive in 2009 and the other on the Novel Foods Regulation in 2011. (Prior to the Amsterdam Treaty, under Maastricht, if the conciliation committee could not reach an agreement, Council could adopt a text unilaterally which would become law unless Parliament rejected it within six weeks by a majority of its members. In fact Council only tried this once, in 1994 on a complex proposal relating to voice telephony; Parliament found the necessary majority and Council never tried this again!). The need for agreement concentrates the minds of those involved in seeking to find an acceptable compromise about legislation which, by this stage, both have accepted the need for, even if they don't yet agree on its terms.

At the outset Parliament examined two models when deciding how to compose its delegation to the conciliation committee. One was that of the

United States where, for conference committees seeking to reconcile differences on the content of legislation between the Senate and the House of Representatives, each side composes its delegation on an ad hoc basis for each item of legislation, drawing heavily from members of the responsible committee. The other was the German model for conciliation between the Bundesrat and the Bundestag where the conciliation committee is set up with permanent members who handle each and every item coming to it. Parliament chose a compromise, providing for three permanent members to be drawn from among the Vice-Presidents of Parliament (able to become experts in the procedures, practices and precedents of conciliation and to keep an eye on horizontal issues that arise) and for the remaining members to be drawn predominantly from the committee responsible and including automatically its chair and rapporteur (bringing their expertise on the subject matter based on the discussions in committee at first and second reading). There have been attempts to modify this system and go more towards the German model but the advantages of the present structure in guaranteeing very broad participation in conciliation have so far prevailed.

In addition, the delegation as a whole must reflect the political balance in the Parliament. Since the 2009 elections, following a decision of the Conference of Presidents, the delegation must normally comprise eleven EPP-ED members, nine S&D, three ALDE, two Greens, two ECR and one each from the GUE/NGL and EFD Groups. Each Group may nominate an equal number of substitute members, who can take a full part in the proceedings of the delegation but can only vote in the absence of the full member from their Group.

For the 2009-2011 period, the permanent members are two from the EPP-ED Group and one from the PES Group. One of the permanent members chairs Parliament's delegation unless the President of Parliament himself is present (which only occurs on a very exceptional basis). On Council's side a minister from the country holding the Council Presidency always chairs the delegation at the conciliation committee. The rest of the delegation is usually composed of deputy permanent representatives (from Coreper I), despite regular appeals from the Parliament to increase participation by ministers. The relevant Commissioner usually represents the Commission.

The conciliation meetings are formally co-chaired and in practice chaired alternately by the leaders of the Parliament and the Council delegations. If the Council first chairs a conciliation on one subject in a Council meeting room, the next conciliation on another subject will normally be chaired by the Parliament on Parliament premises.

At the very first conciliation meeting, the Parliament and Council delegations initially sat opposite each other. In subsequent meetings the two chairs have sat next to each other with their delegations to their right and left respectively and the Commission sitting opposite them. The new arrangement was chosen to emphasise the fact that the conciliation committee is indeed a single committee with equal responsibilities among all its members.

Negotiations with 27 on each side of the table are of course impractical. Indeed, as each participant on Council's side is normally accompanied by two or three other officials, Parliament's own delegation is accompanied by several advisors and assistants and the Commission always has a substantial number of staff to provide support to the Commissioner present, there can often be over a hundred people in the room when the full conciliation committee meets. As early as 1994-95 a trend emerged of preliminary contacts being taken between the Parliament representatives (usually the delegation chair, the committee chair and the rapporteur) and the Council Presidency, represented either by the minister or the Deputy Permanent Representative, with the Commission represented at Director or Director-General level. These meetings, known as "trilogues", described in more detail below, have become an essential part of the conciliation process, with each side able to negotiate more freely and more speedily in the search for compromise than is possible in the full conciliation meeting.

The full conciliation meetings tend to be lengthy, especially since they are frequently interrupted to give time for the Parliament and the Council delegations to meet on their own to decide whether they can accept compromises that have been put forward in the meeting. Each side will also hold preparatory meetings. Parliament's preparatory meeting usually involves the delegation chair and/or rapporteur reporting back on the contacts taken with the Council Presidency, and discussion of the strategy to follow in the committee. A typical sequence of events emerging from the initial meetings is as follows:

–   Council informs Parliament that it cannot accept all of its second reading amendments, hence triggering the conciliation procedure,

–   The Parliament's delegation is chosen and holds a first preparatory meeting to decide on its strategy and to give a negotiating mandate to the delegation chair, committee chair and rapporteur for their informal contacts with the Council Presidency,

–   An informal trilogue meeting is held to explore the differences between the positions and to consider possible compromises,

–   Each side reports back to a meeting of its full delegation (in Council's case, Coreper).

For less controversial dossiers, a procedure can sometimes be resolved by a series of trilogues and delegation meetings and in such cases, the agreement is submitted for formal approval, without debate, at the next meeting of the conciliation committee, which may be on a different subject. Where the disagreement is more profound, the two sides will eventually agree to set a date for a full conciliation committee meeting.

There is no such thing as a typical conciliation meeting. Some can last many hours through the night, others may end very rapidly with both sides agreeing to meet again; nonetheless, the following offers a flavour of how such an event can mix full meetings of the committee with trilogue and delegation meetings:

5.00pm -   separate meetings of Parliament and Council delegations

6.00pm -   trilogue between the negotiators of the two delegations

7.00pm -   further meetings of each delegation to consider new offers

8.00pm -   second trilogue to examine how close the positions are

10.00pm - further meetings of each delegation to consider new offers and/or to consider possible compromise

11.00pm - possibly 3rd trilogue and further delegation meeting

11.30pm - full conciliation meeting to approve an agreement or to note that no agreement has been reached and to agree on a date for a new meeting within the 6-8 week deadline.

Each conciliation must reach an agreement within the deadline of six weeks, which may be extended at the initiative of either institution to eight weeks. In order to maximise the time effectively available, conciliation is always officially opened on the same day as the first meeting of the conciliation committee.

Once agreement has been reached in the conciliation committee, or earlier at first or second reading, the "jurist-linguists" (translators with special legal qualifications) examine the texts. When finalised, they are submitted to the Parliament and the Council for approval, by a simple majority in the former and normally a qualified majority in the latter. If approval is forthcoming, the text is signed by the Presidents of the Parliament and the Council, published in the Official Journal and thereby becomes a piece of Community legislation, which both sides have from then on to defend, notably if there is a legal challenge in the Court of Justice.

Avoiding conciliation: first and second reading agreements

Conciliation casts a backward shadow over the whole co-decision procedure. The inevitability of negotiations at some stage, unless the Parliament and Council have identical positions at the outset, means that conciliation is not seen as the only mechanism for this. The sheer volume of co-decision procedures means that both institutions have an interest in not allowing all disagreements to wait until the conciliation process before being resolved. This realisation has led to much more intensive contact and negotiation between the institutions earlier in the procedure. Between 1999 and 2004, 115, or 28 per cent, of all co-decision procedures were concluded at first reading and by no means all of them were uncontroversial proposals. Even more (200 or 50%) were agreed at second reading, leaving 84, or 22%, to be negotiated to a conclusion in conciliation. This tendency was accentuated still further in the 2004-9 legislature, with 72% concluded at first reading and only 5% in third reading after conciliation.

The phenomenon of early informal negotiation was pioneered in 1997 on a proposed directive on biotechnological inventions. It was a proposal with a history, as in 1995 this same issue had provided the first case where an agreement made by the Parliament's delegation in conciliation was rejected by Parliament as a whole. When a revised version of the same directive came back for consideration in 1997, there was a strong desire on both sides to avoid a similar outcome. The rapporteur, Willy Rothley, made contact with the Council even before first reading, to see how Council could accommodate Parliament's concerns and how the latter could be formulated in a way acceptable to Council. The relative success of this strategy was seen in the willingness of the Council to accept, in its first reading, almost all of the Parliament's 40 or so amendments. As a result, when the Parliament came to vote its second reading, a majority felt there was no need for any further amendments.

In another early case, the two institutions were confronted with a treaty obligation to reach an agreement by May 2001 on the rules governing public access to the documents of the European institutions. In November 2000 Parliament adopted a set of amendments but did not conclude its first reading by voting on the legislative resolution. These amendments did, however, indicate to the incoming Swedish Presidency at the beginning of 2001 the general character of Parliament's demands. The Presidency entered into lengthy negotiations with a delegation from the Parliament with a view to adjusting the package of amendments to make them acceptable to both institutions. Some argued that Parliament should look for a better result later in the procedure in conciliation. However, a majority felt that it would be difficult to find a more favourable Presidency on this specific issue and decided to accept a deal that could enter into force before the treaty deadline. As with biotechnological inventions, the sensitivity of an issue served to shorten rather than lengthen the co-decision procedure.

These and other early cases set a precedent for reaching agreement at first or second reading stage, even on sensitive issues. It became a rush in the run-up to the 2004 elections when there was an understandable wish to complete as many issues as possible before both enlargement (with a set of 10 new actors as well as new languages) and the lengthy legislative break caused by the elections. In the last three part-sessions before enlargement at which legislative texts were considered (March and April 2004), there were around 80 first and second reading agreements. By the 2004-09 parliament, the practice became routine, with a total of 72% of procedures concluded at 1st reading during those five years. Admittedly, these included many "technical" matters, such as codifications, repeals and alignments of past legislation to the new Comitology Decision, and again an important number were concluded towards the end of the legislative term. On the other hand, on many sensitive and important matters, there was often a consensus at the highest political level to conclude the negotiations in first reading (e.g. climate change package).

This growth in inter-institutional negotiations led to the gradual emergence of a new practice, drawing on experience in the budgetary procedure, known as the trilogue.

The Trilogue and its handling in Parliament

Trilogues consist of a meeting, normally in order to negotiate, between a Parliament delegation, the Council Presidency and the Commissioner responsible. Trilogues are now taking place at all stages of the legislative procedure. At the conciliation phase, they prepare agreements for purely formal approval by the conciliation committee, as the latter is now so large (27+27+Commissioner) that it is difficult for negotiations to take place in the full committee.

Parliament's delegation was initially just the committee chair and the rapporteur, but it soon became apparent that it would be useful if they were accompanied by the co-ordinators or the shadow rapporteurs from other Groups. This was welcomed by the Council in a letter from its President,

Anna Lindh, in April 2001, which referred to this as an "enlarged trilogue", a term now fallen into disuse as it has now become the standard format.

On the side of the Council and Commission, representation can also vary, even at different stages of the same trilogue, in terms of the seniority of officials or politicians present. The fluid nature of the procedure is further illustrated by the informal contacts that can also take place between participants, with it not always obvious whether a particular meeting is considered by all sides to be a trilogue or not. Contacts can take place also by telephone and email and it is not unknown for two out of the three institutions to have bilateral meetings during the process. Each side, especially the Parliament and the Council, will of course have internal discussions to adjust their position or tactics, and each side may seek to influence those internal discussions: just as Council will try to play off one EP Political Group against another, so Parliament will try to play off one national representative in Council against another.

The emergence of the trilogue, and concerns about its transparency, prompted Parliament to formalise aspects of the practice and its preparation, first in a Code of Conduct (adopted by the Bureau in September 2008) and then in Rule 70 and Annex XXI of its Rules of Procedure (Corbett Report, May 2009). This has made the trilogue a semi-formal procedure, albeit one that is not provided for in the treaties. The rules lay down the main framework for preparing, conducting and following up trilogues, though much detail has been left to practice.

The rules specify that a decision to seek an agreement early in the legislative process "shall be a case-by-case decision, taking account of, for example, political priorities, the uncontroversial or 'technical' nature of the proposal, an urgent situation and/or the attitude of a given Presidency to a specific issue". The possibility of entering into negotiations is presented by the rapporteur to the responsible parliamentary committee (in practice, this often follows a prior discussion among coordinators) and the committee's "decision to pursue such a course of action shall be taken either by broad consensus or, if necessary, by a vote" (by a majority of its members). The rules specify that as a general rule, "the amendments adopted in committee or in plenary shall form the basis for the mandate of the EP negotiating team. The committee may also determine priorities and a time limit for negotiations. In the exceptional case of negotiations on a first reading agreement before the vote in committee, the committee shall provide guidance to the EP negotiating team".

In practice, in the case of first reading negotiations, the decision is usually taken by the committee together with the vote on the amendments. Three main practices have developed regarding the initial negotiating mandate. One is to hold an "orientation vote", that is a vote on all amendments which does not yet constitute the formal committee vote, and then to pursue trilogue negotiations ahead of the committee vote. A second is to hold a formal vote and negotiate in the phase between the committee vote and plenary. A third is to go to plenary, to vote the amendments without a final vote on the legislative resolution, and to negotiate at that stage. In the case of second reading negotiations, some committees wait until the committee vote before starting negotiations with the Council, and others start negotiations earlier, taking the first reading plenary vote as a mandate.

The decision by the committee to enter negotiations also includes a decision on the composition of the negotiating team. As a general principle, "political balance shall be respected and all political groups shall be represented at least at staff level in these negotiations", though of course, everyone is aware of the respective strength of the different Groups. In most committees the trilogue meetings are preceded by a meeting of the rapporteur and shadows, intended to ensure coherence in the negotiations. At staff level the committee secretariat and the Political Groups' advisors are present and frequently the Legal Service and lawyer linguists.

The actual trilogue meetings take place behind closed doors, but are not secret, as Parliament's rules say that "in order to enhance transparency, trilogue meetings taking place within the European Parliament and Council shall be announced". In most trilogues, only the chair and the rapporteur speak for Parliament, but in some cases the shadow rapporteurs are also given the floor to explain specific aspects of the issue or to ask questions. There have been some cases of members contradicting each other in front of the Council and the Commission.

In some cases different items are dealt with in so called "packages" of several legislative proposals. When such packages are negotiated in trilogues, sometimes only the several rapporteurs (without the shadow rapporteurs) are involved in the negotiations to avoid too large negotiating teams.

As a rule, a document in several columns is used for the negotiations. This document is usually prepared jointly by the Council secretariat and the parliamentary committee secretariat, though they do vary in terms of the number and their content.

The rules require that after each trilogue, the negotiating team reports back to the committee on the outcome of the negotiations and make all texts distributed available to the committee. The committee considers any agreement reached (or updates the mandate of the negotiating team if further negotiations are required). If this is not possible for timing reasons, notably at second reading stage, the committee's position shall be taken by the rapporteur and the shadow rapporteurs, if necessary together with the committee chair and the coordinators. There shall be sufficient time between the end of the negotiations and the vote in plenary to allow Political Groups to prepare their final position.

In practice, the formal feedback to the full committee is mainly done only after several rounds of meetings, to report on general progress, or if strategic decisions need to be taken. Due to the sensitivity of revealing negotiating positions, feedback is often given to the coordinators, instead of to the full committee which meets in public. The possibility of *in camera* meetings is also used to give feedback to the committee.

Any agreement between Parliament and Council must be confirmed in writing by an official letter. If the deal is prior to a Parliament reading, the Council Presidency will write to Parliament to say that such an agreement will be confirmed if Parliament adopts an annexed set of amendments which reflect what has previously been negotiated. Conversely, if the deal is prior to a Council reading, Parliament can write to Council saying that there will be a deal if Council accepts a certain text in its own position. Changes can only be made to any agreed texts with the explicit agreement, at the appropriate level, of both institutions.

The way in which the decision on an agreement is taken varies depending on the stage of the procedure and the way the initial mandate was given. In case of first reading agreements where the committee has not yet taken the final vote (but took an orientation vote or did not complete its vote with a final vote), the decision on the agreement is taken by the formal committee vote. If a formal committee vote has already taken place, the outcome of the negotiations is considered in the committee, but in most cases the outcome of the negotiations is brought to the plenary via amendments tabled by the Political Groups (though some committees do table new amendments to the plenary). In case of negotiations between Parliament's first reading and Council's first reading, the decision on the agreement is usually linked to the letter the committee chair is required to send to the Council. These letters are in most cases approved by (a majority of) Political Groups. In the case of negotiations after Council's first reading, but ahead of Parliament's second reading, the matter is usually not considered by the full committee at the end of the negotiations due to time constraints. The Groups table the necessary amendments in plenary.

Advantages and disadvantages of first and second reading agreements

There are potential benefits as well as costs in aiming for first or second reading agreements, both from Parliament's perspective and from that of other stakeholders, including national parliaments and indeed the wider public.

The advantages include:

– speeding up legislative procedures, saving time and energy;

– majorities to adopt amendments within the Parliament are less demanding in first reading than at second reading, (namely a simple rather than absolute majority), possibly facilitating the definitive adoption of some of Parliament's positions where they only have a small majority behind them;

– when Council (or some of its members) consider a matter to be urgent, or even when a Council presidency simply wishes to conclude during its mandate, Parliament can use the offer of a speedy agreement and the threat of requiring extra readings to strengthen its negotiating position.

The disadvantages (at least where negotiations between Parliament and Council take place before a first reading debate, on the basis of the parliamentary committee's position) include:

– a potential lack of transparency;

– that mandates for Parliament's negotiators may be weaker, as they are largely in the hands of the responsible committee (which might have its own nuances that could differ from those of the whole house) to the detriment of Groups and the plenary (and associated committees);

– the implementation of the mandate depends crucially on just a few members, notably the rapporteur and shadow rapporteurs, negotiating on behalf of the committee (and the Parliament), though skilful and informed negotiators can also be an advantage;

– the resulting package of amendments is normally adopted in plenary without further modification, presupposing that all relevant concerns have been fed in at committee stage.

– interpretation is not always available for negotiating meetings, which generally take place in English, disadvantaging some participants.

Further curiosities include:

– that such agreements may involve adoption of large numbers of amendments by the Parliament which are of little importance for the Parliament but which respond to concerns of the relevant Council working group;

– that shadow rapporteurs play a pivotal position within their Political Group, potentially to the detriment of the Group's co-ordinator.

These questions were evaluated again by the Conference of Committee Chairs in autumn 2010. Although they found that, under the new Rules, transparency and accountability of first reading agreements had improved considerably, they considered that first reading agreements should be the exception, reserved mainly for urgent, uncontroversial or technical dossiers, which would reverse the trend of recent years.

They also considered that Parliament should preferably aim to start negotiations with the Council after the vote in plenary; that the chair of the Conference of Committee Chairs should regularly brief the Conference of Presidents on the state of negotiations on key issues and that Groups should set themselves internal guidelines for considering first reading agreements to ensure a transparent procedure. Interestingly, they opined that Council is normally in a stronger position in first reading agreements to obtain a compromise with the Parliament on its terms, a view not universally shared as the keenness of a rotating presidency to get a "result" during its term, or the urgency of some issues, can often lead to a greater willingness to compromise by Council's negotiator.

It is a matter of debate when these agreements are or are not desirable from Parliament's perspective. In some cases Parliament may get the best possible deal at the first reading stage, in others only at second reading and in others again, only after conciliation. What is clear is that a strategic view needs to be taken from the beginning of each procedure, to identify the key issues and at what stage deals can best be struck.

The impact of the co-decision procedure

Since its initial, limited inception in 1994, Parliament and Council, along with the Commission, have devoted considerable time and energy to ensuring that co-decision would be a success. Intensive inter-institutional discussions produced agreements designed to ensure that both sides could operate within an agreed framework. In 1999 Parliament, Council and Commission agreed a "Joint Declaration on Practical Arrangements for the New Co-decision Procedure" that lays down such matters as the holding of conciliation meetings alternately in Parliament and Council, alternate chairing, voting procedures, timetabling and so on, updated in 2007 notably to recognize tri- logues and to lay down the rules on the letters confirming agreement (OJ C145 of 30.6.2007). Since 2003, the Presidents of Parliament and the Council meet to sign publically all legislation adopted under co-decision to increase its visibility. Important pieces of legislation are even signed in a ceremony in the plenary.

Has the co-decision procedure made any difference? At the outset in 1993 one could have been tempted to assume that the behaviour of the Council of ministers would not change fundamentally. The Council had enjoyed a leg- islative dominance for forty years and would be eager to find ways of main- taining its position. But, the fact that legislation cannot be adopted against the will of the European Parliament gives the latter a bargaining position which it previously lacked. It could no longer be accused of lacking teeth. Co-decision has created a new dynamic within the legislative arena of the European Union. The greater involvement of Parliament has also led to an ever increasing participation of outside actors like lobbyists, NGOs, civil society and so on in the legislative process. Many academic analysts con- sider that it was Parliament, far more than Council, which shaped the final content of legislation on several key pieces of legislation, including the con- troversial services directive, the directive on the registration, evaluation and authorisation of chemicals (REACH) and several recent pieces of legislation on regulating the financial sector. But it is above all partnership and com- promise between the two institutions – sometimes after tough negotiations, sometimes through an easily found agreement – that are the hallmarks of the procedure.

Some feared that co-decision would produce deadlock. The results of the procedure over the following years contradict such a view. Since 1999 only some half dozen procedures have failed in the sense of Parliament's inter- vention resulting in no legislation at all. Four proposals have fallen in third reading (proposed directives on takeover bids and on port services both saw the agreement reached in conciliation being rejected by Parliament, while in the case of a proposed revision of the Working Time Directive in 2009 and of the Novel Foods Regulation in 2011, the conciliation committee found no agreement). In other cases Parliament rejected proposals at second (or even first) reading (such as draft directives on voice telephony, on the Securities Committee, on the patenting of biotechnological inventions and on software patents). The vote on takeover bids in 2001 was particularly spectacular, as Parliament declined to ratify the results of the conciliation negotiation on a tied vote.

However, the impact of the Parliament cannot be reduced to the question of whether or not legislation is finally adopted. Parliament's impact is pri- marily on the content of the legislation, where co-decision has made a sig- nificant difference, going well beyond what could have been achieved under previous procedures.

Figure 7: *The ordinary legislative procedure (co-decision)*

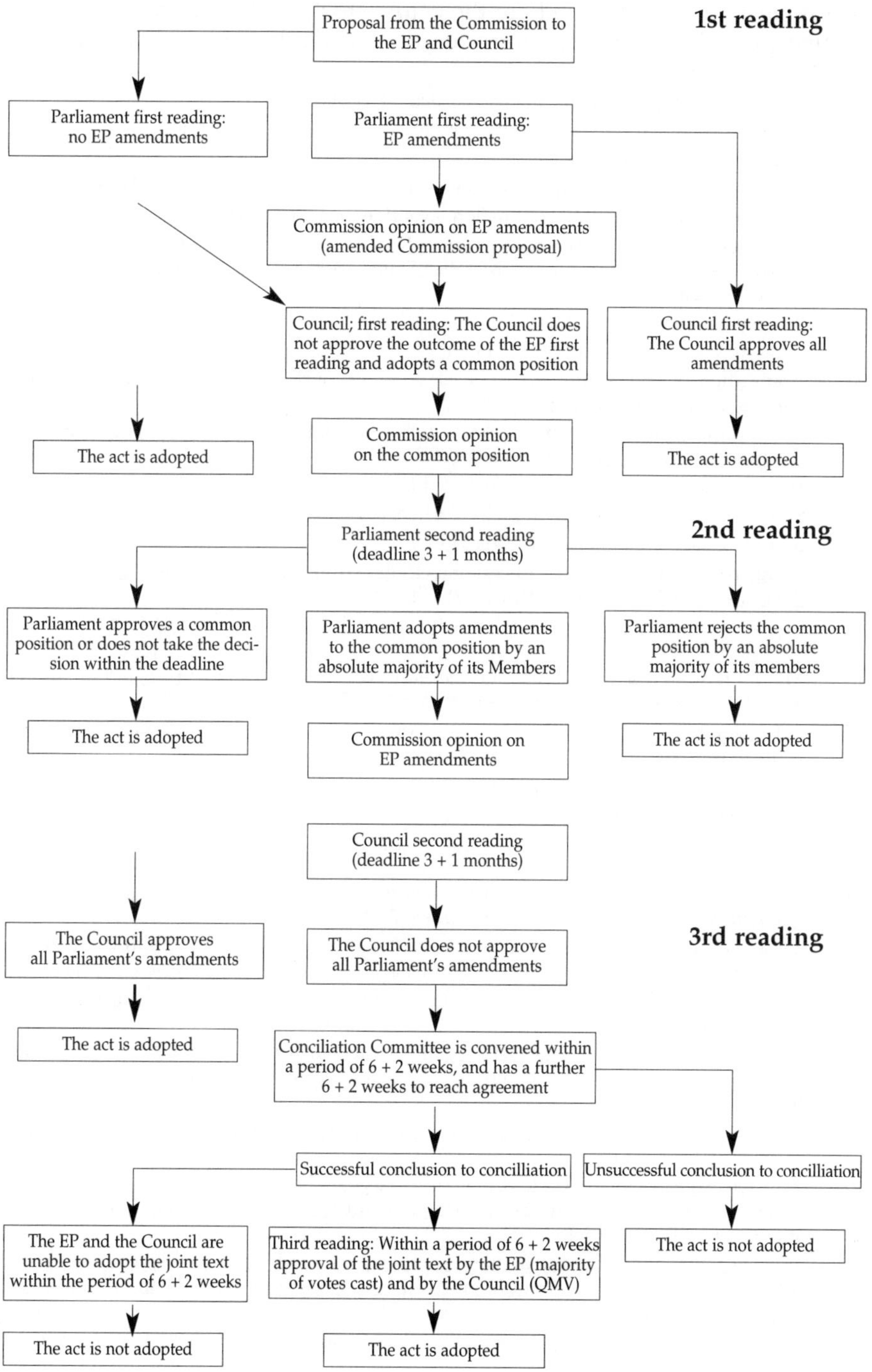

1st reading

Proposal from the Commission to the EP and Council

Parliament first reading: no EP amendments

Parliament first reading: EP amendments

Commission opinion on EP amendments (amended Commission proposal)

Council; first reading: The Council does not approve the outcome of the EP first reading and adopts a common position

Council first reading: The Council approves all amendments

The act is adopted

Commission opinion on the common position

The act is adopted

2nd reading

Parliament second reading (deadline 3 + 1 months)

Parliament approves a common position or does not take the decision within the deadline

Parliament adopts amendments to the common position by an absolute majority of its Members

Parliament rejects the common position by an absolute majority of its members

The act is adopted

Commission opinion on EP amendments

The act is not adopted

Council second reading (deadline 3 + 1 months)

3rd reading

The Council approves all Parliament's amendments

The Council does not approve all Parliament's amendments

The act is adopted

Conciliation Committee is convened within a period of 6 + 2 weeks, and has a further 6 + 2 weeks to reach agreement

Successful conclusion to concilliation

Unsuccessful conclusion to concilliation

The EP and the Council are unable to adopt the joint text within the period of 6 + 2 weeks

Third reading: Within a period of 6 + 2 weeks approval of the joint text by the EP (majority of votes cast) and by the Council (QMV)

The act is not adopted

The act is not adopted

The act is adopted

Table 33: *The ordinary legislative procedure*

The subject areas underlined are those for which co-decision/ordinary legislative procedure has been introduced or extended through the Lisbon Treaty.

1. Services of general economic interest (Article 14 TFEU)
2. Procedures regulating the right of access to documents (Article 15(3) TFEU)
3. Data protection (Article 16(2) TFEU)
4. Measures to combat discrimination on grounds of nationality (Article 18 TFEU)
5. Basic principles for anti-discrimination incentive measures (Article 19(2) TFEU)
6. Measures to facilitate the exercise of the right of every citizen of the Union to move and reside freely in the territory of Member States (Article 18 [21], paragraph 2, TFEU) (Article 18, paragraph 2, TEC)
7. Citizens' initiative (Article 24 TFEU)
8. Customs cooperation (Article 33 TFEU)
9. Application of competition rules to the common agricultural policy (Art. 42, which refers to Article 43, paragraph 2, TFEU)
10. Common organisation of the markets under the common agricultural policy and the common fisheries policy (Article 43(2) TFEU)
11. Free movement of workers (Article 46 TFEU)
12. Social security measures for migrant workers (Article 48 TFEU)
13. Right of establishment (Article 50(1) TFEU)
14. Exclusion in a Member State of certain activities from the application of provisions on the right of establishment (Article 51(2) TFEU)
15. Coordination of treatment of foreign nationals with regard to the right of establishment (Article 52(2) TFEU)
16. Mutual recognition of diplomas and measures concerning the taking-up and pursuit of activities as self-employed persons (Article 53 (1) TFEU)
17. Extending provisions on freedom to provide services to third-country nationals established within the Union. (Article 56 (2) TFEU)
18. Liberalisation of services in specific sectors (Article 59(1) TFEU)
19. Services (Article 62 TFEU)
20. Adoption of other measures on the movement of capital to and from third countries (Article 64(2) TFEU)
21. Administrative measures relating to capital movements in connection with preventing and combating crime and terrorism (Article 75 TFEU)
22. Visas, border checks, free movement of nationals of non-member countries, management of external frontiers, absence of controls at internal frontiers (Article 77(2) TFEU)
23. Asylum, temporary protection or subsidiary protection for nationals of third countries (Article 78(2) TFEU)
24. Immigration and combating trafficking in persons (Article 79(2) TFEU)
25. Incentive measures for the integration of nationals of third countries (Article 79(4) TFEU)
26. Judicial cooperation in civil matters (excluding family law) (Article 81(2) and, potentially (3) (family law) TFEU)
27. Judicial cooperation in criminal matters – measures to facilitate mutual recognition, avoidance of conflicts of jurisdiction, training and cooperation between judicial authorities (Article 82 (1) TFEU)
28. Judicial cooperation in criminal matters – rules for cross-border cases regarding mutual admissibility of evidence, rights of individuals in criminal proceeding and rights of victims(Article 82 (2) TFEU)
29. Minimum rules concerning the definition of criminal offences and sanctions in the areas

of particularly serious crime with a cross-border dimension (Article 83 (1) and, possibly, (2) TFEU)

30. Measures to support crime prevention (Article 84 TFEU)

31. Eurojust – structure, operation, field of action, tasks (Article 85 (1) first subparagraph, TFEU)

32. Arrangements for involving the European Parliament and national parliaments in the evaluation of Eurojust's activities (Article 85(1) last subparagraph, TFEU)

33. Police cooperation (certain aspects) (Article 87(2) TFEU)

34. Europol - structure, operation, field of action, tasks (Article 88(2) first subparagraph, TFEU)

35. Procedures for scrutiny of Europol's activities by EP and national parliaments (Article 88(2) second subparagraph, TFEU)

36. Implementation of the common transport policy (Article 91(1) TFEU)

37. Sea and air transport (Article 100(2) TFEU)

38. Internal market harmonisations (Article 114(1) TFEU)

39. Measures to eliminate distortions in the internal market caused by national actions (Article 116 TFEU)

40. Intellectual property rights, except language arrangements, (Article 118 first subparagraph, TFEU)

41. Multilateral surveillance (Article 121(6) TFEU)

42. Modification of the Protocol on the Statutes of the ESCB and ECB (Article 129(3) TFEU)

43. Measures necessary for the use of the euro (Article 133 TFEU)

44. Incentive measures for employment (Article 149 TFEU)

45. Social policy: health & safety, working conditions, information & consultation of workers, integration of persons excluded from the labour market, equal opportunities, combating social exclusion and modernisation of social protection systems (Article 153(2)(b), second subparagraphs, TFEU)

46. Social policy: equal treatment and equal pay for men and women(Article 157(3) TFEU)

47. European Social Fund (Article 164 TFEU)

48. Education & sport (incentive measures, excluding harmonisation) (Article 165(4) TFEU)

49. Vocational training (measures, excluding harmonisation) (Article 166(4) TFEU)

50. Culture (incentive measures, excluding harmonisation) (Article 167(5), TFEU)

51. Public health – measures to tackle common safety concerns in the health sphere (Article 168(4) TFEU)

52. Public health – incentive measures to protect human health and in particular to combat the major cross-border health scourges, and measures to tackle tobacco and alcohol abuse (Article 168(5) TFEU)

53. Consumer protection (Article 169(3) TFEU)

54. Trans-European networks (Article 172 TFEU)

55. Industry (measures, excluding harmonisation) (Article 173(3) TFEU)

56. Measures in the area of economic and social cohesion (Article 175 (3) TFEU)

57. Structural Funds (Article 177(first sub para) TFEU)

58. Cohesion Fund (Article 177(second sub para) TFEU)

59. European Regional Development Fund (Article 178 TFEU)

60. Framework Programme for Research (Article 182(1) TFEU)

61. Implementation of European research area (Article 182(5) TFEU)

62. Implementation of the Framework Programme for Research: rules for the participation of undertakings and dissemination of research results (Articles 183 and 188(2) TFEU)

63. Supplementary research programmes for some Member States (Articles 184 and 188(2) TFEU)

64. Participation in research programmes undertaken by several Member States (Articles 185 and 188(2) TFEU)

65. Space policy (Article 189 TFEU)

66. Environment, except measures of a fiscal nature (Article 192(1) TFEU)
67. Environment Action Programme (Article 192(2) TFEU)
68. Energy, except measures of a fiscal nature (Article 194(2) TFEU)
69. Tourism - measures to complement the action of the Member States in the tourism sector (Article 195(2) TFEU)
70. Civil protection (cooperation, excluding harmonisation, in combating disasters (Article 196(2) TFEU)
71. Administrative cooperation in implementing Union law by Member States (Article 197(2) TFEU)
72. Commercial policy - implementing measures (Article 207(2) TFEU)
73. Development cooperation (Article 209(1) TFEU)
74. Economic, financial and technical cooperation with third countries (Article 212(2) TFEU)
75. General framework for humanitarian operations (Article 214(3) TFEU)
76. European Voluntary Humanitarian Aid Corps (Article 214(5) TFEU)
77. Regulations governing political parties and their funding (Article 224 TFEU)
78. Creation of specialised courts (Article 257 TFEU)
79. Modification of Statute of Court of Justice, except Title I and Article 64 (Article 281 TFEU)
80. Procedures for monitoring the exercise of implementing powers (Article 291(3) TFEU)
81. European Union administration (Article 298(2) TFEU)
82. Adoption of financial rules (Article 322(1)(a) TFEU)
83. Responsibilities of authorizing and accounting officers (Article 322(1)(b) TFEU)
84. Fight against fraud affecting the Union's financial interests (Article 325(4) TFEU)
85. Staff Regulations of EU officials and other staff (Article 336 TFEU)
86. Measures for the gathering of statistics (Article 338(1) TFEU)

The consent procedure

From assent to consent

The Single European Act introduced (at that point only for association agreements with third countries and the accession of new Member States), a procedure whereby the approval of Parliament is required in a single reading before Council can enact a measure.

This was known initially as the assent procedure, but the Treaty of Lisbon changed its name to consent – and further extended its scope. It had by then already been extended as a result of the Maastricht, Amsterdam and Nice Treaties, to several additional categories of decision (see Table 34), the most frequently used being the approval of various categories of international agreements entered into by the Union (of which more below).

The explicit approval by Parliament by a simple majority of those voting is the normal requirement, but in some areas the approval of the majority of members of Parliament (i.e., abstentions or absences counting against) is required. These are the accession of new Member States, the electoral system for European elections, the multi-annual financial framework, the two ways whereby the European Council may change procedures laid down in the treaties (to switch an area or case from unanimity to qualified majority in the Council or to change from a special legislative procedure to the ordinary legislative procedure), and decisions about (the risk of, or actual) breach of the Union's values by a Member State (the latter also requiring a two-thirds majority of those voting). A majority of members was previously also required under the terms of the Single Act for association agreements with third countries, but the Treaty of Maastricht modified the requirement to a simple majority.

The consent procedure amounts to a crude form of co-decision in that the agreement of both Council and Parliament is necessary. However, there is no scope to bargain over several readings on amendments to the measure in question. This is normal when it comes to international agreements negotiated by the Commission, which, as in national parliaments, have to be dealt with on a take it or leave it basis (see below). It is also understandable for "constitutional" type measures. However, its continuing application to measures that are typically legislative in character, such as measures to combat discrimination, is curious. This used to be the case too for the operational rules for the structural funds, but this was switched to the ordinary legislative procedure by the Lisbon Treaty. The conferral of new tasks on the European Central Bank had also been a matter for parliamentary assent, but is now simply a matter for consultation of Parliament.

There are also three cases where it is the Council that must give its consent to an act adopted by (and, indeed, initiated by) the Parliament. These concern the Statute of the European Ombudsman which lay down the general conditions governing his duties (see Chapter 14), the provisions governing the exercise of the right of inquiry, and the MEPs' Statute.

Making use of the procedure: the growth of Parliament's powers over international agreements

Prior to the introduction of the assent/consent procedure, Parliament had little leverage over international agreements. The original treaties gave Parliament no role at all. As in other matters, its role developed in a series of steps.

A first step came in 1964 when Council, through a letter of its President Luns, undertook to involve Parliament as far as association agreements were concerned. According to this Luns procedure, Parliament held a debate before negotiations opened, the Commission briefed Parliament's responsible committees during the negotiations, and when they were finished, Council's President or his representative appeared before the same committees to brief them confidentially of the contents of the agreement, prior to signature.

In 1971, the Court ruled (AETR judgement, Case C-22/70) that the Community as such is also responsible for the external aspects of its internal policies. This implied that the same treaty provisions would apply in approving external agreements as apply to the policy area in question. These provisions often required the consultation of Parliament. This was particularly important for international agreements in the field transport and agriculture, and also for "cooperation agreements" – a sort of half-way house between commercial agreements and association agreements, combining such things as trade, technical cooperation, aid, loans, etc. Not being specifically provided for under the treaty, these required the use of Article 235 (now 352) as a legal base and therefore consultation of Parliament.

Parliament still had no say in trade and commercial agreements, although these were more numerous and frequently more important (e.g., GATT) than association agreements. This began to change in the early 1970s, partly as a result of the AETR ruling, partly because of the Paris Summit of 1973 agreeing to reinforce Parliament's powers and especially because of a realisation that Parliament's new budgetary powers might enable it to cause problems for the implementation of agreements that had budgetary implications. First, the Commission agreed (Memorandum to Parliament of 30 May 1973), to participate in any debate that Parliament decided to organise in plenary or in committee on the negotiation of such agreements, and to brief parliamentary committees during the negotiations (as in the Luns procedure). Then, in October 1973, Council President Westerterp undertook in a letter to Parliament on behalf of Council, to apply a modified version of the Luns procedure, which became known as the Luns-Westerterp procedure, to commercial agreements. The text of Council's letter was virtually the same as that of 1964, except that it made no reference to the Commission briefing committees (covered already by the Commission's Memorandum) and it undertook to supplement the confidential briefing of Parliament's committees before signature of an agreement with formal and public information to plenary after signature but before conclusion. This was reinforced in 1977 when Council, through a letter of its President, Tony Crosland, agreed that, for "important agreements", the Council President's briefing of Parliament's committees would take place at a special meeting (normally in Brussels) instead of on the fringes of a Strasbourg plenary session, and that the President would submit a written aide-memoire in advance. For other agreements, Council would simply inform Parliament in writing of the opening and the conclusion of negotiations, but Parliament could, if it expressed the wish within two weeks, follow the procedure for important agreements.

In the Stuttgart "Solemn Declaration on European Union", the European Council agreed that Parliament should be formally consulted on all "significant" international agreements before their conclusion, as well as on accession treaties. The Luns-Westerterp procedures were also extended to cover all important agreements (i.e., even those outside the scope of the then Articles 113 and 238 EEC).

None of these early steps forward involved changes to the treaties. As we saw above, it was in 1987 with the Single European Act that Parliament first gained a formal power to grant or withhold assent to agreements, though then only to the accession of new Member States and to association agreements. But these quickly demonstrated how Parliament could make use of this procedure to shape policy.

Accession is not something that arises every month, but the constant pressure to enlarge the Union is a reminder that Parliament could block accession if conditions that it feels are important are not met. This possibility means that the other institutions as well as the applicant states pay considerable attention to Parliament's positions during the negotiations. The importance of this power was evident in the final stages of the negotiations for the accession of Austria, Sweden, Finland and (it was then thought) Norway. A new threshold for obtaining a qualified majority in the Council had to be defined for a larger Union. Most Member States wanted the new threshold to remain the same proportion of votes as before. A minority, including the UK, wanted the same absolute figure (of 23 votes) as a "blocking minority" as before, which would have meant a smaller proportion to block decisions and a higher threshold to adopt them. MEPs made it clear that Parliament would not give its assent to accession if it contained such a weakening of the Union's decision taking capacity. This helped to persuade the Member States to accept to keep the same proportion as a threshold, subject only to the so-called Ioannina Declaration, proving that "if members of the Council representing a total of 23 to 26 votes indicate their intention to oppose the adoption by the Council of a decision by a qualified majority", then "a reasonable time" would be allowed to elapse to see if an agreement could be found with a wider level of support, subject to legal deadlines being met. Parliament felt able to approve the accessions in May 1994 by overwhelming majorities.

As regards association agreements, Parliament's use of the procedure was more significant than had been supposed by some of those involved in negotiating the Single European Act. The then UK Permanent Representative (Michael Butler), for instance, thought that there would be no such procedure "coming forward in the life of this Parliament". In fact, there were over 30 cases just in the remaining two years of that Parliament (1984-89). The large number arose because of the need for parliamentary assent not just for the original agreement, but also for revisions or additions to agreements, such as financial protocols, which may be adopted only for limited periods and require renewal.

Three examples soon showed how Parliament could make use of this power. First, in 1988, unhappy with the conditions imposed on Palestinian producers wishing to export from the occupied territories to Europe, Parliament initially refused to give its assent to three protocols to the EEC/Israel Association Agreement. Council subsequently referred them back to Parliament a second time, and Parliament agreed to put the proposals back on its agenda, but postponed consideration of them for several months while the Commission (and MEPs from various Groups and Parliament's responsible committee) had discussions with Israeli representatives that produced concessions on Palestinian exports. Parliament then approved the protocols.

Second, Parliament refused its assent to financial protocols with Syria and Morocco in 1992 to protest at the human rights situation in these countries. This caused a serious diplomatic rift with Morocco in particular, which refused, in retaliation, to renew a fishing agreement for several months.

Finally, there was a long-running argument in the Parliament about whether or not to give its assent to the EU-Turkey customs union agreement. The human rights situation in Turkey was a source of major concern inside the Parliament and there was a strong sense in the summer of 1995 that there would not be a majority for the agreement. In the end, and after Turkey agreed to change its constitution and legislation (the anti-terrorist law) and also released 81 political prisoners, a sufficient number of members were persuaded that the deal should go ahead, with 343 votes in favour, 149 against and 36 abstentions in December 1995.

But, the Single Act had led to a discrepancy in Parliament's powers. Whereas its assent was necessary for what could often be relatively minor adjustments or additional protocols to an association agreement, it was merely consulted for some major agreements such as the first economic cooperation agreements with Central and Eastern European countries or GATT (now WTO) agreements (and regarding the latter, only informally).

At the time, Parliament sought to overcome this anomaly in two ways. First, it pressed the Commission and Council to define agreements as association agreements wherever there was scope for interpretation. As a result of this, the "Europe" agreements with Central and Eastern European countries and the European Economic Area agreement with the EFTA countries were classified as association agreements. Second, Parliament provided in its own Rules of Procedure to treat any "significant international agreement" according to the same procedures as it applied to association agreements. This meant that Parliament would give or refuse its assent to the conclusion, renewal or modification of such agreements in the same way as it did for association agreements, and that it would expect Council not to conclude an agreement that did not receive its assent.

This approach gained acceptance to the extent that the Member States agreed in the Treaty of Maastricht to change the provisions of the EC Treaty in order to require Parliament's assent for all important agreements. These were defined as any agreement establishing a specific institutional framework, or having important implications for the budget, or requiring the amendment of internal legislation pursuant to the co-decision procedure. There remained some ambiguity about these definitions. Parliament went to the ECJ to test the effective meaning of "important budgetary implications": in case C-189/97 (EC-Mauritania fisheries agreement), the Court found on 8 July 1999 that a sum of €266.8 million over 5 years did not qualify as "important" under the treaty, although a similar but larger-scale fisheries agreement with Morocco subsequently did come under the assent procedure. On the other hand, the criterion of an agreement "requiring the amendment of internal legislation pursuant to the co-decision procedure" was a category that was more precise and which continued to increase with successive treaties such that there are now few areas left that do not require Parliament's consent.

What remained off-limits to Parliament, until the Lisbon Treaty, were the numerous trade agreements under the common commercial policy (CCP), where it was not even formally consulted. It did receive through the Nice Treaty a right to obtain the opinion of the Court of Justice as to whether an agreement envisaged is compatible with the treaty, but it was only with Lisbon that its consent is required for virtually any international agreement of any sort, other than ones relating exclusively to the CFSP, thus including trade agreements. At the same time, the substance of the CCP was extended to include foreign direct investment.

This was complemented by giving Parliament co-decision powers over legislation (under Article 207 (2) TFEU) determining the framework for implementing the CCP and applying trade agreements, a power it first used to provide for a safeguard clause for the 2010 EU-South Korea Free Trade Agreement. Parliament is established as a co-legislator in the field of economic, financial and technical cooperation measures, including assistance, to third countries other than developing countries (Article 212 (1)TFEU).

A spectacular use of Parliament's expanded consent power took place in February 2010 when Parliament rejected the SWIFT agreement between the EU and the USA on the latter's ability to access banking data of EU citizens for purposes of combating terrorism, which a majority in Parliament considered to be lacking sufficient data protection safeguards. Although the agreement was supported by all EU Member State governments, Parliament's rejection meant it fell, and a new agreement had to be negotiated (with care being taken, this time, to square the content with Parliament beforehand). Interestingly, this situation was immediately understood by the US administration, used to similar independent-mindedness of its own Congress, and it rapidly sent Vice President Joe Biden, Secretary of State Hillary Clinton and countless officials to talk to Parliament, while governments of EU Member States were, in some cases, indignant on the side lines.

This gradual strengthening of Parliament's role in the approval of international agreements gave weight to its demands to be more fully informed upstream, notably about the negotiation process (if not in determining the negotiating mandates). This too was eventually recognised in the Lisbon treaty which specified that "the European Parliament shall be immediately and fully informed at all stages of the procedure" (Article 218(10) TFEU).

Parliament interprets "all stages" to include Commission or High Representative recommendations to open negotiations, Council decisions authorising the opening of negotiations and nominating the Union negotiator, directives which the Council may address to the negotiator, the negotiations themselves, initialling of the text of an agreement, signature, possible provisional application, conclusion, suspension of the agreement, modifications to the agreement when the agreement provides for a simplified procedure to do so, and the positions to be adopted in bodies established by the agreement. Council has shown an initial lack of enthusiasm to interpret this quite so widely.

Parliament has even sought to be present at important international negotiations. The Commission had already undertaken in February 1990 (statement by Jacques Delors to Parliament) to include MEPs as observers in its delegations to important multilateral conferences (such as WTO ministerials). In 1998 the Council went further and formally agreed to the principle of MEPs being able to join delegations of the Union at international conferences, subject to a request being submitted at least four weeks in advance by the President of the Parliament. MEPs in such EU delegations attend in an individual capacity, must follow the instructions of the head of delegation, and are given no direct negotiating role.

Such participation has now become common practice, with 15 MEPs, for example, having been present at the 2009 Copenhagen negotiations on climate change. The main point of controversy has been the interpretation of "negotiating role", with this being interpreted as excluding MEPs not just from the direct negotiating sessions with third countries, but also from the internal EU coordination meetings at which the EU's external negotiating stance is discussed. Most MEPs argue that their attendance at such meetings, if only as observers rather than active participants, would facilitate their role in defending and advancing EU positions, notably in contacts with parliamentarians from third countries. The issue has remained deadlocked, with the Council (and Member States) in particular being opposed to such a presence. The negotiations in 2010 to renew the EP-Commission Framework saw intense discussion on this (and the expression of considerable unease by the Council), but no substantial change.

Nonetheless, the growth of Parliament's powers in this area has taken place at a time when the external relations of the Union are of increasing importance. There is an increased perception that trade globalisation and environmental inter-dependence (as well as the development of the CFSP) call for both a more effective coordination and definition of Union and national trade policies and a stronger degree of democratic control.

Table 34: *The Consent Procedure*

I   Council acts, adopted with the consent of Parliament

A.   Unanimity in Council and consent of European Parliament

1.   Accession of new Member States (Article 49 TEU)*
2.   Agreement on arrangements for withdrawal of a Member State from the Union (Article 50 TEU)
3.   Measures to combat discrimination (Article 19(1) TFEU)
4.   Extension of citizenship-related rights (Article 25 TFEU) (national ratification also required)
5.   Decisions on extending Article 82(2) to new aspects of criminal procedure (Article 82(2)(d) TFEU)
6.   Decisions on extending Article 83(1) to new aspects of criminal procedure (Article 83(1), second sub-paragraph TFEU)
7.   Establishment of European Public Prosecutor's Office (Article 86(1) TFEU)
8.   Extension of powers of European Public Prosecutor's Office (Article 86(4) TFEU)
9.   Association Agreements (Article 218(6)(a)(i) TFEU)
10.   EU accession to the ECHR (Article 218(6) (a) (ii) TFEU) (national ratification also required)
11.   Uniform electoral procedure (Article 223(1) TFEU).* (On initiative from, as well as with consent of, EP. National ratification also required)
12.   Multiannual financial framework (Article 312(2) TFEU) *
13.   Action to achieve treaty objectives where they have not provided the necessary powers elsewhere (Article 352 TFEU)

* EP consent by a majority of members of Parliament

B.   Qualified majority in Council and consent of EP

1.   Implementing measures of the Union's own resources system (Article 311(4) TFEU)
2.   Recourse to enhanced cooperation by nine or more Member States outside the field of the CFSP (Article 329(1) TFEU)

C.   Qualified majority in Council, unless certain conditions trigger unanimity, and consent of EP*

1.   International agreements establishing a specific institutional framework (Article 218(6)(a)(iii) TFEU)
2.   International agreements with important budgetary implications (Article 218(6)(a)(iv) TFEU)
3.   International agreements in fields where co-decision or consent procedures apply to internal EU legislation (Article 218(6)(a) (v) TFEU)
4.   Trade agreements under the common commercial policy (Article 207(3) TFEU)

* *Unanimity is triggered if the agreement covers a field where internal EU legislation requires unanimity, or is an economic and financial cooperation agreement with a State that is a candidate for accession to the Union, or is a trade agreement in cultural and audiovisual matters that risk prejudicing the Union's cultural and linguistic diversity, or is a trade agreement in social, educational and health services that risk seriously disturbing the national organisation of such services*

D. *Special majority* in Council and consent of EP by two-thirds majority*

1. Determination of a clear risk of a serious breach by a Member State of human dignity, freedom, democracy, equality, the rule of law and respect for human rights, including the rights of persons belonging to minorities (Article 7(1) TEU)
2. Sanctions in the event of serious and persistent breach of fundamental rights by a Member State (Article 7(2) TEU)

* Four –fifths majority of Council members, on a proposal of the Parliament, the Commission or one-third of Member States, to determine a risk (Art. 7(1)), and unanimity, apart from the Member State in question, and not counting abstentions, for adoption of sanctions (Art. 7(2)).

II European Council decisions, adopted with consent of Parliament

1. Convening an IGC without holding a Convention (Article 47(3) TEU)
2. Transfer of an area requiring unanimity in Council to qualified majority voting (Article 48(7) TEU)*
3. Transfer of a matter requiring special legislative procedure to ordinary legislative procedure (Article 48(7) TEU)*

* EP consent by a majority of members of Parliament

III European Parliament acts, adopted with the consent of Council

1. Statute for Members of the European Parliament (Article 223(2) TFEU): adoption by EP, on its own initiative, after obtaining consent of Council (unanimously as regards taxation regime) and after consulting Commission
2. Provisions governing the exercise of the right of inquiry (Article 226(3) TFEU): adoption by EP, on its own initiative, after obtaining consent of Council and Commission
3. Statute of European Ombudsman (Article 228(4) TFEU): adoption by EP, on its own initiative, after obtaining consent of Council and Commission

Figure 8: *Parliamentary Consent procedure*

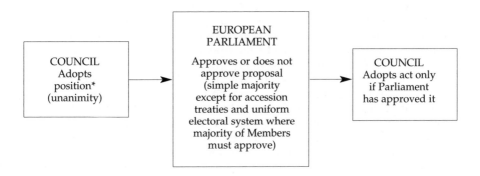

*   Council acts on a proposal of
– the Commission (Articles 105(6), 161, 300 (3) TEC)
– the Parliament (Article 190 (4) TEC)
– the Central Bank[1] or the Commission (Article 107 (5) TEC)
– applicant states, after consulting the Commission (Article 49 TEU)

[1] in which case Council may act by a qualified majority

The consultation procedure

After the Lisbon Treaty, there are still over 30 cases (some half of which can be characterised as legislative in nature) where Parliament is simply consulted by Council. Although many of them are rarely used, some are potentially quite important (see Table 35 below). Yet, as we shall see, the consultation procedure can afford Parliament some influence.

Consultation used, of course, to be the only way Parliament was involved in adopting legislation prior to the introduction of the co-operation procedure (a precursor of the co-decision procedure) in 1986 as a result of the Single European Act. Over time, Parliament had found ways of giving some teeth to the procedure, through agreements with the other institutions and through interpretation of the treaties.

Through successive steps, Council gradually agreed to consult Parliament, even where the treaties did not require it. In practice, by the mid-1970s, Council consulted Parliament on virtually all legislative proposals referred to it as well as on non-legislative texts such as Commission memoranda and Council resolutions, which, whilst not legally binding, nevertheless lay down guidelines, timetables and commitments outlining the framework for forthcoming legislative measures. For its part, the Commission agreed to send to Parliament all memoranda and communications that it sends to Council, thereby reducing what had been an information deficit in the Parliament.

Council also committed itself (through successive letters in November 1969, March 1970 and July 1970) to informing Parliament of the reasons for departing from Parliament's opinion when adopting Community legislation, initially for legislation with financial consequences and subsequently for all important questions. The Paris Summit of Heads of Government, following the first enlargement of the Community in 1973, agreed that Council should justify its opposition to any amendments, either in writing or orally in plenary. In the same year, Commission and Council also agreed that Parliament should be re-consulted whenever significant changes were envisaged to the text on which Parliament initially delivered its opinion.

These developments gave MEPs the opportunity of being involved in all discussions on Community legislation and policy-making. However, until direct elections and the arrival of full-time MEPs in 1979, the practical use made of them was limited. In any case, no matter how extensive the possibilities for parliamentary involvement, the bottom line of being able to block proposals or oblige the other institutions to accept changes was lacking. The European Parliament could make its opinion known at all stages, but it had no bargaining power if the other institutions failed to respond to its views. This situation first began to change following a major ruling of the European Court of Justice in 1980.

The Isoglucose judgment of 1980 and its repercussions

Unlike for the consultation of the Economic and Social Committee, Council could not lay down a deadline within which the Parliament must deliver its opinion. This difference was to prove important.

The 1980 Isoglucose judgment of the Court of Justice (Cases 138 and

139/79) overturned legislation adopted by Council, ruling that Council cannot adopt Community legislation before receiving Parliament's opinion, where this is required under the treaties. The Court made a link between consultation of the Parliament and the democratic character of the Community. It stated that the provisions in the treaty requiring the consultation of Parliament are:

> "the means which allows the Parliament to play an actual part in the legislative process of the Community. Such a power represents an essential factor in the institutional balance intended by the Treaty. Although limited, it reflects at Community level the fundamental democratic principle that the people should take part in the exercise of power through the intermediary of a representative assembly. Due consultation of the Parliament in the cases provided for by the Treaty therefore constitutes an essential formality, disregard of which means that the measure concerned is void".

The Court ruled in favour of the Parliament despite the fact that:

–   Parliament had had a debate in plenary on the basis of a committee report and had finished its examination of the proposal. However, it had not taken a final vote on the resolution as a whole but instead referred the text back to the relevant parliamentary committee.

–   There were objective reasons for taking a quick decision in order to avoid a legal void when previous legislation lapsed.

–   Council maintained that, in the circumstances, it did try to get Parliament's opinion but that "Parliament, by its own conduct, made the observance of that requirement impossible".

–   The Commission intervened in the case on the side of Council.

Parliament included in the arguments on its side of the case the fact that Council had not exhausted all the possibilities of obtaining the opinion of Parliament: for instance it had not requested the application of the urgency procedure provided for by the internal rules of Parliament. Likewise it had not taken the opportunity it has under the treaties to ask for an extraordinary session of Parliament. In its judgment, the Court expressly avoided taking a position on what the situation would have been had Council availed itself of these procedures and had Parliament still not delivered its opinion. Some observers doubted whether the Court would have ruled the same way if Council were to exhaust its procedural possibilities to obtain Parliament's opinion, or if Parliament were to state openly that it was withholding its opinion in order deliberately to block the decision-making process. These doubts were to re-emerge in the mid-1990s after a new Court ruling (see below), but the immediate effect of the judgment was to give some leverage to Parliament to use, or threaten to use, a power to delay when it is not satisfied with the response from the other institutions. It is a mechanism that is more significant for urgent matters, where delay can cause problems, than for items that have been in the pipeline for ten years and could equally well remain there for another ten.

The Isoglucose ruling coincided with a major overhaul of Parliament's internal Rules of Procedure following the first direct elections. Parliament sought to take advantage of the Court's ruling that its opinion was indispensable to the conclusion of the legislative procedure, by adopting a provision, still applicable today in Rule 57, whereby it can decide to postpone the final vote on the Commission's proposal until the Commission has taken a position on Parliament's amendments. Where the Commission refuses to accept these, Parliament can refer the matter back to committee for reconsideration, thereby delaying its formal "opinion" and holding up the procedure. When it gains a sufficient assurance from the Commission, or when a compromise is reached, it can move to a final vote in plenary. The significance of the Commission's acceptance of Parliament's amendments lies in the fact that they are then incorporated into a revised proposal that Council can only change by unanimity.

Parliament was obliged to recognise the limits of the 1980 Isoglucose ruling following a further judgment in 1995 when the Court rejected the Parliament's application for the annulment of a regulation adopted by the Council without Parliament's opinion (Case C-65/93). On 22 October 1993 the Council had requested Parliament's opinion on a regulation for the extension of the system of generalised tariff preferences for 1993, stressing the urgency of the matter as the existing regulation expired at the end of the year. Whilst acknowledging the urgency, Parliament postponed consideration of the proposal twice, the second time at the last session of the year in December, after which Council adopted the regulation, stressing the exceptional circumstances.

The Court argued that the consultation procedure required sincere cooperation between the institutions and that the Parliament had failed in this regard because its second decision to postpone consideration, due to an adjournment motion, was for reasons unconnected with the contents of the regulation. This decision restricts to a certain degree the right of the Parliament to delay giving its opinion by imposing an implicit obligation to have good reasons for such a delay. Parliament must be careful to avoid explicitly blocking decisions by withholding its opinion indefinitely, and instead plead a need to get further information, to investigate the social consequences, to pursue discussions with other institutions or interested parties, to hold public hearings, or to wait for related events.

The 1975 conciliation procedure

In 1975, the (then new) budgetary powers of the Parliament gave rise to a realisation that it might be in a position to use them to prevent the implementation of legislation with budgetary consequences. Council was therefore willing to negotiate and agree on a mechanism aimed at reducing the risk of such conflicts by first seeking agreement with Parliament on the legislation.

Thus, a Joint Declaration of Parliament, Council and Commission was agreed on 4 March 1975. It laid down that, for discretionary acts that would have "appreciable financial implications", either Parliament or Council could request the convening of a conciliation procedure, if there was a divergence of views. (In French it was called *concertation*, which usefully distinguishes it from the later "conciliation", as applicable under co-decision.) The aim was "to seek agreement... normally during a period not exceeding three months" (except in the case of urgency, when the Council could fix an earlier deadline). It specified that "when the positions of the two institutions are sufficiently close, the European Parliament may give a new opinion and the Council shall take definitive action".

As the ultimate power to legislate remained with the Council, the procedure was little more than an opportunity to ask it to think again, with the potential threat of eventually withholding money in the background. Nonetheless, it was seen at the time as a breakthrough and it was the first mechanism to bring MEPs and ministers together in a legislative procedure, laying the basis for the future conciliation phase in what became, 18 years later, the co-decision procedure and is now the ordinary legislative procedure. It established the practice of a joint committee composed of all the members of the Council and an equal number of MEPs (albeit then just 9+9). It made possible direct negotiations between Parliament and Council. Ministers could meet MEPs face-to-face and Parliament could make an input to Council that had not been filtered by the Commission. In this sense it acted as a precursor of the much more developed system of conciliation that exists under co-decision.

That being said, early attempts to build on it without treaty change failed. The initial scope was found to be small (only seven procedures from 1975 to 1982), but a 1981 proposal to extend it to all "important" Community acts fell because of the opposition of the Danish Government. In its 1983 Stuttgart "Solemn Declaration", the European Council undertook to enter into talks aimed at "improving and extending the scope of the conciliation procedure", but subsequently Denmark, alone, continued to block the matter within Council and the other Member States were unwilling to proceed without consensus.

Instead, Council sometimes agreed to interpret the concept of legislation with "appreciable financial implications" flexibly, allowing conciliation, in some cases, on proposals that did not obviously fall in this category, or to hold "informal conciliations" by means of a meeting between the Council President, his successor, two Commissioners, and Parliament's rapporteurs and relevant committee chairs. Council also agreed in 1989 to authorise its Presidents to hold preparatory meetings with the other institutions, prior to conciliation meetings. Such flexibility contributed to a wide range of relatively successful conciliations during the 1980s. However, subsequently, this kind of conciliation became more and more rare. There were meetings on the reform of the structural funds in 1994 and 1999 but the Council showed a decreasing level of interest, refusing, for example, a conciliation on the Cohesion Fund in 1994 on the grounds that Parliament had by that time acquired a power of assent and that conciliation only applied where Parliament was consulted. Only in one area did the procedure continue to be important and that was in revisions to the Financial Regulation, which lays down the details governing the establishment and implementation of the budget and specifically refers to the 1975 Declaration. However, even this special case can be expected to disappear. As a result of the Lisbon Treaty, revision of the Financial Regulation is now subject to the ordinary legislative procedure, making the 1975 variety of conciliation redundant. Even if it has not been repealed, Parliament deleted it from its Rules of Procedure (Corbett Report, 2009).

Table 35: *Council acts adopted after consultation of Parliament*

A.   Unanimity and consultation of European Parliament

1.   Measures concerning social security or social protection (Article 21(3) TFEU)
2.   Citizenship: right to vote and stand for election in Member State of residence in municipal and European elections (Article 22 TFEU)
3.   Adoption of measures which constitute a step backwards in Union law as regards the liberalisation of the movement of capital to or from third countries (Article 64(3) TFEU)
4.   Measures concerning passports, identity cards and residence permits (Article 77(3) TFEU)
5.   Judicial cooperation in civil matters concerning measures relating to family law with cross-border implications, and decision to transfer such matters to the ordinary legislative procedure (Article 81(3) TFEU)
6.   Operational police cooperation (Article 87(3) TFEU)
7.   Conditions and limitations for cross-frontier operations by police and judicial authorities (Article 89 TFEU)
8.   Harmonisation of indirect taxation (Article 113 TFEU)
9.   Approximation of provisions with a direct impact on the internal market not covered by Article 114 (Article 115 TFEU)
10.   Language arrangements for European intellectual property rights (Article 118, second subparagraph, TFEU)
11.   Replacing the Protocol on the excessive deficit procedure (Article 126(14) TFEU)
12.   Specific tasks of European Central Bank concerning prudential supervision (Article 127(6) TFEU)
13.   Social policy: social security and social protection of workers, protection of workers where their employment contract is terminated, representation and collective defence, conditions of employment for third-country nationals – and the transfer of any of these except social security to the ordinary legislative procedure (Article 153(2)(b), final two subparagraphs, TFEU)
14.   Environment: provisions of a fiscal nature, town and country planning, management of water resources, land use and the supply and diversification of energy resources (Article 192(2) TFEU)
15.   Energy: fiscal measures (Article194(3) TFEU)
16.   Association of overseas countries and territories with the Union - rules and procedure (Article 203 TFEU)
17.   Jurisdiction of the Court in the area of intellectual property (Article 262 TFEU)
18.   Modification of the Protocol on the Statute of the European Investment Bank (Article 308 TFEU)
19.   Union own resources – ceiling and creation of new resources (Article 311 TFEU) (national ratification required)
20.   Decision under enhanced cooperation to transfer a matter to ordinary legislative procedure (Article 333(2) TFEU)

B.   Qualified majority and consultation of EP

1.   Measures to facilitate diplomatic protection (Article 23 TFEU)
2.   Measures to ensure administrative cooperation on security and justice issues among Member State departments (Article 74 TFEU)
3.   Provisional measures to help a Member State faced with sudden inflow of refugees (Article 78(3) TFEU)
4.   Competition policy rules (Article 103(1) TFEU)
5.   State aid rules (Article 109 TFEU)
6.   Definitions of overdrafts, loans and debt of Member States for EMU purposes (Article 125(2) TFEU)

7. Certain specific provisions required by Statute of Central Bank (Article 129(4) TFEU)
8. Admission of new members to euro (Article 140(2) TFEU)
9. Research: specific programmes implementing framework programme (Article 182(4) TFEU)
10. Research: setting up of joint undertakings (Article 187 and 188(2) TFEU)
11. Methods and procedures for collecting own resources (Article 322(2) TFEU)
12. Measures relating to outermost regions (Article 349(2) TFEU)

Figure 9: *The consultation procedure*

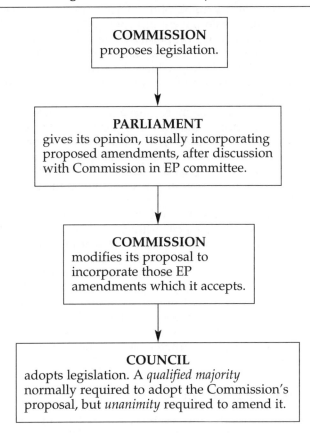

COMMISSION
proposes legislation.

PARLIAMENT
gives its opinion, usually incorporating proposed amendments, after discussion with Commission in EP committee.

COMMISSION
modifies its proposal to incorporate those EP amendments which it accepts.

COUNCIL
adopts legislation. A *qualified majority* normally required to adopt the Commission's proposal, but *unanimity* required to amend it.

The cooperation procedure

The cooperation procedure does not exist anymore, having been superseded by the ordinary legislative (co-decision) procedure, but when it was introduced by the Single European Act in 1987 it played an important part in the development of the powers of the Parliament and was a stepping stone to the full co-decision procedure. From 1987 to 1993, it applied to about one-third of the legislation that Parliament examined, notably the bulk of legislative harmonisation measures necessary for the creation of the single market. It continued to apply in several fields until the entry into force of the

Amsterdam Treaty in 1999, and even after that remained theoretically available for four scarcely used articles relating to monetary matters, until it was finally abolished by the Lisbon Treaty.

The cooperation procedure was the first to introduce a second reading. As compared with consultation (then the sole existing procedure), Council's decision (following Parliament's first reading opinion) returned to Parliament for a second reading at which Parliament could either approve the text (in which case Council had to adopt it), or reject by an absolute majority (in which case it would fall unless Council unanimously agreed within three months and with the agreement of the Commission to overrule Parliament) or propose amendments by an absolute majority of its members, which, if supported by the Commission, were incorporated into a revised proposal. Council could only modify this proposal by unanimity, whereas a qualified majority was enough to adopt it. Council had three or four months to choose one of these two options, failing which the proposal fell. However, any amendments not supported by the Commission required unanimity to be adopted by Council.

This tentative step towards more parliamentary power on legislation helped achieve acceptance of the idea that parliamentary rejection should kill off a text. On most occasions when it was used, Parliament's rejection was sustained, either because Council was unable to find the necessary unanimity to overrule Parliament (e.g. Benzene directive, 1988), or because the Commission withdrew the proposal (e.g. directive on the use of sweeteners in foodstuffs, 1992).

It more frequently gave rise to parliamentary amendments being incorporated into legislation by Council. Although at first sight parliamentary amendments not accepted by Council in first reading seemed unlikely to fare better in second reading, when Council positions were fixed and where Parliament could not act so easily (needing an absolute majority of members and unable to threaten to delay), in practice a Commission-Parliament alliance put a lot of pressure on Council, to choose within a short deadline whether to accept an amended proposal or lose it entirely.

In any case, the second reading gave the impression of a classical bicameral legislative procedure at European level, and helped pave the way towards full co-decision.

Right to initiate legislation

The right to initiate legislative proposals is one that is traditionally associated with parliaments, but in practice, in most countries, this role has been taken over almost completely by governments. In the UK, for example, MPs rely on a lottery system (the ballot for "private members' bills") to introduce a limited category of legislative proposals themselves. In France, the government is given a virtual monopoly in this respect by the Constitution. Even in countries where there are no constitutional or regulatory limitations on Parliament, the detailed and technical nature of much modern legislation means that, in practice, it is the executive that initiates virtually all legislation.

In the European Union the Commission has a near monopoly of legislative initiative. The Parliament does have some formal rights under the treaty to initiate legislation, namely for the purpose of adopting a uniform electoral procedure for European elections, the Statute for its members, the Statute of the Ombudsman, the exercise of its own rights of inquiry and the determination of a clear risk of a serious breach by a Member State of the values of the Union. But in general, the right of initiative lies with the Commission.

As we saw above in the opening paragraphs of the section on the ordinary legislative procedure, these formal provisions do not grant the executive a monopoly on ideas or the right to exercise these powers without due regard to the wishes of Council and Parliament. Council, indeed, was given the right under the original treaties (now Article 241) to request the Commission to undertake studies and to submit any appropriate proposals. The Maastricht Treaty gave the Parliament an equivalent right (now Article 225).

Thus, Parliament can request, by an absolute majority of its members, that the Commission "submit any appropriate proposal on matters on which it considers that a Union act is required for the purpose of implementing the Treaties". Any individual MEP may table such a proposal, which is then referred to the parliamentary committee for further consideration. In practice, Parliament uses this facility sparingly, to give extra weight to specific requests beyond the day-to-day exchanges with the Commission and ordinary requests made in resolutions. If it does so, the Commission has undertaken to respond (as for all Parliament resolutions that call upon it to take action) within three months and either to draw up the corresponding legislative proposal within one year or include it in the following year's Work Programme - or give Parliament a "detailed explanation of the reasons" if it does neither (EP-Commission Framework Agreement, point 16).

In the nearly 18 years since this treaty article came into force, it has been invoked just 29 times (see Table 36) by Parliament.

Table 36: *Parliamentary resolutions to initiate legislation*

- Hotel fire safety (April 1994)
- Environmental damage (May 1994)
- Settlement of claims arising from traffic accidents occurring outside the claimant's country of origin (October 1995)
- Health cards (April 1996)
- Forest strategy (January 1997)
- Network access for renewable energies (June 1998)
- Protection of EU finances (January 2000)
- Improving the legal protection of accident victims (July 2001)
- Cultural cooperation (September 2001)
- Book pricing (May 2002)
- Regional and lesser-used languages (September 2003)
- Heating and cooling from renewable energy sources (February 2006)
- Access to the institutions' texts (April 2006)
- Protecting healthcare workers from infections due to needle stick injuries (July 2006)
- Trans-national succession and wills (November 2006)
- European Private Company Statute (February 2007)
- Limitation periods in cross-border disputes involving injuries and fatal accidents (February 2007)
- Transparency of institutional investors (July 2008)
- Regulation of hedge funds and private equity (September 2008)
- Alignment of legal acts to the new comitology decision (September 2008)

- Supervision of financial markets (September 2008)
- Application of the principle of equal pay (October 2008)
- Authentic acts (November 2008)
- Cross-border implications of legal protection for adults (November 2008)
- e- Justice (November 2008)
- Financing of development aid in certain countries (January 2009)
- Cross-border transfer of the registered office of a company (January 2009)
- Micro-credits (January 2009)
- Implementation of the citizens initiative (February 2009)

The Commission claims that it has "in virtually all cases acted upon them in the manner sought by Parliament" (Answer to PQ E-3086) but in practice the nature of its action has varied considerably. For example, the hotel fire safety proposal resulted only in a study, whereas the traffic accidents proposal led to the adoption in 2000 of the Fourth Motor Insurance Directive. Nonetheless, Parliament has not sought a full right of initiative, underlining the parity between its position and that of the Council, and no doubt wary of such a right being conferred upon the Council.

Article 225 is not the only mechanism available to the Parliament to influence the legislative agenda of the Union. Reference has already been made (in Chapter 7) to Parliament's procedures governing the adoption of reports at its own initiative (either "own-initiative" reports of parliamentary committees, or reports drawn up in response to Rule 120 motions for resolution tabled by MEPs, or indeed resolutions adopted through the urgency procedure or to wind up a debate). Being an independent institution, whose majority is not beholden to the Commission, Parliament frequently uses these opportunities to call on the Commission to take action of one sort or another, and this frequently includes calls for new legislative proposals. Naturally, individual MEPs or Political Groups or indeed parliamentary committees frequently make such proposals in their own right, but those carrying the most weight are own-initiative reports drawn up after due consideration (possibly including public hearings) by the responsible parliamentary committee and adopted after due debate in plenary.

The Commission first responds to such initiatives in the debate in plenary. The Commission agreed in 1982 (in its "report on inter-institutional relations", the so-called Andriessen report, Bulletin EEC supplement 3/82) in principle to take up any parliamentary proposals to which it did not have any major objection. Where it had an objection, it undertook to explain its attitude in detail to Parliament. From March 1983, when it made a commitment to do so through an exchange of letters with Parliament's President (Piet Dankert), the Commission has submitted written reports every six months explaining how it has responded to Parliament's initiatives and what action it has taken. In November 1994, it was agreed to replace this with a more regular report to be examined within the relevant committees.

A famous historical example of how Parliament used this power was the 1982 initiative to press for a ban on the import of baby seal skins into the Community. It was supported by a large amount of public campaigning including a petition with over a million signatures. These efforts resulted in Commission proposals, then backed by Parliament in the legislative procedure, and the adoption of a Council regulation, despite initial reluctance by both the Commission and Council. Another example, this time without much support from public opinion, was the Community's directive on trans-frontier television broadcasts, laying down rules for such broadcasts, which was adopted under co-decision in 1997. This can also be traced back to a Parliament own-initiative report. Similarly, the proposal to ban tobacco advertising, which passed in 1998 under the co-decision procedure, can be traced back to a Parliament initiative of 1990.

The Commission's Annual Work Programme

Another opportunity to influence the initiation of legislation lies in the discussions about the Commission's Work Programme. The fact that (unlike some national parliaments), the European Parliament is master of its own agenda persuaded the Commission of the advantages of seeking an understanding with Parliament about the timetable for dealing with its legislative proposals. This in turn opened the door for Parliament both to influence the priorities in the Commission's programme and to press for the inclusion of new items or even the exclusion of items.

In the 2005 version of the Framework Agreement between the two institutions, an elaborate procedure was laid down for this, substantially revised in 2010. In 2005, it provided that, each year in February, the Commission present an Annual Policy Strategy (APS) for the following year. Following a debate, the relevant parliamentary committees would enter into dialogue with the corresponding Commissioners "to discuss the preparation of the future programme in each of their specific areas". In September, the Conference of Committee Chairs would produce a summary report, which the Commission could use when drawing up its programme for the following year, which must include a list of legislative and non-legislative proposals. The President of the Commission would then present this to Parliament in November, with the whole college of Commissioners present for the debate. The debate would normally be followed by the adoption of a Parliament resolution at the December part-session.

In 2010 it was agreed in the revised Framework Agreement to overhaul this procedure. The APS was dropped, the dialogue between committees and the Commission was enhanced, and a State of the Union speech introduced as a key part of the procedure. It was agreed that the work programme should also include planned initiatives on soft law, withdrawals and simplification. The key elements are set out in Table 37 below.

Table 37: *Timetable for the Commission's Annual Work Programme (summary of Annex 4 of EP-Commission Framework Agreement 2010)*

-   During the first semester of a given year, Commission members and the corresponding parliamentary committee undertake a regular dialogue on the implementation of that year's Work Programme and the preparation of next year's one. The Conference Committee Chairs take stock of this in dialogue with a Vice President of the Commission.

-   In June, the Conference of Committee Chairs submits a report to the Conference of Presidents which includes suggestions for Parliament's priorities for the next programme.

- In July, Parliament adopts a resolution outlining its position and includes particular requests based on legislative initiative reports.

- In September, the President of the Commission introduces a State of the Union debate (and presents an accompanying document), taking stock of the current year and looking ahead to priorities for the following years. Committees subsequently meet with the relevant members of the Commission for a detailed exchange on their policy area, rounded off by a meeting between the Conference of Committee Chairs and the whole college of Commissioners. In case of political difficulties, this is followed up by a meeting between the Conference of Presidents and the President of the Commission.

- In October, the Commission then adopts its Work Programme and presents it to Parliament. Parliament may (presumably if it is dissatisfied) hold a debate and adopt a resolution at the December part session.

Two specific comments can be made about this procedure. First, it creates a certain tension between a broad political programme and a set of specific legislative proposals. At the outset the Commission felt that it could dispense with the need to provide a detailed annual list of activities and that it could provide instead more general indications, backed up by a rolling three-month programme of activities. The Parliament subsequently made it very clear that this was unacceptable and that a proper annual list of legislative and other proposals was an essential complement to the broad political priorities that were being established.

Second, it is a structure that leaves the Council's relationship to the legislative programme uncertain. Back in 1993, in the Inter-institutional Declaration on democracy, transparency and subsidiarity, Council agreed to "state its position on the programme in a declaration and undertake to implement as soon as possible the provisions to which it attaches priority", thereby underlining its desire to remain free to choose the parts of the programme it wanted to act upon. Nearly ten years later, in 2002, the Seville European Council agreed to adopt, on the basis of the Commission's legislative and work programme, an "annual operating programme", the first of which was drawn up by the Greek and Italian governments for their Presidencies in 2003. More recently, there has been agreement to submit Troika working programmes for three successive Presidencies, the first of which was agreed by the German, Portuguese and Slovene Presidencies for 2007-8 – a procedure now contained in the Lisbon Treaty. Again these developments have reflected a wish of Member States to speak to each other in setting EU priorities rather than to submit themselves to the priorities of the Commission and Parliament. Nevertheless, the preparation of these programmes does offer an important benchmark against which the progress of the Council can be judged by both the European Parliament and by national parliaments.

Developments arising from the new legislative procedures

Balance of Parliament's work

The increase in Parliament's legislative work, arising both from the introduction of successive readings and from the growing volume of Union legislation generally, has led to a shift of emphasis in Parliament's work. The

number of legislative resolutions adopted (covering consultation, cooperation, co-decision and assent/consent) has increased substantially: in 1986, just
135 legislative resolutions were considered in plenary but since the early
1990s the figure has consistently averaged between 200 and 250 per year (and
nearly 300 in 2007 and 2008). By contrast, the number of non-legislative
reports remained reasonably constant at a lower figure of around 170 per
year, even falling in recent years to around 140 – and within that category, a
greater number were non-legislative consultations, responding notably to
White or Green Papers, normally the basis of subsequent legislation.

Determination of the legal base of proposals

For a long time, and to a degree still today, the choice of "legal base" (i.e. the
treaty article on which a proposal is based) was crucial. The legal base determines which procedure applies and hence Parliament has been vigilant to
ensure that treaty articles requiring the most favourable procedure are used
in preference to those that do not, wherever there is scope for interpretation.
A procedure for challenging the legal base has been provided for in
Parliament's Rules (Rule 37), whereby the Committee on Legal Affairs, on
its own initiative or after being consulted by the committee responsible, can
invite the plenary to endorse its conclusions as to the suitability of the legal
base chosen by the Commission.

Re-consultation of Parliament

Where, in its first reading position (or in the consultation procedure),
Council departs markedly from the text on which Parliament deliberated in
its first reading, and especially where new elements are incorporated into
that text, Parliament's Rule 59 provides for it to request re-consultation (i.e.
to have a "second first-reading"), if its responsible committee considers this
to be desirable, and if there is also agreement of the Conference of
Presidents. A second reading under the co-decision procedure may thus be
considered not to be sufficient if the changes made to the Commission's proposal are major ones (unless, obviously, they are the changes proposed by
Parliament). This possibility was originally devised in the pre-co-decision
era when Parliament's legislative powers were much weaker but has been
retained in the EP Rules.

Its use is now extremely rare, however, as in the co-decision context an
alternative course of action is to table new amendments in second reading.
Such a re-consultation request arose in February 2005 when the Conference
of Presidents supported a Legal Affairs Committee request for a new first
reading on the Commission proposal for a directive on the patentability of
computer implemented inventions, on which Parliament had given its original first reading in September 2003 and where the adoption of a common
position was blocked in the Council. In the end the issue was resolved later
in 2005 by the rejection of the proposal at second reading in the Parliament.

One special example of re-consultation is where Council amends the legal
base from an article requiring the co-decision procedure to one requiring
only consultation. Council should then re-consult Parliament, which gives a
second opinion under the ordinary consultation procedure (first-reading

procedure) on Council's "common orientation". This is now likely to be exceedingly rare after the entry into force of the Lisbon Treaty.

More dialogue with the Council and Commission

The increase of its formal powers strengthened Parliament's position in the contacts and discussions with other institutions that inevitably accompany the consideration of legislative proposals. The extent of those contacts has increased correspondingly.

All Presidents-in-Office of the various specialised Council configurations now appear before the responsible parliamentary committee at least once or twice during their six-month term. These appearances are normally related to general presentations or reports back of a Presidency's legislative and other priorities but may sometimes consist of an account of legislative decisions at Council meetings or even provide an opportunity to discuss – formally in the meeting or informally in the corridor – the take-up of particular parliamentary amendments to legislative proposals still being considered by Council. However, there is strong resistance by many within the Council, including the Council secretariat, to make systematic presentations of the outcome of Council's legislative readings to committees. This has been a rare event, such as when during the Belgian Presidency in the second half of 2001, the Environment Minister, Magda Aelvoet, a former MEP, did so. A further commitment to appear in committee was made by Council in the Interinstitutional Agreement on Better Lawmaking adopted at the end of 2003, a development which has encouraged Council working group chairs to speak occasionally in committee.

In any case, meetings and correspondence between committee chairs/rapporteurs and Council Presidents-in-Office have greatly increased. Committee chairs are often invited to take part in informal Council meetings. There are frequent contacts between rapporteurs and the chairs of working groups in the Council. Contacts between officials in the committee secretariats and their counterparts in the Commission and Council are also now more intensive. This has been facilitated by the transfer of all parliamentary officials working in the committees from the relative isolation of Luxembourg to Brussels, where virtually all committee meetings take place.

Before a Council Presidency starts, there are meetings at various levels (from officials to committee chairs with ministers) to explore the extent to which a Presidency's priorities and those of Parliament match and what can be done to facilitate their progress. The main Groups also arrange their own such contacts, notably with the corresponding party in the country concerned, especially when it is in government.

Pre- and post- legislative scrutiny

The adoption of Commission legislative proposals does not take place in a vacuum, and the pre- and post- legislative phases are also of crucial importance. The Commission produces a range of Communications and Green and White Papers in the pre-legislative phase, in which it outlines the possible need for legislation and the various policy options available. Individual Parliament committees are closely involved in the consultative phase on these documents, and normally draw up reports on those with important policy implications.

Another issue to assume greater importance in the pre-legislative phase is the need for proper impact assessment of major new legislative proposals, taking account of economic, social and environmental factors. All institutions are committed to taking this much more seriously than in the past. The Commission must carry out thorough assessments of its own proposals and Council and Parliament are committed to doing the same, where appropriate, when amending such proposals. Parliament has set aside a substantial budget for committees to enable them to improve their impact assessments.

Parliament's role is also potentially significant in the post-legislative phase, not just in monitoring national transposition of adopted EU legislation where the Legal Affairs Committee has a specific responsibility, but just as importantly in seeing whether adopted EU legislation is actually working or needs to be amended, dropped or replaced. A number of committees, notably the Environment Committee, now draw up follow-up reports on adopted EU legislation or take up other initiatives, such as the holding of implementation question time in committee. While this activity is part of the scrutiny and control function (see Chapter 15), it is also an essential part of the overall legislative cycle, and is destined to grow in importance.

Overall assessment

The European Parliament's role in the Community's legislative procedure has increased from having, initially, no role whatsoever, to having a consultative role, to being co-legislator with the Council. Parliament has demonstrated its ability to initiate new legislation in areas of concern to the public, to force substantial amendments to major legislative proposals and to adopt or reject the outcomes.

The European Parliament is not a rubber stamp legitimising a government's legislative wishes. It is an independent institution whose members are not bound to support a particular governing majority and which does not have a permanent majority coalition. In this sense it can be compared with the US Congress, with its own identity, independent legitimacy and separation from the executive, whilst seeking to interact intensely with that executive.

The European Parliament is now a clearly identifiable part of an institutional triangle. This fact in itself is remarkable in historical terms. The term "institutional triangle" was virtually unused two decades ago when most commentators referred to a bicephalous Community made up of the Commission and the Council. Now the argument is rather one about preserving and developing the equal status that the Parliament has won with regard to the other two institutions and of making European electorates aware that the content of European laws affecting us all is shaped by their directly elected MEPs in the Parliament.

13. Budgetary powers

About 2 percent of public spending (1 percent of GDP) is carried out at European level through the European Union budget, financing policies that Member States have decided to carry out at this level because of economies of scale or to pool resources or avoid duplication. The budget may be small in relative terms, but in absolute terms (at currently around €130 billion per annum) it is larger than the national budgets of the smaller Member States. Although it has to be balanced, there has been no shortage of debate about its sources of revenue and patterns of expenditure.

With the entry into force of the Lisbon Treaty the Parliament now enjoys a very high level of parity with the Council in determining the shape of the budget. Its position is comparable with that acquired in the legislative area as discussed in the previous chapter. However, the process by which this came about is completely different. Whereas the development of the Parliament's legislative role took place gradually through successive treaty revisions, starting with the Single European Act in the 1980s, the change in its budgetary status has been the product of two sets of treaty changes almost forty years apart. In the intervening period, between the mid-1970s and the end of 2009, the formal treaty provisions governing the establishment of the budget remained unchanged. Lisbon has unfrozen a situation that had appeared immutable and opened up a new era in the budgetary history of the institution and its relations with the other institutions, in particular the Council.

To understand the nature and extent of the changes that have taken place, the chapter will look in turn at the different aspects of budgetary policy making: the definition of the revenue provided to enable the EU to finance its policies, the determination of the multi-annual financial framework within which annual budgets are drawn up, and the procedure for the adoption of the annual budget, including the methods the Parliament uses to influence the shape of expenditure. The chapter will then look at Parliament's role as regards the implementation of the budget, the control of spending and the mechanism set in place to check expenditure after it has taken place, known as the "discharge".

Revenue

In 1970 the Member States decided to replace national contributions as a means of financing Community policies with a system of "own resources", made up of customs duties, agricultural levies and a fraction of VAT receipts. As a result, these resources became collective Community property, collected on its behalf by the Member States and which they were legally obliged to make available. This change led the way to the Parliament acquiring significant budgetary powers in relation to the use made of the revenue – it came to be described as one arm of the "budgetary authority" alongside the Council – but it did not lead to the institution being given any say over the sources of revenue.

Since 1970 the system has been adapted. In 1988 provision was made for the establishment of a fourth resource, consisting of amounts calculated on the basis of the GNP of the Member States and over time this resource has come to be the largest source of EU revenue. The Treaty of Lisbon now specifically provides for the Council to "establish new categories of own resources or abolish an existing category" but such a decision needs to be ratified by every Member State.

Such adaptations have had no effect on the Parliament's role in relation to revenue. It is invited to give its opinion on any changes to the "own resources" structure but the fundamental decisions remain in the hands of the Member States. The one possibility for the Parliament to influence revenue arises from a new provision of the Lisbon Treaty whereby it is invited to give its consent to measures implementing the "own resources" decision. In other words, it cannot decide on the ceiling and provenance of EU revenue but it can hope to influence the detailed way in which the system operates.

The system is one that used to open the Parliament to the charge of "revenue irresponsibility" in that it was not responsible for finding the money that is required to finance EU policies. However, it is the Member States who have never been ready to agree to the Parliament being closely involved in an area which they considered to be too sensitive and too near to an area of national prerogative. Moreover, the revenue system is now combined with a strict mechanism for controlling expenditure, known as the multiannual financial framework, which renders the old charge less significant. The size and shape of EU expenditure is now much more predictable than it used to be.

Multiannual financial framework

In the early years after the Parliament acquired important budgetary rights over the level of expenditure and in particular in the 1980s there was a significant level of conflict between the Parliament and the Council. As a result, the institutions looked for informal ways of channelling their different approaches to the budget by laying down an agreed framework for spending for a number of years. For the Parliament this was seen as a way of protecting its own policy priorities over the medium term and for the Council, it provided a way to ensure that certain levels of expenditure were not exceeded and Member States could plan ahead, with a degree of clarity as to what the size of the budget would be.

As a result, in 1988, Parliament, Council and Commission signed the first of four inter-institutional agreements on budgetary discipline and the improvement of the budgetary procedure (in 2006, this last phrase became "sound financial management"). Each of these agreements included a multiannual financial perspective or framework, laying down expenditure ceilings for a range of policy areas, which all three institutions agreed to respect in the course of the annual budgetary procedure. In addition, the 1999 agreement codified in one document a range of procedures and rules, relating notably to inter-institutional cooperation, the classification of expenditure, the incorporation of financial provisions in legislative acts, the requirement of a legal base and expenditure on the CFSP. Apart from the provisions on legal bases, which have been incorporated in the Financial Regulation (which specifies in detail the rules for establishing and implementing the budget), all these provisions were confirmed in the agreement signed in May 2006, covering all institutions and all expenditure for the period from 2007 to 2013. The 2006 agreement also stresses the importance of sound financial management and budget implementation by the EU institutions and the Member States and includes a requirement that the Member States (responsible for the implementation of around 80% of the budget) have to produce national audit summaries.

Lisbon has now given the multiannual financial framework (MFF) treaty status. It obliges the institutions to incorporate the framework into EU law and provides that the Parliament has to give its consent to the contents of that law. It thereby formalises the practice that had been established in the negotiations over the MFF in the years since 1988. In the same way, it takes over the provision whereby the agreement has to "determine the amounts of the annual ceilings on commitment appropriations by category of expenditure and of the annual ceiling on payment appropriations".

The MFF is designed to last a minimum of five years, thereby opening the possibility of the agreement largely coinciding with the terms of office of the Parliament and the Commission. The Parliament has consistently argued for the idea of the legislative programme of the Commission being underpinned by a financial programme for the duration of its mandate. As it is, both Parliament and Commission are at present obliged to take over a framework that was devised by their predecessors. The introduction of such a new system will now have to wait until 2014 but the detailed discussions over how it will work are likely to dominate the budgetary discussions over the period up to 2013, with Member States all the more sensitive about the shape of EU expenditure, given the difficult economic climate that all of them face, and with the Parliament determined to make the most of the powers it has acquired under the Lisbon Treaty.

The annual budgetary procedure

Within the framework set by the multiannual framework the institutions are obliged to agree an annual budget which authorises expenditure by each of the institutions. Lisbon has significantly changed the character of this procedure in two important respects:

-      it has abolished the procedural distinction between compulsory and non-compulsory expenditure whereby a large fraction of the budget was effectively considered to be determined by treaty obligations and therefore not subject to much revision via the budgetary procedure. Prior to Lisbon the Parliament had a limited say over such "compulsory" expenditure and was restricted to amending, within clearly-defined limits, the "non-compulsory" sector. Now Parliament and Council decide the whole budget on equal terms;

-      it has reduced the budgetary procedure from two readings to one and
       introduced a formal conciliation procedure. As a result, the level of
       cooperation required between Parliament and Council is increased,
       with both sides placed under pressure to find an agreement in a way
       comparable to the conciliation mechanism established under the ordi-
       nary legislative procedure (co-decision).

These two changes have profoundly altered the framework within which
the institutions are obliged to act which can now be summarised as follows:

Summary of Article 314 – the formal rules for establishing the annual budget

*Not later than 1 September the Commission presents a draft budget for
the following year containing the estimates of all the institutions (with
the exception of the European Central Bank). The Council then has to
adopt its position on the draft budget and forward it to the Parliament
by 1 October.*

*Parliament must then adopt its position within 42 days. If it
approves the Council's position as it is or does not adopt a position, the
budget is deemed adopted. If it adopts amendments (by an absolute
majority of its members), the amended draft is forwarded to the Council
and the Commission.*

*In the latter case, the President of the Parliament, in agreement with
the President of the Council, "immediately" convenes a meeting of the
Conciliation Committee. However, if within 10 days of the draft being
forwarded, the Council informs the Parliament that it has approved all
its amendments, the Conciliation Committee does not meet, as the
budget is deemed adopted as amended.*

*The Conciliation Committee, which must be composed of "the mem-
bers of the Council or their representatives and an equal number of
members representing the European Parliament", then has 21 days to
reach agreement. The Commission takes part in the committee's proceedings and must take "all the necessary initiatives with a view to reconciling the positions of the European Parliament and the Council".*

*If the Conciliation Committee does not reach agreement within 21
days, the budget is deemed not to have been adopted and a new procedure must begin with the submission by the Commission of a new draft
budget.*

*If the Conciliation Committee does reach agreement on a joint text,
the Parliament and the Council have 14 days in which to deliver an
opinion on the text. Thereafter there are various possibilities:*

*–Parliament and Council both approve the compromise or both fail to take
a decision or one of the institutions approves the text but the other fails
to take a decision. In all three cases, the budget is deemed adopted in
accordance with the joint text.*

*– Parliament, acting by a majority of its component members, and the
Council both reject the joint text or one of the institutions rejects the
text, while the other fails to act. In either of these cases, the Commission
has to submit a new draft budget.*

–Parliament, acting by a majority of its component members, rejects the

joint text while the Council approves it. In this case, the Commission has to submit a new draft budget.

−Parliament approves the joint text, whilst the Council rejects it. In this case, the Parliament has 14 days to from the date of rejection by the Council in which it can, acting by a majority of its component members and three fifths of the votes cast, decide to confirm all or some of the amendments it adopted at first reading. Where an amendment is not confirmed, the position agreed in the Conciliation Committee is retained. The budget is deemed definitively adopted on this basis.

If the procedure ends in a positive conclusion, the President of the Parliament declares the budget finally adopted and signs it into law (as was already the case before Lisbon).

If the procedure is not completed in time before the beginning of the financial year, expenditure is frozen at the previous year's level on a month-by-month basis, a system known as "provisional twelfths".

The precise impact of this new framework will only emerge in the lifetime of this Parliament. In November 2009 Parliament adapted its rules to implement the new procedure, including the operation of the conciliation committee but informal consultation mechanisms with the Council (and Commission) will need to be developed and a new inter-institutional agreement devised to guarantee the success of the procedure. However, some features of the procedure are clear.

(For those who wish to compare to the old procedure, it ran as follows:

The pre-Lisbon rules, former Article 272 – the old budgetary procedure

The Commission would present a preliminary draft budget which it sent to Council. Council, acting by a qualified majority, would adopt a draft budget, which it would forward to Parliament.

Parliament had 45 days in which to act. If it failed to do so or if it approved the Council draft, the latter would stand as finally adopted. Otherwise, the Parliament had the right to:
– Adopt "modifications" to "compulsory expenditure" by a simple majority of those voting;
– Adopt "amendments" to "non-compulsory expenditure" by a majority of its members.

The budget would then be referred back to Council, which had 15 days in which to complete a second reading. If it did not do so, the Parliament version was deemed adopted. To amend Parliament's "modifications" to compulsory expenditure, the Council needed:
– A qualified majority to approve any modification that increased expenditure;
– A qualified majority to overrule any modification that did not increase expenditure (reductions or transfers from one area to another).

Council could also modify Parliament's "amendments" to non-compulsory expenditure, but only by a qualified majority. Such modifications were referred back to Parliament, which had 15 days to amend them at its second reading. To do so, it required three-fifths of the vote cast and at least a majority of members.

For non-compulsory expenditure, the institutions were obliged to respect a maximum rate of increase fixed annually in the light of the growth of the Member States' GNPs, the variation in national budgets and the trend in the cost of living. Regardless of the level of NCE in the draft budget of the Council, Parliament retained the right to increase NCE beyond the figure in the Council's draft budget by half the maximum rate.

The level of the maximum rate itself could be increased if there was agreement between Council, acting by qualified majority, and Parliament, acting by a majority of its members and three fifths of the votes cast.

Parliament could also, by a two-thirds majority, reject the draft budget as a whole, in which case the whole procedure had to start again, with expenditure in the meantime being frozen at the previous year's level on a month-by-month basis, a system known as "provisional twelfths".)

Preparing for the draft budget

The Committee on Budgets takes the first step by nominating two rapporteurs. One has responsibility for the Commission's administrative and operational budgets, which include all spending on EU policies and amount to over 95 per cent of the total Union budget; the second examines the administrative budgets of the other institutions, including that of the Parliament itself. Normally these appointments are made in December, thirteen months in advance of the financial year under discussion. (In the Union, the financial year runs from January to December.) These posts are much sought after and subject to long negotiation within and between the Groups. As Table 38 shows, the EPP-ED and PES Groups have provided most, but not all, of the rapporteurs, over the last decade.

The work on the next year's budget starts as soon as the previous budget comes into force. The rapporteur for the administrative budgets of the institutions other than the Commission has responsibility in the first half of the year for establishing priorities for all these institutions at the March session and especially for guiding the estimates of the Parliament itself through the plenary. This involves discussions extending beyond the Budgets Committee: the Bureau and the Group chairs also play a major role. The Bureau draws up the first version of the Parliament's spending plans for the following year, known as the preliminary draft estimates. It also decides upon the number of new posts to be created in the establishment plan, with the Budgets Committee able to determine when the related appropriations should be granted. The Group chairs have a specific responsibility in relation to budgetary matters affecting the Political Groups.

Table 38: *Budget rapporteurs since 2000*

Commission budget	Other institutions
2000 Jean-Louis BOURLANGES (EPP)	Kyösti VIRRANKOSKI (ELDR)
2001 Jutta HAUG (PES)	Markus FERBER (EPP)
2002 Carlos COSTA NEVES (EPP)	Kathalijne Maria BUITENWEG (Greens/EFA)
2003 Göran FÄRM (PES)	Per STENMARCK (EPP)
2004 Jan MULDER (ELDR)	Neena GILL (PES)
2005 Salvador GARRIGA POLLEDO (EPP)	Anne JENSEN (ALDE)
2006 Giovanni PITTELLA (PES)	Valdis DOMBROVSKIS (EPP)
2007 James ELLES (EPP)	Louis GRECH (PES)
2008 Kyösti VIRRANKOSKI (ALDE)	Ville ITÄLÄ (EPP)
2009 Jutta HAUG (PES)	Janusz LEWANDOWSKI (EPP)
2010 Laszlo SURJÁN (EPP)	Vladimir MANKA (PES)

During the same period in the first half of the year the rapporteur for the Commission budget prepares a report on the budget priorities for the following year, having met with the rapporteurs of the specialised parliamentary committees. This document indicates to the Commission what priorities to take into account when drawing up the draft budget.

To give greater weight to this resolution, a trilogue meeting is normally organised between delegations of the three institutions, the Parliament's led by the chair of the Budgets Committee, the Council's by the President of the Budgets Council and the Commission's by the Commissioner responsible for the budget. This meeting discusses possible priorities for the budget in advance of the Commission publishing its plans, with a view to enabling it to take account of the positions of the two branches of the budgetary authority.

Although the treaty does not oblige the Commission to present the draft budget before 1 September, it has always traditionally anticipated this date, normally coming to Parliament's plenary in early May. The draft is made up of the consolidated estimates of revenue and expenditure of all the institutions and is at present divided into five main headings. The draft distinguishes between "payment appropriations", relating to expenditure restricted to the year in question, and "commitment appropriations", which authorise expenditure over a number of years for multi-annual programmes. The amounts proposed for 2011, for example, are shown in Table 39 below.

The draft reflects the spending priorities of the Union established over previous years but the Commission still enjoys a significant power of initiative, comparable in many respects to that which it enjoys in the realm of legislation. Its proposals serve as an important reference point for Parliament and Council throughout the procedure. Moreover, under the Lisbon Treaty the Commission can amend its draft at any time up to the moment when the Conciliation Committee is convened, underlining its pivotal position. Comparison of the draft with the budget finally voted reveals that a large part of the initial proposal made by the Commission usually survives.

Table 39: *Commission preliminary draft budget for 2011 (billion euros)*

Heading	Commitments	Payments
Sustainable Growth	**64.4**	**54.6**
Competitiveness	*13.4*	*12.1*
Cohesion	*51.0*	*42.5*
Preservation and Management of Natural Resources	**59.5**	**58.1**
(of which market-related expenditure and direct payments)	*43.7*	*43.7*
Citizenship, Freedom, Security and Justice	**1.8**	**1.5**
Freedom, Security and Justice	*1.1*	*0.9*
Citizenship	*0.7*	*0.6*
The European Union as a global player	8.6	7.6
Administration	8.3	8.3
TOTAL	**142.6**	**130.1**
% of EU 27 Gross National Income (GNI)	1.15	1.05

At the same time, Parliament and Council exercise a significant influence over the proposals put forward and can modify substantially the political direction of the different parts of the budget in the course of the rest of the procedure. As in the legislative arena, it is the interplay between the two arms of the budgetary authority that determines the ultimate shape of the budget.

Responding to the position (formerly draft budget) as adopted by the Council

Unlike the legislative procedure where it is the Parliament that responds first to Commission proposals, in the budgetary procedure it is the Council that is called upon to make the first formal response to the Commission's draft. The treaty prescribes that it must adopt its position on the draft by the beginning of October. However, the Council, too, follows what is called the "pragmatic calendar" and anticipates this date, normally presenting its text before the end of July. Only on one occasion in EU history has the Council failed to respect the deadline laid down in the treaty. In 1987, due to the severity of the revenue crisis then faced by the Community, it did not adopt a draft until February of the following year. Both Parliament and Commission took Council to the Court of Justice for failure to respect the treaty but by the time the Court ruled, the procedure had been resumed. The one sanction applied to the Council was to oblige it to pay the costs of the case!

A second trilogue and a conciliation take place in advance of the Council's adoption of its position on the draft budget. (This system was largely formalized in the 1999 agreement referred to earlier.) The meeting provides an important opportunity for the two sides to explain their respective priorities and to narrow the range of differences in advance of the Council's own deliberations. Hitherto these meetings have not proved very satisfactory from the point of view of achieving concrete results. Under Lisbon, with the disappearance of the distinction between compulsory and non-compulsory expenditure and the reduction to a single reading, both Parliament and Council have felt the need to improve the quality of these advance negotiations. Hence Parliament adopted a resolution in June 2010 to set priorities for the negotiations with the Council.

After this meeting Council adopts its position on the draft budget and forwards it to Parliament. Council has historically seen its role as reducing the budget presented by the Commission to what it considered more reasonable proportions. However, such an approach is tempered by existing policy commitments. Council can be bound by formal and informal commitments to leave some appropriations intact. For example, successive agreements on the size of the structural funds have meant that it has normally had to leave the overall amount (if not the detailed breakdown) in this part of the draft untouched. In addition, in areas where a legislative act adopted has included a figure for the level of funding, there is only limited scope to modify the figures proposed.

Despite such constraints, the first new procedure under the Lisbon provisions, covering the budget for 2011 saw the Council decide, not least in light of major cuts by governments at the domestic level, to cut the budget by €3.5bn, with seven governments even pressing for further reductions and an effective freeze at 2010 levels.

The draft budget in Parliament

Following adoption of the Council's draft at the beginning of July, it is for-warded to Parliament. In practice this normally takes place by the end of July by informal agreement between the two institutions but it does not take place formally until the beginning of September, so as to give the Parliament time to establish its position at the October session, using the 42 days pro-vided for under the Treaty. The period from the end of August to the October plenary is one of intense activity, particularly within the Budgets Committee, the committee which co-ordinates Parliament's response and mediates between the different interests within Parliament.

It is the task of the two rapporteurs to propose the main lines of response to be given to the Council and to suggest how the Budgets Committee should choose between the competing demands presented by the commit-tees of the Parliament that deal with policy areas involving EU expenditure. Both are the subject of considerable lobbying, particularly from within Union institutions. The Commissioner responsible for the budget will be in close contact with the rapporteur for the Commission's budget, although this will not stop approaches from other parts of the Commission, including those who may have been disappointed by its internal decisions incorpo-rated in the original draft. And, although the budgets of the other institu-tions are very much smaller than that of the Commission, contacts with the rapporteur responsible can be very intense.

Parliament also remains in close touch with the Council during this period. In the past a third trilogue meeting took place before the first read-ing in Parliament. The meeting provided for an exchange of views on the state of implementation of the current budget. It could also serve as an occa-sion to discuss any further budgetary requests (contained in supplementary budgets or amending letters) that may have proved necessary due to unex-pected circumstances. The discussion on implementation is normally fol-lowed in October or November by a Commission proposal, known as the "omnibus transfer", for the redistribution of appropriations between budg-etary lines that are underspent and those that risk being overspent.

The ideas of the rapporteurs, based on these various consultations, are presented to the Budgets Committee in a series of detailed working docu-ments designed to justify their proposed treatment of the individual lines in the budget. At the same time, the Political Group co-ordinators discuss the general guidelines presented by the rapporteurs, and in particular the one dealing with the Commission budget, and seek to develop an agreed strat-egy in advance of the vote in committee. This is particularly important when it comes to the amendments that are tabled by the other standing commit-tees, individual members of the Parliament (draft amendments require the signature of at least 40 members) or Political Groups. There is strong pres-sure to develop a broad consensus within the committee and thereafter in the Parliament as a whole. Failure to reach such a consensus seriously endangers the chance of amendments being adopted.

Although absolute majorities in the Parliament can be obtained by various political combinations, the budgetary procedure is comparable to the second reading of the legislative co-decision procedure in that it places particularly strong pressure on the EPP and Socialist Groups to reach agreement. If they can, then it is most probable that the necessary majorities will be gained. However, if either of the two main Groups is unwilling to go along with a particular amendment, then it is far less likely that it will be adopted in plenary. The success of this process of mediation and consensus-seeking in the Budgets Committee can be measured by the fact that the proposals of the committee are defeated on relatively few occasions in the plenary. All recognise the vital role of the committee in establishing an overall coherence in the position of Parliament, even if its individual decisions may be less well received.

The vote on the Parliament's position on the budget takes place at the October session. It is complex, not least because the number of amendments can total more than one thousand. Great care is taken to ensure that the vote proceeds smoothly. In view of the absolute majority required, the Groups usually issue "three line whips" to their members in advance of the plenary. Thereafter the vote proceeds at a considerable pace, with members frequently agreeing to vote en bloc on series of amendments proposed by the Committee on Budgets. If the work of the committee has been successful, the majorities are usually clear, votes are by a show of hands and the procedure can be concluded in as little as an hour. However, where there is uncertainty, there will be an electronic check. And if a Group wishes to see how its members or those of another Group have voted on a particular amendment, then there can be a Roll Call Vote.

Conciliation and agreement... or otherwise

The amendments voted by Parliament are collated and sent to Council which then has ten days to inform the Parliament whether it accepts all of them. If so, the budget is deemed adopted but in the more likely event of a difference of opinion, preparations continue for the meeting of the Conciliation Committee which the President of the Parliament is obliged to convene straight after the Parliament's reading of the budget.

The committee has 21 days in which to reach agreement on a joint text. If it fails to do so, the procedure must start again with a new Commission proposal. If it does agree, both Parliament and the Council must approve the joint text within a further 14 days (though in the event of one institution not taking a position, it is deemed to have acquiesced with the position of the other). Only if Parliament explicitly rejects the joint text does it automatically fall: in that case the whole procedure must start again with a new Commission proposal. If Council rejects the joint text, while Parliament approves it, then the procedure continues with Parliament able, within another 14 days, to amend the joint text by re-adopting its initial amendments by a majority of its members comprising a 3/5 majority of votes cast. This latter possibility is, however, extremely unlikely, as it assumes that a qualified majority of Council members would agree the text in the conciliation committee and subsequently reject it in the Council meeting itself. In practice, it is the negotiations on a joint text, and the final vote in Parliament to approve or reject the outcome, which counts.

The structure of the Conciliation Committee bears a strong resemblance to that of the same kind of committee provided for under the ordinary legislative procedure (co-decision) and is confronted with similar challenges. It is composed of an equal number of representatives of Member States and of the European Parliament (27 on each side at present), a number that is likely to generate the need for smaller trilogues, given the difficulty of taking decisions in very large groups. On the Parliament side, the Rules of Procedure (Rule 75d) specify that the members of the delegation should be appointed by the Political Groups, preferably "from amongst the members of the committee responsible for budgetary issues and other committees concerned". The rules also provide for the President of the Parliament to be able to delegate the role of co-chair to "a Vice-President having experience in budgetary matters or to the Chair of the committee responsible for budgetary issues" but on the first occasion the new procedure was used, President Buzek decided to chair the meetings himself. On the Council side the issue of the level of representation also arises and in particular, whether the committee should include ministers rather than only senior civil servants from the Permanent Representations. The importance of the first meeting in 2010 was underlined by the Belgian Prime Minister, Yves Leterme, acting as co-chair with President Buzek.

The Conciliation Committee provides a forum in which the different approaches of Parliament and Council become very apparent. It is also a venue where brinkmanship in the negotiations, which have a fixed deadline, can easily cause the whole budget to fall. In 2010, on the 2011 budget (the first to be dealt with under the new Lisbon procedure), both sides had agreed on the figures and were separated only by a disagreement about the procedures for involving Parliament in the discussions on the next financial perspective – yet neither side wanted to compromise on this. As a result, the draft budget was not adopted and the Commission was invited to prepare a new draft in accordance with the provisions of Article 314. This it did very quickly (as there was no longer a dispute about the figures) and a new procedure was completed speedily, even before the end of the year.

Even if agreement cannot be found before the start of the budgetary year, such a rejection does not bring the whole Union to a standstill. A complex arrangement comes into force on 1 January if no budget is voted by that time. It allows the Commission to spend each month the equivalent of one-twelfth of the expenditure included in the previous year's budget. This allows the Union to function but prevents it from starting any new activity or adapting existing expenditure to inflation. It has happened on three occasions in the past: most famously, in December 1979 during the budgetary procedure that followed the first direct elections to the Parliament; in 1982, in relation to a supplementary budget, designed to finance the British rebate; and in December 1984 following the second direct elections.

Conflicting priorities

Parliament has always been eager to use the budget to promote new policies. It has defended itself against charges of profligacy by arguing that joint spending at European level can often save money at national level by avoiding duplication or by economies of scale.

Many budgetary arguments took place outside the budgetary procedure, with the legislative procedure becoming the place where the amounts provided for new programmes were determined, particularly in areas where Parliament enjoys joint legislative powers. Budget experts were sceptical about the ability of Parliament to do better in the legislative than in the budgetary procedure and feared a lack of prioritisation of the various interests of the institution. As a result, in the negotiations on the financial framework for 2007 to 2013, the trade-offs between the various multiannual programmes were effectively resolved in advance of the related legislative procedures. In addition, legislative committees are now obliged to ask the Budgets Committee for its opinion on the availability of finance for any modification in the annual amount foreseen for a particular programme.

Even with co-decision on legislation, there is still plenty of scope for the Parliament to develop policy through the budget and it is likely to remain an important feature of every budgetary procedure. In some cases, Parliament acts to defend policies that Council has under-funded. Parliament has, for example, consistently entered substantial funds to induce Council to develop transport policy, notably to finance the Trans-European Networks that Council had itself approved but subsequently seemed reluctant to fund. Similarly, it has strongly supported multiannual programmes for Small and Medium-sized Enterprises (SMEs), increasing the budget much more sharply than Council proposed. In other cases, Parliament has acted together with Council to promote a shared concern. A good example of the latter is the Northern Ireland "Peace" Programme where the EU institutions have acted to supplement the financial efforts of the British and Irish governments.

Parliament also continues to want to use the budget to develop new policies and policies which may not be of specific concern to Council. Examples from the last decade include the KONVER programme for the post-Cold War conversion of the arms industry and military sites to other uses and the URBAN programme as new initiatives within the structural funds, and the environmental programme LIFE. Yet the status of such initiatives continued to provoke conflict with the Council as long as there was no legal base. Here too, though, an agreement was reached which was incorporated in the 1999 and 2006 Inter-institutional Agreements and has been in the Financial Regulation since 2002.

Under these arrangements, Parliament accepted that implementation of appropriations in the budget for any Union action requires the prior adoption of a basic legislative act. However, Council has agreed that no basic act is needed for the implementation of four specific kinds of appropriations:

– those designed to finance pilot schemes aimed at testing the feasibility of an action, the total amount being restricted to €40m in any budget year;

– those relating to preparatory actions intended to pave the way for specific legislative proposals, the total being restricted to €50m per year with no more than €100m actually committed;

– those linked to actions carried out by the Commission by virtue of prerogatives specifically conferred on it; and

- those intended for the administrative operation of each institution.

There is still plenty of scope for disagreement between the institutions, particularly given the growing range of instruments available to the Union with the Lisbon Treaty. The creation of the External Action Service was one of the first elements of the Lisbon Treaty to provoke a strong reaction from the Parliament, which was determined to retain a say over the size and shape of the service and not to be excluded from this instrument of the EU's foreign policy.

For its part, Council showed signs during 2010 of not wishing to continue, or at least wanting to renegotiate the long-standing "Gentlemen's agreement" that Council and Parliament would not touch each other's own internal budgets. The wish of the Parliament to increase further its own staff on the grounds that this would enable it to be better able to face up to its new responsibilities under the Lisbon Treaty (incorporated into an amending budget in spring 2010) met with little sympathy from governments who were all facing tough economic times at home. They also noted the moves by the Parliament to challenge the 20% ceiling on its own administrative expenditure which has been a self-imposed restriction since 1988: the Parliament indicated that it could go up to 22% given its new Lisbon responsibilities. At the same time, the Council criticised the 2008 discharge procedure and the negative stance taken towards the Council by the Parliament and in particular, the Budgetary Control Committee. It remains to be seen whether this irritation will in fact lead to a change in the agreement.

Implementation of the budget

Once the budget is voted, it is then the duty of the Commission, in cooperation with the Member States, to implement it. This does not mean that Parliament's involvement ceases. Rather the nature of its role changes to one of scrutiny and control. This role has been reinforced by the Lisbon Treaty. In particular, the Financial Regulation, laying down the detailed rules for budget implementation, is now subject to the ordinary legislative procedure, whereas previously it was adopted by Council by unanimity after consulting the Parliament.

In the course of the financial year the Commission (and the other institutions) can transfer appropriations from one part of their budget to another within a set limit and need only inform the budgetary authority. Such transfers are deemed approved if they provoke no reaction. However, if the limit is exceeded (in other words, the amount is substantial), then the institution concerned has to submit a transfer request for approval to the budgetary authority (i.e. Council and Parliament).

Such requests can concern transfers between the various chapters of the budget or from the reserve. In the first case, Parliament and Council are invited to agree in the light of changes of priority or circumstances in the course of the year. In the case of items entered in the reserve, it is accepted practice that, where the legislative base for expenditure has not yet been agreed, the related appropriations should be entered in the reserve, only to be released when the legislation is passed. Entry in the reserve is also often used as a discreet form of bargaining, whereby Parliament and Council can get assurances on the use to be made of particular budget lines and the implementation of programmes before agreeing to release the money. This is mostly done during the budgetary procedure itself, without much controversy.

Parliament does not only wait for transfer requests but also scrutinises the implementation of the budget with great care to see whether its wishes are being adhered to, and if not, why not. A particular procedure (known originally as the "Notenboom Procedure" after the Dutch MEP who first proposed it) exists for the Commission to comment on the level of implementation of appropriations voted in the budget in the autumn of the financial year. This has regularly led to the preparation of an omnibus transfer request that also contributes to the debate on the appropriate level of appropriations for the following year. More generally, the Commission provides monthly data on the use of appropriations as well as reports on agricultural spending, known as early warning reports, designed to indicate whether agricultural spending is likely to exceed the financial envelope provided for it. In addition, in 2006 it introduced a new tool, the "Budget Forecast Alert" to try to identify lines with poor implementation.

Control of expenditure and the discharge procedure

Parliament can put pressure on the Commission (and sometimes other institutions) by freezing items in the budget and only releasing them when certain conditions have been met. However, budgetary control is a much broader concept linked to the power that Parliament has to grant annual discharge to the Commission (and other institutions) for their execution of the budget. It is a power that came to assume much greater importance after the major crisis that led to the downfall of the Santer Commission on the Ides of March of 1999.

At the end of each financial year, all the institutions must draw up their audited accounts for submission to the European Court of Auditors (ECA). The Court, set up by the 1975 treaty and made a full institution of the Union in the Maastricht Treaty, is responsible for examining the legality, regularity and sound financial management of all revenue and expenditure of the Union. On the basis of its findings and in accordance with Article 287 TFEU, the Court draws up:

(i)   an Annual Report containing its findings in relation to each of the institutions over the financial year (incorporating its own observations and the replies of the institutions),

(ii)   since the Maastricht Treaty, a "statement of assurance as to the reliability of the accounts and the legality and regularity of the underlying transactions" (widely known by its French acronym "DAS"), which can be found in the annual report, and

(iii)   a series of discretionary ad hoc special reports, dealing with specific areas of budgetary management.

These documents are submitted – the Annual Report with the DAS each November, special reports as they are published – to the European Parliament and the Council for consideration under the annual discharge procedure. The DAS has proven to be controversial, as the Court of Auditors will not grant a positive DAS unless every element of the accounts is in order – and in recent years it has withheld it not so much because of problems with the Commission's accounts, but because of problems with the handling of EU money by Member State governments. As a result, the DAS itself is not looked on by most MEPs and governments as being crucial

– rather, its component elements and reasons behind any shortcomings are what matter in evaluating whether to give discharge.

Responsibility for developing Parliament's approach to discharge, including its response to the Court's reports, rests with its Committee on Budgetary Control. Its most fundamental task is to discuss whether the Commission should be granted discharge at all. Granting discharge is a formal statement that Parliament is satisfied with the implementation of the budget by the Commission. It is the political acceptance of the Commission's stewardship of the Union's budget and formally signs off the financial year under consideration. Parliament uses this to look in some detail at all issues of financial management and difficulties of budgetary implementation and makes recommendations for improvement.

While the power to grant discharge to the Commission derives directly from the Treaty (Article 319 TFEU), the Committee on Budgetary Control has also developed a practice of granting (or postponing and potentially refusing) discharge to all the other institutions including the European Parliament itself as well as the Council. In addition, in accordance with Article 185 of the Financial Regulation the Parliament also draws up discharge reports on the more than 20 decentralised agencies and "joint undertakings" (public-private partnerships with separate legal personality). On the basis of these provisions the Parliament voted for the first time to refuse discharge to an agency in the autumn of 2010, considering that the European Police College, based in the UK, had not responded adequately to criticisms made by OLAF, the EU anti-fraud office.

The practice of extending the purview of discharge to include other institutions than the Commission has been generally accepted by the bodies concerned, with the notable exception of the Council. It cites the "Gentlemen's Agreement" of 22 April 1970 as excluding the possibility of Parliament or Council scrutinising the other's budget. The ongoing sensitivity of this issue was revealed in April 2010 when Parliament voted against the nearly unanimous recommendation of the Committee on Budgetary Control to postpone the discharge to the Council for the 2008 financial year, when it became clear that such a move would have significant unfavourable consequences for relations between the two institutions in the wider budgetary field. (Council was at the time holding up a supplementary budget that increased the size of Parliament's staff to cater for the Lisbon Treaty.)

The right to grant discharge to the Commission can be traced back to the treaty of 22 July 1975, which gave the European Parliament on its own the right of discharge. Between 1970 and 1975, Parliament had shared the power of discharge with the Council, whilst before 1970, the decision lay exclusively with the Council, Parliament only making a recommendation. Nowadays the Council discusses the Court of Auditors' reports and gives its opinion in the form of a recommendation to Parliament, but that opinion is usually couched in general terms and leaves Parliament with considerable scope for defining its response.

The right to grant discharge is the basis of Parliament's powers of budgetary control. Discharge is more than the necessary final act in adopting the Communities' accounts. It enables Parliament to lay down requirements for future conduct by the Commission. Article 319(3) TFEU lays down that: "The Commission shall take all appropriate steps to act on the observations in the decisions giving discharge and on other observations by the European Parliament relating to the execution of expenditure, as well as on comments accompanying the recommendations on discharge adopted by the Council (...) At the request of the European Parliament or the Council, the Commission shall report on the measures taken in the light of these observations and comments and in particular on the instructions given to the departments which are responsible for the implementation of the budget. These reports shall also be forwarded to the Court of Auditors."

The discharge to the Commission and other institutions takes the form of a decision adopted by Parliament in plenary sitting on the basis of a report by the Committee on Budgetary Control consisting of a proposal for a decision, a proposal for the closure of the accounts and a motion for resolution containing a detailed assessment by the institution concerned during the period under review, together with (in the case of a postponement of discharge) shortcomings which must be addressed within six months in order to avoid an outright refusal of discharge.

However, the vote in plenary is in some senses merely the formal conclusion of an appraisal process spread out over a period of six months. This appraisal is based in particular on the annual report by the ECA but also on the Commission's accounts and its follow-up report on the previous year's discharge resolution (which appears in September/October) as well as the investigative work by OLAF and the activity reports drawn up by the individual Directors-General. Moreover, in recent years the committee has increasingly relied on oral discharge hearings between November and January in which the Commissioners responsible for specific sectors are called upon to answer questions before the committee on the financial management of the sectors under their responsibility.

Article 319 makes it clear that discharge is as much a power as a procedure. Over the years, Parliament's Committee on Budgetary Control has pressed more and more its right to be fully informed as to all matters affecting expenditure from the Union's budget. In practice, this has entailed probing with ever-greater insistence into specific allegations of financial mismanagement, irregularity, fraud and corruption both in the Member States and in the Commission itself. The ultimate outcome of this insistence was the crisis of 1999 – a crisis with its roots not only in the specific cases and dysfunctions which came to light, but also in the very processes by which they did so, with a central dispute being over the reluctance of the Commission to provide certain kinds of information requested for the purposes of discharge.

Consequences of a refusal to grant discharge, and the fall of the Santer Commission

The political and legal ramifications of a refusal to grant discharge on the part of Parliament have never been clear. The events of 1999, during which the Parliament rejected a motion to grant discharge to the Commission for the implementation of the 1996 financial year, though underlining and reinforcing the political status of the discharge decision, in fact did little to clarify the legal situation. What is, and was, obvious is that a refusal to grant discharge represents a major political reprimand for the Commission. It is a public statement by Parliament that the Commission has failed in one of its central tasks: its management of the budget has either been irregular and/or uneconomic or has failed to respect the political objectives set when the budget was adopted. Notwithstanding the significance of such a statement, neither the treaties nor the Communities' Financial Regulation deal with the consequences of a refusal to grant discharge. Prior to 1999, the only formal statement by the Commission on the matter dated from 7 July 1977, when Budget Commissioner Tugendhat stated to Parliament that "refusal to grant discharge is a political sanction which would be extremely serious; the Commission thus censured would, I think, have to be replaced".

It was generally believed that Parliament would feel bound to follow a refusal of discharge with a motion of censure should the Commission fail to resign. In November 1984, Parliament did refuse discharge for the 1982 financial year, but the Commission was at the end of its term and due to leave office a few weeks later. In 1999, no such coincidence allowed the consequences for the Commission to be obscured in this fashion. At the same time, however, the politics of the Parliament combined with procedural ambiguities to muddy the waters somewhat.

In its vote of December 1998 on the 1996 discharge, Parliament rejected its committee's report proposing the granting of discharge. For this, only a simple majority was required. However, for Parliament explicitly to refuse discharge, its own Rules of Procedure at that time required the support of a majority of its membership, i.e. then 314 votes. Given the official pro-discharge position of the then largest group, the Socialists, this majority was effectively unattainable. In effect, Parliament risked falling into a procedural limbo between the two options of granting and refusing discharge. In an attempt to clarify the situation, the Socialist Group tabled a motion of censure with the paradoxical intention of using it as a confidence motion by voting against it (as a confidence mechanism is not foreseen in Parliament's procedures).

Events to some extent overtook this plan, with new allegations about financial mismanagement being made by a Commission civil servant, Paul Van Buitenen (who was subsequently elected to the European Parliament and served from 2004 to 2009). At the January 1999 part-session, the Socialist Group withdrew its motion in favour of a compromise negotiated with some other Groups appointing a "Committee of Independent Experts" to examine the allegations against the Commission and to report its findings six weeks later. Crucially, the Commission undertook to accept the findings of the committee and to act accordingly. Nonetheless, at the same time, another motion of censure (introduced by Hervé Fabre-Aubrespy of the Europe of Nations Group) obtained 232 votes in favour, with 293 votes against and 27 abstentions. It was by far the closest that Parliament has come to adopting a motion of censure (118 votes being the previous record), and this despite the adoption of the compromise resolution immediately beforehand.

The report of the Committee of Independent Experts absolved the Commission of fraud but its criticisms of mismanagement were much more sweeping than had been expected. The leader of the Socialist Group, Pauline Green, announced that her Group would now vote in favour of a motion of censure, thereby making it clear that there was now the necessary majority

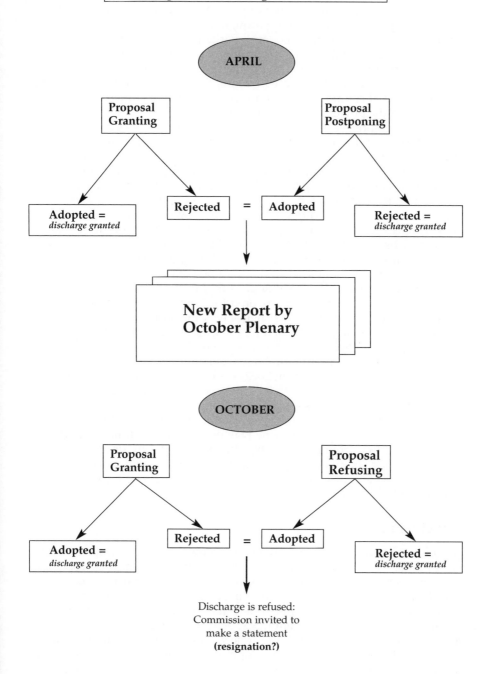

Figure 10: Discharge Procedure

in Parliament for censure. Faced with this prospect the Commission decided to tender its resignation.

These events were seen as marking a turning point in the institutional "balance of power" and as having brought to an end an era of complicit co-existence between Commission and Parliament. Though doing little to resolve the legal ambiguities surrounding a refusal of discharge, they nevertheless significantly boosted the perceived significance of the discharge procedure. The power of censure too, though not exercised in a legal sense, was an essential component in the process and demonstrated its close connection with the power of discharge.

The combination of circumstances that occurred in 1999 was, of course, atypical. In the normal run of events, the discharge procedure is less dramatic. It remains true, for example, that the effectiveness of parliamentary control is limited by the time gaps involved, and by the fact that many discharge decisions concern preceding Commissions. Parliament has, therefore, generally concentrated on extracting concessions and undertakings from the Commission through its "comments" on which the Commission is obliged to act, and, if necessary, by delaying discharge in order to extract extra information. The Budgetary Control Committee attempts to enhance the continuity and consistency of its monitoring by allocating specific sectors to the Political Groups, which appoint one of their committee members to follow that sector. It also works with the parliamentary committees responsible for the policy areas covered by Community spending policies. Some of these committees have themselves introduced systems whereby every few months they are briefed by the Commission officials responsible for the implementation of their areas of the budget.

Following the procedural problems encountered in 1999, Parliament revised its Rules of Procedure in 2002. Under the new discharge procedure (see Figure 10), Parliament first votes in April (or by 15 May at the latest) on whether to grant or (if dissatisfied) postpone discharge. If it is postponed, Parliament votes again in October on whether to grant or refuse discharge. In both cases, a simple majority one way or the other is sufficient to choose between the two options, avoiding the possibility of deadlock within Parliament. The six-month period between expressing initial dissatisfaction and the final vote is designed to put maximum pressure on the Commission to respond before the final vote.

Conclusion

The Lisbon Treaty has opened up a new era for the Parliament in the budgetary arena. The old arguments about the balance between compulsory and non-compulsory expenditure have ceased, to be replaced by a more balanced dialogue with the Council covering all EU spending. The long-drawn out negotiations between the institutions have now been transformed by the creation of a Conciliation Committee specifically designed to find an agreement between the institutions after one reading by each institution rather than two. Together these two developments are likely to modify radically the shape of bargaining between the two arms of the budgetary authority and the Commission. The Parliament continues to be kept at arm's length from the arena of determining the sources of EU revenue but its new powers, when combined with its continuing ability to use the discharge to hold the various institutions to account, provide it with a highly effective set of tools for exercising an ever greater role in the fixing of EU spending and its control.

Table 40: *Budgetary matters (procedure and voting rules)*

SUBJECT	LEGAL BASE	PROCEDURE	VOTING RULE IN COUNCIL
Definition of Own Resources of the Union	Article 311 TFEU	Council Regulation European Parliament consultation	Unanimity + national ratification
Multiannual Financial Framework	Article 312 TFEU	Council Regulation European Parliament consent	Unanimity
Annual Budget	Article 314 TFEU	Joint agreement between European Parliament and Council (Special legislative procedure)	Qualified majority
Financial Regulations	Article 322 TFEU	European Parliament and Council Regulation (Ordinary legislative procedure)	Qualified majority
Discharge	Article 319 TFEU	Council recommendation. European Parliament decision.	Qualified majority

14. Appointment and dismissal

Introduction

Parliament was originally given no formal role in the EU appointments process, which was essentially an inter-governmental one. Each country put forward its own nominees on the basis of domestic rather than European considerations, with Member States accepting each other's nominees on a consensus basis. Even individual appointments, such the President of the Commission, not made on a national basis, did not involve Parliament.

Parliament did always have a treaty right to dismiss the Commission as a whole, but the very powerful nature of this weapon meant that the Parliament was, until 1999, reluctant to even attempt to use it. Changes in procedure, the growing confidence of the Parliament, and a combination of specific circumstances in 1998–99 and 2004 combined to change this situation dramatically.

The development of the Parliament's formal powers

A first step in relation to the power of appointment was taken with the creation of the Court of Auditors in 1975, when Parliament was given the right to be consulted on the appointment of its members.

The major breakthrough, however, came with the Maastricht Treaty. First, Parliament was given an important role as regards appointment of the Commission, being consulted on the nominee for President and being asked to give its approval to the entire College of Commissioners. Second, Parliament was given the right to be consulted on the nominee for the then President of the European Monetary Institute, and subsequently the President, Vice-President and other members of the Executive Board of the European Central Bank. Finally, the treaty gave Parliament alone the power to appoint the EU Ombudsman.

The Amsterdam Treaty introduced one further change, in that it gave the Parliament the power not just to be consulted but to approve the nominee for Commission President.

Besides these, which arose from formal treaty changes, Parliament is now also involved in a number of appointments relating to certain decentralised EU bodies and agencies and also plays a part in the appointment of the Director of the European anti-fraud office (OLAF).

Parliament and the appointment of the Commission

Prior to 1993 (Treaty of Maastricht), the Commission was appointed by the governments of the Member States for a four-year term of office. The

Table 41: *Votes of confidence on incoming Commissions and incoming Commission Presidents (formalised in Treaty since 1993)*

Incoming Commissions		
February 1981	Thorn Commission	155 votes for, 31 against
January 1985	Delors I Commission	209 votes for, 34 against
January 1989	Delors II Commission	Votes not recorded, overwhelming majority in favour
January 1993	Delors III Commission	256 votes for, 84 against
January 1995	Santer Commission	417 votes for, 104 against
September 1999	Prodi Commission (for unfilled portion of Santer term)	427 votes for, 138 against (29 abstentions)
September 1999	Prodi Commission (for full 2000–5 term of office)	404 votes for, 153 against (37 abstentions)
May 2004	Ten new members of Prodi Commission	531 votes for, 18 against (39 abstentions)
November 2004	Barroso I Commission (after modification)	449 votes for, 149 against (82 abstentions)
February 2010	Barroso II Commission	488 votes for, 137 against (72 abstentions
Incoming Commission Presidents		
July 1992	Jacques Delors (third term)	278 votes for, 9 against
July 1994	Jacques Santer	260 votes for, 238 against (23 abstentions)
May 1999	Romano Prodi (vote by out-going European Parliament on Prodi for unfilled portion of Santer term)	392 in favour, 72 against, (41 abstentions)
September 1999	Romano Prodi (vote by incoming European Parliament on Prodi for unfilled portion of Santer term)	446 in favour to 123 against (32 abstentions)
September 1999	Romano Prodi (vote by incoming European Parliament on Prodi for full 2000–05 term of office)	426 in favour to 134 against (32 abstentions)
July 2004	Jose Manuel Barroso (first term)	431 in favour to 251 against (44 abstentions)
September 2009	Jose Manuel Barroso (second term)	382 in favour to 219 against (117 abstentions)

President of the Commission was nominated for a two-year period from among the members of the Commission. In practice, the President was agreed on first by the Member States and was automatically re-appointed mid-way through the Commission's term of office.

Once the Parliament became directly elected, it unilaterally introduced into its own procedures provisions for a debate and a vote of confidence on an incoming Commission when it presented itself to Parliament for the first time with its programme. This became an established practice and was recognised by national governments in the 1983 Stuttgart Solemn Declaration on European Union. Parliament followed this procedure for the appointment of the Thorn Commission in 1981 and the three Delors

Commissions in 1985, 1989 and 1993 (see Table 41). On these last three occasions, the Commission waited until it had received the vote of confidence from Parliament before taking the oath of office at the Court of Justice. This was an important gesture and precedent, showing that the Commission accepted that without the confidence of Parliament it should not take office.

Also in the 1983 Stuttgart Declaration, the Member States agreed that the Enlarged Bureau of the Parliament should be consulted on the choice of President of the Commission. In 1984 and 1992, the Presidents of the European Council (respectively the Irish and Portuguese Prime Ministers) carried out this consultation by attending a meeting of the Enlarged Bureau to discuss the issue. In 1988, this consultation was done through the President of the Parliament, who attended the relevant part of the European Council meeting and acted in consultation with the Enlarged Bureau. The Treaty of Maastricht built on these existing practices. First, it reinforced the consultation of Parliament concerning the choice of the President by providing for consultation of Parliament as a whole rather than just its Enlarged Bureau. This meant that there was now a public vote by the whole Parliament on the President-designate. This was politically much more significant, although still short of a power of formal approval.

In July 1993 when the nomination of Jacques Santer, the Luxembourg Prime Minister, was under discussion (and looked under threat, partly owing to resentment at the UK's veto of the candidacy of Jean-Luc Dehaene), he made it clear that he would withdraw if the vote in Parliament went against him. This view was also expressed by the President of the European Council, Chancellor Kohl, when he met the Conference of Presidents of the Parliament to consult them on the nomination.

The nature of the debate on Santer in July 1994, following his statement to the House, and the meetings he held with the three largest Political Groups, illustrated the character of the procedure as one of building up a parliamentary majority for the confirmation vote. The Amsterdam Treaty later recognised this by turning the vote on the President into a legally binding one and giving the President thus approved the right to choose the remaining Commissioners jointly with the Member State governments. Second, the Maastricht Treaty formalised the vote of confidence in the Commission as a whole, but reinforced it by providing explicitly for it to take place prior to the Commission taking office.

Parliament sought to expand on this. In its Rules of Procedure it provided for the vote to be taken only after the proposed Commissioners had appeared in confirmation hearings before the parliamentary committees corresponding to their prospective fields of responsibility. In the autumn of 1994, this Rule was duly invoked for the first time. Despite initial reluctance (the outgoing President Delors was opposed, for example), the proposed Commissioners agreed to participate in the exercise, not least because President-elect Santer wanted to show goodwill to the Parliament after the close vote in Parliament on his nomination in July 1994, and because Parliament would otherwise have simply postponed its vote of confidence until they did. The hearings procedure also required the Commission President to allocate portfolios before the Commission took office (and Member States to complete their selection of nominees for Commissioner much more swiftly than in the past), another break with previous practice.

Third, the Maastricht Treaty provided for the Commission to have a five-year term of office instead of four, linked to that of the Parliament. The procedures for appointing the President and the rest of the Commission were designed to begin after each European election and the new Commission, if approved, would take office the following January (later changed to November by the 2002 accession treaties). The coincidence of term of office facilitates parliamentary scrutiny as well as the feeling of Commissioners that they are accountable to Parliament.

Taken together, these three changes were a dramatic move in strengthening the accountability of the Commission to the Parliament.

The Parliament's approval of the Prodi Commission in 1999 came after the collective resignation of the Santer Commission in March 1999, with the public spotlight being more on the Parliament than during the previous exercise, and Parliament further refining the hearing procedure. All the nominees were now asked to reply in advance to a prior written questionnaire, with the (often lengthy!) replies being put on both the Commission and Parliament websites. Each of the hearings lasted for three hours, and there were no overlaps between them.

It was, however, the appointment of the Barroso Commission in 2004 that brought the procedure dramatically alive. Already Barroso's own election had been a contested one, with the EPP Group claiming that the European Council's choice of him reflected the fact that they had emerged from the European elections as the largest Group. This, and perceptions of his record as Portuguese Prime Minister, led the (bulk of) the Socialist, Green and GUE groups to oppose him in a vote that was more political than any previous vote on a prospective Commission President.

When it came to the vote of confidence on the Commission as a whole, it became clear that there would be a majority against, largely because of concerns about individual Commissioners that emerged during the hearings. Criticism focussed notably, but not exclusively, on Rocco Buttiglione, former MEP and nominee of the Italian government, whose comments on the role of women and on gays caused many in Parliament (notably on the left and centre) to query his ability to perform properly his designated task of Commissioner for justice and home affairs issues, which included responsibility for non-discrimination. Initially, Barroso appeared to want to brazen it out and count on a narrow victory, but when it became clear the night before the vote that he would lose, he instead announced the next morning (27 October 2004) in Parliament that he was withdrawing his team and would come back as soon as possible with a new proposal.

Following consultations with national governments, Barroso presented a revised team to Parliament in time for a vote the next month (with the Prodi Commision remaining in office in a caretaker capacity in the meantime). The new team saw Buttiglione replaced with a new Italian nominee, foreign minister Franco Frattini, a new Latvian nominee, and a reshuffling of the Hungarian nominee to a new portfolio, thereby meeting the bulk of Parliament's concerns.

The whole episode achieved massive media coverage across Europe. It showed that the parliamentary hearings were not a mere formality. It revealed dividing lines that were political, not national, and that much of the public could relate to. Above all, it highlighted the fact that the

Commission was a political executive, requiring the confidence of a parliamentary majority to take office, making the relationship between the Union's executive and its elected parliament rather more like that familiar to European citizens at national level.

This was again confirmed during the confirmation of the subsequent Commission in 2009-2010. Barroso was again put forward as President by the Member States, and was easily confirmed by the Parliament. The Lisbon Treaty had still not been ratified at this stage, and uncertainties over this delayed the formation of the rest of his team. Once the Treaty had been approved, the list of Member State nominees was finally completed, and the confirmation hearings were held in early 2010. While a number of nominees were the subject of critical speculation, the main attention focussed on the initial Bulgarian nominee, Rumiana Jeleva, who, during her hearing, was the subject of aggressive questioning on her business dealings and also performed weakly in answering questions on the substance of her prospective portfolio. Once it became clear that a majority in the Parliament would not support her, her nomination was withdrawn by the Bulgarian government. The new nominee, Kristalina Giorgieva, then performed very well in her hearing. The new Commission as a whole was subsequently confirmed by the European Parliament in February 2010, with most members in the bigger Groups voting in favour, but with the Greens, GUE and EFD Groups generally opposed, and with the ECR Group abstaining.

The four times the procedure has now been used (1994, 1999, 2004 and 2009-10) have also brought other advantages. Nominees' suitability for the post of Commissioner is better and more publicly scrutinised than before, with their personalities and views becoming clearer at an earlier stage. Wider issues relating to the organisational structure and policy priorities of the Commission are also being more thoroughly explored, and benchmarks are being established to judge subsequent Commission performance. Moreover, while domestic political considerations still loom large as regards the choice of Member States' candidates, the whole appointments process has also raised pan-European considerations, such as the need for better overall gender balance: the last four Commissions contained more women than would have been the case without pressure from Parliament. (There had been no women at all in any Commission until 1989!) The new Amsterdam Treaty right of the President of the Commission to choose the Commissioners jointly with governments has reinforced this trend. Finally, the hearings process has made a contribution to increasing the transparency of the EU institutions as a whole. The 2010 exercise included 22-language coverage of each hearing on a special hearings website, and could be followed not just live in Brussels or Strasbourg, but also in each Member State. Use of social media such as Twitter magnified the effect, and provided for rapid reaction to developments at the hearings. While interest was very variable from one country to another, it was very considerable in certain Member States, notably and not surprisingly in Bulgaria.

Parliament has no formal power to weed out individuals but only to approve or reject the Commission as a whole. After each individual hearing, letters from the relevant committee are sent to the President of the Parliament and then published. When these letters contain sharply critical comments there is inevitably public pressure on the Commissioners concerned and on the President of the Commission. Ultimately, Parliament can do nothing about an individual unless it is prepared to vote down the Commission as a whole – but the 2004 and 2009-10 procedures showed that a threat to do so can produce results. However, even before that, in 1994, sharp criticisms of an individual nominee (Padraig Flynn) by the committee did lead to the President adjusting his portfolio.

Some MEPs would like the treaty to give them the possibility of voting on individuals, though others point out that few national parliaments can vote to confirm individual members of governments – the principle of collective responsibility of the executive prevails. Parliament has therefore never pressed for such a change in any of the treaty-revising IGCs over the years, and the now ratified Lisbon Treaty does not change that situation.

Nor does the Lisbon Treaty include many other changes of substance as regards the appointment of a new Commission. What it does contain, however, is a change of emphasis regarding the choice of President of the Commission. It is still based on a proposal of the European Council, but they in turn are required to take account of the results of the elections to the European Parliament and to make the necessary consultations to ensure that their candidate will obtain the necessary majority. The vote by Parliament is also now referred to as an "election" of the President (a term that was already used in Parliament's Rules of Procedure). Of particular significance, however, is that as a result of the Lisbon Treaty, the European Parliament now votes on the nomination by absolute rather than simple majority of its members. Barroso, for example, was re-elected in September 2009 by 382-219 votes with 117 abstentions, a seemingly handsome majority, but only 13 votes above the needed absolute majority. Moreover, Jacques Santer would have been rejected under this provision in July 1994. The necessary threshold is thus much more difficult to achieve, and contentious nominees will find it more difficult to be elected.

A further change in the Lisbon Treaty is that it is explicitly stated that if the European Council's candidate is rejected, they must make a new proposal. This new emphasis makes the procedure more visibly like the choices made in many countries by their head of state, who has to see who is capable of commanding a parliamentary majority.

As a consequence, the idea has been put forward in recent years that the European political parties could, before the Parliament elections, each propose the candidate that they would like to see elected as President of the Commission, and the European election campaign would then focus in part on those candidates. The results of the elections would then have a direct effect on the executive, which is what the electorate is used to in national parliamentary elections in most European countries. A direct linkage of this kind has still not occurred, but the main European political parties have stated that they will indeed propose candidates ahead of the 2014 election.

Reshuffling of the Commission during its mandate

A related issue to that of the appointment of the Commission is that of the role of the Parliament when new Commissioners are appointed in the course of a Commission's mandate, or if a President decides to reshuffle his team, by swapping their portfolios, or carving out new or modified portfolios. It is understandable, in the light of the individual confirmation hearings held at the beginning of a Commission, that Parliament has also sought to have a role in such cases.

The departure of Commissioners before the end of their term of office, and their replacement by another nominee of their own nationality, is a not infrequent occurrence, especially towards the end of the term of office of a Commission. Reshuffling, on the other hand, has not yet occurred on any scale, apart from in the context of adjusting existing portfolios to make space for Commissioners from new Member States, as when Bulgaria and Romania joined the EU in the middle of the 2004-2009 Commission's term of office.

Parliament's position is weaker in these circumstances than at the outset of a Commission, but Parliament has insisted on holding hearings for such new members of the Commission. This whole matter is covered in Rule 106-6 of the EP Rules of Procedure, which states that: "In the event of a substantial portfolio change during the Commission's term of office, the filling of a vacancy or the appointment of a new Commissioner following the accession of a new Member State, the Commissioners concerned shall be invited to appear before the committees responsible for the areas of responsibility in question ..."

These matters are now also covered in points 6 and 7 of the section on Political Responsibility in the updated October 2010 Framework Agreement between the Commission and the Parliament. This seeks to achieve a balance between giving the European Parliament an enhanced role, and not tying the hands of the Commission President. In the case of replacement of a Commissioner, point 6 states that "the President of the Commission will seriously consider the result of Parliament's consultation before giving accord to the decision of the Council". For its part, "Parliament shall ensure that its procedures are conducted with the utmost dispatch, in order to enable the President of the Commission to seriously consider Parliament's opinion before the new member is appointed". With regard to any proposed re-shuffle, under point 7, the Commission's President undertakes to "inform Parliament in due time for the relevant parliamentary consultation". However, the "President's decision to reshuffle the portfolios can take place immediately." These new procedures are yet to be tested.

Appointments to the European Central Bank

The treaty provides for Parliament to be consulted on the appointment of the President, Vice-President and the members of the Board of the European Central Bank. Given the significant powers of the Board of the Central Bank, these appointments are of great importance.

Parliament's role is only consultative, but is potentially crucial. When it comes to a public vote in an elected Parliament on an individual, it would be surprising if that individual wished to take office should Parliament reject his or her candidacy. It is also doubtful that the Member States would retain the necessary majority to proceed with the appointment.

In exercising its new rights, Parliament again decided to organise public confirmation hearings at which candidates were invited to defend their suitability for office. This first occurred in November 1993, when Alexandre Lamfalussy, the nominee for President of the European Monetary Institute

(EMI, the predecessor of the European Central Bank), appeared before the Parliament's Economic & Monetary Committee. He had replied in writing beforehand to a series of specific questions and answered detailed oral questions for three hours at the public hearing. Subsequently, Parliament gave its approval for his nomination. A similar hearing was later held when Wim Duisenberg replaced Lamfalussy as President of the EMI.

In May 1998, when it came to consultation of the Parliament on the appointment of the first President, Vice-President and other members of the Executive Board of the newly established European Central Bank (ECB), the staggered terms of office established for individual members of the Board meant that this would be the only occasion when all the members of the Board would be up for appointment at the same time. Parliament used the opportunity to ensure that, not only the President (again Duisenberg), but also all the other candidate Board members agreed to attend such hearings, and to reply in advance to written questionnaires, thereby setting an important precedent.

The preparations made for the hearings were thorough, as the credibility of this new powerful institution was at stake. The Socialist Group, for instance, went so far as to organise a video-conference between certain of its members in Strasbourg and Alan Blinder, former Vice-President of the US Federal Reserve in Washington, at which he was asked for his views on possible lines of questioning of the ECB nominees. For their part, the ECB nominees also met up in Frankfurt to discuss their handling of the written questionnaires and of the hearings.

The hearings of 7–8 May 1998 were held in public and resulted in all the nominees being approved by the plenary on 12 May 1998 by substantial majorities.

There were a number of positive results to this process. Duisenberg, who had appeared to have agreed to stand down before the end of his official term of office in favour of a French nominee, succeeded in getting across the message that there was nothing automatic about this promise and that he retained a personal margin of manoeuvre. He also committed himself to a regular dialogue with the Parliament, and to appear before its Economic Committee on at least a quarterly basis. Perhaps most importantly of all, MEPs (and journalists and others attending the hearings) were able to get a much clearer idea of the personalities and views of the different candidates, including those who would not normally be appearing in the future in front of a parliamentary committee. Without the Parliament's involvement in the process, such knowledge would have been limited to a much more restricted group of insiders. Another – limited but still significant – breach in the traditional EU appointments model had been made.

Subsequent appointments to the Board of Governors have, as foreseen in the treaties, been staggered, but based on the precedents set in 1998, there has always been a hearing and a vote in Parliament, including on the appointment of Mr Duisenberg's successor, Jean-Claude Trichet in 2003. The most recent such vote was on 24 March 2011 on the appointment of Peter Praet to be a member of the Executive Board of the ECB. Parliament's relevant Rule (109-4) provides that "If the opinion adopted by Parliament is unfavourable, the President shall ask the Council to withdraw its nomination and to submit a new nomination to Parliament". Up to now, however, such votes have all been positive.

Appointments to the Court of Auditors

As pointed out above, consultation in respect of appointments to the Court of Auditors became, in 1975, the first example of the Parliament being given such a role. A first significant step was taken in 1981 when the Parliament's Budgetary Control Committee began the practice of inviting the nominees to a hearing where they were cross-examined on their expertise and views.

The bottom line of such a consultative procedure is what happens when Parliament gives a negative opinion on a proposed candidate. Such a case first occurred in November 1989, when Parliament was consulted on the appointment or reappointment of six candidates. Parliament approved four of them but felt unable to give a favourable opinion in respect of two of them, the French and Greek candidates. The French government immediately responded by withdrawing the nominated candidate and putting forward a new candidate who, after he appeared before Parliament's Budgetary Control Committee, was approved by Parliament at its next part-session and duly appointed. The Greek government, which was in the middle of a government crisis and between two general elections in succession, claimed to be unable to find a more suitable candidate. Parliament chose not to fight, being pleased enough with the French reaction, and merely regretted the Greek government's position. In contrast, in 1993 the Council ignored the reservation of the Parliament on two candidates, one an incumbent member of the Court.

In 2004, when examining the ten candidates put forward by the new Member States, Parliament followed the recommendations of its Budgetary Control Committee and voted to approve the appointment of eight of the nominees, while giving a negative opinion regarding Julius Molnar of Slovakia and Constantinos Karmias of Cyprus. Karmias's nomination was withdrawn before the vote in plenary and Cyprus proposed another candidate who was subsequently confirmed. The Slovak government, however, maintained the candidacy of Mr Molnar, despite Parliament confirming the committee's negative opinion, and Council duly appointed him. Since that experience the standard questionnaire drawn up by the committee for new appointments contains the question "Will you undertake to withdraw if the Control Committee delivers a negative opinion?"

Parliament's relevant Rule (108) states that: "If the opinion adopted by Parliament on an individual nomination is unfavourable, the President shall ask the Council to withdraw its nomination and to submit a new nomination to Parliament." Experience up to now suggests that a negative opinion by Parliament is quite likely to lead to, but does not guarantee, the withdrawal of the candidate in question.

Appointment of the Ombudsman

The most far-reaching change of all to the traditional EU appointments model was that introduced by the Maastricht Treaty as regards the new post of EU Ombudsman. Article 195 TEC provides for appointment by the Parliament after each parliamentary election for the duration of its term of office. The Member States are given no say at all in the nominations process, which is left entirely to the Parliament.

Parliament provides in its Rules for a call for nominations to be published in the Official Journal of the European Union and for nominations to have the support of a minimum of 40 members who are nationals of at least two Member States. The competent committee (the Petitions Committee) then holds public hearings of the candidates and submits a list of admissible nominations in alphabetical order to the full Parliament, which takes the final decision by secret ballot on the basis of a majority of the votes cast. A quorum of at least half of Parliament's component members have to be present. If no candidate has been elected after the first two ballots, the two candidates obtaining the largest number of votes go through into a final third ballot.

On the first occasion when the Parliament exercised its new powers in 1995, the Rules of Procedure provided for only one name to be submitted to the plenary. This resulted in stalemate when there was a tied vote in the relevant committee between two candidates (Siegbert Alber, a former Vice-President of Parliament, and Gil-Robles, Ombudsman of Spain), without a means of breaking any such tie. The Rules were then modified to provide for the committee to submit a list of names in alphabetical order to the plenary, and for the eldest candidate to prevail in the event of any tie there. A Finnish candidate, Jacob Söderman, was elected by Parliament after nominations had been reopened to allow candidates from the three countries that had joined the EU in the meantime.

All subsequent appointments have been under these rules (see Table 42). Söderman was narrowly re-elected on 27 October 1999, beating former MEP (and long-serving Parliament Vice-President) Giorgios Anastassopoulos. Söderman's announcement of his forthcoming retirement led to a new appointment procedure in the autumn of 2002, with several serving Ombudsmen as candidates: Pierre-Yves Monette, Herman Wuyts (both Federal Ombudsmen of Belgium), Giuseppe Fortunato (a regional Ombudsman in Italy) and Nikiforos Diamandouros (the Ombudsman of Greece), the latter winning against Roy Perry MEP, Vice President of Parliament's Petitions Committee, in the final ballot. Mr Diamandouros served out the remaining period of Mr Söderman's term and was then re-elected by the new Parliament in January 2005. He was again elected for a further term in January 2010, obtaining 340 votes to 289 for his main rival, Pierre-Yves Monette of Belgium and 19 for the Italian Vittorio Bottoli. (See Chapter 16 for further discussion of the relationship between the Parliament and the Ombudsman.)

Table 42: *Ombudsman elections*

Candidates	1st round	2nd round	3rd round
July 1995			
Söderman	139	195	241
Alber	183	193	221
Veil	113	133	
Robles	50		
Vayssade	17		
Newton-Dunn	withdrawn		

	1st round	2nd round	3rd round
October 1999			
Söderman	269		
Anastassopoulos	256		
January 2003			
Diamandouros	238	294	
Perry	159	215	
Monette	73		
Fortunato	35		
Wuyts	11		
January 2005			
Diamandouros	564		
Fortunato	45		
January 2010			
Diamandouros	340		
Monette	289		
Bottoli	19		

European Parliament role in appointments to EU agencies

In addition to its main institutions, the European Union has created a large number of decentralised agencies located in practically all the older Member States, and now in some of the newer ones as well. Without counting purely executive agencies (which are also of great interest to Parliament's budgetary committees), or the very specific agencies dealing with common security and defence policy or police and judicial cooperation in criminal matters, there are now 23 other Community agencies, distinct from the main Community institutions, with their own legal personality, and set up by an act of secondary legislation to accomplish specific tasks. These are very different in character, with some primarily gathering technical or scientific data, but others having important regulatory functions. The European Parliament had no formal or even meaningful informal role in the appointments process when the first such agencies were created in the 1970s, but has gradually developed an increasingly important, if still very uneven role, as regards many of these agencies. This has particularly been the case since the European Parliament became involved in co-decision in the founding regulations of new agencies, or when these regulations were amended or recast. Attempts are now being made to provide a more systematic and consistent approach to European Parliament involvement in this process.

Whatever their functions, practically all of these Community agencies have Management (or Administrative or Executive) Boards, who help to choose the agency's director, and to advise on the strategic direction for the agency. The Member States are always represented on these Boards, as is the European Commission. Certain agencies also contain other bodies as well, such as scientific committees. The European Parliament now also selects representatives on the Boards of some of these agencies, and is playing a growing role in the selection of certain agency directors. In a few more limited cases the Parliament also chooses representatives to scientific or other committees.

There are still a number of agencies where the EP has no specific role, either in the choice of the Director or of the Management Board. Some of these are first generation agencies, such as the European Centre for the Development of Vocational Training (Cedefop) and the European Centre for the Improvement of Working and Living Conditions (EUROFOUND), or more recent agencies, such as the European Agency for Health and Safety at Work (EU-OSHA), the Community Plant Variety Office (CPVO), the European Agency for the Management of Operational Cooperation at the External Borders (FRONTEX) or the Trade Marks Office (OHIM), where the EP was only consulted on their founding regulations. There are also cases where the EP was involved in the founding regulation through co-decision, such as the European Maritime Safety Agency, but where the EP still has no direct role in the appointments process.

(i)   EU nominees to agency Boards

There are, however, many other cases where the Parliament now plays a role in the appointments process. It was first given the right to have nominees on the Management Board of an agency in the case of the European Environment Agency, set up in 1990 on the basis of the then cooperation procedure, whereby the Parliament had two readings on the final legislation, but did not have the same weight as in the co-decision procedure. In 1993 the EP also obtained two nominees on the Management Board of the European Monitoring Centre for Drugs and Drug Addiction, and in 1997 one nominee on the Board of the European Monitoring Centre on Racism and Xenophobia.

In the light of these developments, procedures to choose the Parliament nominees were drawn up within the Parliament, and were then codified by the Conference of Presidents on 5 March 1998 in the form of new rules on the designation by the European Parliament of members of the management boards of the specialised agencies and bodies. Pursuant to these rules, candidates are to be initially designated by a Political Group or 40 members and are then sifted by the committee responsible. Candidates are also asked to disclose to the committee any relevant financial interests or incompatibilities. The committee then adopts a list, in the order of votes obtained, of persons eligible to be appointed as full members and as alternates. The final decision is then taken by the Conference of Presidents.

The rules also require the appointee to make a written undertaking to carry out their duties impartially and independently of any private body or public authority. They contain provisions for subsequent scrutiny of the appointees and for withdrawal, after a prior hearing, of the mandate from any appointee who fails to fulfil his or her obligations, or who violates the principles of impartiality or independence. This has not yet been necessary.

The members designated by Parliament must report back, via the relevant committee, on any developments of interest to Parliament and should also put forward Parliament's views on the operation of the agency. Parliament's designated members of the EEA Board, for example, have played an important role in the Board's discussions during the process leading up to the nomination of the Executive Director of the Agency, as have Parliament's nominees on the Boards of the EMEA and the ECDC. They also often accompany any EP committee delegation visiting the agency. (The relevant committee must send a three-member delegation to visit the agency every two years.)

Some have argued, even within the Parliament, that it should not have nominees on the Boards of agencies that it is trying to scrutinize. The Parliament's internal rules thus stipulate that EP nominees on a Board cannot be sitting MEPs, thus avoiding any such direct conflict of roles. Moreover, the EP nominees, unlike the Member States and Commission representatives, are not formal representatives of the EP. Instead a key aspect of their role is to take an independent look at the way in which an agency is functioning, and to back up the relevant Parliament committee in the latter's task of scrutinizing the work of the agency.

To do this job, it has become increasingly clear that Parliament's choice of its nominees needs to be prepared as carefully as possible. In September 2004 Parliament's Environment Committee innovated in this respect by holding nomination hearings of the various candidates who had been put forward for the two posts to represent the Parliament on the ECDC Management Board. As a result of these hearings the committee put forward the names of two of the nominees, and these were subsequently confirmed by the Conference of Presidents. One of them (Ms Malliori, a former MEP) was later chosen as the Vice-Chair of the full Board. This precedent has since been followed in other cases, for example for hearings for EP nominees on the Boards of the European Environmental Agency (EEA) and the European Chemicals Agency.

In recent years the EP has also linked the issue of its own nominations to agency Management Boards, with that of the size of those Boards. If they are reduced in size, and if not every Member State is represented on the Board, the EP would be prepared to give up its nominees. Where this is not the case, the EP should keep its own nominees. Both of the EP general resolutions on agencies (in 2003 and 2005) have raised this issue, with the latter reiterating the EP's longer term aim "of reducing the size of the Board of Directors for reasons of efficiency". On the other hand, the same resolution goes on to state that "as long as the number of representatives on the board of directors corresponds to the number of Member States, Parliament, for its part, should designate two members of the board of directors".

(ii)   Evolving EU role in appointment of agency directors

Besides this involvement in making its own nominations to the Boards of agencies, Parliament has also carved out a new role in the choice of the agency directors themselves. The key precedent for this came during the co-decision negotiations on the structure of the new European Food Safety Authority (EFSA). Here Parliament's negotiators opted for a different model, whereby it would have no representatives on the EFSA Board but would be given, instead, a direct say in the designation of the members of the Management Board and in the subsequent appointment of the Executive Director.

Parliament was thus given, in April 2002, a Commission-filtered shortlist of 30 candidates for the 14 available places on EFSA's Management Board. Parliament's Environment Committee then set up a small working group of its coordinators or their representatives to look through the candidates' CVs and to establish criteria and make recommendations to Parliament's President. They then put forward a recommended list of nominees for the approval of the full committee, and subsequently of the Conference of Presidents. No formal criteria were adopted by the working group, but they did agree on a number of informal principles, such as the need to avoid having heads of national food safety authorities on the Management Board, as they were better placed on the Advisory Committee on which all Member States were represented. The working group was also concerned about the limited number of consumer representatives on the list submitted by the Commission. They also, in a couple of cases, deliberately put forward two nominees from a single Member State, as these were both justified on the merit of the nominees, and also underlined the principle that the EU was moving away from the old model of one nominee per Member State. Its subsequently reduced shortlist of 17 names was endorsed by the Conference of Presidents. Parliament's recommendations were not binding, however, and the Council agreed with some of Parliament's suggestions and rejected others.

Parliament was then asked to consider the Management Board's designated candidate to be EFSA's first Executive Director in October 2002. A two-hour long hearing was held at which members of Parliament's Environment Committee cross-examined the candidate (Geoffrey Podger of the UK Food Standards Agency). They subsequently recommended that his candidacy be endorsed, and wrote a letter to the President of the Parliament to this effect. By analogy with the 1998 rules on choosing EP nominees to Management Boards, the final decision was then taken by the EP Conference of Presidents.

In light of resistance from the Member States to a reduction in their role on Management Boards, it is perhaps not surprising that the proposed new EFSA model had only limited success. An attempt was made, for example, to apply the new model in the far-reaching 2004 revision of the European Medicines Agency (EMA), but the Member States insisted on keeping their national representatives on the Board. The EP then ended up with a hybrid system, namely having both a role in the appointment of the Director and with its own nominees on the Management Board.

What has survived from the EFSA model, however, is a more generalised EP involvement in the appointment of agency directors, either combined with EP nominees on the agency Board, or without such nominees. Examples of the former are the European Centre for Disease Prevention and Control (ECDC), the European Chemicals Agency, the European Monitoring Centre for Drugs and Drugs Addiction (each with nominees on the Board, and a say in the Director's appointment) and the Agency for the Cooperation of Energy Regulators (ACER), whose 2009 founding regulation provides for 2 Commission, 2 EP and only 5 Council nominees on its Administrative Board, as well as an EP say in the Director's appointment. Examples of the latter are the European Network and Information Security Agency (ENISA), where the EP was given a role in the choice of the Director, but no nominees on the Management Board; and the European Fundamental Rights Agency (FRA), established in 2007, where the EP's role also concentrates on the appointment of the Director. Three other recent examples concern the appointments of the Executive Directors of the three new bodies set up as part of the European Supervisory Body, namely the European Banking Authority, the European Insurance and Occupational Pensions Authority, and the European Securities and Market Authority. The European Parliament is given the power to "confirm" the Executive Directors in all three cases, a power it first exercised on 24 March 2011. The European Parliament is also given the power to "object" to the designation of the Chairperson of each authority.

The EP role in the choice of agency directors tends to be cautiously worded in the founding regulations of the concerned agency, with a typical wording being that, before being appointed, the candidate nominated by the Management Board may or shall be invited to make a statement before the competent committee of the European Parliament and to answer questions put by its members. In practice, as pointed out above, this has been interpreted as requiring a hearing of the nominee, with an evaluation by the committee, and a final decision by the Conference of Presidents.

One exception to this informal model has been in the case of the Fundamental Rights Agency (FRA), where the EP has been given formal equality in this process with the Council, with hearings before both institutions, and an order of preference established by both before the final formal decision by the Management Board.

(iii)   EP nominees on other agency bodies

There are a few agencies where the EP is also consulted on other nominations, for example to the FRA Scientific Committee, as well as on representatives of patients, doctors and vets on the Management Board of EMA. When this latter consultation was first applied it was again on the basis of a filtering exercise by a working group in the responsible committee.

(iv)   Issue of reappointment of Agency Directors

A final related question is the procedure to be followed in the case of the reappointment of agency directors, and the nature of the EP's involvement in such a decision. There has been concern expressed in recent years, both within individual agencies and in the European Parliament, that the Commission has been proposing too much of a role for itself in this regard, that this was inappropriate for an allegedly independent agency, and that the final decision should be left to the Management Board of the agency concerned. The December 2005 resolution of the EP on the Inter-institutional Agreement on Agencies made the EP's position clear in this respect: "A decision to extend the term of office of a director should be taken solely by the board of directors, on the basis of an evaluation of the director's first term of office."

The role of the EP itself in the reappointment process has not yet been clarified, but it is to be expected that it will be seeking a stronger involvement in the future. A very important precedent in this respect has been set in the case of the FRA, where the EP is given the possibility of a re-confirmation hearing in the relevant committee in the case of re-appointment of the sitting Director. The European Parliament is also given the power to re-confirm the reappointment of the Chairpersons of the three new bodies of the European Supervisory Authority. In an even more remarkable development, the Chairpersons of these same authorities "may be removed from office only by the European Parliament following a decision of the Board of Supervisors".

(v)   The outlook

It is too early to judge how these different models will work out in the longer run. Parliament has expressed concern about the multiplicity of structures. In 2004 it adopted a resolution in which it supported a general review of the structure of agencies. Parliament took the view that such a multitude of different forms was not transparent or comprehensible and it thus supported efforts to arrive at a limited number of models. The Commission responded with a draft inter-institutional agreement on this issue, to which Parliament responded in December 2006, but further developments have been slow. An Inter-Institutional Working Party was later set up in March 2009, with 5 representatives from the European Parliament in order to look at the role of regulatory agencies.

In the meantime, the EP has continued to argue forcefully for a more systematic role in the choice of all agency directors, and for better internal procedures to implement its own new powers in this respect. This was restated in the October 2010 Framework Agreement on relations between the European Parliament and the European Commission which contains a section on regulatory agencies. Point 32 of the Agreement thus states that: "nominees for the post of Executive Director of regulatory agencies should come to parliamentary committee hearings. In addition, in the context of the discussions of the inter-Institutional Working Group on Agencies set up in March 2009, the Commission and Parliament will aim at a common approach on the role and position of decentralized agencies in the Union's institutional landscape, accompanied by common guidelines for the creation, structure and operation of those agencies, together with funding, budgetary, supervision and management issues."

Other appointments

Besides the appointments mentioned above, Parliament has a role as regards certain other appointments; for example, it is formally consulted on and holds public hearings with the candidates for the post of the Director of the EU's anti-fraud office (OLAF).

Parliament has also sought to have a role in the choice of external representatives of the EU. In the absence of formal treaty changes, the 1999 revision of Parliament's Rules of Procedure (Corbett/Palacio/Gutierrez report) provided for the possibility of inviting certain new appointees to hearings and, potentially, having a vote on them. Parliament's Rule 95 on "international representation" now states:

"1.   When the head of a Union external delegation is to be appointed, the nominee may be invited to appear before the relevant body of Parliament to make a statement and answer questions.

2.   Within three months of the hearing provided for in paragraph 1, the committee responsible may adopt a resolution or make a recommendation, as appropriate, relating directly to the statement made and the answers provided."

The whole issue again emerged in the difficult negotiations on the future shape of the new European External Action Service, and on Parliament's role in this regard. In September 2010 the Foreign Affairs Committee started to examine the first batch of 27 nominations by High Representative Catherine Ashton to head up EU delegations. It also had to decide which of these nominees to invite to the Committee in the light of the "strategic importance" of their posts. The first such hearing was held at the end of September 2010 with Rosalind Marsden, the new European Union Special Representative for Sudan, and was followed by one with the nominee for the EU Delegation to Japan.

A limited role regarding appointments to the Courts

Parliament has historically played no role in the appointment of judges at the European Court of Justice or its subsidiary Court of First Instance (CFI), now renamed the General Court.

In the run-up to the Maastricht and Amsterdam IGCs, Parliament asked for the right to give its assent to all nominations to the Court of Justice and the CFI. The Court of Justice was dismissive of the idea, considering that it would prejudice the independence of judges. The CFI adopted a less dismissive stance, considering that any projected intervention by the Parliament in the procedure for appointing judges should be confined to the initial appointment, for the obvious reason that it could not extend to a review of the manner in which judicial functions have actually been carried out. Moreover, any such intervention by the Parliament should be solely for the purpose of ascertaining whether the prospective nominees possessed the qualifications required by the treaty in order to exercise their functions. A footnote cited with approval a working document on behalf of the Parliament's Institutional Affairs Committee which had called for the Parliament approval process to avoid political considerations and to concentrate on verifying the qualifications required in the treaty, namely that a nominee could demonstrate his or her independence and that they had held high judicial office or otherwise shown outstanding legal abilities. Thus the CFI considered that appropriate parliamentary involvement could actually enhance the judges' independence.

In the event, the Maastricht IGC and subsequent treaty revisions left the Court appointment procedures almost unchanged. Unlike the US Supreme Court, appointed by the federal institutions, the European courts continue to be appointed exclusively by the Member States. The Lisbon Treaty does, however, provide that, prior to the appointment of a judge or Advocate-General of the European Court of Justice or of the General Court, a panel of seven former European Court or national supreme court judges, one of whom will be selected by the European Parliament, shall give an opinion on the candidate's suitability. This is now covered in Rule 107a of the EP Rules. Parliament's first nomination to this panel was Ana Palacio, a former MEP (indeed, former chair of the Legal Affairs Committee) and former Spanish Minister of Foreign Affairs.

The right of censure

One of the Parliament's oldest powers is to be able to dismiss the Commission. Indeed, only Parliament, not the Council nor national governments, can force a Commission to resign before the end of its term.

Table 43: *Motions of censure on the Commission tabled within the European Parliament*

| December 1972 | Spénale (French Socialist) | EP power of control over the EC budget | Withdrawn (in favour of compromise resolution) |

Table 43 (continued) : *Motions of censure on the Commission tabled within the European Parliament*

June 1976	Kirk (British Conservative)	Incorporation of skimmed milk powder in animal feed	Votes cast: For: Against: Abstentions:	131 18 109 4
December 1976	Aigner (German EPP)	Parliament's right of control - access to documents	Withdrawn (Commission agreed to provide	
15 February 1990	Group of the European Right	The CAP and the Commission's competences	Members Votes cast For Against Abstentions	567 264 16 243 5
11 July 1991	Group of the European Right	Commission and Council policy on Yugoslavia	Members Votes cast For Against Abstentions	567 219 8 206 5
17 December 1992	Lannoye (Belgian Green) and 71 other Members	Position adopted by the Commission during the GATT negotiations	Members Votes cast For Against Abstentions	567 357 96 246 15
20 February 1997	Happart and others	BSE	Members Votes cast For Against Abstentions	626 459 118 326 15
14 January 1999	Fabre-Aubrespy and 69 other Members	The 1996 discharge	Members Votes cast For Against Abstentions	626 552 232 293 27
March 1999	Commission resigns in anticipation of a motion of censure			
4 May 2004	Bonde and 64 others	Eurostat scandal	Members Votes cast For Against Abstentions	788 666 88 515 63
8 June 2005	Farage (UKIP) and 76 others	Gift received by President of Commission	Members Votes cast For Against Abstentions documentation)	732 659 35 589 35
March 1977	Cointat (French RDE)	Butter sales to Eastern Europe	Votes cast: For: Against: Abstentions:	111 15 95 1

The ECSC Treaty only allowed Parliament to censure the Commission ("High Authority" as it was then) when the latter presented its annual report. This limitation was not included in the EEC and Euratom Treaties. When a single Commission for these Communities was set up in 1965, the treaty provided for a general right of censure, which, if carried by a two-thirds majority comprising half the members of Parliament, would force the Commission to resign.

Parliament has to date never adopted a censure motion, but in March 1999 the Commission resigned when faced with the near certainty of the adoption of one. This came about after Parliament declined to give the Commission discharge on its 1996 budgetary accounts at its December 1998 plenary, triggering a series of events described in the previous chapter, which eventually led to the collective resignation of the Santer Commission, within hours of the Political Groups making it clear that there was a majority for censure.

Prior to this only nine censure motions (see Table 43) were tabled in Parliament, though a few more were threatened, and all were rejected or withdrawn. Four of these pre-dated direct elections in 1979. Four motions were tabled by smaller Political Groups, and were all decisively defeated (Conservative Group in 1976 on milk powder, Gaullists in 1977 on butter sales, European Right in 1990 on the Commission's agricultural policy and 1991 on the Commission's conduct in external relations).

A slightly higher level of support for a censure motion was obtained in December 1992 for a motion tabled by various members, including the Greens and the extreme Right, on the issue of the GATT talks on the grounds that the Commission's negotiating tactics had given too much away in the agricultural sector. In February 1997, 118 members voted for a motion of censure tabled by José Happart (Belgian Socialist) on the Commission's handling of the BSE crisis.

Two motions of censure have been tabled since the events of 1999. One was in the last part-session of the Parliament prior to the 2004 elections and was widely seen as an electoral gimmick. Tabled by members of the then EDD (now EFD) Group and other Eurosceptics, it sought to censure the Commission on the ground that it had not dealt adequately with financial irregularities in the EU's statistics agency, Eurostat. Most press interest centred on the position of the UK Conservative MEPs, most of whom initially signed the motion and then withdrew their names after a lively debate in their Group. Seven of them nevertheless maintained their signature. The other motion was tabled in 2005, by the ID Group and other Eurosceptics concerning alleged unethical behaviour of President Barroso. Following the debate and Barroso's explanations, most of them wished to withdraw the motion, but it was too late and Parliament voted anyway, defeating it by a very large majority.

In general, dismissal of the Commission is considered to be a last resort to be threatened sparingly. The Parliament has in practice forged a close working relationship with the Commission, and has had growing influence on its proposals. When conflicts have broken out between the two institutions they have normally been resolved in other ways than by censure. It remains a reserve power, but just as national parliaments only rarely make use of their power to dismiss governments, the fact that they can do so is enough to encourage the executive to pay attention to their viewpoint.

A motion of censure can only be addressed to the Commission as a whole, reflecting the doctrine of collective accountability. Although a vote of censure cannot be passed on an individual Commissioner, there is nothing to prevent Parliament adopting a resolution criticising an individual Commissioner or, indeed, calling upon him or her to resign. Such a resolution would carry even more weight if it were implied that Parliament might move to censure the Commission as a whole if the Commissioner concerned did not resign. Such a course of action was proposed in January 1999 by the Liberal and EPP Groups at one stage in the events which led to the resignation of the Santer Commission.

The idea has since been included in successive Framework Agreements between the EP and the Commission. The most recent such Framework Agreement, that of October 2010, thus states in point 5 of its section on Political Responsibility that: "If Parliament asks the President of the Commission to withdraw confidence in an individual Member of the Commission, he/she will seriously consider whether to request that Member to resign, in accordance with Article 17(6) TEU. The President shall either require the resignation of that Member or explain his/her refusal to do so before Parliament in the following part-session." A formal treaty change to permit individual dismissal of a Commissioner has been supported by some members, but has not won majority support because of the potentially adverse implications for the collegial nature of the Commission. The Parliament does not have any other formal powers of direct censure other than that concerning the Commission. The one limited exception is provided by Article 195–2 of the TEC, which allows for the Ombudsman to be dismissed by the Court of Justice at the request of the European Parliament, a power that has not been used.

15. Scrutiny and control of the executive

What the Americans call "oversight" has always been a major function of parliaments. As the sheer size of administration has grown, and governments have assumed greater powers, so the importance of parliamentary oversight has grown to ensure democratic accountability. In the European Union, similar trends can be observed. The powers exercised at European level, although limited, have expanded and include a significant degree of executive decision taking.

Just as national parliaments have a distinct role in ensuring scrutiny and control of their own governments, so the European Parliament has a responsibility to ensure scrutiny of the executive, primarily the European Commission, but also aspects of the work of the Council, European Council, the European Central Bank and the various agencies that have been set up from time to time.

The Commission is not only responsible for drafting and proposing new legislation, but also for implementing aspects of legislation once it is adopted (through delegated legislative powers or through implementing measures) as well as taking decisions on some matters where the Treaty itself gives decision taking powers to the Commission. Thus, in 2008, the Commission adopted 1,368 binding instruments, three times the number (though not necessarily the importance) of the binding measures (420, mostly legislation) it forwarded for adoption by Parliament and Council.

The Commission can also take Member States to the Court of Justice for failing to apply European law; and it is the competition authority empowered to ensure fair play in the single market. Moreover, although the number of civil servants working for the Commission is often exaggerated (fewer than most major UK city councils or the BBC, for example – and a good third of them dealing with translation or interpretation), it has grown considerably: in 1980, the number of permanent posts in the Commission as such was 8,435, but by 2009 there were 25,728 such posts.

The Commission can thus be considered to be the executive branch of the Union. Yet, the Council is often perceived as such, a misperception reinforced by the usage of the term "Council of Ministers" which (like "Cabinet" in the UK) is the term used for the government in some countries such as Italy and France. But, unlike the Commission, it has no general right of legislative initiative, no power to implement the budget, and its permanent staff is relatively small (3,476 in 2009). Nevertheless, it does exercise some limited executive responsibilities: it may, in specific cases, reserve implementing powers to itself (Article 291 TFEU), it conducts macroeconomic co-ordination of national economic policies and it determines EU positions in the Common Foreign and Security Policy. The exercise of these latter powers is largely outside the reach of judicial review by the European Court of Justice, making political oversight all the more important. The carrying out of the policy is by the EU's High Representative, with the help of the External Action Service. The High Representative is a Vice President of the Commission.

As to the European Council, this is still less a day-to-day executive, but it does, according to Article 15 TEU, "define the general political directions and priorities of the Union". Its strategic importance is therefore considerable.

The European Central Bank was established under the terms of the Maastricht Treaty to manage the euro, with a view to maintaining price stability. It sets the interest rate for the eurozone, has the exclusive right to issue euro banknotes, conducts foreign exchange operations and manages the foreign reserves of the participating states. Its supervisory powers over the financial sector are being increased as a result of the 2008-09 crisis.

The growth of executive power in the European Union has prompted a vigorous response from the European Parliament. It was originally granted only limited supervisory powers by the treaties: the right to receive and debate an annual report of activities, the right to receive oral and written replies to parliamentary questions and, as we have seen, the right to dismiss the Commission by a vote of censure. Over time it has succeeded in extending these powers and in this chapter we will complement the discussion in the previous chapter, on appointment and dismissal, by looking at its general power of scrutiny through debates, questions and reports, alongside the more particular instruments of control over expenditure and secondary legislation, committees of inquiry and judicial review.

General EP – Commission relations: the Framework Agreement

In the course of Parliament's scrutiny and control of the Commission, a host of horizontal problems have arisen, such as access to Commission documents, early communication of information, presence of Commissioners in Parliament, timetables and procedures for a prompt response to Parliament's criticisms or requests. Ad hoc arrangements over the years have been codified into overall agreements with the Commission. A first "Code of Conduct" was negotiated in 1990 and revised in 1995, then replaced in 2000 by a more far-reaching Framework Agreement (itself revised in 2005 and 2010) that sets out general terms of political cooperation between the two institutions. It is appended to Parliament's Rules of Procedure (Annex XIV) and covers a number of headings:
–   "political responsibility" to Parliament of the Commission, its President and its members at the time of appointment, reshuffles and during their period in office
–   "constructive dialogue and flow of information", on the flow of information and documents, response to parliamentary initiatives and criticisms, presence of MEPs at international negotiations, scrutiny of agency appointments and other matters
–   "cooperation as regards legislative procedures and planning", regarding the elaboration of the Commission's annual Work Programme and various aspects of the legislative procedure

- the "Commission's participation in Parliamentary proceedings" specifying when and where the attendance of Commissioners is expected
- "Commission meetings with national experts" (Annex 1)
- procedures for the "forwarding of confidential information to the
  European Parliament" (Annex 2)
- Parliament's involvement in "the negotiation and conclusion of international agreements" (Annex 3)
- the "timetable for the Commission work programme" and its handling
  in Parliament (Annex 4)

The precise commitments entered into are described, as appropriate, throughout this book under the relevant subject. But the overall impact of the 2005 and 2010 revisions was such as to provoke a degree of consternation in the Council, which considered that the agreement involved too many conces- sions by the Commission to the Parliament and upset the institutional balance to the detriment of the Council. It reserved the right to challenge in the Court any decision taken pursuant to the Framework Agreement which infringed its own prerogatives, though at the time of writing, no such challenge has been forthcoming. The Commission, too, criticised the content of a resolution Parliament adopted when it approved the 2010 revision as interpreting the agreement in a way that it disagreed with. The Agreement is thus controver- sial, stretching the bounds of parliamentary powers to the edge of what is pos- sible under the treaties. For its part, the Parliament pointed out that the Council was invited, but declined, to take part in the negotiations.

Scrutiny through debates, questions and reports

The European Parliament has followed national parliaments in seeking to exert greater control over executive decisions by obliging those responsible for such decisions to come and take part in debates in the Parliament, answer questions from members, either in oral or written form, and submit reports on their activities. Some of these mechanisms are laid down in the treaties but others have been established by practice over time and accepted as part of the parliamentary system at European level.

Debates on statements

The Commission is expected to come before Parliament and explain its actions on a very regular basis, and to ensure that major policy initiatives be announced in Parliament before they are made known to the press. This includes the Vice President of the Commission who is the Union's High Representative for Foreign and Security Policy.

More generally, Parliament regularly asks the Commission (and/or Council) to make a statement in plenary on important issues of current interest. The procedure is not unlike the requests in national parliaments for statements by departmental ministers, followed by a short debate. Such statements feature in most part-sessions, and Parliament can, if it so wishes, wind up the debate with a resolution.

Debate with the other institutions is not restricted to plenary, but also takes place in parliamentary committees. The presence of individual members of the Commission, including the Vice President/High Representative, at committee meetings is a routine event. A major committee will often have one or even two Commissioners speaking and answering questions for periods of up to two hours at its bi-monthly meetings. Commission civil servants are also regularly questioned.

The presence of ministers from the country holding the Council Presidency has also become a normal part of the work of the Parliament. For instance, during the Spanish Presidency of 2010, some 10 ministers took part in 25 debates (including the Prime Minister twice, and the Europe Minister 14 times). At committee level too, there are a large number of ministerial appearances, to speak and answer questions on their sphere of responsibility. These are particularly common at the beginning of a Presidency, in order to present the Presidency programme, and to get to know the members with whom the Presidency will be working (not least on negotiating compromises between Council and Parliament), but also occur at the end of a Presidency. Thus, there were 19 ministerial appearances in committee during the first committee week of the 2010 Spanish Presidency (and 5 more in the next few weeks) and 12 during (or just after) the last month of their Presidency. During the 1998 UK Presidency, Jack Cunningham, the then Agriculture Minister, pointed out that in his first month as President, he had appeared more times before EP committees than he had before House of Commons committees during the whole of his ministerial tenure.

The President of the European Central Bank (ECB) also appears before Parliament in plenary and before the Economic and Monetary Affairs Committee. During the hearings that preceded his appointment, Wim Duisenberg, the first President, agreed to appear at least four times a year in public meetings of this committee to keep it informed on the work of the ECB and to answer questions. This has been continued by his successor, Jean-Claude Trichet, and has become the most important mechanism for scrutiny of the actions of the Bank.

The heads of various decentralised agencies (such as the European Environment Agency, the European Medicines Agency and the European Food Safety Agency) also appear regularly before the relevant committees. The Director of the European Investment Bank speaks in plenary in the annual debate on its work. Heads of EU Representations (EU Ambassadors) in third countries can also be invited before committees.

Parliamentary questions

Written and oral questions are an opportunity to obtain precise information on particular points or to force a policy statement to be made. The treaty itself provided for written and oral questions to the Commission. Council accepted to answer questions as well, an arrangement formalised in 1973 and entered into the treaty (as far as CFSP matters are concerned) in 1993. In 2002, Parliament extended the written question procedure to the Central Bank.

Parliament has developed three different procedures to take advantage of its right to put questions:
-       **Written questions** may be tabled by any member. The question and the replies are published in the Official Journal. Questions requiring an immediate answer are to be answered within three weeks, with each

member entitled to put one such priority question per month. Non-priority questions are to be answered within six weeks. If the question is not answered within the time limit, the issue can be placed on the agenda of the next meeting of the committee responsible, at the request of the member.

– **Questions at question time** is a procedure introduced in 1973, following British parliamentary practice. Any member may table a question two weeks in advance, and the President of Parliament decides on their admissibility and on the order in which they are to be taken. Answers are given during a 90-minute "question time" period. One such period at each part-session is for the Commission, and one for the Council. Each member may only table one question to each institution per month. The author may ask a supplementary question following the reply, and further supplementaries may be taken from other members (on average, there are two supplementaries per question). Questions not reached are answered in writing. Question time rarely has the cut and thrust of the Westminster highlights of the Leader of the Opposition questioning the Prime Minister. It is more like Westminster question time for a departmental minister – not an exciting media event, but none the less useful.

– **Questions for oral answer with debate** may be tabled only by a committee, a Political Group or at least 40 members. The Conference of Presidents decides whether and in what order they should be taken. Questions to the Commission must be referred to it at least one week before the sitting on whose agenda they are to appear and questions to the Council at least three weeks before that date. The reply of Commission or Council is followed by a debate and Parliament may decide to follow this by the adoption of a resolution. If so, a Political Group, a committee, or 40 members may propose such a resolution, which is put to the vote on the same day.

Table 44: *Parliamentary questions tabled during the sixth legislature 2004-2009*

Destination	Oral questions with debate	Question Time	Written questions	Overall total
Commission	405	3,122	27, 823	31,350
Council	203	1,933	2, 688	4,824
Total:	608	5,055	30,511	36,174

These three traditional procedures have now been supplemented by a periodical "Question Hour" with the President of the Commission during which, on a totally spontaneous basis, the Political Group leaders or members deputising for them, may put questions to the President for half an hour, followed by a further half hour in which other members may put questions, but on a subject agreed the previous week. This was agreed in the 2010 revision of the Framework Agreement, but revives a practice used during Jacques Delors' presidency. The Agreement specifies that it can also be used for other Commissioners, including the Vice President/High Representative.

In addition, some committees have introduced a formalised question time to the Commission as regular events in their committee. This often involves the Commission civil servant specialist on an issue rather than the Commissioner, is more informal, and gives more chance for follow-up questions than its plenary equivalent.

Answers from the Commission tend to be more rewarding than those from the Council. After all, executive tasks lie mostly with the Commission (though the Council Presidency had until 2009 responsibilities for implementing the Common Foreign and Security policy, which are now transferred to the Vice President of the Commission/High Representative, who will henceforth answer questions on such matters). The Council is now essentially co-legislator with Parliament, and questions from one branch of the legislature to the other are considered by many to be an oddity.

It is therefore not surprising that the most numerous category of questions (see Table 44) is written questions to the Commission: these far exceed the number of written questions to the Council. Oral questions and questions raised at question time that are addressed to the Commission also outnumber the same categories addressed to the Council but by a lower percentage. Some 87% of all questions (91% of written questions) were tabled to the Commission during the 2004-09 parliament.

During recent years, there has been a decline in the number of questions for oral answer with debate (from 411 in 1990, to 203 in 1998 and to an average of just 100 per year in the 1999-2004 parliament and 122 per year in the 2004-09 parliament) and a reasonably stable level of questions at question time (fluctuating around 1,000 per year). On the other hand, the number of written questions rose from about 3,300 per year (1990-93) to around 4,000 per year from 1996 to 2004, before shooting up to about 6,000 per year during the 2004-09 Parliament.

This increase was partly due to the increased number of MEPs following the 2004 enlargement, but also in part due to the prolific number tabled by a handful of MEPs. Robert Kilroy Silk, a member with one of the lowest rates of attendance in Parliament, tabled over 2000 written questions, prompting discreet complaints from the Commission that many of them were nothing to do with the EU, were statements of opinion disguised as questions or were simple demands for statistics already publicly available. This resulted in a small change to Parliament's rules (Corbett Report A6-197/2008) in June 2008, giving the President of Parliament more discretion to rule on the admissibility of questions and laying down guidelines to the effect that written questions must fall within the competence and sphere of responsibility of the addressee, be concise, contain an understandable interrogation, and not contain offensive language. It also allowed questions concerning related matters to be answered together and provided that, if a question seeks factual or statistical information that is already available to Parliament's library, the latter shall inform the member, who may withdraw the question.

It is interesting to note that there is a marked political divergence in the use of this parliamentary tool. During the 2004-09 parliament, the average number of written questions per member was between 25 and 35 for MEPs from the larger Groups (roughly 25 for EPP-ED MEPs, 28 for Socialists and 35 for ALDE), but much higher for those in smaller groups (roughly 76 for the Ind/Dem Group and 87 for GUE) and 146 for the non-attached members.

Commission answers are given by the responsible Commissioner, who has his departmental services to help him prepare. Council answers are given by the rotating President-in-Office, who is not a specialist, and anyway cannot easily take positions on behalf of a body that represents the Member States. The initial draft replies are, indeed, prepared and circulated to all the Permanent Representatives of the Member States and to the Commission for comments or objections (hence the longer deadlines for Council replies). If there are comments, the draft reply is discussed in Coreper. The Commission, too, sends copies of its draft replies to the Permanent Representations when they may be sensitive for national governments, allowing them 48 hours to comment (and a further 48 hours if a national government requests a translation of the draft), but the Commission has the final say over its own answers. The Council President does not.

Besides questions, members may, of course, enter into correspondence with the Commission. There is an ever-growing volume of such correspondence, which can sometimes elicit a quicker reply than a written question. The Commission's internal rules provide for MEPs' letters to receive an acknowledgement immediately. A detailed reply should follow within no more than one month. MEPs also have access to many Commission databases (e.g. on Regional Fund spending).

Reports

The treaties always provided for an annual report of activities to be submitted by the Commission to Parliament for debate. This has now been complemented by further reporting mechanisms for the Commission, as well as for the Council, the Court of Auditors, the Ombudsman and the European Council. These reports provide formal, public, quotable information, the essential raw material for adequate control and scrutiny.

In addition to its annual general report, the Commission now submits (and is often required to by law) to Parliament a very wide variety of regular reports, such as:

- monthly reports on the implementation of the budget (introduced in 1988 as a result of Parliament's pressure to limit agricultural spending, but of more general use monitoring expenditure);
- an annual report on the application of Union law;
- an annual report on competition policy;
- an annual report on the agricultural situation in the Community;
- an annual report on social developments within the Community;
- an annual report on the functioning of the internal market;
- an annual report on the application of the principle of subsidiarity ("better lawmaking");
- an annual report on research and technological development activities;
- a three-yearly report on the application of the citizenship provisions of the treaty;
- a three-yearly report on economic and social cohesion (and use of structural funds).
- an annual statement on the euro area

Besides annual and periodic reports, the Commission often produces communications on the situation in particular sectors, follow-up reports on how a specific piece of legislation is working, etc. Such communications are often called for in the relevant legislation, and/or at the specific request of Parliament. They are useful for parliamentary oversight and sometimes give rise to Parliament reports on the same theme.

The other institutions also present a wide variety of reports to Parliament, some of which are provided for in the treaties and others that have developed as a practice over time:

− the European Council of Heads of State or Government presents an annual written report on the progress achieved by the European Union;

− the President of the European Council must, after each of its meetings, present a report to Parliament

− the Council submits an annual communication on foreign policy and an annual report on human rights;

− the Court of Auditors draws up an annual report after the close of each financial year as well as special reports on specific questions, both designed under Article 248 of the treaties to assist the Parliament and the Council to exercise their powers of control over the implementation of the budget. The annual report constitutes the first stage of the budgetary discharge procedure (see below);

− the President of the European Central Bank is required under the treaty to present an annual report to Parliament.

− the Ombudsman must present an annual report on the outcome of his inquiries.

Parliament studies, STOA and external research

Parliament does not wish to depend entirely for information on the very executive it is supposed to control. Its own services therefore produce background briefings and notes on a broad range of issues. It can draw on a network of researchers in parliaments across Europe, known as the European Centre for Parliamentary Research and Documentation (see Chapter 16). It also commissions studies from external organisations such as universities, research institutes, etc, as well as some EU agencies, such as the European Food Safety Authority. It has provided a substantial budget for committees to commission external expertise. However, it cannot easily match the Commission and national governments in terms of providing an alternative, but equally detailed, viewpoint on controversial complex subjects.

In the scientific field, Parliament decided to address this weakness by establishing in 1987 a unit known as the office for "Scientific and Technical Options Assessment" (STOA). This office, supervised by a panel of MEPs, is designed to help committees and MEPs who increasingly find themselves having to take positions on matters with a scientific or technological component. It was an attempt to respond to the rise in public interest in the social, cultural and political consequences of the application of new technologies. STOA maintains a network of contacts with university departments, research institutes and others. Consultation takes the form of commissions for studies, which are remunerated, and invitations to submit evidence, which are not. It has, therefore, a vocation similar to that of the POST (Parliamentary Office of Science and Technology) in the UK Parliament and the Office Parlémentaire des Choix Scientifiques et Techniques (OPECST) in the French National Assembly. Both of these were established after STOA, but like it, took their inspiration from the now defunct Office of Technical Assessment (OTA) attached to the US Congress.

A permanent staff of three administrators working in Brussels carries out STOA's programme. Additionally, visiting unpaid researchers and scholars work with the permanent staff on the basis of 5 month scientific scholarships (known as Ramon y Cajal scholarships). Hence the work has consisted essentially of managing an external research budget, in contrast, for example, with POST which generally produces studies in-house using its own small but expert staff.

Nevertheless, STOA has produced a number of reports, for example on thermonuclear fusion, BSE, and the ECHELON international telecommunications surveillance system, which have attracted widespread attention. Indeed the last of these reports prompted Parliament to set up a temporary committee on the matter.

STOA now seeks to concentrate its work on larger-scale and longer-term projects of significance for several parliamentary committees, or indeed for Parliament as a whole, such as the implications of biotechnology or nanotechnologies or possible technology solutions to problems of climate change. While it may do some shorter briefings as well, these are more likely to be produced by Parliament's policy departments, or, when there is no in-house expertise, within the context of individual EP committees' budgets for external expertise (see below).

Scrutiny in committees

We saw in Chapter 7 how committees are used for the oversight of Commission departments and for cross-examining both Commissioners and civil servants, and (above) how some have a quasi-formal question time at committee level. Other ways and means include follow-up reports on the implementation of specific items of EU legislation (such as the nitrates and habitats directives), or even highlighting and monitoring the payment of fines by Member States (Greece's fine by the Court for non-compliance with EU environmental law as a result of long-term dumping of waste in the Kouropitos Gorge was a standing item on the Environment Committee's agenda for several months until it was paid and the dump closed). The Environment Committee uses part of its committee question time to the Commission exclusively on problems of implementation of EU directives. Questions of implementation of the EU habitats directive have proved particularly frequent, for instance about the Spanish national water plan and the Odelouca Dam in Portugal.

Despite constraints, such as other demands on committee time, the further development of committee scrutiny of the Commission is likely to become a more important part of the Parliament's overall activities, and new methods are likely to develop. Perhaps the most important aspect will concern the scrutiny of the use of implementing powers and of delegated legislative powers by the Commission (see below).

Parliament's Economic and Monetary Affairs Committee has established (and maintained) two panels of external experts providing short term briefings and notes in the very technical fields of monetary affairs and financial services. This has been especially useful in the context of the short time limits provided for Parliament to react as a result of the "Lamfalussy Procedure" (see below).

Control of expenditure and the discharge procedure

One of Parliament's strongest tools for exercising scrutiny and control over the Commission and sometimes other institutions is its budgetary powers, both during the adoption of the budget (such as by freezing items in the budget and only releasing them when certain conditions have been met) or through its power to grant annual discharge to the Commission (and other institutions) for their execution of the budget. These powers are described in Chapter 13.

Scrutiny of delegated legislation and implementing measures

It is, of course, commonplace for legislatures to confer secondary powers on the executive. Just as national legislation often empowers the government to adopt secondary legislation in the form of "statutory instruments" (UK) or "decrees" (several continental countries), so European legislation frequently gives the Commission the right to adopt implementing measures, or to adapt legislation to technical progress, through Commission regulations, directives or decisions.

For example, when the Union adopts a directive on common rules for the single market, for, say, authorising food additives or labelling dangerous chemicals, it is often up to the Commission (subject to the rules and procedures described below) to decide subsequently which new additives can be approved or which new chemicals fall under a particular category for labelling purposes. Clearly, such measures can be controversial and major commercial interests are often at stake.

The Lisbon treaty provides for the possibility of legislative acts to delegate powers to the Commission enabling it to adopt further "acts of general application to supplement or amend certain non-essential elements of the legislative act" (Article 290 TFEU), known as delegated acts, or to "confer implementing powers on the Commission" (Article 291), known as implementing acts, the latter being for measures that are, presumably, not of general application (such as individual decisions). In the case of the former, the legislation may provide for Parliament (or Council) to veto a Commission act or even recall the delegation of powers. Control mechanisms in the case of the latter were left by the treaty to be decided by a subsequent regulation, eventually adopted by Parliament and Council in December 2010. This is based on an adaptation of the pre-existing and controversial "comitology" system that had evolved over the years and is described below, culminating in the post-Lisbon system.

The emergence of "comitology"

Prior to the Lisbon Treaty, such delegation of powers was not divided explicitly into two categories, but was based on an article of the EC treaty (Article 145, later re-numbered 202) that gave Council the right to delegate implementing powers to the Commission, but allowed it to determine the "conditions" for the exercise of such powers. The practice grew up over the years, initially on an ad hoc basis, but codified by a Council decision in 1987, to oblige the Commission to work with committees of national representatives at civil servant level, with such committees sometimes having the power to block a Commission decision and refer the matter to the Council. Such was the variety of committees and procedures set up over the years that the term "comitology" was coined to describe it.

In 1987, as a result of a requirement of the Single European Act, the Council adopted an overall, codified system for the exercise of implementing powers by the Commission. It established three main types of procedure, known informally (later formally) as:
– *Advisory Committees* (where the Commission must simply ask for an opinion and take account of it)
– *Management Committees* (where a qualified majority in the committee can oppose a decision and thereby refer it to Council)
– *Regulatory Committees* (where the Commission needs the support of a qualified majority, failing which the matter is referred to Council)

When a measure was referred to Council, the latter had a period, normally of three months, to take a decision, failing which the Commission could proceed with its decision (except under a "variant B" of the Regulatory procedure where the Council could, by a simple majority, continue to block the Commission even when it could not agree on an alternative measure).

Parliament objected to these arrangements for three main reasons:
– Only committees appointed by Council (or, technically, Member States) could scrutinise Commission decisions and refer them to the legislative authority; Parliament was given no such right despite the fact that the Commission is, under the treaty, responsible to Parliament (indeed, the 1987 Council decision did not even provide for Parliament to be informed about the Commission's proposals);
– Decisions that were blocked were referred back only to one branch of the legislative authority, namely to Council alone and not to Parliament.
– The whole system, with hundreds of committees, was complex and lacked transparency, with little information provided about comitology meetings.

For two decades, Parliament pressed for reform to this system, gradually achieving it step by step. It was a long and arduous battle.

Initially, Parliament attempted to challenge the 1987 decision in the Court of Justice, but the Court ruled that Parliament did not (then) have the right to bring this type of case, so the substance was not considered.

Parliament did obtain an agreement with the Commission in 1988 to send it draft implementing measures at the same time as they were forwarded to the relevant comitology committee. This was known as the Plumb-Delors procedure after the then Presidents of the Parliament and Commission who signed the agreement. It gave the Parliament the chance, even without formal powers, to take up matters coming up for decision, something it did, for example, in a celebrated case concerning infant formula milk. (A Commission measure to implement a directive on foods for particular nutritional uses, where Parliament was keen to apply WHO principles that manufacturers should not be able to distribute free samples to young mothers without any independent medical advice, and that advertising of such products should be limited to medical journals – Parliament eventually badgering the Commission into submission.) But, in general, the system did not work well. Whether because of the exceptions in the Plumb-Delors procedure (it did not apply to "routine management documents with a limited period of validity and documents whose adoption was complicated by considerations of secrecy or urgency"), or because of ignorance of the procedure in some of the Commission services concerned, many draft implementing measures were not forwarded to the Parliament. Moreover, there was often little time available for Parliament to react. When it wished to do so, it lacked any formal powers.

The "Modus Vivendi" of December 1994

With the entry into force of Maastricht, Parliament was in a stronger position politically to argue its case with Council as the two institutions from then on sometimes jointly adopted legislation, including any provisions for implementing powers.

Parliament maintained that a new system must be agreed such that Council and Parliament not only jointly delegate but also jointly scrutinise and, if necessary, call back, implementing decisions. It put forward a proposal to this effect in December 1993 (De Giovanni Report). The Commission responded with a proposal for an Inter-institutional Agreement along similar lines. The Council, however, continued to claim that co-decision acts were still acts of the Council, and that the 1987 decision was, therefore, fully applicable.

In the absence of agreement, disputes between Parliament and Council over comitology became a feature of most of the first co-decision procedures. Attempts to find ad hoc solutions (for instance, by deleting all comitology provisions) were not always successful and in one case (ONP voice telephony) the newly re-elected Parliament in July 1994 rejected the legislation entirely over the issue of comitology.

Fears of legislative gridlock meant that serious inter-institutional talks over comitology finally took place in the autumn of 1994. The positions of the Parliament and the Council remained far apart, however. In the end, it was agreed that, pending examination of the matter in the forthcoming (Amsterdam treaty) IGC, a temporary truce would be called. The consequent "Modus Vivendi" provided that Parliament would receive all draft implementing measures for general application and the timetables relating to their adoption. The Commission would be obliged to "take account to the greatest extent possible" of the views of the Parliament and to inform Parliament of how it had done so. Where a matter was referred to Council as a result of the deliberations of a comitology-type committee, the Commission would brief Parliament's committee. Council could only adopt a measure after having informed Parliament and given it a reasonable deadline to give its opinion. If Parliament's opinion was negative, an attempt would be made "within the appropriate framework" to find "a solution". What that framework might be was not defined.

Although it was a step forward, the Modus Vivendi did not fully meet Parliament's concerns, and did not prevent further disputes over comitology in co-decision legislation. In 1998, for example, a proposed directive establishing a Securities Committee fell when negotiations between Parliament and Council broke down over the comitology arrangements.

Besides these agreements of general application there were a number of ad hoc sectoral agreements. In July 1993 a code of conduct was negotiated on the implementation of structural policies by the Commission (the so-called Klepsch-Millan agreement), replaced by a new agreement (the Gil Robles-Santer agreement) in May 1999. These codes contained provisions for informing and involving the Parliament on the structural and cohesion fund implementing measures. A Samland-Williamson agreement was reached in 1996 between the then chair of the Parliament's Budgets Committee, and the then Secretary-General of the Commission. The Parliament had been using its budgetary powers to obtain concessions in the field of comitology (including temporary blocking of the funds for comitology committee meetings). The new agreement went further than the others in certain important aspects. In particular, its last indent stated that "if the Parliament, or a parliamentary committee, wishes to attend the discussion on certain items on the agenda of a committee, the chair will put the request to the committee. If the committee does not accept the request, the chair must duly justify the decision". In practice this latter procedure was never used because of systematic objections from the representatives of certain Member States.

The reform of 28 June 1999

The 1994 Modus Vivendi had referred comitology to the 1996-97 Amsterdam IGC (see Chapter 18), but all the IGC managed was to invite the Commission to put forward a new proposal to replace the still contentious 1987 Decision. Parliament was not satisfied with the ensuing Commission text, and called for major amendments. After lengthy discussions, a new Council Decision (1999/468/EC) was adopted in June 1999.

The new decision went further than its predecessor. It established criteria for the choice of a particular type of committee procedure, helpful in preventing undue recourse to the regulatory committee procedure (indeed, on this basis, the Court subsequently annulled legislation imposing a regulatory committee – case C-378/00, January 2003). It removed a "Variant B" of the Regulatory Committee procedure which had allowed the Council to block measures by a simple majority even if it could not agree an alternative: this would now only be possible by qualified majority. And although it did not give Parliament the full equality with Council that it had sought as regards scrutiny of implementing measures, it did reinforce the Parliament's right to receive information and give its views. It provided for

Parliament to "receive agendas for committee meetings, draft measures submitted to the committees for the implementation of instruments adopted by co-decision, and the results of voting and summary records of the meetings and lists of the authorities and organisations to which the persons designated by the Member States to represent them belong. The EP shall also be kept informed whenever the Commission transmits to the Council measures or proposals for measures to be taken" (Art 7.3). The right of Parliament to receive information on committee meetings thus applied in all circumstances, but the right to receive the draft implementing measures themselves is specified only as regards measures implementing co-decision legislation. For other measures, Parliament had to specifically request the relevant documents.

It also created a right (Art 8) (usually known by the French term of *droit de regard*) for Parliament to request re-examination of a draft implementing measure, but only where it is implementing co-decision legislation, and only when Parliament considered that such a measure "would exceed the implementing powers provided for in the basic instrument." In other words, Parliament could formally contest the decision as *ultra vires*, but not if it simply disliked the substance of the measure.

Parliament accepted that the new decision represented a step forward as regards its rights to full information, simplifying comitology procedures, making them more transparent and limiting the rights of Council to block an implementing measure when it could not agree on an alternative. However, the restriction of Parliament's right to formally challenge an implementing measure to those cases where it considered the measure to be *ultra vires*, was considered unsatisfactory – after all, Parliament could always go to Court if such were the case. An explicitly recognised right for Parliament to consider and object to (or "call back") the substance of a measure was still missing.

Practical application of the decision was by means of an agreement reached on 17 February 2000 between the Parliament and the Commission, an important feature of which was that the Parliament was normally given a period of one month to comment on a draft implementing measure that falls under the scope of Article 8 of the decision. Draft measures were to be sent electronically and referred to the relevant parliamentary committee for further scrutiny. All measures forwarded to Parliament have since then been made available in a register that, since December 2003, is accessible to the public on the Europa Internet server.

In the 2002 revision of Parliament's Rules of Procedure, the rule concerning comitology was re-written to better reflect the EP's new rights. The revised rule permitted a decision to be delegated to the EP's responsible committee when there is insufficient time to raise it at plenary level, and also allowed resolutions to be tabled not only when the EP seeks to exercise its formal *droit de regard*, but also when it has concerns about matters of substance. If Parliament objects to the measure, the President must request the Commission to withdraw or amend the measure or submit a proposal under the appropriate legislative procedure. It was first used in September 2002 when a resolution was tabled by the Environment Committee, opposing the Commission's proposed measure to postpone the coming into force of a ban on animal testing in an EU cosmetics directive.

The "Lamfalussy procedure"

In 2001, there was much discussion in the EU of how to deal with financial services legislation: complex and specialised rules requiring frequent updating and adaptation. A report commissioned from an expert group of "wise persons" chaired by Baron Lamfalussy, former President of the European Monetary Institute (forerunner of the Central Bank), concluded that the full legislative procedure would be too cumbersome for the regular speedy updating of such legislation. It suggested that, once the basic principles were adopted by co-decision, substantial implementing powers should be delegated to the Commission, working under comitology procedures with specialist regulatory and advisory committees.

This proved controversial within the Council, where some Member States were unwilling to delegate such substantial powers, now that comitology procedures no longer made it so easy to block the Commission entirely. They only agreed to do so when the Commission undertook, at the Stockholm European Council in March 2001, that it "would not act against the prevailing view within Council".

Similarly, Parliament was reluctant to delegate such substantial powers unless it obtained a right to call them back if it were dissatisfied: the *droit de regard* was not sufficient. Parliament insisted on being treated in an equivalent way to the Council.

This led to further inter-institutional negotiations which resulted, in February 2002, in a formal undertaking from the Commission, read out to Parliament by President Prodi and recorded in the minutes, whereby the Commission accepted that:

- in this field, Parliament's period to examine the draft implementing measures should be three months instead of one month;
- the Commission will take "utmost account" of Parliament's position (i.e. on the substance) and (also) any resolution that the Commission had exceeded the powers granted – for the first time acknowledging that Parliament had a formal role on the substance and not just on the scope as laid down in the 1999 *droit de regard*; and,
- that Parliament could incorporate a "sunset clause" in the legislation such that the delegation of implementing powers ceases after four years, unless renewed by Parliament and Council, thereby giving Parliament a guarantee that if it were not satisfied with the operation of this procedure, it could refuse to renew it.

More generally, the Commission stated that it now accepted that the Council and Parliament "should have an equal role in controlling the way the Commission carries out this executive role" and that it would "endeavour that the Parliament benefits from equal treatment" with the Council.

Operation of the 1999 decision

Following these agreements, a large number of implementing measures began to flow to the Parliament. In 2002, for example, 118 draft or finalised implementing measures were submitted to the Environment Committee alone but by 2004-5 this already high total had risen further, and there were no less than 235 transmissions to the same committee between 1 September 2004 and 1 March 2005.

None the less, Parliament's committees did not challenge many implementing measures. The nature of Parliament's scrutiny is a safeguard, able to challenge the odd objectionable decision, rather than trying to take over implementing decisions itself.

The cases raised tended to concern the substance of a specific measure, rather than because they triggered Parliament's formal *droit de regard* by exceeding the Commission's powers. Thus, concerns were raised about dioxin levels in Baltic Sea fish, BSE and animal nutrition (the feeding of fishmeal to ruminants), in which the Parliament called on the Commission to withdraw its proposal. Sometimes, the mere threat of a parliamentary resolution on a comitology issue appeared to lead to a re-assessment of the proposed measure within the Commission (e.g. in the context of animal testing in cosmetics).

But there were problems with the application of the agreed procedures. In February 2005 the Environment Committee discovered that a considerable number of comitology texts were either not being transmitted to the Parliament at all, or were being transmitted in the wrong context or in an incomplete way. In one case a measure not submitted to the Parliament had been formally adopted and published in the Official Journal and the Commission had to withdraw the adopted measure and to submit a new one with full respect of Parliament's rights. The problems seemed not to be the result of deliberate action, but still posed important questions about the procedures that had been developed. It also showed the importance both of re-evaluating the existing system, and coming up with a more definitive solution as regards the EP's role.

The 2006 breakthrough: the regulatory procedure with scrutiny

As discussions on a proposed new EU Constitution got underway, Parliament put forward a draft providing that: "implementing measures for which responsibility is conferred on the Commission should be forwarded to the Council and to the European Parliament. Should the Council, acting by a qualified majority, or Parliament, acting by a majority of its Members, object within three months to an implementing measure, then the measure in question would be the subject of a legislative procedure (co-decision) to confirm, amend or repeal the measure, unless the Commission withdraws it." (Bourlanges Report, A5-0425/2002, Dec. 2002). At the same time, Parliament accepted that a distinction could be drawn between measures of general scope that implement aspects of the basic legislation or adapt it, (i.e. what could be called delegated legislation), which would be subject to this new procedure, and measures that only have an individual scope, or concern procedural or administrative arrangements, which would be subject to call-back by neither Council nor Parliament.

The Commission, now seemingly very close to Parliament's position, put forward a proposal in December 2002 to amend the 1999 Council decision. Making the same distinction as Parliament between different categories of measure, it proposed, for measures of general scope, to revise the regulatory procedure by introducing two distinct phases. In the initial "executive"

phase, the Commission would consult a committee of Member State representatives. It would then finalise its draft and send it, in the second "control"
phase, to the European Parliament and the Council. Either institution would
be able, within a set deadline, to express opposition to it, in which case the
Commission would have to either submit a legislative proposal or proceed
to adopt the implementing measure, "possibly" amended in the light of the
positions of Parliament and the Council. An urgency procedure would
allow the implementing measures to provisionally enter into force before
the legislator's controls take place. For administrative, procedural measures,
it proposed that these be subject only to an advisory committee procedure,
with neither Council nor Parliament having a call-back right. The management committee procedure would disappear.

The proposal fulfilled the requirement that Council and Parliament be
equal partners in overseeing Commission implementing powers. It took up
Parliament's precise formula of allowing Council, by a qualified majority, or
Parliament, by a majority of its members, to object to an implementing measure within a deadline (albeit of a maximum two instead of three months). It
recognised that Parliament may have a say on the substance of the draft and
not just a right to object that the measure exceeds the powers delegated.
However, the use of the word "possibly" in defining the Commission's
response to a rejection of an implementing measure seriously undermined the
significance of such rejection.

Parliament (Corbett Report, A5-266/2003) approved this new Commission
proposal, subject to changes to clarify that, in the event of rejection by
Parliament or Council, the Commission had to (deleting the word "possibly")
either amend it, withdraw it, or submit a legislative proposal to Parliament
and Council. After lengthy negotiations with Corbett, the Commission
accepted these amendments, leaving the two institutions, at last, supporting
the same basis for a definitive compromise solution to the comitology issue.

This seemed to have an impact on the Convention drafting a new constitution for the EU. It prepared a draft, finally agreed by all Member State governments in the subsequent IGC (and retrieved later for the Lisbon treaty) that
was based on the Parliament – Commission deal. It provided for two categories of Commission decision. Under the first, called "delegated regulations",
both Parliament (by a majority of its members) and Council (by a qualified
majority) would have the right to object to implementing measures, thereby
blocking them. Furthermore, either institution could revoke the delegation of
powers to the Commission at any time. Under the second category, "implementing acts", it was provided simply that a future law, to be approved under
co-decision, would lay down in advance the mechanisms for control.

However, the rejection of the constitutional treaty in referenda in France
and the Netherlands in May-June 2005 meant that the problem of comitology
remained unresolved, whilst problems and conflicts surrounding it continued unabated. In the autumn of 2005, under a UK presidency initiative, suggested by the Parliament's British rapporteur, Council agreed to negotiate
with Parliament on a solution to the comitology problem on the basis of the
Commission's revised 2002 proposal. Parliament appointed Richard Corbett,
the rapporteur (PES) and Joseph Daul, the chair of the Conference of Committee Chairs (EPP-ED) as its negotiators. After seven months of bargaining
with the Council, terminating under the Austrian Presidency which suc-

ceeded the UK Presidency, an agreement was reached which represented the biggest breakthrough for Parliament ever achieved in this field and the only major increase in Parliament's powers during the 2004-09 parliament.

The new system created a new comitology procedure, the regulatory procedure with scrutiny (RPS), giving Parliament a right to block each individual Commission/comitology decision on delegated legislation. It gave Parliament a period (normally of three months) to examine proposals that had been through a comitology committee. If Parliament objected to a proposal, then the Commission (or the Council) could not enact it. Instead, the Commission could either make a new proposal, taking account of the reasons for the objection (in which case the clock is re-set and Parliament can again block), or it could propose new legislation under the co-decision procedure.

The system applied whenever Council and Parliament, under co-decision on the basic legislation, chose to confer powers on the Commission to adopt implementing measures of general scope that could be described as quasi-legislative in nature (delegated legislation), but not to administrative or purely executive decisions. Nor did it apply when the original legislation was not co-decision legislation.

The three month deadline runs from the moment Parliament receives the text in all the official languages. As it anyway receives texts beforehand in some languages, this means that in practice the deadline is longer.

The agreement considerably strengthened Parliament's position. Previously, it could comment, discuss and debate measures that go through the comitology system, but, at the end of the day, it could be ignored. Even under the Lamfalussy procedures for delegated legislation on financial services, where the Commission had conceded enhanced rights of information and discussion with Parliament, the bottom line was that Parliament could be overridden. Under the RPS procedure, a parliamentary objection could not be overruled.

Over 500 measures were considered under the RPS procedure between 2008 and late 2010. Only three were blocked by the Parliament, showing that the procedure is a safeguard, not an attempt by Parliament to systematically intervene in such decisions. For example, in May 2010, Parliament voted by 370 votes to 261 (just one vote more than the 369 required for a majority of members) to veto a proposal to authorize the use of thrombin ("meat glue") in food. This was initiated by Åsa Westlund MEP (Sweden, S&D) in the Committee for the Environment, Public Health and Food Safety, which had backed her objection (31 votes to 21) and submitted it to plenary. An earlier example was in October 2008, when a draft measure on airport body scanners was vetoed by Parliament.

In some cases, Parliament used its new powers to win concessions from the Commission without formally blocking the measure. An example of this was on a proposal on test methods submitted by the Commission pursuant to the REACH Regulation. The Environment Committee had threatened to reject this, and there were then negotiations with the Commission, whose outcome was then enshrined in a Parliament resolution adopted in May 2008.

Delegated and implementing acts under the Lisbon Treaty

As pointed out at the start of this section, a new system of delegated and implementing acts, initially put forward in the draft Constitution, was then taken up in the Lisbon Treaty (Articles 290 and 291 TFEU). As with the RPS procedure, it makes a distinction between delegated acts (under the direct control of the co-legislators, but now without a network of comitology committees) and implementing acts.

Article 290 TFEU covers the new category of "**Delegated Acts**" whereby "the power to adopt non-legislative acts of general application to supplement or amend certain non-essential elements of the legislative act" – a definition equivalent to that used for the above mentioned RPS procedure – might be delegated to the Commission. The European Parliament and the Council would be on an equal footing to express an objection to (and thereby block) any such act within a time limit set down in the legislation, or even decide to revoke the delegation of powers entirely. Parliament would have to act by a majority of its component members, and the Council by a qualified majority. As a general rule, delegated acts cover matters that have fallen under the RPS Procedure set out above. The Commission would be free to consult experts as it wished, but would retain responsibility for the decision, subject to Parliament's and Council's control.

Article 291 TFEU covers "**Implementing Acts**". It lays down that "Member States shall adopt all measures of national law necessary to implement legally binding Union acts but that those acts shall confer implementing powers on the Commission (or in certain limited cases on the Council) in those cases "where uniform conditions for implementing legally binding Union acts are needed". No explicit role is laid down for the Parliament pursuant to this article, apart from enabling it to decide by co-decision with the Council on "the rules and general principles concerning mechanisms for control by Member States of the Commission's exercise of implementing powers." Reaching agreement on this proved difficult, with the final vote only taking place in December 2010.

Under this new regulation for implementing acts, unlike for delegated acts, the old comitology procedures are kept but re-packaged. The previous advisory, management and regulatory procedures are replaced by two such procedures, an advisory and examination procedure. The latter is, in fact, a combination of the former management and regulatory committee procedures, so that, in some cases, the Commission may act if there is no qualified majority against it in the committee, in some cases if there is not a simple majority against it, and in other cases (notably measures concerning taxation, financial services, the protection of health, or safety of humans and animals or plants) it requires the approval of a qualified majority. Any measure blocked at the committee stage is referred, not to the Council as before, but to an Appeals Committee, also composed of Member State's representatives, which must seek to "to find solutions which command the widest possible support". If there is no consensus, then the Appeals Committee votes. If it approves the Commission proposal, then the latter must adopt it; if it rejects it, the measure falls, and if it cannot reach a qualified majority either way, the matter is left to the Commission's discretion (with some exceptions in the fields of trade). There are provisions for urgent procedures, notably whereby Commission decisions enter into force pending confirmation under these procedures.

The Parliament's role here remains a weaker one, but it would still have the old *droit de regard*, being given the possibility (as would the Council) to indicate to the Commission that it considers that a draft implementing meas-ure exceeds the implementing measures provided for in the basic act. In such cases the Commission is to review the draft measure, and must inform the co-legislators as to whether it intends to maintain, amend or withdraw the draft implementing act. An accompanying declaration by the Commission states that its review will take place "immediately", and that before it takes its final decision, it will inform the Parliament and the Council of the action it intends to take and of its reasons for doing so. In addition to this, the reg-ulation contains elements designed to help Parliament (and the public) to be informed of what is going on, including, as before, a public register of infor-mation on committee proceedings containing, inter alia, a list of committees and their composition, their agendas, the drafts transmitted to them, the summary records of their proceedings and the results of any votes. The reg-ulation also provides for a review clause after 5 years.

The distinction between the two new categories of delegated and imple-menting act is by no means obvious and will remain controversial, not least because the choice of act in individual cases has very different implications for the respective powers of the Parliament, Council and Commission. Parliament is now given a powerful role as regards delegated acts, but much less so as regards implementing acts, which will still come under a modified version of the old comitology system. In its role as a co-legislator Parliament will thus be confronted by hard choices as to what to delegate, and what not, which act should apply, and how much importance it should attach to these points in its legislative negotiations with the Council and Commission. It is likely to try to get as many measures as it can classed as delegated acts and not as implementing acts. If implementing measures are used, the Parliament will also have to decide how to exert its more informal scrutiny role. In tack-ling these issues, it will be faced by a considerable organisational challenge.

Consequently, the transition arrangements to the new regime of dele-gated and implementing acts is also difficult. It involves examination of existing legislation to determine, on a case-by-case basis, which procedure will now apply. It entails alignment to the new system of delegated acts, not only from the regulatory procedure with scrutiny, (including cases where the process of aligning measures from the old comitology to the RPS had not yet been completed), but also from other cases, not always a matter of evi-dent agreement between the institutions.

It is still early days to judge the new Lisbon Treaty system of delegated and implementing acts, but it is already becoming clear that the objective of replacing the old and complex comitology provisions by a new and simpler system is not proving easy to achieve, and that a number of the criticised features of the old system remain, albeit restricted to the category of imple-menting acts.

Committees of inquiry

Committees of inquiry can enable a wide-ranging investigation of a partic-ular issue, putting the public spotlight on it and placing it on the political agenda. They can also be used for investigatory purposes to look at cases of maladministration in the institutions or by Member States. Parliament used them for both purposes until 1991, when the Maastricht Treaty confined them to the latter purpose.

Parliament first established a committee of inquiry soon after the first direct elections in 1979 when it set up one on the **situation of women in Europe**. This committee led to the creation of a permanent committee on women's affairs – the only instance of an inquiry committee being converted into a permanent committee.

Apart from this case, the following committees were set up in the ten-year period before the entry into force of the Maastricht Treaty:

Committee of inquiry into the **treatment of toxic and dangerous substances** by the European Community and its Member States (1983–84): this committee looked in particular at the trans-frontier shipment of dangerous waste, in the light notably of the scandal surrounding the waste from the Seveso accident. Its report stimulated new legislation in this field. This committee also set the precedent of all national governments except one agreeing to send officials to testify before the committee, despite the lack of any legal requirement to do so.

Committee of inquiry into the **rise of fascism and racism in Europe**: this was set up following the 1984 European elections and the entry into the Parliament of sufficient members to form a "European Right" Group led by Jean-Marie Le Pen. It led to the adoption by Council, Commission, Parliament and the Member States of the Joint Declaration against racism and xenophobia on 11 June 1986.

Committee of inquiry into the **drugs problem** (1985–86): this compared the methods used by Member States to deal with this problem and examined the problem of extradition of drug traffickers. It also looked at the problems facing developing countries where drugs are produced. It stimulated the interest of Member States to co-operate in this field, eventually given a legal base in the Maastricht Treaty.

Committee of inquiry on **agricultural stocks** (1986–87): this investigated the causes and ramifications of agricultural overstocks at a time when debate on the reform of the CAP was at a crucial juncture. Its conclusions contributed to shaping the reformed CAP and the de-stocking policy.

Committee of inquiry on the **handling of nuclear materials** (1988): this investigated the Mol/Transnuclear scandal. Its investigations concluded that Community officials were not involved in the scandal, but that there were lacunae in Community regulations pertaining to the trans-frontier shipment of nuclear waste. This inquiry initially had some difficulties in obtaining testimony from some officials in the Belgian government. As a result, the problem of inquiry committees was discussed in Council, which adopted a statement emphasising that, while there was no legal obligation on national authorities to attend Parliament's hearings or inquiries, they were invited nonetheless to do so on a voluntary basis, bearing in mind the duty of mutual cooperation enshrined in the treaties. Council accepted that invitations to national authorities from the Parliament could be sent through Council.

Committee of inquiry on **hormones in meat** (1988–89): this investigated another important aspect of Community policy and one which had recently sparked off a trade war with the USA. It endorsed the continuation of the Community's restrictive policy on this matter.

Committee of inquiry on **the application of the joint declaration against racism and fascism** (1989–90): a follow-up to the previous committee of inquiry on the same subject attempting to investigate what progress had been made, and making suggestions for further action.

Committee of inquiry on **trans-frontier crime linked to drug trafficking** (1991): compared the divergent legal situations and general approaches of governments to trans-frontier criminality and drug trafficking and made proposals for concerted European action, at a time when the Member States were discussing new forms of such cooperation which were ultimately included in the Treaty of Maastricht. Although a broad majority agreed on the main recommendations, the committee split almost equally on the question of whether possession of soft drugs should be de-criminalised. Thus, a minority report was also presented (and signed by the rapporteur who had been outvoted on this point).

The setting up of committees of inquiry was given formal recognition in the Treaty of Maastricht, but the Treaty defined their scope more narrowly than the Parliament had done since 1979. A new article (now Article 226 TFEU) was created, specifying that the Parliament has the right to set up such committees to investigate "alleged contraventions or maladministration in the implementation of Community law, except where the alleged facts are being examined before a court and while the case is still subject to legal proceedings".

This restriction on the scope has meant that subjects such as the **Echelon electronic surveillance system, foot & mouth disease, human genetics, maritime safety and CIA rendition flights** – all of which might have been dealt with by committees of inquiry before Maastricht, were instead dealt with through temporary committees (see Chapter 7).

The treaty article also specified that detailed provisions governing the exercise of the right of inquiry were to be determined by common accord of the Parliament, the Council and the Commission. After hard negotiations between the three institutions, an agreement was reached in April 1995, paving the way for the Parliament to set up committees of inquiry governed by this new inter-institutional agreement. The agreement lays down the ground rules. It does not give the Parliament a general power of summons but does provide a mechanism for it to invite EU and national officials as well as other individuals to appear before it.

Under the treaty such committees can be requested by a quarter of Parliament's members but such a request is not enough by itself to establish a committee of inquiry. (This contrasts with the situation in, say, the German Bundestag where it is obligatory to set up a committee if a quarter of members request it.) Once a proposal has been put forward, it has to win majority backing in the Conference of Presidents, which then submits a proposal for approval by the plenary. Without such majority support, no proposal can be put to the plenary regarding the committee's establishment and composition.

During 1995 a minority suggested that French nuclear tests in the Pacific should be the subject of the first committee of inquiry under the new treaty article but it was a proposal that did not win majority support. Later in the year, at the December plenary in 1995, the Conference of Presidents supported the creation of a committee of inquiry to examine the **Community**

transit system. Parliament voted in favour and this first committee, made up of 17 full members and 17 substitutes, came together at the beginning of 1996. It was chaired by the British Labour MEP, John Tomlinson, with a British Conservative MEP, Edward Kellett-Bowman acting as rapporteur. It finally adopted its report in February 1997 and presented it to the plenary the following month.

In the meantime, in July 1996, Parliament decided to set up a second committee of inquiry on the **BSE crisis**. This committee was chaired by a German Christian Democrat, Reimer Böge; a Spanish Socialist, Manuel Medina, was rapporteur. It was originally set up for three months but its life was extended by three months, with the result that it was able to adopt its report in advance of the first committee and to present it to plenary one month earlier in February.

In both cases, unlike the practice with standing committees, Parliament is presented with the committee's report as a finalised text that is not further amended in plenary. None the less, there were debates in each case, with votes on a draft recommendation addressed to the Community institutions and the Member States in the case of the transit report, and on a resolution drafted by the Groups for BSE.

The success of these committees was fourfold. First, despite the lack of any sanctions to oblige witnesses to appear, only one person, Douglas Hogg, the British Agriculture Minister, refused to attend, arguing (correctly, in strict legal terms) that he was not under any obligation to come and that his Permanent Secretary could speak on his behalf (though his successor in the subsequent Labour government, Jack Cunningham, reversed this position and agreed to appear). The Transit Committee scored a notable victory in that it persuaded American executives of Philip Morris, Europe, based outside the EU in Switzerland, to come before the committee, though they insisted that the meeting take place behind closed doors.

Second, although there were no sanctions for perjury, both committees went to considerable lengths to ensure that the evidence given by witnesses was widely publicised, with much of the material being put on the Internet site of the Parliament. The Transit Committee sent every witness a copy of their evidence, inviting them to sign it and indicate that it was a true record: all did so, thereby contributing to the credibility of the record.

Third, the work of the committees had a visible impact on the institutions investigated, in particular the Commission. In its resolution of February 1997, Parliament warned the Commission that if the recommendations of the BSE committee were not carried out within a reasonable time and, in any case, no later than November 1997, a motion of censure would be tabled. This led directly to the reinforcement of the Directorate-General for Consumer Affairs and its taking over of responsibility from the Agriculture Directorate-General for seven scientific, veterinary and food committees advising on pubic health.

Fourth, and more generally, the committees served to show that the Parliament could serve as a focus for public concern on issues transcending national boundaries and could organise the collection of evidence from witnesses from across Europe in a way that few, if any, national institutions or parliaments could hope to match.

Despite these successes in improving the scrutiny role of Parliament, many members felt that the powers of these committees remained too weak, in particular in relation to the obligations imposed on witnesses. Hence there was some expectation that the Parliament elected in June 1999 would seek to activate the review clause in Article 6 of the 1995 Inter-institutional Agreement, which specified that "at the request of the European Parliament, the Council or the Commission, the above rules may be revised as from the end of the current term of the European Parliament [i.e., June 1999] in the light of experience". In fact, such a review did not occur until the Lisbon Treaty came into force. It provided for the Parliament to adopt the rules of such committees on its own initiative, provided Council and Commission gave their consent. A corresponding review is now in progress.

Meanwhile, a new committee of inquiry was set up in January 2006 with Mairead McGuinness, an Irish EPP member, in the chair and Diana Wallis, a British Liberal member, as rapporteur. Its task was to examine the financial difficulties of the **Equitable Life Assurance Society**, which had proved unable to honour commitments to policy holders, notably in Britain, Ireland and Germany. It concluded that the EU life insurance legislation was transposed into British law in an unsatisfactory fashion and asked the UK government to devise an appropriate scheme to compensate the victims. It also called for stricter rules on insurance supervision.

Judicial review

Parliament has always operated within a constitutional framework where the European Court of Justice may be called upon to ensure that the different institutions act legally, do not exceed their powers and respect the inter-institutional balance laid down by the treaty. Hence the Parliament is able, under certain circumstances, to turn to the Court to ensure the correct application of the treaties by the other institutions, including defending its own interests. At the same time, its own actions are subject to judicial review by the Court of Justice or, where the complainant is an individual or company, the Court of First Instance (now the General Court).

This was not always as clear as it is now as regards the Parliament. The original EEC Treaty did not expressly confer on Parliament the right to take annulment proceedings against acts of the other institutions, although the 1951 European Coal and Steel Treaty did allow for the possibility that the High Authority (Commission) or the Member States could take such proceedings against acts of Parliament. In its capacity as an "institution", Parliament was nonetheless entitled to take proceedings for the illegal failure of another institution to act, as well as to "intervene" (i.e. present its views to the Court) in annulment cases brought by others, or in other direct actions, and to provide the Court with any information the Court requested in the framework of the preliminary ruling procedure (whereby national courts request rulings from the Court). But in practice, before the first direct elections in 1979, Parliament participated in proceedings before the Court of Justice only once (other than as a defendant in staff cases), and then only by virtue of answering questions from the Court regarding the opening and closure of the annual parliamentary session (Case 101/63).

This limited participation in legal proceedings was to change dramatically after direct elections in 1979. By a quirk of history, the first episode in the long saga by which Parliament sought first to exploit, then to extend, its capacity to initiate judicial review proceedings arose directly as a result of the organisation in 1979 of the first direct elections. At the last session before parliamentary activities were suspended in the run-up to the elections themselves, Parliament decided not to deliver a consultative opinion on a proposed agricultural regulation concerning the artificial sweetener isoglucose; it therefore reminded the Council that if it considered the matter urgent, it (the Council) could invite Parliament to hold an emergency session to adopt the opinion. The Council did not do so, but adopted the regulation instead, merely noting that it had requested Parliament's opinion which had not been delivered. After a certain amount of soul-searching – some members preferred to seek to resolve any difficulties with the other institutions exclusively on the political plane and/or considered submitting to the will of the Court beneath the dignity of the institution – the newly-elected Parliament decided to intervene in proceedings commenced by two private companies to challenge the validity of the regulation, inter alia, because the Council had not waited for Parliament to adopt its opinion.The Court upheld the challenge on this ground alone, in two materially identical judgments in the Isoglucose cases (178 and 179/79). The judgments established three points of fundamental importance:

–   as an "institution", Parliament is entitled to intervene in legal proceedings before the Community court;
–   the Council's obligation to consult Parliament is not a purely formal requirement, as it is the reflection of a fundamental democratic principle that the peoples take part in the exercise of power (see Chapter 12);
–   the Treaties should be interpreted in such a way as to allow the Court to ensure respect for the balance of powers between the institutions laid down in the Treaties.

The second episode in the saga also arose from cases brought by private individuals, and was also connected with parliamentary elections; this time a national political party – the French ecology party Les Verts – objected to the size of its share of the funds Parliament had made available for an information campaign for the 1984 elections. In its legal challenge to the validity of the decision apportioning the funds, it argued that, while the Treaty did not grant the Court jurisdiction to review acts of Parliament, a literal interpretation of the relevant provisions would prevent the Court from carrying out its overriding duty "to ensure the law is observed". With a sharp eye for the main chance, Parliament did not contest this line of argument, which the Court in turn embraced with enthusiasm, declaring grandly that the Community was one based on the rule of law in which neither the Member States nor the institutions could avoid the judicial review of their acts which had legal effects for third parties. The Court first ruled that it could hear the complaint submitted by Les Verts, and then that this was well-founded. A matter of weeks later, it agreed to rule on a second annulment action against Parliament, this time taken by the Council concerning the 1987 budget which Parliament had adopted.

Parliament in turn relied on this extensive interpretation of the relevant jurisdictional clause of the Treaty in two subsequent annulment actions it brought against the Council. In a surprising volte-face, the Court initially refused to admit that Parliament could take such actions (Case 302/87 comitology), but in the second judgment (Case 70/88, Chernobyl) acknowledged that Parliament was indeed entitled to take annulment proceedings in order to defend its prerogatives in the decision-making process. The latter case concerned the choice of the legal basis for legislation, which determines the extent of Parliament's formal input and powers, and the judgment recognised that Parliament could take annulment proceedings to ensure procedures were properly applied and that the Council fully respected Parliament's prerogatives.

Following this judgment, Parliament brought a number of other annulment actions against Council on legislative matters, for example, for failure to consult Parliament (e.g., Lomé convention financial regulation, Case C-316/91), to reconsult Parliament (e.g., harmonisation of vehicle taxes, case C-21/94), to apply the assent procedure (Mauritania fishing agreement, Case C-189/97), and for adopting an implementing measure that went beyond the terms of the original directive (on plant protection products, Case C-303/94). It also took annulment proceedings against the Commission (Case C-156/93), and against both institutions to defend its budgetary prerogatives (Joined Cases C-184/91 and C-248/91).

The Treaty provisions on annulment proceedings were amended by the Maastricht Treaty to incorporate the Court's case-law and thus to allow Parliament to take legal action, though only in order to defend its own prerogatives; the Nice Treaty removed this last restriction. As a result, Parliament may take annulment proceedings without restriction, and may do so, for example, to ensure the protection of fundamental rights in legislation (Case C-540/03). Although this initially did not apply to the area of freedom, security and justice, this restriction was in effect lifted by the Lisbon Treaty. Parliament therefore enjoys the same rights to initiate or participate in legal proceedings before the Union courts as the Council. Although it cannot initiate infringement actions against the Member States, Parliament may intervene in such cases and may be invited by the Court to state its views on general questions of principle which arise in such cases. It may submit observations on requests for preliminary rulings. It may initiate, or submit observations on, requests for the Court's opinion on international agreements the Union intends to conclude with third States.

The different circumstances in which Parliament participates in court proceedings may be seen in Table 45.

Table 45: *Parliament and the Court: examples of proceedings*

(a) Annulment proceedings by Parliament

Case C-166/07 Parliament v Council : choice of the legal basis for legislation on the transfer of waste

Case C-14/06 Parliament v Commission: implementing act outside the scope of the delegation of powers

Case C-189/97 Parliament v Council: applicability of the assent procedure

(b)   Annulment proceedings against Parliament

Case C-217/04 United Kingdom v Parliament and Council: scope of the internal market legal basis
Case C-299/05 Commission v Parliament and Council: validity of social security regulation
Case C-122/04 Commission v Parliament and Council: choice of procedure for the adoption of implementing legislation
Case C-393/07 Italy v Parliament: decision on the election of an MEP
Case T-222/99 Martinez and others v Parliament: application of Parliament's rules of procedure
Case C-308/07 Gorostiaga Atxalandabaso v Parliament: financial rights of MEP

(c)   Action for illegal failure to act

Case 13/83 Parliament v Council: failure to establish a common transport policy
Case C-41/92 Liberal Democrats v Parliament: failure to propose a common electoral procedure

(d)   Action in damages against Parliament

Case T-383/00 Beamglow v Parliament, Council and Commission: damages allegedly caused by the adoption of a regulation on the market in bananas

(e)   Intervention in Preliminary rulings (referrals to the Court from national courts)

Case 149/85 Wybot: duration of the annual parliamentary session
Case C-408/95 Eurotunnel: proper application of the consultation procedure
Case C-479/04 Laserdisken: validity of Parliament and Council directive on copyright

(f)   Opinions of the Court on proposed international agreements

Opinion 2/00: conclusion of the Cartagena Protocol on Biosafety (observations submitted by Parliament)
Opinion 1/04: conclusion of EU/US agreement on passenger name records (Parliament request for an opinion, subsequently withdrawn).

Although Parliament is not a particularly litigious institution, Court action has enabled it to clarify and defend its powers and sometimes to obtain significant progress in advancing its interpretation of the treaties. But in recent years, as predicted in previous editions of this book, Parliament now appears before the Courts primarily as a defendant, as co-decider of legislation that is being challenged. Judicial review will therefore apply ever more to decisions to which Parliament itself has contributed.

Parliament and the application of European law in the Member States

Another indirect way in which Parliament contributes to the correct application of European law is by drawing to the attention of the Commission any infringements (such as non-application or incorrect application of directives) by Member States. Under the treaties, it is up to the Commission to initiate infringement proceedings against Member States (1097 letters of formal notice in 2009) and, if the situation is not remedied, to bring cases before the Court of Justice (134 in 2009), many of which are settled before a Court ruling is given. These procedures are essential in ensuring the homogeneity and primacy of European law in the Member States.

The difficulty for the Commission is in finding out about infringements; it has, after all, no police force or inspectorate at its disposal and has a relatively small staff. It has to rely on complaints from the public. In this respect, Parliament, through its members receiving complaints from constituents and from the petitions it receives, is furnishing an increasing number of complaints to the Commission, particularly in the fields of the environment, internal market, freedom of movement and transport.

Overall assessment

Parliament's powers of scrutiny and control have, like its legislative and budgetary powers, developed both by treaty change and by agreements reached with the other institutions. Its general powers of scrutiny are now similar to those of national parliaments but in the very particular environment of the Union, Parliament is developing its own style of control. As a result it has at its disposal a selection of instruments which increasingly give it the means it needs to oversee executive activity, whatever its source.

16. A political forum and a channel for communication

Another classical parliamentary function performed by the European Parliament is that of a political forum and channel for communication. With its high level of autonomy, it not only undertakes the tasks that the treaties impose upon it but can take a wide range of political initiatives, many of them in response to the concerns of European citizens. It is part of a network of contacts extending well beyond the European institutions. It proclaims a determination to make the European system more accessible and visible to European citizens as part of the effort to improve the legitimacy of the EU. Much of this role is undertaken as part of its legislative, budgetary and scrutiny duties, but many other aspects are particular. This chapter will illustrate this role by looking at the ways in which the Parliament seeks:

– to broaden the agenda of political discussion through debates, resolutions, hearings, activities in relation to human rights and in response to petitions;
– to enhance its network of contacts with other EU institutions as well as with national governments; and
– to ensure a high level of openness and transparency in its work and to increase public awareness of its role in the EU.

Parliament broadening the agenda

Set-piece debates

The political forum role of any Parliament is most clearly seen in its public debates. This is true for all debates, but some set-piece debates give members an opportunity to take a wider view that may not fit easily into the more specialised discussions that we have looked at in previous chapters. Following the adoption of the Lisbon Treaty, the number, range and shape of these debates has significantly changed.

First, the transformation of the post of President of the European Council into a full time and longer term position means that the results of European Councils are no longer presented by the Prime Minister or President of the country holding the Presidency of the Council of Ministers, often just as part of their general report on activities of the Council. Now Parliament receives and debates a presentation from the President of the European Council on the outcome of each meeting, normally now six times per year.

Second, the position of the President of the Commission has also evolved. In September 2010, for the first time, the President made a State of the Union speech outlining the priorities of the Commission for the coming year. On the basis of the Framework Agreement agreed between Parliament and Commission in October 2010 this speech will in future always precede the adoption of the work programme of the Commission, thereby giving the Parliament the opportunity to debate and influence the shaping of the programme.

Third, the Prime Minister or President of the country holding the Council Presidency retains the opportunity in January and July to put forward the "programme" of the Presidency and subsequently to report on the outcome of the six months during which her or his country was responsible for managing the agenda of the Council of Ministers. The exchanges with MEPs that have followed the speeches of Heads of State and Government, a practice initiated by Mrs Thatcher in 1981, have in the past often proved very lively and memorable affairs. It remains to be seen how the practice will evolve, now that the presentations no longer relate to the outcome of European Council meetings, nor to the conduct of foreign policy (a function that now falls to the High Representatives/Vice President of the Commission), but is largely just a report from one branch of the legislature to another.

Resolutions adopted at the Parliament's own initiative

"Own-initiative" reports by parliamentary committees (see Chapters 7 and 12) are often intended to influence specific policy issues under discussion but they can equally be used as part of Parliament's "forum" role to debate common problems facing the Member States, to discuss external issues (foreign policy, human rights, etc.) or to raise subjects in response to public concerns.

Motions for Resolution tabled by individual members only occasionally give rise to a report from a parliamentary committee, but do allow individual MEPs to raise issues. Such motions are translated into all the Union languages and distributed and are therefore useful, even if no follow-up takes place within Parliament, for the individual MEP concerned to demonstrate his/her activities on behalf of constituents, to place a viewpoint on record, to draw attention to a particular problem or to contribute to discussions in other frameworks (and are therefore comparable to early-day motions in the House of Commons).

Another mechanism allowing MEPs to raise issues is Written Declarations. If they are signed by a majority of members of the Parliament, they are forwarded to the institutions named in them, without debate in committee or plenary. Few such declarations used to obtain the requisite number of signatures but there has been a tendency for the number to increase. Thus there were just 13 such declarations adopted in the three legislatures between 1989 and 2004 but during the 2004-09 Parliament alone the figure rose to 37. Recent examples signed by a majority of members concerned the setting up of a European early warning system for paedophiles and sex offenders, establishing a European Year of Combating Violence against Women, the fight against breast cancer in the EU and the transportation of horses for slaughter.

Hearings

Public hearings of expert witnesses or sectoral representatives provide an opportunity to seek independent expertise and advice; to enter into a dialogue with interested parties; to attract media attention to a particular issue; to obtain endorsement from third parties (such as public figures, other institutions or academic bodies) of particular points of view; and/or to provide a platform for groups that may not otherwise have easy access to decision-takers. Some hearings bring together virtually the whole range of companies, trade unions and consumers concerned with a particular industry. This was the case, for example, with the major hearing on the REACH proposals relating to chemicals held in January 2005, which was attended by around 1,000 people. Committees are free, however, to invite less conventional witnesses: those present will not forget the hearing in October 1999 when the Environment Committee invited a Swedish dog with a unique ability to sniff for mercury, a skill it duly demonstrated at the hearing. At a more serious level, hearings can be conducted with remarkable witnesses who are themselves under threat. In November 2007 Hu Jia, a Chinese internet activist, spoke via a conference call to a hearing of the Human Rights sub-committee. As a result, he was arrested and sentenced to three and a half years in prison, thereby being unable to collect the Sakharov prize that he was awarded the following year.

Since the first elections in 1979, Parliament's committees have held an increasing number of hearings every year. In 2010 more than 50 such hearings with outside experts were held. Hearings are almost always conducted in the context of drafting a report, either on behalf of a standing committee or a committee of inquiry. In October 2010, for example, the Employment Committee held such a meeting to examine the results of an impact assessment of the costs and benefits of paternity and maternity leave in advance of the issue being submitted to the plenary. In practice, committees invite outside experts without reference to the Bureau if no expenses are incurred, but request the Bureau's permission beforehand if there are expenses. Since 1995, an annual programme of hearings has been submitted by committees to the Bureau for approval. Each committee may invite up to 16 paid experts per year from outside Brussels but many outsiders prove to be willing to come to put their point of view without payment.

Some committees have experimented with an open hearing format, inviting anyone interested to send in a written contribution and to present it to the committee in a speech of no more than three to five minutes. More commonly, committees establish in advance the experts they wish to invite. The selection is carried out by procedures determined within each committee. In some it is left to the chair, in others the Bureau, and in others again, a meeting of co-ordinators from all the Political Groups decides. A final vote on the choice is sometimes taken in the full meeting. The response of invited experts has generally been good, given that there is no obligation to attend. There is widespread interest in being able to present evidence to the Parliament.

Once the participants are selected they are normally invited to present written evidence, preferably in advance. When they come before the committee, they make an official statement, which is followed by questions from MEPs. The rapporteur is normally given a predominant role in this. The

Anglo-Saxon tradition of "cross-examination" of the witness has developed widely, with members putting questions one-by-one and having the opportunity to ask a supplementary if not satisfied with the answer.

The other institutions attend hearings in the same way as they attend the normal course of committee business. The Commission is frequently called upon to react to views expressed by expert witnesses. Most committees publish a summary of the results of their hearings in the relevant report or in a specific committee document for this purpose. It is unusual to have an *in extenso* report in the style of the House of Lords or the US Congress, the main constraint being the multilingual nature of Parliament's hearings that normally precludes the preparation of verbatim reports on cost grounds. Occasionally a brochure or booklet has been produced, but it has been rare for evidence received to be made available in all languages, owing to the length of time required for translation and printing. One exception was the evidence received by the Committee of Inquiry into the Community Transit Regime which had all sixteen sessions of evidence that it held translated into all languages, published in a separate volume and put on the Internet. Such a solution required a major investment in resources and has not been repeated. Instead, more recently the tendency has been to make a video recording of the proceedings in the original language and to make it available on the web for those unable to attend.

Activities in the field of human rights

Parliament has put considerable effort into being a channel through which questions of human rights can be raised. Besides dealing with general human rights issues, it is one of the few parliaments that carry out casework on individual human rights violations. For many years this work was dealt with by a specific administrative unit but in 2004 it was decided to upgrade the activity by creating a subcommittee for Human Rights inside the Foreign Affairs Committee. During the subsequent legislature consideration was given to converting the subcommittee into a full committee but for the time being it has been agreed to keep the structure established in 2004.

The role of Parliament in this field was traditionally seen as "informal", since it derived mainly from the Parliament's role as a mirror of public opinion rather than from specific legal competences. Today this is no longer the case; revisions of the treaties have created a solid *acquis* in this area.

As discussed in Chapter 12, the treaties give Parliament a right of consent (known prior to Lisbon as "assent") to many kinds of external agreements. Parliament has rarely voted to reject an agreement, but it has often purposely delayed ratification – almost always because of human rights considerations. In the early 1990s, Parliament delayed financial and technical protocols to the agreement with Israel and to an agreement with Syria. It also blocked some financial provisions relating to the Customs Union with Turkey because of reservations about democracy and human rights. And during the 2004-2009 legislature the Conference of Presidents consistently refused to put the adoption of a trade agreement with Turkmenistan on the plenary agenda because of well-documented violations of human rights in the country. Only right at the end of the legislature was it finally decided to approve the agreement.

As a result of Parliament's insistence, the EU's external agreements have, following the fourth Lomé Convention in 1989, always included human rights clauses. Since 1992 (first in agreements with Brazil, the Andean Pact, the Baltic States and Albania) they have generally provided for a clear legal base to suspend the agreement in the event of serious human rights violations. Even if suspension remains an ultimate and rarely used sanction, its implicit threat adds weight to lesser actions, which range from low-level (*démarches*, public criticism) to procedural sanctions (suspension of high-level and ministerial contacts) to financial and economic sanctions. The last have been used, for instance, with reference to Haiti, Zaire, Malawi and Zimbabwe.

Many EU external agreements also provide for inter-parliamentary contacts. As a result Parliament delegations meet regularly with parliamentarians from third countries, and human rights issues are frequently raised. The largest such meeting, the EU-ACP Joint Parliamentary Assembly, has developed a special mechanism for raising individual cases and appointed a Vice President in charge of human rights.

Successive Presidents of Parliament have also taken up individual cases, both directly with high-level visitors and ambassadors, and in correspondence with governments. They have also been in the forefront of the Parliament's efforts to abolish the death penalty, giving particular support to the World Congress against Capital Punishment which has met four times since 2001, most recently in 2010. They have consistently promoted the "World Day Against Capital Punishment", as in October 2010 when President Buzek stated that: "the European Parliament strongly opposes the death penalty in all circumstances. We condemn all executions wherever they take place. We call on all nations to enforce the implementation of the UN resolution on a universal moratorium on executions".

Since 1983, Parliament has adopted an Annual Report on Human Rights in the World. These reports have increased awareness of patterns of human rights violations across geographic boundaries and have highlighted issues such as the rights of minorities, modern slavery, women's and children's rights and freedom of expression. Many of the innovations in the Commission's treatment of human rights issues have been prefigured in these reports. In 1999 the Council accepted two innovations long sought in Parliament's reports. These were the inauguration of an annual EU report on human rights, including developments inside as well as outside the Union, and the convening of a policy forum where representatives of the EU institutions can discuss human rights issues with NGO representatives and academic experts.

Parliament's Rules of Procedure (Rule 122) provide for a monthly human rights debate. A short-list of situations for inclusion under this heading is drawn up in the preceding week, and the Political Groups may table draft resolutions on the nominated subjects. Every effort is made to verify the details in each case, with all the relevant information available from the many NGOs active in the field of human rights being circulated. Governments naturally dislike being criticised in these resolutions and devote considerable efforts either to stop them being debated, to deny their veracity or to claim they were not properly consulted. However, claims against the truth of the allegations are rarely proven and the resolutions provide an important basis for the subsequent work of the Human Rights sub-committee. It monitors the follow-up by EU institutions as well as by the relevant authorities in the countries concerned, with fact finding delegations being one way of pushing a matter further.

In 1994 Parliament created an item in the Commission budget entitled "The European Initiative for Democracy and Human Rights". This item, transformed by legislative act in 2007 into a European Instrument for Democracy and Human Rights (EIDHR), now provides for well over 150 million euros a year from 2010 to 2013. The Parliament has played an active role in establishing the priorities for this expenditure, which covers: enhancing respect for human rights and fundamental freedoms in countries and regions where they are most at risk; strengthening the role of civil society in promoting human rights and democratic reform; support to areas covered by EU Guidelines on key human rights concerns; supporting the international framework for human rights, and EU Election Observation Missions.

Every year since 1988, Parliament has awarded the **Sakharov Prize** for Freedom of Thought for "achievements in the defence of human rights and fundamental freedoms, in safeguarding the rights of minorities, respect for international law and development of democracy and implementation of the rule of law". The prize, worth 50,000 euros, was named after Andrei Sakharov, who was seen as an outstanding embodiment of these ideals. Three past winners, Nelson Mandela (1988), Aung San Suu Kyi (1990) and Kofi Annan and the United Nations staff (2003) have also received the Nobel Peace Prize. The prize is awarded by the Conference of Presidents in October of each year on the basis of a shortlist of three drawn up by the Foreign Affairs and Development Committees, which examine any nomination supported by 40 MEPs or a Political Group.

The prize-giving ceremony is normally held during the December part session in the presence of the winner. However, it is not always possible for the winner to receive the prize in person. Leyla Zana, for example, was only free to come to the Parliament in October 2004, nine years after she was awarded the prize and this in part due to the pressure exercised by the Parliament in the framework of its human rights activities. In 2008, the twentieth anniversary of the prize, all living previous winners were invited but several were unable to attend. The Ladies in White and Oswaldo Paya were denied travel permits by the Cuban government; the 1990 laureate, Aung San Suu Kyi remained under house arrest in Burma; and the winner of that year, Hu Jia, was still in prison and was indirectly represented by his wife who recorded a message on her computer that was movingly screened in the plenary. The prize can certainly provide moral support to individuals who are often living under very difficult circumstances but it does not always protect them from further difficulties. For example, in October 2010, Oleg Orlov, one of the members of the Russian civil rights defence organisation, Memorial, which won the prize in 2009 was arrested to the consternation and concern of MEPs of all parties.

Table 46: *Sakharov Prize winners*

Year	Winner	Country
1988	Nelson Mandela and	South Africa
	Anatoli Marchenko	Soviet Union
1989	Alexander Dubcek	Czechoslovakia
1990	Aung San Suu Kyi	Burma
1991	Adem Demaci	Albania
1992	The mothers of Plaza de Mayo	Argentina
1993	The Sarajevo daily paper Oslobodjenje	Bosnia
1994	Taslima Nasreen	Bangladesh
1995	Leyla Zana	Turkey
1996	Wei Jingsheng	China
1997	Salima Ghezali	Algeria
1998	Ibrahim Rugova	Kosovo
1999	Xanana Gusmao	East Timor
2000	The Basque peace movement Basta Ya	Spain
2001	Nurit Peled-Elhanan & Izzat Ghazzawi;	Israel & Palestine;
	Zacarias Kamwenho	Angola
2002	Oswaldo Jose Paya Sardinas	Cuba
2003	Kofi Annan and the staff of the United Nations	
2004	The Belarusian Association of Journalists	Belarus
2005	Damas de Blanco, Reporters without Frontiers	Cuba, Nicaragua
	and Havwa Ibrahim	and Nigeria
2006	Aleksandar Milinkievic	Belarus
2007	Salih Mahmoud Osman	Sudan
2008	Hu Jia	China
2009	Memorial	Russia
2010	Guillermo Fariñas	Cuba

Petitions

Much lip-service has been paid by governments and politicians to the need to bring European institutions closer to the citizen. One way of fulfilling this need is by providing people with the direct means to comment upon, complain about, or contest the application of European policy and law. This is a right that only received formal recognition in the Maastricht Treaty that entered into force in 1993. The treaty not only created "European citizenship" but also the right to petition the European Parliament, thereby giving treaty status to a right already provided for in Parliament's internal Rules of Procedure since 1953. Since the entry into force of the Lisbon Treaty it can now be located in Article 227 of the Treaty on the Functioning of the European Union (TFEU).

It was a right that was little known and little used until the mid-1970s, with, for example, only 20 petitions in 1977–78. This figure rose substantially after the first direct elections in 1979, reaching 1,352 petitions in 1994–95. Since then the figure has varied but the enlargements of 2004 and 2007 served to push up the average which is now close to 2,000 (1,924 in 2009). The number of signatories to petitions has also continued to grow, with several campaign-type petitions exceeding one million. The most active petitioners come from Germany, Spain and Italy, who together have regularly made up more than 40% of the yearly total of petitions.

Petitions may be submitted either in writing by regular post or by means of the internet through Parliament's website, with electronic submissions constantly increasing and reaching 60% in 2009. They are deemed admissible if they are formally in order (are signed by a petitioner who indicates his/her name, nationality and address within the EU) and if the subject matter falls within the sphere of activity of the Union (a concept that is usually interpreted liberally). However, there are certain circumstances where the committee cannot consider a petition, for example, when the issue is subject to national court proceedings; nor can it review the outcome of such proceedings.

Since 1987, petitions have been dealt with by a special Committee on Petitions (having been dealt with initially by the Legal Affairs Committee and subsequently by the Committee on Rules of Procedure). The committee has the authority to draw up reports which it may approve itself or, subject to a decision of the Conference of Presidents, have debated and voted in plenary. It uses this latter option sparingly when matters of a particular importance justify such treatment.

The Petitions Committee may also organise hearings or decide to investigate matters in relation to specific petitions, in conjunction with the interested parties. More generally, it deals with the substance of petitions by requesting a preliminary inquiry by the services of the Commission or Member States. Matters may be forwarded, usually after discussion in the committee, to specialised committees with a particular competence in the issue. Occasionally they are invited to provide a specific opinion, in which case they are obliged to respond in writing, or more often the petition is sent for information only, in which case the subject can be integrated into the specialist committee's general legislative work.

When dealing with some of the more complex petitions, and after holding a full debate, the Petitions Committee occasionally organises fact-finding visits to investigate issues on the spot. It will send a delegation made up of two or three members (not from the country concerned) and secretarial support staff. In 2010, for example, there was a visit to Campania in Italy in response to petitions received concerning the acute problem of waste management. There have been previous visits to investigate industrial pollution in Huelva in Spain and proposals to build a trans-European highway through the Raspuda Valley in eastern Poland. The latter proposals were eventually cancelled, in part as a result of the committee's activity.

The Petitions Committee prepares an annual report on its work for debate in plenary. This allows the committee to provide Parliament with a general overview of its activities. The 2009 report, for example, details the number of petitions which were declared admissible and highlights some of the more important issues raised. It notes that 54% of all the petitions received that year were declared inadmissible, usually because they did not fall within the areas of EU responsibility. Many were referred to national authorities or competent agencies; some were passed on to petitions committees in national parliaments where such committees exist; and several were referred to the European Ombudsman, who deals solely with complaints concerning maladministration within the EU institutions (see below).

Although the number of petitions received is considerable, and therefore requires a large amount of work in assessing each individual case, each one's integrity is respected whether signed by one or one thousand people. In general, where the preliminary investigation has been conducted by the Commission or the committee secretariat on an admissible petition, members are informed of the result and the petition is then placed on a meeting agenda. Because of the numbers of petitions involved, and depending on the results of the investigation, some may be dealt with more quickly and closed using, essentially, a written procedure. Others, more complex, or perhaps controversial, are debated in public at meetings of the Petitions Committee which take place every month. The same petition may be debated more than once if further information is required by members before making their decision on action to be taken. Importantly, petitioners themselves are allowed to participate in the debate and the committee may also invite other interested parties to give their views.

Petitions fall broadly into one of two categories. The first are complaints of a general nature, often relating to environmental problems, free movement or difficulties with the internal market. They are often presented by associations or groups of citizens who attach growing importance to this course of action. Such petitions frequently have a very large number of signatories.

The second type of petition is concerned with obtaining redress for a particular grievance. Such petitions, usually from individuals, cover a range of issues such as disputes with customs authorities at internal Union frontiers, welfare entitlements on taking up residence in another Member State (transfer of pension rights, dual taxation, access to health care, etc), problems with importing and registering motor vehicles from another Member State, access to employment in the public sector, civil law, double taxation and residence permits. In such cases the Commission provides valuable help in clarifying whether there may have been a violation of Community law, and may be asked by the committee to take up the matter with the Member State and, if necessary, beginning infringement proceedings, leading possibly to a case before the European Court of Justice.

In the more high-profile recent cases dealt with by the committee – such as the adoption of abandoned Romanian children by foreigners, the impact of extensive urbanisation in Spain, the Lloyds' Names Affair, and the testing of animals in scientific experiments – a lot of work was carried out with the objective of obtaining a constructive solution in conjunction with national or local authorities. In spite of this, "happy endings" are hard to obtain in the absence of any treaty provision aimed at providing a clear non-judicial means of redress for the petitioner through the parliamentary process.

One particularly delicate problem for Parliament in the past has been to know exactly what rights it has to approach Member States for information or assistance. More than twenty years ago, in April 1989, the Presidents of the Parliament, Commission and Council signed a solemn declaration concerning the rights of European citizens to petition the European Parliament and encouraging Member States to give "as clear and swift replies as possible to those questions which the Commission might decide, after due examination, to forward to the Member States concerned". They pointed to the principle of "sincere cooperation" enshrined in what is now Article 4 TEU, requiring the Member States and Union institutions to "assist each other in carrying out tasks which flow from the Treaties." In the early days, progress was very slow, with the assistance of Member States being sporadic and with the Council declining to respond to the call for its officials to attend committee meetings on a regular basis. However, the situation has undoubtedly improved more recently and there is now more pragmatic cooperation between the institutions, with representatives of national authorities regularly attending the committee.

In addition to receiving petitions directly from citizens, Parliament has very close ties with the **European Ombudsman**, who is empowered to receive complaints from any EU citizen or any natural or legal person residing in the Member States concerning instances of maladministration in the activities of the Union institutions or bodies (other than the Court in its judicial capacity). Such complaints may be forwarded directly or through an MEP. The Ombudsman has the right to conduct inquiries at his or her own initiative, except where court cases are underway.

As we have seen (Chapter 14), the Ombudsman is elected by Parliament, in a procedure organised by the Petitions Committee, normally for a five-year term following each European election. The rules governing the performance of his or her duties were established by Parliament after seeking an opinion from the Commission and with the approval of the Council. Parliament's decision of 9 March 1994 on this is now contained in Annex XI of the Rules.

The Ombudsman presents an annual report to the Petitions Committee, which then reports to the plenary. An agreement between the Ombudsman and the Petitions Committee allows some cases submitted by citizens, not necessarily aware of the different remits of the two institutions, to be forwarded from one to the other. The committee may draw up a report on cases of maladministration reported to it by the Ombudsman in his so-called "Special Reports" and did so in response to the Ombudsman's inquiry into the transparency of the EU institutions.

The first Ombudsman, from 1995 to 1999 was Jacob Söderman who developed close relations with Parliament, operating out of the buildings rented by Parliament in Strasbourg. He was succeeded in 2003 by Nikiforos Diamandouros, who had previously been the Greek National Ombudsman. He was re-elected for a full further term first in January 2005 and again in January 2010.

Finally, it is worth recalling that the Lisbon Treaty offers an additional means for European citizens to engage with the institutions. Article 11 TEU provides for the creation of the **European Citizens' Initiative** (ECI) whereby the Commission can be invited to prepare a legislative proposal in response to the submission of a million signatures gathered from a "significant" number of Member States. The Petitions Committee was involved for the first time in the legislative procedure when the Parliament examined the regulation designed to establish the ECI and the committee sought to make the provisions as user-friendly as possible for citizens. Once these provisions take effect, one of the tasks of the Petitions Committee will be to improve awareness of the distinction between such initiatives and petitions, which are not specifically designed to generate new legislation.

A network of contacts

Besides the formal proceedings in Parliament itself, MEPs have a variety of ways and means of pursuing an issue with other EU institutions as well as with national governments. Some of these involve the representation of Parliament as such, notably through its President, whereas others are open to any member. All underscore the importance of Parliament as part of a network linking the actors involved in EU policy making.

Contact channels to the other EU institutions

The development of the role of the Parliament has gone hand-in-hand with an increased variety and depth in the contacts it has with the other EU institutions. It is now hard to believe that there was a time when MEPs hardly had an opportunity to enter the Council building. By contrast, representatives of the Council are now to be seen on a daily basis inside the Parliament, eager to learn the positions of the different Political Groups and to negotiate with rapporteurs on their legislative work. Such changes are visible at all levels.

Since 1988 the President of Parliament attends the meetings of the European Council of heads of state and government. This started during Lord Plumb's presidency of Parliament in 1988. It met strong resistance from some governments but has now become an established feature of the meeting. The President does not normally attend the whole of the European Council meeting, but always presents Parliament's views on the issues to be discussed at the opening. As these meetings are becoming more frequent, the President's opportunities to meet heads of state and government have grown correspondingly. Nor are the meetings purely formal: when President Buzek spoke at the October 2010 European Council about the 2011 budget, it prompted a debate in which 12 of those around the table took part, even though the budget was not a formal item on the agenda.

Besides the President, Group chairs regularly meet with Commissioners, ministers and Prime Ministers, especially those of their own political family. Commissioners attend some meetings of the Political Group with which they have political links. They will normally have informal contacts too with their political family. For example, Socialist Commissioners have traditionally held a regular working dinner with the leaders of the Socialist Group. Group leaders or co-ordinators are in regular contact with ministers from their party, especially prior to Council meetings.

Committee chairs maintain close contact with the minister responsible for chairing Council meetings in their area. They will often meet just before Council meetings. Ministers from incoming Presidencies now seek meetings to get to know them before their Presidency. Moreover, while practice varies from sector to sector, European Parliament committee chairs are increasingly being invited to informal Council meetings, sometimes for only part of the meetings, sometimes for the whole session.

The origins of these increased contacts can be traced back to the time of the 1991 intergovernmental conferences which led to the Maastricht Treaty. At that time, an "inter-institutional conference" was set up composed of ministers from every Member State on Council's side, an equivalent number of MEPs on Parliament's side and Members of the Commission. It enabled ministers to remain in touch with Parliament's views on revision of the treaties throughout the IGCs. It was recreated after the IGCs were over, in order to negotiate agreements on issues arising out of the new treaty. Thus, inter-institutional agreements were reached in October 1993 on the Statute of the Ombudsman, a Declaration on democracy, transparency and subsidiarity, measures to apply the principle of subsidiarity and the operation of the Conciliation Committee. Further agreements were reached in December 1994 on the rights of committees of inquiry and the question of implementing powers ("comitology") for acts adopted under the co-decision procedure. The inter-institutional conference format offered a vehicle for reaching agreement on the detailed application of procedures and it has continued to serve this purpose, even though used much more sparingly over the intervening years. It made it possible, for example, to reach agreement in 2002 on access to sensitive documents in the area of common security and defence policy, in 2003 on "better lawmaking", in 1999 and in 2007 on Joint Declarations on Practical Arrangements for the Co-decision Procedure and more recently, in 2010 on the opening of negotiations on an inter-institutional agreement concerning access by the Parliament to classified parts of international agreements subject to its consent.

The most frequent day-to-day contacts are those between Parliament and the Commission. One Commissioner has traditionally had specific responsibility for coordinating relations with the Parliament; this link was upgraded by Romano Prodi, since when a Commission Vice-President has done the job (Loyola de Palacio 1999-2004, Margot Wallström 2004-10, when the remit was broadened to cover institutional relations in general, and Maros Sefcovic, since 2010).

The extent of the cooperation between the two institutions was significantly deepened by the revised Framework Agreement that they negotiated in 2010 and which was adopted in Parliament in October of that year. It is a very wide-ranging document and, as we saw in Chapter 15, one that provoked some eyebrow-raising in the Council, where some felt that the Parliament had gone further than the Lisbon Treaty would allow. However, a central theme of the agreement is that it provides for more institutionalised contact at all levels. In particular, it provides for:

– the President of the Commission to speak in an annual State of the Union debate to be held in the first September session each year, "taking stock of the current year and looking ahead to priorities for the following years";
– the President of the Commission to meet the Conference of Presidents at least twice a year to discuss matters of common interest;
– the President of the Commission to have a regular dialogue with the President of the Parliament, including issuing invitations to the latter to attend meetings of the College of Commissioners;
– the Vice-President responsible for inter-institutional relations to report regularly to the Conference of Committee Chairs on the implementation of the Commission Work Programme;
– a new Question Hour with individual Members of the Commission to be established, following the model of the Question Hour with the President of the Commission;
– the Members of the Commission to hold a regular dialogue in the first

semester of the year with the corresponding parliamentary committees
on the implementation of the Commission's Work Programme; and
–   the Commission to facilitate the inclusion of a delegation of MEPs as
     observers in international conferences and to keep the delegation fully
     informed about the negotiations.

The implementation of these commitments will also require a tightening of
contacts at the service level. The Commission can call on the comprehensive
internal structure it has for maintaining contacts with Parliament, designed to
ensure Commissioners and their departments are well informed as to parliamentary opinions and the state of play in Parliament. Each Commissioner has
at least one member of his private office (known by the French term "cabinet")
who deals with inter-institutional relations, usually covering both Parliament
and Council. These officials meet each week, together with members of the
Commission's legal service and secretariat-general, in what is called the GRI
or Group for Interinstitutional Relations. The GRI examines, in particular, legislative matters that are being considered in Parliament and Council, to ensure
collegiality and consistency in the Commission's approach. The group also
reports through the weekly meeting of heads of private offices to the College
of Commissioners, enabling them to react quickly if there is a risk of political
difficulties. The GRI's meetings are prepared by the coordinators in each
Directorate General responsible for relations with Parliament and Council.
     It is relatively easy for meetings to be arranged between MEPs and indi-
vidual officials within the Commission: most MEPs have their own individual array of contacts with Commissioners and their civil servants.
Correspondence from MEPs is given priority treatment. The Commission is
a relatively open bureaucracy and this structure ensures that MEPs can take
full advantage of that openness. The personal link between the two institutions is also reinforced by the fact that there have normally been a number
of former MEPs in the Commission (currently over a quarter, see Table 47)
and former Commissioners among the MEPs, of which there are currently
three (Danuta Hübner, Sandra Kalniete and Louis Michel).
     At staff level, Commissioners sometimes include in their cabinet officials
recruited from the Parliament, notably from the Political Groups. Antonio
Preto and Maria Åsenius, heads of the private offices of Commissioners
Tajani and Malmström, worked in the Parliament as officials of the EPP and
Liberal groups respectively. Commissioners have also taken former MEPs
into their cabinets (in the Santer Commission, John Iversen with Ritt
Bjerregard, Luis Planas with Manuel Marin and Ollie Rehn with Erkki
Liikanen; in the Prodi Commission, Luis Planas and Ollie Rehn stayed on,
the former with a new Commissioner, Pedro Solbes, and Raf Chanterie
joined the cabinet of Viviane Reding; and in the first Barroso Commission,
Bartho Pronk joined the Reding cabinet).
     Conversely, 1999 saw the election to Parliament of former cabinet mem-
bers (José Ignacio Salafranca, Spanish EPP and ex-deputy head of cabinet of
Abel Matutes; Nicholas Clegg, UK Liberal and now Deputy Prime Minister,
who worked with Sir Leon Brittan; and Lousewies van der Laan, Dutch D66
member from the Hans van den Broek cabinet). In 2004 Paul van Buitenen,
the Dutch official who worked in Financial Control in the Commission,
became a member of the Green Group and in 2009 Marta Andreasen, former

Chief Accountant of the Commission, became a UKIP member of the Europe of Freedom and Democracy Group.

General contacts at civil servant level were long handicapped by the formal location of Parliament's secretariat in Luxembourg. However, the transfer to Brussels of the staff that work directly on political matters (i.e., committee and Group staff), and the presence there of members' assistants, has largely overcome that handicap. It has become much more straightforward to organise meetings such as the inter-institutional co-ordination group (GCI), formerly known as the Neunreither Group after the Parliament official who established it. This brings together officials of Parliament, Commission and Council (as well as the Economic and Social Committee and the Committee of the Regions and a member of the cabinet of the President of the European Council) every month, notably to monitor progress in current legislative procedures and to try to anticipate difficulties. At individual committee level, contacts in Brussels between the staff of the different institutions for legislative planning and other purposes, such as exploring the extent to which Council Presidency objectives match those of Parliament committees, is gradually becoming more systematic. For these purposes, Parliament committee staff not only have intensive contact with the officials in the Permanent Representations, but are sometimes invited to national capitals to meet the relevant government officials.

Table 47: *Former MEPs in the Commission*

Commission	Year	Commissioners	No. of former MEPs
Hallstein I	1958-1962	9	1 (Caron)
Hallstein II	1962-1967	9	2 (Caron, Rochereau)
Rey	1967-1970	14	3 (Rochereau, Martino, Sassen)
Malfatti	1970-1972	9	1 (Malfatti)
Mansholt	1972-1973	9	1 (Scarascia Mugnozza)
Ortoli	1973–1977	13	2 (Scarascia Mugnozza, Lardinois)
Jenkins	1977–1981	13	1 (Vredeling)
Thorn	1981–1985	13	3 (Thorn, Dalsager, Pisani)
Delors I	1985–1989	14	3 (Delors, Ripa di Meana, Varfis)
Delors II	1989–1993	17	6 (Delors, Bangemann, Ripa di Meana, Scrivener, McSharry, Van Miert)
Delors III	1993–1995	17	5 (Delors, Bangemann, Van Miert, Scrivener, Oreja)
Santer	1995–1999	20	7 (Santer, Bangemann, Van Miert, Oreja, Papoutsis, Cresson, Bonino)
Prodi I and II	1999–2005	20	4 (Reding, Vitorino, Palacio, Busquin)
Barroso I	2005-2009	25	3 (Reding, Rehn, Tajani)
Barroso II	2010-2014	27	7 (Barnier, De Gucht, Lewandowski, Malmström, Tajani, Reding, Rehn)

Finally, Parliament sessions in Strasbourg are an opportunity for an intense round of contacts as MEPs are joined by the entire Commission (which holds its weekly meetings in Strasbourg during plenary sessions), ministers of the Council, officials, lobbyists, journalists, visiting national MPs and so on. This relatively open week-long "conclave" enables MEPs to "collar" Commissioners and ministers in a more informal atmosphere. All concerned are virtually obliged to socialise as none of them is rushing home straight after work, everyone being "away from home".

Contacts with individual governments

Parliament attracts a stream of ministerial visits, particularly during sessions, with ministers generally holding a series of meetings with individual MEPs, a general meeting with those from their own party or country and perhaps a working dinner on a particular subject with a small group.

Day-to-day contact is through the staff of the Permanent Representations of Member States in Brussels. Each of the representations has at least one official with particular responsibility for links with the Parliament. They meet in a Council working group, the General Affairs Group (known by its unfortunate French acronym as the "GAG") and their job includes approving replies to parliamentary questions to the Council. Such officials (or more frequently their colleagues from Council's sectoral working groups) also attend plenary and the more important committee meetings, where they may sit in the seats reserved for Council, and report back promptly to their ministries on what is happening. Most Council Presidencies designate officials in a specific sector as liaison officers with the relevant EP committee. This is almost universal now, for example, within the environment field where one official follows the work of the committee on a day-to-day basis, while his or her colleagues chair the Council working groups and only attend the committee meeting when their minister is present or when there is a particularly important debate or vote within their policy area.

Moreover, a number of other members of the relevant Council working group besides those from the Presidency country will also often attend particularly significant committee debates. Journeys to Strasbourg have thus also become an integral part of the work of the Permanent Representations. For the UK, for instance, several officials from UKREP travel to Strasbourg for the whole or part of each session, where they are often joined by others from the Foreign Office in London for part of the week. Strasbourg provides a good opportunity for national officials to brief MEPs, especially those of their own nationality, on particular concerns of their government as well as for MEPs to contact them for information or to ask for their own views to be passed on.

Some governments provide a written briefing on issues before Parliament, at least for MEPs from their own country. For the UK, Whitehall departments send, through the Permanent Representation, "a written briefing on all new legislative proposals" to UK MEPs and "further briefings on key dossiers at crucial stages in the Parliamentary process" as well as "briefings" on third countries for MEPs who are travelling as part of a delegation. Each Whitehall department has designated an official as "coordinator on EP business" to follow Parliament committee work and be available as a contact point for MEPs.

Contacts also take place, on a party or all-party basis, at the highest political levels in the Member States. In Italy, for example, there are regular working sessions of all Italian MEPs with the Prime Minister. In France, the then former MEP and European Affairs Minister Alain Lamassoure, instituted back in 1994 regular all-party monthly meetings. In the UK there have been periodic meetings for all UK MEPs with the Foreign Secretary or Minister for Europe and occasional seminars with a variety of ministers at the Foreign Office.

Personal links between the Parliament and Member State governments is also reinforced by the fact that there are often a number of former MEPs in government, as we saw in Chapter 4. Many go straight from the Parliament to a ministerial position (see Table48), in many cases becoming Minister for Europe or Foreign Affairs.

The strongest political links and most regular contacts with national governments are likely to be those of MEPs from the same political parties as those in government. Chancellor Kohl met his CDU/CSU party MEPs every three months (usually in Strasbourg). In the UK, up to 2010, the Labour government agreed with the EPLP (the Labour MEPs) a "link system" whereby the MEPs designated a member in each EP committee to act as the contact point with the corresponding UK minister. The link members were regularly invited to ministerial team meetings in Whitehall, enjoying a status similar to a PPS (parliamentary private secretary to a minister) in the House of Commons. Over time, MEPs have been granted equal or similar status to MPs by their national administrations. In the UK, letters sent to ministers by MEPs on behalf of constituents are treated in the same way as those of MPs, and there is equal access to government publications, government receptions and briefings from embassies abroad, for instance.

Table 48: *Sitting MEPs leaving to become Minister,
Prime Minister or President of a Member State*

Parliament	*No. of MEPs*	*Some notable examples*
1979-84	28	Craxi, Prime Minister, Italy; Colombo, Foreign Minister, Italy; Tindemans, Foreign Minister, Belgium; Olesen, Foreign Minister, Denmark; Flesch, Foreign Minister, Luxembourg; Delors, Economy Minister, France; Bangemann, Economy Minister, Germany; Cresson, Agriculture Minister, France
1984-89	12	De Mita, Prime Minister, Italy; Jospin, Education Minister, France; Juppé, Economy Minister, France; Lizin, Europe Minister, Belgium; MacSharry, Finance Minister, Ireland
1989-94	17	Christodoulou, Europe Minister, Greece; Dankert, Europe Minister, Netherlands; Lamassoure, Europe Minister, France; Colombo, Foreign Minister, Italy; Romeos, Economy Minister, Greece
1994-99	13	Matutes, Foreign Minister, Spain; Kranidiotis, Europe Minister, Greece; Moscovici, Europe Minister, France; Guigou, Justice Minister, France; Vitorino, Defence Minister, Portugal; Brinkhorst, Agriculture Minister, Netherlands
1999-04	26	Berlusconi, Prime Minister, Italy; Palacio, Foreign Minister, Spain; Haarder, Europe Minister, Denmark; Costa Neves, Europe Minister, Portugal; Fontaine, Industry Minister, France; Ries, Europe Minister, Belgium

Table 48 continued

Parliament	No. of MEPs	Some notable examples
2004-09	22	Ilves, President, Finland; Pahor, Prime Minister, Slovenia; Dombrovskis, Prime Minister, Latvia; D'Alema, Foreign Minister, Italy; Stubb, Foreign Minister, Finland; Berger, Justice Minister, Austria; Fotyga, Foreign Minister, Poland; Malmström, Europe Minister, Sweden; Wuermeling, Europe Minister, Germany; Bonino, Trade Minister, Italy; Hortefeux, Local Government Minister, France; Costa, Interior Minister, Portugal; Peijs, Transport Minister, Netherlands
2009-14		Schmitt, President of Hungary; Papakonstantinou, Minister of Finance, Greece

Finally, the President of Parliament traditionally makes an official visit to each Member State during his or her term of office, which is normally used to meet the head of state and government and relevant ministers. The President also normally visits the Member State holding the Presidency of Council at the beginning (or just before) its term of office, as do delegations from the larger Political Groups, holding a series of meetings with ministers.

Formal sittings: addresses by Heads of State or similar

Parliament receives many official visits by Heads of State, these often including an address to a formal sitting of the Parliament as well as one or more other events, such as a meeting with the Conference of Presidents, bilateral meetings with the President and other political leaders, and an official lunch or reception.

The Heads of State of EU countries have a standing invitation to address a formal sitting of Parliament. Up to late 2010, as Table 49 shows, all but two EU Member States (Cyprus and Sweden) had availed themselves of this opportunity. Indeed, some Heads of State addressed Parliament more than once (e.g. President Kwasniewski of Poland, President Havel of the Czech Republic, Grand Duke Jean of Luxembourg and King Juan Carlos of Spain).

Heads of State from third countries can also be invited to address formal sittings. Parliament has also used formal sittings to promote dialogue with a particular region as evidenced in the presence of Balkan leaders from Yugoslavia/Serbia and Montenegro, Macedonia and Croatia between 2000 and 2004. The Parliament, perhaps more conscious of its capacity to offer a pan-European platform to those addressing it, has moved quickly to invite newly-elected democratic leaders as with President Kostunica of the then Yugoslavia in 2000 and President Yuschenko of Ukraine in February 2005.

While an address to a formal session is usually reserved for Heads of State, the honour has also been accorded to major religious leaders such as the Patriarch of the Eastern Orthodox Church and the Dalai Lama. It was also agreed to allow the Vice-President of the United States, Jo Biden, to speak to the plenary in May 2010. In a break from the normal practice, the leaders of the Israeli Knesset and the Palestinian Legislative Council, Mr Avraham Burg and Mr Ahmed Qurie (Abu Ala) were invited jointly to make a short address to Parliament in September 2000.

Table 49: *Heads of state or government or similar who have addressed the European Parliament in a Formal Sitting since the first elections*

17/04/1980	Luis HERRERA	President of Venezuela
10/02/1981	Anouar El SADAT	President of Egypt
14 - 15/09/1983	Constantin KARAMANLIS	President of Greece
15/12/1983	King HUSSAIN	King of Jordan
16/02/1984	Queen BEATRIX	Queen of the Netherlands
24/10/1984	Raul ALFONSIN	President of Argentina
12/02/1985	Chaim HERZOG	President of Israel
08/05/1985	Ronald REAGAN	President of the USA
11/06/1985	Sandro PERTINI	President of Italy
23/10/1985	Richard von WEIZSÄCKER	President of Germany
14/05/1986	King JUAN CARLOS	King of Spain
09/07/1986	Mario SOARES	President of Portugal
08/04/1987	King BAUDOUIN	King of Belgium
08/07/1987	Queen MARGRETHE II,	Queen of Denmark
14/10/1987	Patrick HILLERY	President of Ireland
11/10/1988	Pope JOHN-PAUL II	Head of State, Vatican
15/11/1988	Christos SARTZETAKIS	President of Greece
15/02/1989	Jean Pascal DELAMURAZ	President of Switzerland
04/04/1990	Virgilio BARCO	President of Columbia
22/11/1990	Grand Duke Jean	Head of State, Luxembourg
13/03/1991	Yoweri Kaguta MUSEVENI	President of Uganda
16/04/1991	Patricio AYLWIN	President of Chili
11/09/1991	King HUSSEIN	King of Jordan
20/11/1991	Mohammed Hosni MUBARAK	President of Egypt
12/02/1992	Carlos MENEM	President of Argentina
12/05/1992	Queen ELIZABETH II	Queen of UK
15/12/1992	Thomas KLESTIL	President of Austria
22/06/1993	Zin El Abidine BEN ALI	President of Tunisia
16/11/1993	Maauro KOIVISTO	President of Finland
18/11/1993	Oscar Luigi SCALFARO	President of Italy
13/12/1993	Yasser ARAFAT	President of Palestine(OLP)
08/03/1994	Vaclav HAVEL	President of Czech Republic
19/04/1994	Patriarch BARHOLOMEW	Orthodox church
03/05/1994	Albert ZAFY	President of Madagascar
16/05/1995	Mary ROBINSON	President of Ireland
10/10/1995	Roman HERZOG	President of Germany
14/11/1995	Boutros BOUTROS GHALI	Secretary General, UN
17/02/1998	Jorge SAMPAIO	President of Portugal
11/03/1998	Thomas KLESTIL	President of Austria
17/06/1998	Martii AHTISSAARI	President of Finland
07/10/1998	King JUAN CARLOS	King of Spain
18/11/1998	Aleksander KWASNIEWSKI	President of Poland
08/03/1999	Blaise COMPAORE	President of Burkina Faso
26/10/1999	Andres PASTRANA	President of Columbia
14/12/1999	Jacques CHIRAC	President of France
16/02/2000	Vaclav HAVEL	President of Czech Republic

12/04/2000	Thomas KLESTIL	President of Austria
17/05/2000	Milan KUCAN	President of Slovenia
04/10/2000	Carlo Azeglio CIAMPI	President of Italy
15/11/2000	Vojislav KOŠTUNICA	President of Yugoslavia
04/04/2001	Johannes RAU	President of Germany
16/05/2001	Rudolf SCHUSTER	President of Slovakia
24/10/2001	DALAI LAMA	Spiritual leader of Tibet
11/12/2001	KIM Dae-jung	President of Korea
15/05/2002	Vicente FOX	President of Mexico
12/06/2002	King ABDULLAH II	King of Jordan
22/10/2002	Ferenc MADL	President of Hungary
07/12/2002	Alejandro TOLEDO	President of Peru
07/04/2003	Boris TRAJKOVSKI	President of Ex Yugoslavia
14/05/2003	Aleksander KWASNIEWSKI	President of Poland
03/06/2003	Abdelaziz BOUTEFLIKA	President of Algeria
23/09/2003	Ion ILLESCU	President of Romania
09/10/2003	Vaira VIKE-FREIBERGA	President of Latvia
21/10/2003	Abdoulaye WADE	President of Senegal
05/11/2003	Rolandas PAKSAS	President of Lithuania
19/11/2003	Mary McALEESE	President of Ireland
13/01/2004	Svetozar MAROVIC	President of Serbia & Montenegro
29/01/2004	Kofi ANNAN	Secretary General, UN
10/02/2004	Álvaro URIBE VÉLEZ	President of Columbia
26/02/2004	Stjepan MESIĆ	President of Croatia
26/10/2004	Queen BEATRIX	Queen of the Netherlands
17/11/2004	Thabo MBEKI	President of South Africa
23/02/2005	Victor YUSCHENKO	President of Ukraine
10/05/2005	Hamid KARZAI	President of Afghanistan
11/05/2005	Grand Duke Jean	Head of State, Luxembourg
05/07/2005	Carlo Azeglio CIAMPI	President of Italy
25/10/2005	Ricardo LAGOS ESCOBAR	President of Chile
15/02/2006	Heinz FISCHER	President of Austria
14/03/2006	Horst KÖHLER	President of Germany
05/04/2006	Edward FENECH-ADAMI	President of Malta
15/05/2006	Juan Evo MORALES	President of Bolivia
16/05/2006	Mahmoud ABBAS	President of Palestinian Nat Authority
17/05/2006	Karolos PAPOULIAS	President of Greece
05/09/2006	Tarja HALONEN	President of Finland
26/09/2006	Ellen JOHNSON SIRLEAF	President of Liberia
25/10/2006	Laszlo SOLYOM	President of Hungary
14/11/2006	Mikheil SAAKASHVILI	President of Georgia
15/11/2006	Sheik Hamad Bin KHALIFA	Sheik of Qatar
31/01/2007	Traian BASESCU	President of Romania
01/02/2007	Georgi PARVANOV	President of Bulgaria
14/02/2007	Giorgio NAPOLITANO	President of Italy
25/04/2007	Abdul KALAM	President of India
04/09/2007	Aníbal CAVACO SILVA	President of Portugal
13/11/2007	Nicolas SARKOZY	President of France
12/12/2007	King ABDULLAH II	King of Jordan

15/01/2008	Sheik Ahmad Badr Al-Din HASSOUNE	Grand Mufti of Syria
11/03/2008	Toomas Hendrik ILVES	President of Estonia
23/04/2008	Danilo TÜRK	President of Slovenia
18/06/2008	Asma JAHANGIR	UN special Rapporteur
03/09/2008	Oscar ARIAS	President of Costa Rica
24/09/2008	Patriarch BARTHOLOMEW	Head of Orthodox church
22/10/2008	Jorge SAMPAIO	UN High Rep for the Alliance of Civilisations
19/11/2008	Jonathan SACKS	Chief Rabbi of the United Hebrew Congregations
04/12/2008	DALAI LAMA	Spiritual leader of Tibet
13/01/2009	Valdis ZATLERS	President of Latvia
04/02/2009	Mahmoud ABBAS	President of the Palestinian Nat Authority
19/02/2009	Václav KLAUS	President of Czech Republic
11/11/2009	Václav HAVEL	Former President of Czech Republic
06/05/2010	Joe BIDEN	Vice President of the USA
07/09/2010	Amadou Toumani TOURE	President of Mali
06/10/2010	José RAMOS-HORTA	President Timor Leste
19/10/2010	BAN KI-MOON	Secretary General, UN
24/11/2011	Mikheil SAAKASHVILI	President of Georgia

Heads of Government (as opposed to Heads of State) or foreign ministers of third countries are, as a general rule, not entitled to address the plenary. On such occasions, usually in Brussels and described as working visits, a meeting of the Conference of Presidents or a joint meeting of the Foreign Affairs Committee and the relevant inter-parliamentary delegation for the country concerned, or some variation thereof, may be held. This procedure was first used for Foreign Minister Shevardnadze of the then Soviet Union and is known as the "Shevardnadze Procedure". Perhaps ironically this procedure was also used when the man who ended Mr Shevardnadze's political career, President Mikhail Saakashvili of Georgia, spoke to members in April 2004. Similarly, the format of a meeting with the Conference of Presidents has been used to accommodate Heads of State visiting between sessions, such as with King Abdullah II of Jordan in November 2004, as well as important foreign figures, such as Hillary Clinton, US Secretary of State, in October 2010.

Openness and transparency

Visibility of proceedings

Parliament has consistently argued in favour of openness and contrasted its behaviour in this regard with that of the Council. The 1999 Rules revision reinforced the commitment to openness with a new chapter on openness and transparency and a statement that "Parliament shall ensure that its activities are conducted with the utmost transparency..." (now Rule 103(1)). Plenary sessions have always been open (the provision to enable it to be closed under exceptional circumstances was never used and was abolished in the 1999 Rules revision). On the other hand, before direct elections, committee meetings were closed. After 1979 a number of committees such as Social Affairs, and later the Environment and Economic Committees, opened their doors. The Rules used to state that committee meetings were not to be held in public unless the committee decided otherwise. In January 1992, the Rules were modified to provide for neutrality on this issue, and since 1999 it has been obligatory for committees to meet in public (Rule 103.3). There are only three exceptions to this rule. First, committees may decide to discuss certain designated matters behind closed doors as long as such a decision is taken at the latest when the agenda of the meeting is adopted. Second, discussions on requests to waive a member's immunity must be held *in camera*. Third, the conciliation committee and the Parliament delegation meetings that precede the committee (see Chapter 12) are not public. Parliament's committees are thus more open than most of their equivalents in the national parliaments of the European Union. The parliaments of Denmark, Sweden and Finland, for example, which otherwise pride themselves on their openness, provide for closed committee meetings for all normal business. Space is provided for visitors at the back of the meeting rooms and in special rows of seats on the side. Visitors generally fall into three categories: lobbyists, the press and casual visitors. The most regular visitors are lobbyists, especially those who are Brussels-based, and who sometimes specialise in particular committees or specific subjects. Members of the press also attend, but normally only for big hearings on controversial subjects rather than for routine meetings. Casual visitors are becoming more common as the number of visitors to the Parliament in Brussels grows (see below). So far there are not the same numbers as in Washington, where congressional committee meetings and their subject matter are listed in the daily press so that political "tourists" can drop in on the committee of their choice.

However, there are limits on the number of people able or wishing to attend committees. In many committee rooms, the increase in the number of interpretation booths following enlargement in 2004 and 2007 has reduced the amount of space available for visitors. In addition, attendance is limited by the more restricted access allowed to casual visitors to Parliament buildings as a result of security measures taken in the light of the events of 11 September 2001, in particular the requirement that visitors are now meant to be invited and then accompanied by committee staff or by MEPs. Moreover, many potential visitors may now prefer to follow a committee meeting on the internet from their office in Brussels or elsewhere rather than devoting time to coming to the institution. All committee rooms now have robotic cameras which make it possible to record the proceedings and transmit them over the internet.

The other main facet of an institution's openness is the extent of public access to its documents. Here too, there has been an evolution. Parliament's debates and minutes, including any texts adopted are, by definition, in the public domain, but the status of "upstream" documents, such as draft reports or working documents, was less clear until the arrival of the internet. Before individuals could go online, the situation was anomalous. Documents were available at committee meetings to that small minority of the public attending such meetings, but this was not satisfactory for the wider public: Parliament lacked any organised system of making its documents available. Following an initiative by the Ombudsman, in which he wrote to all Union institutions and bodies asking them how they were ensuring access to their documents, a code of public access to Parliament documents was established in July 1997. In April 1998 Parliament's Bureau took a further decision on the fees to be paid for delivery of very large documents, now largely superseded by the development of the internet. The Amsterdam Treaty (Article 255) provided for a right of access to documents of Parliament, Council and Commission and for the application of this right to be laid down in legislation. This legislation was adopted by Parliament and Council in 2001 (Regulation 1049/2001) and sets up a generalised system of public access to EU documents, all of which are available unless the institution concerned can justify confidentiality of part or all of a document on a limited number of grounds (testable in court), and Parliament adapted its internal rules and practices accordingly.

As a result of all this, Parliament now maintains a register of all its documents, the categories of which are listed in Annex XV of its Rules of Procedure. In most cases, these documents can be accessed by internet through the register (if not, a form is available for requesting the document, which should be processed within 15 days). Included are, inter alia, all plenary, committee, and delegation documents and amendments, registers of attendance, studies, questions and press briefings. As regards confidential documents of the Council and Commission, MEPs have access to these as described in Chapter 7. However, they may not, by definition, be passed on to the wider public.

One final point can be made about access to documents and that is the willingness of the institution gradually to make links to websites outside the European institutions. In 2009 the Bureau took the decision that the Parliament's website should publish links to a third party website, www.votewatch.eu, which analyses MEPs' voting records and makes it easy for the public to understand the positions that their MEPs have taken. It represents a significant step towards enlarging the scope of transparency.

Lobbyists and representatives of civil society

Access to Parliament for those with a case to make for a particular sectoral, regional or public welfare interest is an important part of parliamentary life. Brussels is very much like Washington in its variety of lobbyists, with an estimated 15,000 individuals employed by around 2,600 private and public interest groups that have a main office based in Brussels. They include an enormous range of large companies, non-profit organisations, law firms, trade associations and regional and local authorities, all of which are interested in influencing the output of the European institutions.

Lobbying takes many forms, from briefings in Brussels or Strasbourg for 100 or more members down to lobbying of individual MEPs in their constituencies. It can be carried out directly, or by consultants acting on behalf of clients. Some lobbyists are specialists in following the European Parliament, attending all or most part-sessions and relevant committees. Parliament's press conferences are also open to non-journalists and are often well attended by lobbyists (and diplomats), who, however, may not ask questions. Lobbying is also done by letter-writing or email (sometimes with mass write-ins, a tactic that can be counter-productive).

Listening to lobbyists on various sides of an issue can be an important source of information for MEPs, but can also give rise to misgivings when a well-financed campaign is run on one side of an argument, such as the tobacco industry's campaigns to prevent Parliament approving the proposal to ban tobacco advertising in 1998 and to water down the tobacco labelling directive adopted in 2001. Occasionally, too, there has been lobbyist overkill, such as back in 2002 when a lobby against a proposed food sup-plements directive bombarded every individual MEP with hundreds of emails, made an unauthorised (and misleading) film of the relevant com-mittee meeting, requested permission to speak at the meeting, and was even accused of intimidation by the committee rapporteur.

Lobbyists certainly believe that they can make a difference. One of the most high-profile and vociferous campaigns fought over European legisla-tion, on the patenting of biotechnological inventions, set biotechnology companies and organisations against some environmental groups, notably Greenpeace. Parliament's initial rejection of the proposal was felt by many to have been influenced by the latter whereas its acceptance three years later was equally considered to have been affected by the former. In fact, the new proposal that the Parliament approved in 1998 was very different from the one that it had rejected three years earlier, having been heavily modified to take account of Parliament's criticisms.

The increase in lobbying stimulated Parliament to introduce a register and code of conduct for lobbyists. The difficulty of defining a lobbyist, together with a feeling that "big" lobbies can find their way through extra procedural requirements more easily than "small" lobbies, inclined many to caution about introducing detailed requirements. A first attempt by the Bureau of Parliament to regulate lobbying failed to reach a conclusion before the 1994 elections. Parliament eventually adopted rules in 1996 on the basis of a report for the Rules Committee by Glyn Ford MEP (a first report having failed to get the necessary majority).

The Rules have since been further tightened up and now (Rule 9(4)) pro-vide for all persons seeking to enter the Parliament frequently with a view "to supply information to Members within the framework of their parlia-mentary mandate in their own interest or those of third parties" to be given a nominative or personal pass for up to one year on condition that they sign a public register kept by the Quaestors and accessible on the website (some 1,913 organisations and 5,098 individuals were on the register in November 2010) and respect a code of conduct. This code, annexed to Parliament's Rules of Procedure (Annex IX), specifies that lobbyists must at all times wear their (visually distinctive) pass, which displays their photo, name and the name of their employer. They must, among other things, state the inter-ests they represent in contacts with MEPs or staff, refrain from any action designed to obtain information dishonestly, not circulate for profit any Parliament documents, satisfy themselves that any assistance provided to members is declared in the register of members' interests, and not offer any gifts. Any breach of the code may lead to the withdrawal of the pass to the persons concerned and even their firms.

To deal with the possibility that members' assistants might be employed by lobbyists, the code also requires the former to complete a declaration of interests. At the same time, the provisions relating to the declaration of members' interests has been strengthened. As described in Chapter 4, this includes a strict requirement to declare outside support.

For the moment the register is restricted to the Parliament but this is likely to change during 2011. An inter-institutional working party was set up in 2009, involving the Commission and the Parliament (the Council having declined to take part directly) to consider a single register for the EU institutions. In November 2010, having consulted widely with outside bodies, it reached a consensus on a draft inter-institutional agreement for a common register for organisations and individuals engaged in EU policy making and policy implementation. This common register, to be known as a "transparency register", is due to be available online in June 2011. It will go beyond the existing registers of Parliament and Commission, in that it will provide additional information such as the number of individuals involved in all the activities relating to the register and the level of EU resources received by the person or organisation registering. The aim is to provide the public with as a clear a picture as possible as to who gets involved in seeking to influence EU policy making.

The media

Parliament devotes considerable effort to ensuring that press, television and radio journalists can have access to the institution. Both in Brussels and in Strasbourg there are pressrooms and facilities for holding press conferences as well as fully equipped TV and radio studios. A press briefing is held every Friday before the session in Strasbourg to give the latest information on the work of the Parliament in the following week, and individual members and Groups also organise meetings with the press when they think it appropriate.

The number of journalists accredited to the European Union expanded considerably over the ten years from 1996 and 2006, rising from 775 to 1,158. As a result, there was growing pressure on the services provided and occasional differences of opinion as to how far access should extend. In consequence, a number of new rules were introduced in 1997 and 2001, notably for photographers and outside television crews. Crews are obliged to obtain a filming permit but can then film plenary sessions at all times and in meeting rooms with the authorisation of the chair of the meeting and of a majority of members present. Filming in restaurants and bars and the use of hidden cameras is, on the other hand, prohibited.

In the past much effort was expended to persuade the media to follow the activities of the Parliament, and with some success. Between 1979 and 1994, for example, the average number of journalists present at Strasbourg sessions almost doubled, reaching 245 per session. More recently, this issue has become less salient. Economic pressures have reduced the number of accredited journalists in Brussels (now around 850 to 900) and encouraged them to come to Strasbourg only for the most important debates. This is reflected in the number of accreditations issued for TV crews in Strasbourg (around 80 per session) and in the number of television stations that come to the Alsatian capital (just under 40). But it is not simply a question of economics. There is also the fact that journalists can now follow the work of the Parliament at a distance. They can watch the plenary on the interinstitutionally-sponsored facility Europe by Satellite (EbS) as well as on the Parliament's own web television, europarltv.

Europarltv was the product of a long-running discussion in the Parliament about the creation of a television channel, comparable to the American C-Span or the parliamentary channels set up in France and Greece. A study was commissioned in 2005 which recommended that the Parliament should not try to use terrestrial or satellite means to carry its own channel but rather that it should turn to the internet. This was seen as the only medium which would allow the institution to produce programmes in all EU languages and that would not be prohibitively expensive. On the basis of the report it was decided to produce a prototype which operated in the second half of 2007 and which was tested on samples of viewers in all Member States, as well as inside the institution. The experiment was sufficiently successful for the Bureau to decide in February 2008 to launch the channel online officially in September 2008 at www.europarltv.eu. It underwent a significant revamp in the autumn of 2010.

What the channel has shown is that it is possible to produce programmes in all EU languages, using subtitles, and to do so in a way that can appeal to different audiences. Thus as suggested above, the channel allows a person who is unable to attend the plenary or a committee to follow proceedings and indeed to switch between meetings that are held simultaneously. It also has created the means for the outsider to find out what is currently under discussion in the Parliament with a daily news programme. It also provides a large range of background programmes on how the Parliament works and can cater for a younger audience in a dedicated section called "Young Parliament". Last but not least, it has been able to overcome the problem of balance between different political positions, in part by means of an Editorial Charter which lays down that the plurality of opinion be respected, in accordance with a "neutral, non-partisan editorial policy".

The creation of a webTV channel showed that the Parliament did not have to rely entirely on the traditional media to explain what it was doing. However, it remains limited in the degree to which it can allow a dialogue with viewers, enabling them to comment on or raise questions about the institution. This issue came to the fore in the run-up to the 2009 elections when it was decided to take a first step towards the social media and to develop interactivity on a new part of the website devoted to promoting interest in the European elections. The site allowed for comment on articles and a weekly poll and opened the way to go further by the creation of a Facebook page, the placing of "viral videos" on YouTube, the opening of a Flickr account for human interest pictures of the Parliament and the start of the use of Twitter and of a blog, entitled "Writing for y(EU)".

There was some nervousness about these experiments, not least because they meant that the Parliament could no longer control the message it was communicating but became but one part of the conversation about its activities. However, the success of the experiment was considerable: the three viral videos were viewed by half a million people on YouTube and the Facebook account had 50,000 friends by the time of the elections (a figure that has since risen to 70,000). Moreover, the new generation of MEPs who arrived in 2009 proved to be very familiar with these new techniques: 55% of the newly-elected Parliament had Facebook profiles, 38% maintained a blog and 31% used Twitter. As a result, there are now regular Facebook chats with MEPs on the website as well as a much greater use of Twitter to comment on events inside the Parliament. The definition of the media and the way the institution relates to them has thereby significantly broadened.

Visitors

Parliament receives a constant stream of visitors. Some come specifically to meet members, Political Group leaders, committee chairs etc., but many more come to see at first-hand how Parliament works, often having a chance to follow a parliamentary session from the public gallery.

In view of the wide geographical dispersion of the European electorate, Parliament makes a particular effort to help visitors from further afield, arranging for groups of between 20 and 45 people to come and see the institution and learn how it works. Such groups may be, for instance, constituency party sections, students or members of professional associations, trade unions, etc. As Table 50 below shows, these visits are drawing an increasing number of people to Brussels and Strasbourg, the total now reaching over a quarter of a million a year.

However, the table is far from exhaustive. It excludes individuals who come unannounced to the Visitors' Centre in Brussels for a multimedia-guided visit (more than 10,000 per year), those who attend the Open Days in Brussels and Strasbourg that are held annually around Europe Day (9 May), estimated at over 50,000, as well as visits made to Strasbourg outside the session periods. In addition, there are several sessions every year of Euroscola, an event which brings together 16-18 year olds from all EU countries to take part in a model European Parliament exercise.   In this way, more than 10,000 children are given a chance every year to discover for themselves how the Parliament works.

Table 50: *Visitors to Brussels and Strasbourg (2005-2009)*

	Brussels	Strasbourg	Overall total
2005	155,038	76,273	231,311
2006	165,795	76,346	242,141
2007	183,032	82,888	265,920
2008	199,645	76,886	276,531
2009	194,862	73,760	268,622

The figures reflect a particularly big increase in visits to the Parliament in Brussels. In 1991 there were about 10,000 such visitors, a total that has grown nearly twenty-fold since, reflecting the growing concentration of parliamentary time and activity in the Belgian capital. It has meant an increasing pressure on the existing visitors' facilities and contributed to the Parliament's decision to establish a new Visitors' Centre in Brussels. It was decided that it should be free and open to anyone, without having to book in advance and accessible at weekends. It will be spread over 6,000 square metres in the

Brandt building, making it the second largest parliamentary visitors' centre in the world, after that of the United States Congress. It is modelled on comparable centres in Sweden and Denmark, with state-of-the-art interactive role play games allowing visitors to simulate the work of an MEP in a mock hemicycle, debating and passing legislation. It will also include a cafeteria, shop, children's area and a "resource area" offering databases of detailed information. It is expected that the centre will open during 2011.

A more specialised kind of visitor comes to the Parliament under the European Union Visitors' Programme (EUVP). This programme was established in 1974 on the initiative of Dutch Senator Willem Schuijt, chair of the first EP delegation for relations with the US Congress, and is jointly administered by the Commission and the Parliament. Each year some 170 visitors are selected amongst young politicians, government officials, journalists, trade unionists, academics, etc. from third countries (initially largely the USA but now world-wide). During their five to eight day stay they meet leading decision-takers in the European institutions.

Opening up to civil society

The Parliament has consistently sought to be linked as closely as possible with European civil society and to make its activities as relevant as possible to the citizens that it represents. It has always provided a platform for artistic, political, scientific exhibitions to be held on its premises in Brussels and Strasbourg under the sponsorship of individual MEPs: 1,102 such exhibitions were organised between 2004 and 2009. However, the Parliament has also made strenuous efforts to become visible beyond the confines of the institution itself and to this end has taken two particular initiatives.

First, the Parliament instituted in 2007 a forum for civil society organisations known as Agora, where the bodies interested are given the opportunity to use Parliament's facilities, to debate a particular topic and to draw up conclusions for submission to the institutions. The first of these meetings in November 2007 concerned the Future of Europe, the second in June 2008 was devoted to Climate Change and a third is due to take place in January 2011 to consider crises and forms of poverty.

Second, the Parliament has introduced a series of prizes designed to reward individuals or groups in different fields of endeavour. Of particular note are:
–   the *Lux Prize*, established in 2007, to finance the subtitling of a film into all EU languages with a view to encouraging European cinema production. Every year three films are chosen by an international jury and are then shown over a number of weeks. The winner is chosen on the basis of the vote of the MEPs who have watched the films;
–   the *Charlemagne Youth Prize*, established in 2008, organised jointly with the Foundation of the International Charlemagne Prize of Aachen, and awarded to young people, between the ages of 16 and 30, involved in promoting understanding between people from different European countries; and
–   the *European Journalism Prize*, also established in 2008 and designed to promote excellence in journalism on EU issues. It is divided into four categories – written press, television, radio and internet – with a

winner chosen for each category. Thus in 2010 the internet prize went to a British blogger for his article entitled "EUtopia-What percentage of laws come from the EU?"

Overall assessment

Having examined this diverse list of instruments available to Parliament to enhance its role as a political forum and channel of communication, it is worth dwelling for a moment on the purposes that they serve. It is possible to discern three directions in which Parliament serves as a transmitter and articulator of ideas.

First, and most obviously, MEPs transmit concerns "upwards". Parliament is a platform where MEPs, often in response to worries voiced in their constituencies or by national political parties, articulate concerns, express viewpoints, communicate reactions and take initiatives. Issues raised may be directed to Union institutions where the Union has a particular role to play, or outside the Union when dealing with foreign policy issues or human rights.

The second, and most distinctive, direction is "sideways". Parliament is an arena for exchanging experiences and transmitting ideas from one national political culture to another. Parliament is a meeting place for members of political parties facing similar problems, for political activists dealing with similar issues in different countries and, often, for members having faced similar governmental difficulties. National experiences can be compared. MEPs come into regular contact with politicians from other countries more often than almost any other politicians.

Third, MEPs have a role to play "downwards" in explaining the European Union to a wider public. They do this within their constituencies (where many of them have circular newsletters reporting back to party members, local employers and trade unionists, local government and others). They spend time explaining their actions and therefore the Union to local media. They are also inevitably caught up in explaining the policies of the Union, within their national political party. It is a difficult but essential task as Parliament takes on greater responsibility.

17. The EP and national parliaments

The complementary roles of the European Parliament and of national parliaments are widely (but not universally) recognised. The European Parliament provides direct representation of citizens at EU level, and has leverage (scrutiny or co-decision) over the other EU institutions. It works full-time on EU matters, but appears more distant from citizens, and its role is less familiar to them. National parliaments are less specialised, can devote less time or resources to EU matters, and have leverage only over their own individual government. On the other hand, they are generally perceived to be closer and more familiar to citizens and they have a role in monitoring the actions at EU level of their own national governments, not least in those more intergovernmental areas of decision-making where unanimity persists and where the European Parliament has fewer formal powers. The EP and national parliaments together ensure that the EU is subject to far more parliamentary scrutiny and debate than any other international structure.

The present chapter looks at the developing role of national parliaments in the wider context of the various formal and informal changes that have taken place over the last 20 years as regards their involvement in the work of the European Union, and their relations with the European Parliament. The new possibilities given to them by the Lisbon Treaty are evolutionary rather than revolutionary, and their real significance for national parliaments may lie less in any new formal powers and more in the general impetus that is given to their closer involvement in the decision-making processes of the European Union. They are also likely to lead to closer links with the European Parliament, although the relationship may not always be a smooth one.

Pre-Lisbon Treaty involvement of national parliaments

Contact channels between the EP and national parliaments

Before the first direct elections to the European Parliament in 1979, all members of the European Parliament were also members of national parliaments. This had the advantage of maintaining organic links between national Parliaments and the European institutions, and there have continued to be siren voices calling for a return to the previous situation on this very ground. However, duplication of roles in national parliaments and the European Parliament posed great difficulties even in the pre-1979 period when the EU's responsibilities were much smaller, and the European Parliament had far fewer powers. It would be completely impossible today, as the European Parliament has become a full-time Parliament (indeed with much shorter recesses than most national parliaments) and as national parliamentary and European Parliament activity overlap in the middle of the week.

For a while after direct elections there did continue to be a considerable number of dual mandate members, but this steadily decreased over time from one in five members in 1979 to one in 40 by 2002. Since then the dual mandate has been formally abolished. While some countries have been more successful than others in developing a variety of other effective links between MEPs and national parliamentarians, formal linkage is inevitably weaker than in the past.

What has grown up over time is a variety of contact channels, some more formalised and regular than others, with new ideas being explored and sometimes abandoned, loosely supervised by regular Speakers' Conferences (meetings between the Presidents of the European Parliament and the Speakers or Presidents of the national parliaments of the Member States, which have taken place since 1981, at first every 2 years and after 2000 on an annual basis) who have periodically (and most recently in 2008) issued "Guidelines on Inter-parliamentary cooperation between parliaments of the European Union".

What has grown up includes the following:

- National parliaments have set up (if they didn't have one already) **specialised committees on European affairs** (see Table 51 below). Their members have been frequent visitors to the European Parliament and, at least in some countries, individual MEPs often give evidence to them. A number now grant MEPs a right to attend and participate actively (without voting). They all meet jointly twice a year in a body known as COSAC (described in detail below).
- Various forms of **ad hoc joint meetings** of parliaments or their committees. These were rationalised in 2005 into:
  - **Joint Parliamentary Meetings** (JPMs), formalised in 2005, jointly organised by the EP and the national parliament of the Council presidency, whose Presidents co-chair the meeting. They focus on major policy issues facing the EU, including those where it does not necessarily legislate but nevertheless can take important decisions, such as foreign policy, security, macro-economic policy coordination and aspects of security and justice. The aim is not to arrive at common positions, but to establish better parliamentary oversight and control over intergovernmental and non-legislative decisions taken at the EU level. Recent years have seen an average of four Joint Parliamentary Meetings per annum.
  - **Joint Committee Meetings** (JCMs), are also jointly organised by the European Parliament and the parliament of the country holding the EU Council Presidency. Recent years have seen an average of three to five Joint Committee Meetings per annum. These are often focussed on particular legislative issues.
  - **Interparliamentary Committee Meetings** (where individual EP parliamentary committees simply invite national colleagues from their corresponding committees with national parliaments), often focussed on particular legislative items. National parliamentary committees can do likewise.

- A whole range of other formal or informal contacts such as those between MEPs and national Parliamentarians within the same national political parties. Indeed, it is probably the **party contacts** that are the most frequent, if not necessarily the most visible.
- **Technical cooperation at the level of staff and services**, notably the ECPRD (the **European Centre for Parliamentary Research and Documentation**), first established in 1977, and with a broader-based membership than the EU alone (involving Council of Europe member countries too). This focused initially on cooperation among libraries and research departments, notably some 200 comparative studies a year on national legislative provisions, but then extended its scope to cooperation on wider projects, such as use of new technologies and parliamentary use of the Internet. Particularly useful has been the establishment of IPEX (Inter-parliamentary EU Information Exchange), a platform for electronic exchange of EU-related information, which has been operational since 2006.
- **Political and Administrative cooperation** has been significantly reinforced by the designation of officials from individual national parliaments based in Brussels, at the European Parliament, and charged with following developments within the EP and the other EU institutions. Starting with a single official from the Danish Parliament in 1991, and then a Finn in 1995, this has now expanded since the late 1990s to include officials from all of the EU Member State parliaments, apart from Malta. The German Bundestag office is particularly large, with its own premises outside the Parliament, composed both of staff of the Bundestag and of the Political Groups represented in the Bundestag. For its part the EP has established its own Directorate for relations with national parliaments.

COSAC

A development of enduring significance was the creation in 1989 of the Conference of European Affairs Committees, known familiarly as COSAC after its title in French. The idea was proposed by Laurent Fabius, who was at the time both a member of the European Parliament and President of the French National Assembly. It brings together on a twice-yearly basis, under the auspices of the country holding the Council Presidency, the specialised EU committees of the national parliaments and a delegation from the European Parliament (six per Parliament).

The role of COSAC was later formalised in the Amsterdam Treaty Protocol on the role of national Parliaments in the Union (see below), and it was authorised to make contributions for the attention of the institutions of the European Union on the legislative activities of the Union. Originally bound by consensus, it can now adopt contributions by a qualified majority of at least three quarters of the votes cast, although its main function has in practice been to provide a networking opportunity for those members of national parliaments across Europe who are the most involved in debating European issues.

Since 2004, it has also had its own small secretariat headed by a permanent member (with a Dane, a Finn and now a Lithuanian in this role) rather than

Table 51: *List of Committees on European Affairs in the Parliaments of the Member States*

Member State & Chamber	Name of the Committee	Number of Members
1. Austria		
Nationalrat	Main Committee on EU Affairs	27 members
Bundesrat	EU-Committee	17 members
2. Belgium		
Chamber and Senate	Federal Advisory Committee on European Affairs	30: 10 each from Senate and Chamber and 10 MEPs
3. Bulgaria		
National Asembly	Committee on European Affairs and Oversight of the European Funds	18 members
4. Cyprus		
House of Representatives	Committee on European Affairs	10 members
5. Czech Republic		
Chamber of Deputies	Committee for European Affairs	15 members, pro rata to party strength in the Chamber
Senate	Committee on European Union Affairs	9 members, pro rata to political caucus strength
6. Denmark	European Affairs Committee	17 members
7. Estonia	European Union Affairs Committee of the Riigikogu	at least 15 members
8. Finland	Grand Committee	25 members and 13 substitutes who attend and may speak
9. France		
Senate	Committee for European Affairs	36 members, pro rata to the party strength in the Senate
National Asembly	Committee on European Affairs	48 members, pro rata to the party strength in the Assembly
10. Germany		
Bundestag	Committee on the Affairs of the European Union	33 members and 15 MEPs without voting rights
Bundesrat	Committee on Questions of the European Union	17 members, 1 from each federal state
11. Greece	Special Standing Committee for European Affairs	31 members
12. Hungary	Committee on European Affairs	21 members, pro rata to party strength
13. Ireland	Joint Committee on European Affairs	17 members, 11 from lower and 6 from upper House
14. Italy		
Chamber of Deputies	Committee on EU Policies	44 members
Senate	14th Standing Committee on EU Policies	27 members

Table 51 (continued): *List of Committees on European Affairs in the Parliaments of the Member States*

Member State & Chamber	Name of the Committee	Number of members
15. Latvia	European Affairs Committee	17 members
16. Lithuania	Committee on European Affairs	min 15, max 25 pro rata to party strength, currently 24
17. Luxembourg	Committee for Foreign and European Affairs, Defence, Cooperation and Immigration	11 members
18. Malta House of Representatives	Standing Committee on Foreign and European Affairs	9 members
19. Netherlands House of Representatives	Committee on European Affairs	27 members from all political parties
Senate	Committee for European Cooperation Organisation	27 members
20. Poland Sejm	European Union Affairs Committee	44 members
Senat	European Union Affairs Committee	18 members
21. Portugal	Committee on European Affairs	21 members
22. Romania Chamber of Deputies Senate	Committee on European Affairs	35 members
23. Slovakia	Committee on European Affairs	11 members
24. Slovenia National Assembly	Committee for EU Affairs	14 members
National Council	International Relations and European Affairs Commission	10 members
25. Spain Congreso de los Diputados Senado	Joint Committee for the European Union	43 members
26. Sweden	Committee on European Union Affairs	17 members, 42 substitutes
27. United Kingdom House of Commons	European Scrutiny Committee	16 members
House of Lords	European Union Committee	18 members

having to rely, as before, essentially on staff from the Council Presidency national parliament. COSAC's bi-annual reports on parliamentary practices and procedures are meant to permit exchange of best practice among Parliaments.

COSAC meetings normally last one and a half days. They discuss topical issues in the Union, exchange views on improving parliamentary scrutiny and invite members of the Commission and the Council Presidency. The Prime Minister and Foreign Minister of the host country normally address the meeting. The agenda and preparations are in the hands of the parliaments of the Member States participating in a "Troika" (current, former and following Presidents of Council), together with the European Parliament (which is thus the one permanent member of the preparatory group). The European Parliament is normally represented in COSAC meetings by its three Vice-Presidents who are specifically responsible for relations with national parliaments (currently Miguel Martínez, Edward McMillan-Scott and Silvana Koch-Mehrin, see Chapter 6), the chair of the Constitutional Affairs Committee and other members chosen according to the subjects on the agenda, making a total of six, the same size as the national delegations.

There have, however, been different conceptions within the national parliaments as to the relative importance to attach to these different mechanisms and as to how they should work. Some have argued for a central role for COSAC, whereas others see it as just one of the means of contact. There have also been differences between those who believe national parliaments can take collective decisions in bodies such as COSAC and those, like the Nordic and UK Parliaments, who believe that national parliament delegations cannot bind their own parliaments. This approach is now reflected in the Lisbon Treaty formulation that "contributions made by COSAC shall in no way bind national Parliaments or prejudice their position". Moreover, the European Parliament has been involved in all these mechanisms, despite the fact that some parliaments would have preferred that they be reserved as a platform for national parliaments alone.

The Parliamentary Assizes and the Conventions

The run-up to the Maastricht Treaty negotiations led to intensified cooperation between the national parliaments, and between them and the European Parliament. In November 1990 a week-long parliamentary conference took place in Rome, with 250 participants, one third from the European Parliament, two thirds from the national parliaments. These so-called "Assizes" ended up adopting a joint declaration giving parliamentary guidance to the subsequent Intergovernmental Conferences that led up to the Maastricht Treaty. It was perhaps the first time in history that the parliaments that would ultimately ratify a treaty met together to discuss its contents before their governments began the negotiations. What seemed at the time, however, to have been a considerable success, both on substance and in form (MEPs and national parliamentarians sat by political families as in the EP rather than by national delegations) ended up as less so in retrospect. Many national parliamentarians felt that the process had been too much dominated by the EP. Although Declaration 14 annexed to the Maastricht Treaty provided for future conferences of this kind, it was never invoked. The nearest comparable approach was the idea of a Convention involving both parliaments and governments, such as the 1999-2000 Convention that drew up the EU Charter of Fundamental Rights and the 2002-2003 Convention on the Future of Europe that drew up the proposed EU Constitution (see Chapter 18 for its significance). In these, the European Parliament had a dozen full members, along with two from each national parliament (28 times 2, as all member and applicant states were included) and one from each government.

The Commission and national parliaments

Originally, contacts between the Commission and national parliaments were sparse. It was up to the government of each Member State to inform national parliaments on European affairs and to transmit relevant documents to them. It is only over the last decade that this changed substantially, with the European Commission putting a greater emphasis on facilitating and strengthening the role of national parliaments, through nomination of a Vice-President responsible for relations with national parliaments, through annual reports on relations between the Commission and the parliaments, and through other means such as visits or even formal addresses by individual Commissioners in national parliamentary committees or even in front of the full chamber.

A particularly important measure was the so-called Barroso initiative, taken in 2006, which not only aimed to send all new Commission proposals directly to national parliaments, but also invited them to respond to these documents. From September 2006 to the end of 2009 no fewer than 618 opinions were received by the Commission from 35 (out of the 40) chambers, some of them very short, but others quite detailed. In 2009 there were 250 opinions. There has been a group of particularly active chambers, in particular the Portuguese Assembly (47 opinions in 2009), the Czech Senate (27), the two Dutch chambers jointly (19), the Swedish Riksdag (18), the Italian Senate (17), the German Bundesrat (16), and the UK House of Lords (14). The 250 opinions issued by national parliaments in 2009 concerned no fewer than 139 Commission documents. Out of these only 10 documents were commented on by 4 or more assemblies (without counting 3 proposals covered by a COSAC-coordinated subsidiarity test).

Treaty changes prior to Lisbon

In parallel to these developments, successive EU Treaties addressed the involvement of national parliaments. The Maastricht Treaty had two relevant declarations: Declaration 14 mentioned above and Declaration 13, in which governments undertook to make sure that national parliaments received Commission proposals in good time to enable them to make their views known to their respective governments. The Amsterdam Treaty went a step further, with a legally binding Protocol on the role of national Parliaments in the Union, and with a minimum 6 week time period for national parliamentary scrutiny between a legislative proposal being made available and the date when it was placed on a Council agenda The whole debate was then subsequently re-kindled in the course of intensive debate in the Convention on the Future of Europe. It led to a new set of provisions on national parliaments first in the draft Constitution, and then in the Lisbon Treaty, as described below

The Lisbon Treaty and the role and powers of the national parliaments

The powers of national parliaments were the subject of lengthy debates in the Convention. Some of the ideas that were put forward, such as a permanent Chamber of national parliaments were not adopted, but a number of important changes were incorporated in the proposed Constitution, and subsequently further reinforced in the Lisbon Treaty. The various changes are outlined below.

(i)   National parliaments are referred to explicitly in the new Title I on the democratic principles of the Union, as well as in two protocols: Protocol No 1 on The Role of National parliaments in the European Union and Protocol No 2 on the Application of the Principles of Subsidiarity and Proportionality.

(ii)   Article 12 TEU now states that "National parliaments contribute actively to the good functioning of the Union". National parliaments are encouraged to have a greater involvement ... "in the activities of the European Union and to enhance their ability to express their views on draft legislative acts of the Union as well as on other matters which may be of particular interest to them", although "the way in which national parliaments scrutinise their governments is a matter for the particular constitutional organisation and practice of each Member State" (preamble to Protocol No 1).

(iii)   Commission consultation documents, the EU's annual legislative programme, as well as "any other instrument of legislative planning or policy", will now be forwarded directly to the national parliaments by the Commission (or by the EP or the Council), as will all draft legislative acts (Articles 1 and 2 of Protocol No 1). Council agendas and minutes of deliberative meetings are to be forwarded directly to national parliaments, as well as the annual report of the European Court of Auditors (Articles 5 and 7 respectively of Protocol No 1). Moreover, the period within which national parliaments can submit comments on legislative proposals before action is taken on them by the Council (the so-called period for "Scrutiny Reserve") is extended from 6 to 8 weeks. No agreement may be reached on a draft legislative act during those 8 weeks except in duly substantiated cases of urgency (Article 4 of Protocol No 1).

(iv)   The national parliaments are given an enhanced role in the evaluation of measures in the field of Freedom, Security and Justice (Articles 12(c) TEU and 70 TFEU). Council decisions on aspects of family law with cross-border applications shall be notified to national parliaments, and it only takes a single national parliament to block such a decision, as long as it makes its opposition known within 6 months of being so notified (Article 81 TFEU). Arrangements for involving national parliaments both in the political monitoring of Eurojust (Articles 12(c) TEU and 85 TFEU) and in the political evaluation of Europol (Article

12(c) TEU and 88 TFEU) shall be laid down in regulations to be adopted by co-decision between the EP and the Council.

(v)   Formal reference is now made to inter-parliamentary cooperation between national parliaments and with the European Parliament (Article 12 (f) TEU and Article 9 of Protocol No 1) and to contributions from the European Affairs Committees of the national parliaments, COSAC (Article 10 of Protocol No 1).

(vi)   The national parliaments are also brought into the process of future treaty change. They are given the right to be involved in any major treaty reform through the Convention method used for the draft Constitution, whereby an intergovernmental conference to revise the treaty must be preceded by a convention composed of members of national parliaments, of the European Parliament, of the Commission and of a representative from each government (Articles 12 (d) TEU and Article 48.3 TEU). They are also given the right to block revision of policies or procedures in Part 3 under simplified revision procedures, even if only a single national parliament makes known its opposition within 6 months of the date of being notified of any such initiative (Article 48.7 TEU as well as Article 6 of Protocol No 1).

(vii)   National parliaments are to be informed of all applications to join the European Union (Article 49 TEU) and they must, in any case, ratify any accession treaty.

(viii) A particular role is given to national parliaments in the field of sub-sidiarity, where they are to ensure that this principle is respected (Article 12(b) TEU), and on which they may now send "reasoned opin-ions" (Article 3 of Protocol No 1). Specific procedures for subsidiarity are laid down in detail in Protocol No 2. Any national parliament may send such a reasoned opinion stating why it considers that a draft in question does not comply with the principle of subsidiarity, and will have 8 weeks to do so. Regional parliaments with legislative powers may also be consulted, where appropriate, by the national parliament.

It is indeed this last change that has attracted the most attention. Under Pro-tocol 2, each national parliament is given 2 votes (two for a unicameral Parliament, one for each chamber in a bicameral system – currently, 13 are bicameral and 14 unicameral).

Under what has been nick-named the "yellow card" procedure, "where rea-soned opinions on a draft legislative act's non-compliance with the principle of subsidiarity represent at least one-third of all the votes allocated to national parliaments" (or one quarter in the case of proposals in the fields of judicial cooperation on criminal matters and police cooperation), the draft must be reviewed by the Commission. The Commission then has to decide whether to maintain the proposal, amend it or withdraw it, and justify its decision.

The "orange card" procedure only applies for legislation under the "ordi-nary legislative procedure". In these cases, and where a reasoned opinion receives a majority of votes of the national parliaments, and if the Commission still maintains its proposal, the whole issue is referred to the Council and European Parliament for a final decision. Either of them can decide to terminate the procedure immediately, the Parliament voting by simple majority and the Council by a majority of 55% of its members.

Finally, national parliaments are given the right to go to the European Court of Justice on grounds of infringement of subsidiarity (Article 8 of Protocol No 2).

Potential significance and possible constraints of the Lisbon changes

The Lisbon Treaty thus offers a number of possibilities for national parliaments to increase their influence in the EU decision-making system. The extent to which this will happen in practice remains unclear. It is also subject to two sets of constraints, one linked directly to the nature of the Lisbon Treaty provisions, the other to wider structural and institutional limitations inherent both in the nature of national parliaments and in their relations with the European Parliament.

The Lisbon Treaty provisions affecting national parliaments are numerous, but their direct scope is relatively limited, especially when compared to the new powers given to the European Parliament. This is the case, for example, with the most obvious change that has been made, namely the new role given to national parliaments on subsidiarity, and, in particular, the new yellow and orange card procedures. Quite apart from the logistics of mustering coordinated objections in the necessary number of Parliaments, the subsidiarity principle is itself more political than legal, and often very hard to define. Indeed, the Finnish national parliament, which has had a mechanism for subsidiarity control since Finland joined the European Union, has never found a Commission proposal to be in breach of the principle. Some would thus have preferred breach of proportionality to have been included, or even an explicit right to comment on the substance of a proposal when subsidiarity is not being infringed – which is likely to be, in practice, the focus of their work.

There are also wider structural and institutional constraints. The powers and resources available to national parliaments are extremely variable, in addition to the different conceptions of their role mentioned above in the context of inter-parliamentary cooperation. They have little time to devote to the nitty-gritty detail of many EU issues. Moreover, many of them have very small staff, whether devoted to substantive issues in the committees or to practical logistical matters, such as capacity for translation of their opinions into other languages. Moreover, should these limited resources be used in holding their government to account on the substance of proposals, or on issues such as subsidiarity which have not, in practice, caused major concerns up to now?

These constraints are evident not just in general inter-parliamentary relations, but more specifically with regard to relations with the European Parliament. The latter operates in a separation of powers system with great autonomy from the executive, whereas most national parliaments in Europe are in a classic parliamentary government structure with a governing majority loyal to the executive and where both majority and minority parliamentarians are constrained to a much greater extent. There is in practice often little or no scope to amend government texts. Not only is there a difference in their respective roles, but other factors which complicate their relations, notably the fact that the European Parliament is working full time on EU matters, and with more staff and other resources, whereas the national parliaments have less time, expertise and staff resources to devote to EU matters.

Contacts between the EP and national parliaments have certainly intensified over the years, but have often tended to be more formalistic than substantive, and meetings between them, especially at specialised committee level have often suffered from a lack of continuity in the parliamentarians and staff attending from one meeting to the next. This has certainly reduced the scope of such meetings to act as networks for collective action.

Moreover, the European Parliament and national parliaments have sometimes had uneasy relations, as shown, in particular, in the aftermath of the 1990 Rome Assizes and in certain discussions on the role of the European Parliament in inter-parliamentary structures such as COSAC. This is often reinforced by the nature of relations between national parliaments and their own governments, with the former often extremely dependent on the latter for relevant information on EU issues, and with the latter reluctant to see the former adopt too independent a stance on EU legislation or other EU-related issues.

On the other hand there are also very differing views on national parliaments within the European Parliament, with some MEPs being very positive about developing closer relations with them, and others being more suspicious, or, probably more often, simply less interested in working with them and thereby further complicating an already cumbersome decision-making process. An example of this is the uncertainty within EP committees as to how to use national parliament views expressed in the context of the Barroso initiative.

Moreover, the successive stages of EU lawmaking make it more difficult for national parliaments to follow what is going on, and thus to have some kind of impact on the process. This is arguably reinforced by the greater emphasis in recent years on first reading deals in co-decision, which involve early negotiations between Council and Parliament that national parliaments find difficult to follow. Indeed some national parliaments have already expressed their concerns on this issue, noting that such agreements are less open and transparent than agreements reached at second reading or in conciliation.

Conclusions

The formal powers given to national parliaments by the Lisbon Treaty are thus useful, but have clear limitations. National parliaments have very different approaches, resources and thus capacities to make full use of the potential of these new powers.

All this might lead one to conclude that the Lisbon powers for national parliaments are only of limited significance. However, such a conclusion may well under-estimate the impact of the treaty. The real significance of the Lisbon Treaty for national parliaments may lie less in any new formal powers and more in the potential dynamic effects, in particular, the general impetus that is given to democratic accountability within the European Union, to closer national parliament involvement in the decision-making processes of the European Union, to practical cooperation between the

European Parliament and national parliaments and above all to more systematic scrutiny by national parliaments over their government.

First, Lisbon gives a new visibility to the role of national parliaments, and
to wider issues of democratic accountability of EU institutions and policies.
Until now the role of national parliaments has been relegated to mentions in
Declarations and Protocols, whereas general principles are now laid out in
a specially dedicated Article 12 right at the beginning of the Treaty on
European Union. By itself this will have no immediate impact, but it could
well give impetus to the process in the longer-term.

Second, the Treaty could lead to closer national parliament involvement in
the decision-making processes of the European Union. An eight week
period is too short to have a big impact on all but a handful of issues, but it
could encourage national parliaments to have more of a say on substance at
all stages of the legislative process, from legislative planning (the
Commission's annual legislative planning, Presidency programmes, etc), to
Green and White Papers, to the passage of EU legislation and even to the
transposition and implementation phases. This process has already been
encouraged by the Barroso initiative from the Commission, and national
parliament contributions are now starting to be better integrated into decision-making. The amount of information to be provided to national parliaments is already quite extensive, and provides an opportunity (but only if
the political will is there, and the necessary structures and resources provided in consequence) for more detailed scrutiny by them of EU legislation.

The Commission has itself recognised that the role of national parliaments
could not be narrowly restricted to subsidiarity control when it invited
"national parliaments to distinguish in their opinions as far as possible
between subsidiarity aspects and comments on the substance of a proposal"
(December 2009 letter from Commission President Barroso to the Presidents
(Speakers) of the EU's 40 upper and lower national parliamentary chambers). That same letter outlined ways in which the Commission intended to
improve the flow of information. This included sending all draft legislative
acts and consultation documents electronically at the same time as they are
sent to the European Parliament and/or the Council; sending at the end of
each week a reminder list of documents that have been sent so that, in the
case of non-receipt of a document by a national parliament having an
impact on the deadline mentioned under the yellow card and orange card
procedures, the deadline (for that parliament) can be adjusted accordingly;
and undertaking not to consider the month of August for the purpose of calculating deadlines.

An important related question is the extent to which a new dynamic will
be created on EU issues between parliaments and their own national governments, and whether the latter see a reinforced role for the former as a
threat, or else as an opportunity.

Third, the Lisbon Treaty provides a clear incentive for further inter-parliamentary cooperation. This objective is mentioned in the Treaty, but its importance lies less in any direct impact than in encouraging a longer-term process,
in terms both of reinforced cooperation among national parliaments on EU
issues, and of more cooperation between the EP and national parliaments.

There are currently no new structures for inter-parliamentary cooperation, although the idea of an Inter-parliamentary agreement (on the lines of

an Inter-Institutional Agreement between EP, Council and Commission) is implicit in Article 9 of Protocol number 1 (on the Role of national parliaments in the European Union) annexed to the Lisbon Treaty). With this in mind, the European Parliament at the end of 2009, set up a steering group to make proposals, as well as to promote internal coordination of EP activities with regard to national parliaments.

The new subsidiarity mechanisms, in spite of their various limitations, will certainly encourage further cooperation. National parliaments will be looking to use the mechanisms to show that they have real meaning, and even if there may be relatively few opportunities to invoke them, cooperation among national parliaments will surely intensify in consequence. The fact that 26 parliaments have officials in Brussels who meet together each Monday will encourage this trend.

Moreover, the European Parliament has already modified its own Rules of Procedure (in November 2009) in order to establish internal EP procedures for examination of respect for the principle of subsidiarity. The new Rule 38a gives guidance on how to proceed when the EP receives reasoned opinions with the necessary yellow or orange card majorities from the national parliaments. In the former case the EP shall not take a decision on the proposal until its author (usually the Commission) has stated how it intends to proceed. In the more far-reaching latter case, the responsible EP committee has to consult the Legal Affairs Committee, and may either decide to recommend rejection of the proposal, or to make suggestions for amendments related to respect of the principle of subsidiarity. The EP only needs a simple majority to reject the proposal, and would thus be given the right of rejection even at the first reading phase, a power it does not currently enjoy in a formal sense.

The new mechanisms will also have another impact on the EP's internal work, in that committees will also have to respect the 8 week deadline within which they will not be allowed to adopt a position. Most important of all is the extent to which the views of national parliaments are taken into account by Parliament's rapporteurs, committees and Political Groups, and the formal as well as informal mechanisms which are put in place to this effect. The EP will have to do this in the case of reasoned opinions on subsidiarity, especially when the orange card procedure is invoked, but how the EP will react to national parliaments' comments on the substance of a legislative proposal could be more significant in the longer term.

The greater involvement of national parliaments could also help to influence the openness of the legislative process within the European Parliament. National parliaments have already expressed concerns on first reading negotiations on legislation, and it will be interesting to see what impact this might have on the Parliament – probably less in terms of discouraging such deals than in improving communication on them.

The instruments of EP-national parliament cooperation are thus likely to be further developed. In the absence of new structures, existing mechanisms, such as the IPEX system for exchanging EU information between parliaments and other e-parliament initiatives, the Conference of Speakers, and COSAC can all be used. So can networks of officials (national parliament officials in Brussels, the service for relations with national parliaments within the EP, and the EP external offices in the various national capitals).

Cooperation between EP and national parliament specialists also offers considerable potential, for example through meetings of specialised committees and inter-parliamentary meetings on special topics (budget, legislative planning, implementation of EU law, etc), or on the lines of recent EP Internal Market Committee meetings with national parliament counterparts in early 2010.

In this context, EP committees have started to reflect on their own internal organisation, such as by establishing a new role for a committee vice-chairman or other members of a committee as a liaison person with national parliaments. Another option would be to send EP rapporteurs in front of national parliament committees to outline their views before the adoption of EU legislation or to explain their rationale once adopted. Cooperation could also be facilitated if the work schedules could be better coordinated, for example by the occasional holding of meetings on Mondays or Fridays specifically designed to encourage dialogue between MEPs and national parliamentarians in their national parliaments. Enhanced use of new video-conferencing facilities might help in this context.

All these processes may develop in an uneven way, and are subject to political will on both sides, but the Lisbon Treaty has certainly provided a considerable spur for their extension.

18. Parliament and constitutional change

The European Parliament, unlike most national parliaments, has never regarded itself as part of a fully developed constitutional system, but rather as part of one in a process of evolution and requiring change. Hence, Parliament has sought not only to influence day-to-day policies, but also to change the basic framework of the Union. This chapter will look at how Parliament has sought to press Member States to revise the treaties which constitute the basic rule-book or constitution of the Union.

Although it is ultimately up to the Member States, by common accord of all of them, to modify the treaties, they recognised Parliament's vocation to draw up proposals for constitutional change at the Parliament's very first session (as the ECSC Assembly) in 1952 when Chancellor Adenauer, on behalf of the Council, invited it to draft a Treaty for a European Political Community. Parliament, designated as the "ad hoc Assembly" for this purpose, proceeded to do so. Although its project fell in the wake of the failure of France to ratify the EDC Treaty in 1954, many of the proposals it prepared were used in the negotiation of the EEC Treaty two years later.

Parliament also had to press constantly for many years for the implementation of the treaty provision regarding its own direct election by universal suffrage. The achievement of this objective in 1979 was in itself a major constitutional change.

Direct elections initially had an ambiguous effect. They conferred upon the Parliament a greater legitimacy as the only directly elected European institution, but at the same time aroused public expectations that were difficult to meet. Voters who, in the national context, were used to parliamentary elections revolving around the choice of government, suddenly found themselves having to vote for a Parliament which could not elect a government, and which did not then even have a decisive say on policies or legislation. This new political animal was all too easily ridiculed in the press and misunderstood by the public, and was a ready target for those opposed to the European project, who were generally also not keen on seeing a stronger European Parliament.

Nevertheless, direct elections were a step forward. They transformed the Parliament into a full-time institution and created a new body of elected representatives in Europe. Within almost every major political party, there was now a small but significant number of politicians focused on the European dimension who, as we have seen, acted as vital go-betweens in explaining the Union and its potential to national parties and in bringing national parties further into European discussions. They helped to shape their parties' attitudes not just to particular policies, but to the process of EU integration itself. And many MEPs initially elected on an anti-European platform, gradually changed their position and helped change that of their party. This was certainly the case, for example, with many of the 1979 and 1984 intake of UK Labour MEPs, and the initial intake of Greek Pasok MEPs.

After the elected Parliament bedded down, it began to work out precise proposals for constitutional change and to set about winning support for them. These changes have, over 30 years, consistently promoted three distinct but related objectives:

First, Parliament has sought to clarify and where necessary strengthen the competences and responsibilities of the EU itself. Parliament has consistently argued that the Union should exercise those responsibilities (but only those responsibilities) that can be carried out more effectively by common policies than by the Member States acting separately. It argued, with varying degrees of success, that competences originally contained in the EEC treaty needed to be expanded to such fields as consumer protection, the environment, cross-border legal issues, monetary union, foreign policy and security – not necessarily to centralise such policies at European level, but to exercise powers on the basis of the "principle of subsidiarity", that is, that Union decisions should be limited to what cannot be sufficiently achieved through national action. It is a measure of how far Parliament has shaped the political debate that this rather ungainly expression of subsidiarity has become part of political vocabulary: it was a term virtually unknown in the English language until Parliament started to use it in the early 1980s.

Second, Parliament has argued that responsibilities exercised at European level should be carried out more effectively. Parliament has been particularly critical of the practice of unanimity in the Council, arguing that, where it has been agreed to run a policy jointly, it makes no sense to give a blocking power to each of the component States of the Union. Parliament has also pleaded for a stronger role to be given to the Commission in carrying out policies once they have been agreed, subject to proper scrutiny and control.

Third, Parliament has made the case for better transparency, democratic control and accountability at European level. Those responsibilities which national parliaments, in ratifying the treaties, have transferred to the Union should not be exercised by Council (i.e. ministers) alone. The reduction of parliamentary powers at the national level should be compensated by an increase in parliamentary power at European level.

From the Draft Treaty on European Union to the Single European Act

The most celebrated of Parliament's initiatives designed to promote these objectives was its proposal in 1984 to replace the European Community treaties with a new Treaty on European Union. Parliament took a lead from Altiero Spinelli, one of the founders of the federalist movement at the end of World War II, former resistance leader, former member of the Commission, elected to Parliament in 1979 as an independent on the list put up by the reformed Italian Communists. In 1982, Spinelli, with colleagues from other Political Groups in the "Crocodile Club" (see Chapter 10), persuaded Parliament to set up a new committee on institutional affairs for this purpose.

The committee appointed Spinelli as general rapporteur. His approach was to use Parliament to thrash out a political compromise among the main political forces in Europe on the grounds that this was more likely to lead to genuine progress than was the traditional method of preparing treaties by working parties of officials from foreign ministries. Parliament adopted the draft treaty on 14 February 1984 by 237 votes to 31. This very large majority reflected the careful work of compromise and consensus building that had taken place among the main Groups.

Generally positive reactions were immediately forthcoming from Heads of Government in Italy, the Netherlands, Belgium, Germany and especially France, whose President, François Mitterrand, addressed the European Parliament on 24 May 1984 as President of the European Council. His speech marked a major turning point in French attitudes towards European integration, which since De Gaulle had been hostile to anything other than an intergovernmental approach. He expressed support for the draft treaty, stating that "France, ladies and gentlemen, is available for such an enterprise. I on its behalf state its willingness to examine and defend your project, the inspiration behind which it approves. I therefore suggest that preparatory consultations leading up to a conference of the Member States concerned be started up". This speech, prepared after a meeting with Spinelli and Piet Dankert, President of the European Parliament, placed the draft treaty firmly on the political agenda.

The subsequent Fontainebleau European Council agreed to set up an ad hoc committee of personal representatives of the Heads of State and Government, modelled on the Spaak Committee which had paved the way to the negotiation of the EEC Treaty in the 1950s. Some Heads of Government nominated MEPs or former MEPs to represent them on the committee. These included Enrico Ferri, who had been the chair of the Committee on Institutional Affairs, and Fernand Herman, who was still a member. The ad hoc committee also had meetings with the President of Parliament (by then Pierre Pflimlin) and Spinelli.

The ad hoc committee, known as the Dooge Committee after its Irish chairman, Senator Dooge, adopted a report agreeing with Parliament on the need for a new treaty establishing a European Union. It recommended that this treaty be "guided by the spirit and the method of the draft treaty voted by the European Parliament". There were striking similarities between the specific proposals of the ad hoc committee and the Parliament's draft treaty. However, three members – the representatives of the UK (Rifkind), Denmark (Moller) and Greece (Papantoniou) – did not accept the main conclusions of the committee's report.

The report was considered at the European Council meeting in Milan in June 1985. By then, some national parliaments had lent their support to the Spinelli draft treaty. In Italy and Belgium, the parliaments had adopted resolutions calling for the draft treaty to be ratified as it stood. In Germany, the Netherlands and in the French parliament their respective governments were urged to open negotiations on the basis of the draft treaty. In the UK, the House of Lords set up a special sub-committee that held public hearings, including one with Spinelli, and concluded that some treaty changes were desirable.

The Milan European Council decided by an unprecedented majority vote

(with the UK, Denmark, Greece voting against) to convene an intergovernmental conference (IGC) to revise the existing treaties in accordance with the
procedures set out in Article 236 of the EEC Treaty (requiring, ultimately,
unanimous support from the Member States for any treaty changes). During
the autumn of 1985, the Member States entered negotiations that eventually
led to the Single European Act, with the three recalcitrant states in the end
willing to negotiate compromises rather than be isolated. The UK was also
persuaded to negotiate by a focus on completing the single European
market, an objective which the UK supported but which was manifestly
held back by the need for unanimity to adopt the necessary legislative harmonisations.

During the negotiations, Parliament's direct involvement was limited.
President Dankert and Spinelli were invited to two of the ministerial level
meetings, but mainly informal contacts were used to influence the discussion. The IGC had agreed to submit the results of its work to the European
Parliament, and this was done in January 1986, prior to the signature of the
text by the Member States. Italy indicated that it would not ratify the Act if
the European Parliament rejected it. Parliament, although considering the
results to be insufficient, nevertheless accepted them.

The Single European Act was signed in February 1986. After national ratification (involving referenda in Denmark and Ireland) it came into force in
July 1987. It notably provided for:

– the completion of the single European market by 1992;
– slightly wider European Community competencies as regards eco-
    nomic and social cohesion, the environment, research and social
    policy;
– an extension of the field of majority voting and a modest extension of
    the executive powers of the Commission;
– a codification in the treaty of the intergovernmental "political cooper-
    ation" on foreign policy.
– an increased capacity of the Court through the creation of a Court of
    First Instance.
– as regards Parliament, the two-reading cooperation procedure and the
    assent procedure discussed in Chapter 12.

Spinelli compared the outcome to the bones of the fish in Hemingway's
"The Old Man and the Sea". It was, nonetheless, the first general revision of
the treaties since 1957, breaking what had become a taboo and thereby paving
the way for the more substantial negotiations on the Maastricht Treaty concluded five years later. The single market programme gave a new sense of
purpose to the EU, a fillip to its institutions, and generated new pressures for
further integration and reform. The Spinelli draft may not have been
approved in one go, but subsequent IGCs would result in the bulk of its proposals being accepted.

From the Single European Act to Maastricht

Between 1987 and the 1989 European elections, Parliament adopted a series
of reports aimed at showing the insufficiencies of the Community's constitutional system, despite the Single European Act. Initially, the Member

States were not interested in reopening negotiations on the treaty so soon. They eventually changed their position as a result of pressures built up as a direct consequence of the Single Act and the creation of a single European market. A majority of Member States came round to the view that a single market ultimately required a single currency and that it was time to move forward on the Community's long-standing commitment to economic and monetary union (EMU). At the time of the 1989 European elections, the European Council in Madrid agreed to the principle of a new IGC on EMU to begin at the end of 1990.

Parliament's reaction was to propose a wider agenda, not just on economic union but on political union. Its proposals were again based on the triptych of broader Community competence, a more effective decision-taking procedure, notably through extending qualified majority voting in Council, and greater democratic accountability, notably through an increase in the powers of the Parliament itself. On this last point, a series of influential reports prepared by UK Labour MEP David Martin spelt out in detail the shape of a new co-decision procedure (with two readings and a conciliation committee) and a mechanism for involving the Parliament in the appointment of the Commission.

Parliament's proposal to widen the agenda gradually gained support. First the Italian parliament, then the Belgian government gave backing to Parliament's requests. In April 1990, Chancellor Kohl and President Mitterrand wrote jointly to the other heads of government calling for a second IGC on political union to run parallel to that on EMU. In June 1990, the Dublin meeting of the European Council agreed to the principle of a second IGC, but without defining in great detail what it should deal with.

The following months were spent filling out the agenda for this IGC, and Parliament's proposals in the Martin reports were crucial in this respect. A conference of parliaments, called the parliamentary assizes, was held in November 1990, the month before the IGCs opened. All the national parliaments participated in the week-long assizes, held in the Camera dei Deputati in Rome in November 1990, where they provided two-thirds of the delegates with one-third coming from the European Parliament. At the end of the meeting a declaration was adopted, by 150 votes to 13, echoing all of the European Parliament's main proposals for treaty revision (see also Chapter 17). This was the first time in history that the parliaments that would ultimately ratify a treaty met together to discuss its contents before their governments began the negotiations. That they endorsed the bulk of the proposals put forward by the European Parliament was highly significant.

During the IGCs, the European Parliament maintained its involvement through an inter-institutional conference, which continued in parallel with the IGCs, involving monthly meetings between the 12 ministers, 12 MEPs, and four Commissioners. Parliament's President was able to address several ministerial level meetings of the IGCs. Parliament's delegation also toured the national capitals holding individual meetings with each head of government.

The resulting Treaty of Maastricht was, of course, a compromise but it again included major steps forward in the direction advocated by the European Parliament. The treaty:

–   set a timetable and procedure for establishing monetary union with a single currency;

- upgraded European political cooperation into a "Common Foreign and Security Policy" (CFSP) to be run through the Community institutions, albeit with a separate legal base and largely intergovernmental procedures, described as a second "pillar" of the Union;
- created "Cooperation in Justice and Home Affairs" as a "third pillar", also outside the Community legal framework;
- added new chapters and articles to the "first pillar" EC Treaty on development cooperation, education, culture, consumer protection, public health, trans-European networks, industry and European citizenship;
- established stronger provisions on social policy (agreed by all states bar the UK, whose opposition meant it had to be added to the treaty as a protocol binding 11 states only);
- provided for a further modest extension of qualified majority voting in Council;
- gave the Court of Justice the power to impose fines on Member States failing to respect its judgments;
- increased the powers of the European Parliament through the introduction of the co-decision procedure, the extension of the cooperation and assent procedures, the involvement of Parliament in the appointment of the Commission, the change of the Commission's term of office to coincide with that of Parliament, and a number of smaller changes increasing Parliament's powers of scrutiny and control.

Finally, part of the overall compromise was an agreement written into the text to re-examine some issues in a further IGC in 1996.

From Maastricht to Amsterdam

After the entry into force of Maastricht, but prior to the 1994 elections, Parliament secured some minor treaty changes via the accession treaties with Sweden, Finland and Austria. These included a Parliament proposal both to change the order of rotation of the Council Presidency and to make it more flexible by permitting Council to make subsequent changes in the order, and, despite British opposition, the adaptation of the threshold for qualified majority voting. Parliament's own proposal concerning the number of MEPs for the new Member States was followed, bar an extra seat for Austria.

Parliament also worked on a draft constitution (Herman Report, A3-64/94). This was partly in response to a referendum held in Italy in 1989 in which 88 per cent of Italian citizens voted in favour of Parliament preparing such a document. This laid down a marker for future reforms and for the consolidation of the various treaties into a single constitutional text.

After the 1994 European elections, Parliament turned its attention to the new IGC scheduled for 1996. The Maastricht Treaty had specified that this IGC should examine, inter alia, the extension of the co-decision procedure to other areas, and whether fully to integrate the CFSP and cooperation in the fields of justice and home affairs into the Community legal system. In practice, it also looked at the whole functioning of the Union, particularly in view of its potential enlargement to 25-30 Member States.

The Corfu meeting of the European Council in June 1994 agreed to set up a "Reflection Group" to prepare the IGC, composed of a representative of each foreign minister and two MEPs. Parliament therefore had an opportunity to participate directly in the preparations for the IGC. It appointed Elisabeth Guigou, former French European Affairs Minister (Socialist) and Elmar Brok, a German Christian Democrat, as its two representatives. Parliament's Committee on Institutional Affairs prepared a set of proposals, with David Martin, Vice-President of the European Parliament (Socialist), who had prepared the proposals for the Maastricht IGC, and Jean-Louis Bourlanges (Christian Democrat) as co-rapporteurs.

The emphasis of Parliament's proposals shifted somewhat from those it made before Maastricht. It did not press for any radical extension of the field of competence of the EU, as most of its objectives in this regard had been fulfilled by the Maastricht Treaty. It restricted itself in this respect to arguing for the integration of the social protocol into the treaty, for partial integration of the "third pillar" and of the Schengen agreement on border controls into the Community legal framework, and for a new Employment Chapter designed to make policies in this area better coordinated and more visible. All these were eventually agreed by the IGC.

Instead, Parliament, aware of the controversies that had surrounded the ratification of Maastricht, emphasised the need to bring Europe closer to its citizens through measures such as greater openness and transparency, simplifying and codifying the treaties, and giving the EU a role in protecting rights and ensuring non-discrimination.

Parliament also reaffirmed its constant commitment to making the Union more effective and more democratic. As regards the former, it focused on extending majority voting (with a special formula for CFSP matters, such that certain joint actions could be taken without the participation of states that voted against); absorbing WEU into the Union; strengthening the powers of the President of the Commission to choose and reshuffle Commissioners; limiting the size of Parliament in an enlarged Union to 700 MEPs; and allowing, if necessary and under certain conditions, a majority of states to proceed further in a policy field without the others participating from the outset.

As regards democracy, Parliament called for EU decision-making to be more transparent and for guaranteed provision of information to national parliaments in good time for them to influence their governments, though it firmly resisted the idea of establishing a congress of national parliaments alongside the EP and the Council, as France proposed. For its own powers, it called for a formal vote in Parliament on the appointment of the President of the Commission, an extension of the co-decision procedure to cover all legislation going to Council, and three crucial changes to the procedure:

–   eliminating the possibility for Council to seek to adopt a text unilaterally if there was no agreement in conciliation;
–   eliminating the need for Parliament first to announce its intention to reject a text before confirming it in a second vote;
–   providing that when Parliament and Council agree in first reading, there is no need for a second.

The Reflection Group, which met from June-December 1995 under the chairmanship of Spanish EU Minister Carlos Westendorp, offered

Parliament a platform to press its positions. Initially, the two Parliament representatives were the only ones to have detailed proposals to put on the table and were able to play a substantial agenda-setting role. The Reflection Group's Report took up many of Parliament's proposals, indicating that they had broad support, but it also showed that there were deep divisions on many subjects and that one participant (David Davis, UK representative) was unable to agree with virtually any proposal, least of all those relating to the Parliament. Instead, he pressed radical suggestions of his own, such as to allow the Council to overrule European Court judgments, thereby underlining the increasing gap between the British Conservative government and other governments in the run-up to the IGC. Few thought that the IGC would be able to complete its work until after the UK general election in 1997, which opinion polls suggested that the Conservative government would lose.

This last aspect meant that it was important to keep the opposition party – and likely new government – in the UK in the loop. The advisor to Elisabeth Guigou was Richard Corbett, the Deputy Secretary General of the EP Socialist Group and Labour party member (subsequently an MEP), who attended every meeting of the Reflection Group (and later the IGC), providing a crucial link, whilst Labour MEPs were able to help shape their party's detailed position on the IGC as described below.

Parliament sought to have its two representatives continue their work after the Reflection Group, by participating in the IGC itself. This met with opposition from the then UK (Conservative) and French (Gaullist) governments. As a compromise, the European Council agreed that they would meet monthly with the IGC negotiating group and that the President of Parliament would have an exchange of views with the EU Foreign Ministers each time they discussed the IGC. In practice, Guigou and Brok were able to discuss every subject with the IGC negotiators, obtain every document, table their own proposals and counterproposals and join in informal dinners and conclaves.

The May 1997 election in Britain of a Labour government with views much closer to those of other EU governments, notably on the role of the Parliament, provoked an intense period of diplomatic and political activity in the six weeks before the Amsterdam summit, due to conclude the IGC negotiations. Labour's position had been formulated in opposition by a working group chaired by the party leader, Tony Blair, and comprising four Shadow Ministers (shadow Chancellor Gordon Brown, Foreign Secretary Robin Cook, Deputy Prime Minister John Prescott and European Minister Joyce Quin) and four MEPs (Socialist Group leader Pauline Green, EPLP leader Wayne David and deputy leader Christine Crawley and EP Vice-President David Martin). The position drafted by this working group differed radically from the Conservative government's position on issues like the Parliament's co-decision powers, the extension of qualified majority voting, the Social Chapter and the Employment Chapter. This change of position was crucial in breaking the deadlock in the negotiations and, at the Amsterdam summit, the Heads of Government again emerged with a new treaty.

Yet again, the new treaty did not go as far as many had hoped. On the crucial institutional changes needed to prevent an enlarged Union of more than 20 Member States from becoming paralysed, the Amsterdam summit was unable to find a solution, agreeing instead, in time-honoured tradition, to

come back to these issues later. And yet there were significant changes including:
- extension of the co-decision procedure to more than double the number of articles that it previously applied to;
- the changes to the co-decision procedure recommended by Parliament (see above);
- turning Parliament's vote on the President-designate of the Commission from a consultative vote to a full legal confirmation;
- establishing the principle of openness, with a treaty-level obligation to publish the results of votes taken in the Council and statements made in the Council minutes, and with a right of public access to EU documents;
- giving the Union the power to adopt anti-discrimination legislation concerning gender, race, sexual orientation, disability, age and religion;
- a provision (originating from the Spinelli draft treaty) enabling the Union to suspend a Member State that ceases to be democratic or to respect human rights;
- a transfer of much of the "third pillar" to the Community pillar, albeit with a unanimity requirement and a limited role for the Court, and absorption of Schengen by the Union;
- the possibility of "flexibility" whereby, if a Member State or a small minority does not wish to proceed further in a policy area, the majority may, subject to a unanimous vote, proceed without it;
- the UK signing up to the Social Protocol which could now be integrated into the treaty as a revised Social Chapter;
- stronger provisions on employment policy (new chapter), public health, consumer protection and the environment.

The new treaty did not, however, resolve several key problems. Above all, it failed to settle three interrelated problems generally seen as central to making the EU fit for enlargement. These were:
- the scope of majority decision making in the Council (which was only increased slightly);
- the weighting of votes per Member State in the Council with a large number of small countries poised to join, and the related issue of whether population size should be taken account of explicitly; and
- the number of European Commissioners and in particular whether each Member State should be guaranteed such a post.

It was agreed that the Union would need to return to these issues, which became known as the "Amsterdam leftovers", before enlargement could successfully take place. Many felt that a new IGC could not be restricted to these three issues alone.

Salade Niçoise

It was therefore agreed to hold a further IGC in the year 2000. Parliament again pushed for close involvement in the IGC (which it eventually obtained along improved Amsterdam lines, with Parliament's two representatives – Elmar Brok and Dimitris Tsatsos –taking part in every meeting of the IGC negotiating group) and for the IGC to address issues beyond the three left-overs, such as the re-allocation of seats per Member State in the Parliament, the integration of the WEU, the size and working methods of the Courts, enhanced cooperation, the statute of European political parties, and the protection of fundamental rights (with the European Council having convened a body composed of MEPs, MPs and government representatives to draft a Charter of Fundamental Rights for the Union). It also pressed for the extension of the co-decision procedure, though this issue had less salience than in previous IGCs precisely because the EP had made so much progress in the last two decades. Despite the initial reluctance of many Member States to widen the agenda, all of these points were eventually dealt with

The compromise agreed in the middle of the fourth night of negotiation in the European Council at Nice in December 2000 was felt by MEPs to be less than satisfactory in at least two respects, concerning Council and Parliament.

Regarding the Council, a new distribution of votes per Member State was agreed, but it also entailed a new and more complex threshold for obtaining a qualified majority. The previous threshold of 71% of the weighted votes was already high – more than a two-thirds majority. Such a high threshold ensured that it was, in practice, impossible to have a qualified majority that did not, at the same time, represent a majority of the States and a majority of the population. Because enlargement meant that this might eventually not be the case, it was agreed to put a population threshold and a requirement for a majority of States explicitly in the treaty. This should have made it possible to eliminate or at least lower the threshold for the number of votes from this very high level. In fact, however, the threshold was potentially raised still further, possibly going up to 74% after enlargement. Furthermore, the population criterion that was added, at 62%, was above the previous de facto threshold of 58%. In the eyes of many, this "triple majority" requirement, with a higher threshold than before for the weighted vote component, would weaken the decision-taking capacity of the Council.

Regarding the European Parliament, the attempt to move towards greater proportionality between seats and population, while at the same time making room for new Member States, was only marginally successful. It was undermined by maintaining six seats for Luxembourg (with a knock-on effect for the new smaller countries due to join), by allowing Belgium, Portugal and Greece to escape with only a small reduction (with the Czech Republic and Hungary – countries with equivalent populations – being allocated fewer seats than them, an anomaly that was later corrected) and by the fact that Spain bargained away seats in the Parliament for extra votes in the Council (see Table 4). The package agreed ignored the previously agreed limit of 700 MEPs on which Parliament's buildings were based.

The Nice Treaty nonetheless introduced a number of measures which Parliament had pushed for. These included:
– the extension of qualified majority voting to 28 new areas;
– the extension of co-decision to five, later ten, new areas;
– granting Parliament the right to bring the other institutions to the Court of Justice;
– reorganising the Courts to cope with a growing number of cases;
– a compromise reached on the composition of the Commission, with the next Commission to have one member per Member State, and the

-       following Commission a fixed number of members with a rotation
        system;
-       the internal reorganisation of the Commission, with the President to
        have the right to nominate Vice-Presidents and to dismiss individual
        Commissioners;
-       the introduction of qualified majority voting to designate the President
        of the Commission;
-       triggering enhanced cooperation without the need for unanimity;
-       strengthening procedures for dealing with a Member State in which
        fundamental rights are threatened;
-       strengthening the article on the statute for European political parties;
-       establishing EuroJust for cooperation between prosecuting authorities;
-       provisions on defence and security, with the virtual absorption of the
        WEU by the Union;
-       a further round of treaty revision by 2004.

Parliament did not specifically endorse the Nice Treaty, but nor did it call
for its rejection. Instead, it took advantage of the highly critical mood about
IGCs as a working method, with complex deals settled late at night by tired
heads of government, to call for the next reform to be prepared by different
procedures.

From the Convention via the Constitution to the Treaty of Lisbon

Parliament pressed for a novel way of preparing the next treaty reform. It
called for a Convention, composed of European and national parliamentarians, national governments and Commission representatives, meeting in
public, to examine the competences and procedures of an enlarged EU and
to reach broad agreement on a new, codified, simplified and improved constitution for it. Although novel in terms of preparing a new treaty, such a
method had been used to prepare the Charter of Rights endorsed by the
institutions at the time of the Nice summit, and tallied with Parliament's traditional tactic of trying to build alliances, notably with national parliaments
and sympathetic governments.

Few governments were initially enthusiastic, but this was turned around
by a year of lobbying by Parliament, notably via national parliaments, in
time for the European Council meeting in Laeken-Brussels in December
2001. The then Belgian Presidency of the Council worked closely with the
Parliament's Constitutional Committee, and especially an informal group of
its leading members (Napolitano, Mendez de Vigo, Corbett, Leinen, Duff,
Frassoni and Kaufman) dubbed the "Friends of Laeken", in drafting a text
approved by the heads of government, which became known as the Laeken
Declaration.

It provided for the Convention to be composed of one representative of
each government and two of each national parliament from all 28 Member
and Applicant states (including Turkey), 16 members of the European
Parliament, two members of the European Commission, a President (former
French President Valéry Giscard d'Estaing) and two Vice-Presidents (former
Belgian and Italian Prime Ministers, Jean-Luc Dehaene and Giuliano Amato).

During the Convention, which took place from February 2002 to June 2003, Parliament pressed notably for:
–   the treaties to be consolidated into a single document with the typically constitutional parts to be in a short first section;
–   the Charter of Rights, agreed at Nice, to be incorporated into the treaty;
–   an end to the "pillar" structure of the Union, notably by incorporating the remaining part of the "third pillar" into the field of Community law;
–   co-decision to apply to all areas of legislative activity;
–   Parliament to elect the President of the Commission;
–   the posts of High Representative for Foreign and Security policy and Commissioner for External Affairs to be merged;
–   comitology to be further reformed.

Parliament's 16 representatives were led by Inigo Mendez de Vigo (EPP), with Klaus Hänsch (Socialist) and Andrew Duff (Liberal) as his deputies. Hänsch and Mendez served on the 12-member Presidium of the Convention, which proposed most of the drafts and thrashed out many of the compromises. Members of the Convention also met as political groups, with the EPP, Socialist and Liberal Groups playing a crucial part in forging the necessary degree of consensus. It approved a draft constitution for the EU which was submitted to the European Council in June 2003.

In the subsequent IGC, Parliament was represented by Mendez de Vigo (later replaced by Brok) and Hänsch at all the ministerial IGC meetings and by its President Pat Cox at the meetings at heads of government level. The draft constitution drawn up by the Convention was left largely intact by the IGC. It did, however, modify the system proposed for majority voting in the Council. The Convention had proposed to have a "double majority" of states representing three-fifths of the population. However, this was strongly opposed by Spain and Poland (who had disproportionately high votes under the Nice Treaty) and was eventually modified to a complex formula normally requiring 55% of the states representing 65% of the population. The IGC was also more reticent about extending the scope of majority voting, and also changed the formula proposed for the composition of the Commission. But for the rest, the Convention's text was accepted with only small or technical adjustments.

The European Parliament approved the Constitution by 514 votes to 135 (Corbett - Mendez de Vigo Report, vote on paragraph 1) in January 2005, but to come into force it needed to be ratified by every single one of the now 25 Member States. However, France and the Netherlands rejected it in referenda (referenda approving it were held in Spain, Luxembourg and, as the basis for its accession, Romania), causing the European Council to call a "Period of Reflection" on what to do. Although two-thirds of the Member States (18) did ratify, others waited to see what the conclusion of the Period of Reflection would be. It soon became clear that the necessary "grand slam" of 27 ratifications could not be assured, and Member States agreed at the Berlin European Council in June 2007 to abandon the idea of replacing the previous treaties by a new constitution, and to instead maintain – but amend – the existing treaties.

They therefore convened a new IGC, which worked during the autumn of

2007, this time with three European Parliament representatives (Brok, Hänsch and Duff), to draft what became the Treaty of Lisbon. Like the Single Act, Maastricht, Amsterdam and Nice, this amended the previous treaties, with the EC treaty re-named "Treaty on the Functioning of the EU" (TFEU). There was consensus that these amendments should also try to salvage most of the reforms to the institutional system that the Constitution would have introduced, dropping those that had proved controversial – at least in some countries – during its aborted ratification. Thus, "state-like" features, such as re-naming directives and regulations as, respectively, "framework laws" and "laws", calling the High Representative "Foreign Minister", and giving treaty status to the European flag and anthem, were not taken up from the constitution. The status of the Charter of Fundamental Rights was clarified (including a special protocol for the UK and Poland on its interface with national law). To please the French government, competition policy was changed from an objective to a means. Britain and Ireland were given a wider right to opt in or out of police and judicial legislation and the introduction of a new voting system in the Council was modified and postponed until 2017 to please Poland.

Even this new package was not ratified without mishap. Reverting to simple treaty amendments rather than a new "constitution" meant that several Member States who were due to have a referendum on the latter no longer felt the need to do so. In national parliaments, there was a clear majority in every single Member State (in total, some 89 percent of national parliamentarians voting on the treaty supported it) as there was in the European Parliament which approved it by 525 to 115 in February 2008 (another Corbett- Mendez de Vigo Report, A6-13/2008).

However, in Ireland (the only country obliged by its constitution to have a referendum) the treaty was initially rejected by a narrow majority in June 2008. This time, the treaty was not abandoned but, as suggested by Ireland itself, an attempt was made to address issues identified by the Irish parliament as having given rise to concern, but without amending the treaty (which would have required renewed ratification in every country). Thus, apart from clarifications that the treaty made no change to the legal situation in Ireland as regards taxation, abortion, neutrality or conscription, it was agreed to effectively abandon one of the reforms that the treaty contained, namely the reduction in the size of the Commission such that each Member State would nominate a Commissioner only to two Commissions out of three. The loss of an "Irish Commissioner" had been a major issue, although this was something that would have occurred anyway under the Nice treaty. Instead, Member States agreed that they would make use of a clause in the treaty allowing the European Council to vary the size of the Commission and revert to one Commissioner per country. Following these commitments, a new referendum was held in October 2009, with the whole of Europe looking on (and with British and Danish eurosceptics descending upon Ireland to urge a No vote). In the event, the Irish people endorsed the treaty by more than a two-thirds majority (67.1 percent to 32.9).

A further delay then occurred while the President of the Czech Republic refused to sign into law the legislation approving the treaty, despite it being adopted by the necessary three-fifths majority in both chambers of the Czech Parliament and its acceptance by the Czech Supreme Court. He was eventually able to secure an undertaking, which his own government and parliament had felt was not necessary, to allow the Czech Republic a similar protocol to Poland and the UK clarifying the status of the Charter of Rights (which, he had claimed, might give the Sudeten Germans the right to re-claim their properties) before signing.

Thus, the treaty eventually came into force on 1 December 2009, some 8 years after the Laeken Declaration. It is unlikely that there will be much appetite for many years to come to re-open the treaties to further substantial negotiations.

What changes though did Lisbon bring to the EU system? Rather than expand the field of competence of the EU, it focussed on trying to make the institutional system more effective and to improve democratic accountability. The most notable changes are as follows:

To make the enlarged EU more effective, it brought in:

– a further increase in the areas in which Council can decide by qualified majority voting rather than by unanimity;
– a new system of voting in the Council as of 2014/2017, replacing the "triple majority" brought in by the Nice Treaty with a "double majority" of states (55 percent) and population (65 percent);
– a two-and-a-half-year President (renewable once), instead of a six-month rotating one, for the European Council of heads of government;
– a merger of the posts of the Council's foreign policy High Representative and Commissioner for External Relations into a single personality, who is a Vice President of the Commission and who chairs the Foreign Affairs Council;
– more flexible arrangements when not all Member States are willing or able to go ahead with certain policies at the same time;
– a merger of the EU and the EC into a single legal entity and legal personality;
– an extension of the Court of Justice's remit to review decisions in the field of the former third pillar and a new emergency procedure to allow the Court to act "with the minimum of delay" when a case involves an individual in custody

To improve checks and balances and provide more *democratic accountability* it required that:

– the adoption of all EU legislation be subject to the prior scrutiny of national parliaments and, with a few exceptions, the dual approval of both the Council and the European Parliament, by making the co-decision procedure the standard legislative procedure – an objective long sought by Parliament;
– the President of the Commission be elected by the European Parliament – still on a proposal of the European Council, but with the latter obliged to take account of the results of the European elections and to consult to see who is capable of securing a parliamentary majority;
– the Council meet in public when debating and adopting Union legislation;
– a modified budgetary procedure needs the approval of the whole of the annual budget, without any exceptions, and the multiannual financial framework approval by both the Council and the European

      Parliament, thus bringing all expenditure under full democratic control;
- the exercise of delegated legislative powers by the Commission (the old "comitology" system) be brought under a new system of supervision by the European Parliament and the Council, entrenching the 2006 agreement between Parliament and Council;
- all significant international agreements will need the approval (now called "consent" instead of "assent") of the Parliament to be ratified by the Union;
- the EU Charter of Fundamental Rights will be binding in the field of EU law, meaning that all provisions of EU law and all action taken by the EU institutions will have to comply with the standards it lays down;
- the EU will also accede to the European Convention on Human Rights, thereby making the Union subject to the same external review as its Member States are;
- the Union facilitates participation by citizens, the social partners, representative associations and civil society in its deliberations and that individuals will have easier access to justice in connection with European Union law. It provides for a citizens initiative whereby a million signatures will require the Commission to draft a legislative proposal or explain why it can't;
- future treaty changes will be prepared, prior to an IGC, by a Convention involving national and European parliament representatives, unless the European Parliament decides that this is not necessary. The Parliament gains a formal right to propose treaty revisions.

    It also contains *provisions to re-assure those who fear that the EU could become too centralised*:
- it obliges the Union to respect the national identities of Member States and underlines the principles of conferred powers (whereby the Union's only competences are those conferred on it by the Member States), subsidiarity and proportionality;
- it spells out that the Union is based on a set of values shared by all EU countries, namely respect for human dignity, freedom, democracy, equality, the rule of law and respect for human rights, including the rights of persons belonging to minorities, along with pluralism, non-discrimination, tolerance, justice, solidarity and equality between women and men.

Conclusion

The successive treaty revisions since Parliament became directly elected were all strongly influenced by the European Parliament. They illustrate that while, like other actors, the Parliament is not able to secure all its wishes, it can have a major influence and is a catalyst for change. The changes made over the last quarter century have transformed the European system as a whole and Parliament's place in it in particular.

    When Parliament proposed its draft treaty in 1984, it was a time of crisis in the Community, when confidence in its future was at an all-time low.

Summits had broken down on the issue of budgetary contributions of Member States, the European economy was in a period of "Euro-sclerosis" and few thought that there was any realistic chance of amending the treaties. Yet, in thrashing out an agreement among the political forces represented in the Parliament and putting forward its position to governments, to national parliaments and via national political parties, Parliament was able to create sufficient political momentum for at least some national governments to press its case, and a majority of them to accept that there was a case to look at. Of course, the bottom line of unanimity among the Member States meant that there were limits as to what could be achieved, but the momentum was sufficient to enable a compromise package to get through.

Similarly, in 1989–90, Parliament was able to persuade at least the more favourably disposed Member States that there was a need for the planned treaty revision to go beyond EMU and to examine broader issues. External events, such as the radical changes in Eastern Europe, helped. But there is no doubt that the new treaty provisions on citizenship, consumer protection, education and culture and on extending the European Parliament's own powers, would not have found their way into the Treaty of Maastricht had it not been for the constant pressure by Parliament.

By the time of the 1996 IGC, Parliament was accepted as a partner in the preparatory process, if only partly in the IGC itself, and set a large part of the agenda of the IGC. In terms of the final result, many called Parliament the big winner from the Amsterdam Treaty, which considerably enhanced its power.

On the eve of the biggest ever enlargement of the Union, the IGC that produced the Treaty of Nice also saw Parliament enjoy some success in widening the agenda and helping shape the compromises that took the Union forward, even if some other issues left the Parliament dissatisfied. Finally, it was Parliament that suggested the creation of the Convention and played an active part in its work drawing up the proposed new EU Constitution, much of which was taken up in the Lisbon treaty which replaced it. The Convention method is now laid down in the treaty for future revisions.

Taking these episodes together, their cumulative results are striking. In what is historically a short period of time, the European Parliament has come a long way. It sought and eventually obtained a power of co-decision with Council on legislation so that the EU now has what amounts to a bi-cameral legislature. It has acquired a central role in the appointment of the Commission and its President, to complement the right of censure it had acquired when the Community was set up. Its approval is needed for international agreements to be ratified by the Union. It now has an effective right of scrutiny and recall over delegated legislation. In short, the rise of the Parliament is the most significant feature of the cumulative reforms of the treaties of the last two decades.

APPENDIX ONE

EUROPEAN PARLIAMENT ELECTIONS

Austria

Party	2009 %	Seats	2004 %	Seats	1999 %	Seats	1996 %	Seats
Social Democratic Party	23.7	4	33.3	7	31.7	7	29.1	6
Austrian People's Party	30.0	6	32.7	6	30.7	7	30	7
Austrian Freedom Party	12.7	2	6.3	1	23.4	5	27.5	6
Greens	9.9	2	12.9	2	9.3	2	6.8	1
Liberal Forum					2.7		4.3	1
Martin	17.3	3	14	2				
Others	6.0	0	0.8	-	2.2	-	2.6	-
TOTAL		17		18		21		21

Belgium

Party	Region	2009 %	Seats	2004 %	Seats	1999 %	Seats	1994 %	Seats	1989 %	Seats	1984 %	Seats	1979 %	Seats
Socialist Party	Flanders	8.2	2	11	3	8.8	2	10.9	3	12.4	3	17.1	4	12.8	3
Socialist Party	Wallonia	10.9	3	13.5	3	13.5	4	11.4	3	14.5	5	13.3	5	10.6	4
Christian Democrats (CVP)	Flanders	14.4	3	17.4 *with NVA*	4	13.5	3	16.9	4	21.1	5	19.8	4	29.5	7
Christian Democrats	Wallonia	5.0	1	5.7	1	4.9	1	7.0	2	8.1	2	7.6	2	8.2	3
Christian Social Party	German region	0.2	1	0.2	1	0.2	1	0.2	1						
VLD (Liberals)	Flanders	12.8	3	13.6	3	13.6	3	11.3	3	10.6	2	8.6	2	9.4	2
MR (Liberals)	Wallonia	9.7	2	10.3	3	10	3	9.0	3	7.2	2	9.4	3	6.9	2
De Decker List	Flanders	4.5	1												
New Flemish Alliance (NVA)	Flanders	6.1	1	*With CVP*											
Volksunie	Flanders					7.6	2	4.3	1	5..4	1	8.5	2	6.0	1
Vlaams Blok	Flanders			14.3	3	9.4	2	7.7	2	4.1	1	1.3	-	0.7	-
Vlaams Belang	Flanders	9.8	2												
Front National	Wallonia			1.5	-	2.9	1								
Groen (Greens)[1]	Flanders	4.9	1	4.9	1	7.5	2	6.6	1	13.9	1	4.3	1	1.4	-
Ecolo	Wallonia	8.6	2	3.7	1	8.4	3	4.8	1	13.9	2	2.9	1	2.0	-
Walloon Rally	Wallonia									1.5	-	2.5	-	7.6	2
Others (combined)		5.3	-	4.4	-	5	-	6.3	-	1.2	-	3.7	-	4.9	-
TOTAL			22		24		25		25		24		24		24

1   Agalev until 1999.

Bulgaria

Party	2009		2007	
	%	seats	%	seats
Citizens for European Development of Bulgaria (GERB)	24.4	5	21.7	5
Bulgarian Socialist Party	18.5	4	21.4	5
Movement for Rights and Freedoms	14.1	3	20.3	4
National Union Attack (ATAKA)	12.0	2	14.2	3
National Movement for Stability and Progress	8.0	2	6.3	1
Union of Democratic Forces	7.9	1		
Other	15.1	-	16.2	-
TOTAL		17		18

Cyprus

Party	2009		2004	
	%	seats	%	seats
Democratic Rally (DISY)	35.7	2	28.2	2
AKEL	34.9	2	27.9	2
United Democrats (DIKO)	12.3	1	17.1	1
"For Europe" list			10.8	1
EDEK	9.8	1		
Others	7.3	-	16.0	-
TOTAL		6		6

Czech Republic

Party	2009		2004	
	%	seats	%	seats
Civic Democratic Party (ODS)	31.4	9	30.0	9
Czech and Moravian Communist Party	14.2	4	20.3	6
Group of Independents-European Democrats			11.0	3
Christian Democrat Union	7.6	2	9.6	2
Czech Social Democratic Party	22.4	7	8.8	2
Independents			8.2	2
Others	23.9	-	12.1	-
TOTAL		22		24

Denmark

	2009		2004		1999		1994		1989		1984		1979	
	%	Seats	%	Seats	%	Seats	%	Seats	%	Seats	%	Seats	%	Seats
Social Democratic Party	21.5	4	32.6	5	16.5	3	15.8	3	23.3	4	19.5	3	21.9	3
Liberal Party (Venstre)	20.2	3	19.4	3	23.4	5	19.0	4	16.6	3	12.5	2	14.5	3
Conservative People's Party	12.7	1	11.3	1	8.5	1	17.7	3	13.3	2	20.8	4	14.1	2
Centre Democrats							0.9	-	8.0	2	6.6	1	6.2	1
Socialist People's Party	15.9	2	7.9	1	7.1	1	8.6	1	9.1	1	9.2	1[1]	4.7	1
Progress Party							2.9	-	5.3	-	3.5	-	5.8	1
People's Movement against the EU	7.2	1	5.2	1	7.3	1	10.3	2	18.9	4	20.8	4	21.0	4
June Movement (anti-Europe)			9.1	1	16.1	3	15.2	2						
Radical Liberal Party			6.4	1	9.1	1	8.5	1						
Christian People's Party							1.1	-						
Danish People's Party	15.3	2	6.8	1	5.8	1								
Others	7.2	-	1.3	-	6.2	-			5.5	-	2.1	-	11.9	-
TOTAL		13		14		16		16		16		16		16

1   The Socialist People's Party was allocated a second seat when Greenland left the EC on 1st January 1985.

Estonia

Party	2009		2004	
	%	seats	%	seats
Social Democratic Party	8.7	1	36.8	3
Estonian Centre Party	26.1	2	17.5	1
Estonian Reform Party	15.3	1	12.2	1
Fatherland Union-Pro Patria	12.2	1	10.5	1
I.Tarand (Independent)	25.8	1		
Others	11.9	-	23.0	-
TOTAL		6		6

Finland

Party	2009		2004		1999		1996	
	%	seats	%	seats	%	seats	%	seats
National Coalition	23.2	3	23.7	4	25.3	4	20.2	4
Centre	19.0	3	23.4	4	21.3	4	24.4	4
Social Democrats	17.5	2	21.2	3	18.0	3	21.5	4
Greens	12.4	2	10.4	1	13.4	2	7.6	1
Left Alliance	5.9	-	9.1	1	9.1	1	10.3	2
Finnish Christian League/True Finns	14.0	2			2.4	1	2.8	-
Swedish People's Party	6.1	1	5.7	1	6.3	1	5.8	1
Others	1.9	-	6.5	-	4.0	-	7.2	-
TOTAL		13		14		16		16

France

Party	2009 %	2009 Seats	2004 %	2004 Seats	1999 %	1999 Seats	1994 %	1994 Seats	1989 %	1989 Seats	1984 %	1984 Seats	1979 %	1979 Seats
UMP[1]	27.9	29	16.6	17	12.8	12	25.6	28	28.9	26	43	41	16.3	15
UDF[1]			12	11	9.3	9			8.4	7			27.6	25
MODEM	8.5	6												
Socialist Party	16.5	14	28.9	31	22	22	14.5	15	23.6	22	20.7	20	23.5	22
National Front[2]	6.3	3	9.8	7	5.7	5	10.5	11	11.7	10	10.9	10	1.3	-
National Movement			3.3	-										
Greens	16.3	14	7.4	6	9.7	9	4.9	-	10.6	9	3.4	-	4.4	-
Communist Party			6.7	3	6.8	6	6.9	7	7.7	7	11.2	10	20.5	19
Left Front	6.4	5												
Trotskyist Left			4.0	-	5.2	5								
Eurosceptic Right[3]	4.8	1	6.7	3			12.3	13						
Chasse, Pêche (pro-hunting)[4]					6.8	6								
'Energie Radicale' (Tapie List)							12.0	13						
Others	13.3	-	7.9	-	5.5	-	13.3	-	9.1	-	10.6	-	6.3	-
TOTAL		72		78		87		87		81		81		81

1 There was one single right/centre list in 1984 and 1994 and two (one Gaullist RPR and one centrist UDF) in 1979 and 1989. In 1999 the mainstream RPR list (allied with Démocratie Libérale) obtained 12.8% and 12 seats. The centrist list of Bayrou (remaining UDF) obtained 9.3% and 9 seats. In 2004, the former RPR dominated list stood as the UMP, and the UDF of Bayrou again stood separately.
2 In 1999 the far right vote was split and two lists were presented – Le Pen's National Front and Megret's National Movement.
3 This was primarily represented by the Mouvement pour la France party of Philippe de Villiers in 2004
4 Included in others for 2004.

Germany

Party	2009 %	2009 Seats	2004 %	2004 Seats	1999 %	1999 Seats	1994 %	1994 Seats	1989 %	1989 Seats	1984 %	1984 Seats	1979 %	1979 Seats
Christian Democratic Union	30.7	34	36.5	40	39.3	43	32.0	39	29.5	25	37.5	34	39.1	34
Christian Social Union	7.2	8	8.0	9	9.4	10	6.8	8	8.2	7	8.5	7	10.1	8
Social Democratic Party	20.8	23	21.5	23	30.7	33	32.2	40	37.3	31	37.4	33	40.8	35
Greens	12.1	14	11.9	13	6.4	7	10.1	12	8.4	8	8.2	7	3.2	-
Republicans							3.9	-	7.1	6				
Free Democratic Party	11.0	12	6.1	7	3	-	4.1	-	5.6	4	4.8	-	6.0	4
Party of Democratic Socialists	-	-	6.1	7	5.8	6	4.7	-						
The Left	7.5	8												
Others	10.7		9.9	-	5.4	-	6.3	-	3.7	-	3.6	-	0.8	-
TOTAL		99		99		99		99		81		81		81

Greece

Party	2009 %	2009 Seats	2004 %	2004 Seats	1999 %	1999 Seats	1994 %	1994 Seats	1989 %	1989 Seats	1984 %	1984 Seats	1981 %	1981 Seats
New Democracy	32.3	8	43.0	11	36.0	9	32.6	9	40.4	10	38.0	9	31.3.	8
Socialist Party (PASOK)	36.7	8	34.0	8	32.9	9	37.6	10	35.9	9	41.6	10	40.1	10
Communist Alliance	8.3	2	9.5	3	8.7	3	6.3	2	14.3	4	11.6	3	12.8	3
Left Alliance	4.7	1	4.2	1	5.2	2	6.2	2	-	-	3.4	1	5.3	1
New Left (DIKKI)					6.8	2								
Centre/Right Alliance							2.7	-	1.4	1				
EPEN									1.2	-	2.3	1		
Political Spring (POLA)					2.3	-	8.7	2						
Popular Orthodox Rally (LAOS)	7.1	2	4.1	1										
Ecologist Greens	3.5	1												
Others	7.4	-	5.2	-	8.1	-	5.7	-	6.8	-	3.0	-	11.4	-
TOTAL		22		24		25		25		24		24		24

Hungary

Party	2009 %	2009 seats	2004 %	2004 seats
Hungarian Civic Union (FIDESZ-KDNP)[1]	56.4	14	47.4	12
Hungarian Socialist Party	17.4	4	34.3	9
Alliance of Free Democrats	2.2	-	7.7	2
Hungarian Democratic Forum	5.3	1	5.3	1
JOBBIK	14.8	3		
Others	4.0	-	5.3	-
TOTAL		22		24

1   FIDESZ fought the 2004 elections with the MPP (Alliance of Young Democrats) but in the 2009 elections was in alliance with the KDNP

Ireland[1]

Party	2009 %	2009 Seats	2004 %	2004 Seats	1999 %	1999 Seats	1994 %	1994 Seats	1989 %	1989 Seats	1984 %	1984 Seats	1979 %	1979 Seats
Fianna Fail	24.1	3	29.5	4	38.6	6	35.0	7	31.5	6	39.2	8	34.7	5
Fine Gael	29.1	4	27.8	5	24.6	4	24.3	4	21.6	4	32.2	6	33.1	4
Labour Party	13.9	3	10.6	1	8.7	1	10.9	1	9.5	1	8.4	-	14.5	4
Progressive Democrats							6.4	-	11.9	1				
Elected Independents	4.6	1	16.7	2			6.9	1	11.9	2	10.1	1	14.1	2
Workers' Party							1.9	-	7.5	1	4.3	-	3.3	-
Green Alliance	1.9	-			6.7	2	7.9	2	3.8	-	0.5	-		
Sinn Fein	11.2	-	11.1	1	6.3	-	2.9	-	2.3	-	4.9	-		
Democratic Left[2]							3.4	-						
Socialist Party	2.8	1												
Others[3]	12.4	-	4.3	-	15.5	2					0.5	-	0.3	-
TOTAL		12		13		15		15		15		15		15

1   Percentage figure is of first preference votes.
2   Labour Party absorbed Democratic Left in 1999.
3   Others include Libertas, who obtained 5.5% of the first preference vote in 2009, but no seats

Italy

Party	2009 %	Seats	2004 %	Seats	1999 %	Seats	1994 %	Seats	1989 %	Seats	1984 %	Seats	1979 %	Seats
United in the Olive Tree For Europe[1]			31.1	25										
Democratic Party[2]	26.1	21												
Forza Italia			21	16	25.2	22	30.6	27						
Popolo della Liberta[3]	35.3	29												
Communist Parties														
Communist Refoundation Party			6.1	5	4.3	4	6.1	5						
Italian Communists[4]			2.4	2	2.0	2								
Communist Party (PCI)									27.6	22	33.3	27	29.6	24
Christian Democrat Parties														
Christian Democracy									32.9	26	33.0	26	36.4	29
Italian Popular Party[5]					4.3	4	10.0	8						
Patto Segni[6]							3.3	3						
Union of the Centre[7]	6.5	5	5.9	5										
CCD					2.6	2								
CDU					2.1	2								
UDEUR-AP[8]			1.3	1	1.6	1								
Right Wing														
National Alliance[9]			11.5	9	10.3[10]	9	12.5	11						
Tricolour Flame[11]			0.7	1	1.6	1								
Mussolini List			1.2	1										
Italian Social Movement -MSI									5.5	4	6.5	5	5.4	4
Regionalist Parties														
Northern League	10.2	9	5.0	4	4.5	41	6.6	61	1.8	21				
South Tyrol Peoples Party[12]	0.5	1			0.5	1	0.6	1	0.5	1	0.6	1	0.6	1
Other Regionalists[13]					0.7	-	1.4	-	0.6	1	0.5	1		
Greens			2.5	2	1.8	2	3.2	3	6.2	5				
Centre and Liberal Parties and Lists														
Centre List									4.4	4				
Radical Party[14]			2.3	2	8.5	7	2.1	2			3.4	3	3.7	3
Republican/Liberal List					0.5	1					6.1	5		
Republicans							0.7	1					2.6	2
Liberals							0.2	-					3.5	3
La Rete							1.1	1						
The Democrats[5]					7.7	6								
RI-DINI[5]					1.1	1								
Di Pietro List (Italy of Values)	8.0	7	2.1	2										
Socialist Parties														
Democrats of the Left-PDS[15]					17.4	15	19.1	16						
Socialist Party							1.8	2	14.8	12	11.2	9	11.0	9
Social Democrat Party							0.7	1	2.7	2	3.5	3	4.3	4
Other Socialists[16]			2	2	2.1	2								
Pensioner Party			1.1	1	0.7	1								
Others	13.4	-	3.8	-	0.5	-			0.5	-	0.5	-	0.9	-
TOTAL		72		78		87		87		81		81		81

1 Alliance of parties of Socialist, centrist and Liberal orientation, as well as some former Christian Democrats.
2 Democratic Party, a centre-left party, which has replaced the Olive Tree Coalition, and Tree Coalition
3 People of Freedom, a merger between the former Forza Italia and the National Alliance
4 Breakaway from the Communist Refoundation Party.
5 Formerly within Margherita component of Olive Tree Coalition
6 Electoral Pact with National Alliance in 1999.
7 Union of the Centre, coalition of parties, whose leading component is UDC, itself a merger of the former CCD and CDU
8 Stood as UDE in 1999.
9 Patto Segni had joined list with National Alliance – ex MSI in 1999.

10 Common list with Patto Segni.
11 Former MSI members not accepting transformation of National Alliance into more mainstream right-wing party.
12 Stood within the Olive Tree Coalition in 2004.
13 Including Unione Valdostana and Sardinian Action Party.
14 Stood as Bonino List in 1999 and 2004.
15 Largest component of the former Olive Tree Coalition, former Italian Communist Party, whose two main components are the former Democrats of the Left and the former Margherita section within the Olive
16 Stood as United Socialists for Europe in 2004, coalition between Socialist Unity and New Italian Socialist Parties.

Latvia

Party	2009 %	2009 seats	2004 %	2004 seats
Fatherland and Freedom	7.4	1	29.8	4
New Era	6.7	1	19.7	2
Human Rights in a United Latvia	9.7	1	10.7	1
People's Party	2.8	-	6.6	1
Latvia's First Party/Latvia's Way)[1]	7.5	1	6.5	1
Civic Union	24.3	2		
Harmony Centre Coalition (LSP/TSP)[2]	19.6	2		
Others	20.2	-	26.7	-
TOTAL		8		9

1 Stood as Latvia's Way only in 2004
2 The Harmony Centre Coalition consisted of the Social Democratic Party-Harmony (TSP) and the Latvian Socialist Party (LSP)

Lithuania

Party	2009 %	2009 seats	2004 %	2004 seats
Labour Party	8.8	1	30.2	5
Lithuanian Social Democratic Party	18.6	3	14.4	2
Homeland Union-Lithuanian Christian Democrats[1]	26.9	4	12.6	2
Liberal Centre Union (LiCS)	3.5	-	11.2	2
Liberals Movement of the Republic of Lithuania (LRLS)[2]	7.4	1		
Union of Farmers and New Democracy Parties (VNDPS)[3]	1.9	-	7.4	1
Order and Justice [4]	12.2	2	6.8	1
Electoral Action of Poles in Lithuania	8.4	1		
Others	12.4		17.4	-
TOTAL		12		13

1 Stood as Homeland Union only in 2004
2 LRLS founded by former members of LiCS in 2006
3 VNDPS stood as LVLS in 2009
4 Order and Justice stood as the Liberal Democratic Party in 2004

Luxembourg

Party	2009 %	Seats	2004 %	Seats	1999 %	Seats	1994 %	Seats	1989 %	Seats	1984 %	Seats	1979 %	Seats
Christian Social People's Party	31.4	3	37.1	3	31.7	2	31.5	2	34.8	3	34.9	3	36.1	3
Lxmbg. Socialist Workers' Party	19.5	1	22.0	1	23.6	2	24.8	2	25.4	2	29.9	2	21.6	1
Democratic Party (Liberals)	18.7	1	14.9	1	20	1	18.8	1	19.9	1	22.1	1	28.1	2
Greens	16.8	1	15.0	1	10.7	1	10.9	1						
Others	13.7	-	11	-	14	-	13.9	-	19.7	-	13.1	-	14.2	-
TOTAL		6		6		6		6		6		6		6

Malta

Party	2009 %	seats	2004 %	seats
Malta Labour Party	54.8	3	49.0	3
Nationalist Party	40.5	2	40.0	2
Others	4.7	-	11.0	-
TOTAL		5		5

Netherlands

Party	2009 %	Seats	2004 %	Seats	1999 %	Seats	1994 %	Seats	1989 %	Seats	1984 %	Seats	1979 %	Seats
Christian Democrats	20.1	5	24.4	7	26.9	9	30.8	10	34.6	10	30.0	8	35.6	10
Labour Party	12.0	3	23.6	7	20.1	6	22.9	8	30.7	8	33.7	9	30.4	9
Freedom & Democracy Party (Liberals)	11.4	3	13.2	4	19.7	6	17.9	6	13.6	3	18.9	5	16.2	4
Green Left	8.9	3	7.4	2	11.8	4	6.1	1	7.0	2	5.6	2		
Calvinist Coalition[1]	6.8	2	5.9	2	8.7	3	7.8	2	5.9	1	5.2	1		
Democrats 66 (Left Liberals)	11.3	3	4.2	1	5.8	2	11.7	4	6.0	1	2.3	-	9.0	2
Socialist Party	7.1	2	7.0	2	5.0	1								
Transparent Europe			7.3	2										
Freedom Party (PVV)	17.0	4												
Others	5.4	-	7	-	1.8	-	2.8	-	2.2	-	4.3	-	8.8	7
TOTAL		25		27		31		31		25		25		25

1 Formerly RPF, SGP and GVP, now CU and SGP

Poland

Party	2009		2004	
	%	seats	%	seats
Civic Platform	44.4	25	24.1	15
League of Polish Families			15.9	10
Law and Justice	27.4	15	12.7	7
Self-Defence			10.8	6
Democratic Left Alliance	12.3	7	9.3	5
Freedom Union			7.3	4
Polish People's Party	7.0	3	6.3	4
Polish Social Democracy			5.3	3
Others	8.8	-	8.2	-
TOTAL		50		54

Portugal

Party	2009		2004		1999		1994		1989		1987	
	%	Seats	%	Seats	%	Seats	%	Seats	%	Seats	%	Seats
Socialist Party	26.6	7	44.5	12	43.1	12	34.8	10	28.5	8	22.5	6
Social Democratic Party[1]	31.7	8	33.3	9	31.1	9	34.3	9	32.7	9	37.4	10
Popular Party (Centre Party)	8.4	2			8.1	2	12.4	3	14.1	3	15.4	4
United Democratic Coalition[2])			9.1	2	10.3	2	11.1	3	14.4	4	11.5	3
Portuguese Communist Party	10.7	2										
Left Bloc	10.7	3	4.9	1								
Others	5.3	-	4.2	-	7.4	-	7.1	-	10.25	-	13.2	1
TOTAL		22		24		25		25		25		24

1   Joint Social Democratic Party/Popular Party list for 2004 elections.
2   United Democratic Coalition consisted of Portuguese Communist Party (PCP) and Greens, but PCP ran on its own in 2009

Romania

Party	2009		2007	
	%	seats	%	seats
PSD+PC (Social Democrat and Conservative Parties)	31.1	11	23.1	10
PD-L (Liberal Democratic Party)[1]	29.7	10	28.9	13
PLD[2]	-	-	7.8	3
Independent (E.Basescu)[3]	4.2	1		
PNL (National Liberal Party)	14.5	5	13.4	6
Hungarian Democratic Union of Romania	8.9	3	5.5	2
Greater Romania Party, New Generation-Christian Democrat	8.6	3		
Independents			3.4	1
Other	2.9	-	17.9	-
TOTAL		33		35

1   Stood as PD in 2004
2   PLD merged with PD in 2008 to form PD-L
3   Elena Basescu rejoined PD-L party just after 2009 elections

Slovakia

Party	2009 %	2009 seats	2004 %	2004 seats
Slovak Christian and Democratic Union (SDKU/DS)[1]	17.0	2	17.1	3
Movement for a Democratic Slovakia	9.0	1	17.0	3
The Direction – Social Democrats (SMER/SD)[2]	32.0	5	16.9	3
Christian and Democratic Movement	10.9	2	16.2	3
Hungarian Coalition Party	11.3	2	13.2	2
Slovak National Party	5.6	1		
Others	14.3		19.6	-
TOTAL		13		14

1   Stood as SDKU alone in 2004, but merged with Democratic Party (DS) in 2006
2   Stood as SMER-SDL in 2004, later merged with SDL and then with other parties, thus standing in 2009 as SMER-SD

Slovenia

Party	2009 %	2009 seats	2004 %	2004 seats
New Slovenia-Christian People's Party	16.6	1	23.6	2
Liberal Democrats of Slovenia	11.5	1	21.9	2
Slovenian Democratic Party	26.7	2	17.7	2
Social Democrats[1]	18.4	2	14.2	1
Zares	9.8	1		
Others	17.1	-	22.6	-
TOTAL		7		7

1   Stood as United List of Social Democrats in 2004

Spain

Party	2009 %	2009 Seats	2004 %	2004 Seats	1999 %	1999 Seats	1994 %	1994 Seats	1989 %	1989 Seats	1987 %	1987 Seats
Socialist Party	38.8	21	43.5	25	35.3	24	31.1	22	40.2	27	39.1	28
Popular Party	42.1	23	41.2	24	39.7	27	40.5	28	21.7	15	24.6	17
Social Democrat Centre Party							1.0	-	7.2	5	10.3	7
United Left	3.7	2	4.1	2	5.8	4	13.6	9	6.2	4	5.2	3
Convergencia Unio – (Catalan and other regionalist coalition)[1]	5.1	2	5.1	2	4.4	3	4.7	3	4.3	2	4.4	3
Europe of the Peoples[2]	2.5	1	2.5	1								
Other regionalists												
Union, Progress and Democracy	2.9	1			9.2	6	5.7	2	7.1	4	3.6	2
Others	3.5	-	3.6	-	5.5	-	2.9	-	13.5	3	12.8	-
TOTAL		50		54		64		64		60		60

1   In an electoral alliance in 2009 (Coalition for Europe) with a number of other regional parties, including the Basque Nationalist Party (PNV), the Catalan CDC (part of Convergencia I Unio) obtaining one seat and the PNV the other.
2   Left wing regionalist parties, their seat in 2009 being won by the Left Republican Party of Catalonia (ERC).

Sweden

Party	2009 %	seats	2004 %	seats	1999 %	seats	1995 %	seats
Social Democrats	24.4	5	24.6	5	26.0	6	28.1	7
Moderate Party (Conservatives)	18.8	4	18.2	4	20.7	5	23.2	5
June List	3.6	-	14.5	3				
Left Party	5.7	1	12.8	2	15.8	3	12.9	3
Liberals	13.6	3	9.9	2	13.8	3	4.8	1
Greens	11.0	2	6	1	9.5	2	17.2	4
Christian Democrats	4.7	1	5.7	1	7.6	2	3.9	-
Centre Party	5.5	1	6.3	1	6.0	1	7.2	2
Pirate Party	7.1	1						
Others	5.6	0	2	-	0.5	-	2.7	-
TOTAL		18		19		22		22

United Kingdom

Party	2009 %	Seats	2004 %	Seats	1999 %	Seats	1994 %	Seats	1989 %	Seats	1984 %	Seats	1979 %	Seats
Conservative	26.9	25	27.4	27	33.5	36	26.8	18	33	32	38.8	45	48.4	60
Labour	15.2	13	22.3	19	26.2	29	42.6	62	38.9	45	34.8	32	31.6	17
UK Independence Party	16.0	13	16.8	12	6.5	3								
Liberal Democrats[1]	13.3	11	15.1	12	11.9	10	16.1	2	6.2	-	18.5	-	12.6	-
Green Party	8.3	2												
BNP	6.0	2	6.2		2	-	5.9	2	3.1	-	14.5	-	0.5	
Scottish National Party	2.1	2	3.0	2	2.5	2	3.0	2	2.6	1	1.6	1	1.9	1
Plaid Cymru	0.8	1	1.1	1	1.7	2	1.0	-	0.7	-	0.7	-	0.6	-
Ulster Unionist Party[2]	0.5	1	1	1	1.1	1	0.8	1	0.7	1	1	1	0.9	1
DUP[2]	0.6	1	1	1	1.8	1	1.0	1	1	1	1.6	1	1.3	1
SF[2]	0.8	1	1	1										
SDLP[2]	0.5	-		-	1.8	1	1.0	1	0.9	1	1.	1	1.1	1
Others	8.9		5.1	-	7.1	-	2.8	-	2.2	-	4.3	-	8.8	7
TOTAL		72		78		87		87		81		81		81

1   SDP Liberal Alliance in 1984, Liberal Party in 1979
2   Northern Ireland parties elected under a different electoral system (STV), and figures reflect first preference votes received

APPENDIX TWO

SOURCES OF INFORMATION ON THE PARLIAMENT

Primary sources

European Parliament Online

In the last ten years access to information about the European institutions has dramatically increased with the growth of the Internet. The Parliament has developed its own site (www.europarl.europa.eu) that provides a large amount of information about the workings of the institution in all the languages of the Union. As it is regularly updated, it offers a particularly good means of checking on changes in the Parliament since this book went to press.

The site is divided into five main sections, all but one organised on three different levels that are designed to cater for different audiences.

The first section is entitled "News" and is the normal point of entry for anyone coming to consult the site. The first level "Headlines" provides the latest news on what is happening in the Parliament for the general reader, with new articles appearing on a regular basis. The second level offers information for the press on recent parliamentary activity, including the top story of the day, and the third level presents an archive of the different publications of the press service on a thematic basis.

The second section is called "Parliament". At the first level there is a welcome to the institution from the President, at the second level more detailed information on the organisation of the work of the institution, including a link to the Rules of Procedure and at the third level, information on the archives held by the Parliament.

The third section entitled "Your MEPs" provides at the first level a chance to find all MEPs by country, at the second level a directory of the members by group and at the third level an alphabetical list of all MEPs since the 1979 elections, with references to their parliamentary activity.

The fourth section "Activities" presents the core legislative business of the institution, enabling the reader to follow the day-to-day work of the members in plenary, committees and delegations. It provides links to documents going back to the 1994-1999 parliamentary term.

The fifth and final section, EP Live, provides a link to live coverage of parliamentary proceedings and press conferences and offers video-on-demand material of previous plenaries and committee meetings.

In addition, the Parliament launched in 2008 its own webTV channel, known as europarltv, with all programmes available in 22 languages. It can be accessed via the general website but also has its own url at www.europarltv.eu. The site is divided into different sections including Parliament News, with interviews, debates and magazines, Parliament and Me, offering an opportunity for European citizens to put their questions to MEPs, Young Parliament, designed to appeal to a younger audience, Discover Parliament with programmes on the history of the institution, the Political Groups and how the Parliament works and Parliament Live, covering the different activities of the Parliament as they happen. In addition, you can subscribe to a newsletter to receive uptodate news of programmes.

Secondary Sources

As well as the online sources prepared by the Parliament, there has been a growing volume of books, studies and articles about the Parliament written by academics and practitioners. The following is a selection (chiefly in English) made by the authors of material, most of which was written since 2000. Those interested in earlier material should consult previous editions of the book and can also obtain from the Parliament library a CD Rom with a bibliography for the period from 1970 to 2003.

General

Books and studies

BOGDANOR, Vernon, *Democracy, Accountability and Legitimacy in the European Union*, London: Federal Trust for Education and Research, 2007

CORBETT, Richard, *The European Parliament's Role in Closer EU Integration*, Basingstoke: Macmillan, 2002

CORBETT, Richard, *The Treaty of Maastricht: From Conception to Ratification: A Comprehensive Reference Guide*, Harlow: Longman, 1993

COSTA, Olivier, *Le Parlement européen, assemblée délibérante*, Bruxelles: Institut d'Etudes européennes, 2001

FONTAINE, Nicole, *Mes combats: à la présidence du Parlement européen*, Paris: Plon, 2002

HOSKYNS, Catherine and NEWMAN, Michael (eds.), *Democratizing the European Union*, Manchester: Manchester University Press, 2000

HIX, Simon, *How MEPs Vote*, Webber Shandwick, E.S.R.C and Adamson, 2002

HIX, Simon, NOURY Abdul and ROLAND Gérard, *Democratic Politics in the European Parliament*, Cambridge, Cambridge University Press, 2007.

HUG, Adam, *Reconnecting the European Parliament and its People*, Foreign Policy Centre, 2010

JUDGE, David and EARNSHAW David, *The European Parliament*, London: Palgrave Macmillan, 2008 (2nd edition)

PLUMB, Lord, TONGUE, Carole and WIJSENBEEK, Florus, *Shaping Europe: reflections of three MEPs*, London: Federal Trust for Education and Research, 2001

PRIESTLEY, Julian, *Six Battles that Shaped Europe's Parliament*, London: John Harper, 2008

RITTBERGER, Berthold, *Building Europe's Parliament: Democratic Representation Beyond The Nation State*, Oxford: Oxford University Press, 2005

RUFF, Andreas, *Das Europaische Parlament: Enstehung, Struktur, Aufgaben und Schwachen des Europaischen Parlament*, Berlin: Mensch und Buch Verlag, 2001

SIEDENTOP, Larry, *Democracy In Europe*, Harmondsworth: Penguin, 2002

STEUNENBERG, Bernard and THOMASSEN, Jacques (eds.), *The European Parliament: Moving toward Democracy in the EU*, Lanham: Rowman & Littlefield, 2002

Articles

BROAD, Roger and GEIGER, Tim, "The British Experience of the European Parliament", *Contemporary British History*, No. 1, 1997, pp. 98–122

CORBETT, Richard, "Representing the People", in: *Maastricht and Beyond: Building the European Union*, edited by A. Duff, J. Pinder and R. Pryce, London: Routledge, 1994

CORBETT, Richard, "A Very Special Parliament: The European Parliament in the Twenty-First Century", *Journal of Legislative Studies* (Frank Cass Publishers), Vol. 8, No. 2, 2002, pp. 1-8

CORBETT, Richard, Francis JACOBS, and Michael SHACKLETON, "The European Parliament at Fifty: A view from the Inside", *Journal of Common Market Studies* (Blackwell Publishing), Vol. 41, No. 2, 2003, pp. 353-373

CORBETT, Richard, "The European Parliament 2004-2009" Lodge, Juliet (ed), *The 2009 elections to the European Parliament*,Basingstoke: Palgrave Macmillan, 2010

CORBETT, Richard, "The European Parliament 1999-2004 in Lodge, Juliet (ed.), *The 2004 elections to the European Parliament*, Basingstoke: Macmillan, 2005

COX, Pat, "Filling the democratic gap", in: *Expanding the European Union: Reassessing the Fundamentals*, edited by J. Weiler, I. Begg and J. Peterson, Oxford and Malden MA: Blackwell, 2003

DANN, Philipp, "European Parliament and Executive Federalism: Approaching a Parliament in a Semi-Parliamentary Democracy", *European Law Journal* (Blackwell Publishing), Vol. 9, No. 5, 2003, pp. 549-574

FØLLESDAL, Andreas and HIX, Simon, "Why There is a Democratic Deficit in the European Union: A Response to Moravcsik and Majone", *Journal of Common Market Studies*, Vol.44, No.3, 2006, pp.533-562.

HIX Simon, Raunio, Tapio, and Scully, Roger, "Fifty Years on: Research on the European Parliament", *Journal of Common Market Studies* (Blackwell Publishing), Vol. 41, No. 2, 2003, pp. 191-202

KONIG, Thomas and Slapin, Jonathan, "Bringing Parliaments Back in: The Sources of Power in the European Treaty Negotiations", *Journal of Theoretical Politics* Vol. 2004, No. 16, pp. 357-394

MATHER, Janet, "The European Parliament: a model of representative democracy", *West European Politics*, Vol. 24, No. 1, 2001, pp. 181-201

MCCOWN, Margaret, "The European Parliament before the bench: ECJ precedent and EP litigation strategies", *Journal of European Public Policy* (Routledge), Vol. 10, No. 6, 2003, pp. 974-995

MORAVCSIK, Andrew, "In Defence of the 'Democratic Deficit': Reassessing Legitimacy In the European Union", *Journal of Common Market Studies*, Vol. 40, No. 4, 2002, pp. 603-24

SHACKLETON, Michael, "Democratic Accountability in the European Union" in: *Economic Policy Making and the European Union*, edited by F. Brouwer, V. Lintner and M. Newman, London: Federal Trust, 1994

SHACKLETON, Michael, "Interparliamentary Cooperation and the 1996 IGC" in: *The Changing Role of Parliaments in the Union*, edited by F. Laursen and S. Pappas, Maastricht: European Institute for Public Administration, 1995

SHACKLETON, Michael, "The Internal Legitimacy Crisis of the European Union" in: *Europe's Ambiguous Unity*, edited by A. W. Cafruny and C. Lankowski, Colorado: Lynne Rienner, 1997

SHACKLETON, Michael, "The European Parliament" in: *The Institutions of the European Union*, edited by J. Peterson and M. Shackleton, Oxford: Oxford University Press, 2002

VOTEWATCH.EU, Voting Behaviour in the New European Parliament: the First Year, website, 2010

Powers

BRADLEY, Kieran St. Clair, "Halfway house: The 2006 comitology reform and the European Parliament", in *West European Politics*, Vol. 31, No. 4, 2008, pp. 837-854

CORBETT, Richard, "Academic Modelling of the Codecision Procedure: A Practitioner's Puzzled Reaction", *European Union Politics*, vol. 1, no. 3, 2000, pp. 73-81

CORBETT, Richard, "The 2006 Comitology Reform: A Perspective from the European Parliament" in T. Christiansen, J.M. Oettel & B. Vaccari (Eds) *21st Century Comitology*

CROMBEZ, Christophe, "Institutional Reform and co-decision In the European Union", *Constitutional Political Economy*, Vol. 11, No. 1, 2000, pp. 41-58

CROMBEZ, Christophe, "Codecision: Towards a Bicameral European Union", *European Union Studies*, Vol. 1, No. 3, 2000, pp. 363-68

FARRELL, Henry and HERITIER, Adrienne, *The Invisible Transformation of Codecision: Problems of Democratic Legitimacy*, Swedish Institute for European Policy Studies, Report No.7, 2003

FARRELL, Henry, and HERITIER, Adrienne, "Interorganizational Negotiation and Intra-organizational Power in Shared Decision Making: Early Agreements Under Codecision and Their Impact on the European Parliament and Council", *Comparative Political Studies* (SAGE Publications), Vol. 37, No. 10, 2004, pp. 1184-1212

GABEL, Matthew and HIX, Simon, "The Ties that Bind: Partisanship and the Investiture Procedure for the EU Commission President" in: M. Hosli, A. Van Deemen and M. Widgren (eds.) *Institutional Challenges In the European Union*, London: Routledge, 2002

HÄGE, Frank and KAEDING, Michael, "Reconsidering the European Parliament's Legislative Influence: Formal vs. Informal Procedures", *Journal of European Integration*, Vol.29, No.3, 2007, pp.341-361

HIX, Simon, "Constitutional Agenda-Setting Through Discretion In Rule Interpretation: Why the European Parliament Won at Amsterdam", *British Journal of Political Science*, Vol. 32, No. 2, 2002, pp. 259-280

JUDGE, David, and Earnshaw, David, "The European Parliament and the Commission Crisis: A New Assertiveness?", *Governance* (Blackwell Publishing), Vol. 15, No. 3, 2002, pp. 345-374

KARDASHEVA, Raya, "The Power to Delay: The European Parliament's Influence in the Consultation Procedure", *Journal of Common Market Studies*, Vol.47, No.2, 2009, pp.385-409

KASACK, Christiane, "The Legislative Impact of the European Parliament Under the Revised Co-Decision Procedure: Environmental, Public Health and Consumer Protection Policies", *European Union Politics* (SAGE Publications), Vol. 5, No. 2, 2004, pp. 241-260

KREPPEL, Amie, "Rules, Ideology and Coalition Formation in the European Parliament: Past, Present and Future", *European Union Politics*, Vol. 1, No. 3, 2000, pp. 340-62

KREPPEL, Amie, "Moving Beyond Procedure: An Empirical Analysis of European Parliament Legislative Influence", *Comparative Political Studies* (SAGE Publications), Vol. 35, No. 7, 2002, pp. 784-813

KREPPEL, Amie, "Necessary but not sufficient: understanding the impact of treaty reform on the internal development of the European Parliament", *Journal of European Public Policy* (Routledge), Vol. 10, No. 6, 2003, pp. 884-911

MAGNETTE, Paul, "Appointing and Censuring the European Commission: the Adaptation of Parliamentary Institutions to the Community Context", *European Law Journal*, Vol. 7, No. 3, 2001, pp. 292- 310

MAURER, Andreas, "The Legislative Powers and Impact of the European Parliament", *Journal of Common Market Studies* (Blackwell Publishing), Vol. 41, No. 2, 2003, pp. 227-247

MUYLLE, K., "Scrutiny: Is the European Parliament a `Legislator'?", *European Public Law* (Aspen Publishers, Inc.), Vol. 6, No. 2, 2000, pp. 243-252

NOURY, A.G., and ROLAND, G., "More power to the European Parliament?", *Economic Policy* (Blackwell Publishing), Vol. 17, No. 2, 2002, pp. 280-319

RASMUSSEN, Anne, "EU Conciliation Delegates: Responsible or Runaway Agents", *West European Politics*, Vol.28, No.5, 2005, pp. 1015-1034

RAUNIO, Tapio, and Wiberg, Matti, "Controlling Outcomes: Voting Power in the European Parliament 1979-2000", *Journal of European Integration* (Carfax Publishing), Vol. 24, No. 2, 2002, pp. 75-90

RITTBERGER, Berthold, "Impatient legislators and new issue dimensions: a critique of the Garrett-Tsebelis standard version of legislative politics", *Journal of European Public Policy*, Vol. 7, No. 4, 2000. pp. 554-575

RITTBERGER, Berthold, "The Creation and Empowerment of the European Parliament", *Journal of Common Market Studies* (Blackwell Publishing), Vol. 41, No. 2, 2003, pp. 203-225

SELCK, Torsten J., and STEUNENBERG, Bernard, "Between Power and Luck: the European Parliament in the EU Legislative Process", *European Union Politics* (SAGE Publications), Vol. 5, No. 1, 2004, pp. 25-46

SHACKLETON, Michael, "The European Parliament's New Committees of Inquiry: Tiger or Paper Tiger?", *Journal of Common Market Studies*, Vol. 36, No. 1, 1998, pp. 115–30

SHACKLETON, Michael, "The Politics of Codecision", *Journal of Common Market Studies*, Vol.38, No.2, 2000, pp.325-42

SHACKLETON, Michael and RAUNIO, Tapio, "Codecision after Amsterdam", *Journal of European Public Policy*, Spring 2003

THOMSON, Robert and HOSLI, Madeleine, "Who Has Power in the EU? The Commission, Council and Parliament in Legislative Decision-Making", *Journal of Common Market Studies*, Vol.42, No.2, 2006, pp. 391-417

Members, Sessions and Activities

ANDERSON, Peter J., and McLEOD, Aileen, "The Great Non-Communicator? The Mass Communication Deficit of the European Parliament and its Press Directorate", *Journal of Common Market Studies* (Blackwell Publishing), Vol. 42, No. 5, 2004, pp. 897-917

BENDER, P., "The European Parliament and the WTO: Positions and Initiatives", *European Foreign Affairs Review* (Aspen Publishers, Inc.), Vol. 7, No. 2, 2002, pp. 193-208

BOUWEN, Pieter, "The Logic of Access to the European Parliament: Business Lobbying in the Committee on Economic and Monetary Affairs", *Journal of Common Market Studies* (Blackwell Publishing), Vol. 42, No. 3, 2004, pp. 473-495

BOWLER, Shaun and FARRELL, David M., "The Organization of the European Parliament: Committees, Specialization and Co-ordination", *British Journal of Political Science*, Vol. 25, No. 2, pp. 219–43

CUTLER, Robert, and Von LINGEN, Alexander, "The European Parliament and European Union Security and Defence Policy", *European Security* (Frank Cass Publishers), Vol. 12, No. 2, 2003, pp. 1-20

FREEDMAN, Jane, "Women in the European Parliament", *Parliamentary Affairs*, Vol. 55, No. 1, 2002, pp. 179-188

JUDGE, David, "Predestined to save the Earth: the Environment Committee of the European Parliament" in: *Environmental policy in the European Union: actors, institutions and processes*, ed. A. Jordan, Earthscan, 2002, pp. 120-40

KAEDING, Michael, "Rapporteurship Allocation in the European Parliament: Information or Distribution?", *European Union Politics* (SAGE Publications), Vol. 5, No. 3, 2004, pp. 353-371

KRAUSS, S., "The European Parliament in EU External Relations: The Customs Union with Turkey", *European Foreign Affairs Review* (Aspen Publishers, Inc.), Vol. 5, No. 2, 2000, pp. 215-237

LAN, Yuchun, "The European Parliament and the China-Taiwan Issue: An Empirical Approach", *European Foreign Affairs Review* (Aspen Publishers, Inc.), Vol. 9, No. 1, 2004, pp. 115-140

LOOS, Eugene, "Composing 'panacea texts' at the European Parliament: An intertextual perspective on text production in a multilingual community", *Journal of Language and Politics* (John Benjamins Publishing Company), Vol. 3, No. 1, 2004, pp. 3-25

LORD, Christopher, "The European Parliament in the Economic Governance of the European Union", *Journal of Common Market Studies* (Blackwell Publishing), Vol. 41, No. 2, 2003, pp. 249-267

MESSMER, William B., "Taming Labour's MEPs", *Party Politics* 2003 9: 201-218

NOURY, Abdul, "Ideology, Nationality and Euro-Parliamentarians", *European Union Politics*, Vol. 3, No. 1, 2002, pp. 33-58

PRIESTLEY, Julian, "L'Administration du parlement européen au service des deputés", *Revue française d'administration publique*, (7-9), 95, 2000, pp. 439-52

PROKSCH, Sven-Oliver, and SLAPIN, Jonathon, "Parliamentary questions and oversight in the European Union" in *European Journal of Political Research*, March 2010

ROEDERER-RYNNING, Christilla, "From 'Talking Shop' to 'Working Parliament'? The European Parliament and Agricultural Change", *Journal of Common Market Studies* (Blackwell Publishing), Vol. 41, No. 1, 2003, pp. 113-135

SCULLY, Roger, *Becoming Europeans: Attitudes, Roles and Socialization in the European Parliament*, Oxford, Oxford University Press, 2005

SETTEMBRI, Pierpaolo and NEUHOLD, Christine, "Achieving Consensus Through

Committees: Has the European Parliament Managed?", *Journal of Common Market Studies*, Vol.47, No.1, 2009, pp.127-151

Direct elections

BUTLER, David and WESTLAKE, Martin, *British Politics and European elections 1999*, London: Macmillan, 2000

BUTLER, David and WESTLAKE, Martin, *British Politics and European elections 2004*, London: Macmillan, 2005

CARAMANI, Daniele, "Is There a European Electorate and How Does It Look Like? Evidence from Electoral Volatility Measures, 1976-2004", *West European Politics*, Vol. 29, No.1, 2006, pp. 1-27

FRANKLIN, M., "How Structural Factors Cause Turnout Variations at European Parliament Elections", *European Union Politics* (SAGE Publications), Vol. 2, No. 3, 2001, pp. 309-328

KOUSSER, T., "Retrospective voting and strategic behavior in European Parliament elections", *Electoral Studies* (Elsevier Science), Vol. 23, No. 1, 2004, pp. 1-21

LODGE, Juliet (ed.), *The 1999 elections to the European Parliament*, Basingstoke: Macmillan, 2001

LODGE, Juliet (ed.), *The 2004 elections to the European Parliament*, Basingstoke: Macmillan, 2005

LODGE, Juliet (ed), *The 2009 elections to the European Parliament*, Basingstoke: Palgrave Macmillan, 2010

QUINLIVAN, Aodh, and SCHON-QUINLIVAN, Emmanuelle, "The 2004 European Parliament Election in the Republic of Ireland", *Irish Political Studies* (Frank Cass Publishers), Vol. 19, No. 2, 2004, pp. 85-95

SCHMITT,Hermann (ed.), *European Parliament Elections after Eastern Enlargement*, London: Routledge, 2010

Political groups and parties

CARTER, Neil, "Mixed Fortunes: the Greens in the 2004 European Parliament Election", *Environmental Politics* (Frank Cass Publishers), Vol. 14, No. 1, 2005, pp. 103-111

DIETZ, Thomas, "Similar but different? The European Greens compared to other transnational party federations in Europe", *Party politics*, Vol. 6, No. 2, 2000, pp. 199-210

FAAS, Thorsten, "To defect or not to defect? National, institutional and party group pressures on MEPs and their consequences for party group cohesion in the European Parliament", *European Journal of Political Research* (Blackwell Publishing), Vol. 42, No. 6, 2003, pp. 841-866

FENNEMA, M. and POLLMANN, C. "Ideology of anti-immigrant parties in the European Parliament", *Acta Politica*, No. 2, 1998, pp. 111–38

FERRARA, Federico, Weishaupt, J. T., "Get your Act Together: Party Performance in European Parliament Elections", *European Union Politics* (SAGE Publications), Vol. 5, No. 3, 2004, pp. 283-306

HINES, Eric H., "The European Parliament and the Europeanization of Green Parties", *Cultural Dynamics* (SAGE Publications), Vol. 15, No. 3, 2003, pp. 307-325

HIX, Simon, "Parties and Elections in the European Union", *European Review*, No. 2, 1998, pp. 215–32

HIX, Simon, "Legislative Behaviour and Party Competition In the EU: An Application of NOMINATE to the Post-1999 European Parliament", *Journal of Common Market Studies*, Vol.39, No. 4, 2001, pp. 663-83

HIX, Simon, Kreppel, Amie, and Noury, Abdul, "The Party System in the European Parliament: Collusive or Competitive?", *Journal of Common Market Studies* (Blackwell Publishing), Vol. 41, No. 2, 2003, pp. 309-331

HIX, Simon, *What to Expect in the 2009-14 European Parliament: Return of the Grand Coalition?* Swedish Institute for European Policy Analysis, August 2009

JACOBS, Francis B., *Western European Political Parties: A Comprehensive Guide*, London: Longman, 1989

JOHANSSON, Karl Magnus, "Party Elites in Multilevel Europe: The Christian Democrats and the Single European Act", *Party Politics* 2002 8: 423-439

KREPPEL, Amie, "Rules, Ideology and Coalition Formation In the European Parliament: past, present and future", *European Union Politics*, Vol. 1, No. 3, 2000, pp. 340-62

KREPPEL, Amie, *The European Parliament and Supranational Party System*, Cambridge: Cambridge University Press, 2002

KREPPEL, Amie, and Hix, Simon, "From 'Grand Coalition' to Left-Right Confrontation: Explaining the Shifting Structure of Party Competition in the European Parliament", *Comparative Political Studies* (SAGE Publications), Vol. 36, No. 1, 2003, pp. 75-96

LEWIS, Jeffrey, "The European Parliament and Supranational Party System: A Study in Institutional Development", *Journal of Politics* (Blackwell Publishing), Vol. 65, No. 3, 2003, pp. 926-928

MURRAY, Philomena, "Factors for Integration? Transnational Party Cooperation in the European Parliament, 1952-79", *Australian Journal of Politics & History* (Blackwell Publishing), Vol. 50, No. 1, 2004, pp. 102-115

POLLACK, Anita, *Wreckers or Builders? A History of Labour MEPs 1979-1999*, London: John Harper

PRIESTLEY, Julian, *European Political Parties: The Missing Link* (Notre Europe, 2010)

RAUNIO, Tapio, "Losing independence or finally gaining recognition? Contacts between MEPs and national parties", *Party Politics*, Vol. 6, No. 2, 2000, pp. 211-224

SCULLY, Roger, "Voters, Parties and Europe", *Party Politics* 2001 7: 515-523

SAGAR, D. (ed.), *Political Parties of the World*, London: John Harper Publishing, 2009 (7th edition)

TAGGART, P. and SZCERBIAK, A., *Opposing Europe? The Comparative Party Politics of Euroscepticism*, Oxford: Oxford University Press, 2004

VIOLA, Donatella, *European Foreign Policy and the European Parliament In the 1990s: an Investigation into the role and voting behaviour of the European Parliament's political groups*, Aldershot: Ashgate, 2000

WATSON, Graham, *Building a Liberal Europe: The ALDE Project*, London, John Harper Publishing, 2010

WHITAKER, Richard, *Party control in a committee-based legislature: the case of the European Parliament*, Journal of Legislative Studies, Vol. 7, No. 4, 2001, pp. 63-88

INDEX

The index does not contain the names of people or political parties mentioned in lists in the individual chapters or the appendices.